Framing the Social Security Debate

Historical and Current Events

Framing the Social Security Debate

Values, Politics, and Economics

R. Douglas Arnold
Michael J. Graetz
Alicia H. Munnell
Editors

NATIONAL ACADEMY OF SOCIAL INSURANCE
Washington, D.C.

Framing the Social Security Debate: Values, Politics, and Economics
may be ordered from:

BROOKINGS INSTITUTION PRESS
1775 Massachusetts Ave. N.W.
Washington, D.C. 20036
Tel: 1-800-275-1447
     (202) 797-6258
Fax: (202) 797-6004
Internet: www.brook.edu

Library of Congress Cataloging-in-Publication data

Framing the social security debate: values, politics, and
economics / R. Douglas Arnold, Michael J. Graetz, and Alicia H. Munnell,
editors.
     p.   cm.
     Papers presented at the tenth annual conference of the National
Academy of Social Insurance, held in Washington, D.C., on Jan. 29, 1998.
     Includes bibliographical references.

     ISBN 0-8157-0153-5 (pbk.)
     1. Social security—United States—Congresses. I. Arnold R.
Douglas, 1950- II. Graetz, Michael J. III. Munnell, Alicia Haydock.
IV. National Academy of Social Insurance (U.S.). Conference (10th :
1998 : Washington, D.C.)
     HD7125.F73 1998
     368.4'3'00973—ddc21   98-25429
                                                                      CIP

9 8 7 6 5 4 3 2 1

The paper used in this publication meets the minimum requirements of the
American National Standard for Information Sciences—Permanence of
Paper for Printed Library Materials, ANSI Z39.48-1984

Typeset in Times Roman

Composition by R. Lynn Rivenbark, Macon, Georgia

Printed by R. R. Donnelley & Sons, Harrisonburg, Virginia

NATIONAL ACADEMY OF·SOCIAL INSURANCE The National Academy of Social Insurance is a non-profit, nonpartisan organization made up of the nation's leading experts on social insurance. Its mission is to conduct research and enhance public understanding of social insurance, to develop new leaders and to provide a nonpartisan forum for exchange of ideas on important issues in the field of social insurance. Social insurance, both in the United States and abroad, encompasses broad-based systems for insuring workers and their families against economic insecurity caused by loss of income from work and protecting individuals against the cost of personal health care services. The Academy's research covers social insurance systems, such as Social Security, Medicare, workers' compensation and unemployment insurance, and related social assistance and private employee benefits.

Preface

TIMELY REFORM of Social Security is important. It is the cornerstone of retirement security for American workers and their families; for more than two decades Social Security has provided more than half of the total income for two-thirds of elderly beneficiaries.

This volume consists of papers and commentary from the tenth annual conference of the National Academy of Social Insurance, which was held in Washington, D.C., on January 29–30, 1998. The purpose of the conference was not to come up with policy prescriptions for Social Security but rather to clarify the nature of the debate.

People's views about how to restore financial balance to Social Security reflect a combination of economic assessments, political predictions, and value judgments. When these three dimensions are combined, it is difficult to have a productive dialogue. Once separated, however, people with very different policy preferences can identify the sources of their disagreements.

The papers and discussion demonstrate that economists differ little on the economic issues surrounding prefunding, investing in equities, and defined-benefit versus defined-contribution plans. The real debate centers on questions of values and politics. These are the areas in which Congress and the American people must find some common ground. Reasoned debate is in everyone's interest because deferring changes until the baby boom starts to retire will be very costly.

Participants entered the conference with a wide array of views about the extent to which Social Security should move from a defined-benefit plan to a system with both defined-benefit and defined-contribution elements. They also left with a wide range of views. Nevertheless the conference was a success—it produced a clear separation of economic issues from questions of values and politics. As policymakers settle down to the difficult business of strengthening

Social Security for the long term, this volume supplies them with a useful background.

Individuals who had served on the Academy's study panel on Evaluating Issues in Social Security Privatization made a valuable contribution. These individuals had explored Social Security privatization issues for more than a year, and their papers and commentary enriched both the conference and the subsequent deliberations of the panel.

Although the editors' names appear on the volume, the inspiration behind this effort came from two people at the National Academy of Social Insurance—Virginia Reno and Kathryn Olson. They were instrumental in framing the theme of the conference, suggesting authors and discussants, and structuring the sessions. Besides providing much help on the substance, they and the rest of the Academy staff did a wonderful job on the logistics, which helped make the conference such a success. We especially acknowledge Terry Nixon, who masterminded the conference logistics with the help of Suzanne Habbyshaw, Brian Montgomery, and Donielle Wells. Allison Watts aided in coordinating the conference and producing this volume. At the Brookings Institution, Theresa Walker edited the manuscript, Carlotta Ribar proofread it, and Sherry Smith prepared the index.

The Alfred P. Sloan Foundation, the AARP Andrus Foundation, TIAA-CREF, and the Actuarial Foundation provided generous financial support for the conference.

The papers and discussions reflect the views of the authors and do not necessarily reflect those of the employers or other organizations with which the authors are associated or of the funders, officers, board, staff, or members of the National Academy of Social Insurance or the Brookings Institution.

R. DOUGLAS ARNOLD
MICHAEL J. GRAETZ
ALICIA H. MUNNELL

Contents

1

Introduction

Alicia H. Munnell

IN HIS State-of-the-Union address on January 27, 1998, President Clinton called for a national conversation about the future of Social Security. Two days later, the National Academy of Social Insurance held its tenth annual conference, "Framing the Social Security Debate: Values, Politics, and Economics." Conference participants addressed several important questions: Why is Social Security on the national agenda? What are the underlying economic issues? What values are at stake? How might political concerns affect Social Security reform?

Social Security is on the national agenda because the system faces a projected long-term deficit. But things are different than they were in 1983 when Congress last acted to restore financial balance; this time the system is not facing a short-term financing crisis. In fact, government actuaries calculate that the system has an adequate flow of revenues until 2032 and can cover three-quarters of promised benefits thereafter. The emergence of a long-term deficit in the absence of a short-term crisis allows policymakers to consider comprehensive reforms as well as incremental adjustments to the system.

In considering both incremental and comprehensive reform, two relatively new considerations are playing an important role. One is the maturation of the Social Security program. Unlike earlier generations who received large benefits relative to taxes paid, today's workers face a sharp decline in the returns that they can expect to receive on their payroll tax contributions (often referred to as the "money's worth" issue). Since raising taxes or reducing benefits will only worsen returns, almost all reform plans involve equity investment in one form or another to provide additional revenue. The second factor influencing the debate is concern about low levels of national saving. This concern, along with the desire to avoid high pay-as-you-go tax rates in the future, has spawned considerable interest in some prefunding.

Most proposals considered at this conference respond to these concerns. Thus, the conference participants do not debate whether to accumulate reserves through the Social Security program in order to increase national saving. Both proposals to maintain the existing defined benefit plan and proposals to institute individual accounts involve a substantial accumulation of assets. Nor do conference participants debate broadening the investment options for Social Security participants. Almost all observers agree that those covered by Social Security should have access to the higher risks and higher returns associated with equity investment. In other words, the questions of prefunding and of broadening the portfolio are not at issue. Rather, the debate is—given prefunding and given the desire to invest in equities—whether this is better done in the central Social Security trust funds or in privatized accounts.

Where conference participants stand on the issue of privatized accounts versus the current Social Security program has far more to do with values and politics than with economics. In fact, remarkable agreement exists regarding economic considerations. The economists all agree that the questions of prefunding, investing in equities, and defined benefit versus defined contribution are separable from an economic perspective. In principle, it is possible to have a large trust fund with a diversified portfolio in a defined-benefit system or a defined-contribution system with no more than our current funding. Everyone agrees that privatizing without prefunding would not raise the return on Social Security contributions, after making appropriate adjustments for risk and the transition costs. Everyone agrees that prefunding can raise future returns, but only by imposing significant costs on those workers who must pay twice—to maintain current benefits and to build up a reserve. Everyone agrees that providing access to equity investment for the entire population would improve the distribution of risk bearing in society. Everyone agrees that benefit promises under a defined-contribution plan are as subject to risk as those under a defined-benefit plan.

Even with this economic consensus in hand, conference participants still disagree over how the Social Security system should be structured. They disagree for a variety of reasons. Participants place different values on individual control versus shared security. They have different assessments of the long-run stability of the current system and that of a combined defined-benefit/defined-contribution approach. They have different assessments of the ability to protect accumulations in the trust funds versus individual accounts from political pressures to use them for other purposes. They put different weights on the risk of social investing and corporate interference if the Social Security trust funds purchased equities versus the additional costs associated with setting up individual accounts and regulating their activities. They have different views about the appropriate size of the defined-benefit and defined-contribution components of the nation's retirement system.

These differences in values and political predictions cannot be resolved at a conference, they must be decided by the American people. It is hoped that a year-long debate on Social Security will move the nation toward reaching some agreement on these important issues. Clarifying that the disagreement is not about economics is an important first step and a major accomplishment of this conference.

Values, Politics, and Economics of Social Security Reform

Michael Boskin begins the discussion by describing Social Security's projected long-term financing problem, which has put the program on the national agenda. According to the Trustees' 1998 Report, between now and 2013 the Social Security system will bring in more money than it pays out. That is, payroll taxes and income tax receipts from the taxation of Social Security benefits will exceed benefit payments. From 2013 to 2021—adding interest on trust fund assets to tax receipts produces enough revenues to cover benefit payments. After that total income will fall short of benefit payments, but the government can meet the benefit commitments by drawing down trust fund assets until the funds are exhausted in 2032. After 2032, if no tax or benefit changes are made, current payroll taxes and income taxation of benefits will provide enough money to cover only about 75 percent of promised benefits.

The debate is over how to close the gap between the 100 percent of promised benefits and the 75 percent financing currently in place. One way to think of this gap is to consider the amount by which taxes would have to increase today to pay full benefits for the next 75 years. While virtually no one argues for closing the entire gap through a tax increase, it provides a useful way to gauge the size of the problem. According to the Social Security Trustees' 1998 Report, the retirement system's projected long-run deficit over the next 75 years is equal to 2.19 percent of total payroll earnings over that period. Thus, if enacted immediately, the required tax increase is roughly 1.1 percentage point for the employee and 1.1 percentage point for the employer.

How to characterize a 2.19 percent deficit is subject to much debate. Some view it as requiring only modest adjustments. Michael J. Boskin is less sanguine. He notes that modest adjustments were made in 1983 and the system was declared solvent for 75 years only to slip into deficit shortly after the 1983 amendments were enacted. He points out, however, that the U.S. Social Security financing gap is much smaller than that faced by other developed nations.

The reasons behind the projected increase in Social Security costs are primarily demographic. Fertility rates have declined for two centuries. At the same time, gains in life expectancy have been significant. In 1935, when Social Security was enacted, life expectancy at age 65 was about 12 years for men and 13 years for women. Today those figures are 16 years and 19 years, respectively, and by 2075 they are now projected to be 19 and 22. Declining fertility and mortality together produce a permanent increase in the ratio of retirees to workers and a significant increase in costs for a pay-as-you-go pension program. Most of this increase occurs by the time the last baby boomer retires around 2030, and costs drift only slightly higher thereafter.

With regard to closing the financing gap, Boskin makes two points. First, Social Security is one of the great success stories. Enacted during the Great Depression, it has served as a savings vehicle through which people provide for retirement. It has served as an insurance program through which people gain protection in the event of disability or death of the family breadwinner. It has served as a mechanism for redistributing income to those with a lifetime of low earnings. The poverty rate for the elderly is now similar to that for the rest of the adult population (10.8 percent versus 11.4 percent) compared with roughly three times that level in the mid-1960s.

Second, Boskin thinks that several changes to the program would be desirable even if it did not have a long-run financing shortfall. He believes that the cost-of-living adjustments should be made more accurate by correcting for upward bias in the Consumer Price Index and that the normal retirement age, now 65 and scheduled to rise to 67 under current law, should be further increased. Most important, he believes the Social Security program should be used as a mechanism to increase saving and capital accumulation. This involves prefunding, which Boskin acknowledges raises difficult issues of intergenerational equity.

Peter Diamond examines what economics has to say about how best to structure a retirement system. He clarifies at the outset that the three main questions—whether the program should structured as a defined-benefit plan or a mixed defined-benefit/defined-contribution arrangement, how much advance funding should be undertaken, and how that prefunding should be invested—are all separable from an economic perspective.

As Boskin suggests, prefunding involves a question of intergenerational equity—putting aside more money in the near term (either in higher taxes or as contribution to individual accounts) in exchange for lower taxes in the long run. In other words, more funding can increase national saving and avoid the need for high pay-as-you-go tax rates down the road, but only by placing a burden on the transition generation that has to pay not only to maintain current benefits but also to build up a reserve. There is no free lunch here. Moreover, this intergenerational equity issue is the same regardless of whether the accumulation takes place in the central trust funds or in individual accounts.

Similarly, Diamond contends that the economics of the investment issue are straightforward. Just as individuals should hold a diversified portfolio, so too should the central fund, be it either a defined-benefit or defined-contribution arrangement. Many young people and others with little wealth are not particularly risk averse, but currently they have no mechanism for taking advantage of the higher risk/higher return of equity investment. Allowing access to equities for those with few assets would raise the return in the nation's basic pension fund and improve the distribution of risk bearing in the economy. Because a defined-benefit plan can spread risk not only across the population but also across generations, Diamond points out that it could take on more higher risk/higher return investments than a defined-contribution plan. Moreover, spreading a given amount of risk more broadly will increase the efficiency of capital markets and lower the risk premiums. With a lower risk premium firms will undertake more risky investments.

Diamond identifies three issues that affect the choice between a defined-benefit plan and a combined defined-benefit/defined-contribution approach—whether individual investment decisions would lead to an adequate accumulation of reserves for most people, whether a given level of accumulation would provide appropriate protection in retirement, and the costs and administrative feasibility of alternative approaches.

With regard to the accumulation phase, the question is whether having individuals make separate investment decisions will produce the accumulations necessary for their basic retirement benefit. The possible gain from individual choice in a defined-contribution plan is that it could create a better match of portfolios with individual preferences for some investors. But success depends crucially on the quality of individual decisions. It could also produce an inferior portfolio for the inexperienced investor or for those who make mistakes or are taken advantage of in the market.

Diamond also examines the potential exposure for both workers and dependents after retirement. The current defined-benefit Social Security system protects workers from outliving their resources and against the erosive impact of rising prices by providing inflation-indexed annuities. It also protects the families of covered workers by providing benefits to dependent spouses after the worker dies. Under some defined-contribution plans, worker and dependent protection would hinge on the choices made by the beneficiaries. The small size of the current U.S. annuity market suggests that, if left to their own devices, retirees do not choose to annuitize their accumulations. Evidence from the

United Kingdom suggests that people do not purchase inflation protection even when they have the opportunity. Finally, pre-ERISA data indicate that, left on their own, many workers select single-life annuities with no protection for surviving spouses. Thus, both workers and surviving spouses—primarily widows—could be put at risk under a defined-contribution plan.

Social Security's defined-benefit plan is relatively cheap to administer because all assets are managed in the central trust funds. Introducing a defined-contribution component for Social Security may be expensive, with the costs and difficulties depending on the particular approach. The IRA (individual retirement account) approach, in which the participant would have total control over the account, is the most expensive, but it leaves most of the decisions in the hands of the individual. The 401(k) approach, in which the government would select the appropriate investment funds and hold the money, is much less costly, but it could give the government a lot of control.

The 1994–96 Social Security Advisory Council estimates that marketing, tracking, and maintaining an IRA-type individual account would cost 100 basis points per year (that is, 1 percent). A 100-basis-point annual charge sounds benign, but it would reduce total accumulations by roughly 20 percent over a forty-year work life. That means benefits would be 20 percent lower than they would have been in the absence of the transaction costs. Moreover, Diamond points out that the 100-basis-point estimate does not include brokerage fees; if the individual does not select an index fund, then transaction costs may be twice as high. Indeed, costs actually experienced in the United Kingdom, which has a system of individual accounts, have been considerably higher than the Advisory Council estimate. Finally, because these transaction costs involve a large flat charge per account, they will be considerably more burdensome for low-income participants than for those with higher incomes.

Diamond concludes that better risk spreading, better protection for retirees and dependents, and lower costs make a well-run defined-benefit plan superior to a mixed defined-benefit/defined-contribution plan. Therefore, he contends that the current debate is not about economics, but rather about different values—the weight given to individual choice versus shared security—and about different political assessments—how to protect accumulations from political pressures that would undermine their usefulness as a source of retirement income. Clarifying the economics, however, is a necessary first step to sorting out the issues of values and politics.

Hugh Heclo agrees with Diamond that values rather than economics are at the heart of the Social Security reform debate. All long-term pension commitments involve risks that cannot be avoided, and the question is "How should these risks be shared?" Do we want a society where individuals look out for themselves? Or do we want a society where people are bound together for mutual benefit? What balance do we want between individual freedom and shared security?

The two approaches not only rest on very different values but also evoke very different political risks regarding their long-run stability. Some claim that the current system is unstable in the long run because the public will not tolerate the tax increases or benefit cuts required to keep it solvent—or will accept tax increases only if they see them going to their individual accounts. Perhaps, says Heclo, but the public tolerated major changes in 1983, opinion polls are ambiguous about the public's willingness to accept further tax increases, and a transition to a privatized system could involve even larger tax increases. Others argue that public support for the current system will erode because of the poor rate of return that workers earn on their contributions. Possible, says Heclo, but he urges that we keep in mind the fact that higher returns can be achieved under either a collective or individual arrangement and that opinion polls suggest support for Social Security does not hinge on rate of return considerations.

Individual accounts face different political risks. First, it may prove difficult to prevent early withdrawal from individual accounts, leaving participants with inadequate retirement income. The experience with IRAs and 401(k) plans suggests this may be a serious problem. Second, those who fare poorly in their investments may push for a guaranteed return as they approach retirement. This might happen, says Heclo, but he believes it would be unlikely to destabilize the system. Heclo views the third risk as more serious—namely, the erosion of the income redistribution component of the current program. That is, while initially reforms might contain some version of the existing system, Heclo believes that over time middle- and higher-income beneficiaries, doing less well under the reduced system than in their individual accounts, would press for further reductions in their payroll tax contributions. This would lead to an unraveling of the redistributional provisions of Social Security and a significant increase in income inequality.

Heclo contends that political risks of both approaches should be taken very seriously. It is not enough to assert that a program is feasible in the short run, it must also be stable over time. The political forces that could be triggered by individual accounts need particular attention given that the proposed system has no track record.

The Defined-Benefit/Defined-Contribution Debate

Shifting from a defined-benefit to a defined-contribution arrangement for Social Security would necessarily introduce investment risk into the worker's basic retirement pension. In deciding whether this is acceptable, it is necessary to assess what other sources of retirement income people will have available. It is also necessary to understand the magnitude of the risks associated with defined-contribution plans and compare them with risks associated with defined-benefit plans.

Dallas Salisbury makes three points about the broader pension environment within which Social Security operates. First, Social Security alone will not provide adequate retirement income for the vast majority of the population. In response, a mature and healthy private pension system provides important supplementary benefits. But its role should not be overstated since fewer than half of retirees now receive employer-provided pension benefits and that number is unlikely to increase significantly in the future. Specifically, today only 24 percent of retirees report private employer pension income and 18 percent report public employer pension income. With regard to the future, the fact that only 44 percent of the civilian workers participate in any form of employer-sponsored retirement plans means that, if current trends continue, supplementary pensions will continue to be available for only part of the population. Moreover, the effectiveness of employer-sponsored plans in providing retirement income is limited by the fact that almost half of pension payments are made in lump sums and 44 percent of lump-sum dollars are not saved for retirement.

Salisbury's second point is that the employer-sponsored pension system is increasingly defined contribution. In 1993, defined-contribution plans accounted for 46 percent of total private pension assets, 66 percent of contributions, and 49 percent of benefits. Roughly 42 percent of pension participants view their primary plan as defined contribution; the comparable number in 1980 was 16 percent. Salisbury views this as good news, not bad, given the increase in job turnover.

Salisbury's third point is that individuals are starting to save on their own. Although this is a positive development, only one-third of workers have done an estimate of how much they need to save for retirement. Governments and employers are undertaking major educational efforts to improve this performance, but they still have a lot of work to do. Moreover, workers consistently underestimate how long they will live after retirement, but want to retire early. Thus, without further education regarding retirement needs and resources, individual saving like supplementary pensions will serve as a backstop for only a fraction of the population.

The conclusions that Salisbury's discussant Regina Jefferson draws from these facts is that one should approach the adoption of a defined-contribution model for Social Security cautiously. To the extent that individuals have supplementary pension coverage, the shift to defined-contribution arrangements means that workers already bear considerable risks as a result of market fluctuations and overly conservative or aggressive investment strategies. To the extent that individuals save on their own, they face the same kinds of risks in their individual saving arrangements. Jefferson points out that low- and moderate-income individuals are unlikely to have any supplementary protection over and above their Social Security benefit. Given the risk of accumulating insufficient assets in the rest of the retirement system, Jefferson concludes, "It is more important than ever for Social Security to provide a guaranteed and definite retirement benefit."

How would a shift to defined-contribution plans affect the risks workers face over their lifetimes? Lawrence Thompson looks at how to provide predictable retirement income in a world that is inherently unpredictable. The goal of any social security program is to present workers entering the work force with a set of promises that they can rely upon, so that they can then make decisions about how much to spend, how much to save, and how long to work. These promises may be affected, however, by demographic, economic, political, and institutional developments. Thompson looks at these four risks under two polar opposite systems—a pay-as-you-go defined-benefit plan and a fully funded defined-contribution plan.

In terms of demographics, both a decrease in fertility and an increase in life expectancy will increase the ratio of beneficiaries to workers, but they will have different impacts on the two systems. A decline in fertility has no direct impact on a defined-contribution plan, since each worker finances his own benefits. In contrast, a decline in fertility will push a defined-benefit system into deficit, which will require some combination of higher taxes and reduced benefits.

Benefit promises under both a defined-benefit and defined-contribution plan are very sensitive to changes in life expectancy. As we know from the current U.S. situation, an increase in the aged dependency ratio from changes due to either fertility or mortality requires higher taxes, a later retirement age, or lower benefits. Technically the only benefit promises in a defined-contribution plan are that retirement income will reflect the assets accumulated by the time an individual retires, and that after retirement the provider of the annuity will actually honor the benefit commitments. But the implicit promise is that contribution rates are set at a level such that the assets will produce enough income to hit a target wage replacement rate. In the defined-contribution model, retirement benefits are just as sensitive to unexpected changes in life expectancy as in the defined-benefit model. Without any change in contribution rates, longer life expectancies will result in lower annual benefits and therefore lower replacement rates.

In terms of economic variables, Thompson concludes that unexpected changes in wages or interest rates more or less wash out for defined-benefit plans, but create major risks for defined-contribution plans. Higher than expected investment returns reduce accumulations required to achieve a target replacement rate. Higher than expected wage growth increases the amount of required retirement income to achieve a target replacement rate and therefore increases the amount of required accumulations. Thus, the relationship between investment returns and wage growth is critical under a defined-contribution plan.

Thompson performs a number of simulations based on the postwar history of wages, interest rates, and stock market returns in Germany, Japan, the United Kingdom, and the United States to get a sense of the magnitude of the risk associated with unexpected economic developments. Wage growth and investment returns have varied significantly for all four countries. From 1953 to 1973, real wages grew very rapidly and real interest rates were quite low. In the post-1973 period, real interest rates were almost always higher than real wage growth.

Thompson first assumes that the government knew in advance average wage growth and investment returns over the entire postwar period and set the contribution rate accordingly. He then simulates the year-to-year buildup using the actual history and the reverse history. Even with perfect knowledge about averages over the period, the system overshoots by 35 to 40 percent with the actual history and undershoots by 12 to 25 percent with the reverse history. Another simulation assumes the government does not have perfect knowledge but rather adjusts contribution rates every ten years. This time the system overshoots by 50 to 80 percent and undershoots by 35 to 40 percent with actual and reverse history, respectively. In other words, knowing averages over a period is not equivalent to knowing year-by-year fluctuation, and even with complete knowledge of average performance, replacement rates turn out to be 90 percent or 30 percent instead of the 50 percent target.

In short, defined-contribution plans cannot be put on automatic pilot. Just like defined-benefit plans, they need adjustments in response to unexpected economic and demographic developments. There is no way to avoid risk; different plans simply face different types of risks. In such a world, diversification is clearly desirable. Fortunately, the United States already has a mixed system: a defined-benefit plan for the basic pension and a supplementary system that has become increasingly defined contribution. Thompson concludes that we should not change that mix appreciably if we care about producing predictable retirement income.

Henry Aaron agrees that moving to a defined-contribution regime would not take Social Security out of the political arena. Moreover, under defined-contribution plans the adequacy of benefits depends crucially on when individuals retire, which Aaron concludes makes them unreliable as the basic source of retirement income for the mass of workers. Defined-benefit plans also have risks, but these risks are diffused broadly among the population. Aaron's only criticism of Thompson's paper is that by comparing a pay-as-you-go defined-benefit plan with a funded defined-contribution plan he overlooks the real policy choice—namely, a partially funded defined-benefit plan versus a partially funded mixed defined-contribution/defined-benefit plan.

Sylvester Scheiber agrees with Thompson's assessment of the relative risks of defined-contribution and defined-benefit plans and acknowledges that our system diversifies risk by combining the two approaches. He questions, however, the relative sizes of the two components and suggests that Social Security may have become larger than desirable. He points to three factors: large subsidies to early generations may have stimulated unwarranted growth in the program; the majority of the population now pay more in payroll taxes than in income taxes; and Social Security will not be a fair deal for younger workers and future generations.

John Geanakoplos, Olivia Mitchell, and Stephen Zeldes (hereafter GMZ) shift the focus from predictability of retirement income to the question whether privatizing would raise the rate of return to Social Security. Frequent arguments in the popular press suggest that projected returns on Social Security are significantly lower than those offered in U.S. capital markets and therefore workers would be better off if they were allowed to invest directly in private securities. GMZ say that this argument is wrong for two reasons: it ignores transition costs, and it does not deal appropriately with risk.

It is true that private market returns are high and Social Security returns are low. The average annual real return on stocks (1926–96) was 9.4 percent; the corresponding return on intermediate term government bonds was 2.3 percent. In contrast, the real return on Social Security contributions is projected to be roughly 1.3 percent. The reason that projected returns on Social Security contributions are low is that, under our pay-as-you-go system, early generations received large net transfers of roughly $9 trillion, and later generations have to pay the bill. This bill can be paid off in any number of ways, but one obvious candidate is that every generation be required to give up the same percentage of its earnings. Based on the existing $9 trillion unfunded liability, roughly 3 percentage points of the current 12.4 percent payroll tax would go toward covering the startup costs. In other words, 25 percent goes to cover the implicit interest costs on the unfunded liability and earns minus 100 percent; 75 percent earns the market rate for bonds of 2.3 percent. This brings the total return on payroll tax contributions close to the projected rate of 1.3 percent.

In thinking about how privatization would affect the return to Social Security, it is important to differentiate, as Diamond noted in his introductory paper, between privatization (setting up individual accounts in individual workers' names) and prefunding (putting aside reserves to offset the $9 trillion liability). GMZ show that privatization without prefunding will not raise returns on Social Security contributions, after taking account of transition costs and risks. First, consider the transition costs. In a world without uncertainty, workers could send all their new payroll tax contributions to private accounts invested in capital markets and earn higher returns. But then some mechanism must be found to pay off the $9 trillion of unfunded liability. One approach would be to issue recognition bonds to workers and retirees for the full amount. The government, however, would have to raise new taxes to pay the interest on these bonds. GMZ show that the new taxes would eliminate all of the higher returns on individual accounts. In other words, the rate of return in the privatized system, net of new taxes, would be identical to the low returns under the existing system.

Next consider the appropriate treatment of risk. Projected returns on privatized accounts might appear higher because contributions were invested in stocks rather than bonds. But stocks involve considerably more risk than bonds, so their returns need to be adjusted for risk before comparing them with the safe returns from a conventional Social Security system. If all households held both stocks and bonds, they should value an additional dollar of stocks the same as an additional dollar of bonds, even though stocks have a much higher expected return. That is, the risk-adjusted return on stocks and bonds would be identical. In this case, GMZ believe it is appropriate to compare the current system to a privatized system in which the individual accounts were invested only in bonds. This conclusion has to be modified to the extent that some households currently do not have access to equity investment.

In short, privatization without prefunding would not raise returns from Social Security. If prefunding were undertaken either in the trust funds or individual accounts, it would eventually raise returns. But higher returns to future generations would be gained at the expense of lower returns to current generations who have to pay twice, first to cover promised benefits and second to build up reserves. Thus, GMZ conclude that "favoring privatization because it would provide higher returns for all current and future workers is inaccurate and misleading." Rather they say the choice involves weighing the greater freedom and control, reduced political risk, and possible reduced labor supply distortions of privatization against the loss of social risk pooling, higher administrative costs, and the costs of allowing workers to make poor investment choices.

Aaron applauds GMZ's analysis, but says they stop prematurely. GMZ correctly conclude that with proper accounting gross rates of return are the same on equally funded private or public accounts, but they fail to note that the net rate of return will be higher in the public accounts. Aaron offers two reasons. First the administrative costs associated with Social Security are far lower than with privatized accounts. Second, left on their own, individuals frequently try to beat the market and end up doing considerably worse than average. The way to get the highest net return, says Aaron, is to minimize administrative costs and achieve market average rates of return.

Scheiber also agrees that privatization without prefunding will not raise the rate of return on the current system. He agrees that prefunding cannot be achieved without incurring costs. Despite the costs, however, he advocates prefunding in order to improve the rate of return for future generations. Since he believes that the government cannot successfully accumulate reserves, individual accounts need to be an element of Social Security reform.

Karen Holden and Cathleen Zick add another factor that needs to be considered when evaluating the merits of the current system versus privatization—namely, protection for nonearners or lower earners, who tend to be women. Widows have significantly lower incomes than aged couples, with poverty rates about four times as high. That makes them a particularly vulnerable group. The economic burden of widowhood can be cushioned for surviving spouses who have access to private pension income in addition to Social Security. But Salisbury notes that only 24 percent of aged households receive private pension benefits, and Holden and Zick report that only half of the widows of men who received a pension prior to death received a pension as a widow. Moreover, private pension benefits are not inflation indexed, and therefore their value erodes with rising prices. With so little supplementary protection available, the future of survivor benefits under Social Security is terribly important.

If greater individual choice were introduced into the Social Security system, what type of survivorship protection would workers select? To answer that question, Holden and Zick look at the selection of survivor protection in the New Beneficiary Survey. As expected, economic and demographic considerations are important: the greater the wife's own resources, the lower the likelihood of selecting survivor protection; when the wife is substantially older than her husband, the husband is less likely to take a survivor pension. But even after controlling for economic and demographic factors, the 1974 ERISA legislation appears to have had a significant effect. Although only 48 percent of the men whose pension benefits began before 1974 elected a joint-and-survivor option, 64 percent who initiated benefits in 1974 or later did so. In other words, Holden and Zick conclude that without some guidance husbands do not make the best selection for their wives.

The implications of these findings for Social Security, according to Holden and Zick, is that if greater individual choice is introduced into the system, regulations requiring annuitization and a default joint-and-survivor option would be critical to continuing survivor protection. An alternative might be to institute a form of "earnings sharing" by designating the privatized accounts as marital property. This approach combined with mandatory annuitization at retirement might be another way to ensure protection for widows.

Aaron and Scheiber have very different reactions to the paper by Holden and Zick. Aaron's response is that as policymakers start imposing increasing regulations in order to duplicate the protections of Social Security they may well ask themselves why they are moving to privatized accounts in the first place. Scheiber's reaction is that protection for surviving spouses could be easily achieved under a system of individual accounts. In fact, he feels that earnings sharing could be more easily achieved with individual accounts than under the current system. He also sees no problem with mandating joint-and-survivor benefits for married couples.

Insights from Social Security Reform Abroad

The United States is not alone in thinking about reforming its public pension system. Kent Weaver summarizes the experiences of other advanced industrial countries and their lessons for the United States, since these countries are ahead of the United States in terms of aging of the population and, in some cases, have already implemented some reforms.

Weaver identifies four intertwined pressures behind the current waves of activity. First, most countries in the Organization for Economic Cooperation and Development (OECD) have pay-as-you-go systems and are experiencing an aging population. Second, the rising pension costs are eating up an increasing share of public budgets across the OECD. In Europe, this problem has been exacerbated by high unemployment, which has caused contributions to fall and outlays to increase as more people retire earlier. Third, high payroll taxes to finance public pensions have created concern over countries' ability to compete in international markets. Tax rates of up to 50 percent are creating more unemployment and incentives for industry to flee to areas with lower taxes. Fourth, a very strong conservative critique of payroll-tax financed systems has grown up across the OECD. The critics claim these plans discourage saving and do not provide adequate returns for retirees.

Given the high costs of public pensions in the other OECD countries relative to the United States and the fact that these countries are much further along in the demographic bulge, one might expect enormous change. But pressure for change has been moderated by political factors. Politicians in all countries want to avoid or, at least, diffuse blame. Therefore, policies with long lead times and nonobvious technical fixes are particularly appealing. Politicians are constrained also by the "past heritage of policy choices." Having a well-entrenched public pension system makes it almost impossible for countries to start afresh with a dramatically different system or to eliminate tiers of pensions. Public pension programs also create their own constituencies with a stake in preserving benefits. Finally, political institutions also have an important impact on the degree to which compromises have to be made to secure enactment of an initiative.

Political forces have meant that change has been mostly incremental. Most other OECD countries have retrenched slightly on benefits, by cutting indexation at the margin, raising retirement ages, which were very low by U.S. standards, and clawing back some benefits paid to upper-income retirees. On the revenue side, governments have been more willing to raise payroll taxes than appears to be true in the United States, and some have increased the general revenue contribution. The restructuring that has taken place has involved some movement toward partial advanced funding of the earnings-related pension (Canada and Sweden), encouraging private supplementary pension funds through favorable tax treatment and other means (Italy and France), creating a closer link between contributions and benefits for the individual, and linking initial benefits to life expectancy. Only the U.K. has allowed an opt-out from the earnings-related pension plan.

Weaver offers three general conclusions for the United States based on the politics abroad. First, governments face a clear trade-off with regard to making program changes transparent. On the one hand, individuals need explicit information about benefit cutbacks so that they can adjust their behavior. On the other hand, the more clearly cutbacks are portrayed, the more difficult they are to enact. As a result, most of the reforms have been enacted through obfuscation, by tinkering with the benefit formula or phasing in changes in the retirement age over a long period. Second, the other OECD countries have not come up with any magic bullets; they are working with the same kind of incremental adjustments considered in the United States in 1977 and 1983. Third, very little generational politics has been evident. Fourth, taxes are less taboo abroad than one would have concluded based on the current debate in the United States, suggesting that they may be more politically possible in the future than they appear now.

John Myles is not persuaded by Weaver's list of demographic, budget, and competitiveness concerns, and a shift to conservative ideology to explain the near universal rush to reform public pensions. First, governments on the left as well as the right have introduced pension reform. Indeed, most large European reforms have taken place not only with the participation of organized labor but with their approval. Second, enthusiasm for reform appears unrelated to the current and projected level of pension costs. For example, as a percent of GDP, U.S. outlays for Social Security are scheduled to rise from 4.6 percent to 6.8 percent; this is very different from the European situation, where costs are scheduled to go from 10 percent to 16 percent. The real concern appears to be the projected increase in those costs. Myles hypothesizes that the increase is important because most OECD public pension systems are financed by a payroll tax on the bottom two-thirds of the wage bill.

Myles also notes that the late 1980s and early 1990s was a period of expansion as well as retrenchment in public pension systems. Australia, Denmark, Ireland, the Netherlands, and New Zealand had basic universal flat pensions, but no second tier of earnings-related pension. By the mid-1990s, three of the five—Australia, Denmark, and the Netherlands—had developed universal or near universal contributory employer pensions. These pensions were very different than earlier versions. They tended to be funded, and responsibility for variation in benefits did not rest with government. For example, Australia and Denmark adopted the defined-contribution approach so that future benefit changes depend on market returns, and the Netherlands placed responsibility for meeting their defined-benefit commitments on employers.

The new pension systems look very much like the structure advocated by the World Bank. Under this structure, the government provides a first tier of basic security aimed at preventing poverty. Second-tier provisions are earnings related and fully funded. Does this mean that all systems will tend to converge to the World Bank format? Unlikely, says Myles. Existing programs put real constraints on the degree of possible change.

Finally, Myles views the changes taking place in Europe as frequently mischaracterized as a shift from defined-benefit to defined-contribution plans. In countries like Italy and Spain the change is more appropriately characterized as a separation of the income redistribution and insurance functions. First, benefits are made increasingly proportional to contributions with an imputed return linked to the rate of economic growth and annuitized based on cohort-specific life expectancies. In addition, final earnings formulas that redistribute income from those with many years of contributions to those with few years of contributions at high earnings, such as women, are being eliminated. Second, provisions are introduced to provide pension credits for parental leave and for periods of training and education. The redistributive elements are not being entirely eliminated but are being made more visible and targeted. The objective of making these components more visible is to divide financing responsibility. Labor is supportive of this approach because it eases some of the pressure on the payroll tax. Governments like it because its responsibility for future changes is limited to the redistributive portion of the program.

Commentators from the U.K., Germany, and Canada related Weaver's and Myles's general assessments to developments in their own countries. Richard Disney notes that the U.K. social security system has developed very differently from those in the rest of Europe. It provides quite modest benefits, which as a percent of GDP are much closer to U.S. than to European levels. Moreover, unlike almost any other country, U.K. social security expenditures are expected to be lower relative to GDP in 2030 than they are today. The U.K. system conforms to the World Bank scheme of a flat floor benefit, an earnings-related second tier, and a third tier of tax-favored savings vehicles. A particular feature is the ability to opt out of the second tier State Earnings Related Pension Scheme (SERPS) into private pension arrangements. The second tier is now largely privatized, with less than 20 percent of the eligible work force remaining in SERPS. As a result, Disney says that three-quarters of pensioners in the future are likely to receive three-quarters of their pensions from private sources. The U.K. has made the transition to a largely funded pension system without any public outcry, but the contracting-out scheme is very complicated and transaction costs are very high. Some observers also worry that the basic floor of protection is too low and that low-income workers who may receive little from private pensions will end up with inadequate replacement.

Disney attributes the unique development of the U.K. pension system to Weaver's notion of "past heritage of policy choices." The U.K. had very little experience with a public earnings-related pension scheme. The important institutions in the U.K. were the floor benefit emerging from Beveridge's welfare state in the late 1940s and supplementary private pension plans. SERPS was really an experiment, begun in 1975 and cut back substantially in 1986. Because SERPS was never viewed as an important national institution, it did not impede the movement to a largely funded, privatized system. Institutional factors also played a role, particularly a strong private pension lobby. But Disney cautions against adopting too mechanistic a link between institutions and processes on the one hand and the evolution of pension reform on the other.

Winfried Schmähl says that Germany is at a crossroads in pension policy; it is moving away from a system that combines insurance and income redistribution to a system with a close link between contributions and benefits. The new approach could be described as individual accounts within a defined-benefit pay-as-you-go scheme. A stronger benefit-contribution link increases the political acceptability of the benefits, allows the separation of financing for the insurance and redistributional components of the plan, and avoids paying for some of the social costs of German reunification with a tax on only labor income. The link was strengthened by reducing credits for years of schooling and of child care, by introducing an actuarial reduction for early retirement, and by adjusting the benefit formula to reflect changes in life expectancy. (The value-added tax was then increased 1 percent to pay for explicit redistributional provisions.) The demographic adjustment is the most controversial, particularly since, unlike in Sweden where only new cohorts will receive lower pensions if life expectancy increases, it will reduce the benefits of current retirees. Not only will the adjustment reduce benefits (by roughly 1.5 percent of taxable payrolls in the long run), it will also create uncertainty about future benefits levels. Shifting the risk to retirees may create problems, but the difficulties may not be evident for some time since like most pension changes the effect will be felt only very gradually. The relevance of the German experience for the United States, as Schmähl sees it, centers on the issue of determining the appropriate roles for insurance and income redistribution in a national pension plan.

In discussing Canadian pension developments, David Walker shifted the focus from plan structure to process for reform. The Canadian Pension Plan (CPP) is the second tier of a three-tier system, with a flat guarantee below and tax-favored individual savings instruments and private pensions above. The CPP is quite like the U.S. Social Security program, providing earnings-related benefits as well as benefits in the case of disability or death of a breadwinner. Moreover, there are other similarities. Both countries are facing the retirement of the baby boom, albeit earlier in Canada than in the United States. Both have financed their plans on a pay-as-you-go basis and invest surpluses in government bonds. Both countries have well-developed private pension plans, which have shifted sharply from defined-benefit to defined-contribution arrangements. Individuals have become enthusiastic about accumulating their own funds and critical of the national plan's low returns. In both countries, intellectuals, think tanks, and investment houses have been promoting funded defined-contribution options from countries like Chile, Singapore and, more recently, Mexico, which have never had well-functioning pay-as-you-go plans.

While the plans and environments are similar, Canada's political structure lends itself much more easily to dramatic public action than the United States. Because political bargaining after a bill has been introduced is rare, consensus is absolutely necessary at the beginning of an initiative. Since the provinces had to approve any changes to the CPP, officials of the federal government worked with those in the provincial capitals to develop a common base of knowledge and a common approach. The ministers of finance then produced a cautious paper that provided information and laid out options. This differs sharply from the U.S. experience where the Advisory Council handed the president a report with three distinct proposals that immediately created supporters and detractors.

The Canadian government then used the paper as a basis for discussion in meetings (33) throughout the country. These meetings, which produced the principles for any comprehensive reform, combined with both internal and external consultations, led key strategists to propose three changes: a near doubling of payroll tax contributions within five to seven years; a 10 percent cut in disability and retirement pensions over the next twenty years; and a shift in the investment strategy from provincial bonds to a more diversified portfolio. According to Walker, this package satisfied those in the private pension industry who had argued that an investment strategy similar to private pension plans could improve returns. It muted the criticism from those who thought the CPP was about to disappear. It satisfied contributors who recognized that higher returns would stem the need for future rate hikes. Even those who supported the Chilean approach viewed this solution as a step in the right direction. Walker concludes that, although the specifics may differ for the United States, the tripod on which to build the case for reform—benefit cuts, contribution increases, and changes in investment policy—will be the same.

Public Investment in Private Markets

One important factor driving all types of reform proposals is the maturation of the Social Security program and the sharp decline in return on payroll tax contributions (the so-called money's worth issue). Since raising taxes or reducing benefits will only worsen returns, almost all reform plans in one way or another attempt to capture additional revenues through the higher returns associated with equity investment. Some proposals suggest investing in equities through individually managed IRA-type accounts, others involve the Social Security program. Social Security investment in equities can be done either directly through the trust funds or indirectly through the creation of a separate 401(k)-type component. Although the two Social Security managed approaches may sound quite different, both involve the government designating the investment options and maintaining control of the money.

Critics of broadening investment options for Social Security raise several concerns. The two most frequently mentioned pertain to pressures for "social investing," whereby investments would be selected for social or political goals rather than for their risk/return profiles, and the potential for the government to interfere with corporate governance through its role as a shareholder. Theodore Angelis explores these concerns and assesses their seriousness by examining the experience of state pension plans and the Federal Thrift Savings Plan (TSP).

Angelis identifies three issues that arise under the heading of social investing. The first is avoiding firms that are perceived to be unethical; in the 1980s this took the form of selling shares of companies that did business in South Africa, and more recently it has involved eliminating tobacco holdings. The second is targeting neglected investments, such as low-income housing or small business. The third is spending on empowerment zones or public infrastructure. State pension funds have engaged in all these activities. They have not lost huge sums of money, but they have conflated the regulator and investor role of government, added a moral component with no clear boundaries, and eroded confidence in public investing.

To avoid these activities, proponents of investing in equities through Social Security have supported the Thrift Savings Plan model. TSP designers insulated investment decisions from social investing by setting up an independent investment board, narrowing investment choices, and requiring strict fiduciary duties. The TSP also operates in a political culture of noninterference. Its creation involved five years of open forums and debate designed to create strong bipartisan support. Its creators made clear from the beginning that economic, not social or political, goals were to be the sole purpose of the investment board. The TSP has perpetuated this norm by refusing to yield to early pressure to invest in "economically targeted investments" or to avoid companies doing business in South Africa or Northern Ireland.

The question is whether Social Security could duplicate TSP's performance. One obvious difference is size; TSP equity holdings in 1996 amounted to only 0.1 percent of the market value of equity outstanding, whereas the Social Security reform proposals would lead to holdings closer to 5 percent of the market by 2020. Size could cut either way: on the one hand, a larger fund may make it a more attractive target; on the other, its importance to millions of Americans could deter noneconomic activities. Another consideration is that TSP was only established in 1986 and therefore has had limited experience with equity investment. A further concern is that because Social Security is a defined-benefit system rather than defined-contribution, participants might be less vigilant in guarding against social investing. Nevertheless, the TSP offers an example of a public plan that has avoided many of the difficulties inherent in public investing by creating strong institutional safeguards and a political mandate for independence.

The second major concern discussed by Angelis is that the government could become a significant force in corporate decisionmaking. To avoid this problem, proponents suggest that the government shares either not be voted or be required to be voted in a pattern that reflected other common shareholders. This approach is intended to ensure that government ownership does not disrupt corporate control in any way. The problem is that large investors lack the ability to exit a stock by selling its shares, and eliminating their vote might make capital markets less efficient. An alternative strategy would push proxy decisions down to the individual portfolio managers as is done in the case of the TSP. This strategy would allow portfolio managers to exercise voting rights to maximize share values. Other alternatives involve auctioning voting rights to other investors or limiting the amount that the trust fund could hold in any one company to, say, 5 percent. Each approach has strengths and weaknesses that would need careful assessment.

One issue that might be more troublesome at the federal level than at the state level is international investments. For example, if the trust fund held equities in Mexican companies, selling off these shares at the time of the Mexican peso crisis would have signaled U.S. lack of confidence, and exacerbated the problem. Although proponents have called for the use of global indexes, limiting investments to domestic companies is an alternative. Such a limitation may not be that restrictive in an era when many domestic companies have offices around the globe and derive much of their earnings from international activity.

Howell Jackson is optimistic that buying a broad index and delegating voting to fund managers should allow the Social Security trust funds to invest in equities without disrupting capital markets or corporations. Moreover, he points out that the alternative route—namely, IRA-type personal accounts—is fraught with perils of its own. The potential for abuse and overreaching by financial intermediaries is great, given the large number of people involved—many in the market for the first time—and the enormous sums of money. In addition, without some constraints, many individuals would take on substantial financial risk, which could produce big variations in outcomes not only across the population but also across generations.

In order to protect participants, the government is likely to introduce regulation. It probably will not want to deal with 6–7 million employers, so it will turn its attention to the financial firms that could provide services to privatized accounts. But Jackson points out that the financial service industry is highly fragmented; it consists of tens of thousands of firms in different sectors subject to varying degrees of regulation. For example, banks, insurance companies, and money market mutual funds are subject to strict investment restrictions and mandatory capital requirements. Privatized accounts invested through these intermediaries would involve minimal financial risk. In contrast, registered broker dealers, investment advisers, and investment companies are subject only to fiduciary standards and disclosure obligations. Accounts invested through these intermediaries would involve greater financial risk. In order to ensure uniform oversight to these varied organizations, Jackson believes that the government would seek to limit the number of players to, say, fifty entities, perhaps those with the best regulatory records.

It would be possible to rely on existing industry regulation for each of the selected firms, but a more likely option to ensure consistency and uniformity would be to introduce overarching legislation for all providers. At a minimum, this would involve disclosure of fees and perhaps could include fiduciary responsibility on the part of providers to recommend only "suitable" investments. This could involve the requirement to steer participants toward broad diversified pools of equities or toward low-risk instruments such as inflation-indexed bonds, bank CDs, or regulated annuities. Providers might also be required to deter participants from adjusting their accounts too frequently— perhaps limiting adjustments to once a year. To protect against long-term swings in investment returns, providers might even urge participants to purchase insurance that guarantees a minimum return on privatized account investments. Supervisory responsibility for ensuring that these requirements would be met could rest either with the Social Security Administration or be delegated to the primary regulators. Jackson favors the more centralized approach in order to ensure uniformity.

Jackson concludes that privatized IRA-type accounts may not be worth the effort. A full array of regulatory restraints would leave very little room for market competition and would involve substantial costs. It makes more sense to Jackson simply to have the government designate the investment funds as in a 401(k) approach. Moreover, to the extent that Social Security participants were required to purchase insurance against intergenerational variations in return, it may be even more sensible to stick with today's defined-benefit plan and simply broaden Social Security's portfolio.

Francis Cavanaugh agrees, based on his experience as executive director of the TSP, that broadening Social Security's portfolio to include equities is desirable and feasible. This was not always his view. As a career Treasury official he repeatedly advised against proposals from private financial institutions who wanted to manage the trust funds and improve their returns by investing in stocks. He viewed equities as too risky and believed that government ownership would give government control over corporate business. He accepted the TSP job because Congress structured the federal plan in a way that totally addressed these concerns. In Cavanaugh's view, requiring investment through broad indexes reduces the risks of equity investment, and prohibiting the government from voting its shares virtually eliminates the potential for government control of individual corporations.

Moreover, the TSP is insulated from political interference. It is administered by five part-time board members, who are appointed by the president and by a full-time executive director. The board members and employees are subject to strict fiduciary rules, which if breached would make them civilly and criminally liable. The board is not dependent upon the congressional appropriation process, since it can make necessary expenditures from the fund. The money in the TSP fund is owned by the participants, who are solely entitled to the contributions and earnings. Even though Social Security is a defined-benefit rather a defined-contribution plan, Cavanaugh is optimistic that the assets would be viewed as belonging to Social Security participants as a group and thereby insulated from congressional meddling.

Cavanaugh favors direct investment by the trust funds rather than trying to duplicate the TSP for Social Security. The TSP works well because the federal agencies distribute forms, educate employees, and transmit data on a timely basis regarding payroll deductions, investment choices, and so on. This would be a daunting task for the millions of small employers who are currently required to transmit Social Security tax information only once a year. Moreover, the Social Security population has considerably lower earnings than federal employees, which would make the transaction costs much more burdensome as a percent of annual contributions.

Ian Lanoff also supports direct equity investment by the Social Security trust funds, since this approach best addresses the risk raised by Angelis. Lanoff believes that investing in a broad index and applying ERISA fiduciary standards to the board should preclude any form of social investing, which, in any event, has occurred in only a few plans at the state level primarily in response to pressure from state legislatures. Like the TSP, the Board of the Social Security funds should shift the voting responsibility to portfolio managers, which is common practice among public and private funds with the exception of the California Public Employees' Retirement System (CalPERS) and a few others. It would be perfectly reasonable for Congress to prohibit overseas investment given the concern about interference with foreign governments.

The 401(k) approach might be a viable option, but because names are attached to individual accounts it raises more concerns about voting shares. Even though the assets are pooled, individual account holders could be put under pressure to vote their shares in specific ways in the event of corporate takeovers or downsizing. Moreover, as soon as individuals have discretion over their investments, the government will have to devise a way to educate participants on how to make wise investment choices. Lanoff dismisses the IRA privatized approach because it would produce " a broker in every living room" and subject individuals to excessive risk. Individuals would be solicited to vote their shares, and they would end up holding foreign equities. In response, Lanoff expects government to intervene to limit the investment options, so both brokers and the government, as Jackson suggests, would end up in people's living rooms.

Despite the apparent success of the TSP and the endorsement of other panel members, Warren Batts, reflecting the position of the National Association of Manufacturers, views the possibility of equity investment by the Social Security trust funds as a minefield. The easiest way to avoid the problems is to set up individually managed IRA-type accounts, so the investments occur outside government. Batts is sanguine about the transaction costs associated with managing these accounts because he believes that competition between potential fund managers should keep them low.

Public Opinion and the Politics of Reforming Social Security

It is fine for academics to sit around and think about clever ways of reforming the system, but in the end the public's views on these issues and the politics associated with enacting legislation are going to dominate.

Lawrence Jacobs and Robert Shapiro contend that the press often reports opinion polls results in a haphazard fashion and out of context. They argue, based on a comprehensive review of polling data on Social Security over the last 20 years, that many of the common assumptions about what the public knows and thinks regarding Social Security are often wrong or based on half-truths. For example, policymakers often assume that the public does not know very much about Social Security. In fact, in surveys since 1973, roughly 50 percent of respondents have described themselves as "very" or "fairly" well informed. These self-assessments, the authors contend, seem correct. Not surprisingly, those who are better educated and more affluent have a better understanding of the program.

In terms of thinking about how public opinion will play into reform efforts, it is important to differentiate between confidence in the system and support for the system. Third Millennium (a group of conservative young people interested in privatizing Social Security) issued a startling (and incorrect) report that people had more confidence in the existence of UFOs than in Social Security's future. This report left the impression that confidence in the system had suddenly collapsed and that the public no longer supported the program. In fact, confidence in the future of the program stood at 65 percent in 1975, dropped steadily to 32 percent by 1982, and has remained there since. Thus, weak confidence is not a new development.

Despite weak confidence, survey questions indicate sustained and very strong support for Social Security. Nine out of ten Americans say that spending on Social Security is "about right" or "too little." Over the past fifteen years of surveys, two-thirds of Americans have opposed cutting Social Security as a means of reducing budget deficits. Further polling suggests that Americans support the

Social Security program not because it satisfies a simple calculation of money's worth but because it provides insurance against the risk of low income in retirement and a protection from bearing the burden of financially drained parents.

Contrary to press reports, Jacobs and Shapiro conclude that the public is not eager for major change in its Social Security program. Balanced surveys—that is, surveys where questions reference the greater risk as well as greater return—reveal significant resistance to proposals to replace the current system with individual accounts invested in the stock market. In terms of the need for some change to restore financial balance to Social Security, the results are mixed. Although 83 percent of respondents in a 1997 poll agreed that "major changes" will be necessary at some point to "guarantee the future financial stability of the system," the public does not consider Social Security's financing problems an urgent crisis. Of possible incremental reforms, Americans are open to the idea of reducing the cost-of-living adjustment and of scaling back benefits of upper-income individuals, but resist hiking the retirement age. When the public is forced to wrestle with the trade-offs facing policymakers, they prefer tax hikes to benefit cuts. These mixed reactions to even incremental types of benefit cuts suggest that enacting Social Security legislation will require concerted and bipartisan efforts.

The future course of public opinion will be shaped by Americans' distrust of government and the material reported to them by journalists, say Jacobs and Shapiro. As politicians launch campaigns to sell their favorite proposals, journalists will help the process if they present both sides of issues and report an accurate picture of public opinion itself.

Discussants questioned Jacobs and Shapiro's optimistic assessment of the public's understanding of Social Security. Edward Gramlich felt that achieving 56 percent success on self-reports was not that impressive. He was discouraged by results showing that only 33 percent of respondents understood that Social Security was one of the two largest federal programs. He also found the discrepancy between low confidence and strong support puzzling and attributed it to asking blunt questions like, "Do you support Social Security?" Such questions will inevitably elicit positive responses since virtually everyone recognizes the important social protections provided by the program. Gramlich argued that pollsters would gain more information by asking about competing options. Similarly, in terms of the public's views on specific incremental changes, it would be better to ask focus groups how they would restore balance rather than asking respondents if they supported a particular benefit cut or tax increase.

Based on reaction from her readers, Susan Dentzer is also less confident than Jacobs and Shapiro about the public's understanding of Social Security. She offers three suggestions for how the press could improve the situation.

First, the press could clarify the important role that demographics play in the Social Security debate—not just the baby boom-baby bust phenomenon but also the great gains in life expectancy. This might make the public more receptive to the notion of extending the retirement age.

Second, the press should avoid taking sides. She feels that "yuppified" journalists have been unduly enthusiastic about proposals to privatize the system. Third, the press should acknowledge the uncertainties and resist doom-and-gloom prognostications.

Social Security reform will depend not only on what the public thinks about the program but also on how politicians behave. What are the chances that Congress will tackle Social Security and enact reforms in the next few years? What is the likelihood of a comprehensive new system as opposed to modest adjustments to the existing one? Are some reforms more politically attractive than others? Douglas Arnold addresses these important questions. He begins by noting two implications that result from the fact that Social Security's problem is long term and that it faces no immediate crisis. First, no action-forcing event compels politicians to act and, second, policymakers can consider a broader array of reforms.

Against this background, Arnold explores the issue of advance funding, common to all reform proposals in various degrees. Although advance funding has merits, various estimates suggest that the generation caught in the transition would have to pay taxes of up to 8 percentage points to achieve a fully funded system. This is a politician's nightmare—highly visible short-term costs for benefits that will accrue only to generations in the future. Of course less ambitious advance funding would require smaller transition costs, and Arnold argues that some prefunding is not necessarily out of the question. But for politicians to be willing to enact costs-now/benefits-later legislation, they have to believe it is in their self-interest. This can occur only if large majorities of Americans acknowledge the gains of advance funding and indicate a willingness to pay the transition costs.

It is in the interest of Congress to make costs as imperceptible as possible. Although Congress has raised the Social Security tax over the history of the program from 1 percent each on the employee and employers to 6.2 percent each, it has done so in twenty separate steps averaging 0.26 percent per step. As a prime violator of this traditional congressional preference, Arnold cites Gramlich's proposals to raise taxes immediately to finance individual accounts and place all the additional costs on the employee. Although the plan was designed as a moderate alternative between the two other Advisory Council options, Arnold views it as the "least graceful in imposing new taxes."

Although past congressional responses provide some guide to the prefunding issue, they offer no clue to how Congress will respond to the dramatically different proposals about how to structure the system. The alternatives represent very different philosophies about the trade-off between universal retirement security and the importance of individual choice. All the Advisory Council groups advocate equity investment, but they split sharply on the desirability of the government undertaking such activity. One group viewed the potential of government interference in corporate affairs as extremely serious and proposed personal security accounts as an alternative to trust fund investment. Congress will have to decide whether it is worth the additional costs to establish, administer, and maintain millions of personal security accounts, rather than maintain a single centrally managed trust fund. Similarly, Congress must decide whether it makes sense for millions of workers to make their own investment decisions in a public pension system. Some workers will do well, but others will fare poorly. Gramlich's plan occupies the middle ground among the Advisory Council plans on investment decisions, annuitization, and the trade-off between individual choice and retirement security. It does so, however, by allowing government continued control over the assets.

In the end, Congress is unlikely to accept any of the plans currently on the table, but rather will draft its own plan from the vast array of available options. Proponents of comprehensive reform face an uphill battle in this effort, since the status quo is familiar and popular. Individual control also brings individual risk and any move toward prefunding involves those large transition costs. Blocking dramatic change is easy in our political system. In any event, all students of Social Security are convinced that early action is desirable. Changes in taxes and benefits are modest if made in the next few years, but become very large if reform is postponed for thirty years. Moreover, stalemate is not neutral; the price of advance funding soars as reform is delayed.

Edward Gramlich responds to Arnold's criticism regarding the political packaging of his proposal, arguing that Advisory Council members have different roles than politicians. If increasing saving is viewed as a high priority, then Advisory Council members have a responsibility to make it clear that raising contributions to individual accounts immediately—before the baby boomers start to retire—is the appropriate response. Phasing in such a change is at variance with good policy. In contrast, phasing in benefit cuts in order to give people time to change their plans is both good policy and good politics. Gramlich suggests that the inelegance of his proposal could be softened by the harmless move of splitting the tax between employer and employee or by achieving the additional saving through inducing employers to cover more workers in their supplementary defined-contribution plans. But selling proposals should be the job of politicians; the responsibility of council members is to define the problem clearly and offer well-defined solutions.

Paul Light, using his extensive knowledge of the 1983 Greenspan Commission, speculates whether the process inaugurated by President Clinton could produce an agreement by the end of the year. He makes four points. First, the lack of a clearly defined immediate problem makes the challenge harder today than in 1983. Second, agreements require backroom bargaining, so a purely public process is unlikely to produce a plan. Third, politics played an important role in 1983 and will certainly be important this time around. Finally, the public was engaged in 1983, so beginning a national conversation on Social Security is an important development.

Conclusion

The conclusion that emerges from this conference is that important values are at stake in the debate over how to structure the program in the future. It is on questions of values and assessments of political risks that people disagree; the economics, while interesting, complicated, and often misreported, is not controversial.

Hugh Heclo says that the public is particularly ripe for manipulation in the debate about the future of Social Security. He views most people as misinformed about important features of the Social Security program, fearful about their economic future, and distrustful of government. In this vulnerable condition they face a range of options for Social Security that is beyond anything in their living memory and an environment that is highly politicized. Given the difficulties faced by the public, everyone engaged in the debate has a responsibility to lay out both the pros and cons of their options and not oversell their ideas.

Reasoned debate is in everyone's interest. Conference participants agree that early action on Social Security is desirable and that deferring decisions until the baby boom starts to retire is costly. The sooner changes are made, the more modest the required tax increase or benefit cut, and the more time workers will have to adjust their behavior. Achieving congressional action, however, requires finding common ground on values and some comfort about political dynamics. The participants in this conference moved the debate forward by clarifying the consensus on the economics and explicitly elevating questions of values and politics.

2

Values, Politics, and Economics in Social Security Reform

T HE SOCIAL SECURITY debate raises questions of economics, politics, and values. Remarkably, as the papers summarized in this chapter indicate, economists are in general agreement on the economic issues. The disagreements about the future of the program hinge on values—individual control versus shared security—and political judgments.

A Framework for Considering Social Security Reform
Michael J. Boskin

SOCIAL SECURITY is a large and growing share of federal government spending. It also is a large and growing share of federal taxes. By 1960, already two and a half decades after its start, Social Security accounted for 14 percent (excluding the interest on the debt) of the then much smaller federal budget. Today (excluding interest on the debt) Social Security and Medicare account for 40 percent. Although there is a tendency to separate Social Security and Medicare, to the point of creating separate reform commissions, we must think of resolving the problems in these programs in a close and coordinated fashion because of their combined impact on the budgets of their elderly beneficiaries and their aggregate levels of spending and taxes.

Back in 1960, Social Security tax collections were only 16 percent of the federal tax burden; today, they are over a third. Including the employer contribution to social insurance taxes, the typical family in America pays as much or more in payroll taxes as in income taxes.

The first principle to recognize in discussing Social Security reform is that whatever reforms we make in Social Security—or will be forced to make for fund balance or other reasons—will be intimately tied up with other interests on both the spending and tax sides of the budget. For example, those who are concerned about the alleged regressivity of the tax system point to payroll taxes, looking only at the tax side of the budget, ignoring the outlay side of the budget. But the distributional consequences of social insurance outlays on balance are progressive, because of the progressivity of the formula for paying benefits to recipients.

Social Security and the Economic Status of the Elderly

Social Security also has been significantly responsible for one of the greatest achievements of our society: the tremendous decrease in poverty among the elderly. In 1966, three decades ago, the overall poverty rate was about what it is now. However, the poverty rate of the elderly has declined from almost three times that of the general population to about the same as the general population—maybe slightly below, maybe about the same, depending on whether one looks at families or individuals (obviously, this varies among subgroups within the elderly population; the poverty rate of elderly widows is very high). What would have happened to the poverty rate of the elderly had Social Security not been expanded substantially in this period, both in coverage, in real benefits, and indexing? My own view is that a sizable part of this decline in poverty is attributable to the growth of Social Security, but when we look at the role that Social Security plays on the income side of the elderly, we have to recognize that it has, in part, replaced continued earnings and private savings.

Consider, for example, what has happened in the labor market. In the past three decades, the labor force participation of men 65 and over has gone from a little under 30 percent to 16 percent or so. There has also been a very sharp decline in labor force participation of men 55 to 64 years old. There are many causes of this decline in labor force participation of the elderly. They include structural issues in the labor market and preferences of workers for early retirement. But many studies, my own included—document that Social Security availability and the benefit structure have contributed to this trend to early retirement.[1]

This implies that whatever Social Security reforms we might consider must be evaluated in part based on what they would do to the labor market behavior of the elderly and the young (if taxes are changed, for example), and to private

---

1. Hurd and Boskin (1984).

Figure 2-1. *Medicare HI Is Projected Insolvent by 2008*

Percentage of medicare HI taxable payroll

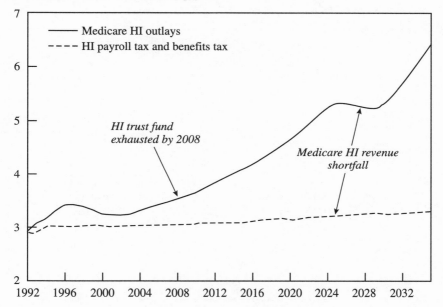

Source: OASDI and HI Board of Trustees, *1998 Annual Reports.*

savings behavior. These all are important matters to the Social Security program itself and to the overall health of the economy.

The Future of Social Security

Next, let us consider the long-run projected future of Social Security. Let us start with Hospital Insurance (HI). It is currently taking in about 1 percent less of taxable payroll than it pays out. Prior to the 1997 balanced budget amendments, the modest reserves in the trust funds were projected to be exhausted by the year 2001. The 1997 legislation pushes that date out a few years but still leaves a large long-run actuarial imbalance (figure 2-1). The gap becomes larger and larger over time, partly owing to projected Medicare inflation, partly to demography.

Social Security faces a similar future. We all know Social Security has been running a cash, so-called operating, surplus. But if we used accrual accounting for Social Security, it would be in deficit if we took the current

Figure 2-2. *Social Security Tax Collections Exceed Current Benefits,*
But Are Not Enough to Fund Future Projected Benefits

Percentage of OASDI taxable payroll

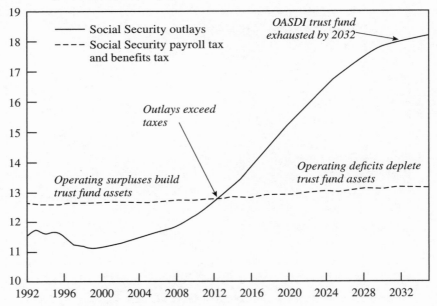

Source: OASDI and HI Board of Trustees, *1998 Annual Reports.*

program benefit structure and projected how much it projects in benefits from
the taxes paid today.

In a few years outlays will start to exceed receipts (figure 2-2). People can
debate when exactly that will occur; that is not my point. Whenever that occurs,
that is the year in which the Treasury has to do something.[2] The Treasury has
to start redeeming the federal government bonds held in the Social Security
trust fund when Social Security shows up and says: "We need them. We need
the cash to pay benefits." Either the federal government has to raise taxes, cut
benefits, or issue debt—new debt—to redeem the Social Security obligations.

Thereafter, there is a large and growing deficit in cash terms. For the remainder of the seventy-five year period, 72 percent of the benefits could be paid by
projected taxes. Some people look at these figures and conclude this is a minor
problem, that a tax increase today of two and one-quarter percentage points

2. Actually, a few years later because of the interest payments earned on the surplus.

Figure 2-3. *Projected OASDI Trust Fund Accumulations in Current Dollars*

End-year asset value (billions of dollars)

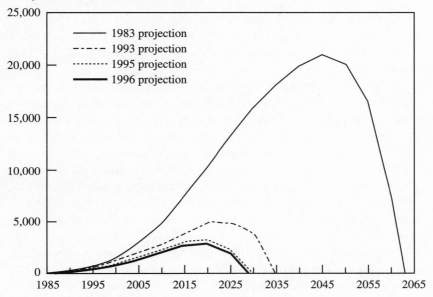

Source: OASDI Board of Trustees, *Annual Reports.*

would take care of this problem for the next seventy-five years. While, technically, that is correct, placed in perspective, that is a substantially larger amount than the Reagan defense buildup, which was only temporary, lasting a few years! It is also true that it is very hard to consider such a tax increase at a time when the general public thinks Social Security is flush in cash and that its surplus is being raided for other purposes. Worse yet, there is an equally large gap beyond the seventy-five years. To put Social Security in actuarial balance already requires almost a 5 percentage point tax increase immediately, much larger if we wait.

Following the Greenspan Commission and the 1983 Social Security reforms, Congress projected that Social Security would build a surplus of 22 trillion dollars, and the trust fund would not be exhausted until about two-thirds of the way into the next century (figure 2-3). Since then, the projections have become progressively more pessimistic in terms of the size of a surplus that we will build up and how long it will last before it is exhausted (until this year when there was a slight improvement).

Demography

There are three important parts to the demography story behind these issues: mortality rates, fertility rates, and the population bulge of the baby boom. At the turn of the century, about 40 percent of Americans could expect to reach age 65. By 1990, that number was 80 percent, and almost a third of Americans could expect to reach age 85.

Many people talk about the gain in life expectancy in pessimistic terms, as a cost. And, certainly, it will put many strains and burdens on our society. However, anybody who thinks that a large gain in life expectancy of the elderly population (most of which is in relatively good health) is a bad thing because it will entail some sizable costs is missing the forest for the trees. Whenever I ask: "Who would like to exchange gaining a month a year in life expectancy for the remainder of your life for paying a little more taxes or having lower Social Security benefits?" Nobody volunteers! People unanimously favor the gains in life expectancy. The gains in life expectancy are unambiguously a very good thing.

The changing demography will affect everything about our economy and society, not just our budget and Social Security and private saving and labor market activity, but where people live, how they choose to communicate, the savings and private insurance vehicles they are going to need to deal with various contingencies, and more.

Future demographic pressures come in a variety of guises, and an overlooked fact is that demographic conditions have been one of the three reasons we have been able to balance the budget. The other two are the peace dividend—and the accompanying sharp reduction in defense spending—and the robust economy we have enjoyed for most of the past fifteen years—by the way, not just since 1993.

We have enjoyed a remarkably benign demography. The ratio of the elderly to the working age population has been essentially flat for many years and will be for another ten years or so before it starts to rise due to the retirement of the baby boomers, after which it will increase by about 50 percent (figure 2-4). Then, it will be common for four generations within families to be alive simultaneously.

I believe the economic projections for the medium term are a little bit pessimistic, but the demographic projections are likely to prove optimistic in terms of trust fund balances. The Census Bureau, along with many private demographers, projects three or four times as many people over the age of 100 and more over the age of 85 than does the Social Security Administration.

Figure 2-4. *Future Demographic Pressures*

OLD-AGE DEPENDENCY RATIO

Persons aged 65+/Persons aged 18–64

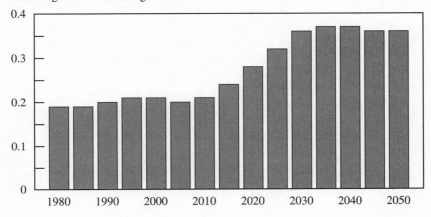

PROJECTED GROWTH IN POPULATION BY AGE GROUP

Percent, 1980–2030

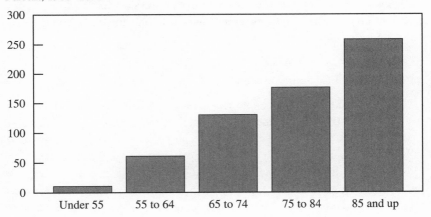

Source: Bureau of the Census.

International Comparisons:
A Window on the Future and an Opportunity

The same issues we face confront the other G-7 countries. In all the G-7 countries, the old age dependency ratios are going up substantially. We are going from one retiree for every three and a quarter workers to one for every two.

Germany is moving toward one retiree per worker. So, for those of you who believe in privatization of Social Security, Germany should have the easiest time doing it. They can just buddy-up. Note that despite our large projected deficit in Social Security and the analogous gap in Medicare, our major competitors will have even greater fiscal burdens associated with their demographic transitions.

These large projected deficits in Social Security and Medicare will lead to very large overall budget deficits, which the CBO projects to amount to 15 to 20 percent of GDP, a quarter of the way into the next century.

Over the past quarter of a century, America had 44 million more working age people, more than that join the labor force, small increases in unemployment and government employment in this period, and a huge number of private sector jobs created.

In sharp contrast, during this period, there were large increases in the working age population in Europe, many fewer people entering the labor force, huge increases in unemployment and government employment, which in Europe may be less distinguishable from unemployment than in the United States, and fewer private sector jobs. Surely part of the explanation for the superior performance of the American economy is the far smaller role of the government in taxes, spending, regulation, mandates, and industrial policy.

Thus, doing something soon to prevent the pressure for large future tax increases that would crush the economy and exacerbate the funding problem is an urgent priority.

The Political Economy of Reform

It is often said that when people start receiving Social Security benefits, for example, when the baby boomers retire, that their own narrow self-interest will make it harder for us to make changes because they will resist changes that reduce their projected benefits. However, if people treat the taxes that they have already paid in during their life as sunk costs, and then ask how much they will get in the present value of benefits in the future if the current system is maintained, compared with the additional taxes they will pay, narrow self-interest in favor of maintaining the status quo and tax increases to fund the actuarial deficit may kick in as early as the mid-forties.

Of course, many other things affect how people will vote. They care about their parents and grandparents. They care about their children. My main point is simply this: the way these demographic pressures may work through the voting process requires the nation to get on with Social Security reform soon, far sooner than hypothetical trust fund exhaustion dates.

Reforms

Because of those long-term actuarial problems, there is going to be intense pressure to reform Social Security sometime soon. It will probably occur at the latest as the baby boomers are beginning to retire. That will be a bad time to undertake reform. It would be much better to build a consensus and make reforms in the relatively near future so people will have an opportunity to do their own planning with some assurance about the Social Security system they will have when they retire. Even if we did not have these long-run actuarial problems, it would be important to make some nontrivial changes in Social Security. I have outlined some of these in my previous writings.[3] Among the variety of reforms that should be considered are more accurate cost-of-living adjustments (COLAs)—preferably accomplished through improvements by the BLS—increases in retirement ages, and changes in the benefit and tax structure. We should also consider more fundamental changes in the tax structure, some of which people call "privatization," that is, giving people additional opportunities that they do not have now to invest some of their payroll taxes privately. I believe some such set of reforms would be desirable to prevent a drain on saving and growth in the future, as well as to improve the efficiency, fairness, and financial soundness of the system.

The Transition Problem

The transition issues are very important. Nobody is suggesting that the benefits of people who have already retired or will retire soon be radically altered. For younger people, whatever reforms are made should gradually phase in more fully.

The total current unfunded liability of Social Security promises in round numbers is 10 trillion dollars—double the current national debt. Some have suggested that these promises and expectations are already incorporated into private behavior and that issuing 10 trillion dollars in recognition bonds, or raising taxes a like amount in present value, would have no impact on the economy, it would just be a wash with the unfunded liabilities. My view is that we cannot be sure what impact issuing such sizable explicit debt, or increased taxes or annual deficits that cumulate in present value to this amount, would have on the economy. It would not be wise to assume this step would be a nonevent.

---

3. Boskin (1986); Boskin and others (1987); Boskin, Kotlikoff, and Shoven (1988).

Conclusion: The Importance of Economic Growth

Finally, a large and underappreciated part of the story is the role of economic growth in dealing with these issues. Economic growth is the single most important factor in thinking about intergenerational equity. If people a generation or two from now will be much richer than we are, that would be a very different environment in which to be worried about the intergenerational transfers in Social Security than if they are going to be only slightly richer. Economic growth and reform of Social Security and Medicare are closely interrelated, with each affecting the other in important ways. A significantly higher growth rate would make many things more affordable, including future costs of these entitlements. But the ability of the economy to generate strong growth is likely to be severely impaired without serious sensible Social Security and Medicare reform. Economic policy must seek to remove barriers to growth. The types of Social Security reforms mentioned above are a major part of that agenda.

The Economics of Social Security Reform
Peter A. Diamond

SOCIAL SECURITY reform proposals raise economic and political questions. The economic questions center on how well a particular reform would deliver retirement, survivor, and disability benefits, and how the reform would affect the overall workings of the economy. Political questions center on what might be legislated now and how a particular plan would evolve over time—changes could occur in response to changing political forces or as a political response to economic and demographic developments. This paper concentrates on the economic questions, identifying places where political arguments are important but not exploring them.[4]

Economic analysis of reform proposals centers on three questions—whether the program should be structured as a defined-benefit plan or a mixed defined-

I have learned a great deal from my colleagues while serving on the Technical Panel on Trends and Issues in Retirement Security of the Advisory Council on Social Security and the Panel on the Privatization of Social Security of the National Academy of Social Insurance. I am grateful to these colleagues. I am also grateful for discussions with Henry Aaron, Courtney Coile, and Virginia Reno, and for financial support from the National Science Foundation under grant SBR-9618698. The views expressed here are my own and not necessarily those of any individual, group, or institution with which I am or have been associated. The same goes for any mistakes in the analysis.

4. More detailed analyses of the economics of reform proposals as well as analyses of the politics of reform proposals can be found in other papers presented at this conference and in Diamond (1997). Since all proposals call for restoring actuarial balance, the paper does not review the size

contribution/defined-benefit plan, how the funding for the retirement income program should be invested, and how much funding the system should have.[5] To organize the issues for these three questions, the paper begins with a discussion of a funded defined-contribution plan with no individual choice about either the portfolio or the form of retirement income. This type of plan is then contrasted with a funded defined-benefit plan, which also has no individual choice. The paper then considers individual choice about the form of retirement and survivor benefits, with particular attention to the possible effects on widows, who are, on average, much poorer than elderly couples. After considering portfolio choice for a central fund, the paper considers individual choice of portfolio, with particular attention to the costs of implementing different methods of individual choice. The paper then considers the implications of having greater funding. Then, the implications of system design for the labor market are examined.

The major economic issues in Social Security reform are, by and large, not controversial. More funding for Social Security involves higher taxes (or lower benefits) in the near term in order to have lower taxes (or higher benefits) in the long run.[6] More funding can reduce the frequency of needed adjustments to Social Security and can increase national savings (beyond the increase that would occur with a traditional Social Security reform). More funding can improve the net financial position of future generations, but only at the cost of worsening the net financial position of current generations (referred to as "money's worth").[7] These economic effects are similar whether the system has individual accounts or not, although the politics will differ.

Just as individuals should generally hold diversified portfolios, and not just Treasury bonds, so too should a central fund. This applies to a defined-contribution system and to a defined-benefit system. Indeed, a defined-

---

of the imbalance nor the case for addressing it sooner rather than later. For the latest estimate of the actuarial deficit, see Board of Trustees, Federal Old-Age and Survivors Insurance and Disability Insurance Trust Fund (1997). For discussion of the importance of addressing the imbalance soon, see Advisory Council on Social Security (1997b).

5. The focus is on alternative proposals that preserve the basic role of Social Security, not the logic of filling such a role. The paper does not consider proposals that eliminate redistribution within Social Security. The paper does not consider proposals to means-test (or affluence-test) Social Security. Such proposals, which relate Social Security benefits to annual income with large implicit taxes, represent taxation of individual savings. Significant taxation of savings does not seem to be a useful part of proposals to increase national savings. Moreover, such proposals would change the basic political status of Social Security.

6. The often-used term "transition costs" does not convey the underlying issues of intergenerational equity implicit in the timing of tax increases and benefit cuts.

7. For a discussion of money's worth calculations and the difficulties in their interpretation, see chapter 3, Geanakoplos, Mitchell, and Zeldes, in this volume.

benefit system that adjusts well to changing circumstances is better able to handle risk than is a defined-contribution system. Portfolio diversification has economic advantages for Social Security participants and for the economy generally. Economically, the case for diversification is clear; but political questions arise about the ability of Social Security to invest well and to avoid improper interference in corporate governance. Introducing individual choice of portfolios and expanding the options beyond a set provided by the government are both responses to these political concerns. It also allows diversity in individual portfolios. In turn, such a move adds to administrative costs and raises questions about the quality of individual investment decisions. It also raises the political question of being able to maintain a mixed system with any given level of redistribution. People hold different values when assessing the importance of different levels of income redistribution and when assessing the importance of allowing additional elements of individual choice. It is unclear whether individual accounts would make the labor market more or less efficient.

My bottom line is that the economics of a well-run defined-benefit system is better than the economics of a mixed defined-contribution/defined-benefit system.[8] The real issue then becomes how well the U.S. government can run a defined-benefit system relative to how well it can run a mixed defined-contribution/defined-benefit system. That is, the basis for genuine disagreement on system design rests on different values and different political expectations, not different economic evaluations.

Benefit Determination with a
Funded Defined-Contribution Plan

In order to clarify the differences in risks between defined-contribution and defined-benefit systems, it is useful to start with the concept of a funded defined-contribution system without any individual choice about the portfolio.[9] For comparison purposes, assume that the accumulations in individual accounts are used to finance real annuities after retirement, given interest rates

---

8. To be "well run," a social security system needs more than just to be "well administered." A well-administered system is a social security institution that administers the legislated social security system well. A well-run system is well administered and also has initial and subsequent legislation that are timely and of good quality for the underlying purposes of the social security system. The Social Security Administration has given the United States a well-administered system. Congress has a mixed record for making Social Security well run.

9. A defined-contribution system without any individual portfolio choice is called a provident fund system. A number of countries (including Malaysia and Singapore) have had provident funds.

and mortality expectations at the time of conversion of an account into an annuity.[10]

The goal of such a system is to accumulate a sufficient fund to support a target income for participants during retirement. The target is generally expressed as a replacement rate that gives the ratio of real benefits to real earnings toward the end of a worker's career. The required rate of savings for a given replacement rate depends on the rate of interest and the rate of growth of wages. Since both wage growth and real interest rates have varied greatly over time, so too has the savings rate required for adequate benefits. Thus a defined-contribution system needs periodic adjustment in savings rate if it is to fulfill its social goal.

Once a savings rate is selected, a defined-contribution system places the risks associated with fund accumulation squarely on the workers.[11] Their ultimate benefits will depend on the growth in their earnings and on the returns earned on the portfolio held in their accounts.[12] In addition to the risk during the accumulation process, workers also face a risk as they convert accumulated reserves into an annuitized flow of income during retirement. The value of the real annuity that can be financed by a given accumulation will depend on the mortality table and interest rate used in the conversion of the accumulation into a promised benefit flow. The mortality table expresses the probability that payments will still be made at different dates in the future, and the interest rate

10. Other options include lump-sum withdrawals, phased withdrawals (where monthly amounts are limited by a formula), choice of different types of annuities, and combinations of the above.

Another dimension of variation is whether benefits are available at some "retirement age" or only if satisfying a retirement test. Moreover, individuals might have some choice as to when benefits begin, with some adjustment of benefits for the age at which they start.

Changing to a partially defined-contribution system also requires adjustment of disability benefits. This is complicated since disability is an event that needs insurance and is not adequately dealt with by simple accumulation. The Advisory Council on Social Security (1997a) has two proposals that have individual accounts and so a need to adjust disability benefits. Both the Individual Accounts (IA) and the Personal Security Accounts (PSA) proposals reduce disability benefits relative to retirement benefits, compared with current law. It would be good to have a detailed analysis of the merits of such a change.

11. This paper does not review different simulations and calculations that describe the magnitude of the risks and the variations in outcomes with different portfolios. For stochastic simulations, see Goodfellow and Schieber (forthcoming) and Olsen and others (1998). For calculations directly based on historical data, see Burtless (1997) and Thompson (1998).

12. Redistribution can be added to such a system by doing transfers among accounts either when deposits are made or when the accounts are annuitized.

One also needs rules for the accounts of workers who die before reaching retirement age. Using the 1991 period life table, 81 percent of 20-year-old males and 89 percent of 20-year-old females would survive until age 62. With a defined-benefit system, the lack of benefits for workers dying before retirement age is used to increase the benefits of those who do survive. A

is used to discount those payments back to the date when the accumulation is converted into a promised benefit flow.

With a defined-contribution system, the risk of interest rates at the time of annuitization is squarely on the individual worker. For a given accumulation, workers who retire when real interest rates are high will receive a larger real annuity than those who retire when real interest rates are low. This risk can be somewhat attenuated by annuitizing part of the fund in successive years near retirement age or by allowing the worker some choice as to the date of annuitization.[13] Also the risk can be hedged by moving the accumulation portfolio to one predominantly of long-term bonds, which matches the portfolio used by insurance companies when pricing annuities.[14]

While the interest rate involves risk for the individual, mortality assumptions involve risk for society, as a cohort of workers might turn out to live longer than expected on average.[15] Mortality improvements have been uneven over decades in the past, and projections for the future are highly controversial. A defined-contribution system leaves that risk with the government if annuities are provided publicly, or with the market if annuity provision is privatized. Either way, a risk premium has to be paid, implicitly (by the government) or explicitly (through privatization).

Besides consideration of mortality of the entire cohort, the question arises of whether to have different annuity prices for different members of a cohort. For example, one might use different tables for men and women or for healthy and unhealthy workers. Any decision about different prices for different risk classes (either allowing them or not allowing them) contains implicit redistribution.[16]

The evolution of mortality rates has two aspects—the response of retirement benefits to the trend in mortality and to the uncertainty about the trend. If

---

defined-contribution system could imitate this pattern, although the natural political response is to give the accounts to the estates of the deceased workers.

13. A more extreme version would have rolling annuitization on an annual basis, as was proposed by Boskin, Kotlikoff, and Shoven (1988). Currently, after retiring, U.S. workers can delay claiming Social Security benefits until age 70 in order to receive a larger annuity, and some do. See Coile and others (1997).

14. I am grateful to Stewart Myers for this point.

15. Blake, Burrows, and Orszag (1998) have proposed that the government issue mortality bonds, bonds with a payment that varies with aggregate mortality, to help insurance companies bear this risk.

16. Combining men and women in a single risk class redistributes from men to women on average. However, having separate risk classes for men and women implies that a man with a given life expectancy has a higher benefit than a woman with the same life expectancy. If annuity pricing varies with health, then, young workers do not know what risk class they will be in when older, an additional source of risk.

the savings rate and the retirement age are both fixed, a decreasing trend in mortality rates—that is, longer life expectancy—will require lower annual benefits. In other words, with increased longevity, a defined-contribution system has steadily declining replacement rates unless it adjusts the savings rate or the retirement age or both.[17]

How the system should respond to the trend in mortality depends on the trend in the ability and interest of participants to continue working. This will vary with developments in health, in job availability, and in lifetime earnings (since better-off cohorts are likely to prefer earlier retirement).[18] Presumably, both ability to work and interest in working should increase along with increased life expectancy, but not necessarily in lockstep. Thus an optimal response to an increasing trend in life expectancy is likely to be a less-than-proportional increase in retirement age and therefore an increased need for savings for retirement. Thus a defined-contribution system would have an increasing early entitlement age and a tax rate that increases across cohorts.[19] This raises a number of issues. Although the economics of steadily increasing tax rates is straightforward, the politics of it may not be.[20]

Separate from adapting to the trend in mortality is responding to the uncertainty in this trend. Over time, more is learned about the trend as it affects a particular cohort. If tax and early entitlement ages do not change, then only expected retirement benefits change as this uncertainty is played out. In other words, a well-run defined-contribution system would adapt to changing circumstances and so would require periodic legislated changes. Although a defined-contribution system can be left unchanged, it is not likely to do a good job of providing retirement income without legislative adjustments.

Benefit Determination with a Funded Defined-Benefit System

In order to appreciate the differences across systems, this section describes how a funded defined-benefit system responds to returns on the Trust Fund portfolio and to both the trend in mortality and the resolution of uncertainty in

17. Increasing the normal retirement age for Social Security is a method for cutting benefits; it may not change the average age at which benefits are claimed.

18. Costa (1998).

19. A separate question is whether a given cohort should have an age-varying tax rate, as is the case in Switzerland.

20. With positive interest rates, increases in life expectancy require less-than-proportional increases in tax rates to finance a given replacement rate. Varying cohort-specific tax rates would complicate tax collection. In addition, a steadily increasing early entitlement age would result in increasing use of the disability program.

mortality.[21] With a defined-contribution system, workers bear risks of accumulation and annuitization. As the system moves toward a defined-benefit arrangement, it shifts risk from the retirees to other participants in the system. And since the past is always history, it also shifts risk forward in time.[22] The central question for a defined-benefit system is how benefits and taxes are adjusted over time in response to economic and demographic developments that affect trust fund size.

Defined-benefit systems can be structured in a variety of ways. At one end of the spectrum, a defined-benefit system can be legislated to be the same for all future cohorts until new benefits or taxes are enacted. An intermediate position is to legislate a set of future adjustments in benefits and taxes for later cohorts, who are presumed to have longer retirement lives. This has been the usual status of the U.S. Social Security program. And, at the end of the spectrum closest to a defined-contribution system, benefits could be indexed to life expectancy as each cohort reaches early entitlement age.[23] These systems would respond differently to both the trend in mortality and information about the uncertainty about that trend. Thus, different defined-benefit systems spread risks in rates of return and in mortality uncertainty differently from each other and from a defined-contribution system. With a defined-benefit system, the risks can be spread more widely, with the economic advantages that come from wider pooling of risks.

Currently legislated indexing for inflation and wage growth has decreased the frequency of significant Social Security legislation. Indexing of retirement ages to life expectancy would decrease it even further. Incorporating future tax and benefit changes into current law also can reduce the frequency of legislation. Nevertheless the program would still need periodic adjustment, even if infrequent, in response to economic and demographic developments. Thus a central issue is how well a defined-benefit system adjusts to economic and demographic realizations that are different from what was planned on. Legislative responses to deviations of trust fund outcomes from trust fund expectations can vary in several dimensions. One is the frequency in response—one can consider infrequent large adjustments and more frequent smaller adjustments. One can have phased-in adjustments or abrupt adjustments. One might have asymmetry in benefit increases and decreases (and also for taxes).

21. Many studies have compared defined-benefit and defined-contribution systems; see, for example, Bodie, Marcus, and Merton (1988) and Diamond (1995).

22. The analysis assumes that the already retired do not bear significant risk from benefit adjustments after retirement.

23. Sweden is enacting such legislation.

As a program for the entire working population (and their dependents), Social Security needs to avoid large abrupt changes in benefits. Given the magnitude of the program and the need for gradual changes, Social Security must be insulated from the short-term fiscal needs of the government and must take a forward-looking approach to legislation needed for actuarial balance. The political mechanisms currently contributing to these outcomes are an earmarked tax and trust fund for Social Security and a highly visible, professional annual projection of the financial position of the program by the Office of the Actuary.

Thus there is a common theme—all systems need adjustment to fulfill their social role. How well such adjustments are made is an important dimension in evaluating arrangements. A defined-contribution system does not require adjustment to avoid insolvency, but any well-run defined-contribution system should be adjusted from time to time.[24] Even an indexed defined-benefit system will require periodic adjustment. If these adjustments are done well, a defined-benefit system is better for spreading risks than a defined-contribution system. But the quality of the political adjustment of the system is central to the comparison of different systems. Without any adjustments, as mortality rates fall, a defined-contribution system has shrinking replacement rates, while a defined-benefit system has growing revenue needs. The quality of both systems as providers of retirement incomes depends on political responses in terms of frequency and quality of adjustments.

Annuitization and Family Protection

In the comparison just made, it was assumed that annuitization rules were set by the government. A proposal might allow individual choice about annuitization, or a proposal that tried to mandate annuitization might find it politically impossible to implement.[25] Thus, it is important to consider the types of decisions that people are likely to make about annuitization of their accumulations.

24. This statement needs to be modified by recognizing the potential for insolvency in the funds paying for annuities, whether held by private insurance companies or publicly through an earmarked trust fund.

25. The Advisory Council on Social Security (1997a) has two proposals that allow individual choice in the form of benefit receipt. The Personal Security Accounts (PSA) proposal places no restriction on the form of benefit receipt. The Individual Accounts (IA) proposal mandates annuitization and allows a choice between single- and joint-life annuities. An intermediate position on annuitization, similar to the approach in Chile, could limit the size of monthly withdrawals for any part of the retirement account that is not annuitized.

Table 2-1. *Poverty Rates of the Elderly by Age, Sex, and Marital Status, 1992*

Item	65 and over	65 to 74	75 to 84	85 and over
Male				
Total	8.9	8.1	9.7	13.2
Married	6.6	6.0	7.5	10.5
Widowed	15.0	13.7	15.7	16.7
Divorced/separated/never married	17.6	18.1	16.5	n.a.
Female				
Total	15.7	12.7	18.9	22.7
Married	6.4	5.6	8.0	n.a.
Widowed	21.5	18.9	23.2	23.8
Divorced/separated/never married	26.0	25.6	27.0	n.a.
Total	12.9	10.7	15.3	19.8

Source: House Committee on Ways and Means, "Overview of Entitlement Programs," *1994 Green Book* (Washington, 1994), p. 860; March 1993 *Current Population Survey* (CPS). Table prepared by Congressional Research Service.

n.a. Not available owing to unreliability of estimate. Percentage base represents fewer than 250,000 persons.

This raises two issues. One is the extent to which people make good choices for themselves. The second is how annuity decisions will affect the longer-lived family member, most commonly a widow. Any movement toward individual choice needs to have its impact on the economic position of widows assessed very carefully. The poverty rates of widows are already much higher than those for couples, and women who become widows have a sharp fall in their ratio of income to needs (table 2-1).[26] Indeed, many analysts have called for greater protection of widows within the current Social Security structure.[27]

Left to their own devices, people do not take much advantage of annuities. The current individual annuities market in the United States is extremely small.[28] Adverse selection is part of the explanation, but the market is smaller than can be explained by adverse selection alone. Moreover, evidence from the U.K. suggests that people purchasing annuities do not purchase inflation protection when they have the opportunity. Even though real government bonds

26. Holden (forthcoming).
27. See, for example, Burkhauser and Smeeding (1994).
28. Friedman and Warshawsky (1990); Mitchell, Poterba, and Warshawsky (1997); Poterba (1997). It is important to distinguish between the actual purchase of a payment flow conditional on survival and "variable annuities," which are tax-favored savings vehicles with insurance companies that include an option to annuitize. This option appears to be infrequently taken, although I know of no published data to support this proposition. See Joseph B. Treaster, "The Money Keeps Rolling in for Variable Annuities," *New York Times*, January 11, 1998, p. 62.

and real annuities have been offered for some time in the U.K., individuals overwhelmingly choose nominal annuities.[29]

Similarly, left on their own, many workers tend to select single-life as opposed to joint-and-survivor annuities, which would continue payment to a worker's spouse after the worker's death.[30] Single-life annuities were very popular in employer-provided retirement plans prior to the 1974 Employment Retirement Income Security Act (ERISA). This pattern began to change when ERISA provided for a 50 percent joint-life annuity as the default provision. Karen Holden estimates that 48 percent of men with pensions beginning before 1974 had joint-and-survivor pensions, while 64 percent of those beginning after 1974 did so. Similarly, the General Accounting Office estimates that the percentage selecting a single-life annuity dropped by 15 percentage points after the 1984 Retirement Equity Act (REA), which required notarized spousal approval before selecting a single-life annuity.[31] Thus, the degree of joint-life annuitization is very sensitive to system design.

The effects of annuitization choices can be seen in the New Beneficiary Data System.[32] A sample of new Social Security beneficiaries was interviewed in 1982 and reinterviewed in 1991. Although the median value of real pension income fell 23 percent for intact couples between the interview dates, the median value of real pension income fell by 75 percent for those couples in which the wife was widowed between the interview dates.[33]

In short, when evaluating a shift from today's defined-benefit system to a defined-contribution approach, it is important to consider not only the effect on the worker but also on the worker's family. Although there has been considerable discussion of changing the treatment of the family within Social Security,

29. "The majority of annuities sold in the U.K. are fixed rate. Contacts of the Bank of England have told them that while there are no aggregate data, it is likely that more than 90 percent are fixed-rate. In particular, where individuals have discretion as to the type of annuity to buy, they appear to prefer fixed-rate annuities. Legal and General, one of the U.K.'s largest insurers, sold no index-linked annuities to individuals in 1996, and less than 1 percent of their individual annuities in force are index-linked." Alex Bowen, personal communication, 1997.

30. Mitchell, Poterba, and Warshawsky (1997) report on an unpublished LIMRA International 1993 survey of twenty-six companies selling these products. They report that only 7 percent elected a joint-and-survivor option.

31. Holden (forthcoming); U.S. GAO (1992); using data from TIAA-CREF, King (1996) found that the percentage selecting single-life annuities fell from 44 in 1978 to 26 in 1994, with nearly half the decline occurring between 1984 and 1986. While some parameter estimates, though large, are not statistically significant, Tegen (1997) finds drops from both ERISA and REA.

32. Courtney Coile prepared these tabulations.

33. The median in the percentage change in real pension income was 20 percent for intact couples and 69 percent where the wife was widowed. This was a period over which the real value of a dollar fell by 29 percent.

changes seem much more likely with a shift to individual accounts.[34] Thus it seems important to highlight the fundamental contrast between a defined-benefit system with auxiliary benefits and a defined-contribution system in which the annuity protection for the family is paid for by the worker and may involve choice.[35] Without explicit redistribution to reflect family structure, such an individual account system would be a large change from our current structure, even if benefits were the same on average.[36] Any large change in structure will imply a different pattern of benefits across families, a difference that needs to be studied carefully.

Portfolio Choice for a Central Fund

Consideration of portfolio choice for a central fund involves two steps. One is the implication for the level and riskiness of benefits. The second is the impact on the rest of the economy. This issue is considered first for a funded defined-contribution plan without worker choice; then for a funded defined-benefit plan.

The role of the government as portfolio planner for a defined-contribution system should be to select the single portfolio that is best for the workers (on average). Current thinking of both academic and industry analysts would suggest a diversified portfolio with significant holdings of both stocks and bonds. In a closed economy, finance theory suggests as a first approximation holding the "market portfolio," which is the same fraction of all assets issued by capital using firms.[37] It would be very expensive to track down portions of all capital investment in the United States; one can do reasonably well with a portfolio restricted to widely traded assets. One thing is clear—such a fund should not hold a portfolio exclusively of U.S. Treasury securities.[38]

Unlike a funded defined-contribution plan, the risks in the portfolio for a defined-benefit system are spread over successive cohorts of workers. Thus, a possible stock market decline is spread more widely than just over the workers then invested in the market. As a result, workers covered by a defined-benefit plan that adjusted well to market outcomes would be less averse to market risk than

34. See, for example, U.S. Department of Health and Human Services (1985) and U.S. House of Representatives, Select Committee on Aging (1992).

35. A similar issue arises in the treatment of divorced spouses.

36. In the mixed defined-benefit/defined-contribution proposals of the IA and PSA plans, the family structures of the defined benefit portions are similar to current law, but the defined contribution portion is different.

37. Since the United States is an open economy, some investment abroad is desirable.

38. Political issues in fund selection are discussed in other papers at this conference, as are political concerns about government involvement in corporate decisionmaking.

workers in a defined-contribution plan. Thus, the portfolio should be at least as risky as that appropriate for a defined-contribution plan. Again, it is not sensible for such a fund to hold a portfolio exclusively of U.S. Treasury securities.

One can ask whether the size of Social Security relative to the economy argues for deviating from this rough guideline.[39] The argument has not been that such investments would be economically harmful to the economy. Rather, the argument has been that having the Social Security trust fund hold a balanced portfolio similar to those typically held by private plans may not be worth the trouble.[40] Alan Greenspan has testified that "unless national saving increases, shifting Social Security trust funds to private securities, while likely increasing income in the Social Security system, will, to a first approximation, reduce non social-security retirement income to an offsetting degree. Without an increase in the savings flow, private pension and insurance funds, among other holders of private securities, presumably would be induced to sell higher-yielding stocks and private bonds to the Social Security retirement funds in exchange for lower-yielding U.S. Treasuries. This could translate into higher premiums for life insurance, and lower returns on other defined-contribution retirement plans. This would not be an improvement to our overall retirement system."

This testimony does not acknowledge the dramatically different distributions of Social Security income, private pensions, and asset income among the elderly.[41] The differences can be seen by looking at the sources of income by quintile of the income distribution. For the bottom quintile, 81 percent of income comes from Social Security, while only 6 percent comes from pensions plus income from assets. For the top quintile, 23 percent comes from Social Security, while 46 percent is from pensions and assets—dramatically different percentages. Either Chairman Greenspan is arguing that those with little other wealth are so risk averse that their pension funds should not be invested in equities, or he is suggesting that the distribution of retirement income among rich and poor is of no consequence. Neither of these propositions is right.

Greenspan's "first approximation" also does not recognize that spreading a given amount of risk more widely in the economy increases the efficiency of the capital markets, lowering the risk premium. The risk is spread not only by adding low-income and young workers to the risk-bearing pool, but also by being able to shift risk to future cohorts. This increase in efficiency lowers the

39. For discussion of these issues, see Munnell and Balduzzi (1998).

40. For example, those with large portfolios might simply alter the rest of their portfolio in response to a change in the Social Security portfolio, remaining with the same overall risk.

41. See Mitchell and Moore (1997); Social Security Administration, Office of Research, Evaluation and Statistics (1997).

risk premium—that is, the excess over the safe rate of interest that a borrower must pay because of the risk that the lender must bear. With a lower risk premium, borrowers are more willing to undertake risky investments.

In conclusion, funded defined-contribution and funded defined-benefit systems should both have widely diversified portfolios. If the defined-benefit system adjusts well to portfolio realizations, the defined-benefit fund should have a higher risk/higher expected return portfolio than is optimal for a defined-contribution system.

Worker Choice of Portfolio in Defined-Contribution Plans

Following the trend in private retirement arrangements, the two partially defined-contribution proposals coming from the Advisory Council on Social Security allow workers to have some choice over their portfolios.[42] The proposals differ in scale and in the form in which worker choice is provided and constrained. The Individual Accounts (IA) proposal models its defined-contribution element on current 401(k) rules.[43] That is, the government selects a small number of funds and allows workers to allocate their accounts among them. The Thrift Savings Plan (TSP) for federal employees works this way. In contrast, the Personal Security Accounts (PSA) proposal models its defined-contribution element on current IRA rules.[44] That is, individuals may choose among a wide variety of investment alternatives in the market, subject only to current restrictions on IRA investments. Since some reform proposals have more regulation than current IRA rules, the analysis also considers a more heavily regulated version of the IRA model, an approach that would be closer to the system in Chile.[45]

Allowing workers to determine their portfolios increases administrative costs. The increase can be small as long as the government continues to hold all portfolios and provides limited services.[46] This approach allows different work-

42. Advisory Council on Social Security (1997a).

43. The IA plan has 1.6 percent of payroll going into individual accounts, with the accounts automatically annuitized when the owners reach retirement age. To preserve roughly the current degree of progressivity in the system, the remaining defined-benefit system is adjusted to recognize the removal of a linear (nonprogressive) portion.

44. After the transition, the PSA plan has a two-tier system—a flat benefit and individual accounts that receive 5 percent of taxable earnings. The proposal places no restrictions on the form of retirement income once the worker reaches retirement age.

45. For descriptions of the system in Chile, see Diamond (1994); Diamond and Valdes-Prieto (1994); Edwards (1998).

46. The Advisory Council assumed an additional charge of 10.5 basis points of accumulated assets.

ers to hold different portfolios and individual workers to vary their portfolios as they age. Insofar as workers understand the principles of sound investment (which are themselves under dispute), they will be able to select portfolios better suited to their degree of risk aversion. Insofar as workers do not understand risk-return trade-offs, they will make some investment decisions that can significantly lower the benefits of investment. Evidence on worker choice in 401(k) plans implies that individuals will differ greatly in portfolio allocations, ranging from completely in bonds to completely in stocks.[47] Since higher-income workers are more likely to hold higher-risk/higher-expected-return portfolios, they will usually receive higher returns and so have even higher retirement incomes relative to low-income workers.[48]

Some analysts are concerned that government selection of available portfolios—that is, the 401(k) approach—leaves too much of the investment decision in the hands of the government. Shifting to the IRA model significantly lowers the role of the government in the capital accumulation process, but it also increases administrative costs and the scope for very poor investment choices.[49] One possible response to both of these concerns is greater regulation of financial intermediaries handling the accounts, which is considered below.

The Advisory Council assumed that the administrative charges for accounts with the PSA plan would be 1 percent of assets under management per year. The council also assumed that the same percentage would apply for workers with different account levels. Yet a large part of the cost of account maintenance is a fixed cost per account—record keeping and communication with account holders. Collection and processing of deposits has a large fixed-cost component as well. Thus, one would expect that, without subsidization, charges would be higher relative to assets for low earners than for high earners, as has been the case in Chile.[50] Moreover, if allowed, some workers would have accounts with several intermediaries, adding to total costs and reducing the average size of accounts.[51] Workers with multiple jobs (simultaneously or

47. For evidence on 401(k) holdings, see U.S. General Accounting Office (1996) and Yakoboski and VanDerhei (1996).

48. These differences may generate political pressure for adjustment.

49. The two models may be different political environments for legislating rules about early access to accumulations and government mandates on annuitization.

50. Currently, many mutual funds have minimum size accounts, keeping out small accounts. Also, some mutual funds have higher charges for small accounts (by waiving some of the fees for larger accounts).

51. With the IA plan, the Social Security Administration would have a single account for each worker. Unless all revenues flow through the government, the PSA plan has no mechanism to combine accounts that workers might have placed with different intermediaries. Some people have argued that diversification across mutual funds is itself of value.

Table 2-2. *Distribution of Annual Earnings under Social Security, 1993, Wage and Salary Workers*

Earnings level	Number of workers (in millions)	Percent distribution
Total	128.2	100
Less than $8,400	42.1	33
$8,400–$13,199	15.4	12
13,200–17,999	14.0	11
18,000–22,799	12.2	10
22,800–27,599	10.0	8
27,600–32,399	7.8	6
32,400–37,199	6.2	5
37,200–41,999	4.8	4
42,000–46,799	3.6	3
46,800–51,599	2.7	2
51,600–57,599	2.5	2
57,600 (maximum)	7.0	5

Source: "Annual Statistical Supplement," *Social Security Bulletin*, 1996, p. 190.

with short employment spells) are particularly liable to start multiple accounts.[52] Indeed, this has been a problem in Australia. To see the magnitude of multiple jobs even within a year, note that in 1993 employers filed 223 million W-2 reports for 128 million wage and salary workers.

The importance of these fixed costs relative to the size of deposits is highlighted by the fact that the distribution of Social Security earnings has considerably more low earners than does the distribution of earnings of full-time adult workers (table 2-2).

To gain some idea whether the assumption of 1 percentage point per year is a reasonable estimate for the IRA approach, it is useful to look at the experience of other countries. Although many commentators have noted the high charges in Chile, the experience in the U.K. may be more relevant.[53] In the U.K., workers can opt out of the earnings-related portion of the government defined-benefit

52. With multiple accounts, one would expect that some would get "lost," with intermediaries unable to locate the owners.

53. See, for example, Diamond and Valdes-Prieto (1994); Edwards (1998). Although some people have argued that it is the nature of regulation in Chile that has caused the high costs, I am skeptical of this conclusion. I have not seen a formal equilibrium model that would show that regulating the structure but not the level of charges leads to an equilibrium with high charges and high sales costs. Moreover, the charges are lower in Chile than in the United Kingdom, where similar regulation does not exist. I think that the high costs are inherent in reliance on individual choice in this kind of market.

Table 2-3. *Charges in the United Kingdom*

Expense loadings	A review of the charges levied by providers on unit-linked APPs indicates the following typical range of charges:
	Initial charge: 5% to 10% of the invested rebate.
	Annual charge: 0.25% to 1.25% of the invested monies, with most providers levying an annual charge in the range 0.75% to 1%.
	Flat-rate charge: £1.50 to £3 a month irrespective of whether rebates are continuing to be paid to the APP account. This charge will generally increase each year in line with an index of prices or an index of earnings.
	It is noted that not all providers levy all these charges: in particular, a number of providers levy no flat-rate charges.
	Having regard to the range of charges levied on APPs, I consider that it would be reasonable to take the charges levied by a typical provider to be:
	Initial charge: 8% of the invested rebate.
	Annual charge: 0.9% of the invested monies.
	Flat-rate charge : £2.50 a month.

Source: United Kingdom Government Actuary and Secretary of State for Social Security, 1996, p.7.

plan (SERPS) for an "appropriate personal pension."[54] The charges for these accounts are not regulated and appear in a wide variety of forms, not all of them visible to the workers. The pattern of charges has been described by the Government Actuary (table 2-3). In addition to initial commissions, management fees, and monthly charges, costs are also associated with early surrender, which David Blake reports can be very large.[55] Costs include a sizable fixed component and are higher than assumed by the Advisory Council, although they have been declining somewhat lately, perhaps in response to the recent entry of index funds.[56] The complexity and magnitude of charges would create

54. Having an optional defined-contribution plan replace part of Social Security has been suggested in the United States. In the United Kingdom, the option has resulted in high-pressure sales tactics, leading some people to switch inappropriately. Some suppliers have been reprimanded and have had to pay compensation. See Blake (1997).

55. "We found that surrender values for with-profits endowment schemes were on average 27 percent below maturity values when cashed in just 1 year to maturity." Blake (1997, p. 289).

56. With limited data, Blake and Orszag (1997) use a nonlinear regression to estimate the contribution charges and fund management charges of a typical worker. Using these estimated values, they calculate that a typical worker would pay about 20 percent of the value of the pension in charges, lower than the figure that the Government Actuary would find and roughly the same as would follow from the 0 contribution charge and 1 percent fund management charge assumed by

Table 2-4. *Charge Ratio*

Interest rate (percent)	Wage growth (percent)	Career length (years)	Front load (percent)	Management fee (percent)	Charge ratio (percent)
4	0.1	40	0	1	21.6
4	1.1	40	0	1	20.7
4	2.1	40	0	1	19.6
4	3.1	40	0	1	18.6
4	4.1	40	0	1	17.5
4	2.1	40	0	1	19.6
4	2.1	40	0	0.5	10.5
4	2.1	40	0	0.1	2.2
4	2.1	40	0	1	19.6
4	2.1	30	0	1	14.8
4	2.1	20	0	1	9.9
4	2.1	10	0	1	5.0
4	2.1	40	8	0.9	24.5
4	2.1	40	1	0	1
4	2.1	40	10	0	10
4	2.1	40	20	0	20

Source: Author's calculations. See Appendix.

considerable logic and pressure to regulate the form of charges.[57] This would be similar to the experience that led to regulation of allowable Medigap policies.

The wide variety of charges for fund management can be put into a common frame by comparing the ratio of the pension accumulation available at retirement with a given set of charges to the pension accumulation that would be available if there were no charges.[58] The charge ratio is defined as the percentage decline in account value as a result of the charges. As shown in table 2-4, the charge ratio depends on the contribution history of the worker and the rate of return on the portfolio as well as the structure of charges.[59] For a worker with a forty-year career, annual wage growth of 2.1 percent and a portfolio that earns 4 percent a year, a 1 percent management fee reduces the value of the account by 20 percent. Higher wage growth reduces the charge ratio, since more contributions are made later in the worker's career and thereby subject to the man-

---

the Advisory Council for the PSA plan. Blake and Orszag are currently redoing their estimate using a more complete data set.

57. Describing U.K. experience, Blake (1997, p. 289) writes: "Charges can be imposed in a bewildering variety of ways."

58. Blake and Orszag (1997).

59. Derivation of the equations used to calculate the table is in the Appendix. In considering a rate of return, one needs to adjust for costs, such as brokerage commissions, that are normally deducted from reported returns rather than bundled with other charges.

agement fee for fewer years. A lower management fee reduces the charge ratio roughly proportionally over the relevant range. A shorter working career, ending at retirement, also lowers the charge ratio.

The next line in table 2-4 shows that the charge ratio of a "typical provider" in the U.K. (not including the flat charge of 2.5 pounds per month) is 24 percent, higher than the 20 percent that would result from the 1 percent annual management fee assumed by the Advisory Council for the PSA plan.[60] The last three lines in the table 2-4 illustrate that front loads result in a charge ratio that is equal to the front load.

Table 2-4 indicates the importance of comparing front-load charges to annual management fees in a consistent framework, since they differ greatly in importance for the same percentages. For example, the total administrative costs of the Social Security Administration are less than 1 percent of annual taxes collected. If all of this cost is attributed to the collection of contributions and record keeping, ignoring the cost of providing annuities, this can be considered a front load of 1 percent. This would result in a charge ratio of 1 percent. In contrast, a 1 percent annual management fee has a charge ratio of 20 percent.[61]

Besides increased costs, the IRA approach also raises the issue of policing of funds to hold down misrepresentations and outright fraud. Fraudulent investment schemes have long existed and a large influx of inexperienced investors might result in a surge of both misselling and fraud.[62] In the U.K., individuals face a variety of complex arrangements for their opt-out accounts. The attempt to use the market to serve a heterogeneous population will inevitably create the potential to confuse and take advantage of some of them.[63] Whatever restrictions are introduced to protect consumers would be expected to be larger in a setting of mandated purchase rather than voluntary purchase.

Administrative costs could be held down by limiting them as a condition of accepting such deposits.[64] The government could introduce a cap on administrative charges as a percent of the size of the account. However, different types of funds have different cost structures, and would need different caps (stock versus bond, index versus nonindex, domestic versus foreign investments,

60. This calculation also does not count other costs, such as the bid-ask spread, that are not quantified by the Government Actuary.

61. In comparing defined-contribution and defined-benefit systems, one needs to include a charge for the conversion of an accumulation into an annuity as well.

62. In addition to the impact of misselling and fraud on retirement incomes, they could affect the political stability of a privatized proposal.

63. Just as we do not want a nirvana theory of government behavior, we should not use a fantasy theory of the workings of markets.

64. Dickson (1997); Goodfellow and Schieber (forthcoming).

direct investment versus holding financial assets). One would also need to be diligent about the different ways in which charges can be introduced into portfolio management; for example, the charges on certificates of deposit (CDs) are built into the interest rate offered. With a restriction on charges, firms may try to refuse to accept particular (small) accounts. This would be likely to become a political issue as well as affecting economic outcomes.

More generally, it might be possible to ease both the administrative cost and the poor choice of investment problems by much tighter regulation of allowable portfolios. For example, the government might restrict allowable investments to widely diversified mutual funds agreeing to low administrative charges. But moving in this direction reintroduces the concerns that have been expressed about direct government selection of available funds. It is not clear whether the political issues would be larger or smaller with heavy regulation than with direct government design and holding of portfolios.

In addition to the administrative costs that would be borne by the workers, additional costs would arise in getting withheld funds from employers (and the self-employed) to the financial intermediaries.[65] Although these transfers could be tacked onto existing 401(k) plans for roughly one-quarter of the population at any time, rules for mandated savings are likely to differ from current 401(k) provisions. In any event, new arrangements would be needed for the rest. The cost of these arrangements would depend on how frequently the deposits were made into individual accounts.[66] At present, neither the Social Security Administration (SSA) nor employers need to track individual payroll taxes more than once a year.[67] Yet individuals are likely to want their withheld payments deposited more quickly. If payments to funds were done privately, then firms would need to send payments to many institutions, although clearinghouses would probably arise to handle payments.

Currently the IRS and SSA are responsible for assuring that withheld taxes reach the Social Security trust funds and that individual taxable earnings are correctly recorded. Each year SSA processes W-2 reports for roughly 220 million employees from about 6.2 to 6.5 million employer reports. Of these reports, more than 5 million are on paper, with employers filing on paper averaging about twelve employees. SSA finds mismatches between what employers report as names and Social Security numbers of their employees and what

65. Pozen (forthcoming).
66. Charges by financial instituions will also depend on the frequency of deposit into the accounts. Many mutual funds have minimum deposit amounts as well as minimum account sizes.
67. Although employers make frequent tax payments, they only need to allocate those taxes to individual workers once a year. Until 1978, quarterly reporting of individual records was required. This was changed to annual reporting to ease administrative burdens on employers.

Social Security has in its records. SSA has computer routines to pick up common mistakes—transposed digits in the Social Security number or common variations in spelling names. After this, SSA ends up with 6 million cases (out of about 220 million, roughly 3 percent) each year of W-2 reports with missing information or an inability to match. In these cases SSA corresponds with the employee or employer. A question is who would play this role in a system of individual accounts if payments to funds were done privately.

Another issue arises with tax payments that are not made, as is the case with some firms approaching bankruptcy. Currently, the cost falls on the Social Security, not on the individual workers, since benefit determination is based on taxable earnings, not on tax payments received. Presumably a similar guarantee would not be present with private payment mechanisms. So someone would need to police this system. Unless the money flowed through SSA, some of the economies of scope now present would be lost.

Besides the costs of generating and monitoring the flow of money, a system of individual accounts with worker choice would need worker education. Many firms that have 401(k) plans provide education in investment for their workers. Such education does affect worker portfolio choices.[68] Who will control the nature of the education offered and who will pay for it are issues.

A further issue comes from the interaction between Social Security and the SSI program. The SSI program guarantees a minimum income to the elderly, subject to an asset test. Thus a poor worker near the point of eligibility for SSI has little to lose and much to gain from holding a high-risk portfolio. Without further regulation, the PSA plan places no limit on the risk that can be found in the market. Such activity could raise the cost of SSI, making it more difficult to increase the basic support level, a move that some analysts think would be worthwhile.

To summarize, adding individual portfolio choice to a defined-contribution plan without choice involves additional costs, large ones if the government does not hold the portfolios. The possible economic gains from such a change depend on the balance between a better match of portfolios with individual preferences for some investors and an inferior portfolio choice by some people who are inexperienced, make mistakes, or are taken advantage of in the market.

Building a Larger Trust Fund

It is possible to build and maintain a trust fund considerably larger than has been the experience with Social Security either within the current structure or

---

68. Bernheim and Garrett (1996).

within a system of individual accounts.[69] Interest in a larger fund comes from two sources. From the perspective of Social Security, a larger fund implies a more favorable return on Social Security for later generations at the expense of a less favorable return on Social Security for current workers (and possibly retirees).[70] From the perspective of the entire economy, building a larger fund is a way to increase national savings by having a larger net flow of revenues to Social Security.

Building a fund requires taxing some workers (or retirees) now in order to benefit other workers who come later.[71] Anyone pointing out the benefits of a higher trust fund and then softly saying that there will be some "transition costs" is not giving equal weight to the two sides of this tax and transfer. Building a fund makes Social Security financially more valuable to workers coming later, at a cost of making Social Security financially less valuable for those paying the tax to build the trust fund. This is the mirror image of the historical fact that Social Security has been made less valuable for current workers as a result of having been made more valuable for earlier cohorts.

Within a defined-benefit system, any additional amount of funding can be selected. If the defined-benefit portion of a mixed system is continued on a contingency reserve basis, then the degree of funding overall in a mixed defined-contribution/defined-benefit system depends on the size of the defined-contribution portion. The larger the degree of funding, the greater the combination of benefit cuts and tax increases needed to accumulate such a fund. The larger the benefit cuts, the smaller the tax increase needed. In addition to the size of funding sought, the speed with which the fund is built up affects the size of initial tax increase needed and the distribution of the cost of building such a fund across different cohorts. For example, the PSA plan, which allocates 5 percent of

69. As is well known, in a steady state the rate of return to participants in a strictly pay-as-you-go Social Security system is the rate of growth of the economy, while the rate of return in a fully funded system is the rate of interest. With a funded system, if the rate of growth exceeds the rate of interest and is expected to remain higher for the rest of time, then the economy is oversaving and can have a Pareto gain by decreasing funding. It is important to note that the converse is *not* true. Having the rate of growth be less than the rate of interest does not imply an opportunity for a Pareto gain by increasing funding. Indeed, in this case, the simple comparison of the rate of growth and the rate of interest is not a sufficient statistic for considering the advantages of increased funding. When considering funding, one must consider both the generations paying to build the fund and the generations benefiting from the existence of a fund built earlier.

70. A larger trust fund would also alter the economics and the politics of future adjustments of the system. Different institutional designs may affect the political stability of maintaining a larger fund.

71. It is the building of a trust fund that is relevant here, not the form of Social Security or of asset management. Insofar as the trust fund is able to earn a higher rate of return by changing its portfolio (beyond the necessary compensation for bearing risk), this additional return can also be saved to benefit future generations and to increase national savings and so wealth.

the 12.4 percent FICA tax to individual accounts, calls for a 1.52 percent payroll tax increase for seventy-two years (along with borrowing $1.9 trillion from the Treasury and repaying it with interest). If the proposal had a different pattern of benefit cuts, it would need a different tax rate. If it had a shorter "transition period," it would need a larger tax increase. If the funded portion were smaller, the tax increase needed would be smaller.

When considering how much additional net revenue to accumulate in Social Security, it is important to consider the trade-off, per dollar, between costs to those paying additional taxes or receiving lower benefits and the benefit to those receiving a better funded Social Security system. One way to put this question is how much a trust fund buildup now can reduce the steady-state payroll tax in the future, benefits held constant. A number of factors will influence that trade-off.[72] Moreover, the trade-off can be considered within the context of Social Security and then in the context of the entire economy. As a starting place, assume that Social Security tax changes and the induced fund buildup do not change labor supply, wages, or the interest rate. In this simple model, each dollar of trust fund accumulation reduces steady-state taxes by the excess of the rate of interest over the rate of growth of the economy. That is, the additional amount in the trust fund earns the rate of interest. However, the trust fund must grow by the rate of growth of earnings in order to maintain the trust fund relative to benefit expenditures. Thus the steady-state payroll taxes are reduced by the difference between these two rates times the amount of increase in the trust fund. In an economy with a rate of interest of 4 percent, average wage growth of 1 percent and labor force growth of 1 percent, an additional dollar placed in the fund will earn four cents, of which two cents are needed to keep pace with economic growth, while two cents can be used to lower taxes.

Since some of any steady-state payroll tax reduction is saved, capital is increased by more than one-for-one with the increase in the trust fund. This tendency is diminished to the extent that some people do not save, to the extent that corporate pensions might decline (beyond any offsetting private savings), and to the extent that other government spending increases net of other taxes. Indeed the politics of the response of the rest of the government budget to changes in Social Security is likely to be the single most important element in determining the impact of Social Security changes on national savings.

Whatever the size of the capital increase after adjusting for these factors, the increased capital will increase wages and decrease the interest rate. These feedbacks directly change government revenues and change savings propensities. A

72. A natural starting place for this analysis is a two-period overlapping generations model. For details, see Bohn (1997a, 1997b); Diamond (1997).

decline in the interest rate lowers the return on the trust fund, decreasing the gain to Social Security. The increase in the wage increases payroll tax revenue and the cost of supplying benefits for a given replacement rate. Net, these two effects lower the gain to Social Security from the simple effects described above. Without detailed computer-simulated modeling, it is hard to evaluate the full impact on Social Security, and one should be very skeptical of calculations without the full set of feedbacks.[73]

A trust fund buildup and induced drop in the steady-state payroll tax rate also has an impact on the rest of the economy. So let the United States examine the impact on the rest of the government budget, continuing to assume no direct response in the rest of the government spending or in tax rates.[74] Three pieces are central in considering the rest of the government budget (and these three pieces each involve feedbacks on equilibrium). Any increase in capital accumulation as a result of the trust fund buildup will increase revenue from the taxation of capital income. In addition, the increase in capital reduces the interest rate, which decreases both income tax revenue and the interest burden of the national debt. Increased capital raises the wage, increasing revenue from the income taxation of earnings. Thus the impact on the unified budget and the impact on Social Security are quite different. Since Social Security is a system financed by an earmarked revenue source and since the burdens of Social Security taxes and of other taxes are distributed differently, this distinction is important. Moreover, this raises the obvious point that if the nation wants to increase national savings by raising taxes, this can be done through the income tax as well as through the payroll tax.

A larger trust fund is a way of making Social Security more valuable for future generations at a cost of making it less valuable for current generations. It is also one way, among many, of increasing national savings by raising taxes

73. Feldstein and Samwick (1997) use a 9 percent rate of interest in their calculations for individual accounts. The analysis in their paper applies as well to the buildup of a trust fund, with the exception that a central trust fund would have lower administrative costs and so a higher rate of return. They estimate that a temporary increase in the payroll tax to fully fund the system would permanently lower the payroll tax rate to 2.02 percent. One can quarrel with their quantitative estimates. It seems to me unreasonable to make the combination of assumptions that all of marginal savings end up in the corporate sector, that a 34 percent increase in the capital stock has no effect on the rate of interest, that there is no market power in the corporate sector (so that the average and marginal returns to capital are the same), that the federal government can obtain the property tax revenues of local government for Social Security, that the administrative costs of individual accounts (under the IRA model) would be only thirty basis points, and that real annuitization can be accomplished by the private market using average mortality and the same 9 percent interest rate. Moreover Disability Insurance is ignored in their calculations, both disability benefits and the payment of OAI benefits to retired workers who were previously receiving DI benefits.

74. Alternative models of the behavior of Congress will naturally produce different levels of long-run capital accumulation.

or cutting benefits. Any restoration of actuarial balance is likely to reduce concern about whether Social Security will be there for young workers. The greater the degree of funding, the more the concern will be reduced.

Implications for the Labor Market

Some claim that switching from a defined-benefit to a partially defined-contribution system will improve the efficiency of the labor market by "tightening the link" between taxes and benefits. However, it is not simple to compare labor market effects of different types of social security systems, and consideration of the effects of all components of proposals provides little support for the contention. Labor market concerns arise on two fronts—retirement decisions and the labor supply of younger workers who pay Social Security taxes.

Social Security affects retirement decisions. Perhaps the largest impact is that the availability of retirement income permits retirement for those who would not have saved enough otherwise. Indeed the large fraction of workers retiring and claiming benefits as soon as they can supports the importance of this effect. The fact that the implicit taxation of continued work is small (and for some even a subsidy) at age 62 is evidence that income availability and not labor market distortion is critical for many 62-year-old workers.[75] Nevertheless, the earnings test certainly affects the labor market behavior of some workers.[76]

An earnings test provides less in benefits for those who are still earning substantial incomes, in order to finance larger benefits for those who have stopped earning and for the later years of those still working.[77] Some of the people retiring early have had a loss of good earnings opportunities, while others are choosing to retire early despite the continuation of good opportunities. Naturally, this source of insurance against the loss of good earnings opportunities distorts the labor supply of some who still have good opportunities, just as all insurance with asymmetric information distorts some decisions. But the goal is not to avoid all labor market distortions, but to balance the labor market distortions with the improved insurance that is only possible with some distortions. Estimates of the impact of changing Social Security on average retirement ages

75. Diamond and Gruber (1998).
76. Friedberg (1998).
77. Individuals differ in work and retirement plans. Any individual faces uncertainty about future health, job satisfaction, and job opportunities. Both individual differences and stochastic realizations result in an enormous variation in lengths of working life. Just as we are concerned with both redistribution and insurance for earnings levels, we are concerned with both issues relative to the length of working life. Thus a retirement system has considerable scope for providing redistribution and valuable insurance of this risk.

generally show small effects. Moreover, one need not have a defined-contribution system just to avoid an earnings test.[78]

With regard to younger workers, economists have raised the issue of the extent to which the payroll tax distorts the labor market. Suggestions that switching to a defined-contribution system will produce large efficiency gains are overblown. Distortions depend on the entire Social Security system, not just the portion in a defined-contribution system. Any redistribution will create some labor market distortion, whether the redistribution is located in the benefit formula or in another portion of the retirement income system.

For example, the redistribution in the PSA plan comes from the one-half of the retirement portion of the payroll tax that finances the flat benefit. This half of the tax is purely distortionary.[79] With the progressive benefit formula in Social Security, the redistribution comes from marginal subsidies on low-income people and marginal taxes on high-income people, with different implicit taxes at different ages and for people with different age-earnings profiles.[80] Sorting out the optimal way to balance the distortions imposed at different places in the income distribution is a difficult problem—one that allows no simple assertions as to what system is better. The answer depends on both income distribution needs and elasticities of labor supply at different places in the income distribution.

In addition to the labor market distortions that come from redistribution, defined-contribution systems have two further sources of distortion—one shared with defined-benefit systems and one that is not shared. Society mandates taxation to finance retirement income because it believes that many workers would not save enough on their own for retirement. If some workers would not save, then they may undervalue the savings they are forced to do (whether through taxes or mandatory savings). If they undervalue the savings, then they view part of mandated savings as an implicit tax.[81] If people have high discount rates (whether from myopia or liquidity constraints) a dollar set aside for future benefits that earns a market return is worth considerably less than a dollar. For example, $1.00 compounded for twenty years at an 8 percent market rate and

78. The politics of an earnings test are likely to be different with different social security systems.

79. Similarly, the SSI program has 100 percent marginal taxation of Social Security benefits from the earnings of low earners. A system with greater reliance on a guaranteed minimum pension amount for its redistribution, as in Chile, has a higher distortion on low earners and a lower distortion for the rest of the population.

80. For calculations of Social Security incentives for an additional hour of work, see Feldstein and Samwick (1992).

81. Although shadow prices may not be consistent across different decisions, we would expect some of the distortion to carry over. See Thaler (1985).

discounted back at an 18 percent subjective rate is only worth $0.17. Thus, it is impossible to require higher savings without distorting labor supply, whatever the type of Social Security system.

Calculations of labor market incentives commonly assume that all workers survive until retirement age. Yet, mortality rates in the 1991 period life table indicate that 19 percent of 20-year-old males and 11 percent of 20-year-old females will die before age 62. Many people place a higher value on having consumption should they survive than on their estates. A defined-benefit system gives larger benefits to those reaching retirement age, financed by the estates of those who do not reach retirement age. In contrast, for someone who does not value bequests at all, the accumulation in a mandatory savings account is of no value if he or she dies before reaching retirement age. Thus a defined-contribution system involves distorting taxation of those with lesser interest in bequests.

In addition to variation in the actual links between earnings and future benefits, the form of pension provision may affect the perceptions of implicit marginal taxation. With a complicated benefit formula, people will not have fully accurate perceptions. They may well undervalue the return to work at some ages and overvalue it at others—particularly if the workers have in mind private pensions that are often based on earnings over a short period at the end of working life.

Defined-benefit and defined-contribution systems differ in their economic impact on labor supply but share the necessity of distortions if they are to accomplish our goals for Social Security. There is little reason to think that a switch to individual accounts will significantly improve the labor market.[82]

Conclusion

Americans differ in values, in prognoses of future politics, and in estimates of the economic implications of alternative reform proposals. This paper has argued that the economics of different reforms shows individual defined-contribution accounts to have lower returns (from increased administrative costs) and less satisfactory risk sharing than a well-run defined-benefit system. Thus the heart of the reform debate is based on different values and different prognoses of politics, not substantial economic disagreements.

People give different weight to individual choice relative to shared security. People have different levels of concern for income distribution outcomes and so the level of redistribution desired. People differ in their forecasts of how well either a central trust fund or individual accounts can be insulated from political

82. No significant improvement has been observed in Chile; see James (1997).

pressures that would weaken their role as providers of retirement incomes. People differ in the importance they give to increased national savings and in the forecasts of how well the political process can respond to perceived needs for more national savings. Clarifying the economics of different retirement systems can help identify and frame the discussion on the real issues in dispute.

Appendix

We do the calculation in continuous time. Consider a worker who earns w_s at time s, assumed to grow exponentially at rate g:

$$(1) \qquad\qquad w_s = w_0 e^{gs}.$$

The tax rate on these earnings is t. There is a proportional front-load charge of f, so that $t(1 - f)w_0 e^{gs}$ is deposited at time s. This accumulates until retirement age T. The accumulation occurs at rate $r - c$, where r is the rate of return and c is the management charge per dollar under management. Thus deposits made at time s have accumulated to $t(1 - f)w_0 e^{gs} e^{(r - c)(T - s)}$ at time T. The total accumulation at time T is the integral of this expression from time 0 until time T. Integrating, the accumulation depends on f and c and (for $g + c$ unequal to r) is equal to:

$$(2) \qquad A[f, c] = t(1 - f)w_0 e^{(r - c)T}\{e^{(g + c - r)T} - 1\}/(g + c - r).$$

For $g + c = r$, the accumulation satisfies:

$$(3) \qquad\qquad A[f, c] = t(1 - f)w_0 e^{(r - c)T}T.$$

For r unequal to both $g + c$ and g, the ratio of the accumulation to what it would be without any charges satisfies:

$$(4) \quad AR[f, c] = A[f, c]/A[0, 0]$$
$$= (1 - f)e^{-cT}\{(e^{(g + c - r)T} - 1)/(e^{(g - r)T} - 1)\}\{(g - r)/(g + c - r)\}.$$

The charge ratio is one minus the accumulation ratio:

$$(5) \qquad\qquad CR[f, c] = 1 - AR[f, c].$$

Sample calculations are shown in table 2-4.

A Political Science Perspective on Social Security Reform
Hugh Heclo

BY CONSTITUTIONAL DESIGN, the American system of government requires a public debate dispersed across many separate power centers before major public policy choices can be made. This imperative of government-by-discussion has become even more dependent on public opinion in the past two generations, owing in large part to changes such as the growth of scientific polling, development of electronic media communications, and the declining power of the two parties to organize voters, nominations, and political campaign strategies.

Here it is prudent to begin with a warning about the current state of public thinking: at present the public mind regarding Social Security reform is especially ripe for error and manipulation. People are not stupid, but on this subject there is now a distinctive mixture of public ignorance, misinformation, fearfulness, and distrust. This volatile cocktail renders ordinary citizens vulnerable to all sorts of pandering, exploitation, and other mischief. In today's public mind, Social Security reform is an issue that now blends four very dangerous ingredients.[83]

—*Ignorance is combined with misinformation.* Despite extensive media coverage of the system's problems, two-thirds of Americans have not followed recent proposals to put Social Security money in the stock market, and the same proportion has not even attempted to determine how much money they need to save for their retirement. Misunderstanding compounds this ignorance so that when asked about what the much publicized "trust fund exhaustion" means, 42 percent either think incorrectly that the system will be completely broke with no money to pay any benefits (30 percent) or do not know (12 percent). Younger Americans (almost one-half of generation X'ers) have the highest level of misunderstanding in thinking trust fund problems mean no money to pay benefits, a mistake that helps explain why young Americans have especially low expectations that Social Security benefits will be there for them. As one expert summarized the data, "Today the public does not have a clear enough understanding of the program to make informed judgments on reform alternatives."

---

83. The following examples use data from Employee Benefit Research Institute (1997); Public Agenda (1997); and U.S. House of Representatives (1997). A somewhat more sanguine view of public opinion than the one reported here can be derived from survey data, but the title of one recent review makes the essential point. Blendon (1998, pp. 45–48).

—Ignorance and misinformation are combined with deepening anxieties about the whole subject. Between 1994 and 1997 the proportion of people worrying about their ability to live the way they want to in retirement rose from 29 percent to 39 percent. Surveys have consistently found that the vast majority of Americans view Social Security as one of the nation's most important programs. In recent years, however, more than 80 percent of the public has also lost some faith in its future. In 1994, 43 percent of the public thought that when they retire it was very likely Social Security will be severely strained in paying benefits, but by 1997 that proportion had climbed to 58 percent. The number expecting that they will not get any Social Security benefits at all rose in these three years from 25 percent to 32 percent.

—Stirred into the mixture of ignorance, misinformation, and fearfulness is a poisonous measure of distrust that explains policy troubles by blaming government and politicians. Of Americans who think the Social Security program should be changed or even eliminated, 62 percent believe the program faces problems mostly because of mismanagement and waste. Problems of an aging population (25 percent) or of benefits set higher than the program can afford (9 percent) come in a distant second and third as reasons for Social Security's problems. More than 8 in 10 of all Americans (84 percent) believe the government is mismanaging the program so badly that money is going to waste. Many Americans seem to understand their leaders' debates on Social Security reform as demonstrating that the whole mess can be blamed on other politicians.

—The result is illogical, unstable structures of public opinion regarding the subject matter of Social Security reform. Although public confidence in Social Security has been shaken, people have not responded by accumulating greater personal savings for retirement or paying more serious attention to the policy trade-offs involved in reforming Social Security. More than half of the members of the working-age public (56 percent) now predict that most of the money to finance their retirement will come from their own savings rather than Social Security or pensions; yet roughly 75 percent of all current workers have no idea how much they need to accumulate for retirement.[84] For the one in three Americans who say they expect to get nothing from Social Security when they retire, there appears to be the same lack of prudent savings for retirement that

84. The 1997 Public Agenda Survey suggests that around 85 percent of nonretired individuals 22 to 61 years old have less than $100,000 put away, counting all their retirement vehicles, and two in three baby boomers 33 to 50 years old have less than $50,000 in retirement savings. At a macro level, the period of declining public confidence in Social Security since the early 1980s tracks with a substantial and counterintuitive decline in personal savings as a percentage of personal disposable income.

characterizes the rest of the working population. A similar inconsistency infects people's thinking about public policy. The vast majority of the public strongly supports the fundamental principles underlying Social Security. Most Americans (84 percent) like the idea that virtually everyone is required to participate, forcing those who might not otherwise save enough to obtain a basic security of benefits. And yet there is also support for reform undermining those principles, for example, with the 41 percent who favor making participation voluntary.

The features summarized above are characteristic of preliminary, poorly formed stages of public thinking on a subject. In contrast to issues such as welfare reform and crime, public views surrounding Social Security reform show little sign that many people have reasoned public judgments.[85] But yet unlike so many other policy issues, the fears surrounding security in old age are inherently personal and inescapable. In short, one is dealing with a subject where the fields of anxiety and confusion in the public mind are ripe to harvest.

Nor is this the full danger. Forces at work in the larger environment both nourish and feed off this vulnerable condition of public opinion. A brief summary follows:

First, the options now open to serious public debate have expanded beyond anything most living Americans have had to think about earlier. In contrast to the last major discussion of Social Security's "crisis" in the 1980s, far-reaching proposals to privatize or even eliminate the Social Security program are now part of the mainstream of policy debate. This is not to say that such proposals are unworthy of consideration, but they do complicate public deliberation in a way not experienced since the mid-1930s turmoil over the Townsend plan, Huey Long's Share the Wealth program, and the like—which is to say, not in almost anyone's living memory.

Second, we live amid a political process that is now predisposed to magnify differences on opposing sides of virtually any major public policy issue. The reasons for demonization instead of reasoned debate are intertwined. To gain attention, raise funds and be newsworthy, problems need to be framed in terms of dramatic, black and white conflict, diminishing the role for non-doctrinaire, moderate, and workable policy solutions. The public chooses leaders who are more extreme than they themselves are and who tend to exaggerate their differences with opponents, thereby encouraging a self-fulfilling prophecy of adversarial conflict.[86] In this environment, it is difficult

85. Yankelovich (1991); Public Agenda (1997).

86. This and other relevant evidence is discussed in McCarty, Poole, and Rosenthal (forthcoming); Richard Morin, "A Nation of Extremists," *Washington Post,* January 11, 1998, p. C5; and was anticipated in Dionne Jr. (1991).

for Social Security reform to avoid the trend toward scorpions-in-the-bottle politics.

Third, without an immediate Social Security crisis, partisan prevarication is a live option. Today's long lead times, which may diminish political resistance to change, also create less political urgency to enact tax increases or benefits cuts to bring Social Security into financial balance thirty years from now. In 1983 short-term pressures—the fear that checks soon would not be mailed— pushed leaders into bipartisan cooperation, and offered the chance to include some long-term improvements in the program. With Republicans and Democrats in agreement on the essentials and eventually on the same reform package, the public was encouraged to trust that the changes were generally desirable. Today by contrast, long-term pressures allow politicians ample opportunity for short-term maneuvering for temporary advantage. Such opportunism encourages a deeper uncertainty among citizens about what, if anything, being said is true or in their interest.

Finally, the expansion of policy options creates huge commercial incentives to mislead public opinion. There is an immense allure in dangling half-truths before people from whom much money is to be made. Hence financial companies are simply doing what comes naturally when they solicit business by enlightening the public with the half-truth that "*Fortune* recently reported that the Social Security system will be paying out more than it brings in by 2013— and is presumed to run out of money completely by 2030."[87] Businesses' vast profit-making possibilities, combined with politicians' short-term incentives to bash opponents rather than find common ground, produces a nasty setting for educating an already distraught public.

The moral of the policy story to be written in the period ahead should be clear. Given the confused public and the stakes for millions of Americans for decades to come, there is an immense fiduciary responsibility confronting political leaders, group spokespersons, media figures, and others engaged in the debate over Social Security. Telling difficult truths and refusing to oversell one's case may seem foolish in the short run. In the long run, however, it is the seriousness in accepting responsibility—as well as any fact shaving, half-truths, and lies—that posterity will remember about our *fin de siècle* efforts at Social Security reform.

What then are the foundational political values and risks at stake in the Social Security debate?

---

87. John Hancock Company letter of solicitation for retirement planning, Robert M. Olshan, registered representative, Washington-Patten Agency, Bethesda, Md., 1998.

The Inevitability of Government

Wide-ranging as they are, all of the major proposals being debated today seek to reform, not abolish, government's role in retirement policy. Amid the swirl of complex details, it is important to recognize this common ground because it reveals a de facto agreement most Americans share about the basic purpose of government retirement policy.

To be sure, the term "privatization" is now widely used to characterize prominent Social Security reform proposals. However no major initiatives advocate a *total* government withdrawal from the problem of financial insecurity in old age; none would rely solely on do-it-yourself provisions within a world of strictly "private sector" retirement arrangements. There are two major reasons for this.

The first reason is that there is no government-less private sector in sight to withdraw to. Voluntary, market-based retirement plans have been created and spread within a federal policy framework of tax incentives and nationally uniform rules (for example, fiduciary responsibilities, diversification requirements, and so on).[88] Moreover virtually all existing "private" pensions, including employer-sponsored pension plans, are designed by taking account of promised government Social Security benefits.[89] Thus any dismantling of the current Social Security program will itself affect virtually all operations and expectations within this system of voluntary retirement plans. Likewise, even the most "private" individual market investments for retirement depend on a framework of government laws and regulations for their protection in orderly markets. In one form or another, national policy—which is to say, government—is an inescapable reality of our complex modern society.

Second and more fundamentally, there is a general consensus underlying the Social Security reform debate that the goal of public policy should be to promote financial security in old age for all Americans. Of course there are other subordinate goals, such as redistributing resources efficiently, encouraging national savings, and so on. But the existence of subgoals should not cause us to lose sight of the larger functional objective. Just as the essential objective of buying a house is not to minimize one's mortgage payments but to provide physical shelter, so the essential objective of government pension policy

---

88. Provisions in the Internal Revenue Code began encouraging private retirement provisions in the 1920s but became especially prominent in World War II and flourished in subsequent years. In 1974 federal policy further encouraged private retirement plans with the protection of national standards enforced under the Employee Retirement Income Security Act (ERISA).

89. ERISA (1996, p.12).

is to provide a financially secure shelter to older Americans who are no longer working.

Thus even today's reform option known as "full privatization"—while entirely eliminating the current Social Security pension program—would use government bureaucracies to compel workers to contribute a given percentage of their earnings to a qualified retirement plan; regulate the retirement plans available for workers' contributions; regulate conditions for the withdrawal of those contributed funds; and operate means-tested government programs to provide some minimum level of income to all elderly persons who cannot support themselves. Labeling all this as a strictly "private" system (rather than a different form of government retirement policy) obscures the consensus about essential purpose presupposed in the reform debate.

This basic purpose is exposed if one asks why reformers assume there should be *any* compulsory government role at all in retirement policy.[90] First, left to their own devices, people are often myopic about their future; by the time they realize they should have been setting aside more of their earnings to provide for adequate consumption in retirement, it is too late to correct their error. Second and relatedly, without government compulsion for all, prudent savers are vulnerable to having to support those who are imprudent. Third, there are unknowns—such as unanticipated inflation and foreknowledge of one's own lifespan—that individuals find it difficult to insure against and that profit-making companies have little reason to insure for masses of people. Even the prudent may outlive their savings. Fourth, with the growth of modern industrial life, families have found it necessary (or highly advantageous) to have government socialize the support for aging parents that otherwise would have to occur within the family or other charitable relationships. Fifth, employers have not reliably been able to sustain large portions of the population through old age pensions that are offered in return for employees' long-term loyalty.[91]

Although these are among the common reasons sheer voluntarism fails, it is the nation's widely shared objective of financial security for all in old age that leads these conditions to be perceived as "failures." Thus, any pension program (public or private) exists to provide some assurance of adequate income in retirement. And government-sponsored pension policy exists, first and foremost, for the purpose of making this assurance more secure for more people than would be the case if one relies only on voluntary individual worker and market decisions.

90. Diamond (1977).
91. Sass (1996).

Political Risks Are Inescapable

If government is inevitable, political risks in retirement policy cannot be avoided. Retirement policy will depend on America's political process, whatever is done. If public distrust of government is a problem for the existing system, it is a problem also for any privatized system of individual accounts. Whatever policy approach is chosen for retirement, there remains an inescapable reliance on our government and political process to guarantee that approach and its integrity through time. Any reform depends on government keeping its promises over the long haul.

The term "political risk" means a given approach's vulnerability to being destabilized as time passes, unexpectedly rendering the plan's original design unsustainable in its promised operations and purpose. Such riskiness is not the same as uncertainties about the future in general. Uncertainties—for example, an unexpected change in the economy or demographic trends—can of course beset any policy. The forces of "political" riskiness have to do with pressures that are fashioned and put into play by a particular policy approach. Rather than being like trying to predict the weather, assessing political risk is like evaluating the structure of a vessel and its capacities not only to stay afloat but to maintain its course amid inevitable but unpredictable storms.

Different approaches to retirement policy are in effect sociopolitical precommitments. They do not rule out future political conflicts but rather shape what the conflicts will be about.[92] To repeat, no reform extracts government retirement policy from permanent dependence on our much maligned political process and the politics of promise keeping over the long haul. Thus, not only is politically immaculate conception excluded; so too is politically immaculate sustainability of pension policy.

At a fundamental political level, every approach to retirement policy has the qualities of a chain letter from one generation to its predecessors and successors. Each retired generation must as a practical matter have much of its consumption supported by means of the resources of the younger generation that is continuing to work.[93] The main thing any generation contributes to its retirement welfare is babies. The necessary purchasing power transferred from

92. Patashnik (1997).

93. In theory the retired population's consumption could be wholly supported by returns they receive from capital they own. Even assuming all retirees always had sufficient income flows from their returns on capital, there is the problem of assuring that capital ownership (and its attendant income rights) matched up exactly with whether or not the individual is retired. Communism sought to solve this problem by socializing all capital. Capitalism doesn't try.

working to retired persons generally results from a combination of three sources.

First is informal transfers from working members of one's family or other charity-minded persons. Since this form of chain letter often fails, government-sponsored transfers are a second mechanism (through mandatory contribution-benefit, tax-transfer programs). A final method of transferring purchasing power from the working to the retired is for the elderly to gain income by selling things of value—real estate, financial assets, precious metals—they have accumulated during working years.

Whatever the mechanism, the reality is that each generation represents an obligational presence backward to its parents and forward to its children. Fortunately for their moral well-being, Americans of every age show very little willingness to define Social Security reform as a matter of generational disengagement or conflict.[94]

Political Equilibrium Is Essential

Retirement plans—whether operated by government, employers, or individuals alone—are long-term commitments. Long-term stability and predictability cannot be achieved in individuals' lives if public policy is vulnerable to short-term pressures and veers off path. Retirement security depends on a program structure that enjoys a politically stable equilibrium. In other words, to endure over time, retirement policy must be self-conscious of the political dynamics produced by its own operations. Experts may be able to design technically correct plans. The more important concern is what happens over time when a plan meets politics.

Thinking about political risks is particularly important now because the current reform debate is grounded in what are typically half-articulated theories and assumptions about American politics. For example, the strictly economic advantages claimed for "privatizing" Social Security can also be achieved by modifying the existing system to provide for higher rates of return on collectively held funds and by requiring more accumulation in those funds to increase national savings.[95] The different positions of advocates for individual or collective savings depend heavily on questions, not of economics, but of values and political feasibility. Hence the politics of reform and anticipated public reactions deserve extremely careful scrutiny.

94. Strahilevitz (1997).
95. Burtless and Bosworth (1997).

Social Values Are at Stake

Fundamental issues of purpose are at stake in the Social Security debate because any given policy reform may over time change the meaning of financial security in old age as well as redefine who has a reasonable assurance of such security. In other words, change in "mere" means can subtly but decisively alter policy ends as time goes on.

Choosing among pension reform alternatives is not simply a matter of individuals' dollar and cents calculations because the results inevitably involve people's rights and responsibilities toward one another. This "values" dimension entails judgments about the intrinsic worth—the goodness—of our social and economic arrangements. All pension plans involve long-term risks that cannot possibly be avoided. How should those risks be shared? What should we want American society to be like? To debate what to do about the Social Security program is to debate different visions for American society. In short, whatever else it may be, our public conversation on Social Security reform is inherently a deliberation on "oughts" and "ought nots" of obligation—which is to say, a moral conversation about the nature of the good society.

Although specific reform proposals are embedded in deeper normative commitments, these values are rarely explicitly spelled out and argued before the public. Even in the best of circumstances, "value" issues are difficult to articulate. They are especially easy to dismiss today when political rhetoric focuses on the economic bottom line. Nevertheless, we must recognize that value commitments are invariably contained within the text of public policies. Although public policy never has *the* agreed-upon answer, when it comes to social values and the kind of society we want, neither is public policy ever entirely neutral. Public policy is always living *some* answer to value questions. This is especially true in any discussion of Social Security reform, where huge long-term patterns of social organization are at issue. Hence before considering the specific issues of political risks, the competing normative implications of the major reform alternatives deserve further attention.

Two principles: individual freedom, on the one hand, and shared security, on the other, are the dominant normative perspectives undergirding the Social Security reform debate. The first perspective places the highest priority on individual freedom of choice and control over one's own personal affairs. The second gives priority to securing a common social protection against the vicissitudes of life. The emphasis on freedom of the first perspective points to a retirement policy in which individuals make unimpeded choices in a marketplace of consumption and investment options. The focus is on getting one's money's worth regardless of the choices others might make for themselves, as the saying goes, each tub resting on its own bottom. The emphasis on security of the second perspective looks toward collective means for people to enhance each other's security, people struggling for security in the same boat. The first normative position celebrates a free society of aggregated individuals looking out for themselves; the second celebrates a society of one people organizing mutual social protection for each other. The first beckons people toward self-sufficiency, the second toward group cohesiveness.

Since norms of both personal freedom and shared security are highly valued in American culture, advocates on each side often try to steal one another's clothes. Pro-liberty advocates may point out that security is enhanced by ownership and management of one's own assets, thereby avoiding dependence on political third parties. Pro-security advocates can respond that freedom is enhanced by avoiding a go-it-alone approach in favor of collective arrangements that limit people's dependence on economic uncertainties and charity. Despite such acknowledgments of each other's attractiveness, freedom and security remain in tension with each other. They are core values embedded in the deep structure of public opinion whenever ordinary people think about their lives and the kind of society government policy should promote.

No reform proposals being seriously debated today lie at either of these two polar extremes. All are hybrid middle-range positions trying to combine desires for both individual freedom and collective social protection. This is as it should be in a democracy where people cherish two opposing but unrelinquishable values. The purpose in contrasting the two core values is to recognize that, though hybrids, the various reform options do point in one or the other of these two directions. A fundamental normative choice is at issue in deciding whether to move from a compulsory collective provision to a system attaching greater value to compulsory individual saving for one's own account. This difference deserves to be taken seriously, not dismissed as mere "philosophy."

If Americans decide to maintain some modestly revised version of the existing Social Security system, they are in effect asserting a normative emphasis on social protection through mutual provision, a norm of social solidarity. There is, after all, good reason why the current Social Security program is termed "social" insurance. Risks of financial insecurity in old age are pooled in one national program where people stand together by paying in earmarked taxes and receiving back standardized benefits.[96] Maintaining some version of the

96. That all are in the same program of pooled risks does not imply all are treated in an exactly uniform way. The point is that in social insurance any differences in treatment are justified by claims of serving a social purpose and not strictly claims of individual equity. In private insurance the latter claims legitimately sort people to favor those who are healthier, higher paid, more regu-

status quo would mean that at the center of retirement policy would be a commonly shared pension program that seeks to provide a basic retirement income for all Americans. The current Social Security system is aptly pictured as a safety net protecting all with the same basic security package. This common security takes the form of a given array of retirement benefits, earned through a work history (not a direct return on one's own contributions) and paid however long one lives (with upward adjustments for inflation). Within that common coverage, each person can pursue added coverage, such as tax-favored retirement savings (IRAs, 401(k) plans) and voluntary employment-based plans that each worker owns individually (again, in a regime of supportive government policy and regulations). The essence of the Social Security program itself, however, is the priority of a common social bond with a common security package for all citizens. Money's worth calculations are not decisive because they ignore the existing system's social solidarity mission—that it is not a purely cash-and-carry economic transaction but a "social" program. Thus the existing Social Security program has sought to promote what proponents regard as a fairer society than would otherwise exist.[97] Behind all the details is the moral contention that the better off should help the worse off—in this case, helping with financial security in old age among people socially bonded as equal citizens, not givers and recipients of charity.

If one decides to reform Social Security by replacing all or a substantial portion of the current system with some version of personal savings accounts, the main emphasis of retirement policy would be reversed. Privatization would put individually owned and managed accounts at the center of retirement policy, accompanied by more residual social protections. Privatization alternatives would not abandon the aged who do not save enough or invest wisely to the sole support of family and friends; minimum government pensions and a means-tested welfare program would no doubt remain. But the emphasis would be on individualized security and freedom of choice rather than on shared security of a predefined benefit (related in part to past earnings but covering all Americans under roughly the same terms). The emphasis would shift from the "one net" security of the current social insurance approach to a more individualized

---

larly employed. By contrast the rationale of social insurance is a forced uniting of people at different risk levels.

97. This motive has for half a century been expressed in two features of the existing system. First, financial resources for consumption are transferred from better-off persons to lower-paid workers of the same generation; this occurs in the formula by which benefit entitlements are related to prior earnings contribution records. Second, generations made wealthier by economic growth have transferred resources to their less wealthy parents' generation when they have gotten old. See Myers (1985).

system of many different security packages, with each person much more the weaver of his or her own safety net. Below that would lie the public provision of means-tested transfers, which opponents of this approach regard as stigmatizing charity and proponents regard as a more efficient use of resources. Be that as it may, the essence of the individualized accounts approach is the priority of individuals freely obtaining their own returns for retirement income. The prospects for great variability in those results is judged acceptable for sake of the larger cause of promoting individually responsible free choices.

Behind all the details, Social Security reform asks Americans to consider this choice of a more individualistic or solidaristic vision of their evolving society. Academics and other experts have no special authority for telling other people what that choice should be.

A Political Risk Assessment of Reform Alternatives

Risk assessment invites attention to the prospects for political pressures to destabilize a given approach over time, rendering the plan's original design unsustainable in its promised operations and purpose. The following sections consider political risks that seem plausibly associated with the central alternatives of maintaining the current policy structure versus introducing reforms based on individual accounts. A fuller consideration would have to pay greater attention to degrees of privatization in more detailed alternatives, as well as consider how likely a little bit of privatization is to lead to a lot of privatization. The reality of history is that slippery slopes point in many different directions. Here we confine ourselves to considering how slippery the biggest of the slippery slopes might be.

Maintaining the Current System

Continuing the current Social Security system requires elimination of a future imbalance between promised benefits and the revenues available to pay them. Proponents of major reform argue that its looming problems render the current system politically unsustainable. There appear to be four central issues in considering the political riskiness and viability of the status quo.

—*Issue 1: the public and its elected representatives may not tolerate the tax and benefits changes needed to keep the current Social Security program solvent.* The strength of this argument depends heavily on the timing and scale of the changes needed. If solvency depends on very large tax increases and/or benefit reductions in the near term, the political difficulties could be very great indeed. However, if the required pain from tax and benefit changes is small and need occur only in the distant future, the contention should carry little weight.

The reality falls somewhere in between.[98] Current estimates expect revenues of Social Security to fall short of expected benefit spending by 14 percent over the next seventy-five years. If the present payroll tax rate remains unchanged, benefit payments currently promised would need to be reduced nearly one-quarter by 2030 in order to keep the current system solvent. Contrariwise, if promised benefit payments are to remain unchanged into the distant future, the payroll tax—now 6.2 percent for employers and employees alike—would have to rise to about 7.3 percent for each by about 2020, to about 8.5 percent by 2035 and about 8.8 percent by around 2060. On a pay-as-you-go basis this would, according to current projections, eliminate the future gap between Social Security payments and revenues. A compromise would entail some combination of benefit reductions and payroll tax increases.[99]

Is the required scale of benefit and tax changes, phased in over a period of decades, politically feasible? There are several reasons for regarding this as an open rather than a closed question. First, the Social Security reform of 1983 managed to gain political acceptance for a significant package of benefit cuts and tax increases.[100] Compared to requirements of the current situation, the scale of needed adjustments was similar but the lead time for making some of those sacrifices was shorter.

Second, evidence from public opinion polls and focus groups appears at least ambiguous. Opinion research indicates most Americans consider Social Security taxes to be a "fair" form of taxation. The majority of Americans (60 percent) continue to support the idea that a part of every worker's income goes to support the Social Security program (19 percent neutral and 17 percent oppose), and given the choice 63 percent say they would prefer to implement some tax increases now to lessen tax increases on future workers.[101] Focus groups have found workers are surprised to discover that their Social Security

98. Board of Trustees Federal Old-Age, Survivors and Disability Trust Fund (1997, pp. 110, 122).
99. Since the early 1970s the automatic indexing for Social Security benefits relative to inflation rates has constrained politicians' freedom to adjust the program to ongoing economic and demographic changes. The result is that today's pressures for fundamental change are probably greater than they might otherwise have been if the nonindexing flexibility had been retained. Although relevant, changing the political calculus by revising Social Security's indexing policy is beyond the scope of this paper.
100. In the 1980s, amid a deepening sense of crisis, Congress found it politically feasible to delay cost-of-living adjustments, initiate income taxes on Social Security benefits for high income groups, and reduce the general level of future benefits (by scheduling increases in the age of normal retirement two decades hence).
101. EBRI (1995, questions 8 and 13).

tax rate is no higher than it is and that the tax increase needed to cover the future financing gap in Social Security is so small.[102]

Finally, the presumption of public resistance to future tax increases and benefit reductions cannot be regarded as a decisive argument against the status quo. This is because any transition to a "privatized" system will also require some version of tax increases, benefit restraints, or combinations of the two. If promises to current retirees and older workers are to be kept, their pension bills must be paid at the same time as workers contribute to any new type of their own compulsory savings account. The combination of the sense of moral obligation of most Americans and the voting power of the elderly compel this outcome politically.

The issue thus becomes refined to asking if there is reason to believe Americans will be significantly more likely to support and sustain tax increases and/or benefit restraints in pursuit of privatized accounts than for purposes of maintaining the established Social Security system.

—*Issue 2: compulsory savings may be more politically popular if people have their own individual retirement accounts.* In effect, this argument is that it would be less risky politically to move to a privatized system than to make needed financial adjustments within the current Social Security program. The basic claim is that additional taxes needed for the transition to privatized retirement will be more politically sustainable than simply raising payroll taxes to cover the looming Social Security financing gap. The contention is that people will be more willing to accept tax increases and benefit reductions as a means of accumulating their own private accounts than as a collective feature of today's public retirement system. This same logic applies to proposals to increase national savings and future economic growth by shifting toward advance funding rather than the current pay-as-you-go financing.

Are people more willing to accept consumption sacrifices if the results are of direct individual benefit to them than if not? On the surface the question would seem to answer itself. But beneath the truism—people usually do not do something unless they get something out of it—lies the deeper fact that people operate from complex motivations. What is seen to be of individual benefit need not necessarily be an exclusively private benefit. Political society, with its everyday restrictions on individual choice and required consumption sacrifices, would hardly be possible otherwise. What Alexis de Tocqueville wrote about nineteenth-century Americans has been repeatedly confirmed by subsequent

---

102. The public perception of impending bankruptcy often implies zero funds left to pay benefits in the near future, but participants in focus groups gain a more realistic understanding when they hear the problem is that current levels of payroll taxes will be able to pay for only roughly 75 percent of benefits at a time some thirty years from now.

historical experience.[103] In this country, persuasive political arguments are typically framed, neither in terms of narrowly privatized benefits nor social altruism, but in terms of "enlightened self-interest." In other words, the appeal that often succeeds is that the individual will benefit by doing something for a worthwhile common purpose. Thus the true argument, that people expect to see benefits from consumption sacrifices, does not necessarily imply that earmarked contributions to personal retirement accounts are ipso facto more politically viable than nonearmarked alternatives. Many Americans clearly worry about Social Security in terms of "will it be there for me." That does not mean they are indifferent about whether it will be there for others.

—*Issue 3: the current system may continue to lose public support because of the poor rate of return workers earn on their contributions.* Acccording to this view, political risks arise because Social Security is an increasingly bad bargain for its contributors. In terms of its future pension benefits, the rate of return on workers' payroll contributions is significantly less than individuals could reasonably expect to achieve by saving and investing for retirement on their own account. Support for the current system will continue to erode as people realize they are not getting their "money's worth" from government and realize they could do better in managing their own compulsory savings for retirement.[104]

A strong variant of this argument predicts future "generational warfare" when today's younger Americans experience an especially low rate of return on their contributions in order to support the large cohort of aging baby boomers early in the twenty-first century. As this conflict is predicted to unfold, boomers defending their economic interests in Social Security will come into sharp conflict with younger generations resenting the high payroll taxes necessary to pay those bills. We could then expect powerful incentives to reduce benefits for the wealthy. The worsening financial crisis will encourage increased taxation or means-testing of Social Security benefits, destroying in turn the program's political constituency among high- to moderate-income groups.

In response to this view, four points should be taken into account. First, any demand for higher rates of return speaks in favor of more active investment of mandatory savings, but it does not necessarily argue for either private or public management of such investments. Higher returns could also be obtained for contributors by more aggressive public investment of compulsory savings within the framework of the existing Social Security program.

103. de Tocqueville (1966).
104. The rate of return is also far less for current workers than it was for those born before 1940. But since the World War II generation of Americans are generally seen as deserving of their Social Security pensions and well organized to defend them, the risk of political backlash because of any sense of this retrospective unfairness appears small.

Second, rate-of-return calculations deal with future retirement pensions but do not capture all the benefits that people seem to value in the existing Social Security program. These collateral benefits include the inflation-proof nature of Social Security retirement, disability, and survivors' insurance provided through Social Security, and Social Security's special emphasis on adequate pensions for low-income workers. To disregard these popular features of the current system (which are not included in "money's worth" calculations) is itself a significant political risk for those who would depart from the existing system.

Third, opinion research suggests that Social Security's broad public support does not derive strictly from workers' individual calculations of expected rates of return on the payroll taxes they pay. Popularity of the existing Social Security system has coexisted with the fact that approximately two-thirds of working-age Americans understand that their individual payroll taxes are not set aside especially for their own retirement benefits. Neither does there appear to be a widespread feeling that the elderly are getting too large a share of government benefits.[105] None of this, however, denies that impending financial pressures will preclude everyone from receiving the same high returns on Social Security taxes that were experienced in past decades.

Fourth, there are strong electoral incentives for almost all politicians to avoid framing problems of retirement policy in terms of a conflict between younger and older voters. In all but the smallest demographically homogeneous districts, such divisive strategies are vulnerable to opponents' vote-maximizing strategy of claiming a more centrist position spanning generations (for example, by appeals to shared sacrifice, to the common interest of young and old in retirement security, to the value of maintaining elderly Americans' independence from family support). This strategic vulnerability to counterattack has proven a persistent problem for "generational equity" advocacy groups.

Finally, this argument assumes that politicians will not act in time to prevent generational conflict under the existing system but will do so in producing a privatized system. Hence one is thrown back on the question of timely reform discussed under Issue 1. If the political process is incapable of taking preventive action to avoid generational conflict by adjusting the current system, it is difficult to see why we should assume it capable of adopting preventive privatizing reforms to avoid generational conflict. Only if Issue 2's premise is assumed—that privatized accounts are a necessary condition for the sacrifices

---

105. Light (1985, p. 63). Although this may change in the future, in 1993 a majority of baby boomers felt the elderly were receiving *less* than their fair share of benefits, 37 percent felt the elderly's share was about right, and only 9 percent thought they were getting more than their fair share. (In fact most younger voters erroneously believe seniors receive less in benefits than they contributed during their lifetimes.) Strahilevitz (1997, p. 34).

involved in timely action—does the continuing loss of public support appear inherent in the present system.

—*Issue 4: the current system is being undermined by a general loss of public confidence and risks losing political legitimacy as time goes on.* Unlike the other issues, here the concern is for a broader sense of insecurity on the public's part, not simply the expected low rates of return on Social Security contributions or the unpopularity of any future tax and benefit changes. To a sporadically attentive public, the Social Security policy that had seemed stable and predictable in earlier decades now seems problematic. Public opinion data show that despite strong overall support for the Social Security program, confidence in the program's promises—the expectation that "it will be there for me"—has been ebbing.[106]

In polls, political debates, and everyday conversation, the problem of public confidence is invariably expressed as respondents' feelings that Social Security benefits will not be there when it comes time for them to retire. This opinion is especially evident among younger working Americans. Recurring media accounts of an upcoming financial crisis in Social Security fuel this loss of confidence in a public already predisposed to disbelieve whatever politicians and policymakers are telling them on any subject. This lack of confidence is accompanied by major public misunderstandings of the Social Security system, particularly in exaggerating the current level of payroll taxes, administrative costs, and future financial deficits.

The "it won't be there for me" argument is an important indicator of public distrust. Insofar as this view taps the generalized distrust that now prevails against government and politicians, it colors the background of *any* attempt either to maintain or privatize the current system. This reaffirms how important (and how difficult) it is for policymakers to speak clearly and truthfully about vital policy issues. However, "it won't be there for me" appears to be a way of registering a generalized mistrust about politics and government rather than a focused judgment about the sustainability of the Social Security program in particular. One should not take the "Expect Nothing" view as a guide to any particular policy action. When asked about their expected sources of retirement income, virtually all Americans expect to receive Social Security, and the majority have made little preparation for personal savings in light of the Social Security that "won't be there." None of this mistrust constitutes an argument against reforms that would maintain the current system. Tapping the same generalized public cynicism, polls show nearly half of all Americans think official economic statistics are inaccurate because the federal government deliberately

---

106. Reno and Friedland (1997).

manipulates the numbers to mislead people.[107] This would be a poor reason to abandon the system of official economic reports (though a very good reason to try and ensure they are fair and honest).

In terms of Social Security reform, the essential political risk raised by the confidence issue is a public ignorance that can easily undermine sustainable policy. Already predisposed to distrust anything being said in policy debates, the public may lack the well-informed perspective needed to carry through long-term choices about retirement policy.

The problem of sustaining the confidence of a poorly informed public applies to advocates on all sides of the reform debate, whether it is a matter of maintaining the current program or moving to a privatized system of policy promises. Public opinion polls used by politicians and the media to gauge policy preferences produce superficial off-the-cuff responses to the options presented. They offer little evidence of the serious public judgment needed for weighing the issues and persevering in a course of action. This is crucial in retirement policy, which to be workable must sustain public support across decades. Thus advocates on different sides can use current polls to show that 63 percent of workers would favor reforming Social Security by cutting future benefits for high-income retirees, that 64 percent would favor partially privatizing the system with individually directed accounts, and that 69 percent would favor investing some Social Security trust funds in the stock market.[108] Since these are to a large extent mutually offsetting reforms, such evidence suggests volatile snap opinions rather than the matured public "judgments" needed for long-term confidence in any approach. Opinions typically crystalize as Congress considers passage of policy proposals and issues are "framed" for public attention in the media. But even then, what really matters is whether realistic opinion materializes in the long haul, which is to say, once choices are made and the working out of policy implementation proceeds.

The difficulty of building long-term confidence on firm foundations of public understanding poses a major risk across all parts of the political spectrum for any reform alternatives. This is especially true since so many of today's leaders and advocacy groups now rely heavily on polls, focus groups, and other "short-term" political marketing devices.[109]

107. *Washington Post*, October 13, 1996, p. A.38.

108. EBRI (1997, p.11).

109. The dangers are illustrated by the Medicare Catastrophic Coverage Act of 1988 (MCAA). Quickly repealed under pressure from the elderly themselves, the act's fate indicated that individual calculations of rates of return were not decisive, since some 60 percent of the elderly would have received benefits in excess of their personal costs. Although high-income elderly people were most likely to mobilize in opposing the program, and all elderly misunderstood key aspects of the

In short, without well-informed public commitment, clever politics easily out-smarts itself. The general message is that even though public education about Social Security reform is a long and difficult road, any shortcuts of mere political salesmanship are destined to be self-defeating. Genuine public understanding is necessary for long-term policy stability.

Introducing Individual Asset Accounts

In the Social Security reform debate there are several different versions of what is widely referred to as the "privatizing" options. Although it would retain much of the existing system, one proposal would channel new or existing payroll contributions from workers into personal savings accounts. Individuals would then have discretion in investing this growing fund for retirement. A more far-reaching version of privatization would eventually replace the current form of Social Security pensions (which combine earnings-related and redistributive elements) with a two-tier system. Workers would be required to contribute to individual investment accounts, which would then pay whatever retirement benefits have been earned. At the second tier would be a basic minimum Social Security pension paid as a flat-rate benefit (offering the same sum for everyone after a given period of employment).

Despite their differences, the basic logic is the same in these and other privatization proposals. All would move toward a system focused on compulsory savings accounts that are individually earmarked and managed for one's own retirement. In effect, the policy emphasis would shift from a general social insurance framework to a universalized version of separate, but now compulsory 401(k) accounts. This section considers the general political risks that all such proposals entail.

Special caution is required in assessing the political risks of individual accounts because of the asymmetry of risk between a largely known status quo program and a hypothetical new policy structure. Since there is actual experience with the Social Security program, we are more likely to recognize the political risks associated with existing policy than we are to predict the new politics arising from a more privatized system. The adage of "better the devil you know" is not grounds for rejecting fundamental changes to the status quo,

---

program, it was the lower-income elderly who were most poorly informed. The vast majority did not know that MCAA had an ability-to-pay financing structure, the major provision that should have appealed to low- and moderate-income elderly. Advocates of catastrophic insurance had sold the program as offering significant benefits to all older Americans and downplayed its progressive financing structure. With little solid base of public knowledge about what was happening, informed consent proved lacking for what reformers were doing. Himelfarb (1995).

but it is a good reason to think very carefully about possible ramifications. The one thing certain is that continuing political reactions and adjustments will occur in any new system. What major reform creates is a different institutional context—different rules of the game—that shapes political interactions and that could be shaped in turn by any subsequent political forces that may be set in motion. Hence the point of departure is to recognize that reforming federal retirement policy is a long-term wager with the future, where the political risks of the prevailing system are familiar and the equivalent risks of any not-yet-running system are largely unknown. Thoughtful citizens will want to wager accordingly.

—*Issue 1. It may prove politically difficult if not impossible to sustain personal investment accounts as retirement savings.* Privatization would create a huge new system of compulsory savings accounts involving tens of millions of working Americans. On the surface the terms for restricting early withdrawals from, or borrowings against, these accounts before retirement seem a technical matter. It is certainly difficult to imagine that passage of such a major reform will depend on such legislative details or regulations. But in fact the issue of withdrawal and borrowing is crucial. The central risk in any retirement policy is that sufficient funds will not be present when work ceases and from then until the retiree's death. Sustainable policy requires that restrictions against early withdrawal or borrowing will have to be firmly maintained over a number of decades. If this does not happen, many persons will likely reach retirement age with their personal accounts depleted for all sorts of good causes that occurred during their working lives. The risk is that short-term political responsiveness to constituents' demands for access to their investment accounts could easily turn long-term retirement policy into a shambles.

In response, there is some experience showing that it has been possible to create legislative and regulatory firewalls to insulate long-term policy commitments from short-term political pressures. For example, restrictions on early withdrawals from IRAs and 401(k) plans have been created and maintained. However it is also becoming increasingly common for discretionary contribution plans with employers, including most 401(k) plans, to permit early distributions as loans or for hardship exceptions.[110]

Little of this past experience may be relevant. On the one hand, IRAs and 401(k) plans are voluntary arrangements individuals enter into in return for tax breaks; loss of tax benefits for early withdrawal is an accepted condition in setting up one's plan. Moreover existing restrictions on early withdrawals are largely that, restrictions rather than absolute prohibitions. Without much sterner

110. Perun (1997, p. 9).

measures for privatized investment accounts than now exist for IRAs and 401(k) plans, political erosion of retirement funds for various good causes would likely flourish. Federal Reserve monetary authorities and Social Security administrators are largely insulated from short-term political pressures. However, these authorities now deal with aggregate funds where there is no question of individual access to accounts. The likely politics of individual retirement savings accounts would be different. The greater the emphasis put on individual ownership and management, the more difficult it will be to maintain government-imposed restrictions on the uses of such funds. This is especially likely because individualized accounts—which may look similar to existing IRA, 401(k), and other tax-subsidized savings instruments—will be treated very differently as frozen retirement funds.

In short, the very advantage claimed for the new system—namely, the political attraction of selling forced savings with the idea that "it's your own money"—will make it more difficult in the long run to sustain such nest eggs for retirement. Under a privatized system, elected politicians will have to resist voters, who having been told it is "their money" the government has compelled them to accumulate in these accounts, must also be told they cannot get at it when they and their dependents need it.

Preretirement needs are a very real prospect given that the bulk of Americans not currently accumulating significant individual financial assets will do so under the new system. For example, one estimate is that somewhat over one-half (54 percent) of all married couples with children lack adequate financial assets (savings, investments and the like) to support themselves for three months at a poverty level of living.[111] These and many other households in an economically precarious situation will constitute a large potential constituency for relaxing Washington's rules prohibiting early withdrawals and borrowing from the new privatized accounts. The line of least political resistance will be to allow exceptions for hardship cases. This in turn will provide precedents for continual "thawing" in savings accounts supposedly frozen for retirement income. Adding to this temptation is people's general tendency to overestimate the wealth represented by a fund of X dollars, not recognizing the large nest egg needed to produce an adequate flow of income during one's retirement years.[112]

Experience shows many examples of benefits granted with costs deferred or hidden, but rarely an instance of political costs imposed so that benefits might be deferred. Overall, it is plausible to expect short-term political responsiveness at the expense of long-term retirement policy.

111. Oliver and Shapiro (1995, pp. 87–88).
112. This misperception, a form of "wealth illusion," seems quite common throughout the general public.

—Issue 2. Poorly managed individual accounts may create political pressures for government bailouts and guaranteed returns as retirement approaches. Even if early withdrawal and borrowing pressures are firmly resisted, the returns on individual investment accounts will be quite variable. Such variability is inherent when individuals take over management of their own compulsory retirement savings, given the inherent uncertainties of future economic change. With the right to choose comes the inevitable chance of being wrong. And this creates a political risk that those who have not done well in investing for retirement security will press for redress, producing new instabilities in retirement policy. This bailout tendency is likely to be fueled by the fact that younger generations of Americans—including almost all those now in the media covering Social Security issues—exhibit high, but untested, levels of trust in private financial markets. With their experience limited to a post-1980 Wall Street and with the passing of the Depression era generation, American society has been gradually replacing its collective memory of hard times with a presumption of confidence in private financial arrangements.

Further, the conversion of individual accounts into a stream of retirement income depends significantly on economic conditions at the time of retirement. Thus, someone who retires in one month may, because of interest rate changes in the interim, receive a significantly different payout amount from his neighbor with the same savings who retires only a short time later. This variability may add to the political demands for "fairer" treatment.

The history of public policy is rich with examples of demands for compensatory government action when free choice and competition do not produce the happy endings people expect. As the savings and loan bailouts of the 1980s indicate, much depends on the capacity of would-be bailees to organize and exert political pressure. Given their dispersed and economically weak position, individuals who have not done well with privatized accounts seem unlikely to be in a position to gain infusions of public funds into their personal accounts. It is more likely that the pressures arising from poor individual investment performance will be indirect in nature. There appear to be three such risks.

First, the most immediate indirect pressures could be new political demands for favorable government management of the investment climate. With individual accounts invested in the stock market will come millions of new households tracking the changing value of their holdings annually or perhaps even quarterly and monthly. Washington could face a loud populist voice seeking to restrain authorities such as the Federal Reserve Board from taking unpopular moves, such as interest rate changes that might cause the stock market to fall. Unlike current pension or mutual fund holdings in the market, the new privatized accounts will probably seem less far removed from individuals and thus more prone to demands for short-term responsiveness, particularly since government itself has required such investment savings. (Such pressure might also occur with public investment of Social Security funds in the stock market, but so long as Social Security maintains a defined-benefit structure, this response should be far more muted.)

Second, hundreds of millions of dollars in new personal accounts will create a huge new market for personal financial services. It is reasonable to expect this lucrative market to become crowded with competitors offering advisory services with management fees. It is equally reasonable to expect that some of this advice will prove unhelpful, and perhaps even disastrous, for persons hoping to maintain a decent standard of living in retirement. As investments turn sour, greatly increased political pressure for regulation of the private financial services industry is likely. Proregulation forces are especially likely to gain strength over time. In this new "privatized" arena of retirement policy, conventional public hostility to government regulation will be minimal because the federal government itself has been the central actor in creating this market and putting individual Americans into it. The larger the scale of privatization, the greater the paternalistic regulation that may occur. And because the individual stakes are so direct, visible, and massive, the regulatory regime that emerges will be more highly politicized than anything currently known in the financial services industry.

A final indirect pressure may be one that tries to improve the position of those whose retirement investments have not gone well. As we have noted, "privatizing" reforms would still maintain government's safety net role by providing a small pension as well as a means-tested welfare system to provide some minimum level of income to elderly persons who cannot support themselves under the new system. This pressure would translate into efforts to raise the level of minimum pension/welfare payments to supplement what is available from the return on personal accounts. This would appear to be the smallest of the three possibilities for bailout. Experience shows (as with the failed Medicare Catastrophic Insurance) that those who are most vulnerable in American society are not particularly effective at organizing to exert political pressure. Political risks that such a "revolt from below" could destabilize a system of private retirement accounts seem small. Much more likely is a "revolt from above," the possibility we turn to with Issue 3.

—*Issue 3. A system of privatized Social Security reform may lead to growing disregard for the gap between the haves and have-nots in retirement.* Different approaches to retirement policy supply different frameworks for structuring politics as time goes on. As noted in the earlier discussion of values, the current Social Security system is a collectivist framework that encourages thinking about what outcomes are socially desirable. This existing policy structure puts everyone in the same boat, in the sense that it returns a given benefit package for all similarly situated workers under the same terms. By the program's very nature, individuals asking "will it be there for me" are necessarily asking "will it be there for us." A system of privatized asset accounts creates a different, individualistic framework. It guides attention to what is individually profitable. The required contributions are particularized to separate individuals who are left free to gain whatever return they can for themselves. Obviously there will be collective rules to follow, but individuation is the very essence of privatized accounts.

This creates a risk that over time policy reforms based on personal investment accounts will create a political dynamic for developing first-class and second-class citizens in the public pension system. At the outset, reforms might contain both privatized accounts and some version of the current Social Security pension. However, the concern is that, as time passes, the operational politics of such a system will undermine any sense that Americans share a commitment to adequate retirement pensions for all workers. In effect, privatized accounts will offer a ready-made vehicle for better-off workers to secede from the fate of other workers.

This is a realistic possibility because the basic logic of privatized asset accounts separates more clearly the redistributive elements of public retirement policy from its personal return-on-contribution features, replacing adequacy for all with equity for the individual. Thus individual accounts will encourage a two-tier pension system that can easily evolve into a division of political constituencies between the weak and the strong. Low-earning, irregularly employed workers will not do as well as others in accumulating personal investment accounts. Neither are they likely to have the investment savvy of more privileged portions of the population. At the same time, the economically better-off will have a vested interest, and more political clout, to push for further improvements in the privatized sphere of federal retirement policy. The constituency more dependent on second-tier basic pensions is unlikely to have the power to keep up with this quiet revolt from above.

The real political risk is not class warfare but a soft landing into growing inequality. Despite occasional rhetorical references to class war in the United States, this is not a realistic risk, if only because those disadvantaged lack resources for the fight. The more likely overt tension will be at the bottom of a privatized retirement system. This is because it will be very difficult to maintain a distinction between the government's minimum basic pension and its means-tested welfare payment for the elderly. Each of these residual safety net programs in a privatized system ostensibly is trying to provide poorer retirees with enough to get by on. Those wanting an adequate basic pension without the stigma of welfare will be at odds with those claiming that welfare benefits are inadequate if they fall below the value of basic subsistence pensions.

In sum, the long-term political risk of privatized accounts is that the nation will gradually and subtly, but decisively, abandon the public policy goal of ensuring financial security in old age for all Americans.

Conclusion

Politically speaking, the American public does not blame the elderly for Social Security's problems. The blame is seen to rest largely with the government and politicians. Nor is this surprising since this is what the partisan and imprudent politics of the recent past has been teaching Americans to think.

In any democratic system, for any public policy issue, the great political sin is to fail to teach people about reality. The punishment for such sin is long term and remorseless. The public becomes ever more intractable for leaders to deal with. What should be deliberative talk of democracy becomes frozen by fear, anger, and mutual distrust on all sides. Rather than learning to do the work of citizens and deal with serious policy challenges, people are taught to become simply clients, consumers, or complainants. Hence the greatest risk in Social Security reform is that it will lack the kind of political leadership that is willing to dare losing its position for the sake of honestly telling citizens complex truths. In the end, the politics of national retirement policy gives renewed edge to the ancient warning: where there is no vision, the people perish.

References

Advisory Council on Social Security. 1997a. *Report of the 1994–1996 Advisory Council on Social Security: Vol. 1: Findings and Recommendations.* Washington: Government Printing Office.

_____. 1997b. *Report of the 1994–1996 Advisory Council on Social Security: Vol. 2: Reports of the Technical Panels.* Washington: Government Printing Office.

Bernheim, B. Douglas, and Daniel M. Garrett. 1996. *The Determinants and Consequences of Financial Education in the Workplace; Evidence from a Survey of Households.* Working Paper 5667. Cambridge: Mass.: National Bureau of Economic Research.

Blake, David. 1997. "Pension Choices and Pensions Policy in the United Kingdom." In *The Economics of Pensions*, edited by S. Valdes-Prieto, 277–317. Cambridge: Cambridge University Press.

Blake, David, William Burrows, and J. Michael Orszag. 1998. "Stakeholder Annuities: Reducing the Costs of Pension Provision." London: Pensions Institute.

Blake, David, and J. Michael Orszag. 1997. *Towards a Universal Funded Second Pension*, Special Report. London: Pensions Institute.

Blendon, Robert J., and others. 1998. "America in Denial: The Public's View of The Future of Social Security." *Brookings Review* (Summer).

Board of Trustees, Federal Old-Age and Survivors Insurance and Disability Insurance Trust Funds. 1997. *1997 Annual Report of the Board of Trustees of the Federal Old-Age and Survivors Insurance and Disability Insurance Trust Funds.* Washington: Government Printing Office.

Bodie, Zvi, Alan J. Marcus, and Robert C. Merton. 1988. "Defined Benefit versus Defined Contribution Plans: What Are the Real Trade-offs?" In *Pensions in the U.S. Economy,* edited by Zvi Bodie, John B. Shoven, and David A. Wise, 139–62. University of Chicago Press.

Bohn, Henning. 1997a. "Risk Sharing in a Stochastic Overlapping Generations Economy." University of California at Santa Barbara.

_____. 1997b. "Social Security Reform and Financial Markets." In Social Security Reform Conference Proceedings, Conference Series 41, 193–241. Federal Reserve Bank of Boston.

Boskin, Michael. 1986. *Too Many Promises: The Uncertain Future of Social Security.* Dow-Jones-Irwin.

Boskin, Michael J., Laurence J. Kotlikoff, and John B. Shoven. 1988. "Personal Security Accounts: A Proposal for Fundamental Social Security Reform." In *Social Security and Private Pensions,* edited by Susan M. Wachter, 179–208 (Lexington Books).

Boskin, Michael, and others. 1987. "Social Security: A Financial Appraisal within and across Generations." *National Tax Journal* 40 (March): 19–34.

Burkhauser, Richard V., and Timothy M. Smeeding. 1994. *Social Security Reform: A Budget Neutral Approach to Reducing Older Women's Disproportionate Risk of Poverty.* Policy Brief 2/1994. Syracuse University, Center for Policy Research.

Burtless, Gary. 1997. "Replacement Rate Projections." Brookings.

Burtless, Gary, and Barry Bosworth. 1997. "Privatizing Social Security: The Troubling Tradeoffs." *Brookings Policy Brief,* no. 14.

Coile, Courtney, and others. 1997. "Delays in Claiming Social Security Benefits." MIT.

Costa, Dora. 1998. *The Evolution of Retirement: An American Economic History, 1880–1990.* University of Chicago Press.

de Tocqueville, Alexis. 1966. "How the Americans Combat Individualism by the Doctrine of Self-Interest Properly Understood." *Democracy in America,* edited by J. P. Mayer and Max Lerner, vol. 2. Harper and Row.

Diamond, Peter. 1977. "A Framework for Social Security Analysis." *Journal of Public Economics* 8 (December): 275–98.

_____. 1982. "Social Security: A Case for Changing the Earnings Test But Not the Normal Retirement Age." MIT.

_____. 1994. "Privatization of Social Security: Lessons from Chile," *Revista de Analisis Economico,* 9 (Junio); revised version in *Social Security: What Role for the Future?* edited by P. Diamond, D. Lindeman, and H. Young, 213–24. Brookings, 1996.

_____. 1995. "Government Provision and Regulation of Economic Support in Old Age." In *Annual Bank Conference on Development Economics, 1995,* edited by Michael Bruno and Boris Pleskovic, 83–103. Washington: World Bank.

_____. 1997. "Macroeconomic Aspects of Social Security Reform." *Brookings Papers on Economic Activity* 2, 1–87.

Diamond, Peter, and Jonathan Gruber. 1998. "Social Security and Retirement in the U.S." Working Paper 6097. In *Social Security and Retirement around the World*, edited by Jonathan Gruber and David Wise, University of Chicago Press (forthcoming).

Diamond, Peter, and Salvador Valdes-Prieto. 1994. "Social Security Reform." In *The Chilean Economy*, edited by Barry Bosworth, Rudiger Dornbusch, and Raul Laban, 257–328. Brookings.

Dickson, Joel. 1997. "Analysis of Financial Conditions Surrounding Individual Accounts." In *Report of the 1994-1996 Advisory Council on Social Security*, vol. II, 484–88. Washington.

Dionne, E.J., Jr. 1991. *Why Americans Hate Politics*. Simon and Schuster.

Edwards, Sebastian. 1998. "The Chilean Pension Reform: A Pioneering Program." Working Paper 5811. Cambridge, Mass.: National Bureau of Economic Research, and in *Privatizing Social Security*, edited by Martin Feldstein, University of Chicago Press (forthcoming).

Employee Benefit Research Institute. 1995. "Public Attitudes on Social Security, 1995." Washington.

_____. 1997. *The 1997 Retirement Confidence Survey: Summary of Findings*. December 23. Washington.

ERISA Industry Committee. 1996. "Getting the Job Done: A White Paper on Emerging Pension Issues." Washington.

Feldstein, Martin, and Andrew Samwick. 1992. "Social Security Rules and Marginal Tax Rates." *National Tax Journal*: 45(1):1–22.

_____. 1997. *The Economics of Prefunding Social Security and Medicare Benefits*. Working Paper 6055. Cambridge, Mass.: National Bureau of Economic Research.

Friedberg, Leora. 1998. "The Social Security Earnings Test and Labor Supply of Older Men." In *Tax Policy and the Economy*, vol. 12, edited by J. Poterba, 121–50. MIT Press.

Friedman, Benjamin, and Mark Warshawsky. 1990. "The Cost of Annuities: Implications for Saving Behavior and Bequests." *Quarterly Journal of Economics* 105 (February): 135–54.

Goodfellow, Gordon P., and Sylvester J. Schieber. Forthcoming. "Simulating Benefit Levels under Alternative Social Security Reform Approaches." In *Prospects for Social Security Reform*, edited by Olivia S. Mitchell, Robert Myers, and Howard Young. University of Pennsylvania Press, Pension Research Council.

Greenspan, Alan. 1997. *Testimony before the Task Force on Social Security of the Committee on the Budget*, U. S. Senate, November 20, 105 Cong. 1 sess. Government Printing Office.

Himelfarb, Richard. 1995. *Catastrophic Politics*. Pennsylvania State University Press.

Holden, Karen. Forthcoming. "Women as Widows under a Reformed Social Security System." In *Prospects for Social Security Reform*, edited by Olivia S. Mitchell, Robert Myers, and Howard Young. University of Pennsylvania Press, Pension Research Council.

Hurd, M., and M. Boskin. 1984. "The Effect of Social Security on Retirement." *Quarterly Journal of Economics* 99 (November): 767–90.

James, Estelle. 1997. *New Systems for Old Age Security*. Policy Working Paper 1766. Washington: World Bank.

King, Francis P. 1996. *Trends in the Selection of TIAA-CREF Life Annuity Options, 1978–1994*. Research Dialogues 48. TIAA-CREF. New York.

Light, Paul. 1985. *Artful Work.* Random House.

McCarty, Nolan, Keith Poole, and Howard Rosenthal. Forthcoming. *The Polarization of American Politics.* Harvard University Press.

Mitchell, Olivia S., and James F. Moore. 1997. "Retirement Wealth Accumulation and Decumulation: New Developments and Outstanding Opportunities." Working Paper 97-12. University of Pennsylvania, Wharton.

Mitchell, Olivia S., James M. Poterba, and Mark Warshawsky. 1997. "New Evidence on the Money's Worth of Individual Annuities." University of Pennsylvania, Wharton.

Munnell, Alicia H., and Pierluigi Balduzzi. 1998. "Investing the Trust Fund in Equities." Washington.: Public Policy Institute, American Association of Retired Persons.

Myers, Robert J. 1985. *Social Security.* Irwin.

Oliver, Melvin R., and Thomas M. Shapiro. 1995. *Black Wealth/White Wealth.* New York: Routledge

Olsen, Kelly A., and others. 1998. "How Do Individual Social Security Accounts Stack Up? An Evaluation Using the EBRI-SSASIM2 Policy Simulation Model." EBRI Issue Brief 195. Washington: Employee Benefit Research Institute. March.

Patashnik, Erik M. 1997. "Unfolding Promises: Trust Funds and the Politics of Pre-commitment." *Political Science Quarterly* 112 (3): 431–52.

Perun, Pamela. 1997. "Defined Contribution Accounts: Their Implications for Distri-bution." Washington: National Academy of Social Insurance. October 22.

Poterba, James M. 1997. "The History of Annuities in the United States." NBER Working Paper 6001. Cambridge, Mass.: National Bureau of Economic Research.

Pozen, Robert C. Forthcoming. "Investment and Administrative Constraints on Personal Security Accounts." In *Prospects for Social Security Reform*, edited by Olivia S. Mitchell, Robert Myers, and Howard Young. University of Pennsylvania Press, Pension Research Council.

Public Agenda. 1997. *Miles to Go: A Status Report on Americans' Plans for Retirement.* New York.

Reno, Virginia P., and Robert B. Friedland. 1997. "Strong Support but Low Confidence." In *Social Security in the 21st Century*, edited by Eric R. Kingson and James H. Schulz, 178–94. Oxford: Oxford University Press.

Sass, Steven A. 1996. *The Promise of Pensions.* Harvard University Press.

Social Security Administration. 1996. *Annual Statistical Supplement to the Social Security Bulletin.*

———. Office of Research, Evaluation and Statistics. 1997. *Fast Facts and Figures about Social Security.* Washington: Government Printing Office.

Strahilevitz, Lior Jacob. 1997. *Shades of Gray: Intergenerational Equity in the Era of Entitlement Reform.* University of California, Berkeley, Institute of Governmental Studies Press.

Tegen, Karen. 1997. "Influence of Survivor Pensions on the Income of Widows: Role of Legislation, Rules, and Consumer Information." M.S. thesis. University of Wisconsin, Department of Consumer Science.

Thaler, Richard. 1985. "Mental Accounting and Consumer Choice." *Marketing Science* 4(Summer): 199–214.

Thompson, Lawrence. 1988. *Older and Wiser.* Washington: Urban Institute Press.

United Kingdom Government Actuary and Secretary of State for Social Security. 1996. *Occupational and Personal Pension Schemes*, Review of Certain Contracting-Out Terms, Presented to Parliament, March.

U.S. Department of Health and Human Services. 1985. *Report on Earnings Sharing Implementation Study.*

U.S. General Accounting Office. 1992. *Pension Plans: Survivor Benefits Coverage for Wives Increased after 1984 Pension Law*. HRD-92-49.

_____. 1996. *401(k) Pension Plans: Many Take Advantage to Ensure Adequate Retirement Income*. GAO/HEHS-96-176.

U.S. House of Representatives. Select Committee on Aging. 1992. *Congressional Symposium on Women and Retirement*, Hearing, Comm. Pub. 102-897. 102 Cong. 2 sess. Government Printing Office.

_____. Committee on Ways and Means. 1994. *Overview of Entitlement Programs, 1994 Green Book*. Government Printing Office.

_____. 1997. *Hearings on the Future of Social Security for This Generation and the Next*. 104 Cong. 2 sess. October 23. Government Printing Office.

Valdes-Prieto, Salvador. 1994. "Administrative Charges in Pensions in Chile, Malaysia, Zambia, and the United States." Policy Research Working Paper 1372. Washington: World Bank.

Yakoboski, Paul, and Jack VanDerhei. 1996. "Worker Investment Decisions: An Analysis of Large 401(k) Plan Data." EBRI Issue Brief 176. Washington: Employee Benefit Research Institute. August.

Yankelovich, Daniel 1991. *Coming to Public Judgment.* Syracuse University Press.

3

Pensions and Savings— In What Form?

THIS CHAPTER describes the private pension and saving environment in which Social Security operates. It provides background for the question of whether individuals will be in a good position to take on the additional market risk associated with a shift from the current defined-benefit plan to a mixed defined-benefit/defined-contribution arrangement.

Employers and Individuals Must Do More Today to Allow Retirement Tomorrow
Dallas L. Salisbury

"A REVIEW of the available evidence indicates that, on a total wealth basis and on a pension savings basis, those in the work force today are doing better than previous generations. However, a minority are building the individual and pension savings that will allow them to meet the goal of maintaining final employment income throughout retirement, without using real estate to produce income.

Should the timing and value of Social Security benefits, Medicare, and employment-based defined-benefit and retiree medical benefits continue to be reduced, the levels of necessary saving will increase, not decline. Should the

The mission of the Employee Benefit Research Institute (EBRI), a Washington-based nonprofit organization, is to contribute to, encourage, and enhance the development of sound employee benefit programs and sound public policy through objective research and education. EBRI does not lobby and does not take positions for or against legislative proposals. The goal of the American Savings Education Council (ASEC), a part of EBRI's Education and Research Fund, is to make saving and planning a vital concern of Americans.

movement toward voluntary pension participation and lump sum distributions continue, increases in participation rates and rates of rollover will be necessary to achieve the income levels projected by today's studies."[1]

Given limited space, I want to use data to emphasize a few points that put the situation of the baby boomers in perspective relative to present retirees. The data show that a great deal of mythology pervades the retirement discussion. Importantly, the data show that:

—Social Security has never provided an adequate income. With changes already enacted to increase the retirement age, and an assumption of no payroll tax increases, benefits for baby boomers will be an average of just under 30 percent of income instead of the 42 percent the present retired population now receives. The lower Social Security contribution to retirement income will require individuals to work longer and to save more. Private employers are beginning to communicate these facts to employees in order to encourage them to save more.

—Even though the parents of the baby boomers rarely had full careers with one employer, employer-sponsored pensions earned over the years before 1980 were limited mainly to the approximately 20 percent of workers who spent a full career with one employer. For the present population of retirees, defined-benefit pensions were sponsored by most large private employers to provide retirement income to employees of long tenure. Large employers also generally sponsored defined-contribution savings and 401(k) plans to assist new and short-service employees as well as long-time employees. Before the early 1980s, small employers never sponsored plans on a widespread basis. However, small companies began to sponsor pension plans following the advent of tax-deferred individual salary reduction plans like 401(k) plans (1981) and the Federal Employee Thrift Plan (1984). Moreover, significant legal changes in terms of vesting, funding, and tax rates, particularly the 1986 Tax Reform Act, have made defined-benefit plans much more expensive and difficult to fund in advance. Although employers can, in the absence of a dramatic drop in the markets or a dramatic run of high inflation, afford to continue the defined-benefit plans now in existence, they may choose not to for reasons connected with demographic forces, work force mobility, and employee preference. Despite all the changes, private employers will nevertheless provide more retirement savings for the average baby boomer than they provide to the average retiree today.

—Few of today's retirees have income from a traditional defined-benefit pension plan or enjoy employer-paid retiree medical benefits. It has gone largely unnoticed that only 24 percent of today's retirees report private

1. Salisbury (1994, p. 10).

employer pension income (18 percent more get public employer pension income), and only 10 percent have Medigap protection fully paid for by employers; thus lack of pension coverage for many of today's retirees is a serious problem. Although coverage is very important to those who have it, the advantages of the status quo should not be overstated. Employers have shown that they cannot, on a widespread basis, afford to pay for retiree medical benefits before or after the age of 65. They do not today; they will not tomorrow. However, private employers are now trying to educate their employees about the need to save for the retirement and the medical costs of old age. For this reason, the baby boomers have an opportunity, with employers' assistance, to be better prepared for retirement than today's retirees.

—Few parents of today's workers saved for their own retirement. This fact stands in sharp contrast to the popular view that retirees have saved for retirement and are all on cruise ships and golf courses. Income from assets is important only to a small minority of retirees today; it must play a larger role if the present generation of workers is to enjoy comfortable retirements. Employers can afford to sponsor a retirement savings plan, and stable and profitable companies can afford to make employer contributions as well. Employers can also encourage employees to use these plans to save for all their retirement spending needs, including retiree medical expenses. Though workers are, for these reasons, doing better than their parents at building retirement assets, they still need to save more. They also need to preserve their access to benefits by rolling lump sum distributions into individual retirement accounts (IRAs) or qualified retirement plans when they change jobs. This kind of change in people's retirement savings behavior will require education and understanding. A number of nonprofit organizations, along with help from employers and some government departments, including the Department of Labor, are working to ensure that public awareness of the retirement savings problem keeps growing.

The private employer pension system is in solid financial condition. As table 3-1 shows, asset growth in the system has been steady. Table 3-1 also presents financial trends in private plans from 1975 to 1994, showing that the defined-benefit system has become quite mature (more on this later). The table highlights the changing composition of retirement benefits provided in the form of defined-benefit plans (the employer promises a given benefit and is responsible for funding it) and those provided in the form of defined-contribution retirement plans (the employer sponsors a plan to which the employee may contribute on a pretax basis and to which the employer may also contribute), showing the growing emphasis on the latter. Future retirees will do better than today's retirees owing to this growing "hybrid" retirement savings system. The growing ratio of contributions to benefits is partially a result of significant

Table 3-1. *Private Plan Financial Trends, Selected Years, 1975–94*[a]

Billions of dollars unless noted otherwise

Item	1975	1980	1981	1982	1983	1984	1985	1986	1987	1988	1989	1990	1991	1992	1993	1994
Assets[b,c]	260	564	629	789	923	1,045	1,253	1,383	1,402	1,504	1,676	1,674	1,936	2,094	2,316	2,299
Defined benefit	186	401	444	553	642	701	826	895	877	912	988	962	1,102	1,147	1,248	1,211
Defined contribution	74	162	185	236	281	344	427	488	525	592	688	712	834	947	1,068	1,088
Defined contribution as percentage of total	28	29	29	30	30	33	34	35	37	39	41	43	43	45	46	47
Contributions[b,d]	37	66	75	80	82	91	95	92	92	91	96	99	111	125	154	144
Defined benefit	24	43	47	48	46	47	42	33	30	26	25	23	30	35	52	39
Defined contribution	13	24	28	31	36	43	53	58	62	65	73	76	81	94	102	105
Defined contribution as percentage of total	35	36	38	39	44	48	56	64	68	71	75	77	73	73	66	73
Benefit payments[b,e]	19	35	45	55	65	79	102	130	122	119	132	129	136	152	156	164
Defined benefit	13	22	27	34	37	47	54	68	66	60	67	66	72	78	79	83
Defined contribution	6	13	17	21	28	33	47	63	56	58	65	63	64	75	77	81
Defined contribution as percentage of total	32	37	39	39	43	41	47	48	46	49	49	49	47	49	49	50

Source: Employee Benefit Research Institute (EBRI) tabulations based on Department of Labor, Pension and Welfare Benefits Administration, *Private Pension Plan Bulletin* (Spring 1998).

a. Excludes single participant plans.

b. Due to rounding, sums of individual items may not equal totals.

c. Excludes funds held by life insurance companies under allocated group contracts for payment of retirement benefits. These funds make up roughly 10 to 15 per-cent of total private pension plan assets.

d. Includes both employer and employee contributions.

e. Includes both benefits paid directly from trust and premium payments made by plans to insurance carriers. Excludes benefits paid directly by insurance carriers.

restrictions on plan funding and income limitations introduced into the law since 1982. These limitations have kept employers from providing the amount of benefits they might desire and also have limited employers' ability to fund benefits. These policies have accordingly reduced the retirement income workers might have obtained from employer plans.

Table 3-2 shows the number of plans by type and participants, and the number of primary plans of each type. As the law shortened vesting requirements for defined-benefit plans, inevitably the role of defined-contribution plans became more important. One Census Bureau survey found that nearly 80 percent of federal employees, for example, view the Federal Employee Thrift Plan, the defined-contribution plan for government employees, as their primary retirement plan, not the defined-benefit plan. Figure 3-1 shows why this is true. Because of the way in which benefit value builds in the two types of plans, any worker with fewer than approximately twenty-five years of service would get more benefit from a defined-contribution plan than from a defined-benefit plan.

By contrast, it is important to note that today's retirees did not save for their retirement. Social Security is the primary source of income for most retirees. Those retirees were told that Social Security benefits would allow them to retire at age 62 or 65, but they were not given much information on what their level of Social Security benefits would be. The implication was that Social Security benefits would finance an adequate standard of living during retirement. Today, we know the income replacement rates are modest for most and that the maximum family benefit does not exceed $25,000. Those with employer pensions do better than others, but the level of individual savings has never been high for most Americans. These observations highlight the first challenge for retirement planning: to get good information on what Social Security might provide (recognizing that Social Security alone will provide adequate income for very few), to take action to get more help from employers in providing for retirement income, and finally, proactively to encourage workers to save toward a secure retirement.

Most workers have never spent a full career with one employer, and even fewer will do so in the future. A telling fact is that 50 percent of men 55 to 64 years old have twelve years or fewer with their present employer, and that 50 percent of women in the same age bracket have ten years or fewer with their present employer. Table 3-3 shows that only 12.4 percent of those 55 to 64 report thirty or more years of service. This percentage is dropping as well, even though it takes thirty years to achieve a maximum pension buildup. A system with portability of cash benefits is one solution to this problem. Figure 3-2 underlines the importance of tenure patterns relative to pension vesting and shows that vesting rates rose dramatically when the law moved vesting requirements down to

Table 3-2. *Private Pension Plans and Participants, Selected Years, 1975–94*

Item	1975	1980	1981	1982	1983	1984	1985	1986	1987	1988	1989	1990	1991	1992	1993	1994
							Thousands of dollars									
Total plans[a,b]	311	489	546	594	603	604	632	718	733	730	731	712	699	708	702	690
Defined benefit[a]	103	148	167	175	175	168	170	173	163	146	132	113	102	89	84	74
Defined contribution[a]	208	341	378	419	428	436	462	545	570	584	599	599	598	620	619	616
Defined contribution as percentage of total	67	70	69	71	71	72	73	76	78	80	82	84	85	87	88	89
							Millions of dollars									
Total participants[b,c]	45	58	61	63	69	74	75	77	78	78	76	77	78	82	84	85
Defined benefit[c]	33	38	39	39	40	41	40	40	40	41	40	39	39	40	40	40
Defined contribution[c]	12	20	22	25	29	33	35	37	38	37	36	38	39	42	44	45
Defined contribution as percentage of total	26	34	36	39	42	45	47	48	49	48	48	50	50	52	52	53
Active participants	31	36	37	37	39	40	40	41	42	42	43	42	43	45	45	46
Primary plan is defined benefit[d]	27	30	30	29	30	30	29	29	28	28	27	26	26	25	25	25
Primary plan is defined contribution[d]	4	6	7	8	9	10	12	13	13	14	15	16	17	19	19	21
Defined contribution as percentage of total	13	16	19	22	23	25	30	32	31	33	35	38	40	42	42	46

Source: EBRI tabulations based on Department of Labor, Pension and Welfare Benefits Administration, *Private Pension Plan Bulletin* (Spring 1998).

a. Excludes single participant plans.

b. Due to rounding, sums of individual items may not equal totals.

c. Includes active, retired, and separated vested participants not yet in pay status. Not adjusted for double counting of individuals participating in more than one plan.

d. For workers covered under both a defined benefit and a defined contribution plan, the defined benefit plan's designated as the primary plan unless the plan name indicates it provides supplemental or past service benefits.

Figure 3-1. *Traditional Defined-Benefit versus Defined-Contribution Plan*

PATTERN OF BENEFIT ACCRUALS

Benefit value of pay (0 percent of pay)

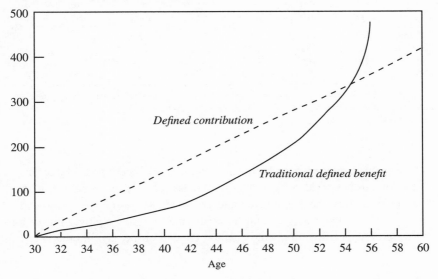

Age

Source: Kelly Olsen and Jack Van Derhei, "Defined Contribution Plan Dominance Grows across Sectors and Employer Sizes, While Mega Defined Benefit Plans Remain Strong," EBRI Issue Brief 190 (Washington: Employee Benefit Research Institute, October 1997).

ten years and then again to five years. As a result of these new requirements, workers' actual entitlements to benefits rose sharply even though pension participation remained steady over the period. In addition, the growth of defined-contribution plans like the Federal Employee Thrift Plan and 401(k)s is very important to workers, as these plans allow workers to build real value even if they change jobs. The popularity of defined-contribution plans thus highlights the second challenge for retirement planning: employees must be careful to save each and every year and must urge employers to provide defined-contribution savings opportunities.

Owing to increasing rates of job turnover, the growing diversity of the pension system is good news. As I have shown, defined-contribution plans have become increasingly popular since 1975. Defined-benefit plans are primarily sponsored by the largest employers in the nation, both public and private. Since employment in organizations with more than 1,000 employees has been relatively steady in absolute numbers, but shrinking as a proportion of the labor force, the number of participants in these plans has remained nearly constant since 1980.

Table 3-3. *Percentage Distribution of Workers, by Years of Tenure at Current Job, by Age, 1996*

Age	Less than 1 year	1–4 years	5–9 years	10–14 years	15 or more years	20 or more years	30 or more years
25–34	25.7	40.5	24.3	8.1	1.3	a	0.0
35–44	14.7	29.0	24.5	14.6	17.2	6.0	a
45–54	11.0	21.7	19.7	14.2	33.5	22.1	3.7
55–64	8.2	19.5	17.5	12.6	42.2	30.5	12.4

Source: EBRI tabulations of the February 1996 Current Population Research Survey research file (final, edited public-use tape will be available in late January 1997).

a. Less than 0.5 percent.

By contrast, defined-contribution plans have always been sponsored by large organizations but are also favored by small ones. These plans generally accrue contributions from both employee and employer. The employer commits to sponsor the plan and may commit to contribute, but the employer makes no promise of a specific retirement benefit at the end of the day. In other words,

Figure 3-2. *Trends in Retirement Plan Sponsorship and Vesting among Civilian Workers, 16 and Older, Selected Years, 1950–93*

Percentage

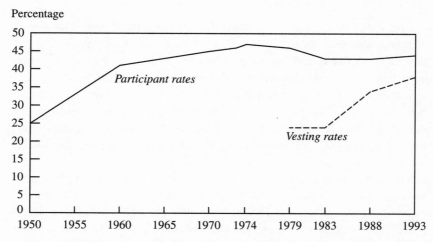

Sources: EBRI estimates of the April 1993 Current Population Survey employee benefits supplement; and U.S. Department of Labor, *Trends in Pensions, 1992* (Washington, 1992).

investment gains and the risk of loss rest with the individual. Since Congress acted in 1978 to allow tax-deferred contributions by both the employer and the employee, the number of defined-contribution plans and participants has grown steadily. The growing popularity of defined-contribution plans highlights the third challenge for retirement planning: workers need to understand what plans are available, how to take advantage of them, and why any plan is better than no plan.

The type of plan is not as important as it used to be for two reasons: all plans are now legally required to pay some benefits in the form of a lump sum distribution, and vesting requirements have accelerated for defined-benefit plans. Figure 3-1 shows the pattern of benefit growth under the defined-contribution and defined-benefit plan approaches. It makes clear that, for the mobile worker (that is, about 75 percent of workers), defined-contribution plans can lead to higher retirement asset accumulations. Both plan types can serve valuable purposes. One plan type does not fit all.

A look at a 1990 snapshot of pension benefit payments reveals that a somewhat startling $107.9 billion was paid in lump sums in 1990, compared with $127.1 billion in annuity payments. This fact raises important retirement security issues: 44 percent of the dollars paid in lump sum distributions are not saved for retirement; and 70 percent of the people who get them do not save them for retirement. Table 3-4 shows simulations of what baby boomer retirement income would look like if all lump sum distributions were rolled over and saved for retirement. Whereas only 36 percent of today's retirees receive private pension benefits, under this simulation private pension benefits would become available to 77 percent of retiring baby boomers, rising to 84 percent in later years. These facts suggest another important component of retirement planning: the need to preserve lump sum distributions now available upon job changes for retirement income.

The data above indicate how important the mandatory system of Social Security and voluntary employer pensions has been in providing income to today's retirees. Table 3-5 gives participation rates in IRAs and 401(k) plans relative to employer pensions. In 1993, 8.1 percent of workers contributed to an IRA (6.3 percent of those without an employer plan). This number compares with 43.7 percent of all workers who were in an employer plan and 64.9 percent of workers who had the option of participation in a 401(k) plan. The low IRA participation rate and the wide availability of 401(k) plans, but for less than universal participation, demonstrates a fifth challenge for retirement planning: we need to find ways to get workers to save on a tax-effective basis when they are given the opportunity.

Table 3-4. *Projected Pension Recipiency with Virtually All
Lump Sum Distributions Rolled Over and Annuitized*

Percentage of aged units with retirement income from various sources, 2018 and 2030[a]

	2018	2030	
Income source	Aged 65 and over	Aged 66–75	Aged 76–84
All retiree families			
Social Security	98	99	97
Employment-based pension	77	81	84
Earnings	20	8	26
Supplemental Security Income	3	1	1

Sources: EBRI tabulations of the Pension and Retirement Income Simulation Model; Advisory Council on Social Security, *Future Financial Resources of the Elderly: A View of Pensions, Savings, Social Security, and Earnings in the 21st Century* (Washington: Advisory Council on Social Security, 1991) (data for 2018); and Lewin-VHI, Inc., *Aging Baby Boomers: How Secure Is Their Economic Future?* (Washington: American Association of Retired Persons, 1994) (data for 2030).

a. Married couples living together where at least one spouse is aged 55 or over and nonmarried persons aged 55 and over.

Retirement planning requires workers to consider the impact of retiree medical expenses. Retirees primarily depend on Medicare and to a lesser extent on employer-provided health benefits. Retirees have frequently acted on their own to purchase supplementation of Medicare where employers have not provided that benefit. Forty-five percent of workers 45 and older will have access to employer-provided health insurance throughout their retirement, but there is wide variation in what the employer will pay. Only 10 to 15 percent of workers will have full Medigap coverage paid for by their employer. The problem of inadequate medical coverage for retirees will become increasingly important as medical costs rise and life expectancies go up.

Conclusion

Today's workers are beginning to save for retirement and will certainly save more than their parents did, but only one-third have yet done an estimate of how much they will need for retirement. As they recognize both the progress made to date and the need for improvement, governments and employers are doing more now than ever before to raise workers' awareness of the need for substantial retirement savings. Workers, like retirees, tend to underestimate how

Table 3-5. *Rates of Pension Participation, 401(k) Participation, and IRA Participation, Civilian Workers Aged 16 and Over, within Earnings Levels, May 1983, May 1988, and April 1993*

Real annual earnings	Number of workers (thousands)			Pension participation (percentage)			401(k) participation percentage of workers offered a plan			IRA participation (percentage)		
	1983	1988	1993	1983	1988	1993	1983	1988	1993	1983	1988	1993
All workers	98,964	113,720	117,874	42.0	42.0	43.7	38.3	56.9	64.9	16.9	12.5	8.1
$1–$4,999	10,294	10,028	7,540	4.9	4.2	2.9	a	22.2	19.9	6.8	4.6	2.4
$5,000–$9,999	11,257	13,502	10,691	16.9	17.2	12.7	a	32.9	34.0	8.0	7.1	3.7
$10,000–$14,999	16,259	16,966	15,409	37.0	38.7	28.8	28.2	41.9	44.5	10.4	7.3	4.6
$15,000–$19,999	14,052	14,700	14,501	55.0	54.0	44.6	32.1	50.5	54.5	13.4	11.3	5.4
$20,000–$24,999	11,993	12,417	12,247	64.7	63.4	60.1	34.7	56.7	60.8	19.1	13.3	7.5
$25,000–$29,999	5,663	8,875	9,817	72.8	71.5	64.2	40.0	58.6	66.8	21.0	17.3	8.2
$30,000–$49,999	11,600	14,377	19,977	73.5	75.4	75.0	47.6	67.0	72.3	32.8	18.0	10.6
$50,000 +	2,948	4,133	8,639	73.3	76.9	79.2	59.3	79.8	83.2	55.8	22.9	14.5

Source: EBRI estimates of the April 1993 Current Population Survey.

a. Sample too small to be statistically reliable.

long they will live once retired, yet they too want to retire early. Government and employer educational efforts are focusing on this problem as well. Although workers are on a better savings path than today's retirees, they have the tools and the opportunity to do even better. The use of both defined-benefit and defined-contribution retirement programs allows all workers in this highly mobile nation to have an opportunity to accumulate sufficient resources for a secure retirement, building on the base of Social Security. However, the primary challenges for governments and employers remains: to provide an environment in which retirement plans will be sponsored and maintained and in which education will be provided to ensure that workers understand the need to become planners, savers, and investors. Choose to save at an early age, or you may have the pleasure of working forever should become the needlepoint in every worker's home, with recognition that the alternative will be a retirement with inadequate income. Workers need to understand the power of compound interest over a long period, to know that a latté saved today may make them retirement millionaires.

Regina T. Jefferson, discussant

A CRITICAL EVALUATION of the private retirement system is useful as changes to the Social Security program are contemplated and the possibility of using the defined-contribution model to replace the traditional defined-benefit model is considered.[2] An identification of the relative strengths and weaknesses of the private retirement system suggests that the adoption of a defined-contribution model for Social Security is highly questionable. Accordingly, any steps to move the Social Security program in this direction should be made very cautiously.

The growth and development of the private pension system are noteworthy. The system's success is evinced by the significant increase in the number of private plans since 1974, when the Employee Retirement Income Security Act of 1974 (ERISA) was enacted. Not only has the number of private plans changed but the composition of the private pension system has also changed. Increasing numbers of employers are establishing defined-contribution plans rather than traditional defined-benefit plans as primary retirement savings vehicles.[3]

The trend to use defined-contribution plans for retirement savings purposes can be explained by two factors. First, defined-contribution plans are less

2. For discussion of recommendations regarding the Social Security system, see Advisory Council on Social Security (1997, pp. 23–30).

3. For statistics relating to this increase, see Silverman and others (1997, pp. 139–45).

expensive and less administratively burdensome for employers to maintain than defined-benefit plans.[4] This is particularly true for 401(k) plans in which contributions are made only on behalf of individuals who elect to contribute portions of their compensation to the plan.[5] Second, defined-contribution plans are advantageous for the members of the labor force who are more mobile because such plans typically vest faster and provide benefits that are easily rolled over into new employer plans or individual retirement accounts (IRAs).[6]

The increasing use of defined-contribution plans does not suggest that they are the best way to maximize retirement income security, however. Their popularity stems primarily from the financial concerns of employers and the changing work patterns of employees.[7]

Although responding to the specific needs of employers and employees can be viewed as a significant and positive development in the private pension system, these concerns are irrelevant to the Social Security program. Unlike the private retirement system, which is voluntary and consists of many different employer-sponsored plans, the Social Security program is mandatory and composed of a single, universal plan.[8] Consequently, there is no need to provide less expensive alternatives as an incentive for employers to participate in the Social Security program or to take affirmative measures to facilitate greater portability for its benefits. Regardless of the positive impact of these developments on the private pension system, they should not be considered in discussions of Social Security reform.

The success of the private pension system notwithstanding, the nation's retirement savings program is not ideal. Its increasing use of defined-contribution plans as primary retirement savings vehicles shifts the risk of accumulating insufficient assets for retirement from the employer to the employee, thereby threatening the retirement security of plan participants. This situation is not easily avoided in the private sector where profit margins, market competition, and employee preferences factor into an employer's decision regarding what type of plan, if any, to offer. It is nevertheless useful to identify the various risks to which defined-contribution plan participants are exposed so that they

4. Scott (1989, pp. 919–20); Halperin (1987, pp. 186–88).
5. The 401(k) plans, also called cash or deferred arrangements, allow the participant a choice between receiving benefits in cash or having the employer make payments directly into that participant's pension plan account. These plans can also allow employee contributions and can include an employer-matching feature. See Canan (1996, pp. 187–89).
6. See generally Langbein and Wolk (1995, pp. 109–14); Halperin (1987, pp. 185–86).
7. Keville (1994, p. 542).
8. For a discussion of Social Security, see U.S. Department of Health and Human Services (1991, pp. 9–10).

can have sufficient information to prepare for their retirements.[9] Moreover, from a policy point of view, it is important to identify the weaknesses in the private retirement system that result from its reliance on defined-contribution plans so that such problems can be fully addressed in the Social Security reform debate.

Defined-contribution plans differ from defined-benefit plans in that the participant rather than the employer assumes the risk of benefit shortfalls. The expected retirement benefits in defined-contribution plans can be estimated by assuming average investment returns on plan contributions. When sudden market fluctuations occur, or when investment strategies that fail to maximize asset performance are selected, actual retirement benefits may fall drastically short of targeted amounts.[10] As a result, individuals who have chosen to save in defined-contribution plans, but whose investment returns are less than average, may not accumulate sufficient amounts for retirement. If these individuals have relied on their expected retirement benefits over their working lives, they may have inadequate personal savings to offset the shortfall in their retirement accounts.

Consequently, the act of saving does not alone ensure retirement income security. The amount of assets accumulated determines the adequacy of one's retirement savings. Thus, the level, timing, and investment returns of retirement savings in defined-contribution plans are of utmost importance to retirees as a variation in any one of them may cause a significant shortfall in a participant's expected retirement benefit.

Another reason defined-contribution plans may fail to accumulate adequate amounts for retirement is insufficient investment information. Some defined-contribution plans require participants to make decisions not only about whether to participate, and the level of contribution to make, but also the manner in which their accounts are to be invested. These plans, known as "participant-directed plans," represent the fastest growing component of the private retirement system.[11]

Participants in participant-directed plans often lack formal investment training. As a result, they typically fail to diversify their portfolios adequately. Accordingly, many participant-directed plans are disproportionately invested in low-risk, low-yield instruments.[12]

A high concentration of low-risk, low-yield investments will often produce insufficient returns over one's working life to provide financial security. Con-

9. Jefferson (1998, pp. 8–9).
10. Keville (1994, pp. 545–46).
11. Silverman and others (1995, pp. 139–45); Jefferson (1998, pp. 37–38).
12. *BNA Pensions & Benefits Reporter* (1990, p. 1243).

sequently, participants who fail to adequately diversify their portfolios need to save greater amounts to be in the same position at retirement as participants who sufficiently diversify.[13] Some employers who sponsor participant-directed plans provide investment education for plan participants to enable them to make prudent investment decisions. Other employers, however, choose not to provide employee education because such programs are costly.

The lack of fiduciary liability in participant-directed plans also contributes to the possibility that participants will not receive their expected retirement benefits. Despite the significant ramifications of investment decisions, employers sponsoring participant-directed plans are not responsible for the investment decisions made by plan participants, as long as the plan provides a broad range of investment choices.[14] Thus, participants in a self-directed defined-contribution plan have no claims against an employer when they do not, or cannot, make prudent investment decisions.

The lack of insurance protection for defined-contribution plans also contributes to the possibility of shortfalls. Defined-benefit plans are insured by the Pension Benefit Guaranty Corporation (PBGC) against benefit losses owing to plan failure.[15] Defined-contribution plans are excluded from the PBGC insurance program because retirement benefits in such plans depend on the investment performance of individual accounts rather than predetermined retirement benefits.[16] Notwithstanding the disparate treatment of defined-benefit and defined-contribution plans with regard to insurance protection, the effects of poor investment performance in defined-contribution and defined-benefit plans are similar.

The similarity of the impact of poor investment performance in defined-contribution and defined-benefit plans can be clearly illustrated if one considers a defined-benefit plan in which all actuarial assumptions used in the funding process have been correct, except for the interest-rate assumption. If such a plan fails with insufficient assets, benefit losses would be solely attributable to unfavorable investment returns. Therefore, to the extent that the PBGC guarantees payment of the retirement benefits, it has effectively insured an average investment return over the working lives of plan participants.[17] In contrast, there is no protection for defined-contribution plan participants when shortfalls occur as a result of less than average investment returns. Providing

13. Jefferson (1996, p. 261).
14. 29 CFR §2550.404(c)-1 (1992); see also Canan (1996, pp. 791–93).
15. ERISA §§4002-03 establish the PBGC. ERISA §4022 governs payment of the benefits.
16. ERISA §3(34) provides that PBGC protection is not available for individual account plans.
17. Jefferson (1998, pp. 69–70).

insurance protection against unfavorable investment performance for defined-contribution plans is controversial. However, designing a defined-contribution plan insurance program that provides insurance protection comparable to that which exists for defined-benefit plans is possible.[18]

In addition to risk-related issues, there are fairness issues to be considered in the use of defined-contribution plans as primary retirement savings vehicles. Although some defined-contribution plan participants experience shortfalls in their expected retirement benefits, others experience windfalls. Individuals who benefit from unexpected market fluctuations, or the use of aggressive but successful investment strategies, receive larger than average retirement benefits from their defined-contribution plans. These individuals are more likely to be high-income employees, since low- and moderate-income employees are less likely to save significant amounts in elective arrangements such as 401(k) plans.[19] Therefore, those who are extremely lucky, have better than average investment skills, or are relatively wealthy tend to accumulate larger amounts in 401(k) plans than other participants. This result is particularly true in light of the recent repeal of the tax on excess distributions from qualified plans.[20]

Another reason shortfalls may occur in defined-contribution plans is because of early distributions. Many defined-contribution plans, including 401(k)s, allow withdrawals before retirement.[21] These distributions permit taxpayers to use retirement funds for nonretirement purposes, such as medical, education, and housing expenses. To the extent that individuals withdraw any funds from their plans prior to retirement, there will be less money available at retirement. It is a complicated exercise to determine how much one needs to save in a defined-contribution plan to ensure retirement income security. Thus, individuals who, for example, fail to take inflation and increasing life expectancies into account may withdraw their retirement funds for nonretirement purposes, erroneously believing that the remaining amount is adequate for a comfortable retirement. Therefore, the ability to take early distributions from defined-contribution plans may adversely affect a participant's retirement income security.

Social Security, personal savings, and the private retirement system are the three most important sources of retirement income.[22] Although these sources are separate and distinct, trends developing in the private retirement system affect the

---

18. Jefferson (1998, pp. 84–100).

19. Karen Ferguson, "Plans Benefit the Wealthy," *USA Today*, November, 25, 1997, p. 13A.

20. See U.S.C.A. 4980A (also 1073 of P.L.105-34, *Taxpayer Relief Act of 1997*, 111 Stat. 788, 948 [August 5, 1997]).

21. See Canan (1996, p. 787); and Langbein and Wolk (1995, pp. 50–51).

22. For a discussion of the "three-legged stool" of retirement benefits, see Keville (1994, p. 532).

role of Social Security. Because the expanded use of defined-contribution plans as primary private retirement savings vehicles shifts the risk of accumulating insufficient amounts for retirement from the employer to the employee, the distinction between personal savings and private pensions is diminishing. As a result, in order for retirees to continue to have access to multiple forms of retirement income, it is more important than ever for the Social Security program to retain its traditional defined-benefit plan structure so that it can deliver a guaranteed and definite retirement benefit to today's workers when they reach retirement age.

References

Advisory Council on Social Security. 1997. *Report of the 1994–1996 Advisory Council on Social Security: Vol. 1: Finding and Recommendations.* Washington: Government Printing Office.

BNA Pensions and Benefits Reporter. 1990. "Diversification Is the Key to Success of Section 401(k) Investments, ASPA Told." Vol. 17, July 16, 1243.

Canan, Michael J. 1996. *Qualified Retirement and Other Employee Benefit Plans.* West Publishing Co.

Halperin, Daniel, L. 1987. "Tax Policy and Retirement Income: A Rational Model for the 21st Century." In *Search for a National Retirement Income Policy*, edited by Jack L. Vanderhei, 159–95. Pension Research Council.

Jefferson, Regina T. 1996. "The American Dream Savings Account: Is It a Dream or a Nightmare?" In *Taxing America*, edited by Karen B. Brown and Mary Louise Fellows, 253–76. New York University Press.

_____. 1998. "Rethinking the Risk of Defined Contributions Plans." Catholic University of America, Columbus School of Law. Mimeo.

Keville, John R. 1994. "Retire at Your Own Risk." *St. John's Law Review* 68 (Spring): 527–56.

Langbein, John. H., and Bruce Wolk, eds. 1995. *Pension and Employee Benefit Law*, 2d ed. Foundation Press.

Salisbury, Dallas, ed. 1994. *Retirement in the 21st Century—Ready or Not.* Washington: EBRI-ERF.

Scott, Peter T. 1989. "A National Retirement Income Policy." *Tax Notes* 44 (August): 919–20. In *Pension and Employee Benefit Law*, 2d ed., edited by John H. Langbein and Bruce A. Wolk, 43. Foundation Press.

Silverman, Celia, and others. 1997. *EBRI Databook on Employee Benefits*, 4th ed. Washington: Employee Benefit Research Institute.

U.S. Department of Health and Human Services, Social Security Administration. 1991. "Social Security Programs in the United States." *Social Security Bulletin* 54 (September): 9–10.

4

Social Security:
In What Form?

T HE PAPERS in this chapter explore risk and return implications of moving from a defined-benefit to a mixed
defined-benefit/defined-contribution plan. The first paper compares how unanticipated demographic and economic developments affect the predictability
of retirement income under a funded defined-contribution plan versus a pay-as-
you-go defined-benefit plan. The second paper investigates whether privatizing
would raise the rate of return to Social Security. The third paper explores the
risk to dependent spouses and widows associated with a move toward a
defined-contribution arrangement.

Individual Uncertainty in Retirement Income
Planning under Different Public Pension Regimes
Lawrence H. Thompson

T HE PROJECTED cost of the baby boom generation's retire-
ment benefits has triggered one of the most vocal debates in six decades about
the structure of the U. S. Social Security program. The wisdom of substituting
privately managed, individual accounts for a portion of the current program is a
prominent feature in this debate.[1] In this context, the individual account alterna-

The author is grateful for the support of the International Social Security Association and the
International Labor Office, who financed much of the analyses described in this paper; his assistant
Adam Carasso, who performed many of the calculations; and to Peter A. Diamond and Stanford
Ross, who made helpful suggestions on earlier drafts.
1. One of the more coherent discussions of this debate is found in U.S. Department of Health
and Human Services (1997).

tive is invariably framed as a series of advance-funded, defined-contribution accounts similar to current IRAs that would replace all or a portion of the defined-benefit package of the current (mainly) pay-as-you-go program.

Thus far, most of the attention has focused on the possible impact of such a change on the implicit rates of return earned by different birth cohorts, the federal budget deficit, national savings rates, and future Social Security contribution rates. Comparatively little attention has been paid to the possible impact on other important attributes of a public pension program. The object of this paper is to begin to fill this important gap in the current debate by focusing on a different issue, the impact such a change is likely to have on the predictability of retirement incomes. At issue is how effective the national pension system will be at helping individual workers formulate their life plans.

Pension predictability has received little attention largely because heretofore the debate has focused on comparisons involving artificial scenarios in which events always unfold in a smooth and predictable manner. For instance, the analyses offered in the current debate almost invariably assume that all workers have a regular and predictable work history (always earning some multiple of the national average wage); rates of growth in economic variables as well as rates of return on investment portfolios are constant from year to year and entirely predictable; demographic parameters will change gradually along a previously predicted trajectory; programs will be enacted and implemented in just the way that their supporters envision; and all the relevant public and private sector institutions will discharge their responsibilities efficiently and effectively.

History tells us that every one of these assumptions is wrong. What is the implication of basing policies on such unrealistic assumptions? How are alternative pension approaches likely to operate in an imperfect world and an unpredictable environment? What happens to retirement incomes when previously unforeseen events occur and things don't work out as planned? Are some approaches more effectively insulated than others from the impact of certain kinds of unforeseen events? Who actually ends up assuming the different kinds of risks in each of the different approaches to Social Security?

The Basic Framework

The paper starts with a discussion of the meaning and importance of predictability in pension plans. It then notes the kind of risks to which pension programs are exposed and the strategy that is used here to analyze the potential impact of these risks.

Predictability as a Pension System Goal

One must start with a clear statement of the objective of public pension policy. The analysis in this paper is based on the assumption that one of the most important goals of any public pension system is to provide a stable, predictable, and adequate source of retirement income to each participant. This need not be the only goal that a society has for its public pension system, and this goal should not be pursued without consideration for other social, political, and economic effects a pension plan can have. A national pension system that doesn't do an acceptable job of producing retirement incomes, however, must surely be judged a failure.

Pension systems operate on the basis of promises made to those working under the system. The promise is that in return for making regular contributions during their working years, the system will supply income during their retirement years. The focus in this paper is on the predictability of that retirement income promise.

In this context, the promise has two important attributes. First, although it is stated in terms of a particular future benefit, it has meaning only in the context of the standard of living that the benefit affords. The reason for supplying retirement incomes to pension system participants is to allow them to maintain a particular living standard after they are no longer able to (or expected to have to) work. To achieve this purpose, the nominal amount of the benefit promise must reflect the cost of maintaining prevailing living standards at the time the participant retires.

Second, the promise represents a long-term commitment issued three decades or more before the participant's planned retirement date. A major reason for making pension promises in advance is to allow people to make intelligent life plans. Such a promise has value, however, only if it can be relied on as people make decisions about how long to plan on working, how much to save, how to finance their children's educations, or how much assistance to offer their own parents.

The Risks and the Approaches

The challenge in delivering predictable retirement income is that the world is inherently unpredictable. Pension systems—and the promises that they make—are subject to a variety of risks. The economy may not behave as expected, demographic trends may alter, political systems may change, and private and public sector institutions important to the pension system may fail to execute the responsibilities they have been assigned. Each of these raises the possibility that pension promises made previously may not be kept.

No national pension system that operates in an unpredictable world can be completely successful in providing a predictable source of retirement income. Some threats to a predictable retirement income may have more serious consequences under one approach to pension provision than under another, however, and some approaches may involve less of a threat in one economic or institutional environment than in another. Our task is to examine each of the major sources of uncertainty that can affect the pension promise and assess how each might affect that promise under the different approaches to organizing a national pension system.

The analysis here focuses on three sources of uncertainty:

—Demographic risk arising from unexpected changes in overall birth rates or mortality rates occurring between the time the pension promise is made and the date of retirement;

—Economic risk arising from irregular or unexpected changes in the rate of growth of wages (or prices) or from irregular or unexpected changes in the rate of return earned in financial markets over the course of the worker's career; and

—Political risk arising from a breakdown in governmental decision processes, allowing politicians to make benefit promises in excess of what society can afford to pay, preventing the political system from making timely adjustments to changing economic and demographic trends, causing adjustments in pension policies that respond to developments not directly related to pension issues or producing ineffective public sector instutions or inadequate regulation and oversight of private sector institutions.

The strategy of the paper is to examine how each of these sources of risk is likely to interact with the two pension models currently being debated in the United States. To avoid being caught up in the details of particular proposals, however, the analysis focuses on relatively pure generic forms:

—A defined-benefit model that involves a centrally managed plan providing retirement benefits scaled to reflect each worker's career average earnings updated to reflect wage levels prevailing at the time the worker retires. It is assumed that pensions are financed on a pay-as-you-go basis entirely from employee and employer contributions.

—A defined-contribution model, which involves a series of privately managed retirement savings accounts. In this model, earners (and their employers) make contributions at a specified rate and these contributions are invested in some mix of financial assets. At retirement, prior contributors receive a benefit based on the current market value of the financial assets in their accounts.

One key difference between the two approaches involves the nature of the promises made to workers. The defined-benefit model makes two kinds of promises to current workers. One involves the benefit they can expect to receive in retirement, and the other involves the contribution rate they will have to pay while employed. In a well-functioning system (such as we have in the United States, but is not so commonly found in some developing and transition economies), detailed projections are made from time to time to see whether these two promises appear to be consistent. At the time they are made (or modified) the two promises are usually consistent, but subsequent changes in demographic and economic conditions often upset this balance. When the promises become inconsistent, one or both must be modified, and the decision about how this will be done must be made through the political process. The unpredictability in the defined-benefit pension promise arises as a result both of the uncertainty of the underlying economic and demographic events and of the need to rely on a political process to adjust the pension promises.

Technically, the defined-contribution model makes only one promise. Retirement incomes will simply reflect the volume of financial assets accumulated at the time the individual retires. All uncertainty involved in not knowing in advance the size of the asset stock needed to provide a given retirement income is borne by the individual worker. A second promise is implicit, however. Those advocating the defined-contribution model focus a fair amount of attention on illustrations of the benefit that illustrative workers can expect to receive under the plan they are advocating. The implication is that the paying of a specified mandatory contribution rate will produce a particular future retirement benefit.

A second key difference is the method of financing. For the purpose of this analysis, the defined-benefit plan is assumed to be financed on a pay-as-you-go basis while the defined-contribution plan is assumed to be advanced funded. The differences in the way that the two approaches handle some of the risks, particularly the first of the demographic risks discussed subsequently, derive from differences in the method of finance rather than the nature of the benefit promise.[2]

The Interplay of the Sources of Uncertainty and the Models

The models differ both in the kinds of risks to which they are vulnerable and in the potential impact of the vulnerability. Some risks pose a greater problem

2. In principle, publicly managed defined-benefit plans could also be partially or fully funded, in which case these particular differences would disappear. Advance funding of such plans has been relatively rare in the last half century but was more common in the first half of this century and is being discussed with increased frequency today.

for one model than for another. Other risks may affect both models but are more likely to upset benefit expectations in one model than in the other.

Demographic Risks

Demographic risks arise from unexpected changes in either birth rates or death rates. A decline in the birth rate means that relatively fewer people will enter the labor force in future years. Eventually, the number of workers will fall relative to the number of retirees, creating problems for pension financing.

A decline in the death rate increases the life span of the average individual. When the decline affects primarily older persons, as has been the case in developed countries in recent years, it means that the average person can expect to spend more years in retirement. The change creates problems for pension financing by raising the ratio of the number of years each individual can expect to spend in retirement to the number of years spent working and by increasing the total number of retirees relative to the total number of workers.

The two sources of demographic change must be considered separately because they differ in how they interact with the two pension models. In considering each case, it is useful to look separately at three different questions: whether a particular pension model is affected by unforeseen changes in the respective demographic element, if so, the likelihood that such unforeseen changes will cause unexpected changes in future retirement benefits, and the likely magnitude of the unexpected alternations in retirement benefits.

CHANGES IN BIRTH RATES. Consider first the case in which birth rates fall but mortality rates do not. Although the life expectancy of the average person reaching retirement age will not change, the number of workers available to support each retired person will eventually decline.

How does this affect the respective pension models? In this case, the impact depends largely on the method used to finance the plan. In a pay-as-you-go system (such as the defined-benefit model being analyzed here), the decline in the number of workers relative to the number of retirees causes the income from worker contributions to fall short of the amount needed to finance retirement benefits. Either the contribution rates have to be increased or the retirement benefits have to be curtailed (breaking either the promise to current contributors or the promise to those about to retire).

The impact of this change in a mature, *advance-funded* system (such as the defined-contribution model being analyzed here) is substantially more complicated and difficult to predict. Once an advance-funded system has reached maturity, the aged support themselves by drawing down their accounts (that is, selling assets) at the same time as the working-age population saves for retirement by adding to their accounts (that is, buying assets). Considering only the transactions that occur within the retirement system, when the number of workers who are buying assets falls relative to the number of retirees who are selling assets, the price of the asset being traded can be expected to decline.

The complication is that these form only one part of a larger set of capital market transactions. Asset prices will be determined not just by what is happening within the retirement income system, but by the aggregate of all sales and purchases in the capital markets. Economists and financial analysts are just beginning to analyze the likely effect on the economy of a major draw-down in pension assets.[3] At this time, it is simply not possible to make a prediction as to whether this is likely to be a problem and how big a problem it may be.

Who bears the risk of unanticipated changes in birth rates? Under the pay-as-you-go model, the exact adjustment to pension promises when birth rates change will be decided through the political process. If the past is any guide, the adjustment is likely to involve some mixture of benefit reductions and tax rate increases, and the benefit reductions are apt to involve some mixture of adjustments that affect only future beneficiaries as well as adjustments that affect both future beneficiaries and those currently receiving benefits.[4] To the extent birth rate changes cause unexpected financial problems in an advance-funded, defined-contribution model, all of the impact is absorbed by unexpected changes in workers' retirement benefits.

How large is the possible benefit adjustment? A change in the birth rate can have a powerful effect over time on pay-as-you-go pension financing, but the effect phases in fairly slowly. The potential magnitudes can be illustrated by focusing on one particularly dramatic historical example. Between the early 1950s and the early 1990s, a time span which represents roughly the working career of someone born in 1930, the crude birth rate fell in Japan by a half.[5] By itself, this would eventually cause that country's aged-dependency ratio to double, which will eventually require either that the average benefit fall to one-half its previous level, the contribution rate double, or some combination of the two.

The changes occur only gradually, however. The annual number of births drifts down over a period of several decades. Moreover, changes in the number

3. For example, Schieber and Shoven (1997).

4. Congress has twice had to adjust the U.S. Social Security program to reduce a gap between projected revenues and expenditures, in 1977 and 1983. In each case, part of the gap was closed through increases in payroll tax rates and part through reductions in benefits for future retirees. In 1983 benefits for current retirees were also reduced through a delay in the cost-of-living increase and the imposition of income taxes on benefit payments.

5. The crude birth rate in Japan was 23.7 in the 1950–55 period, 19.2 in the 1970–75 period, and 12.1 in the 1980–85 period. United Nations (1988).

of births have no effect on pension finances for at least another twenty years, when they begin to influence the size of the labor force. Thus, whereas by itself the birth rate decline after 1950 would eventually cause a doubling in the aged-dependency ratio, it would have caused only about a 25 percent increase in that ratio by 1990, some forty years later.

In summary, changes in birth rates introduce one source of risk that pensions will not actually materialize in the amounts promised. The potential impact on benefit levels and contribution rates under a pay-as-you-go system is large, but the effect phases in quite slowly. Therefore, the long-range social challenge they pose is probably greater than the risk to any particular individual's retirement plans. It is not possible to predict the impact of this kind of demographic change in an advanced-funded, defined-contribution pension system.

CHANGES IN POSTRETIREMENT MORTALITY. Regardless of the pension model employed, an increase in the amount of time that newly retiring workers can expect to live in retirement will raise the cost of providing them with a given monthly income. When this occurs, the choices facing *new entrants* to the labor force are the same under both models. Either they must make higher contributions during their working years, extend their work lives, or accept a lower retirement income.

The models differ in their treatment of those who are currently in *mid-career* at the time that life expectancies increase. Under the defined-benefit approach, the extra cost associated with an unanticipated increase in life spans generates a deficit between projected benefits and projected costs. The gap will be closed through the political process which, if the past is any guide, will spread the cost between rate increases and benefit reductions. Workers who are in the middle of their careers when mortality rates fall will likely suffer some reduction in promised benefits, but far less than the total adjustment that the mortality rate change will eventually cause. In contrast, under the defined-contribution model, the impact of an unanticipated increase in life spans falls entirely on the worker in the form of a lower than expected monthly benefit.

Life expectancies at age 65 have increased substantially in many parts of the world since World War II, causing populations to age and pension costs to rise. From 12.8 years in 1950, male life expectancy at age 65 in the United States had risen 2.2 years (to 15.0 years) by 1990 and is projected to rise another 2 years (to 17.0 years) by 2030 under the Board of Trustees' intermediate assumption set.[6] Under a defined-contribution pension plan, the change between 1950 and 1990 amounts to the equivalent of a 13 percent reduction in planned

6. Board of Trustees of the Federal Old-Age and Survivors Insurance Trust Fund (1997).

benefits. Put differently, a young man starting work in 1950 and establishing a retirement savings plan based on 1950 mortality rates would have found that by 1990 he had accumulated some 87 percent of the amount needed to finance his retirement, given 1990 mortality rates.

Economic Risks

Economic risks arise because of unanticipated changes in wage growth rates and investment returns over the course of a work career. Of the two models analyzed here, the defined-contribution variant is the only one affected by economic risk.

The contribution rate needed to finance a given pension under the defined-contribution model is very sensitive to changes occurring over an individual's work career in both the rate of growth of wages and the rate of return on investments. The rate of growth of wages influences the contribution rate by changing the amount of assets needed to achieve a target replacement rate at retirement. Faster wage growth increases the required contribution rate by increasing the amount needed to maintain preretirement living standards. The rate of return on investment influences the contribution rate by changing the size of the asset stock accumulated at any particular contribution rate. A higher rate of return reduces the required contribution rate.

In contrast, the contribution rates required under the pay-as-you-go model are not particularly sensitive to either of these economic developments. Changes in wage levels tend to influence both the income and outgo sides equally in that faster wage growth simultaneously increases future pensions and provides the additional revenues needed to finance them. Rates of return on investment are of little importance to a pay-as-you-go system since there are few assets to invest.[7]

Economic risks arise because wage changes and investment returns cannot be expected to follow a regular and predictable path over the course of an individual's work career. Every time they change, the contribution rate needed to finance a given retirement pension under the defined-contribution model also changes, leading to changes either in the amount that workers must contribute for a given pension or in the amount of pension associated with a given level of contributions.

Since the economic environment cannot be known in advance, the contribution rate must be set based on the best available information and modified as

7. Even if it were partially or fully advance funded, a defined-benefit plan would insulate workers from most of the economic risk analyzed here. This risk derives mainly from the way that benefits are computed under the two approaches, not the way in which they are financed.

Table 4-1. *Real Wage Growth, Interest Rates, and Implied Individual Account Contribution Rates in Four OECD Countries*

	Germany			Japan			United Kingdom			United States		
Periods	Wage growth	Interest rate	Contri-bution rate	Wage growth	Interest rate	Contri-bution rate	Wage growth	Interest rate	Contri-bution rate	Wage growth	Interest rate	Contri-bution rate
1st 10 years (1953–62)	8.4	3.8	64.2	9.5	5.3	57.7	5.8	1.0	70.5	2.7	1.4	28.6
2d 10 years (1963–72)	6.1	3.9	36.0	7.7	4.3	47.8	5.2	2.5	41.7	1.8	–0.6	39.0
3d 10 years (1973–82)	3.4	3.0	22.4	2.2	2.8	16.6	1.3	–1.2	40.7	–1.2	2.9	5.2
4th 10 years (1983–92)	2.7	5.0	9.8	1.3	3.5	9.9	2.7	4.1	13.1	1.0	5.0	5.7
First 21 years (1953–73)	7.1	3.8	48.5	8.5	4.6	54.2	5.4	1.7	53.5	2.2	0.3	33.4
Next 22 years (1974–95)	2.6	4.0	12.9	1.8	3.0	14.0	1.8	1.9	19.0	–0.1	4.1	5.1
Full 43 years (1953–95)	4.8	3.9	25.5	5.0	3.8	28.1	3.6	1.8	32.2	1.0	2.3	13.5

Sources: International Monetary Fund, *International Yearbook of Financial Statistics, 1996* (Washington); U.S. Bureau of Labor Statistics, Department of Commerce, http://stat.bls.gov, and author's calculations. Interest rates are for 10-year government bonds in each country.

new information emerges. For individual participants, however, this means that the contribution rate actually prevailing during working years may turn out to be either too high or too low to produce the target pension at the point that retirement age is reached. The retiree either overshoots or undershoots the target. Retirees who overshoot the target will have saved too much. They will be able to enjoy higher than anticipated retirement incomes, but at the cost of having made greater sacrifices during their working years than were necessary. Retirees who undershoot will be forced to live in retirement with less than they had anticipated.

THE GENERAL ANALYTICAL APPROACH. The magnitude of economic risk depends on the predictability of actual trends and size and pattern of year-to-year fluctuations. To gain an appreciation for the potential risk from this source, I performed simulations of the impact of the kind of economic variations that actually occurred in the postwar years in four major economies. The historical evidence employed in the analysis is that from the period 1953 through 1995 in Japan, Germany, the United Kingdom, and the United States.

The analysis was based on a simplistic model under which everybody enters the labor force at age 22, is employed consistently at the economywide average wage for the following forty-three years, retires at age 65, and dies on his or her 82d birthday. Each worker's target pension was one-half of the average wage, indexed after retirement to reflect changes in prevailing wage levels. The objective of the exercise was to see how close people came to achieving the target pension under plausible decision rules about how contribution rates would be set.

Several different decision rules were used to set initial contribution rates and to adjust these rates in response to emerging experience. Simulations of economic variations were run using the wage-rate/interest-rate relationship as it actually unfolded and in exactly the opposite order of the way it actually unfolded. The assumption is that changes of the magnitude actually observed historically can easily occur again, and that the trend could go in either direction.

Real investment rates and wage changes in these countries is summarized in table 4-1. It is immediately clear that the contribution rates required to produce the target pension are extraordinarily sensitive to the economic environment. Actual experience at several points in the history of these countries saw wage growth so high relative to real interest rates that the contribution rate required under the simple model runs some 50 percent or more (for example, the 1950s in Japan, Germany, and the United Kingdom, and the 1960s in Japan). At other times, wage growth was so slow relative to the level of interest rates that the target pension could have been produced with a contribution rate of less than

Table 4-2. *Impact of Alternative Strategies for Setting Contribution Rates in Defined-Contribution Systems*

Actual pension as percent of target pension

Item	Germany	Japan	United Kingdom	United States
All bonds				
Simulation 1. Contribution rate set at level appropriate for long-term (43-year) trend				
Actual sequence	137	132	140	138
Reverse sequence	88	80	73	80
Simulation 2. Contribution rate set at level appropriate for first half				
Actual sequence	261	255	233	342
Reverse sequence	41	40	43	30
Simulation 3. Contribution rate adjusted every 10 years (in line with economic conditions of preceding 10 years)				
Actual sequence	163	153	165	181
Reverse sequence	66	68	64	58
50/50 stocks and bonds				
Simulation 4. Contribution rate set at level appropriate for long-term (43-year) trend				
Actual sequence	97	119	132	118
Reverse sequence	113	97	77	85
Simulation 5. Contribution rate set at level appropriate for first half				
Actual sequence	125	173	278	253
Reverse sequence	88	67	35	39
Simulation 6. Contribution rate adjusted every 10 years (in line with economic conditions of preceding 10 years)				
Actual sequence	93	125	188	154
Reverse sequence	100	87	59	66
Basic data				
43-year average				
Real wages	4.8	5.0	3.6	1.0
Real bond interest rate	3.9	3.8	1.8	2.3
Real return on 50/50 portfolio	6.3	6.7	5.6	5.7
Ratio of target accumulation to average wage				
All bond portfolio	9.2	9.5	9.9	7.6
50/50 stocks and bonds	7.5	7.4	7.1	5.8

Source: Thompson (1998).

10 percent (for example, the 1970s and 1980s in the United States and the 1980s in Germany and Japan).

Each set of simulations starts with the calculation of the stock of assets that will be needed at age 65 in order to meet the pension target of 50 percent of the average wage; this value is shown at the bottom of table 4-2. The required asset stock is itself dependent on long-term economic trends and is calculated based on the forty-three-year average of real wage growth and investment returns for each country. For example, in the all bonds scenarios, financing a wage-indexed pension equal to 50 percent of average wages for seventeen years would require at age 65 a stock of assets equal to 9.2 times average earnings in the economic environment that prevailed in Germany, 9.5 times average earnings in the Japanese environment, and so forth.

The next step is the calculation of the stock of assets that would be accumulated if someone actually worked each of the forty-three years at the average wage, made contributions at the rate implied by the long-term economic trends, and received investment returns each year at that year's prevailing rate. This calculation is performed four times for each country, twice assuming the year-to-year fluctuations in wage growth and interest rates that actually occurred, and twice assuming the exact reverse order of the actual year-to-year sequence. One set of calculations assumes that portfolios are held entirely in accounts that earn the ten-year government bond rate each year (but never experience capital gains and losses.) The second set assumes half of the assets are held in a stock portfolio representative of the country's entire equity market.

VARIABILITY WHEN LONG-TERM TRENDS ARE KNOWN. The first set of simulations focuses on portfolios that earn the government bond interest rate. It is based on the assumption that the authorities know how real wages and interest rates will behave in the long run but do not know what kind of year-to-year fluctuations to expect. The results are shown in the first panel of table 4-2.

The results indicate that the timing of year-to-year variations has a significant effect on the size of the asset stock accumulated. In these simulations, the contribution rate that would be appropriate if the 43-year average values prevailed every year produces a stock of assets that is from 30 percent to 40 percent too high using the actual year-to-year variation and produces a stock of assets that is from 15 percent to 25 percent too low using the reverse of the actual sequence. These simulations suggest that, even if the long-term average were predicted perfectly, year-to-year variations in the values that produce the annual average would cause actual pensions to differ substantially from the target. Instead of replacing 50 percent of preretirement earnings, pensions could run anywhere from 37.5 percent to 75 percent of preretirement earnings.

VARIABILITY WHEN LONG-TERM TRENDS ARE NOT KNOWN. The second set of simulations in table 4-2 assumes that the authorities can only predict with certainty how the economy will perform for the first two decades and set contribution rates accordingly. They do not foresee subsequent developments.

This decision rule produces large gaps between the actual asset accumulation and the target. When annual fluctuations are introduced in the actual sequence, the contribution rate established in this way proves to be much too high and results in asset accumulations that are two to three times as much as needed for the target pension. In contrast, when annual fluctuations are introduced in the reverse of the actual sequence, the contribution rate established based on perfect foresight of the first twenty years proves to be much too low and results in asset accumulations that are only 30 to 40 percent of the target. In this simulation, variations in the actual course of economic events causes pensions to range from 15 percent to 170 percent of preretirement earnings.

The third set of results comes from simulating a procedure in which the contribution rate is adjusted each decade to reflect the actual experience of the previous decade.[8] The results indicate that regularly adjusting the contribution rate produces only a slight improvement. When simulated using the actual annual fluctuations, this procedure causes asset accumulations of from 50 percent to 200 percent in excess of the target. When the simulation uses the reverse of the actual fluctuations, the asset accumulations fall short of the target by some 30 to 40 percent.

COMBINING STOCKS AND BONDS. The next three panels in table 4-2 show the results of simulations using the same decision roles but assuming that asset holdings are divided equally between ten-year government bonds and equities. Since equities tend to earn higher returns than bonds, introducing equity returns allows a given pension to be generated with a lower contribution rate. It also introduces somewhat more volatility into the year-to-year pattern of asset returns.

The greater volatility associated with the investment in equities does not necessarily introduce greater variation in the results of these simulations, however. Introducing equities causes accumulations to become somewhat less pre-

8. In this case the initial contribution rate was the rate appropriate at the long-term average rate of increase in wages and of investment returns. Every ten years thereafter the contribution rate was adjusted either upward or downward to reflect the economic environment of the previous decade. The adjustments were assumed to occur at the pace of a 0.5 percentage point change in the contribution rate each year until the new rate is reached (or the decade ends).

dictable in the context of the economic history of the United Kingdom, but become somewhat more predictable in the context of the U.S. economic data. In the context of the economic data from Germany, and to a lesser extent Japan, the introduction of equity returns actually narrows the range of variation substantially. Nonetheless, we see that asset accumulations in the United States would miss the target by some 15 percent to 18 percent even with perfect foresight about the forty-three-year averages. They could overshoot by 80 percent or undershoot by 35 percent when the contribution rate is adjusted each decade.

VARIATION AMONG ADJACENT RETIREMENT COHORT. Equity investment also intensifies intercohort equity problems that are less serious when portfolios are held mostly in bonds. With equity investment, the value of the pension available to a given retiree is quite sensitive to the exact year in which retirement age is reached owing to the greater volatility in the value of the asset portfolio. Those who reach retirement age when asset markets are depressed will find that their assets buy a much more modest pension than those who are fortunate enough to reach retirement age when asset markets are unusually high.

Simulations using these same historical data are reported in table 4-3. They suggest that when retirement portfolios are held entirely in bonds, the retirement pension associated with the portfolios accumulated by the average member of any one retirement cohort can be expected to vary by only about 3 percent from the value of the portfolios accumulated by the average member of an adjacent cohort. When half of the portfolio is held in equities, however, the average variation among adjacent cohorts increases substantially, to just over 9 percent. In this case, if the average worker in one cohort received a pension equal to the target of 50 percent of average earnings, an identical worker in the next cohort could expect, on average, to get a pension that represented either 46 percent or 54 percent of average earnings. In some years, the variance would be less; in other years it would be more.[9]

SUMMARY. In pension plans following the defined-contribution model, actual pensions are quite sensitive to economic conditions over an individual's work career. All of the uncertainty associated with this source of variation is borne by the individual participant. The history of the last half-century suggests that these kinds of uncertainties can easily cause asset accumulations to

9. These results implicitly assume that annuity prices are set to reflect larger-term average rates of return and do not also fluctuate from one retirement cohort to the next. In fact, in many circumstances annuity prices do fluctuate from year to year, which introduces an additional source of intracohort variation not analyzed here.

Table 4-3. *Impact of a One-Year Variation in Year of Retirement*

Mean absolute percentage difference in the ratio of retirement benefits
to preretirement earnings among adjacent retirement cohorts

Item	Germany	Japan	United Kingdom	United States	All four
Bonds only					
Mean difference	3.2	3.6	3.4	2.8	3.2
Standard deviation	1.9	3.4	1.7	1.6	2.2
50 percent bonds and 50 percent stocks					
Mean difference	11.6	9.6	7.6	8.1	9.2
Standard deviation	10.7	6.5	4.6	5.5	7.2

Source: Thompson (1998).

Note: In these simulations, the period over which assets could be accumulated was shortened to 33 years (and the contribution rate each year increased accordingly) to allow a comparison among the experiences of 11 consecutive cohorts. All calculations employed the contribution rate appropriate for the respective long-term average economic environment of the country. Results for the actual sequence and the reverse sequence are combined to produce a total of 22 observations for each country and each investment policy.

fall one-third short of the initial target and, just as easily, come in twice as high as the target. In either case, the amount by which the initial target was missed will be translated directly into retirement benefits that were higher or lower than expected.

These simulations suggest several observations about individual retirement saving strategies that are not reflected in most current discussions of the individual account option. First, the results are influenced by unpredictability of *both* earnings growth rates and investment returns. Variations in earnings growth rates alone are enough to cause errors in estimates of required contribution rates, even if investment returns were regular and predictable. Analyses that focus only on variations in capital returns miss half of the source of unpredictability in setting contribution rates. Second, these results suggest that from the perspective of the challenge in correctly anticipating the correct contribution rate, using equity investments may not introduce any greater uncertainty than using all debt, even though equity investments exhibit greater year-to-year variation in annual returns. Equity investments do introduce greater variation among adjacent cohorts, however. Third, it is not clear that the kind of uncertainty simulated here can be reduced significantly through portfolio adjustments. The results presented already assume portfolios that are indexed to represent each country's equity market, and the mixing of debt and equity does not appear to reduce the uncertainty.

Political Risks

An entirely different category of risks arises out of the political process. By definition, all public pension programs are creatures of the state, whether the state's role is to manage the system directly or merely to establish and enforce the rules under which the system will operate. If the state adopts faulty policies or fails to implement its policies effectively, its actions by themselves may cause pensions promised at the beginning of a worker's career to fail to materialize at the end of his or her career.

Publicly managed pay-as-you-go defined-benefit systems and advanced-funded, defined-contribution systems (whether managed publicly or privately) are both subject to political risk though the type of political failure which gives rise to the risk differs. Political risks arise in a variety of different ways. What follows are six examples of political risks drawn from actual failtures here and abroad in recent years. The first three affect primarily a pay-as-you-go defined-benefit plan, and the last three affect primarily privately managed defined-contribution approaches.

EXCESSIVE PROMISES. Pay-as-you-go, defined-benefit pension plans have proven vulnerable to the problem of excessive promises in those countries where institutions and traditions do not force politicians to consider or acknowledge the future cost of current promises. The problem has been particularly common in Latin America and the former socialist countries of Eastern Europe. It has been far rarer in North America and Northern Europe.

Political risk arises where cost implications can be easily ignored and irresponsible politicians are able to use promises of higher future benefits as an apparently inexpensive way of securing the support of influential groups. Common recipients of such largesse are the military, the police, civil servants, and workers in transportation, mining, and other key export or public utility industries. The problem arises, of course, as the pension system matures and the cost implications of prior promises become clearer. If it is decided that these costs exceed what society is willing to bear, promised benefits will have to be scaled back. Those caught in the middle of their work career when such benefit reductions are finally implemented will have their retirement plans upset as the retirement benefits they had been told they could expect fail to materialize.

The Social Security program has historically been protected from this risk by the tradition of issuing regular long-range cost estimates and the vision that Social Security should be a universal program applicable to all occupations and industries. Because it takes seriously a responsibility to maintain balance in the seventy-five-year cost estimates, Congress has never enacted changes that would cause a long-run deficit to develop or increase the size of one that had already opened. Nor has it ever promised unfunded benefit increases to particular occupational or professional groups within the Social Security program. The deficits that have occurred in Social Security have almost invariably come from changes in the assumptions or methods used in making the cost projections subsequent to congressional action.

POLITICAL STALEMATE. Pay-as-you-go plans are also susceptible to the risk that the political system will find itself unable to enact timely adjustments in the face of unfavorable trends in the underlying demographics of the country. As noted previously, a decline in either birth rates or mortality rates can cause a pay-as-you-go, defined-benefit plan's pension promises to become inconsistent with its contribution promise. Where the political system is unable to come to a consensus about the adjustments to be made, the imbalance may develop into a source of social division and continuing fiscal difficulties for the government.

A political stalemate about how to adjust the pension system introduces an additional risk for midcareer workers. Although they may understand that the current promises must be adjusted, they will not know what kind of adjustments ought to be planned for. Moreover, continued controversy is likely eventually to undermine public confidence in the pension program, compromising its social value and increasing the odds of a major disruption of pension promises at some future time.

In this area, the record in the United States is mixed. Benefit reductions were enacted in 1977 and again in 1983. In the earlier instance, the reductions were preceded by a couple of years of debate and discussion, but were finally enacted on a bipartisan basis in advance of any last-minute financing crisis. The picture in 1983 was not as attractive. Reductions were not agreed to until the pressure to meet regular benefit payments made further delay impossible. The situation may be no better today. Although it is clear that changes will have to be made in the benefit and/or financing schedules, increased polarization in the Social Security debate may make it more difficult to enact such changes far enough in advance to provide individual workers with sufficient notice.

BUDGET ADJUSTMENTS. A third kind of political risk potentially important to any publicly managed plan is that pension benefit adjustments will be enacted for general budget reasons not directly related to pension policy or pension finance. Although no such changes have actually been enacted in this country's pension program, on at least two occasions serious proposals were made to reduce cost-of-living adjustments in order to help balance the budget, despite the fact that such changes were not needed to balance the Social Security program. One was a proposal made in the 1970s by President Ford; another was a proposal developed in the Senate in the mid-1980s but rejected by President Reagan.

A critical element influencing the probability of these kinds of adjustments may be the method of financing. In particular, benefits financed virtually exclusively from a dedicated tax may be less likely to be adjusted as part of general budget policy. This would imply that in the United States this risk is less for pension and hospital insurance benefits than for Medicare part B.[10] Critics of some of the adjustments enacted recently in Europe allege that welfare programs are being curtailed simply to meet artificial criteria for the single currency. It is not clear that any of the changes adopted by European Union countries have reduced benefits in programs that were otherwise adequately financed, however.

The privately managed, defined-contribution model is particularly attractive in those countries that have experienced serious problems of excessive promises or political stalemate involving previous pay-as-you-go plans. It is also attractive to those who fear benefit reductions associated entirely with general budget conditions. Under the defined-contribution alternative, the politicians' ability to use pension promises to reward favored constituents loses its attractiveness since, presumably, each such promise will require an immediate transfer of funds to the private pension manager. The defined-contribution model also eliminates the potential for political stalemate in adjusting to unfavorable demographic developments by removing the adjustment mechanism from the political process. As noted previously, one consequence of this is that working-age people bear a higher risk themselves, particularly of unexpected lengthening in retiree life spans. Where the alternative to this is social division and political stalemate, however, the higher risk may be preferable.

The defined-contribution model suffers from its own set of political risks, however. The nature of these risks is illustrated by experiences in closely related situations in this country or by problems that have developed in other countries.

10. Although a number of changes have been made in the Medicare program as part of various budget reconciliation bills, most have involved reductions in provider reimbursement levels rather than reductions in the coverage offered beneficiaries.

TRANSITION COSTS. Shifting from a pay-as-you-go system to a system based on advanced-funded, individual accounts is a difficult undertaking since the implicit unfunded liabilities of the old system must somehow be paid off. This introduces a new pension financing challenge—how to pay transition costs that can easily amount to 3 percent of a country's GDP every year for a number of years.

Governments that are experiencing fiscal problems traceable, at least in part, to imbalances in their pay-as-you-go pension systems may be tempted to try phasing those systems out as part of a strategy for restoring general fiscal balance. They are likely to find, however, that phasing out a pay-as-you-go pension is a greater fiscal challenge than fixing the system, if the two alternatives are equally feasible.[11] It is even possible that a government trying to undo the effect of past excessive promises in its pay-as-you-go pension system will end up making a new set of excessive promises in the form of future transition payments that it eventually finds it cannot afford.[12]

FAILURE TO PRESERVE FINANCIAL ASSETS. A major disadvantage of the defined-contribution model is that the value of the pension promise depends directly on the effectiveness of the preservation and management of the financial assets.

One challenge is assuring that the assets are preserved until retirement begins and then last throughout the retirement years. In this country, the political system has not previously exhibited the kind of policy discipline needed to force individuals to preserve retirement assets. Currently, funds in many tax-favored retirement savings accounts can also be used for home purchases, medical, or educational expenses or to finance loans to the individual worker, and only very modest penalties are imposed on those who convert funds to unauthorized uses. As a result, a substantial portion of what is set aside in individual retirement savings programs may be dissipated prior to retirement.

Our political system has also not exhibited the kind of discipline needed to ensure that assets are drawn down sufficiently slowly to ensure that the retirement income stream lasts throughout the life span of the worker and any dependent spouse. As a practical matter, this will only occur if people are forced to

11. Chand and Jaeger (1996).
12. The Personal Security Account proposal from several members of the 1994–96 Advisory Council is one of the relatively few "privatization" proposals offered recently in the United States to estimate the size of the transition costs. Under its proposal, these costs would be debt financed with the debt retired by a special dedicated tax (either 1 percent of sales or 1.5 percent of payroll) to be levied for a seventy-year period. The risk inherent in this proposal is that Congress would not enact the full tax or would modify it sometime over the ensuing seventy years, exposing either retirees in particular or the economy in general to fiscal uncertainty. U.S. Department of Health and Human Services (1997).

purchase annuities. Unfortunately, in recent years the trend among private retirement income sources has been in the opposite direction. Among private sector retirement programs, lump sum payments are becoming a more common way of drawing down pension rights while the use of regular monthly payments is declining.

A second issue involves the impact of a major economic or political upheaval. History records many instances in which the value of the assets in individual retirement savings accounts or funded pension plans has been wiped out by hyperinflation, war, or major economic collapse. Since the end of World War II, the countries in the Organization for Economic Cooperation and Development have enjoyed an unusually benign economic environment. The environment has not been quite so favorable elsewhere in the world during the past half century and has not always been so favorable even in OECD countries. The defined-contribution model implicitly assumes, however, that recent OECD experience will continue indefinitely.

A third danger is that competition among institutions for individual account business will lead to excessive risk taking, and, eventually, to financial collapses. So far, the institutional arrangements created in Chile have minimized this danger both through tight regulation of the range of investments allowed and by, in effect, preventing firms from competing on the basis of the rate of return that they promise to earn on pension deposits. As these restrictions are gradually liberalized, however, both the potential for gain and the risk of loss increases.

Experience in many of the commercial banking systems around the world illustrates the degree of risk that is introduced when the regulation of financial institutions is inadequate. The current focus is primarily on financial problems in some of the developing countries in Asia, but problems in recent years have cropped up in both developing and developed countries. They commonly materialize after a particularly sharp run-up in either real estate or stock market prices turns out to be unsustainable. When the financial situation begins to unravel, investment losses aggregating 10 percent of a country's GDP can suddenly appear.[13]

As a practical matter, it is not clear whether the risk of major financial losses such as this should be treated as a risk being assumed by individual participants or a risk that the state will end up assuming on behalf of all participants. In principle, in the defined-contribution model the risk of investment losses is borne by the individual participant. In practice, however, governments have often stepped in to protect individuals from the consequences of

13. *Economist* (1997).

major financial collapses, even when not legally required to do so. Thus, when the U.S. savings and loan industry collapsed in the 1980s, the government assumed liabilities well beyond those it was legally responsible for and in most cases offered each individual depositor a greater guarantee than had originally been promised. The fact that many of these deposits represented the retirement savings accounts of middle-income citizens did not escape the notice of congressional decisionmakers.

INEFFECTIVE ADMINISTRATION. A powerful motive for reform in public pension programs in Latin America (and, to a lesser degree, in the former socialist countries) is the risk that benefits will be lost as a result of incompetent public sector administration. In many of these countries, administrators did not maintain the records necessary to establish benefit entitlements, depending entirely on the individual participant or some third party to maintain records. This is not an acceptable arrangement in a dynamic economy. It increases the chances of fraudulent benefit awards while also raising the possibility that individuals will lack some of the information needed to get all the benefits that have been promised and to which they are entitled.

This kind of ineffective public administration is not, however, a source of uncertainty in the United States or most other OECD countries.

The public sector does not have a monopoly on ineffective administrative practices. Recent experience in the United Kingdom illustrates the potential for losses from incompetence (perhaps intentional in some cases) in the privately managed, defined-contribution model. Apparently, salesmen for personal pensions in that country convinced several hundred thousand people to make financial decisions that were of benefit to the salesmen but harmed the individuals. Whether the result of overzealousness, incompetence, or fraud, the individuals affected have lost pension benefits to which they were otherwise entitled through the failure of adequate political oversight and the irresponsible behavior of private sector institutions.

SUMMARY. Political risks are harder to quantify than are demographic or economic risks. It is more difficult both to evaluate the probability that a given political failure will occur and to predict the consequences of that failure for the future pension benefits of persons caught in the middle of their work careers. Moreover, political risks are affected by the unique traditions and institutions of each country, so that generalizations of possible problems in the United States based on experiences abroad are also more problematical.

The two pension approaches considered here differ in the kind of political failures that are likely to threaten their benefit promises. This difference allows advocates of each approach to minimize the riskiness of the one they favor and maximize the riskiness of the alternative, further confusing an already confused public debate. Perhaps what is most important is the recognition that political risks are an important consideration in assessing pension reliability and that, since public pension programs are necessarily creatures of the state, all of them suffer from one form or another of political risk.

Concluding Comments

This analysis has been based on the premise that an important attribute in public pension programs is their ability to produce predictable pensions. It has focused on the sources of uncertainty that affect individual workers over the course of their work careers to see how each is handled in the two public pension models now being debated in the United States. The uncertainties include those associated with demographic and economic developments and those associated with political and institutional failures.

The two models differ substantially in the way they adjust to different sources of uncertainty. The benefit promises under the classic defined-benefit model are relatively insensitive to unexpected changes in the rate of growth of average earnings or to changes in investment returns, but the benefit promise is exposed to the impact of unanticipated changes in either birth rates or retiree life spans. This model requires overt political intervention to adjust benefits and contribution rates in response to these unanticipated demographic developments. The advantage of political intervention is that it provides an opportunity to spread the impact of the demographic changes among the rest of the population, reducing the risk they pose to the benefit promises of an individual retiree. The disadvantage is that where the political system is not strong enough to make the necessary decisions, the need for overt intervention can lead to policy impasse, social discord, and perpetual government budget deficits.

Retirement benefits under the defined-contribution model are just as sensitive to changes in retiree life spans, but this model transfers the risk of this change completely to the individual retiree. Where the political system is not capable of making overt adjustments, this may actually provide a more predictable result than is provided by the defined-benefit model. Where the political system is stronger, the defined-contribution model involves a greater risk that unanticipated changes in retiree life spans will upset benefit expectations.

Because of its closer linkage to the decision processes of the political system, the benefit promises under the defined-benefit model have been exposed to the risk of irresponsible political behavior in many parts of the world. Excessive benefit promises have been a problem for the public pension programs in many

Latin American countries but have not been a problem in the United States, Canada, or Northern Europe. Generating the political will to adjust defined-benefit programs to changed demographics is a challenge for all countries, however, including the United States.

Where excessive benefit promises and politcal stalemate have been serious problems, the defined-contribution model is attractive precisely because its benefits are more insulated from political interference. Politicians are not the only people who are prone to promise more than they can deliver, however. The defined-contribution model requires sophisticated oversight and regulation to ensure that fraud or mismanagement in the private sector does not lead to the upsetting of retiree benefit expectations or to expensive public sector bailouts of private financial institutions.

A final difference is the rather substantial sensitivity of retirement benefits to unforeseeable year-to-year fluctuations in the economic environment in the defined-contribution model. Were the two approaches similar in their ability to handle all other important risks, this feature alone would argue against relying too heavily on the defined-contribution model as a basic source of retirement income.

Neither of the models is without risk, but the risks are different, suggesting the use of approaches that involve a mixture of the two models as a way of reducing the total risk in a pension system. How one creates such a mixed system will vary from country to country, depending on political and institutional traditions.

In many countries, government previously operated a public pension program whose goal was to provide nearly complete wage replacement to retiring wage earners. In these countries, moving to a mixed approach would require scaling back the public program or splitting it into two different pillars. One way this can be achieved is to shift from a system that relies on one mandatory pillar to one that relies on two mandatory pillars, as has been done in Argentina and Uruguay. Another way is to allow individuals or employers to opt out of a portion of the mandatory state system, as is the current approach in the United Kingdom and Japan. A third way is to simply cut back on the public pillar and encourage the growth of a private pillar, the policy that seems to be emerging in Germany.

None of these approaches is necessarily appropriate in the United States, however. Along with Canada and a handful of other countries, the United States never attempted to provide complete wage replacement through a single public program. Instead, it created a public pension program that, by design, provided insufficient benefits to middle- and upper-income individuals in the hope that they would be encouraged to supplement these benefits on their own. The result has been the growth of a huge private pension and retirement savings industry that appears to be shifting gradually to the defined-contribution model. The United States already has a mixed public/private and defined-benefit/defined-contribution pension system. It does not need to "privatize" its current Social Security program in order to produce one.

Would a Privatized Social Security System Really Pay a Higher Rate of Return?
John Geanakoplos, Olivia S. Mitchell, and Stephen P. Zeldes

As THE U.S. Social Security system has matured, the rate of return received by participants has fallen. In the coming years, around the time the baby boom generation retires, the system will experience a budget shortfall. First, tax revenues will fall short of promised benefits, requiring spending the interest earnings, and then the principal, of the trust fund. Eventually, the trust fund will be depleted. This projected insolvency will necessitate benefit cuts or tax increases, leading to further declines in the rates of return individuals can expect.

Many advocates of reform suggest that an answer to this problem is to privatize Social Security. They argue that the creation of individual accounts invested in private capital markets, and especially in the stock market, will produce better rates of return for individuals than will Social Security. For example, Stephen Moore of the Cato Institute recently claimed that "privatization offers a much higher financial rate of return to young workers than the current system . . . if Congress were to allow a 25-year-old working woman today to invest her payroll tax contributions in private capital markets, her retirement benefit would be two to five times higher than what Social Security is offering."[14] Presidential candidate Steve Forbes criticized Social Security because "the average worker retiring today receives a lifetime return of only about 2.2 percent on the taxes he has paid into the system. Contrast this with

This paper draws on a longer paper by the authors (Geanakoplos, Mitchell, and Zeldes, forthcoming). Useful comments were provided by Jeff Brown, Martin Feldstein, and Kent Smetters.

14. Moore (1997)

the historic 9–10 percent annual returns from stock market investments. . . . The advantages of an IRA-type approach are overpowering."[15]

Our goal in this paper is to challenge the following popular argument: projected returns to Social Security are low relative to expected returns on stocks and bonds, and therefore everyone would receive higher returns and be better off if the United States moved to a privatized system where individuals could directly invest their contributions in stocks and bonds. We argue that for households with access to diversified capital markets, privatization without prefunding would not increase Social Security returns, when properly measured. Privatization together with prefunding would eventually raise the rate of return to future generations of participants, but at the cost of a lower rate of return to early generations.

The real economic benefit to privatization is the diversification that would be made available to constrained households that cannot participate on their own in diversified capital market investment portfolios. The improved rate-of-return argument in favor of privatization thus has no force unless there are constrained households without access to diversified capital markets. However, this group of people is not generally recognized to be key to the popular argument just quoted. Indeed, in the presence of such constrained households, young market-savvy workers, who according to the popular argument should find privatization most appealing, will probably get lower returns as a result of privatization.

We begin by defining what privatization means and by distinguishing that concept from diversification and from prefunding. Next, we ask whether projected returns on Social Security are in fact below those anticipated from U.S. capital markets.[16] Finally, we ask whether low Social Security returns are a valid reason to support a privatization that does not involve prefunding. We conclude that several valid rationales can be offered to support privatization, but taken by itself, the low rate of return on Social Security is not among them.

What Do We Mean by Social Security Privatization?

To begin, it is useful to draw a clear distinction between three terms that are often confused: *privatization* versus *diversification* versus *prefunding* of Social Security. By privatization we mean replacing the current mostly unfunded defined-benefit Social Security old-age program with a defined-contribution system of individual accounts held in individual workers' names. By diversification

---

15. Steve Forbes, "How to Replace Social Security," *Wall Street Journal*, December 18, 1996

16. Although we focus on the rate-of-return concept of money's worth in this paper, additional measures are evaluated in more detail in our longer study (Geanakoplos, Mitchell, and Zeldes, forthcoming).

we mean investing funds (either from the personal accounts or from the Social Security trust fund) into a broad range of assets. These assets might include U.S. private sector stocks and bonds, and foreign securities, in addition to the government bonds now used exclusively by the Social Security trust fund. At the present time, the focus is on diversifying into stocks. By prefunding we mean reducing the sum of the system's implicit and explicit debt (table 4-4).[17]

In the public debate these terms are often linked, but they are conceptually different. It is easy to see why all three categories nevertheless appear together in the public mind. Suppose the Social Security system had begun as a forced saving plan in which all workers were obliged to set aside money for their retirement, which would be put into private accounts invested in a balanced portfolio of stocks and bonds. Then from the beginning the system would have been privatized, diversified, and completely prefunded.

The situation is quite different now from what it was in 1935 when the U.S. Social Security system began. Social security systems in the United States and in most developed economies have amassed substantial unfunded liabilities; assets on hand are insufficient to pay for the present value of benefits that have been accrued and promised to workers and retirees based on contributions already made.[18] In the United States, for instance, the unfunded present value of Social Security promises totals about $9 trillion.[19] Although this Social Security debt is implicit rather than explicit, it is economically significant. The United States will surely not decide to eliminate this implicit debt by ignoring all of the promised benefits.

Our tripartite decomposition is intended to emphasize that Social Security reform could change any one of these three categories without changing the other two. For example, the trust fund could invest in stocks as well as bonds, thus diversifying without privatizing. Alternatively, workers could be given private accounts in which the money was always invested in government bonds, thus privatizing without diversifying. This is the case in Mexico's new individual account system, where the government has required that all pension assets be invested only in inflation-indexed bonds.[20] It is also possible to raise system

17. There is debate over whether prefunding should refer to a change that reduces the total government debt rather than just the Social Security debt. Here we assume that any changes in Social Security do not change the non-Social Security debt or deficit.

18. The concept of unfunded liability is different from that of actuarial imbalance. Actuarial imbalance is defined as the present value of expected benefits over some period (often seventy-five years) minus the present value of expected tax receipts over the same period, minus the current value of the trust fund. The United States currently has a seventy-five-year actuarial imbalance of about 2.2 percent of payroll a year, or about 2.9 trillion dollars in present value. See Goss (forthcoming).

19. Goss (forthcoming).

20. Mitchell and Barreto (1997).

Table 4-4. *Differentiating Privatization, Prefunding, and Diversification of Social Security*

- *Privatization:* Replace existing Social Security system with a system of individual accounts held and managed by individuals.
- *Prefunding:* Raise contributions or cut benefits so as to lower the sum of explicit and implicit debt associated with the system.
- *Diversification:* Invest Social Security funds into a broad range of assets, including equities.

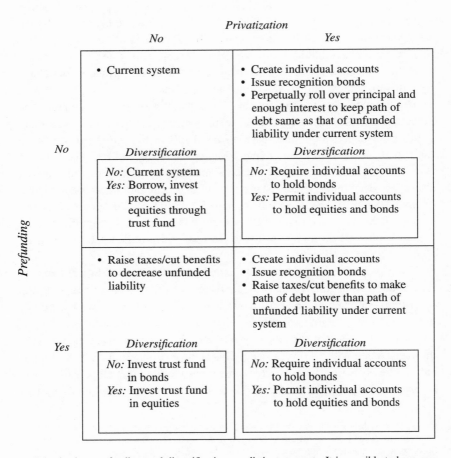

Privatization, prefunding, and diversification are distinct concepts. It is possible to have any one, without either of the other two.

funding without involving individual accounts; taxes could be raised or bene-fits cut and the proceeds could be put into a central trust fund. Singapore's national Provident Fund, for example, is a nonprivatized, prefunded system where the central government collects taxes sufficient to generate substantial assets, which it then invests on the system's behalf. Conversely, people could be given individual accounts without prefunding of benefit promises. A privatized but unfunded pension system has recently been established in Latvia, where payroll taxes are collected by the government, which then credits workers' so-called notional accounts with paper returns on contributions. Chile is the best-known example of a country whose program is both prefunded and privatized: here workers hold assets in individually managed accounts, and debt under the old system is being reduced over time.

Likewise in the United States, privatization without prefunding is quite pos-sible; a Social Security reform that created a national 401(k)-type system of pri-vate accounts could be implemented with no change in Social Security debt. For example, the Social Security system could issue new explicit debt (recognition bonds), guaranteed by the federal government, with payouts set exactly equal to the benefit promises that have accrued to date under the current system. These bonds would be given to current participants in lieu of their accrued future ben-efit payments. All new contributions to Social Security would then go directly into private individual accounts.[21] If the recognition bonds were paid off in full with new government tax receipts, the debt would eventually disappear when the last of today's workers finally died. However, the Social Security system could instead borrow again in the future by issuing new bonds to meet the recognition bond coupon payments, and then again and again to meet the payments on these new bonds. Subject to some limits, the government could choose how much interest and principal to roll over and how much to pay off. If the government were to choose to keep the path of explicit debt equal to the path of unfunded lia-bilities under the current system (the implicit debt), the result would be a Social Security system that was privatized without being prefunded.

In what follows we shall examine the claim that a privatized, diversified Social Security system could deliver higher returns without any additional pre-funding. We do so in three steps. First, we analyze returns in a privatized sys-tem that confines investments to government bonds. Next, we examine returns in a privatized and diversified system in which investments in stocks are per-mitted. Finally, we analyze returns in a privatized and diversified system and allow for the possibility that there are some constrained households who do not currently have access on their own to diversified capital markets.

21. More gradual transitions to a system of individual accounts that leave (implicit plus explicit) debt unchanged are also possible.

Table 4-5. *Annual Inflation-Adjusted Returns on Stocks and Government Bonds, 1926–96*

Percent

Asset	Arithmetic average real return	Standard deviation
S&P 500	9.4	20.4
Long-term government bond	2.4	10.5
Intermediate-term government bond	2.3	7.1
Short-term T-bill	0.7	4.2

Source: Authors' calculations based on data from Ibbotson & Associates (1998).

Are Projected Rates of Return on Social Security Lower Than Those on U.S. Capital Markets?

A starting point for projecting future returns on U.S. capital markets is to examine historical returns. Table 4-5 reports the historical average of inflation-adjusted (that is, real) returns on stocks, bonds, and Treasury bills, as well as their variability. The average annual real return on stocks (as proxied by the S&P 500) was 9.4 percent; the corresponding return on intermediate-term government bonds was 2.3 percent.[22] Whether these provide reasonable forecasts for future years depends in part on one's judgment about whether the past will predict the future.

Cohort-specific rates of return under Social Security, from a study by Dean Leimer, are presented in figure 4-1.[23] Historical data on current and past workers and retirees, as well as projections of future contributions and benefits, are used to compute rates of return, which we sometimes call by their more precise name, internal rates of return (IRRs). We note first that prospective (internal) rates of return depend on a host of predictions, including mortality, population growth, and real wage growth.[24] Second, the prospective IRR data are not those

22. These are arithmetic averages of annual returns from 1926 through 1996 taken from Ibbotson and Associates (1998). The 1994–96 Social Security Advisory Council projected that in the future stocks would earn a 7 percent real return, compared with 2 percent real return on bonds.
23. Leimer (1994).
24. The internal rate of return (IRR) is defined as the interest rate that equates the present value of taxes paid to the system and the present value of benefits received, by cohort. Two other "money's worth" measures sometimes reported are the present value ratio (PVB/PVT), or the present value of benefits divided by the present value of taxes, and the net present value (NPV), or the present value of benefits received minus the present value of taxes paid. The IRR and its companion money's worth measures are appealing because they seek to summarize in a single measure how a household might evaluate the complex multiyear stream of Social Security payments and

Figure 4-1. *Estimated Real Internal Rates of Return on Social Security Contributions*

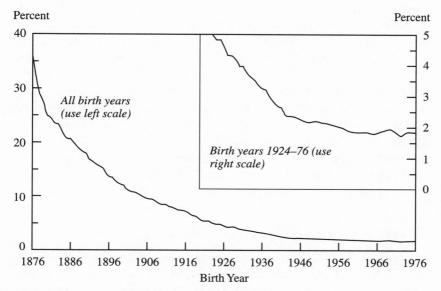

Source: Leimer (1994) tax increase balanced budget scenario.

that would follow from forecasting taxes and benefits under *current* Social Security rules, since that system faces insolvency or actuarial imbalance. Instead the IRR figures for the future assume that taxes will be increased sufficiently so that the system does not run out of money.[25]

Figure 4-1 shows that early cohorts under the program received very high IRRs in real terms. Workers born in 1876 received a real return of over 35 percent a year. Workers born in 1900 received a 12 percent real return. The figure reveals that IRRs fell over time for subsequent cohorts. Leimer estimated the

---

receipts. However the measure's simplicity belies the extensive assumptions and calculations needed to arrive at a single summary number. For example, in order to conclude that workers born in 1930 anticipate a Social Security IRR of 4 percent, it is necessary to compute what that cohort paid in payroll taxes over all years of work (Leimer 1994). Not all those born in 1930 have retired as yet, so future earnings profiles, taxes, and retirement patterns must be forecast. Each group's tax payments must then be compared against the stream of Social Security benefits actually paid out to people of that birth year. Of course, many 1930-cohort members are still living, so future benefit payments and mortality patterns must again be estimated. For details see Geanakoplos, Mitchell, and Zeldes (forthcoming).

25. Leimer also provides estimates under the assumption that benefits are reduced to maintain solvency.

return to be 5.7 percent for those born in 1920, and about 2 percent for those born 1950–70. For workers born in 1975, he forecasted that IRRs would be around 1.8 percent, dropping down to 1.5 percent for those born in 1998.

Young or middle-aged workers listening to the Social Security reform debate today could reasonably ask how their anticipated IRR from Social Security would compare with what could be earned by investing in U.S. capital markets. Leimer's data indicate IRRs of about 1.5 percent for future cohorts; theoretical models of a pure pay-as-you-go Social Security system in steady state suggest that the IRR would be expected to equal the growth of the wage base, which is currently forecast to be about 1.2 percent.[26] Either way, it is clear that projected IRRs are well below expected returns from investment in equities based on historical averages, and fall short of average government bond returns in table 4-5 as well. Thus, the popular rate of return argument in favor of privatization seems to apply whether or not the investments are diversified.

Why Are Projected Social Security Returns Low?

Projected Social Security returns are low, not because of waste or inefficiency, but because the system developed as a primarily unfunded, pay-as-you-go system. In a pure pay-as-you-go system, all contributions received by the system are paid out in the same year as benefits to someone else, and no trust fund is accumulated. This means that there are some early beneficiaries who receive benefits even though they have not made any contributions. The U.S. Social Security system was not started as a pure pay-as-you-go system, because only those individuals who contributed some money to the system were eligible for benefits. Nevertheless, the accumulated trust fund was minimal, so that it was still the case that the present value of benefits received by those retiring soon after 1940 far exceeded the present value of contributions they had made.

The key to understanding why IRRs must fall in our nearly pay-as-you-go Social Security system is to exploit the connection between net present values (NPV) and internal rates of return (IRR). Whenever the NPV for a cohort is positive, the IRR for the cohort will be greater than the market rate, and vice versa. Therefore, stating that early generations received a positive net transfer from Social Security is equivalent to saying that they received above-market rates of return on their contributions.[27]

26. For a discussion of the assumptions used to estimate future wage base growth rates as well as future Social Security benefit and tax paths, see Advisory Council on Social Security (1997).

27. Comparing the present value of a cohort's benefits and taxes is an application of the generational accounting approach to measuring fiscal policy. See, for example, Auerbach, Gokhale, and Kotlikoff (1994).

Figure 4-2. *Social Security Net Intercohort Transfers*

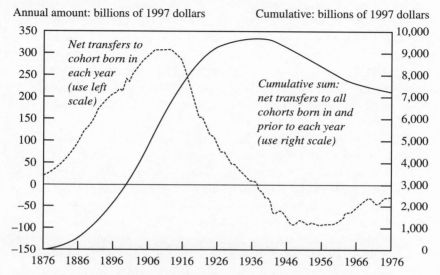

Annual amount: billions of 1997 dollars   Cumulative: billions of 1997 dollars

Sources: Leimer (1994) tax increase balanced budget scenario and authors' calculations. All figures are present values as of 1997.

In figure 4-1, we saw that the real rates of return for early cohorts (birth-year 1876–1900) ranged from 12 to 37 percent.[28] Figure 4-2 presents estimates of cohort net present values, derived from Leimer's study, corresponding to these cohort rates of return.[29] The dotted line (left scale) is the net present value, in 1997 dollars, of all contributions and benefits for individuals born in the indicated year. As expected for the beginning of a pay-as-you-go system, the present value of benefits exceeded taxes for the first wave of retirees. Each birth-year cohort between 1880 and 1900 (those retiring approximately 1945–1965) received a lifetime transfer (in 1997 present value dollars) of between 40 billion and 240 billion dollars. The solid line in figure 4-2 (right scale) is the cumulative sum of all net transfers received by cohorts born prior to and including the indicated birth year. Cohorts born through 1900 received a cumulative net transfer of about 3 trillion dollars.

28. Recall that these are real or inflation-adjusted returns; nominal returns would obviously be even higher.

29. Leimer (1994) used the interest rates on trust fund assets (essentially intermediate-term U.S. Treasury bonds) to convert current dollars into 1989 dollars. We convert the series into 1997 dollars using the corresponding interest rates between 1989 and 1997.

In part because the Social Security tax rates started out low in 1937 (the initial tax rate was 2 percent) and gradually rose over time, the positive transfers to retirees continued well past the first wave of beneficiaries. Those born between 1901 and 1917 received net transfers with present value of about $4.9 trillion. In addition, the twenty age cohorts born between 1918 and 1937 are scheduled to receive a further net transfer of $1.8 trillion, in present value. Adding up the $3 trillion, $4.9 trillion, and $1.8 trillion, we arrive at an estimate of the total net transfer to the first sixty age cohorts of $9.7 trillion, or roughly $10 trillion.

What do the positive net subsidies and high returns for early cohorts have to do with the low returns forecasted for current and future cohorts? It can be shown that the present value across all cohorts (from the beginning of the system forward for the infinite future) of the net transfers received must sum to zero.[30] Inevitably, cohorts born after 1937 must give up in aggregate the whole $10 trillion, discounted back to 1997 dollars.[31]

In other words, since past cohorts received positive net transfers, some present and future cohorts must receive negative net transfers. The connection described above between net transfers and rates of return means that we can

30. To see this, first consider a system that is pay as you go, so that in each year aggregate taxes are equal to aggregate benefits, that is, benefits minus taxes equals zero. Hence, the present value of each year's benefits minus taxes must equal zero, and therefore the sum across all years of these present values must equal zero as well. So long as the present value of all benefits across all years and the present value of all taxes across all years are each finite, which must necessarily hold if the interest rate is on average higher than the rate of growth of the economy, we can rearrange and regroup benefits and taxes however we like. Grouping together benefits and taxes for each birth cohort, it must be, as claimed, that the present values of net transfers (benefits minus taxes), cohort by cohort, sum to zero.

This is also true with prefunding, and even with trust fund borrowing, provided that the trust fund assets are invested at the same interest rate used to compute present values. In this case, the present value of all benefits paid up to and including any year T is equal to the present value of all taxes up to and including year T plus the present value of the year T trust fund. Allowing T to go to infinity and assuming that the trust fund is not allowed to grow increasingly negative at rate r or faster and that the government would not want it to grow increasingly positive at rate r or faster, the present value of net transfers (benefits minus taxes) made to all birth cohorts must equal zero. See Geanakoplos, Mitchell, and Zeldes (forthcoming) for more details.

The difference between a prefunded system and a pay-as-you-go system is that in the latter, the early cohorts must get positive transfers, leaving negative transfers for later cohorts, whereas in a prefunded system, the early cohorts may not get any positive transfers. Our current Social Security system has very little prefunding. The correspondingly small trust fund indeed earns a bond rate of return, so our analysis is relevant.

31. It is important to note that this discounting is at the real rate of interest. If, for example, the real rate of interest is 2.3 percent a year and inflation is 3 percent, and if the $10 trillion were paid back in one lump sum in 30 years, then it would cost $48 trillion in 2027 dollars. The relentless power of compounding interest is what makes the burden of the initial Social Security transfers many years ago loom so large today.

translate this statement about net transfers into a statement about rates of return. Because past cohorts received rates of return greater than market rates, current and future cohorts must receive rates of return lower than market rates.[32]

How big the negative transfer must be for any one cohort born after 1937 depends on how the total transfer is spread across all the cohorts. Observe that according to (our modifications of the numbers in) Leimer, the cohorts born between 1938 and 1977 are scheduled to receive negative transfers of about $2.5 trillion, reducing the total projected net transfer to cohorts born before 1978 to approximately $7.2 trillion. Of course much of this $2.5 trillion transfer has not yet occurred. The young born in 1975, for example, have just begun to work, and so have not had time to make any significant transfers through the Social Security system. Roughly half of the working careers of cohorts born between 1938 and 1977 have passed by 1997. We might guess therefore that subtracting the present value of Social Security taxes already paid by cohorts born between 1938 and 1977 from the present value of Social Security benefits already accrued as a result of these taxes gives about half of $2.5 trillion. That would mean that the sum of the net tax burden on all contributions made after 1997 would equal $9.7 trillion minus $1.25 trillion, or about $8.5 trillion. In fact, the number must be equal to the unfunded liability, which was calculated independently by Stephen Goss at just under $9 trillion, thus providing a check on our numbers.[33]

There is a simple way of estimating the transfers that might be made each year after 1997. Suppose the total negative transfer of $9 trillion is spread equitably among all the cohorts, in the sense that every cohort is (or will be) asked to give up the same percentage of its earnings each year of its working career. In a steadily growing economy, the required annual transfer in year t would then be approximately equal to $(r - g) \times$ (unfunded liabilities at end of year $t - 1$), where r is the riskless real rate of return and g is the growth rate of the economy (approximately equal to the sum of population growth and technological improvement).[34] Assuming that r is about 2.3 percent (as indicated in

32. If the system had instead started as and remained a fully funded system, then early participants would have received market returns, that is, zero net transfers, as would all current and future workers.

33. Goss (forthcoming).

34. The transfer in period $t + 1$ (TRANS_{t+1}) is the amount by which contributions in period $t + 1$ exceed the present value of the benefits accrued as a result of those contributions. Define UL_t as the unfunded liability at time t. It can be shown (Geanakoplos, Mitchell, and Zeldes, forthcoming) that the change in the unfunded liability between t and $t + 1$ ($\Delta \text{UL}_{t,t+1}$) is equal to $(r \times \text{UL}_t) - \text{TRANS}_{t+1}$. In a steady-state economy, the unfunded liability must grow at rate g, i.e., $\Delta \text{UL}_{t,t+1} = g \times \text{UL}_t$. This implies that the transfer must be exactly $(r - g) \times \text{UL}_t$, as claimed in the text.

table 4-5), and that g is about 1.2 percent, and using $9 trillion as the current unfunded liability, transfers in 1997 must be on the order of $100 billion. Measured as a percentage of Social Security taxes paid, which were about $400 billion in 1997, this transfer represents about 25 percent of annual payroll taxes.[35]

Spreading the remaining start-up cost of our pay-as-you-go Social Security system evenly over all cohorts requires each cohort to give up about 25 percent of every annual contribution, or 3 percentage points of the current 12.4 percent payroll tax. In other words, implicit interest payments explain why young workers may expect only 75 percent of their taxes back in (the present value of) benefits over their lifetimes.[36] As long as the Social Security debt is spread out over all subsequent cohorts, returns on Social Security will be lower for every cohort than returns paid by bonds.

Are Low Social Security Returns a Valid Reason to Support Privatization?

The second step in the causal argument supporting privatization seems the easiest and most straightforward—so much so that it is often taken for granted. If projected returns on Social Security are significantly lower than those offered in U.S. capital markets, doesn't it immediately follow that we would all be better off if we were allowed to invest Social Security contributions directly in private securities? Frequent arguments in the popular press and some studies by advocates of privatization suggest that this is the case.[37] Yet, this conclusion is misleading for two reasons: it ignores transition costs (that is, how do we eliminate the implicit Social Security debt); and it does not account for changes in risk borne by participants.

35. This number is, of course, only an approximation. To get it we assumed that the real interest rate would stay constant at 2.3 percent and that the wage base would grow steadily at 1.2 percent. Among other things, both assumptions ignore demographic changes. In the current baby boom era, both real interest rates and growth rates are higher than we assumed. If anything, however, it looks like actual $r - g$ is higher than we presumed, which would imply that the necessary transfers might be even more than we suggest.

36. As a check, consider a hypothetical worker who pays level real Social Security taxes for forty years and receives level real benefits for the next twenty years at an internal rate of return of 1.2 percent (an estimate of g). If instead, his contributions were reduced by 25 percent but his benefits remained the same, then his internal rate of return would be 2.12 percent, which is close to our estimate of r of 2.3 percent.

37. See, for example, Steve Forbes, "How to Replace Social Security," *Wall Street Journal*, December 18, 1996, and Beach and Davis (1998) There are sites on the World Wide Web that calculate for users the benefit stream they will likely receive from Social Security and compare it to the income stream attainable from investing their Social Security contributions in private capital markets. See, for example, the Cato Institute web site at *www.socialsecurity.org/calc/calculator.html*.

Transition Costs

Let us begin by ignoring issues related to risk, such as diversification. Since the rate of return on bonds is greater than the rate of return of Social Security, it would be easy to increase the return for future cohorts by simply ignoring past contributions and not paying any benefits accrued under the current system. The old Social Security system could be shut down, and all new Social Security tax receipts could be put into private accounts invested in bonds. Future cohorts would be able to earn market returns. But then the entire $10 trillion cost of subsidizing the first sixty cohorts would in effect be borne by the current middle-aged and old, who would then have paid into the system for years and received nothing in return.

Alternatively, one could shut down the old system and privatize but continue to pay all the Social Security benefits accrued to date, based on past contributions. As noted earlier, recognition bonds could be issued to workers and retirees for the full amount of the unfunded liability (that is, $9 trillion). If the government did not default on these bonds, new taxes would have to be raised to pay interest on the recognition bonds. Further, if the new taxes were set to keep the path over time of recognition bond debt the same as the path of implicit debt under the current system, then the new taxes would correspond exactly to the transfers we mentioned in the last section.[38] In other words, it can be shown that the new taxes raised would eliminate all of the higher returns on individual accounts.[39] Let us see why.

Consider a steady-state economy growing at the constant rate g with market interest rate r, and with a pay-as-you-go Social Security system begun sometime in the distant past. As pointed out earlier, the implicit tax paid through Social Security in each year is $(r - g) \times$ (the unfunded liability at the end of the previous year). If suddenly at date t Social Security were privatized and transition costs were ignored (for example because accrued benefits were never paid), the IRR on the privatized system in which individual accounts were all held in marketed bonds would be equal to r. If instead recognition bonds were issued, their market value at date t would have to be equal to the unfunded liability in that year. In order to keep the debt growing at the same rate g as the economy, taxes in the next year would have to be raised in the amount $(r - g) \times$ (unfunded liability). The extra taxes needed to finance the payments on the recognition bonds would thus be identical to the transfers made each year in the old Social Security system. By choosing the tax rates appropriately, the tax

38. In a steady state, the required path of debt would keep constant the ratio of outstanding recognition bond debt to GDP.

39. For a further discussion of this result, see Geanakoplos, Mitchell, and Zeldes (forthcoming).

burden could be made to fall exactly on the same people who were contributing more to Social Security than they were receiving in benefits.[40] Aside from the transfers, participants in the current pay-as-you-go Social Security system are in effect earning the bond rate of return on their money. In a privatized system in which households invested their forced saving in bonds, they would have to pay in new taxes exactly what they paid before in transfers.

In other words, the rate of return on a privatized system in which all private investment is in marketed bonds, net of new taxes needed to pay the appropriate interest on the recognition bond debt, would be identical to the low rate of return on the current system. This is true regardless of how large the difference is between r and g—this difference could be 1.1 percent, 3 percent, 10 percent, or even higher.[41] That is why it is fallacious to assume that all future participants in a privatized Social Security system could earn returns equal to those forecast for U.S. capital markets. We thus agree that returns to the current Social Security system are low, but we argue that there is no costless way of improving them for all current and future workers.

Suppose, alternatively, that taxes were raised disproportionately on current cohorts, and receipts were used to buy out some of the recognition bond debt, so that the system reform increased the degree of funding.[42] Then later cohorts would face lower taxes to pay the interest on the remaining recognition bond debt. For these later cohorts, returns on Social Security contributions, net of recognition bond taxes, would be higher than under the current system. But for current workers, returns on a privatized system would be lower than under the current system. Thus, transition costs mean either that returns under a privatized system would be the same as the current system (privatization with no prefunding), or that returns in the privatized system would be lower than under the current system for some or all of the currently alive cohorts and then higher for later cohorts (privatization with prefunding). The debate should be focused on whether this is a trade-off worth making, not on whether there is a free lunch.[43]

40. There are different ways of measuring accrued benefits, and each method would require a different tax scheme to make taxes in a privatized system just equal to transfers in the current Social Security system. We give one example. Suppose accrued benefits are defined on an equal present value basis, that is, suppose each dollar of contributions brings the same present value of accrued benefits (discounted back to the point when the dollar is contributed). Suppose this ratio is .75. Then a proportional tax of $(1 - .75) \times 12.4$ percent = 3.1 percent would leave everyone exactly as well off in a privatized system as he or she was in the current pay-as-you-go Social Security system.

41. Higher r makes privatized returns higher but, as we have just seen, it also increases the interest burden of the unfunded liability.

42. A potential advantage of prefunding is that it would, according to most economists, increase national saving. There is no reason to believe that privatization without prefunding would necessarily increase national saving. See, for example, Mitchell and Zeldes (1996).

43. As argued, for example, by Feldstein (1997).

Risk Adjustment

Advocates of Social Security reform might be tempted to say that people would invest their individual accounts in stocks—earning a higher rate of return—rather than in bonds. By now readers should be suspicious of arguments that promise something for nothing. After all, we just saw that although bonds earn a higher return than the Social Security system, privatizing and investing in bonds would give no higher return once the new taxes needed to redeem the outstanding liabilities of the current system were properly accounted for.

IRR computations usually overlook the fact that workers and retirees bear different risks in a privatized versus a publicly run Social Security system. It is important to keep in mind that when one asset is riskier than another, it should have a higher equilibrium expected market return; this explains why stocks on average should earn a higher return than bonds. As a result, safer returns from a conventional Social Security system cannot be directly compared with riskier returns anticipated from an equities-based system, unless risk adjustment is done to make the programs comparable. By risk adjustment, we mean adjusting downward the expected value of risky returns (for example, stock returns) to recognize the increased risk associated with these securities.

Households that already hold both stocks and bonds in their portfolios and that have the expertise to buy and sell stocks and bonds should value an additional dollar of stocks the same as an additional dollar of bonds, even though stocks have a much higher expected rate of return. If they valued an additional dollar's worth of stocks more than an additional dollar's worth of bonds, they would have already sold some of their bonds and bought stocks with the money.[44] For this type of household, the risk-adjusted rate of return on an additional dollar of stocks is identical to that on bonds. Put differently, when considering a Social Security change that alters a small fraction of such a household's portfolio, it would be appropriate to compare the current Social Security system to a privatized system in which the individual accounts were required to invest only in government bonds.[45] And we have already seen in that case that privatization does not bring higher returns, correctly measured.

For a larger change in Social Security investment policy, such households could simply use their non-Social Security portfolio to completely offset the change in Social Security. For example, imagine a middle-aged household

44. This is not to say that such a household would put its first dollar of saving into bonds instead of stocks, but rather after its (perhaps considerable) investment in stocks, the next dollar of stock would increase well-being no more than another dollar of bonds.

45. In practice, government bond returns are not equal to Social Security returns, and neither is riskless. We ignore these issues here.

paying $5,000 a year in Social Security taxes (including employer contributions), which initially were being placed directly into a personal account (run by the government) in the U.S. Treasury bond market. Suppose the household was also saving outside of the Social Security account an additional $10,000 a year, $9,000 in stocks and $1,000 in treasury bonds. Overall, the household is putting 60 percent in stocks ($9,000 out of $15,000), and 40 percent in bonds ($6,000 out of $15,000). If the government suddenly switched the entire Social Security account into stocks, this household could restore the 60-40 split of its total saving by putting $4,000 into stocks and $6,000 into bonds out of its private saving. In fact, no matter how the Social Security account is invested, this household will be no better or worse off. The appropriate risk-adjusted return to such a household from a Social Security account, no matter how it is invested, is the bond return. For a household that is already diversified, the correctly measured return from a privatized and diversified Social Security system is no higher than the current system.[46]

The real economic benefit to privatization comes from the attendant diversification that would be made available to households that cannot participate on their own in diversified capital markets. According to economic theory, every household whose income is uncorrelated with stock returns should include some stock in its portfolio in order to take advantage of the higher returns stocks provide compared to bonds and other safe assets. The first dollars invested in stocks would definitely raise risk-corrected returns, because they would bring extra returns without adding much risk. Subsequent dollars invested in stock continue to raise returns, but at the cost of more and more risk, eventually lowering risk-adjusted returns. How much money should optimally be invested in stocks depends on the wealth and risk tolerance of the household.

Households that are constrained in their private portfolio from holding sufficient amounts of stock would be helped if a portion of their Social Security returns coincided with equity returns. What type of households would fit into this category and how do we recognize them? First, there are households that will not accumulate any wealth outside of Social Security, but who would like to borrow money to invest in the stock market if they could find a lender to loan

46. This argument holds even if there is an inexplicably large equity premium, as some economists claim there is. Suppose the excess return on stocks above bonds is much more than can be justified by the risk differential, because many households are irrationally underinvesting in equities. In that case, we might be tempted on paternalistic grounds to force these irrational households to hold more stock. However, this is no simple matter. If Social Security were simply privatized, these households would likely choose not to hold any equities in their Social Security accounts for the same reasons they held too few stocks in the rest of their portfolio. If households were instead forced into equities in Social Security, they would likely undo this by reducing their holdings of equities in the rest of their portfolio.

them money at the bond rate.[47] Second, there are households that will invest 100 percent of their private wealth in the stock market and that would like to invest even more in the stock market if they could borrow at the bond rate. Finally, there are households that will accumulate wealth outside of Social Security, but will choose not to invest in the stock market either because they are uninformed about the relative returns and risks or because it is not worth it to them to incur the fixed costs of becoming a stock market investor. Each of these groups would benefit from owning individual accounts invested in the stock market.[48] This provides us with an economic rationale for privatization and diversification.[49]

There remains the issue of how many "constrained" households there are, that do not have sufficient access to the stock market. The second group is probably small. The first and third groups are a subset of the people who own no stocks. Fully 59 percent of the U.S. population (in 1995) did not hold stocks in any form.[50] Some of the nonstockholders, however, are young and have not yet accumulated much Social Security or private wealth. What we really want to know is what fraction of the population is unlikely to hold stock in the future, when they are accumulating Social Security wealth. Although we do not have direct estimates of this, about 50 percent of the population 44 to 54 years old and 60 percent of those 55 to 64 years old held no stock in 1995. But stock-ownership has risen in the past and is likely to continue to rise in the future, so this is probably an upper bound on the fraction of the population that will not hold stock in the absence of Social Security privatization and diversification.

47. Given the chance, these "liquidity constrained" households would prefer to use borrowing to increase current consumption. If borrowing could be used only to purchase other assets, however, these households would choose to borrow and purchase stocks.

48. This assumes that the fixed costs would be lower under an individual account system.

49. This raises the issue of whether diversification into stocks is better achieved through privatized individual accounts or through central trust fund investments. If constrained investors tend to be irrational or myopic in their investment decisions, then it would be more advantageous for them if the Social Security trust fund itself undertook stock investments on their behalf. Unconstrained investors could still keep control of all their asset holdings (inside and outside of their Social Security funds) by compensating in their private accounts for whatever the trust fund did that was not to their taste, as we saw above. However, households such as those who have chosen optimally to hold small amounts of stocks, perhaps because they are risk averse, may be forced to hold too much extra in stocks in their Social Security accounts. These households would be made worse off. The more heterogeneous are constrained households in their tolerance of risk, and the wiser we think constrained households would be in their investment choices, the more attractive is privatization as a means of achieving diversification. The more homogeneous are constrained households in their tolerance of risk, and the more myopic we think constrained households would be in their investment choices, the more attractive is trust fund investment as a means of achieving diversification.

50. This is based on calculations using the 1995 Survey of Consumer Finances. It includes stocks held directly, through mutual funds, and through defined-contribution pensions. See Kennickell, Starr-McCluer, and Sunden (1997) and Ameriks and Zeldes (in progress).

Also, not all those without stock would benefit substantially by holding stocks. For some, their wage income or private business income might be sufficiently positively correlated with the stock market that they are better off not holding any equities. Others, who hold zero stock because they are very risk averse and face a small fixed cost, would only see a small benefit from increased holdings of stock in their Social Security account. Overall, we would guess that significantly fewer than half of households would benefit substantially, and therefore experience substantially higher risk-adjusted returns, from increased Social Security investment in stocks.

If there is a large number of constrained households, then Social Security diversification would have macroeconomic consequences as well. The most important general equilibrium effect of diversification would be an increase in the demand and thus in the price of stocks and a corresponding decline in their expected return. As the value of the stock market increased, current holders of stocks, which disproportionately include the wealthy and older workers who have had time to accumulate stock, would see their wealth increase. Young workers would find that they earned smaller returns on their future stock purchases than they would have in the absence of diversification.[51]

While privatization and diversification may indeed bring benefits to some constrained households, and perhaps some indirect benefits to the economy as a whole, the presence of these households is not part of the currently popular rate-of-return argument for privatization. According to that argument, all households, and especially the youngest (25-year-old workers), are supposed to see higher returns from privatizing Social Security. Yet when properly measured, rates of return for unconstrained households will stay the same or actually decline for young unconstrained households.

Another risk consideration is that the government-run Social Security system provides insurance functions that an individual-account system probably would not provide, including insurance for shocks to earnings, length of life, disability, and inflation. For instance, the benefit formula is structured to provide a higher rate of return to low lifetime earner households than to high lifetime earner households. This is justified on the grounds that a social insurance plan can pool over the entire population certain risks that are difficult to insure privately, particularly disability, unemployment, and poverty. To the extent that

51. Social security diversification would bring some indirect benefits to the economy if there were many constrained households. Unconstrained households would end up holding less stock, because some of it would be in the hands of Social Security accounts held by constrained households who could not buy stock previously. Thus unconstrained households would bear less risk. They would be inclined to shift the mix of investment projects undertaken toward more risky ones. This might in turn raise future GDP.

private equivalents for these forms of social insurance would be more costly or nonexistent, privatizing the program would increase participants' risk exposure. Consequently, to the extent that social insurance affords benefits that private insurance could not, this raises the risk-adjusted return on a government-run Social Security system.

There is another risk factor that must be accounted for as well. A publicly run defined-benefit program incurs political risk. This occurs because current workers cannot effectively contract with and bind as-yet-unborn cohorts of taxpayers to pay for them when they grow old. As a result, baby boomers feel unsure that they will wield the political clout to extract rising payroll taxes from their children and grandchildren, to support them when they are old. This is a risk that cannot be traded, so there is no way for those more willing to bear this risk to trade with those less willing to bear it. Although the simple models described above do not have a good way to price this type of risk, correcting for political risk would probably work in the direction of increasing the risk-adjusted returns and relative attractiveness of a privatized system.

Conclusion

In this paper we argue that privatization, diversification, and prefunding are distinct and should be considered as such. We also argue that it is worthwhile separating a move toward system privatization into three steps. Suppose that individual accounts are created, but that all benefits accrued to date from past Social Security contributions are honored, and that the funding level of the system is held constant (because new explicit debt is issued to cover the unfunded liability of the present Social Security system). In the first step, consider a world with no uncertainty in which individuals are only allowed to invest the individual accounts in government bonds. Although the market return on bonds is greater than that projected on Social Security, once transition costs (to pay interest on the new debt) are accounted for, the rate of return on the two systems would be identical. We estimate that paying for the transition costs would require about a 25 percent tax on all payments into new accounts. This surtax would wipe out all of the extra returns attainable by holding bonds in people's individual accounts. Our 25 percent number depends on forecasts of future growth rates g of the economy, and future real interest rates r. If those forecasts of r and g were to change, the tax would have to change. But the result that all of the gains to privatization would disappear in extra taxes to pay off the unfunded liability is true regardless of the specific values of r and g.

Next, consider adding idiosyncratic risk (for example, shocks to earnings and length of life). If the privatized system contains no special insurance provisions and the private market is unable to provide these, then the risk-adjusted rate of return under privatization would be lower than under the current system.

Third, consider adding aggregate risk and allowing households to invest their individual accounts in equities. For households that already held both stocks and bonds elsewhere, and were thus unconstrained in their portfolio choice, the risk-adjusted rate of return would be no higher than the risk-adjusted rate of return if the individual accounts were held entirely in bonds. For the others, namely, those who do not currently have as much invested in equities as they might like, the risk-adjusted rate of return on a portfolio with equities would be higher as a result of diversification into stocks, thus providing an important rationale for diversification. Nevertheless, this return would not be as much higher as a naive comparison of expected returns would suggest. If this group is large, there will also be general equilibrium effects that will likely lower the expected return on stocks, thus making worse off young households who would have invested in stocks anyway.

Finally, what if the system's funding were increased at the same time as individual accounts were created? Although the increase in funding would likely raise the rate of return on Social Security for future generations (and raise national saving in the process), it must be kept in mind that it would do so only at the cost of lower returns to current cohorts.

We argue that the Social Security reform debate should focus on the trade-off between returns for current cohorts versus future cohorts; the risk-bearing benefits to the economy of enlarging the population that holds a diversified portfolio to include constrained households; and whether diversification is better implemented via privatized personal accounts or through trust fund investments.

We recognize that privatization has several other important benefits, including increased portfolio choice, reduced political risk, possibly reduced labor supply distortions, and an intangible increased sense of ownership and responsibility. It is also possible that privatization may improve the political feasibility of implementing prefunding or diversification, thus increasing the chance of achieving the benefits to future generations and constrained households described earlier.

Indeed some find these overwhelming reasons to favor privatization. These positives, however, must be balanced against the loss of social risk pooling mentioned above, somewhat higher administrative costs, and perhaps the social and personal costs of permitting workers to make "unwise" portfolio choices.[52]

52. See Mitchell (forthcoming) for an analysis of administrative costs.

In any event, our main message is that the popular argument that Social Security privatization would provide higher returns for all current and future workers is misleading, because it ignores transition costs and differences across programs in the allocation of aggregate and household risk.

Insuring against the Consequences of Widowhood in a Reformed Social Security System
Karen C. Holden and Cathleen Zick

WIDOWHOOD remains an economically risky event. As documented in this paper, the average household income of married women falls sharply in the United States when their husbands die, even when income measures are adjusted for the reduced consumption needs of the now smaller household unit. The share of the couple's prewidowhood income that continues to be paid to the widow is a consequence of both the couple's private insurance choices and the way in which social policy protects married women against the loss of a husband's income upon widowhood. The current debate over reforms of Social Security that would include an individual account component is in large part a debate over the necessity of providing income guarantees to widows. In contrast, some argue that individuals understand income security risks and can be trusted to make the most appropriate long-term insurance decisions for their families and survivors.

This paper reviews what we know about the income consequences of widowhood in the United States, the role of Social Security and private pension survivor benefits in insuring against potential income losses when widowhood occurs, and the implications of these findings for Social Security reform. First, we look at survivor benefit provisions in the current Social Security program. Next we explain regulations that govern survivor benefits of employer-provided pension plans and individual account plans (as defined by federal law). This is followed with evidence on the income consequences for married women of their husbands' deaths. These data separate the income change into two components: (1) the change that can be attributed to the presumably "involuntary retirement" through death of husbands who had not yet retired; and (2) the change that can be attributed to widowhood itself. This distinguishes the decline in income upon widowhood that can be attributed to the way in which the system insures against the loss of income upon a worker's retirement from the income change resulting from how the system regulates the inheritance by the widow of a married worker's retirement benefits.[53]

Social Security reform proposals that include an individual account component propose different degrees of autonomy over the disposition of these accounts at retirement and death and thus are likely to lead to a different outcome for widows than does the current program. We estimate these outcomes, drawing on results from recent research on pension option choice, and, finally, draw implications for Social Security reform.

Survivor Benefits: Social Security

The Social Security benefit structure reflects both insurance and income redistribution goals. It accomplishes the former with a defined-benefit pension that replaces a percentage of average covered earnings, paying absolutely larger benefits to higher average wage earners, but it incorporates redistribution by using a formula that replaces a higher percentage of covered earnings for lower-wage workers.[54] Social Security survivor benefits, equal to 100 percent of the deceased worker's retired (or disabled) worker benefits, reflect this same mix of insurance and redistributive elements but are subject to an additional redistributive component—the dual-entitlement provision—that reduces survivor benefits by one dollar for each dollar received from Social Security for any other reason (for example, because the survivor is eligible for retired-worker or disability benefits).

In effect, the dual-entitlement provision shifts survivor benefits from strict insurance against loss of husband's benefits to an insurance settlement that is capped and may be reduced to zero if the survivor receives other Social Security income.[55] This distinction is illustrated by considering two types of couples: a

53. For example, a system may have a high earnings replacement rate for retired workers yet for a survivor replace a small percentage of the worker's retirement benefits. Alternatively, a system may provide a low retirement replacement rate yet have 100 percent survivor benefits. While the latter system may appear to be more generous toward widows, the outcomes in terms of widows' income may be identical.

54. A defined-benefit pension pays a benefit determined by a formula that typically includes as factors in the benefit formula, years of service and average earnings. In contrast, a defined-contribution plan pays benefits based solely on the amount in the worker's account when benefits begin. Social Security is a defined-benefit plan that bases benefits on lifetime earnings. The government bears the risk of contributions falling short of expected benefit payouts.

55. Note that this dual-entitlement provision is analogous to a 100 percent income offset in means-tested programs. It is not like restrictions against double dipping from two private insurance policies covering the same hazard, for example, from two separate health insurance policies covering the same reimbursable health care event. In the case of Social Security, benefits because of one insurable event (for example, death of a spouse) are reduced owing to receipt of benefits because of another unrelated, insurable event (for example, retirement of the surviving spouse).

single-earner couple in which the retired worker receives a retired-worker benefit and the nonworking spouse receives a benefit equal to 50 percent of that
amount, and a two-earner couple in which spouses have identical covered-earnings
histories and, consequently, each spouse receives an identical retired-worker benefit. Upon the death of the worker in the first couple, the widow will be paid a benefit equal to the deceased worker's benefit, or two-thirds of the combined prewidowhood benefit. The widow of the couple in which spouses had identical earnings
histories will continue to receive only her own retired-worker benefit without additional payments to compensate for the loss of the deceased spouse's benefits.[56]
This outcome results from a shared consensus in the early years of the program
that a guarantee of survivor benefits should be provided to women who would otherwise be ineligible for benefits but that survivor benefits were not needed when
her own Social Security income was otherwise assured.[57]

Thus Social Security provides an important guarantee of survivor protection
to women who would otherwise be ineligible for retired-worker benefits, a
group that includes not only widows who never worked but also young widows
with minor children. It also promises a benefit supplement to age-eligible survivors if their own retired-worker benefits fall short of the benefits for which
their deceased spouse would have been eligible.[58]

Survivor Protection: Employer-provided Pensions

The 1974 Employee Retirement Income Security Act (ERISA) required that
when the primary form of plan payout is an annuity, the default payout form to
married workers must be at least a joint-and-one-half survivor annuity that is
actuarially equivalent to the single-life worker pension. Under this provision
[29 USC Sec 1055, (b)] a "qualified joint and survivor annuity" must pay a survivor annuity that:

56. It may seem that the system should be described as offering a joint and one-half option to
dual-earner couples. Although one half of the combined prewidowhood benefits paid to the couple
is paid to the surviving spouse, the joint benefit is based on the earnings records of two individuals
and the widow receives no more than her own retired-worker benefit. In effect she receives no benefit based on the loss of her husband's income. For clarity in drawing parallels to the employer-
provided system, both cases should be described as illustrating a system in which insurance is in
force against the loss of a husband's benefits, but in which means-testing may reduce the survivor's
benefit to zero.

57. See Holden (1996) for a discussion of the redistributive consequences of the dual-entitlement provisions across couples with different degrees of shared earnings efforts.

58. Surviving (including divorced) spouses are eligible for survivor benefits if caring for a child
under the age of 16 or, if not disabled, at age 60. Because wives are on average younger than husbands, the age of earliest eligibility for survivor benefits was set (and remains) earlier than the age at
which a worker is eligible to receive retired-worker benefits. Disabled widows are eligible at age 50.

(1) for the life of the spouse . . . is not less than 50 percent of (and is not greater than 100 percent of) the amount of the annuity which is payable during the joint lives of the participant and the spouse, and

(2) which is the actuarial equivalent of a single annuity for the life of the participant.

This legislation allows married workers to choose some other form of payout—a single-life annuity, a lump-sum distribution, or some other option—instead of the default option or to designate an alternative beneficiary without notification to the spouse. Under the 1974 legislation only survivors of those who died either after reaching the earliest age of pension eligibility or were within ten years of the normal retirement age, whichever was earlier, were covered by the default survivor benefit. Survivors of vested workers who died at younger ages were not required to be paid a survivor benefit.

The 1984 Retirement Equity Act (REA) amended ERISA survivorship provisions in two important ways. It required the spouse's notarized signature when the default joint-and-survivor option was rejected or another beneficiary designated. Further, it mandated that the default benefit be paid to survivors of a vested worker, regardless of the worker's age at death. However, payment of survivor benefits may be delayed until "the month in which the participant would have attained the earliest retirement age under the plan" [29USC 1055 (e), (1), (B)]. Unlike Social Security, which pegs receipt of benefits to the survivor's age (for example, nondisabled women are eligible for benefits at age 60), this provision would result in variation in eligibility date for survivor benefits based on the age of the deceased husbands. Women married to much older men thus would receive benefits at younger ages.

The reach of ERISA's survivor benefit provisions is limited by public employer-provided plans not being covered by ERISA. Further, the survivor provisions need not be met by individual account plans as long as:

such plan provides that the participant's nonforfeitable accrued benefit (reduced by any security interest held by the plan by reason of a loan outstanding to such participant) is payable in full, on the death of the participant, to the participant's surviving spouse (or, if there is no surviving spouse or the surviving spouse consents in the manner required under subsection (c)(2) of this section, to a designated beneficiary), [and] . . . such participant does not elect the payment of benefits in the form of a life annuity.

Thus survivorship protection in the United States is composed of four distinct regulatory components:

—A Social Security system that pays survivor benefits to age-eligible survivors (or those with minor children) of retired or active workers but that may reduce those benefits to zero because of a survivor's labor market earnings or receipt of her own retired-worker benefits from Social Security;

—A private employer pension system mandated to pay survivor benefits as the default form to survivors of retired and active workers but which must allow beneficiaries to choose a single-life benefit. The system may delay benefits to survivors of younger deceased workers, but it may not reduce survivor benefits because of other income received by the survivor;

—A public-employer pension system that is not covered by federal survivor benefit mandates and which varies in its offering of default survivor benefits; and

—An individual retirement accounts system (with tax advantages) that can avoid the survivorship provisions by establishing lump-sum distribution as the primary form of payment.

Widowhood and Income Change

ERISA, passed almost forty years after the Social Security Act, mandated that private, employer-provided pension plans offer survivor benefits. This legislation was motivated by two persistent findings. One, women widowed during the 1970s and 1980s were economically vulnerable.[59] Two, receipt of a pension was associated with higher income levels as a widow and cushioned the income decline upon widowhood. Policymakers expected that requiring pension payout in the form of a joint-and-survivor annuity, unless the worker explicitly rejected it, would increase the share of a couple's resources remaining to a woman after her husband's death.[60] Figure 4-3 documents the continuation of these income patterns among women who became widows over approximately the 1990–93 period.

Figure 4-3 compares one measure of well-being—the income-to-needs ratio—for two groups of women who were interviewed in the 1990, 1991, or

59. Bound and others (1991); Holden and Zick (1997); Burkhauser, Holden, and Feaster (1988); Hurd and Wise (1989).
60. Social Security provisions are sex neutral. Although this paper discusses widow benefits, all conclusions apply to widowers as well. The difference lies in the far higher probability that married women will be the surviving spouse and the still relatively disadvantaged work histories of married women compared with married men.

Figure 4-3. Income Adjusted for Needs: Couples Categorized by Husbands' Survival

Income to needs

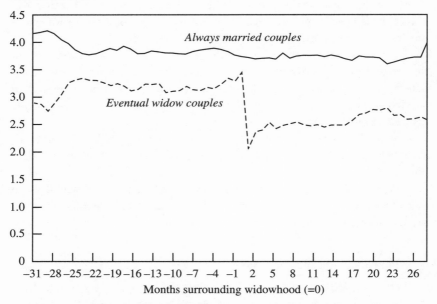

Months surrounding widowhood (=0)

Source: Authors' calculations based on Survey of Income and Program Participation, Panels 1990, 1991, 1992.

1992 Panels of the Survey of Income and Program Participation (SIPP).[61] The eventual widows (whose data are shown with the lower line) include all women who were age 40 or older and married (husband present) at the first SIPP interview and whose husbands died at some point during the thirty-two-month period. All these women were interviewed at least once as a widow. The economic experience of these women is compared with that of married women 40 and older who remained married throughout SIPP (shown by the top line). The graph shows how the ratio of household income to a consumption needs standard changes over the months of the SIPP survey. The standard of consumption used is the U.S. poverty threshold, which varies with family size and, conse-

61. Each SIPP panel is a nationally representative sample of households whose members are interviewed at four-month intervals over approximately thirty-two months. A new panel is introduced each year. The data presented in this paper are from the three SIPP surveys. Sample weights are used to adjust for sampling and response differences. The merging of the samples increases sample size and, consequently, the reliability of our behavioral estimates.

quently, is one indicator of implied changes in household consumption needs as household size changes with the death of a husband.

The monthly data for each eventual widow are centered on the month in which the woman first reported being widowed. Because this may occur at different months during the SIPP interview period, the aggregate data are arrayed over a sixty-four-month period, even though for any single couple we have a maximum of thirty-two months of data.[62] A month of widowhood is randomly assigned to the latter group of couples, but in such a way that the pattern of death across months is in the aggregate identical for the (weighted) samples. Although the continuously married couples are in fact never widowed, an assigned widowhood month allows a comparison of the experience of these two groups of women over a comparable period of time.[63]

Even prior to widowhood, the income-to-needs ratio of eventual widows is about 15 percent below that of their continuously married counterparts, implying that one component of widows' lower income may be attributed to longstanding prewidowhood differences between the two groups. The eventual widows' average income-to-needs ratio was 3.40 in the two months preceding the death and that ratio drops and stabilizes at about 2.7, roughly 70 percent of that of the comparison couples.

Average levels, however, obscure important variation among women—specifically, the consequence of differences in prewidowhood retirement probabilities for observed differences in levels and change in income upon widowhood. Eventual widows include couples in which the husband had already retired before death—and consequently whose prewidowhood income reflects the consequences for the couple of his retirement—as well as those for whom income changes upon widowhood reflect a dual economic hazard—that of the husband's death and by definition his retirement. The observed lower income of eventual widows prior to widowhood arises in part from the not surprising fact that husbands who are about to die are more likely to be out of the work force than are their continuously married counterparts. Conversely, the sharp drop upon widowhood observed on average for some eventual widows comes from the joint effect of the husband's death and his forced retirement.

62. Income for the month in which the husband died is a combination of income received as a wife and widow (Burkhauser, Holden, and Myers, 1986), thus it may not accurately reflect the widow's income. Subsequent months reflect her status as a widow and subsequent adjustments in earning behavior or household composition.

63. Because women widowed in SIPP are on average younger than those who remain married, we weight the married sample such that the age distribution at the time of the first interview is identical to that of eventual widows. Thus, differences in patterns between the two sets of couples are net of differences in age structure.

Figure 4-4. *Income Adjusted for Needs: Retiring Couples*

Income to needs

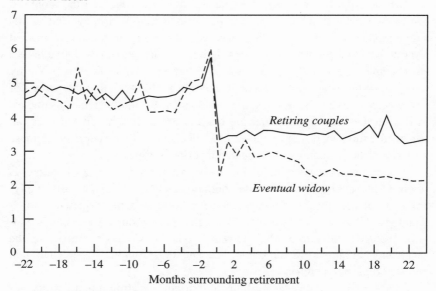

Months surrounding retirement

Source: See figure 4-3.

Figures 4-4 and 4-5 contrast these two groups of couples. Figure 4-4 shows those eventual widows whose husbands continued to work during the prewidowhood period, and figure 4-5 shows those whose husbands had already retired prior to death. Figure 4-4 centers the data around the date of retirement—which is the month in which we actually observe a husband ceasing work for the continuously married couples and which is simultaneous with the month of widowhood for couples in which the husband dies. For the eventual widows, prewidowhood income is comparable to that of their continuously married, working peers and, likewise, a large decline occurs upon widowhood, attributable in large part to the (in this case, presumably, involuntary) retirement of the husband. Nevertheless, widowhood appears to lead to persistently lower income compared with intact, retired couples. Among couples with already retired husbands (whose data are centered around the month of (imputed) widowhood for both groups), the income-to-needs ratio during the prewidowhood period, when husbands in both groups are not working, is comparable. But for the eventual widows, the husband's death leads to a reduction in income at permanently lower levels.

Figure 4-5. *Income Adjusted for Needs: Already Retired Couples*

Income to needs

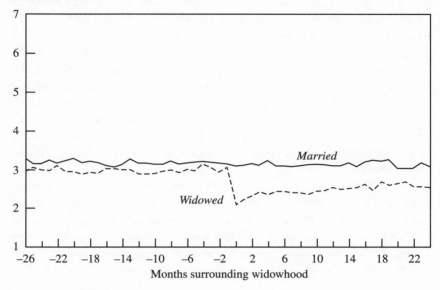

Months surrounding widowhood

Source: See figure 4-3.

The story told by these two figures is that the economic well-being of widows is tied to two insurance components: the insurance provided to workers against the income consequences of retirement; and the inheritance by widows of those insurance rights. The income impact of widowhood is a consequence of both the replacement rate at which preretirement income is replaced when both spouses are alive and the rules of inheritance by survivors of the retirement benefits of their deceased spouses.

Changes in Social Security and Pension Income

From the eventual widows' sample in SIPP we can estimate how Social Security and pension income does change upon widowhood. For this group we do not know the Social Security or pension benefits for which individuals were eligible; the estimates are based on couples who reported prewidowhood retirement income. These are primarily drawn from the group that was already retired. Among couples in which the husband was a Social Security beneficiary before his death and the wife received benefits as a widow, Social Security income fell by about 40 percent. The best estimate of the percentage of a husband's pension that continues to the widow comes from couples in which the husband reported prewidowhood pension income and the wife did not, but in which pension income was reported by the widow.[64] For these couples, postwidowhood pension income was 71 percent of the husband's prewidowhood pension income—implying a selection by husbands on average of a two-thirds survivor benefit. However, only 59 percent of the widows of pensioners received any postwidowhood pension income. Couples in which the husband appeared to reject a survivor pension were worse off in the prewidowhood period than those who appeared to select a survivor pension (income-to-needs ratio of 3.18 versus 3.93), and the average decline in the income-to-needs ratio upon widowhood was larger (to 67 percent versus 78 percent of their prewidowhood period).

Thus while 61 percent of the husbands in the sample of those who eventually died received a pension prior to death, only half that many of the wives of these pensioners report a pension as a widow. It remains the case that some women are better protected against the economic consequences of this dual hazard of widowhood than are others. Women who lost pension income experienced the larger fall in income; it does not appear that other insurance options compensated for the loss of husbands' pensions.

The Choice of Survivor Benefits in Private Pension Plans

The decline in income upon widowhood raises the question of whether in a privatized Social Security system married men would voluntarily extend the privatized retirement protection provided to them as retirees to their widows through the selection of a joint-and-survivor benefit. In a defined-contribution plan the selection of an annuity that continues to be paid to a widow will reduce the monthly benefit paid during the retiree's lifetime (in contrast to the current Social Security system, which exacts no reduction for the protection provided to spouses and survivors). Even if workers' own retirement benefits were higher under a privatized Social Security system, some married workers could be expected to choose a single-life annuity, leaving their widows with substantially reduced protection compared with their status under the current Social Security system. Wives with less favorable work careers could be worse off than under the current system if husbands underestimated the risk and income consequences of widowhood.

64. The ratios are not substantively different for couples in which the wife had prewidowhood pension income. For these couples it is more difficult to separate the share of postwidowhood pension income that is the survivor benefit component from the wife's own retirement pension.

Karen Holden and Sean Nicholson have examined who among pensioners selects an annuity form that would continue pension payments to the widow.[65] Using data from the New Beneficiary Survey (NBS), a panel study that interviewed respondents first in 1982 and again in 1991, they examine the factors that influence married men's choice of a survivor pension and the effect of ERISA's mandate that this be the default option. Their major conclusions are as follows:

—Married men's choice of a survivor pension is shaped by rational economic factors. That is, husbands whose wives are in greater need of survivor protection (as measured by wives' own probable postwidowhood Social Security benefits and pensions) and husbands more able to afford purchasing this coverage (as measured by their own relatively high wealth) are more likely to choose this option.

—Even after controlling for economic factors that shaped husbands' decisions, the ERISA mandate of a default survivor benefit substantially raised the probability of married men choosing a survivor benefit. This suggests that regulations governing the offer and selection of a survivor benefit are necessary to insure widows' receipt of survivor benefits from a privatized Social Security system.

In the 1982 NBS interview, married pension recipients were asked whether, if they died today, their pension would continue to their spouse. In addition, pensioners were asked the year when their pension was first paid, which makes it possible to determine whether their pensions began before or after 1974, the effective date of ERISA. Among the married male pensioners, 62 percent indicated they had elected a pension that would continue to their widow. Although only 48 percent of the married men whose pension benefits began before 1974 selected a survivor option, this was the case for 64 percent of the married men whose pension began in 1974 or later. This is comparable to the 59 percent of widows in our SIPP sample of women who were widowed in the early 1990s whose husband's pension continued after his death. The factors that shaped the pension option choice for these married men is described more fully in Karen Holden and Sean Nicholson.[66] Here the most relevant findings for Social Security reform are described. As hypothesized, wealthier husbands, as measured by their total wealth, including the wealth value of their single-life pension benefit and their own retired-worker Social Security benefits, are more likely to forgo consumption during their own lifetime in return for protecting their wives against the income consequences of widowhood. In addition, the

65. Holden and Nicholson (1998).
66. Holden and Nicholson (1998).

greater the portion of his wealth taken up by his pension (an indicator of how important is his pension in any bequest to the widow), the more likely he is to choose a survivor pension.[67] The greater the need of the wife as a widow for additional income from her husband's pension—because she has less wealth of her own (measured by the value of her own pension, Social Security benefits, and other assets held in her name)—the more likely the husband is to choose a survivor benefit.

Demographic and health effects suggest that husbands consider the relative actuarial value to them of the survivor pension reduction. The husband's own poor health, an indicator of his likely earlier-than-average death, increases his chances of choosing a survivor benefit. The older is the husband than the wife, the less likely he is to choose a joint-and-survivor pension, probably a result of the much larger reduction in the single-life pension for such couples. Finally, men making their pension decision after 1973 are more likely to choose a joint-and-survivor pension; for a representative couple in which the wife has no pension of her own, the estimated probability is 27 percentage points higher than for a similar couple making their pension decision before 1974.[68]

Conclusions and Policy Implications

Studies of widowhood have found that Social Security survivor benefits are important to the economic well-being of widows, as are benefits from private pension plans.[69] In addition, by disaggregating the decline in income upon widowhood into two components, we can see the importance for widows of inheriting some share of the husbands' retired-worker Social Security and pension benefits. The decline in widows' income when husbands were working before death is only somewhat larger than the income decline for intact couples when the men retire. This decline for men is shaped by Social Security retirement

67. The estimate of pension wealth is the actuarial value of the single-life option, adjusting for the actual pension option selection of these men. While we know when a survivor pension is chosen, we do not know what specific choice was made. We assume a joint-and-one-half pension (the minimum required by ERISA) when estimating the actuarial value of the pension of men who chose a survivor option. This is an underestimate of pension wealth for men who in fact chose a more generous survivor pension. This will underestimate the difference in pension wealth between single-life and joint-life beneficiaries, biasing the coefficient on wealth and pension wealth toward zero.

68. In Holden and Nicholson (1998) the marginal effects of the independent variables on the likelihood that a retired male pensioner will choose a survivor option are estimated for a representative couple. The representative husband is white, in good health, has had at least one child of his own (not necessarily living with him), and has only been married once. The representative wife is within three years of her husband's age and is not eligible for her own pension.

69. Holden, Burkhauser, and Feaster (1988).

benefits and employer-provided pensions. The absence of inheritance rights to husbands' retirement income could lead to even more severe income declines upon widowhood.

Social Security survivor benefits guarantee to widows (including divorced survivors) a Social Security benefit at least equal to the retired-worker benefit for which their husbands would have been eligible. For single-earner couples the survivor benefit offer is equivalent to a joint-and-two-thirds annuity. The dual-entitlement provision will reduce that percentage for dual-earner couples. We find Social Security benefits declined by almost 40 percent from the pre- to postwidowhood period among women widowed during the early part of the 1990s. This percentage is likely to increase as two-earner couples become more prevalent and the dual-entitlement provision leaves fewer women in receipt of a supplemental widow's benefit. The diminishing value of Social Security survivor benefits to working women is one point of debate over the structure of the current system. It may be that a system akin to private pensions that allows dual-earner couples to choose a survivor benefit would make some widows better off. This paper has argued for the importance in a privatized Social Security system of regulations that would diminish the chances of widows being left without any survivor pension.

ERISA mandated that private pensions offer a survivor benefit option that can be declined only with the spouse's approval. Estimates based on SIPP and NBS data indicate that about 40 percent of married couples did reject the offer. To some degree husbands' pension-option choice is akin to the Social Security system's dual-entitlement provision, that is, husbands are less likely to bequeath a share of the pension to their wife when she has income and wealth from other sources.

The difference between the Social Security system and the ERISA-governed private pension system lies in the ability of workers in a privatized system to choose against a survivorship option *even when the widow would have no other pension income.* In contrast, the Social Security system assures a postwidowhood benefit at least equal to that of a husband's retired-worker benefit. The question faced by regulators of a private system is what degree of autonomy they should allow workers in making that choice. While a privatized Social Security system could make some women better off by allowing them to receive both their own and their deceased husband's retirement benefits, nonworking wives or those with their own (but small) pensions may be left worse off if the couple has chosen to reject the survivor benefit option. The analysis of men's pension-option choice also suggested that ERISA regulations themselves altered the probability of men's selecting a benefit that would continue to be paid to their widow. Mandates on pension plans to provide the survivor option and to have that be the default form of payout affected the decisions of husbands even when their right to choose against a survivor option was preserved.

What does this mean for Social Security reform? If we move toward a system with greater individual choice, the question arises of what regulations to establish, if any, governing the form in which the accumulations may be distributed. The results reported in this paper suggest that for women, regulations that require annuitization and, in conformity with ERISA, a default survivor option, are important to continuing the survivor protection offered through Social Security.

The analysis suggests that some regulation of payouts from individualized accounts could increase the protection to survivors provided by these accounts. Mandated annuitization, as proposed in the Individual Account plan, and a default survivor payout form would increase the chances that widows would not be worse off under a privatized Social Security system. Alternatively, survivor protection could be achieved through federal law that would define retirement benefits as marital property. Such a system, which would equally divide a couple's accumulated Social Security accounts, would in effect recognize the couple's shared rights to the account contributions and earnings during marriage. Divorcing couples would divide these assets—thus retaining for divorced spouses protection that would otherwise be lost—as would long-time married couples at the earlier retirement of one. This would, in effect, provide protection to surviving spouses, granting a share of all Individual Accounts accumulated through a reformed Social Security program. This would also encode in a major social program an increasingly accepted principle that marriage is a joint economic partnership that ceases upon divorce but continues after the death of one partner and includes shared rights to all property and benefits accumulated during marriage.

Sylvester J. Schieber, discussant

THE DISCUSSIONS COVERED in these three papers are at once quite distinct from each other but with intersecting sets of issues.

Larry Thompson's basic proposition is that one of the most important goals of any public pension system is to provide a stable, predictable, and adequate source of retirement income to each participant. He evaluates the ability of publicly run defined-benefit versus publicly mandated defined-contribution plans to deliver on this goal.

He assesses four risks within this context:

—Demographic risks of changing birth rates and life expectancy;

—Economic risks of changing wage growth and changing asset prices;

—Risks related to the political policymaking process; and

—Risks associated with institutional or regulatory failure.

After assessing each of these he concludes our current system is just fine because it has never attempted to fully provide "adequate" benefits to retirees across the lifetime wage spectrum.

To a significant degree I agree with his assessment of the current system and the conclusions he reaches about many of the relative risks of defined-benefit versus defined-contribution plans. However, I do believe that there is a question of relative sizing of our existing national defined-benefit retirement system that is worthy of public discussion. At the end of his analysis Thompson concludes that our current system is just about the right size even though that particular conclusion does not derive from the prior analysis. I believe that there are indications—some of them historical, some of them current, and some of them forward looking—that suggest our system is larger than a lot of people would like.

Economists have observed that the tax incentives encouraging home mortgages and employer-sponsored health benefit plans have led to potentially excessive direction of our national resources to housing and health care. I believe a similar argument could be made that the significant subsidization of Social Security benefits during the implementation of our national system probably encouraged it to grow larger than it would have otherwise and possibly larger than is desirable. Just as the National Association of Home Builders or the National Association of Hospitals might argue that current tax incentives for home mortgages or health benefits should not be reduced or significantly changed, I would expect the vast majority of members of the National Academy of Social Insurance to argue that our current Social Security system should not be reduced or significantly changed either. Still, I would argue that it may have grown larger than might be desired, even considering the risk criteria that Larry Thompson includes in his analysis.

While Social Security was relatively redistributional even during its early days, the absolute subsidization of retirement income was much larger for middle- and upper-income workers than it was for those with a career of low earnings. The program was such a good deal in its early years that workers had to have been enthralled with their significant windfalls. It is unlikely that they fully appreciated the burden they were creating for future generations. Certainly, larger employers of the day who were creating their own retirement plans to manage work forces had to have understood the tremendous windfall presented them because they had trained actuaries helping to integrate the systems.

During the late 1940s, those concerned about the tendency for the tremendous deal to stimulate public demand for more of the same advocated a two-tier system with immediate provision of benefits for all the elderly. They thought the cost rate of a fully implemented system would act as a governor on benefit demands. These proposals were never successful, and the system as we know it today did not mature until the mid-1970s, the point when the portion of the population over 65 receiving benefits reached equality with the portion of the work force paying taxes.

On a contemporary basis, concerns over the sizing of the program are expressed through observations about the relative magnitude of payroll taxes and income taxes that workers pay, about the intrusion of payroll tax rates on rank-and-file workers' ability to save for their own retirement needs, and on the overall deadweight burden on economic activities.

For the future, there are dual concerns about the expansion of burden rates that many people already find onerous and about whether or not the system is a fair deal for today's younger workers and future generations. This brings us to the second paper by John Geanakoplos, Olivia Mitchell, and Stephen P. Zeldes, who focus specifically on the rate of return issues that seem to be on many people's minds. Once again, I agree generally with their conclusions.

I agree wholeheartedly that privatization and prefunding are distinct and need to be evaluated as such. I am of the opinion, one not universally agreed on, that a central government entity of the sort that our Social Security is will never be an accumulator of private assets. I come to this partly because of my reading of the history of the current system, which was originally intended to be partially funded. I also come to it because of my perceptions about the role of the central government in our society.

I agree that privatization without prefunding will not raise the rate of return on the current system. I also agree that prefunding cannot be achieved without incurring costs and that the assignment of those costs will affect the overall rates of returns differentially for various generations. Despite the costs associated with it, I am driven to the conclusion that we would be better off with some prefunding. I come to this conclusion partly because of the rate of return issue for future generations. I am not the first to come to this conclusion. Indeed, the earliest architects of the program worried about this matter. As evidence, I offer an observation from Arthur Altmeyer, Mr. Social Security during the early years of the program. Of the de facto decision to move the program from its originally intended partial prefunding basis to a pay-as-you-go basis, he testified:

> Therefore, the indefinite continuation of the present contribution rate will eventually necessitate raising the employees' contribution rate later to a point where future beneficiaries will be obliged to pay more for their

benefits than if they obtained this insurance from a private insurance company.

I say it is inequitable to compel them to pay more under this system than they would have to pay to a private insurance company, and I think that Congress would be confronted with that embarrassing situation.[70]

Anticipated rates of return provided by Social Security for future cohorts of retirees are problematic. They are likely to generate increasingly negative assessments of the program, further undermining the faith of the American public in it. This is not an ideological conclusion; it follows from the common sense assessment of Arthur Altmeyer back in 1945. His point merits serious consideration.

When the Committee on Economic Security reported to Congress, Franklin Roosevelt said the goal of its recommendations was to protect workers against "certain hazards and vicissitudes of life." Of the hazards and vicissitudes of life that Social Security covers, the greatest concern over money's worth arises under the Old Age Insurance program. The reason for this relates to the accrual of "wealth" in the form of Social Security benefits during workers' careers and the implied rate of return on that wealth accumulation. The problem Social Security faces is that its ultimate rate of return is limited to the combined rates of growth in wages and the labor force. In a world with slow growth rates in both of these items, cohort-specific returns are bound to be paltry.

Part of the concern about Social Security's returns relates to the hazards that are being "insured" by the retirement program. I believe there are essentially two separate "hazards" being covered. Their muddling has led to significant criticism of the program from a money's worth perspective. One of the hazards is the risk of an unsuccessful work career. The other is the risk of workers' myopia in regard to saving for retirement during their working career. The insurance to cover these two risks raises widely different implications about the importance of Social Security rates of return.

Some workers are unsuccessful over their whole careers and cannot save adequately for their retirement. Others are successful for part of their career but face circumstances at some point that significantly derail their ability to save. Such problems diminish workers' ability to save on their own, and a redistributive social insurance program can help to ameliorate the situation. Private insurance institutions do not provide insurance of this sort.

---

70. I. S. Falk, "Questions and Answers on Financing of Old-Age and Survivors Insurance," memorandum to O. C. Pogge, Director, Bureau of Old-Age and Survivors Insurance, February 9, 1945, p. 16.

Insuring against workers' myopia relative to their own need to save for retirement is completely different than insuring them against career break-downs. In insuring against the problem of savings myopia, the requirement that workers make some provision for their own retirement needs can be achieved through Social Security, as we do now, or by requiring that workers save for retirement through some alternative vehicle.

Current money's worth calculations for the "bad labor market experience" element of Social Security may be misleading because there is no private market counterpart against which the program's operations can be measured. This part of the program provides insurance with similarities to home fire insurance. Just because a homeowner can not make a claim on insurance because there has not been a fire doesn't mean the homeowner has not received value from the insurance. Just because a worker experiences a full successful career does not mean that he or she does not derive some value from insurance against a bad career outcome. There is insurance value in the protection against the contingency of career breakdown even though none occurs in some cases. This value is not recognized in current money's worth analyses.

The difference between insurance against bad labor market experience and home fire insurance is that the latter has a determinable value based on the probability of a fire and the property value being insured. In the case of insuring people against career failure, the actuarial determination of value that can be made on homeowner's fire insurance must be replaced by a social valuation determined in the courts of public opinion and political deliberation. To determine whether the "bad labor market experience" element of the program is providing money's worth, policymakers must weigh program costs against perceived benefits to society. This inexact process is driven by political considerations about relative needs of retirees versus other things that compete for governmental resources.

Relative rates of return to the mandated retirement savings portion of our Social Security system are extremely important. Once again, the reason relates to the point that Arthur Altmeyer made in his 1945 congressional testimony cited earlier. Simply put, it is unfair to compel workers to pay more under this system than they would have to pay under a private alternative. The current system has not been an effective capital accumulation vehicle because of the realities of the legislative process that flows from the political risks that Thompson has outlined within the context of national retirement program financing. The original architects of Social Security in the United States knew that the failure to fund the program would have dire implications for future workers when the system matured. John Geanakoplos, Olivia Mitchell, and Stephen P. Zeldes have estimated the size of the tremendous subsidization of early participants' benefits that occurred because Social Security could not be an effective capital accumulation mechanism. Because of the inability to fund the program during its early years, Social Security is unfair to many current workers according to the criteria its architects specified, and it will become increasingly unfair for future worker cohorts.

If we were to create some form of individual accounts as an element of Social Security reform, it would introduce a different element of risk than exists in the current system as Larry Thompson has pointed out. But in Karen Holden's paper we see that there are ways that some of these risks can be accommodated. In some regards, earnings sharing, or more precisely, retirement accrual sharing could be achieved more readily under an individual account program than under the current system. If men are not inclined to properly make provision for dependent spouses through voluntary joint and survivor provisions, then there would be no limitation preventing policymakers from mandating joint and survivor benefits for married couples.

When I look at these three papers together, it is fairly clear to me that no matter what we do to reform the current system, we cannot eliminate all of the risks that workers and retirees will face in the future. But Franklin D. Roosevelt acknowledged this problem in his presidential statement at the signing of the Social Security Act in 1935 when he said: "We can never insure 100 percent of the population against 100 percent of the hazards and vicissitudes of life." That is as true today as it was then. But the certainty is that we must do something. The practical fact is that we would be better off doing something sooner rather than later. The hope that I have is that we can find a solution that will give people a greater sense of security and fairness relative to Social Security than seems to prevail across large segments of the work force today.

Henry J. Aaron, discussant

THE RELATIVE RATES of return on Social Security and privatized alternatives have been receiving, and will receive, a lot of attention. John Geanakoplos, Olivia Mitchell, and Stephen P. Zeldes (henceforth, GMZ) alert us to some frequent, naive mistakes. I think that their argument is exactly right. I shall make the same argument in a slightly different way.

GMZ begin by pointing out that privatization and funding are distinct issues. The key to privatization is moving from a defined-benefit system to a defined-contribution system. The GMZ grid in table 4-4 shows that the decision about whether to have a defined-benefit or a defined-contribution plan is one thing. The decision about whether to have a pay-as-you-go or a funded system is quite another thing. Two times two is four, and all four combinations are possible.

The current debate about Social Security reform is therefore about two questions. Should we shift from a defined-benefit to a defined-contribution system? Should we move further along the continuum from a pure pay-as-you-go system toward a fully funded system?

GMZ point out the obvious fact that we cannot run away from the unfunded liability. That liability resulted because President Roosevelt and successive Congresses decided to provide more generous benefits to older workers than were justified by payroll taxes paid on their behalf. Maybe this decision was right. Maybe it was wrong. Without doubt it cannot be reversed. The unfunded liability exists and someone is stuck with it. It is logically possible to renege on all promises under the current system. That would impose large costs on current retirees and in varying degrees on current members of the labor force. No sane or compassionate human being advocates such a final solution to the unfunded liability problem. Or we could spread it out over current and future workers by forcing them to pay more than the cost of their own retirements. That way of paying down the unfunded liability is what privatizers call the transition problem. The transition lasts seventy years in the plan advocated by a minority of Advisory Council members. To call a period that lasts a decade more than the entire history of Social Security a transition is, in my view, a truly Orwellian distortion of language.

But I digress. The key point that GMZ point out is that one cannot ignore the costs of paying off the unfunded liability when one calculates rates of return. Some advocates of privatization, including the Heritage Foundation, but not including Sylvester Schieber, do just that. In so doing, they overstate the rates of return under privatized plans. GMZ show that when these costs are taken into account, the gross rates of return are the same on equally funded private or public accounts.

They stop at this point. If they had gone one step further, they would have reached what I believe is the bottom line: the net rate of return available under individual accounts from a given portfolio is *lower* than that available under Social Security. There are two steps to this argument.

First, let us assume that reserves of given aggregate size managed on behalf of all workers collectively are invested in the same portfolio that is held in all individual accounts of a privatized plan taken together. The *gross* returns on individual accounts will be the same as the gross returns to a pooled Social Security account. It has to be the same because the assets are the same. But the *net* returns to the collectively managed Social Security fund will be higher than the net returns realized by all individual investors. The difference is administrative costs that individual management generates.

Second, as Barry Bosworth pointed out a few years ago at a National Academy of Social Insurance conference, the social return from accumulating reserves in either individual accounts or in a pooled Social Security account is the same. It is simply the private return on investment. In either case, an additional $1 billion of saving supports an additional $1 billion of private investment. However, we all yearn to emulate the children of Lake Wobegon and be better than average in our rates of return. Unfortunately, the evidence is fairly clear that when we try, we fail. The average return on individual accounts invested in stocks or bonds or some combination of stocks and bonds has to be approximately the average returns generated on stocks or the average return on bonds, or the weighted average of the two. Some investors seeking better returns will do better than this average. Some will do worse. On the average, they will earn the average.

Well, not quite. If they invest in actively managed funds and try to pick winners and time the market, they will earn less than average. Actively managed accounts do worse than index funds. The reason is administrative costs. Last year 90 percent of mutual funds did worse than market averages. The best people can do on the average is to invest in index funds that minimize administrative costs. Some people will succumb to the temptation to try to beat the market. The only clear gainers from active management are fund managers, brokerage houses, banks, and other financial companies. This fact may explain why they are so active in promoting privatization. Their gain is the average pensioner's loss.

The bottom line is that the best we can do on the average is to invest reserves in ways that minimize administrative costs and achieve market average rates of return.

Alas, Larry Thompson, in an otherwise excellent paper, muddies just this issue. He suggests at the outset of his paper that the choice is between a pay-as-you-go defined-benefit program and a funded defined-contribution program. He thereby links the two policy questions that GMZ argue must be kept distinct. I believe that the choice should and will be between a funded defined-benefit and a funded defined-contribution system. Thompson does not take a stand on this or any other policy choice. But his paper should prove very useful in helping people think about the policy choice. In particular, he points out something that most of us had not thought much about before. It is simply not true that moving to a defined-contribution system would take pensions out of the political realm. His risk chart, alas, seems to ignore the findings of his own paper. The Larry Thompson who wrote this splendid paper has much to teach the Larry Thompson who compiled this table. Defined-contribution plans require periodic legislative adjustment just as defined-benefit plans do. Based on fluctuations in inflation and interest rates and variations in earnings growth, any nation would find that defined-contribution plans were either very much overfunded or underfunded. As a result, legislatures would have to change contribution rates. The changes could be absolutely staggering, halving or doubling contribution rates. This is the stuff of political uncertainty.

Thompson also stops short of an additional implication. The fluctuations in the adequacy of accumulations will depend sensitively on the age of workers. My colleague, Gary Burtless, has mapped out what the replacement rates would have been under a defined-contribution plan. He assumes contributions of 5 percent of earnings each year. All contributions are invested in a stock index fund. Under such a plan, workers retiring in 1969 would have received a 100 percent replacement rate. Workers retiring in 1976 would have received a 40 percent replacement rate under the same plan. A lot clearly depends on when you buy and when you sell. Now consider the implications of another aspect of mandatory defined-contribution plans. Mandatory contribution rates are quite unlikely to vary by age. Let's suppose that the legislature looks at accumulations just before 1969 in the Burtless world. It concludes that accumulations are excessive. As a result of this reexamination, the legislature is likely to lower the mandatory contribution rate. Such a cutback would in all likelihood apply to all workers. The result would be that workers who retire seven years later would receive replacement rates even smaller than the 40 percent rate that Burtless's analysis indicated.

The moral of this story is that we cannot rely on defined-contribution plans for the basic source of retirement income for the mass of workers. Fluctuations in benefits would be economically disruptive and politically insupportable. Let me be clear what this statement does not mean.

First, it does not mean that defined-benefit plans are free of risk and uncertainty. As Thompson points out, risk and uncertainty are inescapable in any long-term contract. The difference between a defined-benefit and a defined-contribution plan is who bears the risk. Under a defined-benefit plan, the political system diffuses risks broadly among the general population. A defined-contribution plan imposes risks on each worker.

Second, it does not mean that defined-contribution saving is a bad idea. Our financial system is built on savings and investment where individual savers and investors bear the risk. Gainers can earn handsome rewards for intelligence or good luck. Losers suffer the consequences of foolishness or bad luck. This system contains admirable and vital incentives. It is the right system for retirement saving beyond what is necessary to provide a basic income. Most of us would consider it unwise for a family of modest means to bet its subsistence in a lottery even if the odds were favorable. But few of us would censure the well-heeled if they blew a bundle in Las Vegas. For the same reason, it is not prudent for the nation to permit individuals to gamble basic retirement income even on a good gamble. And, as I indicated earlier, investing in individual accounts is a bad gamble because administrative costs cut the returns. People who go for more than the average return most often get less largely because they trade too often and generate needless administrative costs.

Finally, Karen Holden reminds us that in evaluating the appeal of individually managed retirement saving, considerations other than the rate of return are important. We are, after all, talking not about individual retirement accounts, Keogh plans, or SEPs, but about social insurance. Poverty rates among aged widows and widowers are about four times as high as among aged couples. Part of this differential is a cohort effect: widows and widowers are older on the average than couples and older people, on the average, had lower incomes than younger people did. Furthermore, the poor die younger and are therefore more likely to be widowed than are the rich. But more is going on. Holden reminds us that we need to attend to regulations to make sure that the interests of non-earners or lesser earners, most likely still to be women, are attended to. When we attend to those interests, for example, by stipulating annuitization under joint-and-survivor rules, we impose regulations. Bit by bit, we impose regulations on initially untrammeled, unregulated individual accounts in the name of making sure that the proposed system continues to perform vital functions that Social Security now performs. At some point, one wonders why we considered making this trip in the first place.

References

Advisory Council on Social Security. 1997. *Report of the 1994–1996 Advisory Council on Social Security: Vol. 1: Findings and Recommendations.* Washington: Government Printing Office.

Ameriks, John, and Stephen P. Zeldes. "How Do Household Portfolio Shares Vary with Age?" in progress.

Auerbach, Alan J., Jagadeesh Gokhale, and Laurence J. Kotlikoff. 1994. "Generational Accounting: A Meaningful Way to Evaluate Fiscal Policy." *Journal of Economic Perspectives* 8 (1): 73–94.

Beach, William W., and Gareth G. Davis. 1998. "Social Security's Rate of Return." Heritage Foundation Study. Washington. January 15.

Board of Trustees of the Federal Old-Age and Survivors Insurance Trust Fund. 1997. *Annual Report of the Board of Trustees of the Old-Age and Survivors and Disability Insurance Trust Funds.* Washington: Government Printing Office.

Bound, John, and others. 1991. "Poverty Dynamics in Widowhood." *Journal of Gerontology: Social Sciences* 46:S115–24.

Burkhauser, Richard V., Karen C. Holden, and Daniel Feaster. 1988. "Incidence, Timing, and Events Associated with Poverty: A Dynamic View of Poverty in Retirement." *Journal of Gerontology* 43 (2):546–52.

Burkhauser, R. V., K. C. Holden, and D. A. Myers. 1986. "Marital Disruption and Poverty: The Role of Survey Procedures in Artificially Creating Poverty." *Demography* 23 (4): 621–31.

Chand, Sheetal K., and Albert Jaeger. 1996. "Aging Populations and Public Pension Schemes." Occasional Paper 147. Washington: International Monetary Fund (December).

Economist. 1997."A Survey of Banking in Emerging Markets." April 12.

Feldstein, Martin. 1997. "Transition to a Fully Funded Pension System: Five Economic Issues." NBER Working Paper 6149. Cambridge, Mass.: National Bureau of Economic Research.

Geanakoplos, John, Olivia S. Mitchell, and Stephen P. Zeldes. Forthcoming. "Social Security Money's Worth." In *Prospects for Social Security Reform*, edited by Olivia S. Mitchell, Robert J. Myers, and Howard Young. Pension Research Council and University of Pennsylvania Press.

Goss, Stephen C. Forthcoming. "Measuring Solvency in the Social Security System." Forthcoming. In *Prospects for Social Security Reform*, edited by Olivia S. Mitchell, Robert J. Myers, and Howard Young. Pension Research Council and University of Pennsylvania Press.

Holden, Karen C. 1996. "A Social Security Policy and the Income Shock of Widowhood: Is Social Security Fair to Women?" In *Social Security in the Twenty-First Century*, edited by Eric Kingson and James Schulz, 91–104. Oxford University Press.

Holden, Karen C., and Sean Nicholson, 1998. *A Selection of Joint-and-Survivor Pensions.* Working Paper. Madison, Wisc.: Institute for Research on Poverty.

Holden, Karen C., and Cathleen Zick. 1997. "The Economic Impact of Widowhood in the 1990s: Evidence from the Survey of Income and Program Participation." *Consumer Interests Annual*, vol. 43, edited by Irene E. Leech, 34–39. Colombia, Mo.: American Council on Consumer Interests.

Holden, Karen C., Richard B. Burkhauser, and Daniel J. Feaster. 1988. "The Timing of Falls into Poverty after Retirement and Widowhood." *Demography* 25 (3): 405–14.

Hurd, Michael, and David Wise. 1989. "The Wealth and Poverty of Widows: Assets before and after the Husband's Death." In *The Economics of Aging*, edited by David A. Wise, 177–222. University of Chicago Press.

Ibbotson, R., & Associates. 1998. *Stocks, Bonds, Bills, and Inflation Yearbook.* Chicago.

Kennickell, Arthur, Martha Starr-McCluer, and Annika E. Sunden. 1997. "Family Finances in the U.S.: Recent Evidence from the Survey of Consumer Finances." *Federal Reserve Bulletin.* January.

Leimer, Dean. 1994. "Cohort Specific Measures of Lifetime Net Social Security Transfers." ORS Working Paper 59. Washington: Office of Research and Statistics, Social Security Administration (February).

Mitchell, Olivia S. Forthcoming. "Administrative Costs of Public and Private Pension Plans." In *Privatizing Social Security,* edited by Martin Feldstein. Cambridge, Mass.: National Bureau of Economic Research (NBER Working Paper 5734, August 1996).

Mitchell, Olivia S., and Flavio Barreto. 1997. "After Chile, What? Second-Round Social Security Reforms in Latin America." *Revista de Analisis Economico* 12 (November): 3–36.

Mitchell, Olivia S., and Stephen P. Zeldes. 1996. "Social Security Privatization: A Structure for Analysis." *American Economic Review* 86 (May): 363–67.

Moore, Stephen. 1997. *Prepared Testimony on the Future of Social Security for This Generation and the Next.* House Ways and Means Committee, Social Security Subcommittee, 105 Cong. 1 sess. June 24. Washington: Government Printing Office.

Schieber, Sylvester J., and John B. Shoven. 1997. "The Consequences of Population Aging for Private Pension Fund Savings and Asset Markets." In Michael D. Hurd and Naohiro Yashiro, eds., *The Economic Effects of Aging in the United States and Japan.* University of Chicago Press.

Social Security Administration, 1996. *Annual Statistical Supplement to the Social Security Bulletin, 1992.* Washington: Government Printing Office.

Thompson, Lawrence. 1998. *Older and Wiser: The Economics of Public Pensions.* Urban Institute Press.

United Nations, Department of International Economic and Social Affairs. 1988. *World Population Prospects.*

U.S. Department of Health and Human Services. 1997. "Report of the 1994–96 Advisory Council on Social Security."

5

Insights from Social Security Reform Abroad

THIS CHAPTER summarizes what Americans can learn from social security reform in other advanced industrialized countries. The paper presents an overview of the forces driving reform initiatives in other OECD countries, and the discussants provide detailed descriptions of developments in the United Kingdom, Germany, and Canada.

The Politics of Pensions: Lessons from Abroad
R. Kent Weaver

PUBLIC PENSION PROGRAMS in the advanced industrial countries are, if not exactly under siege, certainly facing substantial and sustained pressures for change.[1] A sampling of actions considered and taken just during 1997 is indicative. In Germany, the federal government enacted, over the objections of the opposition Social Democrats, legislation that will gradually lower replacement rates for retirees and increase the federal value-added tax rate by 1 percent to pay for rising pension costs. In France, the center-right government passed a law in February that for the first time gave preferential tax treatment to private retirement savings funds.[2] The French Socialist party promised during last year's legislative election campaign to scrap the new law if they won the election, but instead of doing so, they have announced that they will introduce

I would like to thank Keith Banting, John Myles, and Steven Teles for comments on earlier iterations of this paper.
    1. See Myles (1989); Pierson (1996); Pierson (1997).
    2. For a brief description of the legislation, see "France: Retirement Savings Funds" (1997).

new legislation intended to give those funds a place as complements to the state-run pay-as-you-go system.[3] In New Zealand, the government held a referendum in September on a plan to phase out the existing general revenue-financed state pension system and replace it with a system of mandatory contributions to personal pensions.[4] The proposal was rejected, however, by a staggering 92 percent of those voting in the referendum. In Canada, the federal and Quebec legislatures enacted a phased increase in the payroll tax that funds the contributory earnings-related tier of their pension scheme, known as the Canada/Quebec Pension Plan, raising combined employer/employee contribution rates from 5.85 to 9.9 percent by the year 2003. But continuing a two-year delay caused by a fear of political repercussions, the federal government in Canada again postponed (and later abandoned) moving forward with legislation to meld the means-tested and universal tiers of Canada's pension system; a move that would have resulted in lower pension benefits for upper-income seniors and eliminated them entirely for some.[5] In Italy, the center-left government headed by Romano Prodi reached an agreement with unions in November that will cut pension expenditures and require increased contributions from the self-employed, but the government was forced to create numerous exemptions to the reforms for blue-collar and self-employed workers in order to avoid a governmental collapse and get its budget through the Italian parliament.[6] In Britain, the new Labor government of Tony Blair announced tentative plans to create a new tier of pension plans for those who are not in stable employment owing either to caregiving responsibilities or working on short-term contracts. The British government remains divided on how to structure the new pensions and on whether to retain or phase out the second-tier state pension, the State Earnings-Related Pension Scheme, in favor of the privately managed pensions with which SERPS already competes.[7]

3. Andrew Jack, "French About Turn on Private Top-Up Pension Schemes," *Financial Times,* July 9, 1997; "Aides Deny Jospin About-Face on French Pensions," *Reuters Newswire,* December 11, 1997.

4. The plan would have required individuals to contribute 3 percent of their earnings over $NZ96 a week, rising to 8 percent in the year 2003. Beginning in 1999, payments would also have been made on interest, dividends or trusts, and self-employed persons would have paid into the funds on income over $NZ5,000 a year. The government pledged that payments into the new personal pension funds would be largely offset by tax cuts. For a description of the proposal, see New Zealand, Independent Referendum Panel (1997).

5. See Laura Eggertson, "Martin Defends Premium Hike for CPP Security," *Toronto Star,* October 29, 1997. Some upper-income seniors had already lost their OAS pensions through previous "clawback" measures.

6. See Balmer (1997); "Italy PM Says Pension Reform Radical," *Reuters Newswire,* December 19, 1997.

7. See, for example, Larry Elliot, "Top-up Pension Plans Unveiled," *Guardian,* November 20, 1997; and Larry Elliot, Michael White, and David Brindle, "How the Labour Team Fell Out of Step," *Guardian,* November 21, 1997.

Nor is 1997 unique. The amount of pension policy change considered and enacted in the OECD in recent years is simply extraordinary. A detailed, systematic analysis of change in specific countries is a much bigger task than can be covered in a paper of modest length; moreover others have already offered such analyses.[8] What I will try to do in this paper is paint a broad portrait of recurring patterns of pension policy change and pension politics in the industrialized world, the underlying causes of those patterns, and their implications for the United States. I will make only passing reference to pension policies and politics in the industrializing countries and the newly democratizing countries of the former Soviet bloc.[9]

The pension reform experiences of the other advanced industrial countries are not only of great interest in their own right, they also offer tremendous learning opportunities for the United States. Although each country has unique political institutions and a unique program history, they share with the United States accountability of governments to voters and many basic similarities in pension structures. But the other advanced industrial countries have two further advantages that make them even more valuable as sources of information. First, many of these countries, as discussed later in this paper, are much further along in the demographic dip in the ratio of workers to dependents than the United States. Demographically, they allow us to look into the future of the United States in terms of the likely politics of a Social Security crisis. Second, several countries have attempted, and a few have implemented, some of the pension reforms that are currently being advocated for the United States—notably increased reliance on mandatory contributions to fully funded, privately managed pension funds with individual accounts. A look at these experiences allows us to anticipate some of the political battles that are likely to be waged over these reforms in the United States, and, it is hoped, to avoid some of the mistakes made elsewhere.

The basic causal model underlying this paper is shown in figure 5-1. First, a common set of pressures for change—demographic pressures, budgetary pressures, competitive pressures, and conservative critiques—have confronted pension systems in all of the OECD countries. Specific pressures have been felt to differing degrees across those countries, however. Second, these pressures have been mediated in critical ways by political and policy characteristics of those

8. See in particular Myles and Quadagno (1991); Ploug and Kvist (1994); Myles and Quadagno (1997).

9. In many ways, the pension problems of the industrializing countries are even more severe that those of the OECD countries, since public health and medical advances have caused their populations to age rapidly while those countries still have relatively low per capita gross domestic product. See especially the discussion in James and others (1994).

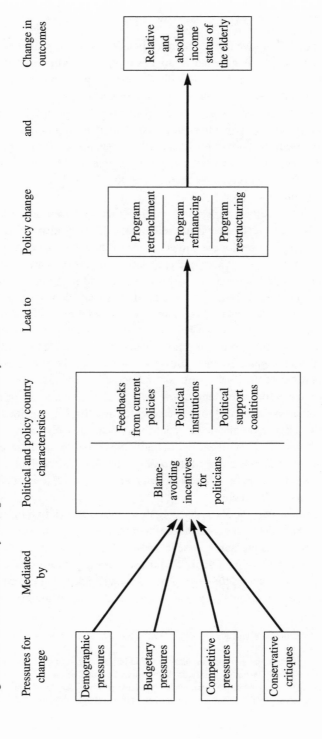

Figure 5-1. *A Causal Model of Changes in Retirement Income Systems*

countries. Most generally, politicians have sought to respond to those pressures in a way that minimizes the blame and electoral retribution that they encounter from organized groups and individual voters. Both the strategies and policy choices that they make to avoid blame and the opportunities that their political opponents have to generate blame are in turn influenced by feedbacks from current policies, political institutions, and political support coalitions. The interaction of these broad pressures for change, politicians' motivations to avoid blame, and country-specific political and policy characteristics are what determine patterns of pension policy change, which in turn affects the relative and absolute income status of the elderly.

The first section of this chapter briefly discusses the major options for organizing public pension programs, and the second section compares the current pension policies of the United States with other industrialized countries. The third section of the paper examines the common economic and political forces enumerated above that have brought pension reform onto governmental agendas across the OECD. The fourth section skips ahead in the causal model to policy changes, arguing that the tremendous pressures for change in pension policies have more often given rise to incremental retrenchment and refinancing than to fundamental restructuring. The fifth section begins by arguing that patterns of policy change cannot be explained solely by cross-national differences in the strength of the four sweeping pressures for pension change. Political factors mediate pressures for pension cutbacks and help to explain patterns of policy change. Strong blame-avoiding motivations for politicians appear to be particularly important in explaining the overall dominance of incremental reform. At the same time, policy feedbacks from existing programs play especially important roles in explaining cross-national differences; political institutions and the structure and organization of political support coalitions play a secondary, but not unimportant, role in determining pension reform outcomes. The final section focuses on the lessons that international experience in pension reform suggests for the United States, both in terms of the general political constraints on reform and the politics of moving toward a fully funded "defined-contribution" pension system.

Varieties of Pension Systems in the OECD

Public pension programs differ in a number of characteristics, most notably in their methods of pension financing and entitlement. Traditionally, pension programs have been divided into three basic types: universal programs that provide benefits to all citizens,[10] usually financed by general tax revenues; means- or need-tested benefits, given only to persons with low incomes, and again financed primarily by general revenues; and social insurance programs, financed largely through payroll tax contributions by employees or employers, with benefit entitlement based at least loosely on contributions history.[11]

Each of these broad categories of programs conceals tremendous complexity and diversity, however. Among means-tested pension programs, for example, the Supplemental Security Income program in the United States contains severe means tests; receipt is limited to the very poor. In Australia, on the other hand, the basic state pension is means tested, but means tests have been so relaxed with exclusions (for example, for homeowners) that it excludes only the well-off: about 84 percent of aged Australians receive at least some assistance.[12]

The general category of social insurance programs contains a particularly diverse set of programs. Social insurance programs vary along at least three dimensions that will be relevant in the discussion of pension reform later in the chapter:

—*Accumulation of funds.* Most social insurance programs have operated on a pay-as-you-go (PAYG) basis, in which today's workers pay for today's retirees, with very little accumulation and investment of funds to pay the future benefits of today's workers. Usually only a small reserve is held to protect the fund against temporary declines in contributions or increases in outflows of benefits (for example, due to a recession). However, some pension systems, including the U.S. Old-Age and Survivors Insurance (OASI) fund at present, accumulate at least some funds to meet future obligations, although rarely following the principles of actuarial soundness followed by private sector pension funds. Once a country has begun to operate its pension system on a PAYG basis, it is extremely difficult to switch to a system of advanced funding, because the transitional generation would have to pay both for its own retirement and that of the generation that preceded it—the so-called double payment problem.

—*Linkage of contributions and benefits.* Public pension funds vary dramatically in the closeness of fit between past contributions and eventual retirement benefits. Some systems have a tight linkage, while others do not. The U.S. Social Security program, for example, replaces a higher share of earnings for

10. Immigrants frequently receive a reduced benefit based on their length of residence during adulthood.

11. See the discussions in Esping-Andersen (1990, chap. 2); Titmuss (1958).

12. Of these, 65 percent receive the full age pension and 35 percent get a partial pension. See O'Sullivan (1997). In 1981, 87 percent of aged Australians received the age pension. Stricter means tests have been imposed in recent years. See Shaver (1991).

workers with low-wage histories than for those with a higher earnings history, and in recent years a portion of benefits for retirees with high incomes has been subject to income taxation.[13] In short, Social Security has veiled partial income tests at both the lower and upper income ranges. Other pension systems give individuals pension credits for military service, for time in education and training, or for time spent as an unpaid caregiver for children, disabled persons or frail elderly parents, for example, regardless of whether social insurance contributions were actually made.

—*Guarantee of benefits.* Traditional social insurance pension programs have generally had "defined benefits," whose value is determined at retirement according to a statutory formula that links an earner's wage history and history of contributions according to a fixed formula. The initial pension benefit replaces some fixed share of the earner's past wages over the reference period (for example, last ten years, highest ten years, or entire working life). In addition, most industrialized countries have over the past three decades indexed wage histories used in initial benefit calculations to reflect increases in both inflation and real wage growth, and indexed benefits to protect retirees' pensions from being eroded by inflation. Many countries index benefits at least partially to earnings or GDP growth rather than prices to allow retirees to participate in overall economic growth. These benefits thus enjoy a high degree of statutory guarantee, although governments can of course change statutory provisions on both replacement rates and indexation. In defined-contribution programs, however, the government does not guarantee benefit levels: whatever contributions have accrued in a retiree's account prior to their withdrawal, along with earnings on those contributions, form the basis of a retiree's pension benefit (usually financed through purchase of an annuity upon retirement).

Defined-contribution pensions are usually found in fully funded pension schemes—most often in the private sector but also in the new Australian mandatory occupational pensions. It is also possible to run PAYG public pension schemes on a defined-contribution basis: each retiree can be assigned a share of incoming pension fund contributions, with individual benefit levels depending on the inflow of contributions and death rate of retirees.[14] This option has not been popular, however, because it increases uncertainty for pensioners, creates a very direct and visible zero-sum conflict between pensioners and workers, and (unless contributions are raised) makes it likely that pensions will decline as the ratio of workers to retirees declines.

13. See Simanis (1994).
14. Reynaud (1995).

Complexity within pension programs is even more evident when the interaction of multiple programs within countries is considered. Most countries offer multiple tiers of public pensions, usually involving some form of minimum guarantee and an earnings-related component. Countries offering "universal" flat-rate first-tier pensions have generally added means-tested and earnings-related tiers as well, while the United States has a main OASI social insurance tier complemented by a means-tested Supplemental Security Income program.

These three categories of pension provision are complicated even further by the growth of a fourth, quasi-state, category of pensions in many countries. These pension funds are not managed by the state, but the state plays an important role by providing special tax benefits (as in the United States), by mandating contributions (as in Australia), or by subsidizing contributions for at least some workers (as in the United Kingdom). Unlike most social insurance programs, quasi-state retirement fund benefits are usually based not on some more-or-less tight linkage to earnings history (defined benefit)[15] but rather to contributions to the fund and to the earnings of the fund prior to retirement (defined contribution). Trying to develop accurate, comparable cross-national measurements of public pension activity is exceptionally tricky, but this fourth tier is even trickier than the others, and most statistical studies do not even try.

The U.S. Pension System in Comparative Perspective

Comparing pension systems across nations is a complex task that requires looking at multiple measures. The United States has traditionally been viewed as a welfare state "laggard" relative to other industrial countries, creating programs to deal with problems of social dependency relatively late, and offering relatively ungenerous benefits once those programs have been created. In comparing the U.S. pension system with those in other OECD countries, it is helpful to compare at least three aspects of pension programs: program structure, program expenditures, and program outcomes.

Program Structure

The United States relies very heavily on a social insurance program, Old-Age and Survivors Insurance, to provide retirement income to its older citi-

---

15. Of course, defined benefits are truly "defined" in the sense that government has a legal obligation to pay them unless it alters that obligation—usually by statute. Governments have often done so. For examples, see James and others (1994, pp. 112–13).

zens. In calendar year 1996, almost $233 billion was paid to retired workers and their dependents, compared with only $4.5 billion paid to the aged under the means-tested Supplemental Security Income program.[16] In the absence of a universal pension, this pension structure tends to produce relatively low pension minimums, even with redistribution built into the Social Security benefit formula.

Overall public pension benefits are relatively ungenerous by OECD standards. The most common measure of pension generosity in public pension systems is the "replacement rate," or percentage of former wage received by a retired worker. This measure statistic can be calculated in several ways, all of which have serious measurement problems, so any conclusions drawn from replacement rate indicators should be done with caution.[17] Nevertheless, a comparative analysis of the generosity and financing of public pensions suggests clear differences across the OECD countries. The United States is relatively ungenerous, especially in its absolute level of minimum guarantee to older retirees (table 5-1). The variation among the advanced industrial countries on retirement ages is much smaller, but the United States is at the high end and will clearly be so when planned retirement age increases are fully phased in (table 5-2). Payroll taxes for social purposes are much lower in the United States than in most other OECD countries: about 18 percent in the United States compared with almost 54 percent in Italy and 42 percent in Germany (table 5-3).

Program Expenditures

Efforts to compare program expenditures are also fraught with difficulties. In particular, countries differ dramatically in the percentage of their population that is elderly. In Sweden, for example, 18 percent of the population was over age 65 in 1990, according to the World Bank; it was only 10.7 percent in Australia, and 11.3 percent in Canada (table 5-4). In general, a higher elderly percentage of the population means a higher pension burden. Countries also differ substantially in the retirement age of their populations: Italy, for example, has long had a lower entitlement age than most of the other OECD countries. Finally, countries differ in the extent to which their pension effort is channeled through "public" systems. If, for example, significant pension effort is channeled through tax concessions to personal or occupational pensions, it will not be counted in the data in table 5-4. And the United States does indeed

16. The SSI figure includes state supplementation. Social Security Administration (1997, pp. 165–288).
17. See in particular Whiteford (1995).

Table 5-1. *Pension Wage Replacement Rates and Benefit Levels in Selected OECD Countries*

Country	Replacement rate of Social Security pension for worker with average earnings in manufacturing, 1980 (as percent of earnings in year before retirement)[a]		Net (after tax) pension as a percentage of net preretirement earnings, 1992[b]		Pension replacement rate, 1995[c]	Minimum benefit for single older person in 1991 $U.S. (Index with U.S. = 100 in parentheses)[d]
	Single person	Couple	National average earner	1.5 times national average earnings		
Australia	28	47	n.a.	n.a.	n.a.	6834 (133)
Canada	34	49	n.a.	n.a.	29.2	7344 (143)
Denmark	29	52	63	87	n.a.	6545 (127)
France	66	75	86	84	60.1	6131 (119)
Germany	49	49	84	74	52.0	4813 (93)
Italy	69	69	89	90	53.9	5770 (112)
Japan	54	61	97	79	19.6	n.a.
Netherlands	44	63	89	92	n.a.	7380 (143)
New Zealand	39	64	n.a.	n.a.	n.a.	6406 (124)
Norway	n.a.	n.a.	80	78	n.a.	6067 (118)
Spain	n.a.	n.a.	88	90	n.a.	3661 (71)
Sweden	58	83	79	70	39.0	5861 (114)
Switzerland	37	55	77	68	n.a.	4897 (95)
United Kingdom	31	47	76	77	17.5	5150 (100)
United States	44	66	65	67	38.5	5160 (100)

n.a. Not available.

a. Whiteford (1995, pp. 3–30).

b. Lowndes (1992). See study for explanatory notes.

c. Average pension benefit as a percentage of the average gross wage. See Chand and Jaeger (1996, p.12).

d. Benefits are in purchasing power parities. For details on programs included, see Whiteford (1995, pp. 3–30 at p. 26).

channel substantial effort through the tax system—close to $113 billion in 1997.[18] The data in table 5-4 nevertheless provide a crude comparative estimate of governmental pension effort across the OECD. As the left hand column of table 5-4 shows, the United States is roughly at the top of the bottom

18. The totals, in outlay equivalents, include net exclusion of pension contributions and earnings ($92.88 billion), exclusion of Social Security ($17.81 billion) and railroad retirement ($440 million) benefits, and an additional tax deduction for the elderly ($1.795 billion). See Office of Management and Budget (1997, p. 82).

Table 5-2. *Retirement Ages in Selected OECD Countries*

Country	Gender	1977	1997	Planned eventual retirement age (as of early 1997)
Australia	Men	65	65	65
	Women	60	61	65 (2013)
Canada	Men	65	65	65
	Women	65	65	65
Denmark	Men	67	67	67
	Women	62/67[a]	67	67
France	Men	60	65[b]	65
	Women	60	65[b]	65
Germany	Men	63/65[c]	63/65[d]	63/65[d]
	Women	63/65[c]	63/65[d]	63/65[d]
Italy	Men	60	63[e]	57–65[f]
	Women	55	58[e]	57–65[f]
Japan	Men	60/65[g]	65	65
	Women	55/65[h]	65	65
Netherlands	Men	65	65	65
	Women	65	65	65
New Zealand	Men	65	62.9	65 (2001)
	Women	65	62.9	65 (2001)
Norway	Men	67	67	67
	Women	67	67	67
Portugal	Men	65	65	65
	Women	62	63.5	65
Spain	Men	65	65	65
	Women	65	65	65
Sweden	Men	65	65	65
	Women	65	65	65
Switzerland	Men	65	65	65
	Women	62	62	64 (2005)
United Kingdom	Men	65	65	65
	Women	60	60	65 (2020)
United States	Men	65	65	67 (2027)
	Women	65	65	67 (2027)

Source: U.S. Social Security Administration, *Social Security Programs throughout the World*, (Washington, various years).

a. 62 for single women; 67 for married women.

b. 60 with 150 quarters of coverage.

c. 63 with 35 years' insurance; 65 with 15 years.

d. 63 with 35 years of coverage; 65 with 5 years of coverage.

e. With 18 years of contributions. Seniority pension also available with 40 years of contributions at any age, or at age 57 with 35 years of contributions.

f. Flexible retirement age for new labor market entrants in 1996 or later. For those with less than 18 years of labor market experience, retirement age rises to age 65 for men and 60 for women in 2001.

g. 60 for employees' pension insurance (except 55 for miners); 65 for national pension program.

h. 55 for employees' pension insurance; 65 for national pension program.

Table 5-3. *Contribution Rates for Social Security Programs,*
OECD Countries, 1997

Percent

Country	Old age, disability, death			All Social Security programs[a]
	Insured person	Employer	Total	Total
Australia	0	0	0[b]	1.25[b]
Austria	10.25	12.55	22.80	44.90
Belgium	7.50	8.86	16.36	37.94
Canada	3.00	3.00	6.00	14.03[c]
Finland	4.50	11.86	16.36	26.76[c]
France	6.65	9.80	16.45	50.65
Germany	10.15	10.15	20.30	41.86[c]
Greece	6.67	13.33	20.00	35.85
Iceland	4.00	9.88	13.88	15.23
Ireland	7.75[d,e]	12.00[d,e]	19.75[d,e]	20.00[c,e]
Italy	8.89	19.36	28.25	53.77
Japan	8.67	8.67	17.34	27.80
Luxembourg	8.00	8.00	16.00	28.20[c]
Netherlands	32.25	0	32.25	55.25[c]
New Zealand	0	0	0[b]	0[b]
Norway	7.80[d]	14.10[d]	21.90[d]	21.90[c]
Portugal	11.00[f]	23.75[f]	34.75[f]	37.75
Spain	4.70[d]	23.60[d]	28.30[d]	38.08
Sweden	1.00	19.06	20.06	35.85[c]
Switzerland	4.90	4.90	9.80	12.94
United Kingdom	12.00[d,e]	10.00[d,e]	22.00[d,e]	22.00[c,e]
United States	6.20	6.20	12.40	18.15

Source: U.S. Social Security Administration, *Social Security Programs throughout the World* (Washington, 1997), p. xlvii.

a. Includes old age, disability, death; sickness and maternity; work injury; unemployment; and family allowances. In some countries, the rate may not cover all of these programs. In some cases, only certain groups, such as wage earners, are represented. When contribution rate varies, either the average rate or the lowest rate in the range is used.

b. The central government pays the entire cost of most programs from general revenues.

c. The central government pays the whole cost of family allowances.

d. Also includes rate for other programs.

e. Range according to earnings bracket. Higher rate is shown, which applies to highest earnings class.

f. Plus flat amount for unemployment.

Table 5-4. *Elderly Population and Pension Effort in OECD countries, 1990*

Country	(a) Public pension spending as percent of GDP	(b) Percent of population over 65 years old	a/b
Australia	3.9	10.7	0.36
Austria	14.8	15	0.99
Belgium	11	15	0.73
Canada	4.2	11.3	0.37
Denmark	9.9	15.4	0.64
Finland	10.3	13.3	0.77
France	11.8	13.8	0.86
Germany	10.8	14.9	0.72
Greece	12.3	14.2	0.87
Iceland	4.8	10.6	0.45
Ireland	6.1	11.4	0.54
Italy	14.4	14.8	0.97
Japan	5	11.9	0.42
Luxembourg	12	13.8	0.87
Netherlands	9.8	13.2	0.74
New Zealand	7.5	11.1	0.68
Norway	10.1	16.4	0.62
Portugal	7.7	13	0.59
Spain	7.5	13.2	0.57
Sweden	11.6	18	0.64
Switzerland	9.9	14.9	0.66
United Kingdom	9.5	15.7	0.61
United States	6.5	12.3	0.53
Average	9.2	13.6	0.68

Source: James and others (1994, pp. 343, 358).

quartile of government tax effort for pensions measured in absolute terms. The right-hand column of table 5-4 shows that the United States ranking is similarly low if we control for the percentage of the population 65 and over by looking at the percentage of GDP devoted to pensions divided by the percentage of the population that is elderly.[19]

19. The pension sector in the United States looks somewhat larger if privately managed pension fund assets are included. In a recent ranking of pension fund assets as a percentage of GDP, the United States placed fourth among nine countries, behind three countries (Netherlands, Switzerland, and the United Kingdom) where contributions are compulsory or quasi-compulsory. See James and others (1994, p. 174).

Policy Outcomes

Similar patterns are evident in policy outcomes, specifically the poverty status of the elderly. Efforts to develop cross-national measures of the well-being of the elderly are fraught with methodological and empirical difficulties, notably how to treat health services, which are provided free in some countries and require substantial out-of-pocket expenses by the elderly in others.[20] The data that are available, mostly data on purchasing power equivalents of family disposable income from the Luxembourg Income Study, suggest that the elderly in the United States are modestly disadvantaged relative to the elderly in other countries, but they fare better than other disadvantaged groups in U.S. society. In a study by Timothy Smeeding, Barbara Boyle Torrey, and Martin Rein of eight OECD countries using LIS data from around 1980, for example, the United States had the fourth-highest rates of poverty among both elderly women and men living alone, third-highest poverty rates among elderly married couples, and the highest poverty rates of elderly persons among elderly persons living in other combinations.[21]

These statistics reinforce the conventional portrait of the United States as a modest welfare state laggard in the provision of public pensions. But the United States is not so different in program structure, expenditures, or program outcomes that the pension reform experiences of other countries can easily be dismissed as not comparable. The implications of historically low U.S. pension effort for a period of pension retrenchment are unclear, however: if the United States is less generous in pension provision because its national values and constellation of interest group pressures are more hostile to government activity than those of other countries, then one might expect that the United States would be a leader in cutting and restructuring pressures once pressures for retrenchment set in. If, however, the outlier status of the United States is because of factors such as fragmented political institutions that make any change from the status quo (expansion or retrenchment) difficult, then the United States might be a laggard in retrenchment as well.

Roots of Retrenchment Initiatives

Four intertwined pressures for change in public pension systems have contributed to the frequency with which pension reform is appearing on public

20. For valuable discussions, see for example Palmer, Smeeding, and Jencks (1988) and Smeeding, Torrey, and Rein (1988, p. 105).

21. Smeeding, Torrey, and Rein (1988). For a recent review of comparative analyses of the poverty status of elderly women, see Siegenthaler (1996).

agendas across the industrialized world. A first source of pressure for change in pension schemes in the advanced industrial countries is demographic change. Most OECD countries operate their pension systems on a PAYG basis, which may lead to a funding crisis when birth rates decline or life expectancy increases, causing an increase in the ratio of retirees to workers.[22] Moreover, as in the case of U.S. Social Security, the first generation of workers in a PAYG retirement system often receives a substantial bonus of benefits relative to their contributions, and benefit promises made when the ratio of retirees entitled to benefits to workers is low become unsustainable later on.

Currently, both the percentage of population over retirement age and the ratio of the elderly to those of working age are increasing dramatically throughout the developed (and developing) world, leaving fewer workers to support the elderly population. Particularly large rates of increase are occurring among the very elderly (those over age 75). Moreover, because of higher life expectancies for women, the population of elderly is disproportionately female. Even with survivors' benefits, elderly women are frequently ill-served by earnings-related pension schemes because their lifetime earnings tend to be lower than men's and because they disproportionately bear costs of living alone and of invalidity in very old age.[23]

Demographic challenges vary significantly across the industrialized countries. A recent IMF study, using relatively optimistic World Bank population projections, argues that the United States will have only modest increases in its 1995 elderly dependency ratio (that is, the population 65 and over as a percentage of the population 15 to 64 years old) of 19.2 through the year 2010, but that ratio will then rise to 35.8 by the year 2030. Germany, however, faces a much more immediate and severe demographic crisis. Its elderly dependency ratio is expected to increase from 22.3 in 1995 to 30.3 in 2010 and 49.2 by 2030. The demographic outlook in Italy and Japan is even bleaker (table 5-5). All other things being equal, countries that experience early, and more severe, increases in their elderly dependency ratios should presumably also make earlier and more drastic changes in their public pension programs than countries like the United States.

A second source of change in pension systems is increased budgetary concerns. In all of the advanced industrial countries, pension and health care costs for the elderly have become a very substantial, and largely fixed, drain on public treasuries. Budgetary pressures posed by pensions have been exacerbated by

---

22. See, for example, Organization for Economic Cooperation and Development (1988); Reynaud (1995).

23. James and others (1994, pp. 29–30).

Table 5-5. *Projected Trends in Elderly Dependency Ratios, 1995–2050*

Population aged 65 and over as a percentage of population aged 15–64

Country	1995	2000	2010	2020	2030	2050
Canada	17.5	18.2	20.4	28.4	39.1	41.8
France	22.1	23.6	24.6	32.3	39.1	43.5
Germany	22.3	23.8	30.3	35.4	49.2	51.9
Italy	23.8	26.5	31.2	37.5	48.3	60.0
Japan	20.3	24.3	33.0	43.0	44.5	54.0
Sweden	27.4	26.9	29.1	35.6	39.4	38.6
United Kingdom	24.3	24.4	25.8	31.2	38.7	41.2
United States	19.2	19.0	20.4	27.6	36.8	38.4

Source: Chand and Jaeger (1996, p. 5).

aging of the population. In many countries, policies enacted during periods of high unemployment to encourage early retirement added to these pressures. In Europe, prolonged high unemployment in the 1990s has further strained social insurance systems both by inflating the number of claims made against the system and by lowering the flow of contributions into the system. Budgetary pressures in Europe have also been exacerbated by the conditions imposed in the Maastricht Treaty for joining the European Monetary Union. In both Germany and Italy, for example, pension retrenchment was seen as necessary to meet the 3 percent of GDP target set for government deficits.[24]

Budgetary pressures and challenges differ substantially across countries, depending both on demographic pressures and the nature of past pension promises made to the elderly regarding retirement ages, wage replacement rates, indexation provisions, and so on. Italy, for example, has faced particularly severe problems: by 1995, its pay-as-you-go pension system was running a deficit equivalent to 4 percent of GDP, requiring a subsidy from the state government equivalent to 26.5 percent of its costs.[25] All other things being equal, countries facing overall high budget deficits or pension system funding crises should presumably be the most likely to engage in pension retrenchment and restructuring. This is consistent with the experience of the United States, where major Social Security reforms in 1977 and 1983 were precipitated by trust fund crises.

24. See Leibfried and Pierson (1995); Gillian Tett, "Lies, Damn Lies, and Statistics: Are EU States Engaging in Creative Accounting to Qualify for a Single Currency?" *Financial Times*, October 9, 1996, p. 2. Similar pressures are being felt in the new democracies of central and eastern Europe that want to join the European Union and the single European currency in the future. See Bertrand Benoit and Matej Vipotnik, "EMU Shadow over Pension Reforms," *Financial Times*, August 20, 1997, p. 2.

25. Robert Graham, "Italy Fails to Obey Pension Arrears Ruling," *Financial Times*, February 1, 1995, p. 2; David Lane, "Pensions to Be Reined In," *Financial Times*, July 28, 1995, p. 102.

Governments could respond to budgetary pressures by raising taxes as well as cutting expenditures. That they have been reluctant to do so is due in part to a third, and related, source of retrenchment pressure: concerns about economic competitiveness. Most economists argue that payroll taxes are borne by workers in the form of lower cash wages and therefore have no impact on competitiveness. But many business leaders and conservative politicians are less sanguine, believing that the high payroll taxes associated with generous pension and other welfare state programs may make firms in the countries providing those benefits unable to compete with firms in lower-cost countries. Labor leaders and politicians on the left, however, worry about second-order effects of competitiveness concerns, notably the possibility of migration of jobs to low-cost countries or a "race to the bottom" in social benefits.[26]

A final critical source of pressure for change in the pension systems of the advanced industrial countries is a conservative ideological resurgence that argues that governmental pension systems are inherently flawed. In particular, critics have decried the tendency of politicians under payroll-tax-funded schemes to rely on pay-as-you-go rather than advanced funding, and the consequent tendency of such systems to lower savings and economic growth. Moreover, the tendency of governments to rely on state pension funds as sources of borrowing at below-market rates reduces the amount of money available to fund pensions. Formal and informal international consortiums of think tanks and advocacy organizations pressing for pension reform based on this critique have emerged during the past decade.

Having conservative critiques of the current system, and even conservative politicians in power, might be sufficient to lead to a retrenchment in pension outlays, but it need not lead to a single consistent direction in restructuring initiatives. In recent years, however, a consistent direction has emerged, focusing on an increased role for personal and occupational pensions that are managed by private companies rather than governments and that invest in equities as well as government securities. Government's role in such systems is limited to requiring a minimum payroll deduction for investment in those funds, and perhaps regulating the risks they take and the accuracy of the claims they make to potential contributors. The star models of these reforms are, of course, the pension fund set up by the Pinochet government in Chile and the reforms of the State Earnings-Related Pension Scheme (SERPS) engineered by Margaret Thatcher in Britain.[27] Perhaps

26. See the discussions in Pierson (1996) and Leibfried and Pierson (1995). See also Michael Cassell, "Business Locations in Europe: Social Packages Can Weigh Heavily," *Financial Times,* October 8, 1996, p. 5.

27. On Chile, see, for example, Diamond and Valdés-Prieto (1994); Kritzer (1996); and Holzmann (1997). On the United Kingdom, see Pierson (1994, chap. 3); and Disney and Johnston (1998).

as important as the example of the Chilean and British experiences is the endorsement of a minimalist role for government pension plans by the World Bank. In its influential study *Averting the Old Age Crisis*, published in 1994, the bank study team endorsed many of the conservative critiques of public pension schemes. The bank study argued that rather than a "dominant public pillar" that combines poverty reduction and earnings-related savings functions, industrialized countries should move toward a three-tier model in which the role of public pensions would focus on a minimal poverty reduction role, complemented by a fully-funded, mandatory defined-contribution savings second tier in which workers would ideally be able to choose between personal, portable pensions and an occupational scheme, and a third tier of voluntary savings.[28] Conservative politicians and business leaders in a number of countries have joined the call for a fundamental restructuring of pensions to increase the role of privately managed supplementary pension funds relative to that of public pensions.[29]

These massive, multiple, and reinforcing pressures in public pension systems might be expected to produce equally massive changes in those systems unless they were offset by equally powerful countervailing pressures resisting retrenchment. In fact, as discussed in the next few pages, changes in public pension programs in recent years have been mostly incremental.

Patterns of Change

Governments can respond to these multiple, reinforcing pressures for pension retrenchment in several basic ways. First, they can try to cut back on the generosity of specific provisions of their pension programs, what will be referred to here as retrenchment. Second, they can refinance pension programs, either by adding dedicated revenues like payroll taxes or general revenues. Third, they can attempt to restructure their pension programs in fundamental ways—for example by adding or deleting tiers of programs. Though countries

28. James and others (1994, chap. 7). For further discussion, see Beattie and McGillivray (1995); James (1996); and Beattie and McGillivray (1996). A 1996 International Monetary Fund Staff paper argues that changing the parameters of current pay-as-you-go systems by increasing retirement ages, altering indexation mechanisms, and so on, and increasing contribution rates to a constant level adequate to provide savings for dips in the worker-retiree ratio "would in most countries suffice to contain adverse fiscal developments" and that "it may be preferable to fix the PAYG system instead of shifting to a fully funded system." Chand and Jaeger (1996, p. 2).

29. See, for example, Eggertson, "Martin Defends Premium Hike." "Rentenerhöhung muß gestrichen werden," *Die Welt*, November 24, 1997; Mahnke (1997); Palme (1994). In addition, the European Commission called for liberalization of member government restrictions on supplementary pensions in a recent Green Paper. See European Commission (1997).

differ substantially, several clear overall trends in pension reform have emerged in recent years: governments have moved toward retrenchment in past pension commitments, drawing on a common repertoire of incremental cutback mechanisms; increased tax effort to pay for pension systems has been less taboo in many other countries than in the United States, even in countries where the payroll tax is already much higher than in the United States; and initiatives to fundamentally restructure pension systems have been much less common than incremental retrenchment mechanisms, and have succeeded even less often. In some countries, however, incremental changes may themselves add up over time to produce something close to a fundamental restructuring.

Common Repertoires and Recurring Patterns of Retrenchment

Faced with aging populations, heightened deficit concerns, exploding health care costs, and a conservative ideological resurgence, all governments are looking at how to cut back on pension expenditures, and most of them have done so. Given the limited number of options available to governments and the even more limited number of politically acceptable options, it should not be surprising that government's menus have many items in common, such as:

—*Adjusting of postretirement benefit indexation mechanisms downward.* Trimming postretirement indexation provisions for pension benefits has been a staple of pension retrenchment throughout the OECD.[30] The Italian reform of 1992 and the French reform of 1993, for example, index pensions to prices rather than to salaries.[31] Finland in 1996 moved from an indexing system based on a 50/50 ratio of prices and earnings to an 80/20 ratio.[32] Germany in 1992 moved to a system of indexing based on changes in net rather than gross earnings, a major difference given tax increases relating to the costs of German reunification.[33] Although most indexation reforms produce modest results in the early years, they compound over time to produce striking results: the Thatcher government's decision in 1980 to index the basic state pension to prices rather than the higher of earnings and prices has eroded the value of that pension from 21 percent of average male earnings in 1980 to 14 percent in 1997; it is expected to shrink further to 9 percent in the year 2008.[34]

30. See Wartonick and Packard (1983, pp. 9–15); Weaver (1988); Vording and Goutswaard (1997). It is also possible to lower pensioners' initial retirement benefit by altering the indexation formula used to adjust their wage history for inflation in a defined-benefit scheme.

31. Babeau (1997, p. 268).

32. International Social Security Association (1996, p. 11).

33. Puidak (1992).

34. "Target Poor Pensioners," *Guardian*, August 20, 1997.

It is important to note the failures and limitations of attacks on indexation as well as the successes, however. Throughout the OECD, the principle and much of the reality of indexation has remained intact in almost all programs that already had indexation provisions. Governments have rarely attempted deindexation or partial deindexation of existing pension programs on a permanent basis. One government that tried, the Mulroney government in Canada in 1985 (proposing to limit indexation of OAS and GIS to inflation over 3 percent), suffered a political defeat that cast a shadow over the rest of its time in office.[35] In the United States, the Social Security reform package of 1983 imposed a "delay" in the cost-of-living adjustment that resulted in a permanent loss of benefits to then-current retirees, but this was possible only because the cut was small in size and did not escalate in real dollar terms over time.[36] Attacks on the principle of indexation have mostly been indirect: rather than phasing out indexation of current direct benefit programs, the role of defined-benefit social insurance programs has instead been eroded relative to that of (generally newer) defined-contribution programs.

—*Increasing retirement ages.* In Europe, where retirement ages in many countries have been lower than in the United States, general movement has been toward higher retirement ages. Japan and New Zealand have also raised their retirement ages (table 5-2). Only Denmark, Norway, and the United States have established a standard retirement age above age 65, however (the Danish and Norwegian standard has always been 67, whereas the United States enacted changes in 1983 that do not begin to increase until the year 2000 and are not fully phased in until the year 2027).

Increases in the retirement age for women in cases where they were lower than those for men have been especially common in Europe (notably Germany, Austria, Italy, and the United Kingdom), and have also taken place in Australia. The gender harmonization in the European Union followed a ruling by the European Court of Justice and a directive by the European Union on gender equality that required equalization of retirement ages by gender. Demographic and budget pressures were used to justify upward rather than downward harmonization, easing for politicians what otherwise would almost certainly have been a politically unpopular and contentious policy change.[37] As in the United States, retirement age increases usually have been phased in over a number of years to lower political resistance and avoid major disruptions in the lives of

35. For a discussion, see Bercuson, Granatstein, and Young (1986, chap. 6); Pierson and Weaver (1993).

36. For a discussion, see Weaver (1988).

37. See "European Court of Justice Orders Equal Treatment in Awarding Pensions," 1991. On the United Kingdom, see Sinfield (1994, p. 133).

those very near to retirement age. The transition periods have generally been much shorter than the incredible thirty-four years scheduled for the U.S. retirement age increase, however.

Several governments have chosen to offer increased "flexibility" in retirement ages rather than a direct attack on retirement ages. Flexible retirement continues to allow early retirement, but with lower benefits. The Italian pension reform of 1996, for example, introduced a flexible retirement age of between 57 and 65, while Sweden's proposed reform allows retirement beginning at age 61. The reality is that those who continue to retire at younger ages will get lower benefits, although both the Swedish and Italian reforms will be phased in over long periods.[38] Similarly, a number of countries have either reduced earnings tests or increased benefits to those who retire later than the standard retirement age to induce workers to work longer, thus reducing the draw on pension systems.

—*Restricting early retirement.* Closely related to the question of standard retirement ages is the question of the conditions under which workers may retire early. In the slow economic growth era that followed the 1970s oil shocks, a number of countries adopted policies that encouraged workers to retire or partially retire early, opening jobs for younger workers. In Germany, for example, older workers who "pre-retired" continued to be paid by their firms, with partial reimbursement by the government if they were replaced by an unemployed worker. Overall, the labor force participation rate of German men age 60 fell from 77 percent in 1977 to 51 percent in 1986.[39]

In recent years, early retirement provisions of pension programs have been expanded in some countries and contracted in others (table 5-6). This pattern reflects conflicting pressures on governments: continued high unemployment in many OECD countries leads governments to try to open up work opportunities for younger workers, while budget deficits and competitiveness concerns cause governments to try to cut back on social commitments. Many of the expansions of early retirement provisions have been through separate financing mechanisms, however, so that they do not impose an additional funding burden on already-overburdened retirement funds.

—*Encouraging delayed retirement.* Complementing initiatives to discourage early retirement, several OECD countries have enacted measures intended to reward people who draw their pensions later. These measures can be especially important in countries where pension replacement rates are high and earnings

38. The Swedish reform will apply in full to those born in 1954 and later, partially, to those born earlier. The Italian reform will not apply to those with more than eighteen years of pension credits in the current system. See International Social Security Association (1996, p. 5); Torgander (1998); Sweden, Ministry of Health and Social Affairs (1998).

39. Jacobs and Rein (1991, p. 251).

Table 5-6. *Selected Changes in Benefits and Eligibility for Old Age and Retirement Pensions in the OECD, 1987–97*

Country and year enacted	Description	Year effective
Changes in postretirement indexation mechanisms		
Germany, 1989	Pensions adjusted in line with net rather than gross earnings.	1992
New Zealand, 1991	Pension indexation, suspended for two years.	1991
Changes in pensionable age		
Germany, 1992	Retirement age raised from 63 for men and 60 for women to 65 for both; flexibility for early retirement retained with reduced pension.	2000–2012
Germany, 1996	Increase in pension age enacted in 1992 accelerated.	Phased in, 2001–2004
Italy, 1992	Normal retirement age rises from 55 for women and 60 for men with 15 years of contributions to 60 for women and 65 for men with 20 years of contributions.	Phased in, 1994–2000
New Zealand, 1993	Retirement age increases from 60 to 65.	Phased in, 1994–2001
Portugal	Retirement age for women increases from 60 to 65.	Phased in over 6 year period
Switzerland	Retirement age for women raised from 62 to 64.	Phased in through 2005
United Kingdom, 1995	Retirement age for women raised in stages from 60 to 65.	Applies only to women born after 4/26/50; phased in, 2010–2020
Years required for full pension		
France, 1993	Years required for full pension raised from 37.5 to 40.	Phased in, 1994–2003
Spain, 1996	Years required for full pension raised from 30 to 35.	
Provisions affecting replacement rates		
France, 1993	Reference period for calculation of pension changed from 10 best years to 25 best years.	1994
Germany, 1989	Period of training counted as labor market participation reduced from 13 years to 7.	1992

Table 5-6. *Selected Changes in Benefits and Eligibility for Old Age and Retirement Pensions in the OECD, 1987–97 (Continued)*

Country and year enacted	Description	Year effective
Germany, 1997	Replacement rate lowered from 70 to 64 percent for a worker with a full lifetime history of work.	2000 to 2030
Greece, 1990	Reference period for pensions changed from final two years of employment to final five years of employment.	1992
Spain, 1996	Pension benefits calculated based on latest 15 contribution years rather than last 8.	Phased in for persons born after 1933 from 1994 through 2008
Changes in early retirement provisions		
Australia, 1994	Mature Age Allowance introduced for unemployed persons over age 60 and under pensionable age.	1994
Denmark, 1991	"Transitional allowance" created to allow early retirement by 55 to 59-year-olds.	1992
Germany, 1989	Workers allowed to combine part-time work with partial pension in year prior to retirement.	
Germany, 1997	Early pension due to reduced earning power can be received only for health, not labor market, reasons.	2000
Quebec, 1997	Workers aged 55+ who reduce working hours allowed to draw on supplementary pensions and continue contributions to Quebec Pension Plan based on prior full salary if employer agrees.	1998
Delayed retirement provisions		
Australia, 1997	Workers who continue to work at least 25 hours per week up to 5 years beyond eligible age can receive lump sum payment upon retirement.	1998
Norway, 1990	Earnings restrictions on persons earning pensions eased.	1992
Norway	Basic and earnings-related pensions of persons aged 67–70 reduced 40 percent (rather than previous 50 percent) for earnings that carry income above pension "base amount."	1997

(continued)

Table 5-6. *Selected Changes in Benefits and Eligibility for Old Age and Retirement Pensions in the OECD, 1987–97 (Continued)*

Country and year enacted	Description	Year effective
Changes in means-testing provisions		
Canada, 1989	Universal Old Age Security pension benefit "clawback" introduced through income tax mechanism.	Phased in, 1989–1991
Denmark, 1993	Old-age pension means-test extended to all ages, not just those aged 67–70.	1994
Italy, 1988	Replacement rate credit lowered for earnings above a specified level.	1988
Italy, 1995	New minimum means-tested benefit created for Italian citizens aged 65 and older to operate in tandem with new contribution-based pension system.	1996
New Zealand, 1990	Income test for National Superannuation pension tightened by raising income tax surcharge and lowering income exemption.	1992
Norway	Retiree whose spouse is still working eligible only for 75 percent rather than 100 percent of base pension.	1997
United States, 1993	Up to 85 percent of Social Security benefits subject to income taxation for recipients whose income plus one-half of benefits exceed $US34,000 (single) and $US44,000 (couple); income thresholds not indexed.	1993
Changes in tax status of pensions		
Denmark, 1993.	Pensions and most other social benefits made taxable, with benefits generally raised at least enough to compensate.	1994
Caregiver provisions		
Germany, 1997	Caregiver credit for old-age pension increased to three years of average earnings for insured population, added to person's earnings up to contribution assessment ceiling.	Phased in, 1998–2000
Norway, 1990	Caregiver credit introduced for old age pension.	1992
Switzerland, 1994	Caregiver credit for old-age pension introduced at 70 percent of median full-time wage	1997

disregards or retirement tests are stringent. Delayed retirement can be encouraged in several ways (table 5-6), including easing of earnings disregards (Norway), increasing pensions actuarially for late retirees, or paying a lump sum that increases in size with the age of retirement to those who delay retirement (Australia).

—Cutting benefits to recipients with higher incomes and assets. Rather than limiting pensions solely to the very poor as a way to reduce funding requirements, policymakers have increasingly resorted in recent years to restrictions on payments to upper-income households. As John Myles and his collaborators have noted, the application of means- and assets-tests have generally been more direct in universal benefit programs (for example, Australia, Denmark, New Zealand) than in social insurance programs.[40] For example, Canada introduced a clawback on its universal Old Age Security universal pension in 1991 that eliminated benefits entirely for upper-income seniors (it does not affect contributory Canada Pension Plan pensions, however). The Canadian government also announced, but eventually abandoned, a plan to combine OAS and the means-tested Guaranteed Income Supplement into a single Senior's Benefit that would have further cut benefits to upper-income seniors.[41] In 1996 Finland began to phase out the universal base pension for recipients whose earnings-related pension is above specified levels.[42]

In contribution-financed social insurance programs, where recipients feel that they have earned their benefits, the normal pattern has been more one of imposing special surtaxes on or weakening prior-law tax exemption for pension benefits of upper-income households, without "clawing back" benefits entirely. Social Security legislation in the United States enacted in 1983, for example, subjected up to half of Social Security income to taxation for high-income households for the first time; 1993 legislation made a higher percentage (85 percent) taxable for those at higher income levels. In both the Canadian and U.S. cases, the percentage of pensioners affected by these tax provisions escalates over time because the clawback thresholds are not fully indexed for inflation.[43] Australia has chosen a somewhat different approach: in 1997 it enacted legislation that imposes a surcharge on the concessional tax treatment given to high-income superannuation contributors.[44]

—Increasing the earnings period over which initial benefits are calculated in defined-benefit contributory pension systems. Since most workers earn more

40. These programs are generally financed by general revenues rather than payroll contributions, but there are exceptions, as in Denmark. See Myles and Quadagno (1997, pp. 248–56); Myles and Pierson (1997).

41. See Shawn McCarthy, "Martin Backs off Seniors' Plan," *Globe and Mail*, Toronto, July 29, 1998; and Jeffrey Simpson, "Waving the White Flag," *Globe and Mail*, Toronto, August 5, 1998.

42. International Social Security Association (1996, p. 4).

43. The phase-in points for Social Security taxation are fixed in nominal terms, while the phase-in point for OAS clawback was partially indexed. Similarly, Australia in the late 1980s indexed the assets component of its means-test for the age pension, but not the income component. See Shaver (1991, p.116).

44. For a brief legislative description and history, see Australia (1997).

in real terms in their later earnings years than in their earlier ones, increasing the number of years over which earnings histories are calculated is likely to lower a pensioner's initial benefit. It also discourages payroll tax evasion, since years for which payroll taxes are not paid do not accrue pension benefits in contributory schemes. Many European countries have enacted legislation that increases the reference period for calculating pension benefits. For example, France in 1993 passed legislation that will, over a ten-year period, increase the reference period on which pension benefits are calculated to the best twenty-five years of earnings rather than the best fifteen years.[45]

—*Increasing caregiver credit.* Although general movement in pension policy has been toward retrenchment and a closer linkage of benefits to contributions, a number of countries have introduced or increased pension credits to caregivers (of children or aged parents) in recognition that those responsibilities lower the pension that a person is likely to receive upon retirement. In part, this may represent a trade-off for the increasing of women's retirement ages as they are harmonized with those of men.

Increasing Taxes

Governments may respond to pressure on their pension systems by increasing revenues (refinancing) as well as cutting back on pension eligibility and benefits. Although resistance to tax increases is formidable almost everywhere, tax increases to increase the solvency of pension funds have also been adopted in a number of countries in recent years (table 5-7). Several patterns are evident in these restructuring moves. First, increases in payroll taxes have been much less politically taboo in other countries than in the United States, even where those levels are already much higher than in the United States. Second, to make these taxes more palatable, they have sometimes been linked to new defined-contribution "tiers" of pension coverage that will be in individual accounts over which individuals will have more control and a stronger ownership claim. Examples include the adoption of mandatory occupational pensions in Australia and the proposed new tier of personal pensions in Sweden. Third, payroll taxes are increasingly being levied on employees as well as employers to increase their visibility. Finally, as payroll taxes rise to very high levels, several countries (for example, Germany) have increased general revenue financing of social insurance programs owing to employer resistance to higher payroll taxes.

45. Babeau (1997, p. 268).

Table 5-7. *Selected Changes to Contribution Rates and Tax Bases for Old Age and Retirement Pensions in the OECD, 1987–97*

Country and year enacted	Description	Year effective
Australia, 1992	Employers required to set aside 3–4 percent of payroll in payments into mandatory private pensions, rising to 9 percent of payroll.	Phased in, 1992–2002
Canada, 1997	Payroll tax increased in stages from 5.85 to 9.9 percent of payroll; shared equally by employers and employees; basic exemption amount below which payroll tax is not assessed frozen at $C3,500.	1997 (retro-active to beginning of year)
Finland	Employee contribution of 3 percent introduced for occupational pensions.	1993
Italy, 1995	Contribution increased from 27 percent to 32.7 percent of wages.	1996
Portugal	Employee contributions increase from 11 percent of salary to 24.5 percent for mandatory system and up to 32 percent for voluntary scheme.	Phased in over 5-year period

Modest and Uneven Movement toward Fundamental Restructuring

Moves toward fundamental restructuring of pension systems can be divided into two broad families. On the one hand, a few countries have tried to improve targeting of universal pension programs through their qualification and even elimination. An example is Canada's recently abandoned initiative to consolidate the Universal Old Age Security and means-tested Guaranteed Income Supplement into a single Seniors Benefit.

Far more important in terms of structural reforms, however, are a broad family of changes to contributory earnings-related pensions (table 5-8). Ranked in rough order from least radical to most radical (some of the options can, and have, been employed together):

—*Encouraging voluntary pensions.* Clearly the least radical reform, encouragement of voluntary private pensions, can take a variety of forms, ranging from lowering the regulatory barriers to pension fund operations to granting tax breaks for such contributions (as is done in the United States). A number of countries have moved to lower existing barriers to pension fund activity and to encourage them by granting favorable tax treatment. The French legislation of February 1997 follows this model; it also includes a requirement that the new

Table 5-8. *Selected Structural Changes in Old Age and Retirement Pensions in the OECD, 1987–97*

Country and year enacted	Description	Year effective
Measures to encourage voluntary pensions		
France, 1997	Statutory framework and tax concessions established for pension funds to be funded by voluntary contributions from employers and employees.	1997
Allowing public pension investment in equities		
Canada, 1997	Up to one quarter of future Canada Pension Plan fund accumulation to be invested in equities.	1998
Require mandatory contributions to private pension funds		
Australia, 1992	Australian Superannuation Guarantee requires contributions to occupationally based defined-contribution pension schemes.	1992

pension funds invest 35 percent of their value in stock shares as a way of encouraging investment in French companies.[46]

—*Advanced funding of pension liabilities in existing social insurance systems.* Widespread recognition of the inability of PAYG financing schemes to deal with demographic bulges like the retirement of the baby boom has led some countries (notably the United States and Canada) to move toward building up at least partial financing in their current public systems. This is politically very difficult in many European countries, however, where payroll taxes are already very high and further tax increases are seen as a potential barrier to job creation and a threat to competitiveness.[47]

—*Allowing investment of public funds in equities as well as government securities.* Critics of public pension funds have long criticized the below-market (in some cases actually negative) return assigned to accumulated pension funds by the governments that control them. One way around this is to allow those fund balances to be invested in the stock market. Historically, allowing such investments has provoked strong opposition among business interests, who fear that it will lead to increased government influence over corporate decisionmaking and even "backdoor" nationalizations. Many governments have in recent years nevertheless moved toward such investments. The Swedish "wage-earner funds" were pioneers in this regard, as was the

46. See "France: Retirement Savings Funds" (1997).
47. For a discussion, see Walrei and Zika (1997).

Quebec Pension Plan. The 1997 revisions of the Canada Pension Plan also call for partial investment in equities.[48]

—*Moving from defined-benefit to defined-contribution principles in a pay-as-you-go state pension.* One of the most important recent trends in European pension systems is a movement toward defined-contribution principles in the reform of existing PAYG programs. If fully implemented, these principles would make pension benefits, or at least retirees' initial benefits, entirely dependent on the "points" accumulated through contributions to a pension program for retirement. Thus rather than a fixed benefit, the benefit would vary based on factors such as changes in life expectancy for a cohort of retirees, changes in earnings, and other factors that affect contributions inflow into the system.[49] No country has moved fully to defined-contribution principles in their existing PAYG systems. But both the proposed Swedish pension reform and the 1997 German pension law will for the first time make future pension benefits partially dependent on increases in life expectancy. Any future increases in life expectancy will in the future result in slightly lower wage replacement rates at retirement. In Sweden, the initial retirement wage benefit will be based on an index of a person's wage-indexed contributions and the average life expectancy for a cohort at age 61, with those who retire later receiving a higher initial benefit.[50] The German law is based on life expectancy at age 65. Only half of any life expectancy increases will be reflected in replacement rate declines, and a replacement rate floor of 64 percent for a worker with a full wage history was placed on declines owing to the demographic factor. This floor is expected to be reached anyway under other reforms in the new pension law, but the demographic factor may allow it to be reached sooner.[51]

—*Allowing opt-out from state earnings-related pensions.* Some discussion of this reform has been advanced in the United States. It has been implemented only in Britain, however, where employees can choose between the state-run SERPS plan, personal pensions, and in many cases, occupational pensions.

—*Requiring mandatory employer or employee contributions to private pension funds.* These reforms have taken a number of forms. In Australia, for example, widespread occupational pension contributions were first achieved through labor negotiations in the 1980s and then mandated by legislation in 1992. The difficulty of moving to advanced funding in most European countries

48. For a general discussion, see Haanes-Olsen (1990). On Canada, see Banting and Boadway (1997).

49. See the discussion in Reynaud (1995).

50. See Smedmark (1994).

51. See Verband Deutscher Rentenversicherungsträger (1997).

is that payroll taxes are already so high that employers, employees, and economists resist making them higher.

Ironically, declining confidence in existing pension schemes may be making personal pensions on the British model a relatively easier sell: if taxpayers do not believe that they will be able to collect public pensions, they may be more willing to take an extra bite out of their earnings for increased assurance that those funds will at least be "theirs."

The overall (and unsurprising) conclusion to be drawn from this review is that incremental retrenchment and refinancing through higher payroll taxes have been much more common than dramatic restructuring. And even when restructuring has occurred, it has more frequently involved the addition of new tiers of pension provision than the elimination of old ones.

Modest Convergence

The combination of continued pressure from workers and retirees for security in retirement and pressures for retrenchment in public pension programs have led to a modest amount of convergence in the benefit structure of pension programs among the OECD countries.[52] Most countries now offer some combination of a basic minimum pension guarantee for those with weak earnings records and an earnings-related pension; mechanisms to claw back some of the pension benefits of high-income recipients are now increasingly common too.[53] But these policies are delivered through varying combinations of programs, and the enormous weight of past policy choices means that countries are unlikely to converge around a single model, be it social insurance, the three-tiered model suggested by the World Bank, or something else in the foreseeable future.

Similarly, substantial cross-national variations in the generosity of pension programs across countries are likely to remain in the future. Most OECD countries have made unsustainable commitments on pensions and are likely to cut back on those commitments. But some countries are likely to continue more generous pensions, and the rank order of countries in terms of pension generosity twenty years from now is likely to be very similar to the rank ordering today.

Is the United States an Outlier in Its Patterns of Change?

The United States is unusual in some of the characteristics of its programs, notably a weighted benefit formula that gives additional weight to the first dollars

---

52. See the argument in Overbye (1994).
53. For an exception, see Overbye (1994, p. 164).

of earnings in benefit calculations and the relatively early point in the demographic trough at which it began major retrenchment initiatives in 1977 and 1983.[54] Perhaps the characteristic that most makes the United States an outlier among the OECD countries in the past fifteen years, however, is the degree to which public pensions have not been on politicians' "action agenda." In countries like Germany and France, pension retrenchment initiatives have been commonplace. In Italy, they are becoming as much a part of everyday life as corruption scandals, cabinet crises, and scantily clad women on television game shows.

In contrast, the silence of both the House Republicans' 1994 Contract with America and the budget negotiations of 1995–97 on the subject of Social Security was absolutely deafening. The reasons for this silence are no great secret: it is a legacy of (1) the relatively favorable demographics of the 1990s, with the baby boom generation in its peak earning years creating a major inflow of funds into the OASI trust fund; (2) prior financing decisions—most notably in 1977 and 1983—that have created temporary surpluses in the OASI trust fund, removing an "action-forcing mechanism" for policy change; and (3) a political history in the early 1980s that caused most politicians to continue to see Social Security as the "third rail of American politics." Whether President Clinton's willingness to raise the issue in 1998 will be followed up by the political risk taking needed to lead to real action in the absence of an immediate funding crisis remains to be seen.

Politics as a Mediating Force in Pension Reform

The patterns of pension policy change observed in the last section of this paper are complex, not simple. Nevertheless, some broad themes emerge: the ubiquity of pension reform on governmental agendas, the predominance of incremental change over fundamental restructuring, and movement toward a tighter contribution-benefit linkage and advanced funding in some countries.

In the absence of comparable cross-national measures of change in pension programs, it is difficult to know how close the relationship is between the demographic, budgetary, competitive, and ideological pressures and the amount and timing of change experienced in individual countries. The similarities and differences in pension outcomes across countries cannot be explained completely by the four common pressures for change outlined earlier, even when taking into account differences in the strength of these pressures across countries. As John Myles argues convincingly in his discussion of

---

54. According to Simanis, only five countries used a weighted benefit formula as of 1993, down from nine in 1977. See Simanis (1994).

this paper, pension restructuring has sometimes been greatest in countries like the United Kingdom and Australia, where the budgetary and demographic challenges posed by an aging population are least dramatic and immediate. And as Myles further notes, major changes have frequently been pursued by Labor or Social Democratic governments as well as conservative ones.

Understanding the four great pressures for change can help to explain some of the general patterns we observed. Most notably, budgetary and demographic pressures help explain why pension reform is so frequently on governmental agendas across the OECD and why retrenchment initiatives appear most frequently and persistently on the agendas of countries that are experiencing pension funding crises. Competitive pressures are helpful to explain why raising payroll taxes (a form of refinancing) is not the sole, or even the preferred, solution to the pension funding problem. Conservative critiques help to explain why defined-contribution plans are at least on discussion agendas, if not governmental action agendas, throughout the OECD.

These pressures also contribute to understanding some national particularities. The long absence of an immediate demographic and budgetary crisis helps to explain the absence of Social Security from politicians' action agenda in the United States. And it is surely no accident that the most dramatic restructuring of an existing pension program—that of SERPS under Margaret Thatcher—occurred under a government with particularly uncompromising conservative beliefs. Overall, however, the four broad pressures for change in pension systems provide limited leverage in understanding both the general patterns or national particularities of pension reforms.

The reason that demographic, budgetary, competitive, and ideological pressures are limited in explaining pension reform in the industrialized world is that those pressures have encountered strong countervailing pressures. As Paul Pierson has noted, even if competitive forces do disadvantage countries with high social costs, that does not automatically lead to reductions in those programs; the policy changes adopted also depend on the political strength and bargaining leverage of forces resisting change.[55] Equally important, policy change is shaped by the desire of those in power to avoid paying the political consequences for making their constituents worse off.

The Blame-Avoiding Imperative

Pension reform politics share broad common characteristics and pose a common set of challenges for politicians in all countries: pressures to avoid or

---

55. Pierson (1996, pp. 149–50).

diffuse blame are strong, and the opportunities for claiming credit are limited. The central imperative of avoiding blame helps to explain many of the most common recurring patterns in pension retrenchment and refinancing, such as the delay and stretching out over long periods of increases in the retirement age, changes in pension replacement rates, and increased contribution rates, as well as highly technical changes in indexation formulas. The more obscure the changes and the longer the delay between when painful decisions are made and when they actually take effect, the better the chances that politicians will be able to avoid blame.[56] Similarly, blame-avoiding incentives help to explain the relative paucity of initiatives to delete existing tiers of pension programs outright: such steps, even where new programs are put in place, are likely to maximize nervousness among pensioners and provide a tremendous opportunity for blame generating by political opponents. Finally, blame-avoiding incentives may help to explain why retrenchment initiatives have frequently been targeted on the better off, both in countries with strong labor union movements and those, like the United States, where labor movements are relatively weak. As researchers on blame have frequently stressed, politicians attempt to offer justifications for their unpopular actions, and saying that painful but necessary retrenchment has been borne disproportionately by those most able to afford it is a justification that is likely to be viewed with sympathy.

The universal pressures for avoiding blame in democratic politics are not felt equally in all political systems, however. Instead, as shown in figure 5-1, they are interwoven with features of specific features of national political systems: policy feedbacks from existing program structures, political institutions, and the structure of political support coalitions. Of these three, policy feedbacks are particularly important. Together, these national contexts affect the types of retrenchment initiatives that are attempted, the strategies used to sell those initiatives and avoid blame, and the eventual timing and scope of pension reform.[57]

Policy Feedbacks

Perhaps the most important influence on prospects for pension retrenchment and restructuring initiatives is the heritage of past policy choices, what Pierson refers to as policy feedbacks.[58] The most important aspects of past policy are the structure and age of the current pension system in a country.

---

56. See Weaver (1985); Pierson (1994, chap. 2); Pierson (1997).

57. As Pierson puts it, "there is no simple 'politics of pensions.' Rather, each country faces the distinctive politics of distinctively constituted systems." Pierson (1997, p. 274).

58. See Pierson (1994).

When a pension system has been in place for many years, people develop expectations about the level of benefits that they should receive. These expectations are especially powerful in contributory systems, where a sense of "entitlement" to a given level of "earned benefits" is likely to arise, even if the ratio of benefits to past contributions is extremely high. Thus the prospects for pension retrenchment are likely to be greatest in "immature" contributory systems, where few people have begun to draw benefits, and political mobilization against retrenchment and restructuring initiatives is therefore likely to be relatively weak.

The same is true of pension restructuring: the weight of past programmatic choices makes it politically almost impossible for countries to start afresh with a dramatically different system of social provision and almost as hard to delete existing tiers of pensions. In the case of Canada's multitiered (universal, means-tested, earnings-related) system, for example, targeting inefficiencies in the universal Old Age Security program were long recognized. But simply abolishing it and relying on the contributory Canada Pension Plan was not an option. Because the CPP was originally designed as a supplement to the universal system rather than as a replacement for it, the replacement rate provided by the CPP is very low. That could be addressed by increasing benefits from and contributions to the CPP, but it once again would create a double payment problem—today's workers would have to pay increased contributions now for themselves plus the cost of the current pension system to current retirees.

The recent trend toward mandatory or near-universal privately managed occupational or personal pensions on defined-contribution principles also shows the effects of policy feedbacks. These plans have made the most headway in Australia and Denmark, countries that had not enacted public earnings-related pension systems before the 1990s.[59] The policy legacy of not having a public earnings-related pension tier appears to have had several effects. First, and most obviously, it created a pent-up demand for earnings-related pensions. Second, it led to the development of sizable occupational or personal pension sectors in those countries, which both made those options more familiar and gave those pension providers a stake in ensuring that they were not squeezed out by a subsequent public scheme. Third, it meant that mandatory private pensions appeared more viable when those countries were considering an earnings-related pension tier. Finally, budgetary and pension funding crises in many countries increased policymakers' awareness of the pitfalls of PAYG defined-benefit earnings-related pensions, making it less likely that this option would be chosen when an earnings-related pension tier was created.

59. On Denmark, see Overbye (1996).

The United Kingdom is an interesting intermediate case for showing the combined effects of timing and pension system structure and age on adoption of a privatized defined-contribution system. Britain's SERPS was not created until 1975 and was thus "immature" (that is, relatively few people were receiving a sizable SERPS pension at the time of the initial Thatcher reform of SERPS). Thus relatively few recipients had a strong stake in it, and the cost of buying off those who did was relatively affordable.[60] It is doubtful that the Thatcher and Major governments could have succeeded in their efforts to largely supplant Britain's SERPS with personal and occupational pensions enjoying government tax subsidies if that system had been in place longer.

A second and related major feature of existing policy structures that frames the politics of pension reform is the dominance of pay-as-you-go principles in pension finance in virtually all OECD countries. Once that principle has been established, it is extremely difficult to abandon PAYG.[61] This is especially true if the initial early generations of retirees in a pension system have been given far greater benefits than they contributed to the system, because it would require double payment by a later generation to move back to full funding. Indeed, Pierson has argued that "the likelihood of privatization declines in direct relation to the scope and maturity of a pay-as-you-go scheme."[62]

While PAYG certainly does constrain later policymaking, recent developments in countries like Australia, Sweden, Canada, and the United States show that a move to partial prefunding and even partial privatization is possible under several conditions, notably: when action is taken relatively early in a demographic downswing, as in Canada and the United States; when political and economic conditions provide leeway for additional payroll taxes, as in Canada and Sweden; and when an existing pension system provides very incomplete pension coverage, as in Australia. Frequently, as in Australia and Sweden, this partial prefunding and privatization involves creation of a new tier of pension coverage—which also helps to legitimate mobilization of new revenues.

A third critical feature of policy that affects the prospects for pension reform is the presence or absence and the nature of "action-forcing" mechanisms that compel policymakers to deal with funding problems. Usually these action-forcing mechanisms are imbedded in the programs: if a pension program relies exclusively on a dedicated revenue source (usually a payroll tax), pension reform will come to the top of politicians' agenda when fund outflow is about to exceed contributions inflow (or when accumulated funds are about to run out, in partially

60. On this point, see especially Pierson (1994, chap. 3).

61. See R. L. Brown, "The Future of the Canada/Quebec Pension Plans," Institute of Insurance and Pension Research, cited in Pierson (1997, p. 286).

62. Pierson (1997, p. 286).

funded systems). If, on the other hand, a pension program's governing statutes permit, or even require (as with most universal or means-tested pensions) general revenue financing, retrenchment and restructuring initiatives are likely to be delayed until a government faces a general budget crisis. But general action-forcing mechanisms such as the deficit targets for accession to the European Monetary Union can also accelerate attention to pension reform.

Indeed, the greater immediacy of pension reform on the agendas of many other OECD countries than in the United States does not reflect "American exceptionalism," but rather the fact that both in the U.S. and abroad, pension retrenchment, refinancing, and restructuring are more likely to be on a government's agenda when a crisis forces immediate response than when it does not. Many European countries face an immediate pension funding crisis; the United States does not.

A comparison of health care and pension sectors reinforces arguments about the importance of action-forcing mechanisms in mobilizing government to deal with exploding costs. In the United States, the Social Security funding crisis was addressed relatively early in the demographic downswing because of the trust fund crisis. The story is very different in the health care sector, where payments are fragmented among many payers, and a very large part of government's financing role is hidden because it takes the form of tax expenditures. Health care costs in the United States have spiraled out of control, and are far higher than in any other OECD country. The reason is that the governing structure of health care finance tends (with the exception of the trust fund for Medicare Part A) to disguise the dimensions of the crisis and discourage governmental action rather than to compel it.

A fourth important feature of programs that can affect the prospects for retrenchment is the rules that govern changes in program standards. If those standards can be changed by executive agencies alone, without requiring legislative action, the prospects for retrenchment are enhanced. Similarly, if negotiations require approval by "social partners" such as employers and trade union confederations, responses to pension funding problems are likely to be delayed. The same is true of changes that require the approval of supermajorities—for example, the requirement that seven Canadian provinces representing two-thirds of the population approve any changes to the Canada Pension Plan.[63]

Political Support Coalitions

The relative power of political support coalitions, especially labor unions and left political parties, has been widely recognized as an important factor

---

63. See, for example, Banting (1995).

influencing the way that welfare states develop. But as Pierson has noted, welfare state retrenchment is not the mirror image of welfare state expansion: levels of welfare retrenchment are not directly related to the decline in left political strength across countries, for example.[64] The reason is that pensions and other welfare state programs create their own constituencies with a stake in preserving the benefits.

Interests are organized in different ways, however. In a number of countries in Europe, centralized bargaining between employers and trade unions, with government as a concerned (and sometimes guiding) third partner, is an important feature of the policymaking process. Myles and Quadagno have suggested that because leaders of these "social partners" can reach binding agreements and allocate costs among their members, such arrangements may facilitate pension retrenchment and restructuring.[65] Recent evidence from Europe suggests little support for this argument, however. Reaching agreement, especially with trade unions, has proven extremely difficult. This should not be surprising, given the reluctance of any leaders who can be held accountable to collaborate in imposing visible losses on their rank-and-file. Even in Sweden, the quintessential organized society, reaching final agreements has been extremely slow since a tentative multiparty agreement was reached in 1994.[66] Even when agreements have been achieved, they have been protested in several countries (for example, France and Italy) by the rank-and-file, sometimes forcing renegotiation. In short, the existence of centralized bargaining mechanisms is likely to affect the process through which pension cutbacks are negotiated, but it is doubtful that their existence increases the capacity of government to achieve such cutbacks.

The power of the "gray lobby" does not appear to have the same strength in other countries that it has in the United States. Even in the United States, the power of the elderly lobbies is more negative than positive. There are many groups, with different perspectives, that claim to represent the interests of older Americans. Thus these groups are more successful at blocking changes from the status quo than at building a consensus on and winning enactment of policy change—especially if that change involves a redistribution of income among the elderly.[67] In countries where politics is more overtly class oriented, control over policymaking is more centralized in government, and centralized bargaining between employers and trade union confederations is common, "gray lobbies," even where they exist, have less leverage to make their distinctive voices

64. Pierson (1996, p. 150).
65. Myles and Quadagno (1997).
66. On the interparty disputes, see for example Tillberg (1998).
67. See Quadagno (1991).

heard as policy is being formulated. Instead, trade unions are likely to be perceived as legitimate representatives for wage earners present and past. And because party discipline is stronger—and interest groups are therefore less able to blame and punish politicians—elder interest groups have less leverage at the end of the legislative process as well.

Political Institutions

The literature on welfare state retrenchment suggests several arguments about how political institutions structure opportunities for retrenchment. Perhaps the most obvious argument is that systems that concentrate power in the executive, with few and relatively weak veto points where retrenchment initiatives can be blocked—single-chamber legislatures with cohesive, executive-dominated single party majorities and no requirement for a supermajority, for example—are more likely to enact pension retrenchment and restructuring initiatives than those that lack these institutions. But as Pierson and Weaver noted in their study of pension retrenchment in Canada, the United Kingdom, and the United States, this advantage of concentrated power is at least partially offset by concentration of accountability in political systems with strong electoral traditions. Voters know that it is the governing party that is imposing losses, and those in power know that they know it, and may therefore to be reluctant to undertake initiatives that are very likely to incur retribution at the next election.[68] Moreover, even governing parties with extraordinarily strong formal powers may face pressures not to use them to maximize their own preferences: the financial stakes in pensions are so high for employers, unions, pension providers, and others that they are likely to view stability and predictability over time as supremely important. Even pension policy changes that serve a group's short-term interests may not be desirable if they pose a high risk of reversal (with the attendant transition costs) by a later government.

The interaction of each of these effects is visible in the clearest case of fundamental restructuring of an OECD pension system that has occurred to date: the Thatcher government's marginalization of Britain's State Earnings-Related Pension Scheme (SERPS). Not surprisingly, this restructuring was enacted by a government that enjoyed strong formal powers, a clear majority in the House of Commons, and an exceptionally weak and divided Labor opposition. Even the Thatcher government was not omnipotent, however: it had to back away from its initial 1985 proposal to abolish SERPS entirely in the face of widespread criticism from its usual allies (employers and pension providers) and a

---

68. Pierson and Weaver (1993).

pledge from Labor Party leader Neil Kinnock to reverse the change when Labor came back into power.[69]

The real world rarely provides polar opposite cases to illustrate the impact of political institutions and conditions, but the attempted New Zealand super-annuation reform in 1997 is about as close to an opposite case to the Thatcher situation as one could imagine. Rather than a single-party majority govern-ment, the New Zealand reform was pushed by the junior partner (New Zealand First) in a National Party-New Zealand First coalition government formed after the 1996 election. The proposal was the result of neither an elec-toral mandate for the reform nor consensus within the coalition for the pro-posal. As a result, supporters of the reform turned to the referendum device—an extraordinarily risky mechanism when new taxes, the phasing out of a popular state pension program of long duration, and increased uncertainty over future pensions are all at stake. The National Party-New Zealand First coalition held a slim majority in Parliament and was widely perceived to be the result of a cynical bidding war between the National and Labor Parties for the support of New Zealand First, and thus was itself extraordinarily unpop-ular with, and little trusted by, the public. The government's superannuation reform proposal itself was publicly opposed by many senior cabinet ministers in the senior coalition partner (the National Party), including Jenny Shipley, who would oust Prime Minister Jim Bolger in a caucus coup shortly after the referendum. It was also opposed by major opposition parties, trade unions, and leading firms in the New Zealand pension industry. And finally, almost comically, a commission of experts appointed by the government reported near the beginning of the referendum campaign that the current tax-financed superannuation system was sustainable at least through 2015, weakening the sense of immediate crisis that helps to promote unpopular reforms.[70] Given this staggering array of unfavorable conditions for fundamental reform, it is no surprise that the "super" reform was crushingly rejected in the September referendum.

Neither the United Kingdom nor New Zealand situations are the norm in the industrialized world, of course. But fear of incurring blame for pension cuts or tax increases is clearly ubiquitous. Even Canada, which had a strong majority Liberal government after the 1993 election, delayed moving its reform of the Canada Pension Plan through Parliament until just after winning (barely) another majority in the summer 1997 general election, not wanting to inflame opposition in the run-up to that election. Moreover, it backed off entirely on the

69. See Pierson (1994, chap. 3).
70. Retirement Income Policies Periodic Report Group (1997).

planned restructuring of its quasi-universal pension tier, Old Age Security, when budget surpluses made cuts in OAS less viable politically.

Most OECD countries use some form of proportional representation and are therefore generally governed by multiparty coalitions or even minority governments. These governments have had to develop different mechanisms for avoiding blame. In Sweden, for example, pension reform has grown out of the 1994 recommendations of an all-party working group intended to shield any particular party or set of parties from blame (this device has been used in Sweden on a variety of policy conflicts).[71] The Riksdag endorsed the working group principles in the summer of 1994, but progress thereafter was agonizingly slow: detailed specifications were not released until the fall of 1997, with legislation finally enacted in the summer of 1998.

Italy's major pension reform in 1995 followed a different path. It was engineered by a technocratic government composed entirely of nonpoliticians and headed by Lamberto Dini that was therefore unconcerned about its future electoral prospects. The Dini government took office in an atmosphere of political and economic crisis after the collapse of the Berlusconi government in December 1994 and made pension reform one of its top four priorities. The new government put forward a severe package of pension cuts but made concessions to the trade unions in tripartite bargaining with unions and employers. It then pushed the deal through Parliament by using a parliamentary tactic that superseded 3,500 proposed amendments and repackaged the debate on legislative passage into three votes of confidence that neither the center-left coalition backing the Dini government nor Berlusconi's opposition, for their own strategic reasons, wanted the government to lose.[72]

The overall conclusion about the effect of political institutions on pension reform suggested by this discussion is that concentration of legislative power is an advantage for cutting or restructuring pensions, and multiple veto points and diffused power is a disadvantage. These effects are very contingent, however, on factors such as the proximity of elections and divisions among the political opposition. Moreover, systems with more diffuse power structures can and do develop alternative mechanisms such as all-party agreements and technocratic governments that allow them to come forward with politically painful pension reform initiatives and enact them. Political institutions, in short, have less effect on *whether* a government responds to a pension funding crisis than on how

71. Smedmark (1994, p. 75); see also Palme (1994).

72. On the 1995 Italian pension reform, see Reynaud and Hege (1996); Robert Graham, "Italy Untangles Its Pension Knot," *Financial Times*, May 10, 1995, p. 2, "Confidence Vote Called in Rome," *Financial Times*, July 13, 1995, p. 2, "Dini Wins Pension Confidence Vote," *Financial Times*, July 14, 1995, p. 3.

deep that crisis is likely to be before a response occurs, the content and severity of the reform initiative, and the degree to which compromises have to be
made to secure enactment of the initiative.

Foreign Lessons for the United States

International experience with pension reform suggests a number of lessons
that can inform debates in the United States. Perhaps the most important overall lesson is the importance of what can be called a "clarity-obfuscation" trade-
off for governments that seek to limit public pension commitments. Lowering
people's expectations of what they can expect from government in the future
requires sending strong, unambiguous signals to individuals so that they can
adjust their behavior. Workers must be made aware of the need to save for their
own retirement if they hope to have the same retirement standard of living as
their parents. If the signals sent by government are not clear and immediate,
when cutbacks do go into effect, individuals will not have changed their behavior to save more for their own retirement, will demand that the existing level of
pensions or other transfers be maintained, and will feel betrayed by government
and politicians, exacerbating already high levels of mistrust about the political
system.

The problem with sending clear signals to recipients and potential recipients
of government programs indicating the severity of proposed retrenchment initiatives, however, is that such signals arouse intense opposition, making it much
more difficult to actually get such initiatives adopted. The most successful pension retrenchment initiatives have taken place when cutbacks were made more
obscure or delayed into the future so that politicians could be at least partially
shielded from the affects of blame.[73] They are, in short, cases of what Canadian
social policy analyst Ken Battle has brilliantly labeled "social policy by
stealth."[74] In the absence of these "stealth retrenchment" mechanisms, retrenchment initiatives have often collapsed or been scaled back. No adequate solution
to this clarity-obfuscation trade-off has emerged.

A second lesson is that the repertoire of incremental pension retrenchment
possibilities is limited. Changes in indexation procedures, lengthening the
employment history base for calculation of initial benefits, increasing retirement ages, and other potential retrenchment initiatives are all well-known by
U.S. policymakers, and most of them have already been employed here—and
may be used again. But expecting any politically viable "magic bullets" to

73. See Pierson (1994); Weaver (1985); and Pierson and Weaver (1993).
74. Battle (1990).

come out of foreign experience is unrealistic. One of the few really new ideas to come out of foreign experience in recent years is the inclusion of defined-contribution principles such as "demographic factors" in initial benefit calculations. This mechanism lowers state pension fund liability for future increases in life expectancy and decreases uncertainty over that liability, but only by increasing uncertainty for pensioners. It is, however, probably more politically viable than making the retirement age itself dependent upon changes in life expectancy, as has sometimes been suggested in the United States, precisely because it is less visible than a change in the retirement age.

A third lesson about pension reform politics is that "generational politics"—political mobilization along generational lines—has been quite muted almost everywhere. Politicians and business leaders throughout the OECD have repeatedly justified pension retrenchment and restructuring as necessary to ensure that such systems are financially sustainable for and maintain the confidence of younger generations. But they have not tried to mobilize the young against the old; pension cutbacks are instead portrayed as a regrettable necessity. The reason is simple, as Hugh Heclo has noted: "Such a politics is likely to be a losing proposition for anyone who would attempt to engage in it, whatever the country."[75] Politicians generally "have a strong incentive to promise benefits and avoid a discussion of unpleasant trade-offs," especially when those who are on the losing side of the trade-off are more likely to remember and be mobilized politically by it than those on the winning side. And younger workers are unlikely to begrudge the payment of adequate pensions to their parents, since it lessens their fears that their parents will become dependent upon them. Outside the United States, and especially in countries where employers rather than employees "pay" payroll taxes, pension politics is more likely to be seen as a zero-sum game of classes than of generations.

A fourth set of lessons from international experience concerns increases in payroll taxes. Increased payroll taxes for Social Security have essentially been off the agenda in the United States since 1983. This has not been the case in other countries, even when conservative governments have been in power. But tax increases have frequently been linked to the creation of new tiers of benefits over which individuals at least theoretically have more control—for example, the creation of personal pensions in Sweden. This suggests two lessons for the United States. First, when a pension funding crisis is imminent—not twenty years in the future, as is currently the case in the United States—tax increases to fund at least part of that shortfall may appear more viable than they do at present. Second, an increase in payroll taxes for Social Security, with

75. Heclo (1988, p. 383).

all of the increase and part of the current payroll tax going into personal pension funds that can be invested in equities, may be a promising way to bridge the differences between advocates for the status quo and those who favor a more highly privatized pension system in the United States.[76]

A fifth lesson is that any effort to get people to retire at higher ages is likely to put increasing pressure on disability insurance systems. As workers are expected to work later in their lives, those with blue-collar jobs in particular will find it increasingly difficult, and may find it more advantageous to claim disability benefits. In fact, in Sweden "a phased increase in the pension age that was to have begun in 1994 was suspended when it was determined that the pension savings would be matched by increased unemployment and disability benefit costs."[77]

A final set of lessons from international experience concerns the use of mandatory private (that is, personal or occupational) pensions. Experience from the United Kingdom, Australia, and elsewhere suggests that such schemes can be an important element in dealing with problems of pension finance and pension politics. But they also suggest that mandatory private pensions have real problems and limitations.

A first limitation relates to the acceptability of mandatory private pensions: except in unusual circumstances, like those obtaining in the United Kingdom under Thatcher, they are more politically sellable as a supplement to rather than as a replacement for an existing pension tier. These pension schemes have generally been introduced where state earnings-related pensions were absent (Australia), immature (the United Kingdom), or had other problems (Sweden). This does not mean that they cannot over time take on a larger role, as the value of state pensions is eroded in a series of incremental cutbacks. But attempting to market them as a replacement for familiar, "guaranteed" public pensions is a recipe for political disaster. The 1997 New Zealand referendum is an important caution about what can happen when governments (especially weak ones) overreach in attempting to impose pension reform.

---

76. It must be recognized, however, that such a "compromise" could not occur in the United States without a major cutback in current "defined-benefit" program benefits. Among the plans considered by the 1994–96 Advisory Council on Social Security, for example, the Gramlich plan, which would maintain existing payroll taxes while adding an additional payroll tax devoted to individual accounts, would eventually cut basic Social Security benefits by about 32 percent for those with a high earnings history and 22 percent for those with a low earnings history. These benefits would be supplemented with income from individual accounts. See 1994–1996 Advisory Council on Social Security (1997, p. 62). The Personal Security Accounts option, which would reallocate almost half of current payroll taxes to individual accounts, would cut basic Social Security benefits even more dramatically.

77. Bolderson and Mabbett (1996, p. 11).

A second limitation is that the "window of opportunity" for moving toward addition of a mandatory private pension tier usually occurs in the years before a country begins to experience a major decline in its worker-to-retiree ratio. Once that slide begins, the experiences of countries like Germany, France, and Italy suggest that governments are likely to (in a mildly mixed metaphor) have their hands full putting fingers in the eroding dikes of an overwhelmed pension system, with little tax room left to create a new tier of substantial size.

Third, administrative costs in mandatory private pensions are increased by having multiple funds and by the advertising that fund managers do to get customers. The problems of the Chilean system have gained much attention of late: the pension funds employ 20,000 salespeople, 2 million people changed pension funds in 1995, and kickbacks to employees who change funds have become common.[78] Given the hard-sell tactics currently employed by telemarketers and mass-mail marketers of credit cards and competing long-distance phone companies in the United States, it is hard to imagine that such techniques would not be employed with regard to pensions, where the monetary stakes are vastly higher and the number of potential purveyors is at least as high. Unless such activities are regulated, it is not hard to imagine potential tie-ins—five thousand frequent flier miles on Trans-Global Airlines to switch to a new pension fund and an additional mile for every dollar you contribute to the new fund—that could induce fund churning and make it difficult for customers to calculate real returns on fund contributions.

A fourth, and even more serious, issue is the potential for misrepresentation and even fraud by fund managers seeking customers. In the United Kingdom, for example, up to 2 million people may have been misadvised by pension management companies in the late 1980s and early 1990s to take personal pensions rather than joining or remaining in occupational pension plans that offered more generous benefits. Compensating the victims of mis-selling may cost more than £2 billion ($3.4 billion).[79] The potential for lawsuits brought by disgruntled pension fund investors in a society as litigious as the United States is clearly enormous. The potential for a new program of personal pensions to be derailed or mismanaged by a Congress responding to the credit-claiming and

78. See Jonathan Friedland, "Chile's Celebrated Pension-Fund System Has Growing Pains as Returns Decline," *Wall Street Journal*, August 12, 1997, p. A10; Queisser (1995).

79. See, for example, Sinfield (1994, pp. 133–35); Christopher Brown-Humes, "Pensions Review Picks Out the Worst Offenders," *Financial Times*, July 10, 1997, p. 30; Charlotte Beugge, "Another 17 Firms Added to Pension List of Shame," *Evening Telegraph* (electronic edition), September 19, 1997; Alex Brummer, "Top Man from PRU Apologizes for Pension Scandal," *Guardian*, November 17, 1997; Rosemary Bennett, "U.K. Pensions Mis-selling to Cost 2.0 Billion," *Reuters Newswire*, November 18, 1997.

blame-generating incentives to redress scandals in such a program should not be underestimated.[80]

A fifth problem is that political battles are likely to emerge over who is allowed to provide personal pensions, under what conditions, and for what purposes. Securities firms, insurers, banks, and established pension providers will undoubtedly fight for such a huge market and try to hobble their competitors or exclude them from the market entirely. In Australia, for example, banks have fought to be allowed to offer Retirement Savings Accounts as part of the mandated superannuation system, while critics have charged that unwary investors who choose RSAs for security too early in their earnings years are likely to suffer a drastic deficiency in savings.[81] Similarly, the Australian housing industry has sought to allow superannuation fund members to make withdrawals for first-time home purchases—a move that would of course stimulate the housing market while cutting stock market investment.[82] Allowing access to retirement savings for education, housing, and other purposes would in many cases also lower the availability of savings for retirement income. In Europe, battles over the use of pension funds have focused on government restrictions on foreign investments by pension funds.[83] Parallel conflicts would almost certainly break out over use of mandatory pension funds if they were introduced in the United States.

A sixth issue relating to personal pensions is that the linkage of pension rights to related programs needs to be thought through very clearly. Even if private sector pension funds increasingly take over pension benefit provision, this does not necessarily mean that other functions, most notably survivor and disability benefits, should be transferred as well. If they are, then the task of ensuring availability of adequate information about alternatives, and about the conditions associated with alternative policies, is essential. In Australia, for example, concern has been raised that persons switching pension plan providers risk endangering disability coverage in the transition.[84] To minimize information costs and the potential for fraudulent claims by providers, it would probably be desirable to require all pension funds to adhere to at least a basic minimum package of disability and survivor benefits established by govern-

80. On congressional incentives to respond to social program scandals, see in particular Derthick (1990, chap. 8).

81. Tim Blue, "Super Law May Cost Retirees $0.5," *Australian* online; James Kirby, "Banks Chase Super League," *Australian*, March 12, 1997.

82. See Ian Henderson, "Super Would Aid Home Buyers," *Australian*, July 7, 1997.

83. See, for example, Andrew Hill, "More Funds in Prospect in Italian Pension Plan," *Financial Times*, April 7, 1995, p. 2.

84. Anne Lampe, "Expert Warns of Catch Over Employee's Insurance," *Sydney Morning Herald*, December 8, 1997.

ment. If these functions remain with government, new principles of contribution rates and benefits may have to be worked out.

A seventh issue associated with personal pensions is that they risk creating a new kind of political football for politicians. Getting pension fund management out of government's hands has long been justified in part by a fear that governments would use those funds for purposes that are politically convenient for the government but harmful to the fund's contributors—bailing out failing public enterprises, for example. But increased reliance on personal pensions with a heavy stake in stock equities may skew government decisions away from actions that impact unfavorably on firms weighing heavily in pension fund portfolios. In the United Kingdom, for example, politicians, pension fund managers, and corporate leaders have all used the claims that tax policy proposals they did not like would unfairly lower benefits or raise uncertainty for pensioners as a vehicle to block those proposals.[85]

Finally, it should be noted that defined-contribution plans are very likely to produce inadequate pensions for persons with low earnings over their lifetimes, or irregular work histories. Thus in any movement toward a contribution system, policymakers must determine how to "top up" pensions for this part of the elderly population. Italy, for example, created a new means-tested, state-financed minimum old-age allowance when its 1995 pension reform law moved toward a pension based more (at least in theory) on defined contributions.[86] Chile also "tops up" pensions for long-time (twenty years) contributors who are unable to accumulate enough funds to finance a minimum pension.[87]

None of these limitations or issues suggest that compulsory personal pension funds are unworkable as a second tier of public pension schemes. But it does suggest that much care must be devoted to resolving these issues before such a tier is put in place and that substantial regulation is likely to be required after they are put in place. Some sort of federal backstop role, as is currently performed by the Pension Benefit Guaranty Corporation for occupational pensions, would be required as well.

Conclusions

Overall, the pension reform experience of other OECD countries sounds themes that should be very familiar to U.S. readers: comprehensive reform is

85. See, for example, Michael White and Ewen McAskill, "Labour to Halve Windfall Tax," *Guardian*, March 19, 1997; Roger Cowe, "Pension Funds Fight Tax Changes," *Guardian*, May 16, 1997.
86. See Reynaud and Hege (1996).
87. See Queisser (1995).

much more difficult than incremental reform, especially when it imposes highly visible losses; overreaching can lead to political stalemate; windows of opportunity for reform can be fleeting and close quickly; in designing and reaching agreement on reforms, the devil is in the details.

These lessons suggest that conservatives in the United States who favor a radical change of Social Security in the direction of a privatized, defined-contribution system may face the same sorts of choices that President Clinton faced in making his health care reform proposals. The temptation is always strong to move as close to your preferred policy position as you can, and it may not be clear what the political limits on reform are. But if proponents of Social Security reform try to polarize debate along generational lines, overreach in their policy proposals, and fail to compromise on more limited reforms when they have a chance, they are likely to miss fleeting windows of opportunity for policy change. And as the experience of countries that are already experiencing dramatic drops in their ratio of workers to retirees suggests, fundamental reform is likely to get harder rather than easier as the United States moves into the twenty-first century.

Richard Disney, discussant

THE UNITED KINGDOM has reformed its pension program at frequent intervals: most recently in 1975, 1986, and 1993. And the process continues—the Blair administration proposed from its inception that welfare reform, including revision of the pension program, was high on its agenda. How, then, has the United Kingdom's program developed and why has pension reform remained high on the agenda for more than two decades when, as Kent Weaver points out, other countries have shown little interest in reform until their immediate crises of financing pension commitments have arisen?

The U.K. Pension Program: A Brief Overview

The United Kingdom has now gone a long way down the road to a largely privatized system of pension provision. As a rule of thumb, under the present system, three-quarters of pensioners in the United Kingdom will in the future receive three-quarters of their pensions from private sources.[88] The United Kingdom has a 'three pillar' scheme of pension provision very similar to that described by the World Bank.[89] It has a floor flat benefit provided by the state,

88. Disney (1998, pp. 157–67).
89. World Bank (1994).

financed on a pay-as-you-go basis from a payroll tax (the National Insurance contribution). It has a second tier of mandatory provision, which can be publicly provided (the State Earnings-Related Pension Scheme—SERPS) or privately provided—whether in the form of company-run defined-benefit or defined-contribution schemes, or in the form of an individual retirement savings account (known as an Approved Personal Pension). And it has a third voluntary tier of tax-relieved savings in retirement saving vehicles.[90]

A particular feature of the United Kingdom's pension program is the ability of private schemes to "opt out" of the second tier of the public program (SERPS). This opting out, known as "contracting out," takes two distinct forms in the scheme. By the procedure established in the 1975 legislation, employees and employers covered by company pension plans (called occupational pension schemes in the United Kingdom) pay a lower rate of National Insurance contribution to the state and in return are required to provide a pension benefit at retirement which, broadly, is at least as good as the forgone SERPS benefit. Since the generosity of projected SERPS benefits was cut back significantly in 1986 and 1993, this requirement to replace the state benefit has become less onerous over time. As a result, the projected size of the "contracted-out rebate" (the difference between the "full" and reduced rates of National Insurance contribution) will fall.

The second form of opting out applies to the individual Approved Personal Pension and was introduced in the 1986 legislation. Here not only is the contribution liability of the employee and employer reduced, but the contracted-out rebate is paid, by the Department of Social Security, directly into the Approved Personal Pension (APP) on behalf of the optant. Since 1996, this contracted-out rebate has been age related, being higher for older people. The rationale is that of compound interest: contributions put in by younger people will compound for longer, and thus a lower contribution will be required to finance a given benefit at retirement. However, the contracted-out rebate applied to occupational pensions of the defined benefit form is not age related, nor is it related to any other measure of scheme-specific financial requirements, such as the pensioner-contributor ratio.

Several consequences flow from this scheme of flat benefits plus contracting out. First, the returns to contracted-out status are almost always greater than remaining contracted-in to SERPS, especially since the cutbacks in projected SERPS benefits in 1986 and 1995. So this second tier of the pension program is now largely "privatized," with less than 20 percent of the eligible work force

90. For further description of the evolution of the program in recent years, see Dilnot and others (1994); Disney and Johnson (1998).

remaining in SERPS. Second, large interpersonal and interscheme subsidies to contracting out result in a trade-off between administrative simplicity and short-run public sector costs, in the sense of forgone contribution receipts. Third, individuals have almost complete freedom of choice within this tier; they can leave and rejoin SERPS, leave occupational schemes and start an APP, or vice versa (not always costlessly). Currently well over one hundred providers of APPs are offering different investment portfolios, structures of commission charges, payment structures, annuitization strategies, and so on.

The New Labor government is now signaling its intention to offer a further alternative: the "stakeholder pension," which is designed to be a low-cost, group-provided defined-contribution alternative. It is not clear whether this option is intended to tempt the remaining members of SERPS into the private sector (these people being largely those with interrupted career histories and low lifetime incomes) or as a long-run alternative to Personal Pensions. Nor is it clear whether the attraction of a "simple" low-cost alternative to the existing scheme outweighs the disadvantage of providing an extra alternative in what is an already overcomplex choice environment.

In the short run, this combination of contribution rebates and tax reliefs has raised the public cost of providing the remaining public pension program by encouraging contracting out. This rise in public sector costs has been offset somewhat by immediate cutbacks, such as the decision to index flat benefits in payment to prices rather than earnings. These cutbacks further reduce the long-term commitments of the public pension program. For example, the projected National Insurance contribution rate in 2030–31, when the baby boom generation is largely retired, is 17.5 percent of eligible payroll. This compares to a rate of 18.3 percent in 1994–95.[91] The United Kingdom faces no future financing crisis; instead some observers are concerned that the future "floor" benefit is too low to provide any sort of income replacement in retirement. Private pensions must deliver on promised benefits for adequate living standards to be retained during retirement. But this process also illustrates how a "double burden" of moving to a largely funded scheme can be achieved by the back door of incremental opting out rather than by a "big bang" reform of the Chilean model.

The Policy Process

How have these reforms come about in the United Kingdom? Here, Kent Weaver's trichotomy of policy feedbacks, political support coalitions, and political institutions offers a useful device for analyzing the policy constraints.

91. HMSO (1994).

POLICY FEEDBACKS. In terms of Weaver's "past heritage of policy choices," the United Kingdom differs from much of continental Europe, with the important exception of the Netherlands, in having had a robust scheme of private occupational pensions for many years prior to the introduction of state earnings-related pensions, albeit only covering a section of the work force.[92] The United Kingdom experimented with comprehensive earnings-related social security only for a short period of its history, from 1978 (when the 1975 act's main features were implemented) until, arguably, 1986, when SERPS was radically cut back and new private pension instruments were given contracted-out status. Thus limited public experience with state-provided earnings-related pensions produced little effective opposition to the severe cutbacks of SERPS in 1986 and 1995.

In contrast, the flat part of the state pension, the basic state retirement pension, is universally popular, partly because of the political resonance of its introduction as part of Beveridge's "welfare state" in the 1945–50 period. Even though the contribution of this component to retirement income is likely to be derisory in the future, any suspicion that the benefit may be means-tested, or replaced, is held to be an unacceptable strategy.[93] For example, the Conservative administration's ingenious proposal in the 1997 election campaign to introduce "Basic Pension Plus," which was intended to replace the pay-as-you-go state retirement pension by a fully funded defined-contribution statutory plan, *but introduced only for each new cohort entering the labor market*, was universally regarded as a political error because it cast doubt on the future (in fact many years hence) of the state pension. Thus Labor has so far been very careful in its attitude toward the basic benefit. Up to this time it has only leaked the possibility of "rebalancing" the basic pension in that its absolute level is (perhaps) raised while the benefit is tapered such that it is withdrawn at some rate from higher-income groups. To an economist, this apparent policy dichotomy by which income testing through the benefit system is "bad," whereas income testing through the tax system may be "good," even if the distributional impacts are similar, is a frustrating triumph of form over substance. But taxing back pensions as opposed to means testing benefits has important political implications in the United Kingdom, and indeed New Labor has spent

---

92. See Weaver's paper.

93. By an administrative quirk, the income-tested welfare payment, Income Support, is actually paid at a higher rate than the basic state pension for this age group. Thus for those past state pensionable age with no sources of private income, there will be entitlement to income-tested benefits in addition to the contributory insurance benefit.

much of its initial energy for welfare reform in replacing income-tested benefits by tax credits, especially for low-income working parents.

POLITICAL SUPPORT COALITIONS. Here, again, the decline of SERPS presents an illustration. The introduction of SERPS arose at the end of a long political battle between those who wanted a state pension scheme that would ultimately supplant private provision and those who wanted to extend private provision to a greater proportion of the work force.[94] In this debate, the existing private pension industry was an influential lobbyist not only against any change that would supersede its own involvement in pension provision, but also against statutory private provision, which might involve it in insuring the "bad risks" at a fixed contribution rate. The compromise reached in the 1975 legislation was essentially backward looking and gained little public support. Although Kent Weaver describes a coalition of interests against abolition of SERPS, the key opponent of full abolition of SERPS in 1985 was the Treasury, which correctly saw extended contracting out as having adverse short-run budgetary consequences, for the reasons described earlier.[95] This again illustrates the relative marginality of SERPS in public debate as to the nature of welfare reform.

One consequence of the range of private arrangements now available is that a variety of private interest groups are involved in pension provision. The interests of the occupational pension sector, usually represented by the National Association of Pension Funds, are by no means coincident with those of the providers of Personal Pensions, which are increasingly banks, the major insurance companies and even well-known "high street" names such as Virgin, and Marks and Spencer. It is not clear whether stakeholder pensions will be provided by an existing subset of providers, perhaps given privileged status by the government in exchange for agreement on low commission charges, or by new providers. At present, statements that these pensions, and the new individual saving accounts (ISAs) will be provided "across the counter" leave it unclear as to whether a greater variety of retail outlets will be invited to provide a product or whether the same counters will offer a different product. It is, in any event, unclear whether new providers with less experience of financial asset provision will in the long run be able to deliver benefits at lower cost, although more simplicity and uniformity of provision (for example, through more "no frills" packages marketed directly by telephone) seems likely. Since the debacle associated with the introduction of Personal Pensions, by which many individuals were persuaded to leave occupational pension schemes in order to join APPs,

94. Briefly described in Dilnot and others (1994); Disney and Johnson (1998).
95. Lawson (1992).

the industry has been noticeably more circumspect in its advertising of competing alternatives.[96] This may, however, reflect the changed marketing environment of the 1990s compared with that of the 1980s.[97]

The large private pension industry has not always been successful in resisting legislation, which was perceived to be against their interests. Despite New Labor insisting on its "new compact" with private industry, one of the first budgetary measures was to abolish a significant tax relief on the earnings of accrued pension funds. Some evidence also suggests that the present administration is interested in moving to a "level playing field," by which it reduces reliefs on assets with disproportionate tax relief, such as private pensions, and ratchets up tax reliefs on other assets, such as accounts held in banks. This seems to be the rationale behind the new proposal for individual savings accounts, which should thereby have positive distributional consequences, depending on behavioral reactions.[98] The reaction of elements of private industry will presumably in part depend on whether individual providers see themselves as entering the market for ISAs and other new, prospective, financial assets.

POLITICAL INSTITUTIONS. Institutional reasons may also explain why change in the United Kingdom has been more rapid and taken place at an earlier stage than in other countries. Although "first past the post" voting arrangements have contributed to large majorities for the governing party in 1983, 1987, and, most recently, 1997, these may not be the only factor. Workable majorities in the late 1960s and 1970s failed to generate successful changes in the pension regime. The 1975 act was passed by a government with a rather small majority. In some cases, "sea change" political victories, as in 1945, 1959, 1979, and 1997, put the elected leadership in an unassailable position. In other cases, sheer will power has played a part, as in Margaret Thatcher's famous conviction that SERPS should be abolished, even though other senior ministers were openly skeptical, pointing out the short-run costs and the fact that the problem would not emerge for many years. New Labor has also emphasized, with almost crusading vigor, that "welfare reform" is high on its agenda, even though it is far from clear what such a process would involve, especially in the pension sector, where much change has taken place in the last few

96. But Kent Weaver's figure that "up to 2 million" APP optants may have been adversely affected is almost certainly too high, not least because individuals often have inflated views of what their occupational pension plan will deliver. See Disney and Whitehouse (1996).

97. Lunt and Disney (1997).

98. For further discussion, see Banks, Dilnot, and Tanner (1997).

99. The overt reason for the concern with welfare reform is the "rising cost of welfare expenditures in the U.K." Quite apart from the fact that social security costs are generally lower in the

years.[99] Much of the dynamic here arises from the tension between the Treasury, which is overtly hostile to any measures that may increase public spending, and the well-articulated ideas on welfare reform, perhaps short on detail, of the minister for welfare reform.[100]

Of more importance in the U.K. context may be the nature of the political process and the reduced scope for major financing crises in Social Security because a coalition can block measures to, say, increase contributions or redistribute welfare resources. Changes in National Insurance contribution rates, and the value of the contracted-out rebate, for example, are based on the recommendations of the Government Actuary concerning the projected balance of expenditure and income of the (notional) National Insurance Fund. Incremental increases in contribution rates need not be attached to budgetary or fiscal measures or passed as explicit legislative measures unless they reach a "trigger" rate increase. Some of these changes, such as the shift to age-related contracted-out rebates, elicited very little debate. Compare this with the equivalent result were the United States to switch from, say, a flat to an earnings-related payroll tax, or vice versa!

Conclusion

The U.K. reform process has delivered an affordable pension scheme, with a transition to largely private funding without great political outcry. The same process has created distributional concerns for those with little private provision, and the scheme of contracting out is overcomplex, largely because the contracted-out rebate which was designed for one task (to relieve contracted-out occupational schemes from paying for SERPS) has been adapted to a second task (as the basic contribution to a system of individual savings accounts). Although the current New Labor government has promised a further radical rethink of pension provision, a defensible case could be made that what is needed is some retuning and simplifying of the scheme rather than yet another drastic restructuring of provision.

The ease by which the transition to a largely funded, privatized, system took place arises in large part because the United Kingdom had little experience of

---

United Kingdom than in other comparable countries, as illustrated in table 5-2 of Kent Weaver's paper, it is interesting to note that social security spending, as a share of GDP, has actually fallen in every year since 1993–94 in the United Kingdom, from 13.6 percent in 1993–94 to 12.4 percent in 1997–98 (I am grateful to my colleagues at the Institute for Fiscal Studies for providing this information).

100. Contained in Field (1997). Frank Field resigned as minister for welfare reform in July 1998, citing differences with Treasury ministers on the direction of welfare reform as his motive.

Table 5-9. *Aging, Work, and Social Expenditures, Seventeen OECD Countries*

Region	*1* Population 65+ 1990	*2* Normal ret. age M/F 1992	*3* Empl/pop. Men 55–64 1995	*4* Pension exp. % GDP 1995	*5* Proj. pension exp. % GDP 2040	*6* Increase (5/4) 1995–2040	*7* Significant reform 1980–97
Nordic countries							
Sweden	17.8	65/65	64.4	11.8	14.9	1.26	Pending
Norway	16.3	67/67	70.0	5.2	11.8	2.27	No
Denmark	15.4	67/67	63.2	6.8	11.6	1.71	Yes
Finland	13.3	65/65	34.9	10.1	18.0	1.78	Yes
Mean	15.7	66/66	58.1	8.5	14.1	1.66	
Continental Europe							
Germany	14.9	65/65*	47.2	11.1	18.4	1.66	Yes
Austria	15.1	65/60	40.8	8.8	14.9	1.69	Pending
Belgium	15.0	65/60	34.5	10.4	15.0	1.44	Yes
Netherlands	13.2	65/65	39.9	6.0	12.1	2.02	No
France	13.8	60/60	38.4	10.6	14.3	1.35	Yes
Italy	14.8	60/55*	42.3	13.3	21.4	1.61	Yes
Mean	14.5	63/61	40.5	10.0	16.0	1.60	
Anglo-Saxon							
Canada	11.3	65/65	54.0	5.2	9.1	1.75	Pending
Ireland	11.4	66/66	59.1	4.1	2.9	0.71	No
United Kingdom	15.7	65/60	56.1	4.5	5.0	1.11	Yes
United States	12.6	65/65	63.6	4.1	7.1	1.73	Yes
Australia	10.7	65/60	55.2	2.6	4.3	1.65	Yes
New Zealand	11.1	61/61	63.0	5.9	9.4	1.59	Yes
Mean	12.1	65/63	58.5	4.4	6.3	1.43	
Japan	11.9	60/58	80.8	6.6	14.9	2.26	Yes

Sources: Population, retirement age, pension expenditures from Organization for Economic Cooperation and Development (1997a); employment/population ratio from OECD (1997b).

publicly provided earnings-related pension schemes. The 1975–86 period is the "experiment" in the United Kingdom, not the period since, and that period of less than a decade provided little time for SERPS to enter public consciousness. Undoubtedly institutional factors were also at work: the existing strength of the private pension lobby (although bifurcated between occupational pension schemes and the new Personal Pension providers), the "first past the post" system of voting, the possibility of "strong" governments enacting reforms, and the institutional procedures that allow quite major changes in, for example, contribution levels, to pass Parliament without debate. But adopting too mechanistic a link between institutions and processes on the one hand and the evolution of reform on the other is dangerous. Politicians may make major interventions, as in Margaret Thatcher's crusade against SERPS, and these may be fallible and counterproductive, as in the Conservative proposals on pension reform before the 1997 election. History has its fair share of accidents, and personal idiosyncrasies, which explain the evolution of welfare systems.

John Myles, discussant

THE POSTWAR EXPANSION of old-age security systems in the developed capitalist democracies was more or less complete by the mid-1970s. Almost from the moment of maturation, however, discussions began over the looming "pension crisis." The intensity, timing, and rhetoric of these discussions varied significantly from country to country. But already by the mid-1980s, the first serious efforts to reform national pension systems and resolve the "crisis" were under way. Cross-nationally, the reform movement gained momentum in the late 1980s and then grew exponentially in the 1990s (see table 5-9, col. 7). It is still under way today with no end in sight. In many countries last year's reforms are superseded by new reforms even before the former can be implemented. What accounts for this near-universal rush to reform? The question is particularly intriguing since the real pension crunch is several decades away. It is unusual for politicians to make painful decisions that will mainly benefit policymakers sometime in the next generation, long after the current leaders are dead.

Kent Weaver suggests four intertwined pressures behind the current wave of reforms: demography, budgetary pressures, concerns about competitiveness, and a resurgence of conservative ideology. Clearly, all of these factors have played a role. It is difficult, however, to explain the timing, extent, or type of reform as simple linear extrapolations of these pressures.

In the United States and the United Kingdom, pension reform has been associated with a resurgent conservatism in political life. However, reform initiatives are as likely to come from the left as from the right. Moreover, in the majority of capitalist democracies (continental Europe, the Nordic countries), the consent of organized labor has usually (though not always) been a necessary if not sufficient condition for pension reform. The reasons are several. First, unlike Canada, the United States, or the United Kingdom, where organized labor is just one "interest" group among many, in the majority of countries organized labor is an "encompassing institution" that represents virtually all employees. In most continental European and some Nordic countries the role of labor is further reinforced by the fact that the pension system is designed on corporatist principles, administered by representatives of labor and employers (the "social partners" as they are called in Europe).

A striking feature of reform is that it seems unrelated to either current or projected levels of expenditure on old-age benefits (table 5-9, cols. 4 and 5). The countries of continental Europe face the highest levels of spending now and in the future because of generous pension schemes and very high rates of early retirement by those under 65 (table 5-9, col. 3). In contrast, the quite modest current and projected expenditures in the Anglo-Saxon countries make one wonder why these countries are bothering with their pension systems at all. Despite these differences, one hears virtually the same rhetoric of "crisis" and "unsustainability" whether one travels to high-spending Italy or low-spending Australia.[101] And, by 1997, the majority of OECD countries had gone through at least one significant effort to redesign their old-age security systems.

The reason why spending *levels* appear to have little to do with reform is highlighted in column 6 of table 5-9: what strikes fear into the hearts of treasury officials is the projected *rate of growth* of old-age expenditures, which on average is projected to rise to about 160 percent of 1995 levels by the year 2040. And the reason this rate of growth is troublesome ("unsustainable" in the jargon of treasury officials around the world) is less true because of the amounts involved than because of the financing mechanism used to provide these amounts. To push the argument a bit, one could say that it is not population aging that is the problem; rather, it is the design of the typical old-age security system that *makes* population aging a problem.

The problem can be stated as follows. The large pay-as-you-go defined-benefit schemes that developed in Western Europe and North America in the postwar decades are financed by governments with a tax on only part of national income, namely, labor market earnings. And in most schemes, this tax

101. When one of the authors pointed out to a senior official in Australia's Department of Social Security that even the most dire projection for Australia's old-age security budget left the country spending only about 4.5 percent of GDP, less than a third of what Italy spends today, he was told, "That won't cut any ice here."

is imposed on only part of the total wage bill, the bottom half or two-thirds of the earnings distribution. As a consequence, virtually all of the increase in expenditures that results from rising pension expenditures must, in this design, be financed by raising payroll taxes, which in turn drives down the relative wages of the workers affected. Small wonder, then, that unions worry as well as treasury officials.

The need for raising revenues and the pension dilemma facing policymakers has a demographic component and a wage component. The demographic component is the changing ratio of wage earners to retirees, which is declining. The wage component is slow growth in average real wages, which most policymakers assume will continue into the future.

The problem is usually framed by comparing implicit "rates of return" in a pay-as-you-go scheme to those in a fully capitalized scheme financed out of returns on investments. The return in a funded model depends on long-term rates of return to capital (real interest rates). The implicit "rate of return" in schemes financed from a payroll tax is the annual percentage growth in total real wages and salaries (returns to labor). Total real-wage growth is a function of the growth in the average wage multiplied by the growth in the number of wage earners. The latter is in turn a function of population growth and the rate of labor force participation.

Quite simply, then, the financial viability of old-age pensions financed from payroll taxes depends on high wage growth, high fertility, and rising rates of labor force participation. Given the values of these parameters in the 1960s most "sensible" treasury officials would have advised their ministers to opt for a pay-as-you-go design.[102] By the 1990s everything had changed. Numbers produced by the Canadian Department of Finance illustrate the turnaround (table 5-10).

Clearly by the end of the 1980s a "sensible" treasury official would be advising her minister that the model put in place in the 1960s was in difficulty. Irrespective of whether projected expenditures represent 5 percent or 25 percent of GDP, the parameters that made the pay-as-you-go design the model of choice in the 1960s—rising wage rates, full employment, and comparatively high fertility—had changed dramatically.

In fact, all cases of major pension system *expansion* since 1980 have been financed on a funded basis whereby returns depend on real interest rates. By the beginning of the 1980s, five countries did not have a large earnings-related pay-as-you-go scheme in place: Australia, Denmark, Ireland, the Netherlands, and New Zealand. All five had a "basic security" system of universal flat benefits in

102. The reasons for a historical bias in favor of a pay-as-you-go design are numerous and complex. The point is that during the years of expansion, from the 1950s to the 1970s, there were also sound financial reasons for this "bias."

Table 5-10. *Real Growth in Total Wages and Salaries and*
Real Interest Rates, Canada, 1960s–90s

Real growth in	1960–69	1970–79	1980–89	1990–94
Total wages and salaries	5.1	4.8	2.1	0.0
Real interest rates	2.4	3.6	6.3	4.6

Source: Canada (1996).

place, but none had a second tier of earnings-related benefits. And in three of the five countries pension politics during the 1980s and 1990s was a politics of expansion, not retrenchment. By the mid-1990s Australia, Denmark, and the Netherlands had evolved a system of universal or quasi-universal contributory employer pensions. And in all three cases the driving force behind the changes was organized labor, not a resurgent neoconservatism.

In each case, however, the design of the new systems avoided the pension dilemma faced by governments elsewhere. In none of these countries do future governments face an obligation of raising payroll taxes to finance guaranteed benefits for future retirees. All three systems are capitalized so that future revenues depend on "returns to capital" rather than "returns to labor." Australia and Denmark have adopted a defined-contribution model so that future benefit changes can be "blamed on" (or credited to) markets rather than governments. In the Netherlands, where a defined-benefit design prevails, responsibility for meeting future obligations lies with employers, not the government.

A sketch of these changes and their implications is presented in an appendix to this paper. Briefly, mandated employer pensions in Australia were the result of a wage accord between the unions and the Labor government in the mid-1980s. The unions agreed to wage restraint in exchange for the pension mandate. Governments were not directly part of the Dutch or Danish expansion because such involvement was unnecessary. Although only 26 percent of Dutch workers are union members, state regulation of the labor market (extension laws) ensures that all benefits negotiated at the bargaining table are extended to nonunion workers and to nonunion firms. In 1980, 60 percent of Dutch workers were covered. By the 1990s, this figure was somewhere between 82 percent and 95 percent of the labor force depending on the source. In Denmark, where the vast majority of employees are unionized, labor went on a pension offensive in the late 1980s with the result that coverage rose from about 35 percent in 1986 to more than 80 percent of the labor force by 1997.

In varying degrees, each of these "latecomers" has evolved a pension design that approximates the model of choice for an aging society advocated by the

World Bank.[103] Governments provide a first tier of "basic security" financed from general revenue and aimed at poverty prevention. Expenditures on this first tier are expected to decline as the second tier matures. Second-tier pensions are fully capitalized, and in Australia and Denmark benefits are determined on a defined-contribution basis, reflecting contributions plus investment returns. Unlike the Chilean model second-tier pensions for the majority are organized on a collective (industrywide) basis rather than on an individual one (personal retirement accounts). Nevertheless, as Fritz von Nordheim Neilsen observes, Denmark has become one of the "darlings" of the World Bank.[104]

The point to emphasize is that in all three countries governments bear no direct responsibility for meeting future pension obligations; rather their role is that of mediator and regulator. They avoid the "blame avoidance" problem identified by Weaver.

What is the likelihood of other nations converging on a similar design? Assuming, as the World Bank contends, such a design represents "best practice" for nations facing an "aging crisis," neoclassical economic theory would lead us to anticipate that convergence is highly probable if not inevitable. Quite simply, in the neoclassical world of negative feedback and declining returns, countries that fail to adopt "best practice" will be uncompetitive in a globalized economy, and will be punished in the international marketplace. No matter how difficult, most countries will attempt to at least approximate such a design.

Like Weaver, I am skeptical about such an outcome. The United Kingdom has made the jump to this model but as Weaver points out, the State Earnings-Related Pension Scheme, implemented in 1978, was not yet mature so that the transition costs of making the change to a mandatory defined-contribution model were comparatively small. As Weaver notes, patterns of reform elsewhere will be shaped by pre-existing program design, policy feedback, and the political coalitions built into the existing design of welfare states. Moreover, Weaver's concept of "blame avoidance" provides a powerful analytical tool for understanding recent reforms. Let me illustrate with a few examples.[105]

The Impact of Program Design: The Politics of "Means Testing"

A readily available moral framework for adjusting to "hard times" is the principle of need. The costs of restructuring should be borne by those most able to afford it, and the weaker members of society should be protected.

---

103. World Bank (1994).
104. Von Nordheim Neilsen (1998).
105. For additional detail see Myles and Quadagno (1997) and Myles and Pierson (1997).

Benefits for high-income seniors should be reduced and the savings used to achieve a number of desirable social goals: cut deficits, raise investment, and improve benefits for low-income groups, whether old or young.

A needs-based rhetoric provides both a justification and a model for pension reform. Cuts will be made by reducing or eliminating benefits for high-income families. Both the Concord Coalition in the United States and the Conservative Party in Canada have used the imagery of benefits going to "wealthy bankers" in their symbolic struggles to implement income testing for old-age pensions. Income testing has been successfully introduced in Canada, but the comparative evidence suggests the proposals of the Concord Coalition and others like it will continue to be unsuccessful in the United States.[106]

The reason is not to be found in politics or spending levels but in programmatic differences in the design of their old-age security systems. Like a handful of other countries in the postwar years, Canada created a first tier of universal flat benefits for which the sole qualifying conditions were citizenship and residency. All of these countries, except Norway, have introduced some form of targeting for these benefits since 1980.[107] Indeed by 1996 the "citizenship" model of the traditional sort was virtually dead. In 1997, the New Zealand government removed the income tests established in the late 1980s and early 1990s, but observers expect this change to be temporary. In contrast, no country has adopted a targeting strategy with respect to benefits for which individuals qualify on the basis of contributions and to which pseudoproperty rights attach as a result.

The Politics of Blame Avoidance:
From Defined Benefits to Defined Contributions

The model of choice of the World Bank to meet the income security needs of retirees is a mandatory, funded defined-contribution plan. For the reasons discussed by Weaver, making the change to a funded design is extremely difficult for the majority of mature pay-as-you-go schemes and the economic benefits of doing so are uncertain. An alternative strategy is to redesign benefit for-

106. A number of countries, including the United States, have begun taxing benefits that were not taxed in the past. An income test such as that introduced in Canada, however, goes further and effectively imposes a "supertax" on social income, that is, a rate of taxation higher than that imposed on other forms of income.

107. Canada and New Zealand adopted an income test. After a brief period of providing universal flat benefits to the elderly, Australia returned to means testing (that is, a test of assets as well as income) in the 1980s. Finland adopted a "pension test" (benefits are tested on the basis of income from public pensions but not other income), and pending legislation in Sweden includes a similar reform. Somewhat less dramatically Denmark adopted an earnings test.

mulas of current pay-as-you-go schemes to emulate the performance of a funded defined-contribution model. Adopting the language of cyberspace, Robert Artoni and Alberto Zanardi describe such a model as "virtually fully-funded."[108] Both the Italian reform of 1995 and the 1994 Swedish reform proposals are usually described in these terms.

The major feature of both the Italian and Swedish reforms is much stricter proportionality between lifetime contributions and expected lifetime benefits. Contributions are assigned an imputed rate of return based on economic growth, and they are "annuitized," on the basis of the expected longevity of the retiring cohort. For Italy and Sweden, these changes are indeed quite dramatic. The reason is that, unlike the defined-benefit plans typical of most countries, the Italian and Swedish plans were final earnings plans, and maximum benefits were calculated on the basis of relatively short contributory periods. In the traditional Swedish formula, benefits were estimated on the basis of the best fifteen years of earnings and a maximum contribution period of thirty years. This had the result of redistributing benefits from workers with many years of employment with high earnings to workers with fewer years of employment at high earnings (for example, women).

Italian benefits were based on the last five years for private sector workers and the last year for public sector workers. Moreover, one could apply for a retirement pension (the seniority pension) after thirty-five years of contribution in the private sector but after only twenty years for employees in the state sector irrespective of age. This produced what is known in Italy as "baby pensioners," employees who retire in their early fifties or even in their forties (and then often go on to other employment). In the new design, benefits will be calculated on total lifetime contributions, and Italy will phase out seniority pensions. Other countries (France, Finland) with final or best earnings formulas have similarly taken steps to lengthen the period on which benefits are based.

At first glance, such changes represent a dramatic transformation in the distributive logic of the income security system in these countries. The aim of the old design was simply that of wage replacement for retired workers with rather limited attention to the proportionality between contributions and benefits. In

---

108. Artoni and Zanardi (1997, p. 253). A pay-as-you-go defined-contribution model has long been the basis for France's compulsory second-tier pension systems (AGIRC, ARRCO). Individuals acquire pension points based on their contributions, and the value of each point is determined only when the entitlement is due based on current and expected contributions. Subsequently, the point's value is reevaluated annually. Plan administrators (in this case the social partners, not the government) then face the problem of keeping finances in balance by deciding whether to raise contributions or to reduce benefits. The difference between this design and the more familiar capitalized version is that whether benefits are allowed to decline as revenues fall or contribution rates are increased is determined by politics rather than the market.

the new model "workers" are being transformed into "savers." Such a conclusion would be misleading, however, or at least premature. Simultaneous with such changes, Italy, Sweden, and a number of other countries are adding or enriching (redistributive) pension credits for periods of maternity, child rearing, and unemployment. The aim of all this, as Emmanuel Reynaud points out, is to make the redistributive role of old-age pension systems increasingly transparent, to introduce a clear division between the contributory and "solidaristic" (redistributive) elements of the welfare state.[109] But why? And, in particular, why would labor embrace such a strategy?

A recent analysis of the Toledo Pact of 1995 negotiated by the Spanish government and the labor unions, which is intended to set the basis for the reform of the Spanish pension system, suggests the answer.[110] The aim of the Spanish unions was to introduce a clear division of financial responsibility between contributors (workers), on the one hand, and the "state" on the other. Payroll contributions will be used to finance "earned" benefits, while the state will finance the redistributive elements of the system from general revenue. For labor, some of the upward pressure on payroll taxes is relieved. For the government, the problem of "blame avoidance" will be limited to future changes in the redistributive elements of the old age budget. This may be an intriguing idea for American policymakers to pursue.

A second important feature of these changes also fits nicely into Weaver's thesis of "blame avoidance." Many of the new design features are intended to make the system "self-equilibrating" by introducing adjustment mechanisms that will stabilize the relation between contributions and benefits without a requirement for new legislation.[111] Thus, indexing benefits to expected cohort longevity makes changes in the normal retirement age into a technical feature of the system rather than requiring a political decision. In a similar spirit, the German reforms of 1992 introduced several automatic-stabilizing mechanisms. When the pension reserves fall below one month of expenditures, contribution rates are raised automatically. Simultaneously, however, benefits are reduced since they are now indexed to net rather than to gross wages and higher payroll taxes reduce net wages.

This strategy is the mirror image of that introduced during the era of expansion when automatic indexing of benefits was adopted to keep benefits in line with price increases so that adjustment was a technocratic rather than a political exercise. In short, in the spirit of "blame avoidance" pension reform is being depoliticized.

109. Reynaud (1997a, p. 11).
110. Tuchszirer and Vincent (1997).
111. Reynaud (1997b).

Conclusion

In recent debates over the future of old-age security, the fear is often expressed that the accomplishments of the past are about to be dismantled, leading to the impoverishment of the elderly. Such an outcome may occur, but it is not what the current debate over old-age security is about, at least not in the first instance. If the share of the elderly population doubles in the next thirty years, then a safe prediction is that their share of national income will also double. The issue confronting most nations is not one of per capita shares but rather about the "delivery system." What is the best way to "deliver" the elderly their per capita shares? Through Social Security? Occupational pensions? Personal savings? Intra-family transfers? Through the labor market? And in what mix?

Will pension systems in various countries converge toward a single model? As Weaver has argued, the answer is "probably not." The policy instruments put in place in the past impose strong constraints on what is politically feasible today. He concludes, correctly in my view, that "the rank order of countries in terms of pension generosity twenty years from now is very likely to be similar to the rank ordering today."

Appendix: Pension Expansion in Australia, Denmark, and the Netherlands

Australia: Until the 1980s, the Australian elderly had access to only a modest flat rate benefit financed from general revenue.[112] For most of its history, the "age pension" had been subject to a test of both income and assets (means testing). During the 1970s, the means test was gradually eliminated, in part a result of electoral victory by the Australian Labor Party in 1972, their first of the postwar era. By the mid-1980s, however, both income and assets tests had been restored. Means testing, Australian style, however, has always been rather different from that found in other countries. It is designed to exclude the "rich" rather than to confine benefits to the "poor." In 1986, for example, 75 percent of couples and 91 percent of single females were receiving benefits.[113] Nonetheless, the majority of Australians were without the earnings-related second-tier benefits familiar to workers in most other countries. In the mid-1970s organized labor began pressing for a national superannuation scheme along the lines of private sector schemes available to civil servants, employees in the financial sector, and senior management.

112. This summary relies extensively on Bateman and Piggot (1993) and Piggot (1997). For a fuller account see Olsberg (1997).
113. Shaver (1995, p. 18).

The first step in this direction was taken in 1986 when the unions and the labor government reached their second major wage accord. An agreement was reached to increase compensation by 6 percent to keep pace with inflation, but half of the increase would take the form of a 3 percent employer superannuation contribution to be paid into an individual account in an industry fund. Between 1987 and 1991, superannuation coverage increased from 32 percent to 68 percent of the work force. This was a classic instance of labor agreeing to wage restraint in exchange for a higher retirement wage, the same phenomenon that drove pension reform in many European countries in the late 1960s and early 1970s. The key difference was that employer contributions were being directed into fully funded, defined-contribution plans under the joint control of unions and employers on an industrywide basis. This arrangement gives labor unprecedented control over a major and growing source of Australian capital.

The absence of complete coverage led to pressure to make superannuating mandatory. This was accomplished with legislation in 1992 through the Superannuation Guarantee Charge. A 9 percent employer contribution is being phased in over the period to 2002, which is to be combined with a 3 percent employee contribution. By August 1995, coverage of full-time workers stood at 90 percent and coverage of part-time workers at 70 percent (up from 8 percent in 1984). The 1995–96 Labor budget also proposed to supplement the 3 percent employee contribution with a matching 3 percent contribution from the government. This decision was reversed by the National-Liberal coalition government in favor of increased tax incentives for individuals to contribute to personal retirement accounts.

The late emergence of mandatory funded, defined-contribution pensions gets current and future Australian governments "off the hook" of the pension dilemma being faced elsewhere in a double sense. First, because no promises have been made about future benefits (they are to be determined by contributions and rates of return on investments), the problem of "blame avoidance" should future revenues fail to meet expectations is bypassed altogether. It will be the "market" rather than future "governments" that will be responsible for future benefit levels. Second, as these plans begin to mature in the next century, demand for the means-tested age pension is expected to decline, thus generating downward pressure on the tax revenues required for its financing. This is not to say that "pension politics" will not emerge as the Australian population ages. Rather the politics will be dramatically different.

Denmark: In the postwar years, Denmark followed the Scandinavian model of developing universal flat rate benefits but not in creating a large second tier of earnings-related pensions.[114] Moreover, coverage under employment-based plans negotiated with employers remained extremely modest. By 1986 only 35 percent of wage earners were covered.[115] In the mid-1980s, providing adequate pensions for the majority of its members without coverage became a central objective of the Danish Federation of Trade Unions (the Landsorganisationen, or LO). Rather than follow the Swedish-Norwegian route of a pay-as-you-go defined-benefit scheme, however, the LO presented a proposal in 1985 for the implementation of mandatory occupational pensions that would be fully funded, defined-contribution plans and, as in Australia, bargained in exchange for lower wage increases.[116] Political debate over the form and type of supplementary schemes continued through the 1980s. Finally, in frustration, the metal workers broke ranks with the LO and negotiated their own settlement in 1991. Other unions soon followed suit. By 1993, 70 percent of Danish workers were covered and by 1997 more than 80 percent. In 1995 a government study concluded that mandating further coverage was unnecessary. Virtually all Danish workers are covered because almost all Danish workers are unionized.

Like Australia, Denmark will enter the next century with comparatively limited government obligations to finance the income needs of the elderly in part because the maturation of these plans will drive down the demand for income-tested supplements in the public schemes. Moreover, future conflicts over pension benefits will be between the social partners.

The Netherlands: The General Old Age Act (AOW) legislated in 1957 created a first-tier, flat rate benefit financed from payroll contributions.[117] Second-tier earnings-related pensions have been provided mainly in the form of funded industrywide schemes providing defined benefits negotiated by employers and unions. In 1980 approximately 60 percent of the labor force was covered by these plans. During the 1980s and 1990s coverage expanded dramatically so that, like Denmark, coverage is now virtually universal. Estimates of current coverage levels vary somewhat. Lei Delsen reports that 82 percent of employees between the ages of 24 and 64 are covered, and Erik Lutjens says that 95 percent of the Dutch working population participates in a supplementary pension scheme.[118]

Unlike Denmark, where high rates of coverage can be explained by high rates of unionization, the mechanism of expansion in the Netherlands would

114. This discussion relies on Hippe and Pedersen (1996) and Overbye (1995).
115. Hippe and Pedersen (1996).
116. Von Nordheim Nielsen (1991).
117. This discussion relies on Delsen (1996), Lutjens (1997) and Blomsma and Jansweijer (1997).
118. Delsen (1996); Lutjens (1997).

appear to be Dutch "extension laws" by virtue of which all employers in an industry are required to extend benefits to all employees irrespective of whether they are union members or not. Thus the government's decision not to make supplementary pensions mandatory in 1991 was no doubt because existing extension laws made such mandating redundant.[119] As Delsen writes, "A separate law makes participation compulsory in the branch pension fund for all businesses. A company can opt out only if it establishes a company scheme with a level of provision that exceeds that of the branch funds."[120]

Though financed on a funded basis, most industry schemes are defined-benefit plans. As a result, future pension conflicts will depend on whether returns on investments are large enough to pay for the benefits that have been promised. Such conflicts, however, will be between the employers and the unions with government's role restricted to that of mediator and regulator. Moreover, through pension integration (second-tier defined benefits must take account of the flat-rate universal benefit) and by allowing the relative value of the AOW to decline, government has effectively transferred a growing share of the pension burden to employer plans.

Winfried Schmähl, discussant

LIKE MANY OTHER countries, Germany is facing several challenges to its Social Security system, particularly regarding pensions and the long-term care of the elderly.[121] Many of the causes of this stress are well known to other industrialized countries. These factors include demographic aging (which is relatively pronounced in Germany), the changing structure of private households, and intensified international competition, particularly as formerly socialist countries have been integrated into international markets. Some challenges are more specific to Germany: these include Germany's relatively high unemployment rate and the economic consequences of German reunification. While coping with these problems, Germany must also shape its Social Security policies to meet the Maastricht convergence and other fiscal policy standards required of all members of the European Monetary Union.

Before discussing strategies and measures to cope with these challenges, some basic information on the structure of old-age protection arrangements in Germany is set forth in the following pages. Here I emphasize the central role of social pension insurance in German old-age security.

119. Blomsma and Jansweijer (1997, p. 240).
120. Delsen (1996, p. 118).
121. In 1995 state-provided long-term care insurance was introduced in Germany; see Schmähl and Rothgang (1996) and Rothgang (1997).

The Present Structure of Old-Age Protection in Germany

Figure 5-2 gives a comprehensive picture of the different forms of old-age protection in Germany. The core of the system is the statutory pension scheme (social insurance) for blue- and white-collar workers, a mandatory scheme. This is the most important component of old-age security. Supplementary occupational pension schemes in the private and public sector form a second tier, while the third tier consists of all types of private saving for old age. The policy and political debate has focused mainly on the social pension insurance. Especially since 1997, the pension scheme for civil servants (which is included in the public budget) has also received public attention.[122]

Table 5-11 gives some information on the quantitative importance of the different pension schemes. It shows the overwhelming importance of the state's social pension insurance system, which pays nearly 70 percent of all expenditures for old-age security in Germany. Expenditures for social pension insurance alone are nearly 10 percent of GNP. More than 80 percent of the West German population is covered by this pension scheme; in East Germany the percentage is even higher.[123] For most retired people social insurance pensions are by far the most important source of income in old age.

The First 100 Years of Germany's Social Insurance Pension Scheme

The origins of the present social insurance pension scheme date from the late nineteenth century, when the chancellor of the newly founded German Reich, Otto von Bismarck, succeeded in creating an additional branch of social insurance for disability and old age. The program was financed mainly by contributions from employers and employees. However, the program also relied on substantial grants from the central public budget (which were also reflected in the pension formula). This arrangement contrasts with the financing of German accident and health insurance, which was not supported by any tax revenues.

122. A dominant feature of Germany's public pension scheme is that pensions are calculated according to the worker's former earnings over his or her lifetime. But the basic public pension scheme takes into account the worker's earnings during his entire "earnings career," while civil servants' pensions are tied to their salary in the last year of work. Both of these schemes also provide disability insurance and benefits to a surviving spouse.

123. In East Germany, private sector occupational pensions as well as life insurance expenditure have been too small to be relevant. Therefore, state-provided pension insurance in East Germany is even more important as an element of old-age protection than it is in West Germany. In the former socialist German Democratic Republic social insurance covered nearly the whole population with some special schemes for certain groups like the military. After the German unification, schemes for special groups of the population (according to the structure of pension arrangements in West Germany, see figure 5-2) were introduced step by step, and the number of people of these groups (like self-employed, civil servants) has increased quite slowly over time.

Figure 5-2. *Types of Old-Age Pension Schemes for Various Groups of the Population in the Federal Republic of Germany*

Type of old-age security	Total working population in the							
	Private sector							Public sector
	Self-employed					Employees		Civil servants[c]
	Agriculture	Professions	Crafts	Artists	Others	Blue- and white-collar workers		
						Mining-industry	Others	
First tier (base)	Old age pension scheme for farmers[a]	Pension schemes of professional associations[b]	Craftmen's insurance (included in statutory insurance)	Artist's social insurance	Compulsory or voluntary membership	Miners pension insurance (part of statutory insurance)	Pension insurance for other blue- and white-collar workers	Civil servants' pension scheme
			Statutory (old-age) pension insurance					
Second tier (supplementary)						Occupational pensions (about 50 per cent of all employees) (voluntary)	Public sector schemes (for all employees) (collective agreement)	
Third tier (additional)	Private old-age pension provisions (life insurance, savings, and so on)							

a. Partly including family workers. This scheme is designed as partial old-age security besides income from the former farm.
b. Partly also for employees of the restrictive branches, with the possibility to contract out of the statutory pension scheme.
c. Civil servants, judges, soldiers.

Table 5-11. *Expenditures of Institutions for Old-Age Security in Germany, 1995*

Item	Billion DM	Percent of the social budget	Referring to GDP (percent)	Percent of the total old-age security
Functional classification of social budget[a]				
Old age	423.938	35.9	12.3	...
Surviving dependents	20.073	1.8	0.5	...
Invalidity	77.897	6.6	2.3	...
Total	521.908	44.3	15.1	...
Institutional classification				
Statutory pension insurance	361.121	30.6	10.4	69.0
Civil servants' pension	55.967	4.7	1.6	10.7
Farmers' pension	6.213	0.5	0.2	1.2
Self-employed pension	2.590	0.2	0.1	0.5
Occupational pension (private sector)	24.080	2.0	0.7	4.6
Occupational pension (public sector)	13.592	1.2	0.4	2.6
Private life insurance (including direct insurance as old-age occupational pension)[b]	60.273	...	1.7	11.5
	0.740	...	...	...
Total old-age security[c]	523.096	...	15.1	00.0

Sources: Breier (1995, p. 136). Private life insurance: Information of Gesamtverband der Deutschen Versicherungswirtschaft (November 5, 1997).

a. Without private life insurance.
b. Not included in social budget.
c. Without double payment direct insurance.

Ever since Bismarck's program, pension insurance in Germany has been based not only on the idea of *insurance*—that is, intertemporal redistribution and risk pooling—but also, through reliance on general tax revenues, on *interpersonal redistribution*. Social pension insurance in Germany is a mix of different strategies for designing a public pension scheme. Although the organizational structure created in the founding period of German social insurance has survived intact to the present day,[124] the precise mix of different elements—

124. For example, there are different regional agencies for blue-collar workers, while there is one central agency for white-collar workers, which was established in 1911. Owing to changes in the structure of employment, there are fewer and fewer blue-collar workers. As the proportion of blue-collar workers in the German economy has declined, innovations to achieve fiscal equaliza-

namely, equivalence and intertemporal redistribution on the one hand, and interpersonal redistribution over the life cycle on the other—was and remains a major topic of discussion.[125]

Bismarck's original idea, however, was quite different from what was ultimately established in 1889: he originally proposed a *tax-financed flat rate pension*, a system in which workers would be treated as "state pensioners."[126] This idea has survived as a serious alternative to earnings-related pension insurance. Thus from Bismarck's era to today, whenever major reforms in pension insurance have become necessary because of changing economic, demographic, or social conditions, a tax-financed flat-rate pension has been discussed in Germany.[127]

Not just the form of payment and source of funds but also the method of financing—pay-as-you-go (PAYG) versus funding—was discussed intensively in the late nineteenth century, taking into account, for example, their differing effects on individual and national saving. Although public pension insurance in Germany originally in principle was based on full funding, over time funding became more and more of a fiction because of inflation, wars, economic crises, and the use of accumulated funds for purposes other than pension financing.[128] But notwithstanding the shift to PAYG financing, PAYG versus funding remains a topic of discussion, one which has been especially prominent in recent public and academic debates in Germany.

In 1957 a major reform in post-war Germany took place with the introduction of the so-called *dynamic pension*. The dynamic pension linked pension calculation as well as pension adjustment to the development of gross wages.

---

tion across different types of employment became necessary, because financing as well as pension calculation was identical for both groups of insured employees. The fact that blue-collar pension agencies have fewer and fewer "clients" has prompted the states (Länder) to demand a reorganization of pension agencies by strengthening the agencies on the regional level and cutting down the central agency on the federal level. The existing organizational structure is a remarkable example of path dependency.

125. This is also linked to the level of social protection in old age: Those who favor a public pension scheme aiming (only) at avoiding poverty in old age, quite often propose a design of the scheme that is dominated by interpersonal redistributive effects. However, in principle a poverty-avoiding minimum pension can also be based on equivalence and intertemporal redistribution. This was proposed, for example, in the well-known *Beveridge Report* of 1942 in England. A flat-rate contribution that results in a flat-rate pension is highly regressive during the period of contribution payment and politically difficult to implement.

126. For the history of the creation of social insurance in Germany (compared with England), see Ritter (1983).

127. An overview of this discussion is given in Schmähl (1993a).

128. Mörschel (1990) describes these developments over time.

And in an important change driven by economic considerations, the method of financing was also shifted toward PAYG. Only a limited reserve, covering pension expenditures for one year, was required. This reserve requirement was reduced in 1969 to three months and finally in 1992 to only one month. The proposal to switch to PAYG financing in the 1950s was based mainly on the argument that because the program was a mandatory scheme and because the state could always raise taxes to pay for the program, large reserves were not required.

In addition, some economists argued that all current social (especially pension) expenditures should have to be covered by current national product and therefore from a macroeconomic point of view no important difference between funding and pay-as-you-go financing exists.[129] In the German debate this argument was important for a long time. However, this argument focuses on a closed economy and relies on pure cross-sectional reasoning, neglecting longitudinal aspects and effects.[130]

The 1957 pension reform was also remarkable from a political point of view:

—The reform was enacted just prior to elections for the German Federal Parliament (Bundestag) and became an important factor in the election campaign, having considerable influence on its results. Pension policy has remained an important political topic ever since, especially during election periods.

—The major political parties tried to find a political consensus on major aspects of the pension reform. This attempt remained relevant in the years that followed. However, the current political environment is characterized by a breakdown of political consensus, at least concerning many of the major elements of pension policy.

The discussion of the future development of the pension scheme dates from the 1960s, when discussion began to focus on the aging of the population. To cope with the expected financing problems, a proposal was considered to accumulate reserves by increasing the contribution rate to a level above what was needed to balance the current budget. The idea was to use these reserves later to avoid a subsequent steep increase in contribution rates. The metaphor of

129. This argument was especially advocated by the German economist and sociologist Gerhard Mackenroth. However, Mackenroth's argument, for which he was given credit in public debate on the controversy, had already been published—word for word—years earlier, during the Nazi period. Mackenroth never indicated that he was quoting others in his work; see Schmähl (1981).

130. Not only the history of this argument, but also its limitations are discussed in Schmähl (1981).

"digging a tunnel into the pension mountain" was frequently used to illustrate this attempt to avoid large shortfalls in the future.[131] However, not only was any increase in reserves rejected but the politics of the 1960s instead produced a *reduction* in reserve requirements.

The early 1970s, before the first oil price crisis, were characterized by forecasts of huge surpluses in the state pension scheme, based on optimistic projections for future economic growth. Accordingly, competition developed among the political parties proposing alternatives for increasing pension expenditures. The reforms were enacted just before the 1972 parliamentary elections. An emblematic change wrought by this legislation was the introduction of an option that allowed workers to retire at age 63 instead of 65, without any offsetting actuarial deduction from their pensions.[132] However, a few years later the oil crisis shocked the economy and several ad hoc measures were taken to reduce pension expenditures.[133]

The 1992 Pension Reform

Demographic scenarios showing dramatic changes in the age structure of the population led to an agreement on November 9, 1989 (the same day the Berlin Wall was opened) to reform the state pension scheme. Most elements of this Pension Reform Act were to be implemented in 1992, and for this reason the agreement became known as the 1992 Pension Reform. At the time of the 1989 agreement, the scope of the reform measures was limited to West Germany alone.[134] No one expected the imminent unification of Germany, which meant that reforms would apply to East Germany as well as West Germany.

After a series of ad hoc interventions stretching back for approximately the previous fifteen years, the 1989 agreement was designed to establish again a set of clear rules, to introduce a self-regulating mechanism to stabilize the pension scheme's finances, and to reduce the burden on future workers. The other major objective was to maintain an appropriate level of pension support relative to an individual's earnings.

131. The focus therefore was not mainly on additional saving, investment, and economic growth, but rather on intertemporal aspects of sharing the "burden" between generations.

132. Under the new system, retiring at age 63 was allowed if the worker had made contributions for thirty-five years or more. This new regulation became relevant in fact only for men, because even before this change, women and the unemployed (subject to several requirements) were allowed to retire at age 60 without any reduction in their full pension. Handicapped persons were also allowed to retire early. See Jacobs and Schmähl (1989).

133. The political process for German pension policy from 1975 to 1989 (and the 1992 Pension Reform, discussed in the next section) is described and analyzed in Nullmeier and Rüb (1993).

134. For a detailed discussion see Schmähl (1993b).

A closer examination of some of the basic elements of the German pension system helps put the 1992 pension reform into context and also illuminates subsequent changes made to the system in 1996 and 1997. As I mentioned earlier, social pension insurance in Germany is, like general social insurance, a mix of a pure insurance scheme (aiming ex ante at intertemporal redistribution plus risk pooling) and a tax-transfer scheme (aiming at interpersonal redistribution, also over the life cycle). The "insurance approach" predominates in Germany, resulting in a (relatively) close link between individual contributions and future benefits. However, this basic scheme is modified by rules that have some redistributive effect: for example, years spent in school, during illness, as well as during parental leaves, and periods of unemployment are all counted as years of insurance and result in a crediting of pension claims.[135] The levels and methods of funding such redistributional aspects of pension policy have for many years been a major political topic in Germany, and the 1992 pension reforms, as well as changes made in 1997, have produced larger transfers from general revenues to pay for social pension insurance.

Specifically, the German public pension scheme is earnings-related because
—Each individual's pension is calculated based on the worker's historical earnings (compared with the nationwide average earnings) for each single year of his working career.

—The *absolute* amount of the individual's pension at time of retirement is based on the national average gross earnings for all workers, calculated just prior to the individual's retirement.

—The amount of an individual's pension during retirement fluctuates with average national earnings.

These principles can be stated in mathematical terms: the individual's gross earnings (W) are compared year by year to the average national gross earnings for all employees (W^a) for that year. This ratio is the individual's pension points (or earnings points, EP) for that year: $W/W^a = EP$ for a given year of work.

If, for example, individual gross earnings are equal to average gross earnings in one year, the result is one EP for that year. When claiming the pension, an individual's EPs for all years are taken into account (including EPs credited according to special rules connected to child care, schooling, or unemployment).

To calculate an individual's pension benefit, the sum of the person's EPs over his or her working life are multiplied by a conversion factor known as ARW (the value in DM for one EP in year t), which is tied to growth in average

135. There is no general minimum pension in Germany. To avoid poverty in old age a means-tested social assistance exists. But less than 2 percent of all pensioners claim additional social assistance.

earnings: total $EPs \times ARW$ = the individual's pension in DM in a given year. As the formula suggests, ARW is the dynamic factor of the German pension system, because it changes year by year depending on the growth in average earnings.

The calculation of ARW was changed in an important way by the 1992 Pension Reform. From 1957 until the 1992 reform, ARW had been calculated based on growth in average gross earnings, but beginning in 1992 the formula was changed so that ARW reflects changes in average net earnings. (Net earnings is defined as gross earnings, minus the income tax on earnings, minus the employee's contributions to statutory pension insurance, health insurance, and unemployment insurance.)

Annual changes in ARW affect the pensions not only of persons retiring in the current year but also of everyone else receiving a pension. In this way, the pensions of everyone in the system fluctuate with ARW, and all retirees with the same number of EPs receive the same size pension in any given year, regardless of when they retired.

As noted earlier, the German pension scheme has allowed individuals to retire at 63, but an early retirement decision did not greatly affect the calculation of annual benefits, even though early retirement will produce benefits for a greater number of years. This creates an obvious incentive to retire early.[136] Accordingly, since the introduction of the "flexible retirement age" in 1972, male labor force participation rates have dropped dramatically: today approximately 20 percent of 63-year-old men work, compared with 67 percent in 1972. Although incentives in the pension scheme are not the only reason for this development, they clearly were a major factor influencing this trend. The lower retirement age for pensions also affected expectations in the population about when it is appropriate to retire.

One of the goals of the 1992 Reform Act was to postpone retirement. After a long controversial discussion, some pension reductions were planned to be phased in beginning in the year 2001, over the next ten years for those retiring before age 65. Age 62 was made the earliest retirement age for all participants in the pension scheme, male and female alike. However, the reduction for retiring early was set below an actuarially fair rate, with a rate of 3.6 percent in the

---

136. The pension is reduced only to the extent that the number of years of contributions (and therefore EPs) is lower. Retirement age, however, is not identical with exit from the labor force for older workers. There exist several other possibilities to end official gainful employment without claiming an old-age pension, namely a disability pension (the number of disability pensions is to a certain degree also linked to labor market conditions) and several preretirement agreements. A detailed discussion of existing possibilities as well as of the changes included in the 1992 Reform Act is given in Schmähl (1992b) and in Schmähl and others (1995).

annual pension for every year of retirement prior to age 65. Disability pensions, however, were not burdened by any early-retirement penalty. (It became clear that the rules for claiming disability pensions would have to be changed in the future, to prevent disability pensions from becoming a loophole for early retirement.)[137]

Another element of the 1992 reform package was a new formula designed to stabilize the amount of federal grants to the pension system at about 20 percent of pension expenditure. This change in the computation of the federal grant, in combination with the change in the *ARW* factor (converting earnings points into actual pensions based on growth in average net earnings), has formed a self-regulating mechanism for the pension insurance scheme.[138] This has been important politically as well as economically: since 1992 no parliamentary decision about the pension adjustment rate or the federal contribution rate has been necessary. Changes are made automatically by the government based on clearly defined statistical data produced by the Federal Statistical Office.

This self-regulating mechanism is based on two cornerstones:

—A minimum reserve equal to one month's pension expenditure has to be maintained. If for the coming year it can be expected that the reserve would fall below the reserve equal to one month's pension expenditure, the contribution rate will be increased to meet the reserve requirement (the contribution rate will be lowered, if the reserve is expected to exceed the requirement).

—A politically decided link between present wages and individual pensions exists: for example, for a so-called standard pension with forty-five earnings points the pension is set at about 70 percent of present average net earnings of all employees.[139] Because pension adjustment rates are linked to the increase of average net earnings, the individual net pension relative to average net earnings remains constant over time.

Taken together, these elements produce a mathematical relationship between the minimum reserve requirement, the contribution rate, and the pension adjust-

137. Another new element was the introduction of a partial pension. This option, which involves a phased retirement, has not been a success, mainly owing to unfavorable labor market conditions as well as other possibilities (pathways) to leave the labor force early. Only a negligible number of pensioners claimed such a partial pension. It is possible to claim either one-third, one-half, or two-thirds of the pension and supplement earnings from part-time employment. Viebrok (1997) analyzes in a very differentiated manner the labor supply effects of the German social security scheme, theoretically (taking into account the institutional arrangements) as well as simulating effects based on a dynamic programming approach.

138. For a more detailed analysis see Schmähl (1993a).

139. For employees with lower pension claims, this percentage is lower and vice versa. For example, for a pension based on 40 earnings points the target pension level is 40/45 times 0.7, or 62.2 percent, instead of 70 percent.

ment rate. For example, if for the coming year, projections show that the minimum reserve requirement is not going to be fulfilled, then the workers' contribution rate is automatically increased. This means not only higher contribution revenue but also higher payments from the federal public budget, because federal payments are linked beside earnings development also to the development of the contribution rate. The higher contribution rate lowers the increase of the average net wage, and, according to the adjustment formula, lowers the pension adjustment rate (which is linked to the growth in net wages) and therefore lowers the increase of pension expenditure as well.[140]

The 1992 Pension Reform Act resulted from a broad political consensus among the governing coalition parties and the major opposition party in the German Parliament, as well as among employers' organizations and trade unions.[141] Such consensus has been a common element of all major pension policy reforms in Germany, and the tendency to build comprehensive coalitions when making sweeping reforms of such long-term policies was an important element of Germany's overall political culture. Germany is somewhat different from the United States and some other countries in that the biggest political parties (Christian Democrats and Social Democrats) both have favored the "social state" and share many basic values.[142]

The 1996 Reform: Slowing Down the Growth of Pension Expenditures

For many years there was a broad consensus among employers, trade unions, and government to reduce unemployment by encouraging older workers to exit early from the labor force in order to give younger people more jobs. A low youth unemployment rate in Germany compared with many other European countries seemed to validate this policy. But as pension costs and the costs of unemployment insurance rose, this consensus broke down. Since the summer of 1995, proposals to discourage early exit from the labor force have been considered, even though overall unemployment has remained

---

140. One effect of this mechanism, not anticipated in the decision process, is that the contribution rate changes every year. This is mainly because the contribution rate has to be fixed at such a percentage, that—based on assumptions for employment and earnings development—the minimum reserve requirement is realized. I have therefore proposed that the reserve be allowed to fluctuate within a corridor, so that the contribution rate can remain stable for some years. In 1997 this recommendation was incorporated into the latest reform.

141. The "social partners"—unions and employers' organizations—also work together in the self-administration bodies of the social insurance system.

142. The term "social state" (*Sozialstaat*) is used in Germany instead of "welfare state"; *Wohlfahrtsstaat* is the German literal translation. In German, Wohlfahrtsstaat has a different meaning than Sozialstaat.

high.[143] The growing consensus is that the effect on contribution rates and consequently on nonwage labor costs makes a pro-early exit policy too expensive, particularly as international economic competition intensifies.

In February 1996, the federal government adopted measures intended to stop the growing number of early retirees claiming an old-age pension at age 60 after a period of unemployment. First, although the 1992 reforms had postponed until 2001 the phase-in of the 3.6 percent annual deduction in the pension of those workers who retire before age 65, the new law advances the phase-in of these deductions to 1997 and accelerates the phase-in. For pensions after periods of unemployment (which can start at age 60) the reference retirement age will be increased to 63 by the end of 1999; thereafter for all types of old age pensions by 2001 up to age 65.[144] For the female retirement age (at 60) this reduction of benefits will (after strong resistance by several organizations) start in 2000, and the reference retirement age will become 65 at the end of 2004. Figure 5-3 compares the original and new path of increasing the reference retirement ages.[145]

Second, an option was added allowing part-time work between ages 55 and 60 without forgoing the pension system's treatment of unemployed early exiters (for example, retirement allowed at 60). Participants can work part time between these ages and, at least under certain conditions, are supported by supplementary benefits from unemployment insurance. However, in Germany there is a lack of part-time jobs, especially for men.[146] The rule was intended to be used in the following way: working full time but only for half the time up to age 60, while the working time was set at zero for the remaining years.[147] The 1996 law also reduced the number of school years which count as years "worked" for pension purposes even if no contributions are made.

143. A widely used measure for preretirement has been the layoff of older workers. In these instances, employer payments supplement the unemployment benefits, so that the net income of the now unemployed person remains nearly the same as in the period of employment. After a period of unemployment, the old-age pension can be claimed at age 60. There was a sharp increase in the use of this type of pension. In 1994 about 20 percent of all male pensioners claiming a pension used this pathway into old-age pension; in East Germany this percentage was much higher, more than 40 percent. Large companies in particular used this measure extensively.

144. This means that also the existing "flexible" pensions which can be claimed from age 63 will be "burdened" by deductions.

145. According to the 1996 reform, old-age pension can still be claimed at age 60 at the earliest, however, with a deduction from the full pension by 18 percent (five times 3.6 percent) after the phase-in of the deduction is completed.

146. This is also the main reason why the "partial pension" introduced in 1992 has not been effective. In 1994 only 0.15 percent of all new pensions were partial pensions.

147. For a detailed discussion of early retirement, see Gatter and Schmähl (1996). In 1998 the time span for part-time work arrangements for older workers was extended from age 55 to age 65 (instead of age 60).

Figure 5-3. *Increase of Early Retirement Ages (Introduction of Deductions) according to Decisions in Pension Reform Act, 1992 and 1996*

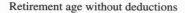

Retirement age without deductions

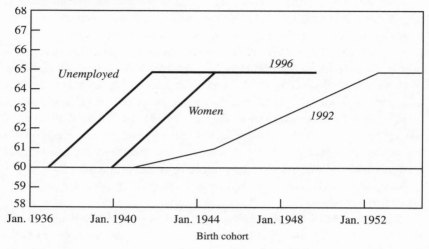

All these measures were worked out in 1996 very quickly and with a surprising lack of public attention. The reduction of the number of credited years of schooling, as well as the introduction of deductions from the full pension in case of early retirement, can be interpreted as elements of an underlying strategy to reduce pension expenditure but at the same time to strengthen the link between an individual's contributions and the level of his or her benefits. The government appears to have become convinced of this strategy in the past few years, principally as a reaction against proposals to shift public pension policy to a flat-rate approach.[148]

The 1997 Reforms (the 1999 Pension Reform Act): Social Pension Insurance at the Crossroads

Some politicians and leading members of employers' organizations proposed another reform to the pension system in the summer of 1996, even though the long-term financial prospects of the system had changed very little since November 1989 when the 1992 Pension Reform was debated, as can be seen

---

148. For a detailed discussion of arguments in favor of a strategy aiming at a closer contribution-benefit link see, for example, Schmähl (1985).

Table 5-12. *Necessary Contribution Rate, Social Pension Insurance in Germany, according to Projections for Different Years*[a]

| Year | 1989 West Germany only | | 1994 | 1996 | | 1997 |
	Without 1992 pension reform	With 1992 pension reform	With 1992 pension reform	With 1992 pension reform	With additional measures 1996	With 1999 pension reform
2000	22.0	20.3	19.7	20.4	20.1	19.7
2010	24.5	21.4	21.5	21.6	20.6	19.1
2015	25.5	21.6	22.1	22.2	21.4	19.2
2020	28.1	22.8	23.1	23.2	22.6	20.0
2030	36.4	26.9	27.0	26.2	25.5	22.4

Sources: Sozialbeirat (1996, p. 219); draft 1999 Pension Reform Act, German Federal Government, June 24, 1997, p. 82.

a. Contribution rate necessary to balance the budget and to meet the reserve requirement (pension expenditure for one month).

from table 5-12.[149] These actors in the political arena argued that more needed to be done to avoid the consequences of Germany's "demographic time bomb" and the expected future increase in contribution rates. During this period, the mass media began to play a greater role in setting the political agenda.

Although the projection of contribution rates based on demographic and economic assumptions was hardly novel, the political climate had dramatically changed. Several major events now shaped the terms of any social policy debate. Optimistic political forecasts about German reunification proved mistaken; German reunification had taken longer than expected and had large economic and social consequences, including high unemployment. Meeting the Maastrict convergence criteria, a process urged by economists as a supply side measure and supported also by pressure groups from industry, led to a policy of retrenchment in some areas of social policy. Relations between the labor unions on the one side, and the government and employers' organizations, on the other, worsened, particularly after the government (with the approval of the majority in Parliament) decided to change the rules for continued wage payments in case of illness of employees—a highly sensitive topic for trade unions because the prior rule had resulted from a severe strike in the past.

149. The contribution rate is about 1 percentage point higher because of transfers from West to East Germany. Also, about 2 percentage points are used to finance redistributive measures (instead of financing by taxes) and at least 1 percentage point is because the pension scheme was used as an instrument of labor market policy.

Mass media (especially newspapers and television) pushed the idea of a "collapse" of the pension scheme. Banks and insurance companies also threw their weight behind this argument. As is common in such periods of upheaval, radical proposals surfaced for abolishing the social pension scheme and introducing flat-rate pensions or at least reducing the pension level drastically. Although the argument often focused on giving people more scope for "self-reliance," these proposals were nevertheless often advanced by self-interested parties in the business community.

The proposals for radical change in the social pension scheme implicated several basic controversies in old-age security: public versus private provision for old age; financing by funding versus pay-as-you-go; and mandatory versus voluntary participation. These topics received growing public attention as well as consideration in academic discussions.

As this debate got under way, the government initially reacted very passively, saying only that pensions were secure. However, in the summer of 1996, in response to the growing public debate, the federal government appointed an expert commission, chaired by the minister of labor, charged with proposing a new pension reform and required to deliver a report by the end of 1996. At the same time, another commission chaired by the minister of finance was formed to develop proposals for a major income tax reform.[150] Both projects were to be fulfilled by the end of 1997 at the latest, a time near the end of the election period (the next parliamentary election was scheduled for September 1998).[151] While the government had a majority in the Bundestag (the federal parliament), the Bundesrat (representing the states, the Länder) was dominated by the major opposition party.[152]

The debate in the commissions and the public debate concentrated on two main areas: possibilities for a further reduction in the growth of pension expenditures, aiming at a reduction of the financing burden for "future generations," and a "fair" distribution of "burden" in financing the current pension expenditures, taking into consideration the different distributional targets (intertemporal versus interpersonal redistribution), and especially attempting to reduce nonwage labor costs so that the German labor market might become more internationally competitive.

150. In addition the Christian Democratic Party and the Christian Social Party also established party commissions.

151. There was hardly any direct contact and coordination between the two reform commissions or the two reform projects as a whole. For a discussion see Schmähl (1997b).

152. It is not useful here to describe in detail the process of passing a law in Germany. Suffice it to say, if the states are affected, they have to approve the law as well. Even if this is not the case, a time-consuming process is necessary if there are different majorities in the Bundestag and Bundesrat.

The proposals of the expert commission were to maintain the concept of an earnings and contribution-based defined-benefit pension scheme. The commission rejected the concept of tax-financed flat-rate pensions. These views were also backed by the majority in the political decision process.

In addition to previously enacted changes in retirement ages for old-age pensions, the new plan introduced deductions from the full pension for disability pensions, too. This development was linked to some additional changes for old-age pensions: starting in 2012, the earliest age to claim an old-age pension is scheduled to be 62, equal for men and women, but only for those having made contributions for thirty-five years. The full pension would be reduced by 3.6 percent for each year prior to age 65, or three times 3.6 percent (10.8 percent) for someone retiring at age 62. This 10.8 percent reduction was also made applicable to disability pensions.[153]

However, the new law also provided for additional pension expenditures by adopting a more liberal policy of crediting contributions for years devoted to child care. This measure is generally an element of family policy and results in interpersonal redistribution that should be financed from general public revenue rather than from earnings-based contribution payments. This is discussed further below.

The most important change affecting pension expenditure levels was the introduction of a so-called demographic factor into the formula for calculating and adjusting all pensions. The underlying argument was as follows: life expectancy will continue to increase, and pensioners will live longer. If this development is to have no impact in increasing the contribution rate, a reduction in the level of pensions is required. The solution proposed by the majority of the expert commission of the government and subsequently enacted by the federal Parliament is a moderate version of more radical proposals—a compromise—which takes changes in life expectancy into account, along with changes in the growth of average net earnings, in determining the amounts of pension that retirees receive. This change may have severe consequences for the pension scheme over the long run.

Under this feature of the new law, the development of the *ARW* factor, which determines the pension level, will be influenced by two elements: one is the rate of change of average net earnings,[154] discussed earlier; the other is the demographic factor. The demographic factor lowers *ARW* proportional to half the

153. There are some other technical changes not discussed here as well as changes for pensions for certain handicapped people.
154. This also reflects increases in life expectancy insofar as this increases the contribution rate of the pension scheme.

annual (further) increase in life expectancy of people at age 65, with a time lag built in so that the annual increase is calculated as of eight years ago.

The parameters of this demographic factor formula were chosen so that the so-called standard pension level (for pensions based on forty-five earnings points) would gradually be reduced from 70 percent of net average earnings today to 64 percent by the year 2030.[155] Additionally, the law provides that in any event the standard pension level is not to fall below 64 percent.[156]

Apart from the official argument in favor of such a change in the pension formula, at least five separate concerns should be taken into account in evaluating the new policy:

—Owing to its additional complexity, the participants in the insurance program are less likely to understand how the formula works.[157]

—The introduction of the demographic factor is a first step in uncoupling pension payments from earnings growth.

—An individual's specific level of earnings points does not provide sufficient information to calculate her pension relative to average net earnings. Planning for one's old-age provision, including, for example, estimating how much additional personal savings will be required, becomes more complicated.

—The reduction in the pension level owing to the demographic factor may have remarkable consequences on the income of the insured.

—The general reduction of the pension level may have the effect that a great number of employees will receive a pension that is only slightly higher than social assistance, even after long periods of paying contributions to the pension scheme. This could undermine the legitimacy and acceptance of the mandatory contributory scheme.

The last two points can be best understood in light of some facts.[158] At present, based on the existing rules for calculating and adjusting pensions, the "standard pension" (for a retiree with forty-five earnings points) is about 70 percent of average net earnings (of all employees). A full claim for social assistance (if no other income exists) is 40 percent of average net earnings. A pension can be based on different combinations of the number of years of

155. It was assumed that life expectancy of people age 65 will increase from 16.9 years (1996) to 19.0 years in 2030 (average for men and women).

156. When this percentage will be realized, however, depends on the development of a great number of factors. One is the development of life expectancy in the future. If a pensioner has forty EPs his present pension level is 40/45 times 0.7 = 0.62 and will decrease to 40/45 times 0.64 = 0.53.

157. In my view it would be preferable not to make pension insurance directly dependent on the development of other variables (like the different contribution rates to social insurance and income tax), but to limit these variables. This is discussed in Schmähl (1997a).

158. For a more detailed discussion as well as of alternatives, see Schmähl (1997a).

Figure 5-4. *Number of Insured Years for a Pension in the Same Amount as Social Assistance*

(= 40 Percent of Average Net Earnings)

Number of insured years

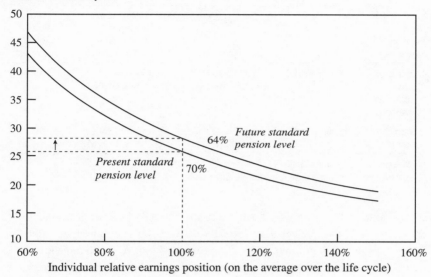

Individual relative earnings position (on the average over the life cycle)

insurance and the relative earnings position of the worker over the life cycle.[159] As can be seen from the Iso-pension-curve in figure 5-4, somebody who was (always or on the average of his working career) an "average earner" at present needs twenty-six years of insurance to receive a pension equal to the social assistance level. By contrast, someone who earned two-thirds of the average needs forty years of insurance. If the pension level is reduced generally,[160] more years of insurance contributions are needed to obtain a pension above the social assistance level.[161]

While factors unrelated to individual contributions have been added to the formula, the number of EPs a participant can accumulate during her working life continues to be of decisive importance. Here the following facts are

159. Or the average number of EPs a contributor acquired over the whole period of coverage during his or her working life.

160. For the standard pension (equal to forty-five EPs) reduced from 70 to 64 percent of average net earnings.

161. For the standard pension (equal to forty-five earning points) reduced from 70 percent to 64 percent of average net earnings.

Table 5-13. *Effects of a Reduction in the Standard Pension Level on Pension Benefits and Realized Pension Level*

Basis 1996, West Germany (1 Earnings Point = 46 DM)

	Standard pension in percent of average net earnings			Realized pension level (percent)
Pension based on	70	64	Retirement at age 62 (deduction 10.8 percent)	
45 earnings points (standard pension)	2083 DM[a]	1904.50 DM (= −178.50 DM)	1698.80 DM (= −384.20 DM)	57.1
40 earnings points	1852 DM	1693.30 DM (= −158.70 DM)	1510.40 DM (= −341.60 DM)	50.7

Source: Author's calculations.
a. Absolute amount of pension in DM per month.

significant: (a) today about 50 percent of male and 95 percent of female old-age pensioners have fewer than forty-five EPs; (b) certain changes, such as the reduction in the number of school years credited, will make it more difficult to obtain forty-five EPs, even though this number will remain the basis of the standard "full" pension; (c) in the future, only whose who retire at age 65 will be eligible for a "full" pension. Those who retire earlier will suffer a reduction in their pension amount irrespective of the number of EPs they have accumulated (10.8 percent for a worker who retires at 62).

Table 5-13 shows the effect of a reduction in the standard pension level from 70 percent to 64 percent. If, as a hypothetical example, we apply the 64 percent pension level to the other 1996 figures, the resulting pensions for different persons exhibit a remarkable effect.[162] If the pensioner claims his pension at age 62, and if he is owed a standard pension, his pension is equal to just 57.1 percent of average net earnings. A pensioner with forty EPs receives less than 51 percent of average net earnings. Remember the social assistance level is currently 40 percent.

In the long run, the introduction of such a "demographic factor" enacted in 1997 and the reductions of the pension level could undermine the legitimacy of the social pension scheme, which requires employees to pay substantial contributions for many years without providing them pensions substantially higher than they would receive through social assistance.

162. In reality it will be phased in over time.

Figure 5-5. *Deductions from the Full Pension and Increase of Retirement Age in Case of Increasing Life Expectancy*

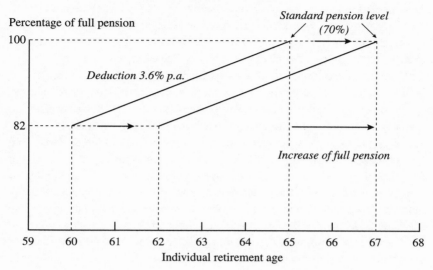

There are alternatives to a general reduction in pension amounts. If life expectancy increases, thereby increasing the number of years retirees will receive pensions, "there is a natural merit in extending retirement ages and discouraging earlier retirement."[163] Reference retirement age could be linked to changes in life expectancy, with the pension formula left constant (as proposed in Schmähl 1997a). Figure 5-5 gives an example of such a strategy, assuming a deduction of 3.6 percent a year and the earliest retirement five years before the reference retirement age.

Such an increase in retirement ages might start, for example, around 2010 to 2015, or whenever labor market projections show a change in labor market conditions (which is often connected to larger demographic trends). Such a policy would show workers very clearly the underlying economics of the longevity problem: by working longer for the same pension level as today, a worker would receive a pension at today's standard annual level for a retirement period of about the same length; by retiring early a worker would receive a pension for a longer time but at a reduced annual level (because of the deductions from the full pension). This alternative, however, did not enjoy support of a political majority.

163. Chand and Jaeger (1996, p. 31).

The government was able to enact the changes on the expenditure side of the social insurance budget through their majority in parliament (the Bundestag). The opposition parties, however, have been strongly against changing disability pension rules as well as against the new pension formula. They have announced their intention to cancel these reform measures if the government changes hands in the 1998 elections. The new rules may not survive.

Moreover, the political conditions for increasing transfers from the general public budget to social pension insurance were less propitious. Here the government also needed the acceptance by the Bundesrat, with its opposition majority, in order to cover to a larger extent than today those elements of pension expenditures involving interpersonal redistribution (and therefore to avoid finance-linked contributions, which would increase labor costs).[164] Although all political parties—along with employers' organizations and trade unions—wanted such a change in the structure of financing,[165] it took a process of many months of negotiation and debate to obtain opposition agreement to increase the value-added tax.[166] The agreement was ultimately precipitated by continued weakness in the labor market, particularly by a downward trend in the number of contributors and a slowdown of contribution revenue. The result would have been an increase of the contribution rate in 1998 from 20.3 percent to 21 percent. This has been avoided now by additional transfers from the federal budget financed by an increase of the value-added-tax rate by 1 percentage point from April 1998.

With the enactment of the 1999 Pension Reform, the contribution rate necessary to balance the budget of the pension insurance compared with calculations without these additional measures has been projected (see table 5-12).[167] In 2030 the contribution rate—according to this projection—will be 3.1 percent lower attributable to the following factors (percentage points in round figures):

—The "demographic factor": –1.5 percentage points
—Changes in disability pensions: –1.0 percentage point
—Additional credits for child care: +0.3 percentage point
—Additional "federal grant": –1.0 percentage point

164. I do not discuss here different shifting assumptions for employers' contribution payments.

165. A detailed discussion of the financing structure, its effects and the arguments for change is given in Schmähl (1997d).

166. Revenue from the value-added tax finances state as well as federal expenditures.

167. It is not possible to discuss here the underlying assumptions, especially concerning the labor market and economic development in general. Such assumptions, however, can always be questioned.

Tasks and Topics for the Future

The steps taken during recent years to reduce pension expenditures and restructure the finances of the pension system have had an underlying goal of achieving a closer contribution-benefit link. This can in principle legitimate the system, so long as insured people are aware of the link (understandable information is a precondition), and if they believe in the long-run stability of the scheme. The public discussion in Germany during the last years gave the people neither adequate information about the strategic aspects nor the feeling of "security."

The government has announced a second stage of pension reform that it would begin after the 1998 election, which would focus on pensions for widows and widowers and old-age security for women.[168] Representatives of employers and industry organizations have already demanded additional cuts in the pension level. As mentioned above, the reductions already agreed to in the general pension level have the potential (in my view) to undermine the legitimacy of the present scheme in the long run. A strategy to draw a closer link between contributions and benefits should be tempered by consideration of the overall effect any reductions in pensions may have in lowering benefits below or close to the income provided by ordinary social assistance.

Especially for employees in the middle- and lower-income brackets, there is a reduced chance to accumulate enough pension claims (EPs), even after a long period of contributions, to maintain a consumption pattern in old age similar to that enjoyed during the worker's last years of employment. Taking into account, first, that in the private sector only about 50 percent of all employees have supplemental pensions provided by their employers, second, that the overall long-term trend is for employers to reduce or eliminate these supplemental pensions, and third, that the distribution of these pensions is highly unequal (concentrated in big firms and relatively more on employees with higher earnings as well as higher social insurance pensions), the future problems become obvious.[169] This pension gap exacerbates the problem poorly qualified workers face in finding employment in the German labor market, which is increasingly oriented toward more highly skilled workers.

At the present time, there is no indication that occupational pensions will become more generous. The tendency is toward more defined-contribution

168. These measures are closely linked to the interaction of labor market developments, family structure, family policy, and old-age security. For an overview of proposals under discussion in Germany, see Horstmann (1996).

169. A detailed analysis is given in Schmähl (1997c).

plans and for more employee financing of occupational pensions. Taking into account the fiscal stress on the public sector, no changes in tax policy to stimulate firms to introduce or extend occupational pension schemes should be expected during the coming years. However, the government does plan to subsidize specific saving plans. Whether this will actually happen and how effective it will be remains an open question. Taken together, the current political and economic circumstances demonstrate the limitations of demanding more self-reliance in old-age provision. The most important factor is income during a person's working life; therefore, an expanding and dynamic labor market is critical.[170]

Increasing political pressure to introduce minimum standards for old-age protection can be expected. Moreover, in many countries with flat-rate or means-tested benefits, or with public old-age protection arrangements with only a low pension level, mandatory additional schemes have sooner or later been introduced. If the tendency to reduce the pension level in Germany continues, the demand for supplemental mandatory schemes might arise.

We can also expect further discussion about a shift from pay-as-you-go financing to more capital funding—even within the public sector. There have meanwhile been political decisions to accumulate some reserves in the pension scheme for civil servants, which are financed from the general public budgets. There are also proposals to accumulate reserves in the social insurance scheme. It is not possible here to explore the micro- and macroeconomic effects of such a strategy, but one must be particularly concerned about the effects over a relatively long transition period if the pension level in social insurance is reduced further in order to lower the contribution rate to the program, at least in the long run.[171] There exist some doubts (also based on prior experience) whether capital funding in the public sector is a strategy to recommend, taking into account that big reserves can stimulate "temptations" for politicians. In general, a worldwide tendency toward funding of public expenditures on pensions can have destabilizing effects on capital markets and instability in capital markets in turn increases risks of inadequate protection in old age.[172]

Other topics remain on the agenda regarding additional reform measures within the present defined-benefit social insurance scheme. The first relates to compliance with financing requirements. Employees as well as employers have demonstrated a tendency to avoid making contribution payments. Aside from the unknown quantitative effect of the underground economy, it is possible to

---

170. "In examining the requirements of a greater role of self-help, nothing is as important as a big reduction of European unemployment from its enormously high level." Sen (1997, p. 25).

171. For example, if the contribution rate will be higher than necessary to balance the budget.

172. Schmähl (1997d).

be employed without paying contributions if earnings are below a certain amount (one-seventh of average gross earnings; in West Germany in 1998 this is 620 DM per month). There has long been discussion about whether these jobs should be subject to contribution requirements.

Another related development—in my view more important in the long run—is the outsourcing by firms of production and services to "self-employed" vendors (whether really self-employed or not is a question which often cannot be answered clearly). There are many different types of self-employment. Two effects concerning old age are linked to this development: the base for financing social insurance is weakened, and, of possibly greater importance in terms of social policy, these self-employed people can become a social problem during their retirement, if they do not save for their old age and if periods of being self-employed constitute a substantial portion of their working lives. Therefore, one can imagine a general obligation for self-employed people to make contributions to social insurance if they are not required to make contributions to another institution which provides old-age security.[173] The required contributions might be quite limited, for example, only up to some number of earnings points (EP) sufficient to protect the self-employed from poverty in their old age.

If the contribution-benefit link is very close in a pension scheme, then the attraction of not being covered will be reduced along with the "tax wedge."[174] The desirability of the a closer benefits-contribution link suggests the following reforms:

—The scope of problems addressed by the pension system should be limited to income loss in case of old age, the death of an earner, and disability. Other tasks like family policy, labor market policy, and poverty policy should be dealt with by other specific institutions. One institution should not be overburdened by too many tasks and different objectives. This is a strategy for a *lean pension scheme*.

—If certain other activities are nonetheless to be incorporated into the pension scheme, then adequate financing should be provided from general public revenues. For example, if child care or years of schooling are to be credited as years worked under the pension scheme, because they are regarded as activities that should be promoted, then payments should be made from the public budget equivalent to the pension claims created.

—A general rule for pension insurance therefore is suggested: *no pension claim without a contribution payment*—whether in the case of gainful employment with contributions paid by employer and/or employee, in the case of

173. As was pointed out in figure 5-2, several groups of self-employed have their own specific pension schemes or already participate in the social pension insurance program.
174. For a detailed discussion, see Schmähl (1997d).

unemployment with contributions paid by unemployment insurance, or in the case of child care with contributions paid from general public revenue (to name the more prominent examples).[175]

Finally, I want briefly to address two defects in the German pension policy-making process. First, there is still a lack of information about the effects policy changes will have on household income and on the personal distribution of income both over the life cycle and for different cohorts. When changes in pension policy are discussed, typically only the effects on the amount of employer and employee contributions, on the size of transfers from the general public budget, and on the level of the standard pension are considered.

Second, the political decision process is characterized by a fragmented approach. For example, the reform projects for income taxation and for pension policy have for the most part been considered in isolation from one another, discussed in separate circles with hardly any exchange of views on common matters. In general the discussion in Germany is largely dominated by a confrontation of actors in the area of "economic policy" on the one hand, and "social policy" on the other. Because the border between social policy and economic policy is hard to identify and each relates to the other, an integrated approach is needed. This compartmentalization is an important obstacle to adequate decisionmaking, a special disadvantage for an area that is of central importance for the whole population during most of their lives.

David Walker, discussant

THE PURPOSE OF this paper is to explain how Canada came to reform its national pension plan and to suggest what lessons others might glean from the Canadian experience. Like so many situations in public policy across industrial nations, countries can learn much from one another. However, the particular nature of each country's political institutions can also produce very different outcomes.

Canada and the United State have a lot in common. The demographic structures in the two countries are mirror images of each other. The only exception is that Canada's post–World War II baby boom was more immediate and more pronounced than that in the United States. Consequently, Canadian policymakers are totally focused on the abrupt growth in the over-65 age group that begins in 2011. Canadians explicitly frame their retirement income debate around public and private strategies that ready the nation for that year.

175. In Germany, such contributions are already paid under certain conditions for unemployed persons and for persons helping others who need long-term care.

Second, both Canada and the United States created their public pension schemes when pay-as-you-go structures were endorsed and thought to be quite workable. Both countries decided to invest surpluses in nonnegotiable government bond instruments. Both extended benefits and made changes more generous to recipients rather than payers. Both countries left their plans unchanged for too long and now face difficult and somewhat unpopular choices.

Third, the two countries have important private pension industries with numerous products. These products have evolved during the past thirty years. For example, private plans outside the national pension system have shifted sharply from defined-benefit to defined-contribution arrangements. At the same time, the baby boom generation, as it prepares for retirement, is generally more interested, more sophisticated, and more critical of public and private options than earlier generations. Many prefer individually oriented rather than government/collectively oriented approaches. As a consequence, both consumers and the industry have been critical of the national pension plans in both Canada and the United States.

Fourth, several North American intellectuals, think tanks, and investment houses have promoted public pension options from nations that never had the pay-as-you-go schemes of North America and Europe. For example, they cite the experiences of Chile, Singapore, and, more recently, Mexico with their various individualized accounts for pension savings. This challenge by those who are opposed for strategic and intellectual reasons has made reform much more difficult despite the urgent need for immediate action.

Finally, and this will make most of you smile, Americans and Canadians share the same gene pool of reluctant politicians. Pension reform involves difficult issues and attracts very few heroes.

The Canadian Experience

It will come as no surprise to anyone involved in pension research and reform that this is indeed one of the most difficult areas in public policy. Pension policy is difficult to understand, to communicate, to build coalitions and to establish long-term solutions for. And even when legislation is finally enacted, years must pass to provide the hard evidence for evaluation and historical judgments.

The Canadian case serves as an interesting example of pension reform. Like most Western industrial societies, Canada in the last decade of this century had to face the need to reform its national pension plan.

The Canada Pension Plan was launched on January 1, 1966, after extensive federal-provincial negotiations. The CPP is a federal-provincial partnership with both levels of government acting as stewards of the plan on behalf of current and future beneficiaries. The province of Quebec has its own pension plan.

The CPP allows all working Canadians to provide for their retirement through their own mandatory contributions. It also provides disability and death benefits as well as survivors' benefits. The plan was the last of the three pillars of Canada's retirement income system to be introduced. At the time the plan was started, two other pillars were already in place: Old Age Security (OAS), which provided a flat benefit to seniors, and employer-sponsored pension plans and personal retirement savings plans (RRSPs).

Another element of the retirement income system, the Guaranteed Income Supplement (GIS) for lower-income seniors, was added to the OAS when the CPP was introduced. Together, the OAS and GIS are one pillar, financed from the general revenues of the federal government. The OAS provides a basic pension to seniors, and the GIS provides supplements for those in need.

Tax assistance for employer-sponsored pension plans and personal savings accounts (RRSPs)—the third pillar—encourages Canadians to save enough to avoid serious disruption in their living standards at retirement. Overall, the Canadian systems fit the description of a three-pillar, integrated, private and public system as now advocated by international organizations. It combines elements of direct government payments, private pension plans, individual savings, and tax-assisted programs.

The political structures in Canada do, in an odd and deceptive fashion, lend themselves to very dramatic public action. In Canada consensus is an absolutely necessary condition in the beginning of an initiative. Since deals among legislators after a bill has been presented by the government are very rare, every effort is made to line up support beforehand. This, in part, explains how the CPP was reformed.

The Canadian pension system required a consensus within the provincial and federal governments. Two territorial governments (the Northwest and the Yukon) participated in discussions but did not have a vote. Although pensions were formerly a provincial domain under the Canadian constitution, all except Quebec had ceded this domain to the federal government by the time the CPP was launched in 1966. However, the provinces continued to be involved in two important respects. First, they negotiated that any surplus in the CPP account would be loaned to the provinces at the current twenty-year government of Canada bond rate. Since most provinces did not enjoy such a favorable rate in the bond market, they gained access to lower-cost long-term financing. Second, the provinces retained the right to approve changes in the CPP. In fact, the process for changing the CPP is more rigorous than for changing the Canadian constitution inasmuch as amendments (benefits, contributions, and investment of surplus funds) require the support of at least two-thirds of the provinces with two-thirds of the population.

As a consequence of the need for consensus, the federal Department of Finance had to spend considerable time with senior officials and politicians of the provincial governments to help them become more familiar with the CPP and to share the same analysis. As most provincial governments are small (six provinces have a population of 1 million or fewer), most provincial officials had only limited knowledge of the CPP. Ottawa handled the cash flow through its national tax collection system, delivered the monthly checks, and administered the complex disability component.

Thus, to return to a point made earlier in this paper, the real work had to be done in the provincial capitals to ensure that these governments could support the proposed changes. The education process went on intensely for twelve months (1996–97), and devising the ultimate plan took three years 1995–97. The strategy had three separate components: to build and solidify support in the federal government, to persuade the public that changes were inevitable for the survival of the CPP, and to develop a consensus among the provinces.

The federal team was led by the Department of Finance, since its officials controlled contribution rates and provincial access to surplus funds for borrowing. However, since the day-to-day management of the CPP, including the distribution of pension checks and the handling of disability claims rested with Ottawa's Department of Human Resources Development, natural tensions between the two departments emerged. The tensions were typical of those between departments of finance at the center and departments responsible for social policy. Other central agencies, the cabinet, and the prime minister's office generally deferred to the minister of finance in the negotiations with the provinces (although key actors were briefed regularly).

The internal workings of Canadian federalism, where joint federal-provincial solutions must be created, occur in the meetings of officials. For example, in the domain of finance, important topics such as reform of the CPP are discussed by the associate deputy ministers, who meet in preparation for their deputy-ministers, who in turn meet before their ministers of finance. Thus by the time that ministers hold their semiannual meetings, issues are well known and positions largely developed. Because of the long history of these meetings, and the sensitive nature of their subject matter (for example, the management of public debt, which in turn affects interest rates and currency markets), these sessions are normally held without press leaks. Indeed a great deal of work goes into postmeeting communications to ensure that political differences do not disturb markets.

The public coalition building began with the publication of a sixty-two-page paper on the CPP, which was approved by the ministers of finance at their February 1996 meeting. By producing a cautious paper (*An Information Paper for Consultations on the Canadian Pension Plan*) that provided information and offered options, Ottawa was able to launch a review of the CPP without making specific recommendations. Later, when different provinces began questioning Ottawa's analysis, they were reminded that they had endorsed this perspective with their original joint publication. The joint release also helped reinforce the idea to the media and Canadians that the CPP was a shared responsibility.

By contrast the American document that launched the Social Security review of 1996 had three separate views and was available only after a long delay. Instead of a consensus-building document, the executive branch was handed a report, which immediately produced supporters and opponents. The president was forced to wait several months before he could launch his own campaign to find a Social Security solution.

The next stage in consensus building in Canada was a public consultation process. Over a three-month period, April through June of 1966, the governments held a series of meetings (thirty-three) in every province and territory (nineteen cities in twelve jurisdictions). Each meeting was chaired by the federal representative and an elected official chosen by each provincial/territorial government. The two-hour sessions featured fifteen to twenty-five representatives from groups as diverse as pension specialists, trade unions, small and large business organizations, social policy coalitions, seniors' groups, and youth leadership organizations. A special meeting was held for young people to explore their need for a nationally organized, government-run, compulsory pension plan. A second meeting was held for disability insurance as this component accounts for 17 percent of expenditures.

Each session was open to the public, and anyone who approached the chair before the meeting was given an opportunity to sit at the table and to participate fully. At the end of the formal session, members of the audience were also given the opportunity to participate, with the simple provision that they identify themselves as all interventions were being recorded. Those who could not attend were invited to submit briefs to the CPP consultation secretariat, which was housed in the Department of Finance in Ottawa. More than two hundred submissions were received.

After briefs were formally presented, a roundtable discussion was pursued. This format forced participants to deal more directly with one another's perceptions than often is the case with witnesses in front of legislative committees. Since the media was invited to attend, it provided extensive coverage in each local market. This coverage reinforced two important messages: Canadians valued the CPP; and Canadians expected politicians to fix it and to fix it right this time to end the prolonged insecurity about the public pension system. The communication strategy emphasized these two themes from coast to coast.

This provided several important benchmarks that contributed to the eventual success of the reform process. Transparency, participation, and openness are key to any successful public policy. Similiarly, officials must be responsive and report back in a manner that reflects views and attitudes expressed during the consultation process.

At the end of the consultations, the deputy ministers submitted a report to the finance ministers in June 1996. It was also made public. Again in the context of these meetings, no decision was sought except for a commitment to find a solution. It was agreed, however, that the joint consultations exercise had been a success. The document clearly laid out the principles that should underpin any comprehensive solution. Once all the governments committed themselves to these principles, the negotiations became more focused as some options could then be quickly dismissed. From that point on, few could argue creditably that they did not have a chance to be heard.

The next step involved internal and external consultations to reach a consensus. Building on these consultations and earlier meetings, key strategists concluded that a successful resolution of the problems of the existing CPP would require action on three issues: contributions (they needed to nearly double from current levels within five to seven years), benefits for both disability and retirement pensions (they would have to be reduced by about 10 percent over the next twenty years), and the investment strategy (it would have to move from provincial bonds to a more nonpolitical, diversified yet conservative market strategy with a real return of 3.8 percent annually).

Several provinces over the next seven months expressed their priorities (some wanted more aggressive benefit cuts, others wanted to introduce greater progressiveness into the social insurance structure), but in the end the negotiations came to a successful conclusion. Two provinces, Saskatchewan and British Columbia, with strong ties to the trade union movement, publicly dissented and eventually refused to sign the agreement. However, because a majority approved the deal, their dissent had no consequence for the residents of these two provinces. The changes applied directly to all Canadians living outside of Quebec; significantly, the Quebec government changed the Quebec Pension Plan to essentially parallel the amended CPP legislation.

The Canada Pension Plan Investment Fund in the end provided the proponents of change a vehicle for building public support. It brought on board those in the pension industry who thought that a national pension plan with an investment strategy parallel to private plans could produce better returns than the current system. It muted the criticism of recipients who were worried that CPP was about to disappear unless dramatic action was taken. Contributors were not interested in a payroll tax increase as the only solution, so they supported the new investment strategy in order to get better returns and stem future premium hikes. It quieted the provinces who saw that public opposition was too strong for their maintaining exclusive access to surplus funds. Even some of the critics who wanted an entirely new approach, such as that adopted in Chile, concluded that this was at least a step in the right direction.

The new legislation also provided for a regular three-year review of the CPP. Canadians had left their plan alone for the first twenty years as no review was automatically triggered by the original legislation. The subsequent five-year reviews, which were agreed upon in 1986, had produced a climate of increasing anxiety. It was decided that a more regular review with a publicly discussed agenda would allow the CPP to evolve and change without a crisis environment. Similarly, more rigorous reporting procedures would give Canadians a more regular and accurate assessment of the security of the CPP. Once this CPP deal was agreed to, it was up to Ottawa to draft the necessary legislation to ensure its passage. The provinces stepped back after the February 1997 announcement, and Ottawa took over. After the legislation was passed in Parliament, the provinces simply had to pass cabinet level approvals to ensure it became law on January 1, 1998.

A federal election occurred last spring and the CPP was not a major issue, despite earlier protests by opposition parties. In the September "Speech from the Throne," when the government signaled its priorities, it stated that CPP legislation was the highest priority. The legislation took two months (October and November) in the House of Commons including hearings in the Finance Committee. Since draft legislation dealing with the new CPP Investment Board and Fund had been circulating for several months, the pension industry was comfortable with the proposals as they had had easy access to finance officials to discuss the details of the new fund. Benefit reductions were diffuse enough and within the realm of expectations that no real opposition was mounted on these points. It helped enormously that current beneficiaries were not affected by the changes. Opponents of the new contribution rates (read taxes), however, offered very real and sustained criticisms, especially as the new rates affected young workers. Given that this age group largely wrote off the CPP before the debate began, it was relatively easy to play on the fear of increased taxes with no guaranteed benefits. Yet this debate in the end did not delay the legislation.

In the Senate, the debate shifted to questions about the new investment fund. With the clock ticking down, the government-dominated (but not controlled) nonelected body expressed serious reservations about the new fund mainly on the grounds that senators had had no time to call expert investment witnesses. In a rare legislative conference between the Minister of Finance and the opposition senators on the committee, the government agreed to postpone for three months implementation of those sections of the legislation dealing with the investment fund. In return the government was able to meet its timetable. It gave the provinces enough time for their approvals and was able to implement changes due less than two weeks later, on schedule.

The work that made the reform of the CPP possible was done at the front end. Criticisms raised later, while disruptive, did not force any of the governments to retreat from their original accord.

Conclusion

In the end, the United States and Canada have reached the same crossroads at the same moment in history. Actions are required just as much in the United States as they were in Canada. Although the specifics may turn out to be different, the tripod on which to build the case for reform is very much the same; it will take action simultaneously on benefits, contributions, and investment policies. It is possible to build an effective coalition. However, as in the case of the health care debate earlier this decade, the public must support politicians willing to work on this problem, or those who simply want to wish it away will again win the day. To build a consensus means working carefully with an extremely broad-based coalition, who are committed to protecting the nation's public pension plan. In this context, Canadians found that it was essential to build a consensus early in the process. Without consensus building, the equation of lower benefits and higher contribution rates can quickly sour a debate.

Similarly it helped the Canadian debate to provide for more regular reviews of the CPP which could lead to further reforms. Opponents then thought that this was not the last chance to put forward their ideas to make the plan more workable.

It is hard to imagine an industrial nation without such a plan for its work force. But it is also hard to find such a plan that is both sustainable and affordable. Canadians found that waiting to reform its public pension only prolonged the agony.

References

Advisory Council on Social Security. 1997. *Report of the 1994–1996 Advisory Council on Social Security: Vol. I: Findings and Recommendations*. Washington: Government Printing Office.

Artoni, Robert, and Alberto Zanardi. 1997. "The Evolution of the Italian Pension System." In *Comparing Social Welfare Systems in Southern Europe*, edited by Bruno Palier, 243–66. Paris: MIRE.

Australia, Commonwealth of, Parliamentary Library. 1997. *Bills Digest No. 61 1997–98: Superannuation Contributions Tax (Members of Constitutionally Protected Superannuation Funds) Assessment and Collection Bill 1997*.

Babeau, André. 1997. "The Problems Raised by the Introduction of Pension Funds in France." In *Comparing Social Welfare Systems in Southern Europe: vol. 3–Florence Conference*, edited by Bruno Palier, 267-80 (Paris: Mission Recherche et Expérimentation, July).

Banks, J. A., W. Dilnot, and S. Tanner. 1997. *Taxing Household Saving: What Role for the New Individual Savings Account*. Commentary 66. London: Institute for Fiscal Studies.

Banting, Keith. 1995. "The Welfare State as Statecraft: Territorial Politics and Canadian Public Policy." In *European Social Policy: Between Fragmentation and Integration*, edited by Stephan Leibfried and Paul Pierson, 269–300. Brookings.

Banting, Keith G., and Robin Boadway. 1997. *Reform of Retirement Income Policy: International and Canadian Perspectives* (Kingston, Ontario: Queens University School of Policy Studies).

Bateman, Hazel, and John Piggott. 1993. "Australia's Mandated Private Retirement Income Scheme: An Economic Perspective." Sydney: University of New South Wales, School of Economics.

Battle, Ken [under the pseudonym Grattan Grey]. 1990. "Social Policy by Stealth." *Policy Options*, vol. 11(2):17–29.

Beattie, Roger, and Warren McGillivray. 1995. "A Risky Strategy: Reflections on the World Bank Report *Averting the Old Age Crisis*." *International Social Security Review* 48 (3-4): 5–22.

———. 1996. "Rejoinder." *International Social Security Review* 49 (3):17–20.

Bercuson, David, J. L. Granatstein, and W. R. Young. 1986. *Sacred Trust: Brian Mulroney and the Conservative Party in Power*. Toronto: Doubleday Canada.

Blomsma, Martin, and Roel Jansweijer. 1997. "The Netherlands: Growing Importance of Private Sector Arrangements." In *Enterprise and the Welfare State*, edited by Martin Rein and Eskil Wadenjo, 220–65. Cheltenham: Edward Elgar.

Bolderson, Helen, and Deborah Mabbett. 1996. "Cost Containment in Complex Social Security Systems: The Limitations of Targeting." *International Social Security Review* 49 (1): 3–17.

Breier, Bernd. 1997. *Sozialbudget 1995*. Bundesarbeitsblatt 3: 136.

Bundesministerium für Arbeit und Sozialordnung, ed. 1997. Vorschläge der Kommission "Fortentwicklung der Rentenversicherung." Bonn.

Canada. Department of Finance. 1996. *An Information Paper for Consultations on the Canada Pension Plan*. Ottawa.

Chand, Sheetal K., and Jaeger, Albert. 1996. *Aging Populations and Public Pension Schemes*. Occasional Paper 147. Washington: International Monetary Fund (December).

Delsen, Lei. 1996. "Gradual Retirement in the Netherlands." In *Gradual Retirement in the OECD Countries*, edited by Lei Delsen and Genevieve Reday-Mulvey, 111–32. Aldershot.

Derthick, Martha. 1990. *Agency under Stress*. Brookings.

Deutsche Bundesregierung [German Federal Government], ed. 1997. "1999 Pension Reform Act." *Draft June 24*: 82.

Diamond, Peter, and Salvador Valdés-Prieto. 1994. "Social Security Reforms." In *The Chilean Economy: Policy Lessons and Challenges*, edited by Barry P. Bosworth, Rudiger Dornbusch, and Raúl Laban, 257–320. Brookings.

Dilnot, A. W., and others. 1994. *Pensions Policy in the U.K.: An Economic Analysis*. London: Claredon Press.

Disney, R. 1988. "Lessons from Overseas: The United Kingdom." In *Social Security Reform: Links to Saving, Investment and Growth*, edited by S. A. Sass and R. W. Triest, 157–67. Boston: Federal Reserve Bank of Boston.

Disney, R., and P. Johnson. 1998. "The United Kingdom: A Working System of Minimum Pensions?" In *Redesigning Social Security*, proceedings of Kiel Week Conference, 207–32. Tübingen: Mohr Siebeck.

Disney, R., and E. Whitehouse. 1996. "What Are Occupational Pension Plan Entitlements Worth in Britain?" *Economica* 63 (May): 213–38.

Esping-Andersen, Gøsta. 1990. *The Three Worlds of Welfare Capitalism*. Princeton University Press.

European Commission, Director General XV, Single Market and Financial Services. 1997. *Supplementary Pensions in the Single Market: A Green Paper*. Brussels: The Commission, June 5.

"European Court of Justice Orders Equal Treatment in Awarding Pensions." 1991. *Social Security Bulletin* 54 (2): 14–16.

Field, Frank. 1997. *Reforming Welfare*. London: Social Market Foundation.

"France: Retirement Savings Funds." 1997. *Trends in Social Security*, 3/1997, pp. 16–17.

Gatter, Jutta, and Winfried Schmähl. 1996. "Vom Konsens zum Konflikt—"Die Frühverrentung zwischen renten—und beschäftigungspolitischen Interessen." In *Massenarbeitslosigkeit durch Politikversagen*, edited by Bremer Gesellschaft für Wirtschaftsforschung, 183–204. Frankfurt am Main: Lang.

Gesamtverband der Deutschen Versicherungswirtschaft, ed. 1997. "Private Life Insurance." *Information of Gesamtverband der Deutschen Versicherungswirtschaft, November 5*.

Gutachten des Sozialbeirats zum Rentenversicherungsbericht. 1996. In *Bundestags-Drucksache* 13/5370, 215–20.

Haanes-Olsen, Leif. 1990. "Investment of Social Security Reserves in Three Countries." *Social Security Bulletin* 53 (2):2–8.

Heclo, Hugh. 1988. "Generational Politics." In *The Vulnerable*, edited by John L. Palmer, Timothy Smeeding, and Barbara Boyle Torrey, 381–411. Washington: Urban Institute.

Hippe, Jon Mathias, and Axel West Pedersen. 1996. "The Growth of Private Pensions in Two Scandinavian Welfare States: A Comparison of Denmark and Norway." In *The*

Privatization of Social Policy: Occupational Welfare in America, Scandinavia and Japan, edited by Michael Shalev, 187–210. London: Macmillan Press.

HMSO Pensions Bill. 1994. *Report by the Government Actuary on the Financial Provisions of the Bill on the National Insurance Fund*, Cm2714. London.

Holzmann, Robert. 1997. "Pension Reform, Financial Market Development, and Economic Growth: Preliminary Evidence from Chile." *IMF Staff Papers* 44 (2): 149–78 (June).

Horstmann, Sabine. 1996. *Kindererziehung und Alterssicherung*. Grafschaft:Vektor.

International Social Security Association. 1996. *Social Protection in Europe: Outline of Social Security Programmes*. Geneva.

Jacobs, Klaus, and Martin Rein. 1991. "The Future of Early Retirement: The Federal Republic of Germany." In *States, Labor Markets, and the Future of Old-Age Policy*, edited by John Myles and Jill Quadagno, 250–67. Temple University Press.

Jacobs, Klaus, and Winfried Schmähl. 1989. "The Process of Retirement in Germany: Trends, Public Discussion and Options for Its Redefinition." In *Redefining the Process of Retirement—An International Perspective*, edited by Winfried Schmähl, 13–38. Heidelberg: Springer.

James, Estelle. 1996. "Providing Better Protection and Promoting Growth: A Defense of Averting the Old Age Crisis." *International Social Security Review* 49 (3): 3–17.

James, Estelle, and others. 1994. *Averting the Old Age Crisis* (Oxford: Oxford University Press).

Kritzer, Barbara E. 1996. "Privatizing Social Security: The Chilean Experience." *Social Security Bulletin* 59 (3): 45–55.

Lawson, Nigel. 1992. *The View from Number 11: Memoirs of a Tory Radical*. London: Bantam Press.

Leibfried, Stephan, and Paul Pierson. 1995. "Semisovereign Welfare States: Social Policy in a Multitiered Europe." In *European Social Policy: Between Fragmentation and Integration*, edited by Leibfried and Pierson, 43–77. Brookings.

Lowndes, Noble. 1992. *The 1992 Guide to Pensions and Labour Laws in Europe*. Surrey, U.K.

Lunt, P., and R. Disney. 1997. "Interpreting Financial Service Adverts." London: Department of Psychology, University College. Mimeo.

Lutjens, Erik. 1997. "The Netherlands." In *Social Europe: The Outlook on Supplementary Pensions in the Context of Demographic, Economic and Social Change*. Luxembourg: Office for Official Publications of the European Community.

Mahnke, Hans-Jürgen. 1997. "DIHT fordert Deutsche zum Umdenken auf." *Die Welt*. November 25, 1997.

Mörschel, Richard. 1990. "Die Finanzierungsverfahren in der Geschichte der gesetzlichen Rentenversicherung." In *Deutsche Rentenversicherung*, 619–61. Frankfurt.

Myles, John. 1989. *Old Age and the Welfare State*, rev. ed. University Press of Kansas.

Myles, John, and Paul Pierson. 1997. "Reforming Public Pensions." Paper presented to the Conference on The New Politics of the Welfare State, Center for European Studies, Harvard University, December.

Myles, John, and Jill Quadagno, eds. 1991. *States, Labor Markets, and the Future of Old-Age Policy*. Temple University Press.

Myles, John, and Jill Quadagno. 1997. "Recent Trends in Public Pension Reform: A Comparative View." In *Reform of Retirement Income Policy: International and Canadian Perspectives*, edited by Keith G. Banting and Robin Boadway, 247–71. Kingston, Ontario: Queens University School of Policy Studies.

New Zealand, Independent Referendum Panel. 1997. *Understanding the Compulsory Retirement Savings Scheme*.

Nullmeier, Frank, and Friedbert W. Rüb. 1993. *Die Transformation der Sozialpolitik*. Frankfurt/New York: Campus.

Office of Management and Budget. 1997. *Budget of the United States Government: Analytical Perspectives*.

Olsberg, Diana. 1997. *Aging and Money*. St. Leonards, NSW: Allen and Unwin.

Organization for Economic Cooperation and Development. 1988. *Reforming Public Pensions*. Paris.

————. 1997a. *Aging in OECD Countries*. Paris.

————. 1997b. *Employment Outlook*. Paris.

O'Sullivan, Paul. 1997. *Testimony presented at the Hearing for the Subcommittee on Social Security of the Ways and Means Committee in the United States Congress on 18 September 1997*, Australian Department of Social Security. 105 Cong. 1 sess. (http://www.dss.gov.au/international/18sep.html).

Overbye, Einar. 1994. "Convergence in Policy Outcomes: Social Security Programs in Perspective." *Journal of Public Policy* 14 (2):147–74.

————. 1995. "Different Countries on a Similar Path: Comparing Pension Politics in Scandinavia and Australia." Paper presented to the International Sociological Association, RC 19 seminar on Comparative Research on Welfare State Reforms, Pavia, Italy.

————. 1996. "Pension Politics in the Nordic Countries: A Case Study." *International Political Science Review* 17(1): 67–90.

Palme, Joakim. 1994. "Recent Developments in Income Transfers in Sweden." In *Recent Trends in Cash Benefits in Europe*, edited by Niels Ploug and Jon Kvist, 39–59. Copenhagen: Danish National Institute of Social Research.

Palmer, John L., Timothy Smeeding, and Christopher Jencks. 1988. "The Uses and Limits of Income Comparisons." In *The Vulnerable*, edited by John L. Palmer, Timothy Smeeding, and Barbara Boyle Torrey, 7–27. Washington: Urban Institute.

Pierson, Paul D. 1994. *Dismantling the Welfare State? Reagan, Thatcher and the Politics of Retrenchment*. Cambridge: Cambridge University Press.

————. 1996. "The New Politics of the Welfare State." *World Politics* 48: 143–79.

————. 1997. "The Politics of Pension Reform." In *Reform of Retirement Income Policy: International and Canadian Perspectives*, edited by Keith G. Banting and Robin Boadway, 273–93. Kingston, Ontario: Queens University School of Policy Studies.

Pierson, Paul D., and R. Kent Weaver. 1993. "Imposing Losses in Pension Policy." In *Do Institutions Matter? Government Capabilities in the U.S. and Abroad*, edited by R. Kent Weaver and Bert A. Rockman, 110–50. Brookings.

Piggot, John. 1997. "Australian Retirement Income Provision." Sydney: University of New South Wales, School of Economics.

Ploug, Niels, and Jon Kvist, eds. 1994. *Recent Trends in Cash Benefits in Europe*. Copenhagen: Danish National Institute of Social Research.

Puidak, Peter. 1992. "Recent Developments in Germany." *Social Security Bulletin* 55 (2): 78–79.

Quadagno, Jill. 1991. "Interest-Group Politics and the Future of U.S. Social Security Policy." In *States, Labor Markets and the Future of Old-Age Policy*, edited by John Myles and Jill Quadagno, 36–58. Temple University Press.

Queisser, Monika. 1995. "Chile and Beyond: The Second-Generation Pension Reforms in Latin America." *International Social Security Review* 48 (3-4): 23–40.

Retirement Income Policies Periodic Report Group [Todd Task Force] 1997. *1997 Retirement Income Report*, Wellington. July.

Reynaud, Emmanuel. 1995. "Financing Retirement Pensions: Pay-as-You-Go and Funded Systems in the European Union." *International Social Security Review* 48 (3-4): 41–57.

_____. 1997a. "L'avenir des Retraites en Debat." *Chronique International de l'IRES* 58: 5–16.

_____. 1997b. "Reforme des Reatraites en Italie: Principaux aspects et questions soulevees." *Revue D'Economique Financiere* 40: 65–84.

Reynaud, Emmanuel, and Adelheid Hege. 1996. "Italy: A Fundamental Transformation of the Pension System." *International Social Security Review* 49 (3):65–74.

Ritter, Gerhard A. 1983. *Sozialversicherung in Deutschland und England*. München: Beck.

Rothgang, Heinz. 1997. *Ziele und Wirkungen der Pflegeversicherung*. Frankfurt/New York: Campus.

Schmähl, Winfried. 1981. "Über den Satz "Aller Sozialaufwand muß immer aus dem Volkseinkommen der laufenden Periode gedeckt werden." In *Hamburger Jahrbuch für Wirtschafts-und-Gesellschaftspolitik*, vol. 26, 147–71. Tübingen: Mohr.

Schmähl, Winfried, ed. 1985. *Versicherungsprinzip und soziale Sicherung*. Tübingen: Mohr.

Schmähl, Winfried. 1992a. "Transformation and Integration of Public Pension Schemes—Lessons from the Process of the German Unification." In *Public Finance in a World of Transition, Public Finance, Supplement*, vol. 47, edited by Pierre Pestieau, 34–56.

_____. 1992b. "Changing the Retirement Age in Germany." In *The Geneva Papers on Risk and Insurance*, 81–104. Association de Genève.

_____. 1993a. "Proposals for Flat-Rate Public Pensions in the German Debate." In Jos Berghman and Bea Cantillon, eds., *The European Face of Social Security*, 261–80. Aldershot and other places: Avebury.

_____. 1993b. "The '1992 Reform' of Public Pensions in Germany: Main Elements and Some Effects." In *Journal of European Social Policy*, vol. 3, 39–51.

Schmähl, Winfried, Rainer George, and Christiane Oswald. 1996. "Gradual Retirement in Germany." In *Gradual Retirement in the OECD Countries*, edited by Lei Delsen and Geneviève Reday-Mulvey, 69–93. Aldershot: Dartmouth.

Schmähl, Winfried. 1997a. "Alterssicherung–Quo vadis?" In *Jahrbücher für Nationalökonomie und Statistik*, vol. 216, edited by Adolf Wagner and Heinrich Strecker, 413–35. Stuttgart: Lucius and Lucius.

_____. 1997b. *Finanzpolitik und Rentenversicherung*. Working Paper 19/97. University of Bremen: Center for Social Policy Research.

_____. 1997c. "The Public-Private Mix in Pension Provision in Germany: The Role of Employer-Based Pension Arrangements and the Influence of Public Activities." In *Enterprise and the Welfare State*, edited by Martin Rein and Eskil Wadensjö, 99–148. Cheltenham: Elgar.

_____. 1997d. *Financing of Social Security—Two Papers on the Instruments and Methods of Financing Social Insurance Schemes.* Working Paper 21/97. University of Bremen: Center for Social Policy Research.

Schmähl, Winfried, and Heinz Rothgang. 1996. "The Long-Term Costs of Long-Term Care Insurance in Germany." In *Long-Term Care: Economic Issues and Political Solutions*, edited by Roland Eisen and Frank A. Sloan, 181–222. Boston: Kluwer.

Sen, Amartya. 1997. "The Penalties of Unemployment." Termi di discussione, N. 307. Banca d'Italia, Rome. Mimeo.

Shaver, Sheila. 1991. "'Considerations of Mere Logic': The Australian Age Pension and the Politics of Means-Testing." In *States, Labor Markets, and the Future of Old-Age Policy*, edited by John Myles and Jill Quadagno, 105–26. Temple University Press.

_____. 1995. "Universality and Selectivity in Income Support: A Comparative Study in Social Spending." Sydney: Social Policy Research Center.

Siegenthaler, Jürg K. 1996. "Poverty among Single Elderly Women under Different Systems of Old-Age Security: A Comparative Review." *Social Security Bulletin* 59 (3): 31–44.

Simanis, Joseph G. 1994. "The Weighted Benefit Formula—A Method of Redistribution." *Social Security Bulletin* 57 (3): 102–03.

Sinfield, Adrian. 1994. "The Latest Trends in Social Security in the United Kingdom." In *Recent Trends in Cash Benefits in Europe*, edited by Niels Ploug and Jon Kvist, 123–47. Copenhagen: Danish National Institute of Social Research.

Smedmark, Göran. 1994. "The Swedish Social Insurance System: A Model in Transition." *International Social Security Review* 47(2): 71–77.

Smeeding, Timothy, Barbara Boyle Torrey, and Martin Rein. 1988. "Patterns of Income and Poverty: The Economic Status of Children and the Elderly in Eight Countries." In *The Vulnerable*, edited by John L. Palmer, Timothy Smeeding, and Barbara Boyle Torrey, 89.Washington: Urban Institute.

Social Security Administration. 1997. *Annual Statistical Supplement, 1997.* Washington, December.

Sweden, Ministry of Health and Social Affairs. 1998. *Pension Reform in Sweden: A Short Summary* (http://www.pension.gov.se/summary.html).

Tillberg, Åsa. 1998. "Nya pensionen klar efter sex års arbete." *Dagens Industri*, January 10, 1998.

Titmuss, Richard. 1958. *Essays on the Welfare State.* London: Allen and Unwin.

Torgander, Mats. 1998. "Pensionera ska följa tillväxten." *Dagens Nyheter.* January 18, 1998.

Tuchszirer, Carole, and Catherine Vincent. 1997. "Un Consensus Presque Parfait Autour de la Reforme du Systeme du Retraite." *Chronique Internationale de l'IRES*, 48: 26–30.

Verband Deutscher Rentenversicherungsträger. 1997. "Sonderausgabe zur Rentenreform 1999: Die Änderungen im Rentenversicherungsrecht durch das

Rentenreformgesetz 1999." *Informationen aus der gesetzlichen Rentenversicherung*, Nr. 4/97. October 10.

Viebrok, Holger. 1997. *Das Arbeitsangebot im Übergang von der Beschäftigung in den Ruhestand*. Frankfurt am Main: Lang.

Von Nordheim Nielsen, Fritz. 1991. "The Politics of Aging in Scandinavian Countries." In *States, Labor Markets and the Future of Old-Age Policy*, edited by John Myles and Jill Quadagno, 127–74. Temple University Press.

_____. 1998. "From Scandinavian Laggard to World Bank Pet: The Transformation of Danish Pensions in the 1990's." Paper presented at World Congress of Sociology, Montreal, July.

Vording, Henk, and Kees Goudswaard. 1997. "Indexation of Public Pension Benefits on a Legal Basis: Some Experiences in European Countries." *Social Security Bulletin* 50(3):31–44.

Walrei, Ulrich, and Gerd Zika. 1997. "Social Protection: An Obstacle to Employment?" *International Social Security Review* 50 (4):7–26.

Wartonick, Daniel, and Michael Packard. 1983. "Slowing Down Pension Indexing: The Foreign Experience." *Social Security Bulletin* 44: 9–15.

Weaver, R. Kent. 1985. "Controlling Entitlements." In *The New Direction in American Politics*, edited by John E. Chubb and Paul E. Peterson, 307–41. Brookings.

_____. 1988. *Automatic Government: The Politics of Indexation*. Brookings.

Whiteford, Peter. 1995. "The Use of Replacement Rates in International Comparisons of Benefit Systems." *International Social Security Review* 48(2):3–30.

World Bank. 1994. *Averting the Old Age Crisis: Policies to Protect the Old and Promote Growth*. Oxford: Oxford University Press.

6

Public Investment in
Private Markets

THIS CHAPTER addresses the implications of alternative approaches to broadening the investment options for Social Security participants. The paper describes issues associated with directed trust fund investments in corporate stocks and bonds, while the commentators discuss the complexities associated with government regulation of individual accounts and the success of the Federal Thrift Savings Plan investing in corporate equities without political interference.

Investing Public Money in Private Markets:
What Are the Right Questions?
Theodore J. Angelis

FACING AN AGING population and a mature, pay-as-you-go funding system, the 1994–96 Advisory Council on Social Security proposed three different plans for Social Security's future. The proposals overlapped, however, in their common attempts to keep future benefit cuts and tax increases to a minimum by capturing the higher returns historically available through investing in equities.[1] One plan, the Personal Savings Account, would accomplish this almost exclusively through individually managed personal accounts similar to IRAs. The other two plans, the Maintain Benefits (MB) and Individual

1. Advisory Council on Social Security (1997a, p. 13) At the time of publication of the report, proponents of the MB plan urged only "further study and examination . . . [of] the possibility of large-scale investment of OASDI Trust Fund monies in the equity market." The previously released description of the MB plan, and most of the technical analysis included in the Advisory Council Report assumed this investment would occur. This paper also assumes that a portion of the built-up trust fund reserves would be invested in the equities markets under the MB plan.

Accounts (IA) plans, both envision investment strategies in which the federal government would retain control and investment authority for the Social Security Trust Fund.

The MB plan would move from the present pay-as-you-go financing to partial advance funding, and it would gradually shift from investing only in Treasury securities to investing 40 percent of the Social Security Trust Fund in the equities markets. If historical rates of return continue, the trust fund's real rate of return would rise from 2.3 percent to 4.2 percent. The increased earnings, together with other structural changes, would keep the system in balance over the next seventy-five years and beyond.[2]

The Individual Accounts plan would reduce guaranteed benefits for future beneficiaries relative to current law or the MB plan, but it would create a new "individual account" benefit by requiring workers to contribute an additional 1.6 percent of their earnings into a government-held account. The government would invest the accounts according to each worker's choice within a limited set of investment options, similar to those available under the Federal Employees Thrift Savings Plan (TSP), which resembles a private 401(k) plan. The IA proponents believe that by giving each individual an "explicit stake" in Social Security, the IA plan would avoid many of the political, economic, and demographic uncertainties that plague the current Social Security system.[3] The IA supporters also believe that individuals' ability to direct their investment choices decreases the chance of "political interference in the operations of private business."[4] They oppose individually managed accounts, however, because government-managed accounts offer lower administrative costs. Because the IA plan would pool small accounts, its administrative costs are projected to be only 10 percent of those of individually managed accounts.[5] Government-managed accounts would also eliminate individual investors' ability to make unwise investment choices.

The Questions

This paper examines some of the background issues that would accompany public investing in private markets under the two plans that envision a prominent government role. It begins with the problem of social investing and asks how federal officials can avoid political pressure to use investment decisions to serve social or political goals. The trust fund is susceptible to three types of

2. Advisory Council (1997a, p. 25).
3. Gramlich (1997, p. 26).
4. Advisory Council (1997a, p. 155).
5. Advisory Council (1997a, p. 36).

social investing: avoiding unethical firms; targeting neglected investments; and funding pet projects. The key question is how much, if any, social investing the trust fund can permit without sacrificing the overall goal of improving returns, and what processes will insulate the trust fund from social investing. The MB and IA plans seek to protect investment choices both from external political pressure—applied by Congress, the White House, and other political actors—and from internal pressure by those with investment power who would wield it for social ends. This paper examines the most commonly proposed insulation techniques as they have been employed by the Thrift Savings Plan (TSP) and contrasts the TSP's experience with that of state government pension plans, whose occasional involvement in corporate governance and perceived inclination toward social investing are often cited as reasons to avoid public investing in private markets.

Second, there are the questions that arise from the government's status as shareholder. By using indexed investments, both plans eliminate the traditional "exit" model of selling equities to indicate displeasure. When faced with similar constraints, other large investors have used "voice" strategies such as proxy battles and corporate monitoring to change companies from within. Business leaders worry that a large federal shareholder would follow suit and involve itself in corporate management.[6] The potential for such involvement raises several questions. If it were done under strict fiduciary rules to act in the best interests of plan participants (and by independent, professional fund managers), would it be harmful? Is the concern that government would dominate other shareholders? Is it that government would inevitably have competing objectives? Or is the worry that the investment managers would follow the lead of some large plans and act more like regulators or politicians than a typical economically driven shareholder? After describing the debate over the proper role of institutional investors, the paper attempts to answer these questions by assessing the impact of four strategies designed to limit the negative effects of government holdings.

Third, the paper returns to the concept of social investing to discuss the special case of international equities, where the available protections are fewer and the political pitfalls more numerous. It assesses whether international investing should be allowed at all, whether other reforms might decrease risk, and how public investing in international markets will complicate foreign and economic policy.

Fourth, there is the question of whether public investing will disrupt other government activity. The Securities and Exchange Commission's difficulties

---

6. Committee for Economic Development (1997, p. 47).

in articulating a clear policy toward institutional investors may become yet harder in the face of public investing. Trust fund investments in equities may lead Congress to displace the split federal and state regulation of corporate activity in favor of federal rules. Public investment might also complicate other federal obligations, such as fiscal and monetary policymaking.

Assessing and Insulating against Social Investing

The most common concern is that officials would select investments to satisfy social or political goals rather than for their risk/return profiles, and that such investments would consequently lower investment returns. Social investing is compatible with the goal of improving trust fund returns only when the socially worthy investments offer better returns than an all-treasuries portfolio. The question, therefore, is which kinds of social investing to allow and to what level. Each category of social investing—avoiding unethical firms, targeting neglected investments, and funding pet projects—presents its own difficulties for trust fund investing.

Avoiding Unethical Firms

Both the MB and IA plans would require the trust fund to invest its equity holdings according to a broad index designed to reflect the overall domestic equities markets. Index investing would force the trust fund to support a variety of corporate behaviors that, while not illegal, might be considered unethical or unpopular. Public pension funds have occasionally divested their holdings in companies that do not match their ethical standards. In the 1980s, they sold shares in companies that did business in South Africa, and more recently, many plans have eliminated their tobacco holdings.[7] Opponents of this practice point out that divestment can cause large losses both at the time of sale, because of brokerage fees and depressed stock prices during a government-mandated sale, and afterward as the narrower selection of stocks increases a portfolio's riskiness.[8] For example, the South Africa divestiture created a bias toward small capitalization stocks. This portfolio performed better than its nondivested counterpart during the early 1980s, but significantly worse from 1985–89.[9]

7. Moore (1995, p. ix). Some state pension funds disallow investments in Iran, in Cuba, in companies that comply with the Arab League's boycott of Israel, and in companies that discriminate based on religion in Northern Ireland.
8. "Divestment Proves Costly and Hard," *Wall Street Journal*, February 22, 1989, p. C1. The New Jersey state pension fund divested itself of all South African linked securities and lost between $313 and $515 million in brokerage fees and lost profits.
9. Smith (1997, pp. 30–31).

Targeting Neglected Investments

Some social investing proponents see pension money as a tool for economic development. They assert that gaps in public capital markets, in areas such as low-income housing and small businesses, offer opportunities for pension funds to receive a competitive return while providing societal benefits.[10] These economically targeted investments (ETIs), proponents claim, are attractive for both economic and noneconomic reasons. ETIs differ from traditional social investing, which involves actually giving up some economic gain for political or social benefits. Though ETIs often provide less liquidity and less information about their risks and returns, they have been approved as an appropriate discharge of fiduciary duties under the Employee Retirement Income Security Act of 1974 (ERISA).[11]

The line between ETIs and traditional social investing, however, remains blurry. Presumably there should be some premium to compensate investors for illiquidity and uncertainty, but no clear standards exist to determine whether an ETI offers the same risk/return profile as a more traditional investment. It also seems difficult to reconcile the valuation of overall social benefits with investors' fiduciary duty to act "for the exclusive purpose of providing benefits to participants and their beneficiaries."[12] The courts, the Department of Labor, and academic commentators have struggled with these difficulties, and the result has been confusing standards.[13] Detractors also emphasize that there is little empirical evidence that gaps in capital markets hinder economically viable projects from going forward and that even if gaps did exist, a public pension system is the wrong venue for funding public goods. A more transparent program would allow easier assessment of the true costs and benefits of the program.[14]

Funding Pet Projects

Some ETIs provide only a general promise of future economic benefits. Programs such as empowerment zones or infrastructure projects, for example, straddle the line between investments and expenditures. In an era of limited discretionary funds, the Social Security trust fund might face pressure to invest

10. Litvak (1981); Cross (1993, p. 931).

11. 29 CFR, sec 2509.94-1. While the trust fund would not be subject to ERISA, that statute tends to be authoritative on the scope of fiduciary duties.

12. U.S. Code, title 5, sec. 8477(b)(1)(A). The "exclusive purpose" requirement is a typical dictate of fiduciary investing.

13. For a review of these decisions and a summary of the debate over whether costless social investing is a workable concept, see Langbein and Wolk (1995, p. 776–85).

14. Romano (1993, pp. 813).

in these projects with the understanding that its investment would provide higher tax revenue in the future. Though this is the least likely form of social investing, opponents note that political leaders have called for this type of ETI in the past.[15]

The Costs of Social Investing

Though each type of social investing could lower investment returns, there are comparatively few instances in which any form of social investing has substantially decreased the investment returns of a public pension plan. Although a few plans have lost significant amounts of money in pursuit of ETIs, these debacles are rare.[16] Confining ETIs and pet projects to a small portion of the overall portfolio should nearly eliminate the risk of serious loss. A formal divestiture mechanism that allowed for an orderly exit also might limit the damage of preferentially selecting companies for political reasons.

Nonetheless, there are reasons to avoid social investing apart from lower returns.[17] Social investing conflates the roles of government-as-regulator and government-as-investor by shifting the venue of political decisionmaking away from broad policy choices to more marginal investment decisions. For example, it invites Congress to regulate tobacco investment policy instead of tobacco itself. Ideally, government actors would establish regulations that reflect a societally approved baseline around which individuals choose their own investments. The practice of avoiding unethical firms, however, would add an ad hoc moral component with no clear boundaries. The MB and IA proponents fear that without an absolute stand against preferential stock selection, ethical targeting would encourage each pressure group to add its priorities on the trust

15. While running for president in 1992, then-Governor Clinton called for states to use pension money to fund infrastructure projects: "We'd be interested in the states coming up with creative financing ideas, including some mechanism that could include use of pension funds." "Campaign '92: Democrats Are Outbidding One Another on Plans to Create Jobs by Rebuilding U.S. Infrastructure," *Wall Street Journal*, July 7, 1992, p. A16.

16. For a discussion of Connecticut's $25 million loss sustained while attempting to save Colt Industries from bankruptcy, see Schwimmer (1992, p. 4). For a description of the more than $100 million in losses Kansas incurred in supporting Kansas businesses, see James White, "Picking Losers: Back Yard Investing Yields Big Losses, Roils Kansas Pension System," *Wall Street Journal*, August 21, 1991, p. A1.

17. In his response to this paper, Howell E. Jackson correctly points out that social investing is estimated to eliminate less than half of the expected difference in returns between current investment practices and the proposed move toward equities. The fundamental question is whether this decrease, when coupled with other drawbacks to social investing, changes policymakers' decisions about how to structure the trust fund investment process.

fund's portfolio. Similarly, selecting ETIs would force an investment board into the same controversies that surround more traditional pork barrel spending such as defense contracts and infrastructure projects. This is doubly true for pet projects. Although these three types of social investing might not substantially harm the trust fund's overall investment returns, their potential to expand beyond set limits and to erode confidence in public investing has led the MB and IA plans to attempt to prohibit social investing altogether.

Insulation

Both the MB and IA plans envision the Federal Thrift Savings Plan (TSP) as a model because it has successfully avoided the problems of social investing. State pension plans, in contrast, have struggled with social investing. The differences examined below suggest that preventing social investing is easiest when the initial program designers want to avoid it; they devise strong procedures to do so; and an ongoing political consensus keeps future politicians from undoing their work.

The Federal Thrift Savings Plan

The TSP's designers sought to insulate investment decisions from the temptation to engage in social investing. To accomplish their goal they created an independent and neutral investment board, strict fiduciary duties, and a narrow universe of investment choices. By regulating both the inputs and the outputs (as well as the composition) of the investment board, this structure provides "double insulation" from political pressure.

The authorizing statute creates an independent management structure. The Federal Retirement Thrift Investment Board is nominally within the executive branch, but it is permitted to determine its own budget and submit it directly to Congress. The president appoints the members of the board and selects its chairman, and the House and Senate each recommend one of the board's members,[18] but once confirmed by the Senate, board members cannot be removed during their four-year terms.[19] The board selects an executive director to implement its guidelines, but the board cannot prescribe particular investments. The board members serve on a part-time basis, but the full-time executive director provides the day-to-day management of the TSP according

18. U.S. Code, title 5, sec. 8472(a)-(b).
19. U.S. Code, title 5, sec. 8472(e)(1).

to statutorily enumerated powers and policies established by the board. The chairman of the board also appoints a fourteen-member Advisory Committee to represent labor, management, beneficiaries, and women employees.

The statute also limits the investment motives of the board. It requires that the plan's fiduciaries discharge their duties "solely in the interest of the participants and beneficiaries [of the TSP]."[20] The statute applies the "prudent investor" fiduciary standard[21] to the board, the executive director, and any other person who exercises discretionary authority over the fund's assets or who might otherwise be considered a fiduciary under ERISA.[22] The statute gives the secretary of labor the authority to enforce these standards by bringing a civil action against any fiduciary except a member of the board or the executive director. The secretary also performs fiduciary audits in addition to the yearly financial audit performed by a private accounting firm.[23]

The statute limits investment choices. The board may create only five broad investment funds,[24] and in the case of the equities funds, the investments must match a "commonly recognized index . . . which is a reasonably complete representation of the United States equity markets."[25] A well-defined, broad-based index eliminates the ability to choose any specific set of companies, industries, or projects for social or political reasons. Although the board chooses the indexes, it selects a private investment manager to invest the funds. The statute also prohibits the board or TSP officials from exercising voting rights linked to its shares.[26] The board's outside investment manager votes the shares.[27]

20. U.S. Code, title 5, sec. 8372(h).

21. The prudent investor standard requires that investors act "with the care, skill, prudence, and diligence under the circumstances then prevailing that a prudent individual acting in a like capacity and familiar with such matters would use in the conduct of an enterprise of a like character and with like objectives; and . . . by diversifying the investments . . . so as to minimize the risk of large losses, unless under the circumstances it is clearly prudent not to do so." U.S. Code, title 5, sec. 8477(b)-(c).

22. U.S. Code, title 5, sec. 8477 (Thrift Savings Plan); U.S. Code, title 29, sec. 1002(21)(A) (ERISA).

23. U.S. Code, title 5, sec. 8439.

24. These are a government securities fund (G), a fixed income investment fund (F), a Common Stock Index Investment Fund (C), a Small Capitalization Stock Index Investment Fund (S), and an International Stock Index Investment Fund (I). The last two funds were congressionally authorized in 1996 but have not yet been offered to plan participants.

25. U.S. Code, title 5, sec. 8438(b)(2)(A). The TSP has used the S&P 500 as its benchmark because it is recognizable to plan participants and because it is easy to hold in its entirety unlike broader funds, which generally require that investors hold a large sample of the index. Francis X. Cavanaugh, telephone conversation with author, January 5, 1997.

26. U.S. Code, title 5, sec. 8438(f)

27. The TSP funds are part of a larger, commingled, passive account that serves hundreds of institutional investors. The need to act for the common benefit of all of these investors further insulates investment activities from pressure from any one fund.

These static protections require a stable political environment to function properly. One dynamic mechanism for achieving political insulation is an ongoing political culture of noninterference. The TSP has captured some of this dynamic protection by creating a strong consensus that it should remain apolitical. Its creation spanned five years of deliberations, open forums, and policy analyses designed to create strong bipartisan support. Its creators took pains to emphasize that economic, instead of social or political, goals were to be the sole pursuit of the investment board.[28] The TSP has perpetuated this noninterference norm by refusing to yield to pressure to invest in ETIs and to avoid companies doing business in South Africa or engaging in religious discrimination in Northern Ireland. The first executive director, Francis Cavanaugh, also attributes some of the TSP's investment independence to its ability to convince pressure groups that the TSP's unique structure would not endanger the social goals of other federal programs. An investment program as large and as symbolically important as Social Security may be less amenable than the TSP to such a strategy. Nonetheless, a detailed study and discussion of investing options, coupled with strong congressional statements of the proper role of public investing, could help to build a similar political culture of noninterference that would prevent future politicians from adding social or political goals.

Finally, the TSP's choice of a defined-contribution system with individual accounts may provide more political insulation than a centrally managed investment system. Shifting investment risk to individuals could increase incentives to monitor investments and to oppose any attempts to fulfill social or political goals with Social Security money.[29] The IA proponents believe that allowing individuals to direct their own accounts will eliminate calls to dump politically unattractive stock from the equity portfolio.[30]

Though often presented separately, these strategies overlap. A rigid indexing requirement, for example, makes strict fiduciary duties and board independence less necessary. Conversely, an independent investment board coupled with a political culture of noninterference should decrease the need for indexing to avoid politically motivated investment strategies. The strategies occasionally conflict, demonstrating the trade-off between insulation and other investment goals. For example, the plan to allow investments only in government bonds

28. U.S. Senate (1985, p. 521). Senator Stevens said, "I don't think that [social investment] should be our function," and that the statute should allow only "strict economic investment." Cavanaugh indicates that he invoked the language of Senator Stevens whenever approached by social investing advocates.

29. This is one of the primary reasons given by Michigan's governor, John Engler, and its treasurer, Douglas Roberts, for the switch from a defined-benefit to a defined-contribution plan for public employees. Roberts and Hanley (1997, p. 21).

30. Advisory Council (1997a, p. 155).

and indexed equities hinders the fiduciary duty to diversify. Limiting the trust fund to two classes of investment goes against the most recent formulations of the fiduciary duties of pension managers.[31] Even if equities often offer a superior return, fiduciary duties under the "prudent investor" standard require diversification unless imprudent.[32] The widespread use of novel investment vehicles such as Venture Capital funds, Real Estate Investment Trusts (REITs), direct investment in individual foreign markets, and various derivatives, raises questions about whether a uniform reliance on equities and treasuries is the most appropriate investment strategy.[33] Second, rigid adherence to a broad index could violate the fiduciary duty to minimize costs. Some stocks, especially in the broadest indexes, trade relatively infrequently. Holding the specified proportion of all of the stocks in the index could require costly transactions. Fund managers typically employ sampling techniques to avoid these problems, but the lack of a clear mandatory index could skew results.[34] The TSP has overcome these problems by choosing the S&P 500 as its index, at the cost of selecting an index narrower than those used by other large public pension plans.[35]

Several important differences between the TSP and Social Security limit the ease with which Social Security could duplicate the TSP's investment insulation. The most obvious is size. As of October 1997, the Thrift Savings Plan had a total of $53.5 billion invested, of which $26.2 billion is in the equities (C)

31. The new Uniform Management of Public Employee Retirement Systems Act (UMPERSA), designed to improve investing practices of state pension plans, subjects "trustees" to strict fiduciary duties but rejects "categoric restrictions on types of investments." UMPERSA, sec. 8(a)(2) & (4). UMPERSA, ERISA, and the Restatement of Trusts: Prudent Investor Rule all rely on "modern portfolio theory," defining risk as either "compensated" or "uncompensated." A well-diversified portfolio contains no uncompensated risk. By choosing only equities and treasuries (at least initially), the MB and IA plans retain diversifiable risk. One explanation is that they are implicitly deciding that the protection against social investing or other government interference is worth more than the additional diversification.

32. Securities offer a better long-term return because they are "riskier" in an economic sense. This means that their value fluctuates from its average more than other investments. Over time, securities have outperformed individual investments, but a well-diversified portfolio decreases the risk of loss at any single point in time.

33. Malkiel (1993).

34. An index is a theoretical construct. No investor can fully match an index's return because of tracking errors such as the need to hold some cash, the costs of acquiring stocks, and the delay in receiving and reinvesting dividends. Occasionally, these tracking errors are quite large. In England, for example, in 1996 the FTSE 100 index grew by 12.2 percent, but the Barclays Unicorn FTSE-100 fund grew at 21.57 percent and the Marks & Spencer UK FTSE-100 fund grew only 8.18 percent.

35. The TSP will begin to offer a fund that invests in smaller capitalization companies in the near future, allowing investors to further diversify their stock holdings.

fund.[36] The MB plan, on the other hand, would hold equities on the order of $1 trillion (1996 dollars) in 2014.[37] Even the estimate for the Individual Accounts plan, $560 billion (1996 dollars) invested in stocks by 2014, would still represent a twentyfold increase over the Thrift Savings Plan's current equity holdings.[38] These estimates may grow larger as reformers see equity investing as a means to avoid other, less popular changes such as increasing the normal retirement age, decreasing cost-of-living adjustments, or including all state and local workers in the Social Security system.[39] One benefit, however, is that under the MB and IA plans, the trust fund's investments would grow slowly, allowing periodic assessment of its operations, and decreasing the disparity in size between it and other large investors.

The TSP is also a new equity investor. Established in 1986, the TSP has been heavily invested in stocks only in the last five to six years. In 1996 and the first nine months of 1997, the common stock (C) fund grew by $16.6 billion. Thus, over 50 percent of the TSP's equity investments are fewer than two years old. It is troublesome to draw conclusions about the ease of investing the Social Security trust fund from a program that has only recently reached the size of other large pension funds.

The effects of size are unpredictable. On the one hand, a large pool of investment money makes an attractive target for government needs. Proponents of the Personal Savings Account plan point out, for example, that the secretary of the treasury borrowed TSP funds to avoid debt-ceiling limits during the budget dispute of early 1996.[40] On the other hand, Social Security's vital importance in millions of Americans' lives might deter attempts to use its investments to meet

36. Peter Mackey, chief financial officer, Federal Employees Retirement System Thrift Savings Plan, telephone conversation with author, October 17, 1997.

37. Hammond and Warshawsky (1997, p. 58). These numbers reflect the Advisory Council's assumptions that an additional 2.67 percent of the trust fund will be invested in equities each year from 2000–2014 to a cap of 40 percent and a real rate of return of 7 percent on equities and 2.3 percent on bonds.

38. There is some debate over the proportion of equities that the trust fund would hold. Hammond and Warshawsky (1997, p. 58) estimate that Social Security equity investments would not exceed 5 percent of total domestic equities. Stanton (1997, p. 423) estimated the likely ownership closer to 15 percent. These figures assume that the trust fund's investments can be invested evenly in all equities. If the trust fund were invested only in a narrower index such as the S&P 500, its percentage ownership of individual companies would be higher.

39. The Advisory Council may have overestimated the ease with which some of its revenue-enhancing reforms might be implemented. For example, the proposal to include all remaining state and local workers in Social Security was first included in President Bush's 1989 budget and has appeared in nearly every budget thereafter, though it has never been approved. For an argument that the exclusion benefits state and local workers, see Even and MacPherson (1997, p. 39).

40. Advisory Council (1997a, p. 127).

other goals. Perhaps the only certain effect of the size of public equities hold-ings will be increased attention to investment issues that are now of interest to a narrower segment of the population.

The TSP—like the investment portion of the IA plan—is a defined-contri-bution plan. Both place the risk of poor performance on the investor. The MB plan, as a defined-benefit plan, places investment risk on Social Security tax-payers as a whole. Both the MB and the IA plan anticipate limiting authorized investments to treasuries and a single index of equities. However, this limit might be less politically stable for the MB plan. First, a single government investor can hold a wide variety of financial instruments more cheaply than multiple pooled-account investors can. Thus, it makes more sense under an MB plan to allow additional investments in the interest of diversification. A broader range of investments would increase the pressure to use some portion of the fund for ETIs or pet projects. Second, when the group bears the investment risk, individuals have fewer incentives to oppose or even monitor political influ-ence on investment choices. This second view, however, may ignore the reality that individual risk does not guarantee that participants will fully consider their choices.[41]

The TSP example, moreover, cannot reveal whether large-scale public investing will affect the independence of markets and accounts when invest-ments go sour. In an IA, defined-contribution plan, a significant market drop could raise an outcry for congressional intervention either to halt the equities losses or to make up lost gains, especially for those nearest to retirement. An MB, defined-benefit plan, could also prompt a stock market bailout if losses significantly alter the long-range-funding financial balance of the trust fund. In general, federal employees offer a poor example of how much risk Congress will allow participants to bear in an Individual Accounts plan. Federal employ-ees under the TSP are relatively well educated, enjoy secure employment, and have powerful unions. They are less likely to suffer from substandard returns because of interrupted work histories or poor investment selection. In contrast, in the Social Security example, these concerns, coupled with the elimination of guaranteed full Social Security benefits, are likely to increase risk aversion,

41. A defined-contribution plan that authorizes an environmentally friendly "E" fund, for exam-ple, consisting of the index minus polluting companies, might find that environmental groups con-vince participants to choose it without a full understanding of the additional risk. If the plan also offered a human-rights based "H" fund, and a majority of investors choose the E or H fund, the investment board might drop the plan index in the interest of administrative efficiency or use one of the socially progressive indexes as a default for those workers who do not choose an asset allo-cation. I owe this insight to Peter Diamond.

especially for the lowest-paid workers.[42] Recent data from 401(k) plans confirm that lower-paid employees continue to invest more conservatively than they should to maximize their long-term returns.[43] If the guaranteed floor of Social Security benefits drops, this risk aversion could increase, and if substandard returns exacerbate income inequalities in retirement, pressure will increase for Congress to offer some form of redistribution or guaranteed income.[44]

Despite these differences, the TSP's success demonstrates that a public plan can avoid many of the difficulties inherent in public investing by employing overlapping insulation techniques and building a political mandate for continual independence.

The State Public Employee Retirement Plans

Large state pension plans offer the main alternative analogy for an equity-based federal retirement system. Despite fiduciary standards almost identical to those of the TSP and ERISA, and the extensive use of indexed investments, state plans are occasionally politically and socially activist.[45] This section examines the differences between state plans and the TSP, how these differences affect investing, and whether they would prove problematic for trust fund investing under the MB and IA plans. Though state plans vary considerably, they have been less committed to the goal of preventing social investing, with some states specifically reserving a portion of their portfolio for social goals. They have also relied upon less rigid means of separating investing from politics and have wavered in their continual support for noninterference.

Critics of public investing point to a variety of problems that have afflicted state pension plans. For example, in times of budgetary crisis, state leaders have attempted to manipulate actuarial accounting or simply to seize "excess"

42. Federal workers are required to sign a statement indicating that they understand the risks of investing in equities before they are allowed to place their money in the C fund. See U.S. Code, title 5, sec. 8477(h). A similar requirement for Social Security investments could exacerbate risk aversion.

43. Employees earning less than $45,000 annually invested approximately 65 percent in fixed income assets and 35 percent in equity, whereas for workers earning over $75,000, the percentages were reversed. Gordon (1997, pp. 1556–57).

44. John Langbein (1997) has warned that disparity will encourage Congress to "stick its big foot in . . . [and] recapture the winners' gains [to redistribute to losers]." This redistribution could be accomplished indirectly. Current 401(k) plans, for instance, limit the annual income from these plans to $150,000 (1994 dollars) per year. See Internal Revenue Code, sec. 401(k)(17).

45. The vast majority of state funds employ a core/noncore strategy in which a percentage of their equities are passively managed in index funds and the remainder are actively traded. I have not encountered a state or local plan that relies on index funds for 100 percent of its equity investments.

earnings out of the pension funds.[46] Judicial protection has remedied some of these abuses,[47] but apart from obvious cases, courts cannot easily determine whether a withdrawal of or decrease in payments is a legitimate reaction to overfunding or an improper attempt to use pension funds as a budgetary safety valve. States have also engaged in some forms of social investing. Several state plans encourage or require investment boards to avoid unethical firms and invest in ETIs, and on occasion, investment trustees have acted on social concerns of their own volition.

The continuing debate over public investment in tobacco stocks, for example, demonstrates that skillful politicians can recast social investing into fiduciary language. In Florida the state treasurer and governor forced divestiture because of the increased risk to tobacco profits owing to the proliferation of lawsuits against major tobacco companies. They relied in part on legal advice from the governor-appointed attorney general who said that tobacco stocks were uniquely vulnerable owing to a series of legal attacks.[48] The dissenting Florida comptroller joined a host of officials from other state plans who cited extensive investment and legal advice indicating that divestment was unsound and a violation of fiduciary duty.[49] The same debate has played out in many states. Massachusetts, Vermont, Florida, Texas, Maryland, New Hampshire, and New York all chose some form of divestment for their pension plans. Other states resisted, claiming that their fiduciary duties prevent them from selling to achieve social goals and often mentioning the difficulty of doing so while maintaining indexed investment funds.[50] No clear statutory or structural features separate the two camps, but all of the funds that chose to divest faced pressure from political leaders pushing for the change. In some cases, the debate over fiduciary duties between pension fund managers and political leaders served as a prelude to future statewide elections.

46. California transferred $16 billion to its general fund, Illinois transferred $21 million, New York changed actuarial accounting to defer $429 million in payments, and California attempted to transfer actuarial decisions to a governor-appointed actuary and away from the CalPERS board. Walters (1992, p. 18).

47. For a discussion of California's mandatory $1 billion repayment to CalPERS, see Debora Vrana, "State Loses Battle over Withholding from CalPERS," *Los Angeles Times*, February 21, 1997, p. D1. For a description of the overturning of New York's actuarial assumptions and deferrals, see Hemmerick and Schwimmer (1992, p. 10).

48. Shirish Date, " Florida May Vote to Dump Tobacco Stocks," *Florida Times-Union*, May 28, 1997, p. A1.

49. Katherine Bloomburg, "Quitting Profitable Tobacco Stocks Is Hard for Pension Funds," *Seattle Post-Intelligencer*, June 10, 1997, p. B9.

50. Don Michak, "Sparring Continues over Tobacco Investments," *Journal Inquirer*, October 3, 1996, p. 25.

Many state plans allow or require investors to consider a wide variety of economically targeted investments. Enabling statutes can list dozens of investments concentrated in areas such as local infrastructure, in-state equity funds, Ginnie Mae and Fannie Mae pools, residential mortgages, small business loans, in-state equity funds and partnerships, and other private placements of capital.[51] Some states without these statutes have adopted internal guidelines that authorize these investments.[52] Fiduciary duties dictate that investors may choose ETIs only if they offer competitive returns for their risk.[53] When evaluating investments becomes difficult, however, the potential for competing motives to emerge increases.[54] There is no easy way to decide whether ETIs tend to be sound or little more than traditional social investments in disguise; for example, rescuing troubled local businesses seems unwise, but even these investments, if properly diversified, can fit within a sound investment policy. Empirical studies indicate that the presence of mandated in-state and other targeted investments only moderately depressed pension funds' earnings.[55] Because ETIs represent a small part of most state portfolios, and because the type of investment affects the long-term investment returns more than any particular choices within each class,[56] it is hard to say whether social investing has overshadowed legitimate goals for choosing these investments.

The causes of these behaviors are easy to discern. Unlike the TSP, state investment boards are not politically independent. Investment boards have three types of members: those appointed by the governor of the state, those elected

51. Examples include Ariz Rev. Stat. Ann., sec. 38-757(B) (1996); Ark. Code, sec. 24-3-414 (1996); Colo. Rev. Stat., sec. 24-51-206(1) (1996); Conn. Gen. Stat., sec. 3-13 (1994); Fla. Stat. Ann., sec. 215.47 (1997); Haw. Rev. Stat., sec. 88-119 (1994); Iowa Code Ann., sec. 97B.7(2) (1995); Kan. Stat. Ann., sec. 74-4921(5)(c) (1994); Ky. Rev. Stat., sec. 161.430(1) (1994); Mass. Gen. Laws, sec. 23(1)(d).

52. The California Public Employees Retirement System (CalPERS), for example, has a target of $5 billion in alternative investments and a detailed Economically Targeted Investment Policy. Romano (1993, p. 809) mentions six states with similar policies: Alabama, Kansas, Minnesota, Oregon, Wisconsin, and Wyoming.

53. Colorado, for example, states that "preference shall be given to Colorado investments consistent with sound investment policy." Colo. Rev. Stat § 24-51-206(1) (1996).

54. Romano (1993, pp. 805–06). In fact, there is evidence to suggest that there is pressure to find that socially desirable investments offer an adequate or favorable return even where evidence is to the contrary. See U.S. House (1983, p. 68); U.S. General Accounting Office (1992).

55. Hsin and Mitchell (1995) found the presence of in-state investments to be significantly negatively related to fund performance in only one of the five years studied. Mitchell and Hsin (1997, p. 109) and Romano (1993, pp. 828–29) found that social investing legislation and policies were also negatively related to performance, but only weakly so, and concluded that board composition overshadowed the effect of social investing.

56. Zorn (1997, p. 62); Ibbotson and Brinson (1987, pp. 257–59).

by plan participants and beneficiaries, and those that serve because of the office that they hold in state government. Boards range in size from three to twenty-eight with an average of eight members.[57] An average of four members are appointed, usually by the governor, and typically two, often the state treasurer and the state controller, serve ex officio.[58] Several empirical studies have examined the link between board independence, as measured by the proportion of members not appointed or serving ex officio, and fund performance. Romano found that independence and earnings were significantly and positively related, and that boards with participant-elected members offered the greatest increases in returns.[59] These results were confirmed by Mitchell and Hsin, who found a statistically significant relationship between pension funding levels and the number of board members elected by plan participants and beneficiaries.[60]

Neither the state plans' provisions for avoiding unethical firms nor their explicit authorization of ETIs poses as much of a threat to a redesigned Social Security system. In several state plans, investment authority rests entirely with elected officials.[61] Elected officials have competing duties to fulfill and must stand for reelection.[62] The federal boards proposed in both the IA and MB plans, on the other hand, place a high premium on independence; no elected officials would retain investment policy authority. Also, both the IA and MB plans rely on strict indexing requirements to augment fiduciary duties. If the ability to select particular investments is removed by law, the question of ETIs and pet projects is moot. Moreover, apolitical boards are far less likely to attract politically motivated individuals, further decreasing the likelihood that board members would use the index to avoid unethical firms.

Internal political pressure is only one side of the insulation dilemma. The state plans demonstrate that external political pressure could affect the selection of an index. There are hundreds of mutual funds that avoid socially unpopular investments such as tobacco, alcohol, nonunion corporations, and environmental violators. Indeed, the Social Investing Forum indicates that "socially respon-

57. Zorn (1997, p. 21).
58. Mitchell and Hsin (1997, p. 92).
59. Romano (1993, p. 825).
60. Hsin and Mitchell (1995).
61. Florida, Connecticut, and New York, for example, employ this model.
62. A recent controversy has erupted in California, where the elected State Controller and Treasurer both received substantial campaign contributions from companies in which CalPERS and CalSTRS, the first and third largest public pension funds in the nation, had investments. See Paul Jacobs, "Donations to Pension Officials Scrutinized," *Los Angeles Times*, August 21, 1997, p. A1. A similar set of stories questioned the campaign contributions received by the elected comptroller of New York, the sole trustee for the Common State Retirement Fund. "Pay for Statewide Campaigns," *Buffalo News*, January 28, 1996, p. F8.

sible investing" is up 85 percent since 1995, to a total of $1.185 trillion.[63] Political pressure on index funds has followed this trend. The New York Common Retirement Fund differentially selects for less tobacco in its index fund, and the largest passive investor, BZW Barclays, which also manages the Thrift Savings Plan's stock portfolio, plans to offer index options that exclude or underweight according to certain social goals. In general, however, tinkering with indexes is less important for federal actors because they have other more powerful and more direct tools to regulate unethical activities.[64] State politics also presents a different political environment. Because state plans cover only a small percentage of the work force, but retain the ability to make up revenue shortfalls by taxing the entire population, they can take greater risks of lower returns without alarming future taxpayers.[65] The federal system, however, would apply to every worker, and the potential for lower returns or higher taxes would add a stronger incentive to forgo political manipulation of the index.

How likely is a redesigned Social Security program to avoid the problems of social investing? The answer depends on the designers' commitment to strong institutional safeguards and their ability to maintain a durable political commitment to independence. The initial signs are encouraging. The Advisory Council's report reflects a strong commitment to preventing social investing that policymakers are likely to adopt. The TSP model offers a preliminary blueprint for the institutions that the designers could adapt for trust fund investing, though Social Security's size, political importance, and defined-benefit structure may lessen their effectiveness. Strong political support should also limit the ability of future politicians to subvert a carefully constructed investment process. The state plans' experience does indicate that some issues have more potential to translate social preferences into investment decisions. Whether the proposal safeguards would prevent all social investing remains an open question.[66]

---

63. Laura Castaneda, "Arcata Looks for 'Social' Investments," *San Francisco Chronicle*, November 18, 1997, p. C1.

64. Douglas Arnold has attributed states' tobacco divestment and lawsuits against tobacco companies to the lack of other means for affecting their behavior. The rush to divest tobacco stocks might also be discounted because of perception that dumping them would help in the recovery of billions of dollars in health care costs paid for smoking-related illnesses.

65. Diamond (1997, p. 38) has called this pattern of attentive politicians and inattentive taxpayers a "natural political equilibrium."

66. Neville Nankivel, "Senate Intervention Helps Widen Debate over Retirement Systems," *Financial Post (Canada)*, December 20, 1997, p. 29, points out that Canada was confident enough in the combination of an independent, professional board, strict fiduciary duties, and indexed investments that it passed a broad reform similar to the MB plan that allows the Canadian Pension Plan to begin investing in equities. For a description of the proposed plan, see Slater (1997, p. 98).

Government as Shareholder

Another worry is that equity holdings could make the federal government a significant player in corporate decisionmaking. The Committee for Economic Development, a pro-business think-tank, stated that "the possibility of federal government influence on private firms . . . is an unnecessary and undesirable risk for the U.S. economy."[67] Responding to this concern, the proponents of the MB plan stated that "in one way or another, the neutrality of Social Security's voting rights should be established."[68] The IA proponents implicitly concurred in this view by endeavoring to protect the "public-private split." Yet the debate over how much power institutional investors, and especially government institutional investors, should have over corporate decisions remains very contentious.

The Role of the Institutional Investor

Large investors usually lack the ability to "exit" a particular company by selling its stock. They are either bound to an index—as would be the case under the MB and IA plans—or cannot sell all of their shares because the large volume would depress the stock price and inflict a loss on the fund.[69] Faced with the elimination of the exit option, other large investors have chosen to rely upon "voice" options, in the form of proxy voting or other more informal relational investing.[70] The elimination of both exit and voice could produce less efficient capital markets or leave the government's shares vulnerable to opportunistic behavior by management or other shareholders. This dilemma is reflected in current fiduciary doctrine on voting. A fiduciary investor must not only select a group of securities, but also monitor the investments for "continuing suitability, . . . and vot[e] the shares."[71] Monitoring involves a wide variety of activities, but voting is the central mechanism for influencing corporate decisionmaking.[72] It is through voting for directors that shareholders set broad

67. Committee for Economic Development (1997, p. 47).

68. Advisory Council, (1997a, p. 26).

69. Bagley and Berger (1997, p. A25).

70. The concepts of exit and voice are developed in Hirschman (1970). Relational investing involves the practice of large investors taking a more active role in corporate management, usually by meeting with corporate executives and suggesting certain structures and decisionmaking processes the firm should use.

71. Langbein (1996, p. 665).

72. The Private Securities Litigation Act of 1995, for example, encourages institutional investors to become lead plaintiffs in lawsuits against corporations for federal securities violations (U.S. Code, title 15, sec. 77a). Though Congress is unlikely to authorize the trust fund investment board to engage in such suits, other public pension funds have done so successfully, and other federal agencies have used private counsel to represent them in civil suits against corporations acting

corporate policy, and shareholder votes are used to ratify significant corporate decision and to make policy where existing legal and corporate rules do not govern.[73] While management might prefer passive shareholders, voting has long been considered a fiduciary duty of share owners,[74] and pension trustees have a duty to undertake actions that will provide benefits greater than their costs. In most large transactions that require shareholder votes, such as buy-outs, mergers, and other business combinations, the cost of investigating and voting proxies is small in comparison to the potential gains, and thus voting clearly falls within the established fiduciary duties. Yet large institutional investors have been increasingly willing to use voice solutions in more routine circumstances to remind companies to place shareholder interests first.[75]

By targeting poorly managed companies, and formulating general rules for favored corporate policies, proponents of voice strategies see increasing returns to monitoring as institutional investors acquire larger holdings.[76] John Pound, for example, sums up this view by stating that pension funds should "undertake active strategies precisely because they have the power to affect the returns that they realize. Returns, in other words, are endogenous to their actions."[77] Some quantitative studies support this view, finding that stock prices can be driven as much by perception as the underlying economic potential of the company, and that voice strategies have led to significant gains over investment benchmarks.[78] Voice proponents believe that a large shareholder has a duty to actively monitor the structure and activity of the corporations in which it invests because "the potential benefits of an activist strategy that targets poorly managed firms are quite substantial relative to the associated cost."[79] On the other hand, there is a similarly large and growing set of scholars that dismisses voice strategies

---

illegally. Lavelle (1991, p. 3). Scott J. Paltrow, "FCIC Seeks $6–8 Billion Damages from Drexel," *Los Angeles Times*, November 15, 1990, p. A1.

73. Easterbrook and Fischel (1983, p. 395).

74. The Department of Labor has explicitly endorsed "shareholder activism" and affirmed the duty to exercise voting rights to maintain shareholder value especially where the ability to exit investments was limited. See 29 CFR, sec. 2509.94-2. Costs must be weighed against the benefits that they produce as compared to the costs and benefits of realistic alternatives. See American Law Institute, Restatement (Third) of Trusts (1992, p. 6).

75. Anand (1997, p. 20) observes that "institutional investors are using noisy, rabble-rousing techniques to cow management into submission."

76. Black (1990, p. 553); Nesbitt (1994, p. 76); Pound (1993a); Roe (1991, p. 1469).

77. Pound (1993b, pp. 39–42).

78. Fama and French (1993, p. 1) and Fama and French (1992, p. 427) cast doubt on the Capital Asset Pricing Model (CAPM) and the notion of complete market efficiency. For an example of this conclusion with regard to CalPERS, see Nesbitt (1994, p. 76) and Gordon and Pound (1993).

79. Biggs (1996, p. 4). For an explicit conclusion that large shareholders have a duty to engage in voice strategies see Koppes and Reilly, (1996, p. 423).

because they offer neither clear proof of significant improvements in investment returns, nor a convincing analytical argument they are superior to rational apathy.[80] In either case, the addition of a large, federal institutional investor would reinvigorate the debate over the role of voice strategies and might leave investment managers with conflicting models for their fiduciary duties.

Structuring Voting Rights

The uncertainty over shareholders' proper role complicates the choice of how to structure voting rights for trust fund investments. Both the IA and MB plan seek to limit government involvement in corporate affairs but take no position on the type of monitoring that private investment managers should exercise. Congress can pursue a variety of strategies to either eliminate or minimize the direct government involvement in corporate decisionmaking. Votes can be completely eliminated by legislative prohibition or automatically voted pro rata ("scored") to match other voters' decisions; exercised by investment managers with strict fiduciary duties to vote them only in the best interests of plan participants; auctioned to other investors; or minimized by limiting the amount the trust fund may own in any one company to a small percentage, perhaps 5 percent. Each strategy, however, differentially affects the ability of shareholders to police corporations.

Eliminating or scoring votes—the first option presented by MB plan advocates—removes government influence on voting decisions, but it might also destroy a substantial part of the value of each share.[81] Though empirical studies indicate that, on average, voting rights constitute a relatively small percentage of a stock's value, these values can "fluctuate wildly, and voting rights can sometimes become as valuable as cash-flow rights."[82] Where control over the firm is contested, the voting premium rises sharply.[83] The existing research, moreover, might understate the value of voting rights for Social Security investments because it focuses on small individual holdings and assigns value based on the pro rata share of benefits available to victors who secure positions on the board of directors. Because neither the IA nor MB plan envisions placing a Social Security representative on corporate boards, even where trust fund holdings would justify a position, the value of the lost votes is the cost of lost oppor-

---

80. See, for example, Romano (1996, p. 277); Wahal (1996, p. 1); Smith (1997); Coffee (1997, p. 1970).
81. Advisory Council (1997a, p. 26).
82. Zingales (1995, pp. 1049, 1059) found that the mean value of the "voting premium" was 10.5 percent of each share, while the median was 3 percent.
83. Shleifer and Vishny (1997, p. 748).

tunity for voice strategies and the increased potential for abuse at the hands of other investors.

Elimination or scoring shares will increase the voting power of other shareholders. To use a stylized example, if the government purchased equities constituting 50 percent of a firm's common stock, a previous 25 percent shareholder would now own 50 percent of the voting shares of available equity.[84] This increased voting power could have several detrimental effects on the ability to police directors' actions. Because incumbent managers and their allies tend to have de facto control of more shares than their rivals, most methods of ousting ineffective managers would become more difficult.[85] Two corporations scholars, Jensen and Ruback, argue that the self-perpetuation of poor managers is already the most expensive problem in corporate governance.[86] Secure managers have engaged in a variety of value-decreasing activities, including reinvesting cash rather than paying dividends, pursuing economically unwise acquisitions in the interest of "empire building," and establishing takeover defenses.[87] One benefit, however, is that the increased value of existing shares would make other investors' holdings more powerful and more conducive to effective monitoring. Yet individual investors tend to own less stock than board members and their allies and are prohibited from acting in concert in most circumstances. In sum, eliminating votes is unlikely to decrease value enough to make equity investing less profitable than an all-treasuries portfolio, but it could exacerbate one of the most difficult problems in corporate governance.[88]

Another option is to allow private investment managers to exercise voting responsibilities with fiduciary duties to vote them to maximize shareholder returns. This is the strategy employed by the Federal Thrift Savings Plan, many state plans, and most private investors. Private fund managers are generally adept at avoiding public pressure. Their professional reputation depends on their ability to focus upon economic incentives. For example, TSP officials

84. Effective control requires a much smaller percentage of stock ownership. The SEC, for example, has stated that control of 20 percent of voting stock in a widely held corporation will in most instances constitute control. See U.S. SEC (1989).

85. Managers rarely own large blocks of shares in publicly traded firms. The inability of ordinary shareholders to control managers' actions, however, gives managers effective control over most of the firm's decisions. Proxy battles, tender offers, and hostile takeovers could all become more difficult when the pool of available shares is decreased.

86. Jensen and Ruback (1983, p. 5).

87. Jensen (1986, p. 323). For a list of several studies detailing this practice, see Shleifer and Vishny (1997, pp. 746–47).

88. As Hammond and Warshawsky (1997) point out, the trust fund holdings are unlikely to constitute more than 5 percent of U.S. equities securities. Though a 5 percent block would make the trust fund a major shareholder, eliminating its voting rights would give other shareholders only a small increase in voting power.

indicate that BZW Barclays International has encountered pressure to vote according to social or political goals. Barclays' standard response is that it believes that other government institutions offer a more appropriate avenue to pursue those goals. The use of private managers seems especially promising if the private investment managers invest on behalf of numerous institutions. By pooling hundreds of institutional investors in a small number of accounts, investment managers at BZW Barclays have minimized political pressure to act on behalf of any single client and have reduced transaction costs because buy and sell orders are matched within the fund.

With a fund as symbolically important as Social Security, however, the attention and publicity surrounding key votes might lead to widespread media attention and political pressure for both the investment manager and the corporation. A broad index would dilute this effect, but the specter of a politically charged corporate decision, such as the elimination of thousands of jobs or the decision to move production abroad, would highlight the government's role in the corporation. Both the corporation and the investment manager might find themselves surrounded by political pressure to preserve jobs.[89] There is also some worry that fund managers would go beyond "legitimate" business goals into regulatory or political priorities. CalPERS's proxy voting strategy, for instance, encompasses not only the basic structure of the corporation but also a broad range of social and political issues.[90]

The line between corporate governance and social investing, moreover, is not a clear one. One issue that keeps resurfacing is the question of executive compensation. It is not clear whether the trend toward strict scrutiny for pay packages is motivated by business concerns or broader issues of ethics and fairness. Public outcry has prompted tax laws designed to limit executives' compensation, but their provisions have failed to curb increases.[91] Indeed, the ten-

89. Similar concerns have led twenty-five states to adopt "constituency statutes" that allow corporate managers to consider the needs of workers, suppliers, and local communities in addition to shareholder well-being. These divided loyalties would not affect investors' fiduciary duties to act in the sole interest of Social Security shareholders, but they do demonstrate the potential clash between politicians' and investors' motives.

90. The social/political issues section of CalPERS proxy policy includes areas such as animal rights, community reinvestment, corporate contribution, political action committees, the environment, infant formula, Israel, Mexico, and occupational health. See CalPERS (1995, pp. 24–32). Each is arguably designed to maximize shareholder returns.

91. The 1993 Omnibus Revenue Reconciliation Act, for example, limited the deduction available for pay to key executives to $1 million. The provisions are so complex, however, that they have not limited executive compensation. Graef Crystal, "CEO's and Incentives: The Myth of 'Pay for Performance' Compensation," *Los Angeles Times*, January 16, 1995, p. D1, points out that executive pay has increased unabated in the years since the limitation was passed and that the added shareholder activism has led to increased pay during good years to compensate for the possibility of lower pay during periods of bad company performance.

uous link between executive performance and executive pay was one of the primary instigators of the move toward voice solutions by large institutional investors.[92] The proxy plans of most of the large state pension funds contain detailed provisions for the approval or rejection of pay packages, and even companies that are performing well can meet with disapproval.[93] A partial list of similarly troubling crossover issues includes takeover resistance plans; workplace training and human capital investment initiatives; marketing restrictions for such products as tobacco, alcohol, and gambling; corporate charitable contributions; environmental issues; and affirmative action.

A third option would have the trust fund set up an auction to sell its votes. The money received would be added to the equity fund and thus would allow fund managers to increase the value of the trust fund's holdings while avoiding the need to participate in corporate decisionmaking.[94] Vote selling has long been controversial with academic commentators and state lawmakers because once votes are separated from share ownership, vote holders can cause the corporation to act in ways that benefit them at the expense of other shareholders.[95] Courts have recognized this danger and forbidden vote selling where it is likely to lead to inequitable consequences. In Delaware, where most corporate law is made, vote buying is a voidable transaction requiring a judicial test of intrinsic fairness or a shareholder approval to uphold its validity.[96] The Delaware courts have placed a high hurdle around vote buying because of its potential to "defraud or in some way disenfranchise the other stockholders."[97] At the same time, however, the Delaware courts and legislature have allowed great flexibility in the construction of voting agreements and voting trusts that provide for long-term vote commitments if not outright sale. Though the law of vote selling is probably too controversial to support such a large-scale plan, the potential for a vote auction highlights both the value and the importance of corporate voting.

A fourth option is to limit the size of the Social Security trust fund's holdings in any one company to some small percentage to minimize government

92. Crystal (1992).

93. CalPERS (1995) establishes ten separate factors to evaluate in deciding whether an investment manager should support an executive compensation package. Even though Disney had posted record profits during his tenure, a coalition of public pension funds "voted against or abstained from approving Disney Chairman Michael Eisner's fat new pay package and the estimated $90 million severance pay package for Disney's failed president Michael Ovitz." Franecki (1997).

94. Lanoff (1997, p. 3).

95. Easterbrook and Fischel (1983).

96. *Schreiber* v. *Carney*, 447 A2d 17 (Del. Ch. 1982). Other states simply prohibit vote selling altogether, for example, N.Y Bus. Corp. Law § 609(3).

97. *Schreiber* v. *Carney*, p. 17.

officials' ability to control the corporation or dominate other shareholders. This strategy is used by the Chilean pension system, and several state pension funds, and can work in conjunction with the other strategies listed above. A percentage limit would decrease the trust fund's ability to overwhelm other investors, but even a 2 or 3 percent block of shares would ensure substantial influence over the largest publicly traded companies. Small holdings, moreover, will not guarantee passivity if voice strategies are used. For example, TIAA-CREF, the largest private pension plan, made headlines and helped to change employee compensation policy by voting only 1 percent of Disney's shares against the proposed executive pay packages.[98] The holdings of notoriously activist CalPERS, moreover, usually constitute far less than the proposed 5 percent ownership cap.[99] The ability to "move the herd" through largely symbolic action can disproportionately magnify the power of small holdings.[100]

The negative features of each voting strategy show that the problems of investing Social Security funds have as much to do with the inherent problems of corporate governance as with the actors who vote proxies and manage investments. The current debate over trust fund voting does not really assess how a large block of federal money will interact with the increasing power of institutional investors, and what level of investor activism will maximize value for the trust fund. If Social Security money is to retain its public character and also to be invested in the private equities markets, institutional designers must decide how much is to be gained and lost from each type of passivity.

Social Investing Revisited

Perhaps the most difficult area in which to constrain political pressure to engage in social investing is in international investments. The MB plan calls for the eventual use of global indexes, and the IA plan would almost certainly establish an international investment option similar to the International Stock Index Investment Fund created under the Thrift Savings Plan.[101] The act of creating an index of acceptable foreign equities is itself political.[102] Even after the

98. "CREF Withholds Support for Disney Compensation Plan and Directors" (1997).
99. Coffee (1994, p. 859) states that "despite their vocal willingness to criticize managements, public funds to date have shown relatively little inclination to 'put their money where their mouth is' by making concentrated investments."
100. Reilly (1997, p. 979).
101. Advisory Council (1997a, p. 26). U.S. Code, title 5, sec. 8438(b)(4)(A). The TSP has decided to use the EAFE stock index representing twenty countries in Europe, Australia, and the Far East.
102. This is not to say that no indexes represent international equities. The problem is that choosing acceptable countries and allocating the proportion of investments is not as simple as in the

index is selected, already complex issues that require weighing of economic prerogatives against human rights, such as whether to renew MFN status for China or whether to support the economy of Indonesia could become more difficult with an agent of the federal government increasingly interested in each of those markets. In the international arena, moreover, the federal government lacks the ability to regulate traditional social concerns, and thus the call to use investment money as a punishment could be quite strong. Recent legislation authorizing sanctions on companies who do business in Cuba and Libya underscores Congress's willingness to use economic and trade tools to realize foreign policy objectives. A passive strategy would also eliminate investors' ability to exit markets that suddenly become unpredictable because of unforeseen political or economic instability, as in the cases of Russia and South Korea. Yet subsequent decision to remove a specific market from the index would itself have important symbolic consequences.

One way to avoid these difficulties is to ignore international investments altogether. Congress could easily require that trust fund investors choose only domestic equities. Recent research into diversification, however, indicates that a large fraction (approximately 39 percent) of a well-diversified portfolio should be invested in international equities, and that investing in domestically traded multinational corporations cannot duplicate these benefits.[103] The problems of international underdiversification are only now beginning to affect the decisions of large institutional investors.[104] As institutional investors move more of their money abroad to diversify their portfolios, the trust fund will face pressure to follow the trend.[105]

---

domestic context, where the concern is simply the number of stocks to include. In Norway, the public oil investment fund has devised a complicated percentage breakdown that lists acceptable countries and the percentage of foreign investments for each. Such a system in the United States could produce foreign lobbying on behalf of native markets as well as ill will from those countries who are excluded or receive a small share of foreign investments.

103. Burton Malkiel, telephone conversation with author, May 9, 1997. The appropriate analysis involves the creation of a 'Markowitz frontier' that looks to the risk and return of each investment. The goal is to maximize return for the chosen level of risk. Since return is an economic 'good' a rational investor should not be indifferent to the choice between a higher and lower return at the same level of risk.

104. State and local pension plans have increased their holdings in international equities by over 95 percent since fiscal year 1994, and international fixed income investments by almost 40 percent. Zorn (1997, p. 92).

105. The problem of underdiversification is separate from the problem of forgone growth opportunities. Some critics have attempted to dismiss the need to diversify by characterizing foreign investment as high-risk/high-return strategies. Malkiel's findings (and those of Modern Portfolio Theory in general), however, demonstrate that for the same amount of risk, a higher return can and should be realized.

A second option is to simply remove the voting rights in foreign securities or to purchase foreign debt instruments that have no voting rights. This too is an imperfect solution. As above, the lack of exit and voice options makes the Social Security shareholders more vulnerable and could depress legitimate monitoring. The elimination of voting, moreover, will not remove the problems of choosing and maintaining a list of approved countries or substantially diminish the impact of international investments on foreign economic policy. During the Mexico peso crisis, for example, the United States extended over $40 billion in loan guarantees to stop a massive outflow of investor capital.[106] The presence of Social Security money abroad might increase the frequency of such bailouts. Similarly, there would be pressure to keep Social Security funds invested during economic crises, even when imprudent, to avoid undermining government stabilization efforts.

A third option is to choose a commercially available international index and allow the private managers to dictate any changes. This strategy would eliminate many of the foreign policy overtones of individual actions but would not necessarily remove the impulse to protect Social Security money from disaster. Delegation could also increase the likelihood that fund managers would be lobbied by foreign governments, and their domestic supporters, for preferential treatment.

Dynamic Uncertainties

Another potential question is whether large sums of public money would complicate federal regulation of securities. The Securities and Exchange Commission (SEC) has had a difficult time regulating large investors in the shadow of increasing tension between institutional investors and the corporate community. The 1992 amendments to the federal proxy rules offer an illustrative case study. In 1991 the SEC announced that it was considering relaxing the proxy rules promulgated under section 14(a) of the Securities Exchange Act of 1934 to allow for greater shareholder control.[107] The comment period produced over 1,700 letters—framing the battle between institutional investors and business groups—each vehemently opposed to the position of the other.[108] Seeking

106. Juanita Darling, "News Analysis: Mexico Traded Sovereignty for Aid, Critics Say Crisis, Bailout Reminds the Country of How Dependent It Has Become on the United States," *Los Angeles Times*, January 16, 1995, p. D1.

107. The SEC acknowledged that "its proxy filing and disclosure rules were widely perceived to 'restrict unduly' shareholder communications and requested comment on specified revisions to those rules." See SEC (1991, p. 6).

108. Coffee (1994, p. 839) recounts the debate between the business community who "feared the new power and activism of the public pension funds, who, led by CalPERS and the Council of

a middle ground, the SEC did eventually relax some of the strict regulations that prohibited communications between shareholders, but over the next several months it strengthened other rules to limit this new communication power.[109] The SEC's quest to be a neutral referee in the great corporate governance debate will become more difficult as it is called upon to articulate policies that affect not only government shares but growing institutional investors of all kinds.[110] One benefit of government holdings, however, is that the IA and MB plans would protect small investors against shady business practices, and thus are less likely to complicate the SEC's procedures for protecting unsophisticated individual investors.[111]

Federally held investments might also disrupt the current state-based corporate charter system. Because there are no federal corporate charters, states regulate the form and practices of corporations. When the federal government does regulate, however, its primacy displaces the existing state law. The result is overlapping requirements for disclosure, voting procedures, and shareholder protection. For example, when corporate directors deal in their own interest, they may immunize the "self-dealing" transaction by disclosing it to shareholders and receiving their approval. While the procedure for doing so is governed by state law, the proxy statements sent to individual shareholders are regulated by both state and federal law. If they are materially misleading, shareholders can seek relief under either federal or state law. Several academic commentators have noted that although competition among states tends to produce benefits for shareholders, federal protections may actually harm shareholder welfare.[112] In the past, perceived inadequacies in state protections have helped

Institutional Investors, seemed intent on reshaping the balance of power between shareholders and managers across the face of Corporate America," and the institutional investors who accused the SEC of capitulating to the business community in "fram[ing] its proxy rules so as to chill and silence dissident shareholders' voices."

109. For a detailed analysis of this process, see Coffee (1994, pp. 876–906).

110. Coffee (1994, pp 876–906) presents a pessimistic view of the SEC's ability to articulate a clear policy for the challenge of growing institutional investors, saying that "in this battle of paradigms, the SEC appears to be zealously and outspokenly—on both sides." Fisch (1993, p. 1131) concurs noting that the SEC was "repeatedly buffeted back and forth between various players in the corporate governance arena but apparently adrift from any predetermined course of its own."

111. The PSA plan, conversely, is more likely to encourage regulatory changes designed to protect private accounts of small investors

112. Romano (1996, p. 318) indicates that share prices increase when corporations move to states with shareholder friendly regimes and that competition for corporate charters increases the expertise and efficiency of courts and legislatures in states, such as Delaware, that attract the most corporations. In contrast, several studies have pointed to detrimental effects of federal regulations designed to *protect* shareholders. See, for example, Easterbrook and Fischel (1983) (proxy regulation); Haddock and Macey (1987, p. 311) (insider trading regulations); Schwartz (1986, p. 229) (tender offers).

to fuel the call for federal reforms and even federal corporate charters. This movement has yet to succeed, but a series of well-publicized abuses—where public shareholders are at the losing end—might reinvigorate the process and cause a crisis of federalism.

Finally, there are a host of related federal decisions that will become more complex as large sums of public money move into the equities markets. The decisions of the Federal Reserve Board may gain more attention and criticism as each interest rate change affects Social Security funding. Federal fiscal policy and government borrowing will also affect the rate of return on equities and will make spending decisions more complicated. The incentive for budgetary games will increase with the opportunity to put the federal equities "on budget" to offset other spending.[113]

Conclusion

This paper attempts to present some of the most important background issues that surround the decision to invest public money in the private equities markets. It finds that the most commonly considered insulation tools provide good protection against the various forms of social investing but occasionally conflict. The contrast between the politically insulated Federal Thrift Savings Plan and state public pension plans indicates that political pressure can gravitate to areas where duties are either not defined or in conflict. The Thrift Savings Plan, by rigidly employing these insulation strategies, has managed to avoid political interference. Its size, recent creation, coverage of only federal employees, and defined-contribution structure, however, offer some limits to its generalizability. The state pension plans present a somewhat less successful model where fiduciary duties offer weaker coverage as a result of divided political loyalties, and where the authorization of hard-to-value investments has led to some privileging of social and political goals. Yet the lack of independent boards, the small ratio of covered workers to taxpayers, and the differences between state and federal politics also limit the negative lessons to be drawn from these plans.

In the corporate governance arena, neither plan envisions allowing public officials to vote proxies appurtenant to Social Security's share holdings. Yet managing voting rights and corporate monitoring presents several problematic choices. Eliminating proxy votes may insulate incumbent managers and render

---

113. A full analysis of the interplay between Social Security and the budget is beyond the scope of this paper.

shareholder monitoring less efficient. External fund managers would provide protection, but these managers might employ some of the same intrusive monitoring strategies that the business community fears from direct government investment. Using private fund managers also moves the political pressure point. These managers have avoided political pressure thus far, but their skills may be tested under public scrutiny of Social Security's investments. Auctioning proxies runs counter to the policy judgments struck by current state law and several academic commentators, and its potential effects remain unknown. Limiting holdings to a small percentage of each company would still allow the trust fund to hold a substantial block in the largest, most widely held companies, and would not necessarily eliminate the temptation to use the voting process as an opportunity to rally other investors for both economic and social gains. Many potential corporate issues, moreover, exist midway between legitimate business concerns and social issues.

International investments offer a particularly difficult arena for social investing, but should not be ignored because they represent an important diversification strategy. Solutions aimed at minimizing the interplay between international politics and Social Security investing are problematic.

Finally, public investing presents the potential to magnify existing tensions within the securities and financial regulatory communities. The SEC already struggles with institutional investors and is likely to have more trouble once Social Security funds are added to the markets. Perceived inadequacies in state corporate regulation could prompt additional federal regulation. Fiscal and monetary policy will affect performance of Social Security funds, and thus decisionmaking by the Federal Reserve and budgetary politics may also become more difficult.

None of these potential problems should preclude the use of public money in private markets. The success of the Thrift Savings Plan and most state pension plans indicates that public investing is a workable concept. By explicitly engaging the most difficult issues, policymakers can minimize the pitfalls that lie ahead.

Warren L. Batts, discussant

LET ME BEGIN by saying that it is a bit awesome to be the only business representative on a panel with so many outstanding experts. I hope that I can adequately represent the viewpoint of employers on the important issue of Social Security reform. I appreciate the seriousness with which the National Academy of Social Insurance is approaching reform, particularly the focus on investment in private markets and the many thoughtful technical, financial, political, and social issues raised in the paper by Theodore J. Angelis.

Public debate on Social Security reform has progressed significantly since my year as chairman of the National Association of Manufacturers. The association's principal theme for 1996–97, and one that continues, is that economic growth is vital to improving the standard of living of all Americans. Over the long term, the greatest threat to our economy is unreformed entitlement programs, particularly Social Security. We have come a long way in the last several years from the characterization of Social Security as the third rail of politics to discussions like these on how to solve the Social Security dilemma.

President Clinton's proposal in his recent State of the Union address to use the budget surplus to strengthen Social Security, as well as the Republican leadership's interest in reform, demonstrates the increasing priority given to this issue. Press interest grows daily, and the topic of investment in private markets appears in many stories.

For more than three years, the National Association of Manufacturers has been committed to reforming the Social Security system. During this time, we came to the recognition that the conventional tweaking of the system would no longer work and that major restructuring was in order. The association was the first major business organization to show leadership on this issue, and I am proud to work with the association in pursuit of this goal.

The National Commission on Retirement Policy, convened last year by the Center for Strategic and International Studies, is examining ways to ensure that Social Security remains strong and available to future generations. I am pleased to serve on that commission. The center is currently drafting a reform proposal that is expected to have strong support from its bipartisan congressional cochairs. It is encouraging to see other public policy groups getting involved in this issue.

There is also strong interest on the part of the general public. Surveys bear that out. For example, a December survey conducted by presidential pollster Mark Penn showed that 73 percent of voters questioned—and this cut across party lines—shared the belief that Social Security will soon face a crisis requiring serious reform. Members of Congress, in turn, need to listen to the American people and realize that major reform is not only the right thing to do, but that people expect it and it is essential to avoid collapse of the system within a generation.

Economic Growth

The nation is currently enjoying one of the longest periods of economic prosperity in modern times. Budget analysts are predicting the achievement of a balanced budget three years ahead of the bipartisan agreement. Before we pat ourselves on the backs, however, some reality testing is in order. Even if we do achieve a balanced budget, it would be a fallacy since the government borrows substantial sums from the Social Security trust fund to pay for current expenses. Last year roughly $100 billion was borrowed in this fashion. We cannot continue to do that indefinitely and expect high economic growth.

After 2012, the government will have to sell new debt for the Social Security trust fund to meet its obligations. By 2030, around the peak in the number of retirees, the national debt will be between two and one-half and three times the nation's GDP. Long before the debt reaches these levels, we will face two options, both unsatisfactory. One is to monetize the debt, leading to hyperinflation. The other is to continue selling bonds, which would raise interest rates and lead to a rapid slowdown or even a decline in our economy.

Policies must be changed soon in order to prevent the national debt from escalating to these levels. If we do not fix Social Security soon, we will bring the economy to its knees. But if we reform the system in a way that is both fair to the work force and economically sound, then American business will find new sources of capital to invest in the American economy, and our standard of living will be maintained and perhaps even enhanced.

Investment in Private Markets

As the paper by Theodore Angelis points out, all three Advisory Council proposals include some type of investment in private markets. Unfortunately, one of these proposals—the Personal Security Account plan—receives little discussion. Angelis focuses on the two plans where the problems of investment in private markets are greatest. But most of these problems would disappear under the Personal Security Account plan because investment of funds would occur outside the government. It is all the more reason to allow individuals to invest directly their own hard-earned money for retirement.

It seems to me that Angelis dismisses the Personal Security Account plan because he believes that direct investment by individuals would be too costly. Economies of scale, however, and competition among potential fund managers should keep those costs low. Even if such costs were high, individuals over time would realize savings, making administrative costs a minor issue. To critics who point out that government management of funds of this magnitude would be less costly than management by the private sector, I note the example of a large mutual fund company that charges its major clients twenty basis points and $25 a participant a year.

If we accept the Personal Security Account plan, the various technical issues raised by Angelis regarding investment of public funds become moot. From a business perspective, I see potential minefields from government trying to invest public funds. The problems of social investing and economically targeted investments are very serious and deserve careful attention. All investments on behalf of employees should be made solely to maximize returns for plan beneficiaries. Selecting investments because they fulfill a particular political or social purpose, while at the same time providing the best yield for retirement purposes, does not work. Moreover, agreeing on what social or political purpose an investment should advance is difficult to achieve. The experiences of public employee plans, which are not shielded from politics, are a good example of such difficulties. Historically, such plans sustain lower earnings than private plans covered by ERISA.

Another troublesome issue arises when government is both an investor and a regulator, as in the case of the Securities and Exchange Commission. The inherent conflicts are obvious. The fiscal and monetary issues are also enormously complicated, as are the foreign policy issues. The recent Helms-Burton Act clearly drove home how fiscal and foreign policy can be so intertwined. We have yet to resolve these problems.

Investment in the private market by individuals is good not only for the economy, it is good for the prosperity of American workers. For example, a married couple in their mid-thirties with combined annual wages of $60,000, who invested 9 percent of their income each year in the stock market, could accumulate a million dollars when they retire in thirty years. This example assumes a 10.5 percent annual return, which is the Standard & Poor's average since 1926. Even a minimum wage worker who invested just six dollars a week in the stock market could retire with a $200,000 nest egg. Compare this figure to a return of a mere 2 percent from Social Security.

Other nations have successfully reformed their public pension systems using private accounts, including Chile, Argentina, Australia, and Great Britain. Several years ago, Britain, a close cultural cousin to the United States, established a two-tiered system that has begun to eliminate their long-term Social Security financing problems. The British economy, at the same time, has blossomed. In the 1980's, Australia's labor government essentially replaced its Social Security system with a tax-subsidized individual savings program. Under this program, individuals must put 9 percent of their earnings into a private pension account that is similar to a 401(k) plan. As a result, their retirement income will be several times greater than promised under the previous system. Equally impressive is the fact that private savings increased over sevenfold in Australia from 1985 to 1997.

A Reform Proposal

The members of the National Association of Manufacturers are convinced that the economic effects of not reforming entitlement programs are unacceptable. We have concluded that our nation has no choice but to reach a consensus solution on significant restructuring of Social Security. This solution must honor past promises, strengthen the safety net, and promote economic growth. Last April, the association's board of directors endorsed general reform principles that would move us toward individual savings rather than a collective entitlement, while retaining a safety net for the truly needy.

According to these principles, a portion of the Social Security program would be transformed into a system of individual retirement savings with a choice of investment opportunities. These savings accounts would be the exclusive property of their owners. The accounts would be managed and invested independently of government control and would allow workers—the owners of the accounts—reasonable flexibility in selecting their own investments. Certain transition provisions would be needed to protect workers and to prevent increased financial exposure for employers.

Many of us in business have been educating our employees, our colleagues, and the general public about the benefits of private accounts and their promise of economic growth and greater prosperity. This helps to account for the boom in 401(k) plans. We believe an even broader educational program is in order. However, time is of the essence for reform. The first baby boomers begin retiring in 2013. More immediately, a presidential election in 2000 means we have a very small window of opportunity to act before politics overtakes us. We believe changes to the existing system should begin promptly. The longer we wait, the sooner we face retirement of the baby boom generation and meltdown of the current system.

Francis X. Cavanaugh, discussant

THEODORE J. ANGELIS raises the right questions. They are essentially the same questions Congress and the Federal Retirement Thrift Investment Board had to deal with in establishing the Thrift Savings Plan (TSP) for federal employees, which provided for substantial public investment in private debt and equity markets.

The TSP was established by the Federal Employees' Retirement System Act of 1986 (FERSA).[114] The TSP is a voluntary savings and investment plan

---

114. P. L. 99-335, 100 Stat. 514 (codified as amended largely at 5 U.S.C. sec. 8351 and 8401-8479).

similar to the defined-contribution plans offered by private corporations under section 401(k) of the Internal Revenue Code.

Before I took the job as executive director of the Thrift Board in 1986, I had spent thirty-two years in the Treasury Department as an economist and federal debt manager. On several occasions I had to respond to proposals from private financial institutions to permit them to manage the Social Security and other trust funds. They proposed to improve the earnings by investing in equities. I advised against such proposals on the grounds that stocks were too risky for government trust funds and government ownership of stocks would lead to government control over corporate business. Then in 1986 I went to the Thrift Board to do what I said should not be done. It's not that I was "born again." My earlier concerns were put to rest by the fact that Congress required that the TSP stock investments be done through the then recently established stock index funds, which reduced risk through diversification and virtually eliminated the potential for government control over individual corporations. Also, in establishing the Thrift Investment Board, Congress enacted several unique management requirements to insulate the TSP from political interference. Were it not for the index fund requirement and the extraordinary degree of agency independence, I would not have taken the job.

TSP Protection against Political Influences

I would like to take credit for establishing the TSP in a politics-free zone, but I cannot. Congress protected the TSP from politics in three ways: the legislative history; the TSP management structure; and the TSP investment structure. Congress itself made the TSP politically untouchable.

INTENT OF CONGRESS. Congressional concern about possible political influence over TSP investments is evident from the following statement in the Conference Report on FERSA:[115]

> Concerns over the specter of political involvement in the thrift plan management seem to focus on two distinct issues. One, the board, composed of presidential appointees, could be susceptible to pressure from an administration. Two, Congress might be tempted to use the large pool of thrift money for political purposes. Neither case would be likely to occur given present legal and constitutional restraints.

115. H.R. Conf. Rep. No. 99-606, at 136–37 (1986), reprinted in 1986 U.S.C.C.A.N. 1508, 1519–20.

The board members and employees are subject to strict fiduciary rules. They must invest the money and manage the funds solely for the benefit of the participants. A breach of these responsibilities would make the fiduciaries civilly and criminally liable.

The structure of the funds themselves prevents political manipulation. The Government Securities Investment Fund is invested in nonmarketable special issues of the Treasury pegged to a certain average interest rate. The Fixed Income Investment Fund is composed of guaranteed investment contracts, certificates of deposit, or other fixed instruments in which the board contracts with insurance companies, banks, and the like to provide it with a fixed rate of return over a specified period of time. The board would have no knowledge of the specific investments.

Finally, the Stock Index Fund is one in which a common stock index such as Standard & Poor's 500 or Wilshire's 5000 is used as the mechanism to allocate investments from the fund to various stocks. . . .

Political manipulation is unlikely and would be unlawful.

As to the issue of Congress tampering with the thrift fund, the inherent nature of a thrift plan precludes the possibility of Congress tampering with thrift funds. Unlike a defined-benefit plan in which an employer essentially promises a certain benefit, a thrift plan is an employee savings plan. In other words, the employees own the money. The money, in essence, is held in trust for the employee and managed and invested in the employee's behalf until the employee is eligible to receive it. This arrangement confers upon the employee property and other legal rights to the contributions and their earnings. Whether the money is invested in government or private securities is immaterial with respect to employee ownership. The employee owns it and it cannot be tampered with by any entity including Congress.

Also, the Senate specifically rejected language in a Senate bill after it was pointed out in a committee hearing that the language could be interpreted as an endorsement of social investing.[116]

I cited those two pieces of legislative history many times in denying requests from special interest groups that were seeking preferential treatment for their constituencies.

---

116. Hearing before the Senate Committee on Governmental Affairs on S. 1527, Senate Hearing 99-754, at 521 (1985).

TSP MANAGEMENT. Because of its unique independence and total dedication to its participants and beneficiaries, the TSP has been broadly accepted throughout the federal government. It has had record growth, with assets now over $58 billion and with 83 percent of FERS employees thus far electing to contribute to the plan. (In six major agencies the participation rate is above 90 percent.) TSP administrative expenses, including investment management costs, are only 7 basis points, a small fraction of the expense ratios of even the best private funds and virtually negligible compared with the average charges of stock mutual funds over the past decade. Such charges were estimated by Vanguard at approximately 200 basis points (including transactions costs).[117] This success could not have been achieved without specific statutory and administrative requirements designed to protect plan participants against political interference and avoid conflicts of interests.

The TSP is administered by five part-time board members who are appointed by the president to fixed terms and by a full-time executive director who is appointed by the board and serves as chief executive officer of the agency. Each of these six named fiduciaries is required to act solely in the interest of the participants and beneficiaries of the TSP and must have "substantial experience, training, and expertise in the management of financial investments and pension benefit plans."[118] The executive director is required to carry out the policies of the board but also has specific statutory responsibilities regarding procurement, contracting, investment management, and plan administration. Vesting these administrative duties directly in the executive director facilitates efficient administration and protects against the appearance of conflicts of TSP interests with the private business and financial interests of members of the board. These unique statutory requirements for the management of the TSP help insulate the TSP from political interference.

Also, the board is not subject to the various processes by which other federal agencies are controlled by the administration or by the appropriations committees of Congress. The board is self-financing in that it has a permanent indefinite appropriation to make necessary expenditures from the Thrift Savings Fund. It is exempt from the requirements imposed on other federal agencies to clear their budgets, legislative proposals, and regulations with the administration.

TSP INVESTMENTS. The investment practices of the board add further insulation from politics and also help ensure that the board will not influence the

---

117. Vanguard Group, "In the Vanguard" (Valley Forge, Pa., 1996), p. 10.
118. 5 U.S.C. sec. 8472(d).

management of corporations whose stock is held by the TSP. The board is required to invest in a broad stock index fund and is prohibited by law from voting the stock. The stock is voted by a private manager of a commingled Standard & Poor's 500 fund hired by the executive director through a rigid competitive procurement process. The commingled fund manager has hundreds of other institutional investors and has a fiduciary responsibility to vote the stock in the interest of all of its investors, not just the TSP. So there is no opportunity for the TSP to buy or sell the stock of any one corporation or to influence stock voting or corporate management. This is a secondary benefit of the commingled fund approach; the primary benefit is that it increases the efficiency of TSP stock investments since it permits cross-trading with other investors in the fund, which avoids the expense of buying or selling securities in the market. Thus, if Congress were to require the TSP to shift from an S&P 500 fund to, say, a new and smaller environmentally friendly fund that excluded polluting companies there could be a substantial increase in the TSP's investment management costs.

TSP as a Model for Social Security

The TSP is a proper model for investing part of the Social Security trust fund in stocks or other private securities. The TSP has demonstrated that such investments can be efficiently made without political interference and without adverse effects on private companies or securities markets. Yet, as discussed below, the TSP is not a proper model for individual investment accounts in the Social Security program.

THE MAINTAIN BENEFITS PLAN. Unlike the TSP, the Maintain Benefits (MB) plan proposed by some members of the Advisory Council on Social Security in its 1997 report would not establish individually owned accounts. Yet the MB stock funds might well be insulated from politics since they would be dedicated to the Social Security trust fund beneficiaries as a group and could not be used for any other purpose. Also, the Social Security trust fund is now uniquely insulated from the congressional budget/appropriations restraints. The continued protection of the Social Security trust fund from competing budget needs or from demands by advocates of social investment, minority preferences, or other special interests would depend, of course, on whether Congress would be more responsive to such special interests than to the legendary third rail of American politics.

Concerning the question of market impact, the proposed MB investments in stocks of 40 percent of the Social Security fund would of course be much larger than the TSP's stock holdings and would total an estimated $1 trillion (1996 dollars) in 2014. Yet the rapid development and growth of a variety of index funds in the United States and abroad should provide ample opportunities for substantial diversified investments of Social Security funds with minimal market impact. The capitalization of the U.S. stock market today is approximately $12 trillion, and at a 7 percent real growth rate it would be close to $40 trillion in 2014. The MB plan also contemplates investment in foreign stocks, which would reduce the estimated impact of MB investments on the U.S. stock market to less than 2 percent. The MB's 40 percent allocation to equities is quite modest—a 50 percent allocation would be more in line with the portfolio mix of other retirement funds. The TSP currently has 51 percent in equities, and *Pensions and Investments* (January 26, 1998) reports that the top thousand defined-benefit plans hold 62 percent of assets in equities and that the top thousand defined-contribution plans hold 65 percent in equities. The Federal Reserve System has had about two-thirds of its $3 billion defined-benefit plan assets in stocks (the Fed apparently has not viewed that as "irrational exuberance"). Based on the Advisory Council's investment return assumptions, a 50 percent allocation to equities in the Social Security fund would slightly more than double the investment earnings of the fund.

THE INDIVIDUAL ACCOUNTS PLAN. The Individual Accounts (IA) plan proposed by other council members would appear to be more susceptible to political interference than the MB approach, since many individuals would not want to have their forced savings accounts channeled into the stocks of corporations that they find socially unacceptable. It would be difficult to resist pleas to give individual investors a choice of environmentally friendly, economically targeted, or other social investment funds. The fund administrator charged with selecting the specific social investments would clearly be under extreme political pressures from the various interest groups.

The IA plan also raises formidable administrative problems, because of its dependence on millions of small businesses and households to perform daunting administrative tasks for their employees. The TSP is a very large and complex record keeping task for 2.3 million federal employees—the largest defined-contribution plan in the nation. In my view, the IA plan, with over 100 million participants, could not be modeled after the TSP. The TSP is dependent upon the federal employing agencies and their expert personnel, payroll, and systems people to handle the "retail" operations of the TSP. That includes the distribution of TSP forms and other materials, employee education and individual counseling, and the timely transmission of data to the TSP record keeper each payday for each employee regarding payroll deductions, investment choices, interfund transfers, loans, loan repayments, withdrawals, error corrections, and other essential information to ensure prompt investment of employee accounts and restoration of employees' lost earnings because of delayed deposits or other employer error. (Although the IA plan does not contemplate emergency loans or withdrawals, I believe that it would be politically impossible to deny emergency access to funds vested in the names of individual account holders.) Private employers are now required to report individual Social Security tax information just once a year. Surely there would be many millions of small employers who would be unwilling or unable to assume the administrative burden of the IA plan and the corresponding financial liability, for example, to make up for the lost stock market earnings resulting from employer failure to process an employee's interfund transfer request on time.

Even if the IA plan were workable, perhaps by adopting (politically unpopular) measures such as exempting small employers or limiting the options of small investors, the net investment earnings would probably be substantially less than would have been earned from Social Security fund investments in Treasury securities. According to the Social Security Administration, 46 percent of Social Security workers, including part-time and temporary workers, earned less than $15,000 a year in 1994. Servicing such small accounts would entail unacceptably high expense ratios. Assuming a current average income of $20,000, the proposed IA tax of 1.6 percent would produce an account of $320 in the first year. Assuming the annual cost of servicing an account is $30,[119] then the expense ratio would be 9.38 percent, or 938 basis points (compared to the TSP actual expense ratio of 7 basis points in 1997 and the 10.5 basis points estimated by the council for the IA plan). That expense ratio would exceed by 2.38 percentage points the IA plan's assumed real return on stocks of 7 percent. Moreover, since individuals with incomes as low as $20,000 tend to be risk averse and thus avoid stocks (less than 9 percent of such individuals invest in stocks according to one survey) in favor of lower-yielding fixed-income investments, their net earnings (after expenses) would likely be negative in the early years of the plan.[120]

Contrary to popular belief, the Social Security trust fund now receives preferential treatment, compared with private investors in Treasury securities, because it is not required to pay any transaction costs, it receives the (higher)

---

119. According to Advisory Council on Social Security (1997a), $30 a year is typical of charges levied for IRAs for flat dollar account maintenance fees.

120. Cavanaugh (1996, p. 103).

long-term interest rate on its short-term investments, and it is insulated from market interest rate risk by being guaranteed par value redemption on securities redeemed before maturity.[121] If the same preferential treatment were offered as an investment option to IA participants, communicating this vital piece of information to unsophisticated investors would be a major challenge to the managing fiduciaries of the IA fund. They would have to overcome the misinformation from U.S. political leaders who have convinced millions of Americans that the money in the Social Security fund "is not there." People have been led to believe that the fund has been "looted" and that it is invested in a bunch of worthless IOUs.[122]

To sum up, the experience of the TSP or of other 401(k)-type plans or IRAs provides no model for the IA plan. We have no experience with programs of mandatory savings for low-income investors administered by small employers. This is uncharted territory, and I do not see how we could get there from here.

THE PERSONAL SAVINGS ACCOUNT PLAN. I would agree with the Advisory Council that the Personal Savings Account plan (PSA) IRA-type alternative proposed by some members of the council would be the least cost-effective alternative, but I would expect the expense ratio to be even higher than the council's estimated 100 basis points. As stated above, the average expense ratio for stock mutual funds has been estimated at 200 basis points, and the PSA accounts would be much smaller and thus relatively more costly to maintain.

The suggestion by some that competition would force financial institutions to lower costs substantially is not well grounded. The market for personal savings and investments is already well established and highly competitive. More aggressive competition will entail more marketing, promotion, advertising, and high-pressure sales costs.

Also, given concerns about the likely exploitation of small investors by the sharp practices of many financial advisers and investment managers, Congress would likely impose new regulatory burdens that would add to administrative costs and cause more political intervention in the market than the IA or MB plans.

Congress specifically rejected PSA-type proposals when it designed the TSP:[123]

> Because of the many concerns raised, the conferees spent more time on this issue than any other. Proposals were made to decentralize the

121. Cavanaugh (1996, p.158).
122. Cavanaugh (1996, pp. 97–98).
123. H.R. Conf. Rep. 99-606, at 137–38 (1986), reprinted in 1986 U.S.C.C.A.N. 1508, 1520–21.

investment management and to give employees more choice by permitting them to choose their own financial institution in which to invest. While the conferees applaud the use of IRAs, they find such an approach for an employer-sponsored retirement program inappropriate. . . .

The conferees concur with the resolution of this issue as discussed in the Senate report (99-166) on this legislation:

As an alternative the committee considered permitting any qualified institution to offer to employee[s] specific investment vehicles. However, the committee rejected that approach for a number of reasons. First, there are literally thousands of qualified institutions who would bombard employees with promotions for their services. The committee concluded that employees would not favor such an approach. Second, few, if any, private employers offer such an arrangement. Third, even qualified institutions go bankrupt occasionally, and a substantial portion of an employee's retirement benefit could be wiped out. This is in contrast to the diversified fund approach, which could easily survive a few bankruptcies. Fourth, it would be difficult to administer. Fifth, this "retail" or "voucher" approach would give up the economic advantage of this group's wholesale purchasing power derived from its large size, so that employees acting individually would get less for their money.

Of course, the conferees were viewing this from the standpoint of the federal government as an employer; it is not clear whether Congress would take a more or less paternal view in the case of Social Security.

Finally, based on my thirty-two years as a U.S. Treasury debt manager, I would advise against the PSA plan to borrow $1.9 trillion (in 1995 dollars) from the Treasury to provide interim financing for Social Security trust fund benefit payments. Such dependence upon general government revenues would compromise the financial independence of Social Security. Moreover, experience with borrowing from Treasury to finance other federal programs has not been good. Treasury loans are often subsidized initially, or later by means of various forms of forbearance. Perhaps the worst cases were the Treasury loans to the Rural Electrification Administration, which were made at subsidized interest rates substantially below Treasury's own cost of borrowing. Then, in 1974, Congress enacted legislation to forgive the loans entirely. Congress at times seems to view interagency financings as some sort of funny money that's all in the family. Given the reluctance of Congress to raise Social Security taxes or reduce benefits, it strikes me as extremely risky to give Congress a third (and politically painless) option of simply reducing or canceling the $1.9 trillion debt to Treasury. Conservatives who support the PSA plan seem to me to be very short-sighted.

Relevance of State Pension Plan Experience

As discussed in the paper by Theodore J. Angelis, the failure of many states to insulate their pension plans from political interference may be attributed to many factors. Unlike the TSP board, appointments to state pension boards are not limited to experts in financial and pension plan management. State boards include political appointees who are state government officials serving on an ex officio basis, which raises serious conflict-of-interest questions. Also, the equity investments of state funds are not limited to index funds, and their direct investments in individual stocks create substantial pressures for social investment as well as interference with corporate management. In the case of the traditional state defined-benefit plans, the states have a financial incentive to manipulate investments or actuarial projections to reduce state contributions to the plans as a way of solving short-term state budget problems. The role of the states in their pension plans is that of employers providing benefits to their employees—which is quite different from the role of the federal government as trustee of a Social Security fund financed by private employer/ employee contributions.

Conclusion

There are no apparent reasons why a portion of the Social Security trust fund should not be invested in stocks. The TSP experience over the past eleven years has demonstrated that the federal government can do what virtually every large private and public retirement fund in the nation has done—enable workers to enjoy a more secure retirement from stock market investments. The TSP has also demonstrated that such investments can be administered without political interference and without adverse impacts on the management of private corporations. Even if a modified PSA, IA, or some other individual account plan were adopted, I believe that, in the interest of fairness to Social Security taxpayers, a substantial portion of the remaining Social Security trust fund should be in equities. Centralized investment, as in the MB plan, is the only way to realize the full benefits of the higher returns from stocks. Those additional returns would be largely diluted by the administrative expenses associated with the IA or PSA plans. To those who say that some sort of individual account approach is needed to change the income redistribution or generational effects of Social Security financing I would say the first priority should be to enlarge the total Social Security pie, through more rational investment policies, so that we may better deal with any equity issues—a rising tide lifts all boats. To those who say that an individual account approach is needed to increase real savings in our economy I would say that such real savings would be significantly reduced by the high administrative expenses associated with small individual accounts—greater real savings would be realized by channeling any increased Social Security taxes into centralized investment in the Social Security trust fund. Finally, the fundamental principle of insurance, social or otherwise, is to shift risk from the individual to the group. The IA or PSA plans would take us in the other direction.

Howell E. Jackson, discussant

HOW SHOULD A PRIVATIZED Social Security system be regulated? Are existing legal structures adequate to police a privatized Social Security system? Or are the problems associated with a privatization sufficiently novel or acute to require new regulatory mechanisms? If new regulations are required, what sort of supervisory controls should be incorporated into reform proposals and what protections can we reasonably expect them to afford social security participants? These are the questions that this essay explores.

Public Interference with Private Capital Markets

As someone who spends much of his time dealing with the regulation of financial intermediaries and capital markets, I greatly enjoyed Theodore J. Angelis's paper. While the expanding body of academic literature on social security reform alludes to the regulatory challenges of privatizing social security, Angelis's paper is one of the first to attempt a careful review of an important aspect of such reforms: the concern that political considerations will interfere with the investment of Social Security funds in public capital markets. This possibility arises whether the trust fund's own assets are invested in the capital market or the investments are made through some sort of individual accounts. In either case, the government may be tempted to intrude into our capital markets in novel and potentially troubling ways.

If a substantial portion of the Social Security assets were invested in the private equity markets, Congress or other government officials might well be tempted to utilize that investment authority to influence the management of private corporations—either directly through the proxy process or indirectly through eligibility requirements for inclusion in the trust fund portfolio.[124] Although it remains a matter of speculation whether Congress or regulatory agencies charged with overseeing trust fund assets would in fact attempt to manipulate the trust fund in this way, the concern is sufficiently serious that it warrants careful consideration before we adopt proposals that would move substantial amounts of private capital under the control of the trust fund or its managers. The critical question is whether Social Security privatization can be structured so as to minimize the risks of disrupting our equity markets without imposing undesirable collateral consequences. Although Angelis refrains from offering a definitive answer to this question, I think it is probably fair to say that the paper is at least susceptible to the interpretation that problems of corporate governance are substantial and not easily resolved.[125] Although I am sympathetic to the concerns he raises, I am somewhat more optimistic on both counts.

As Angelis suggests, a first line of defense against political manipulation of trust fund investments is to move investment control and shareholder voting decisions out of the hands of government officials and under contractual assignment of private investment managers of the sort that routinely manage private pensions today and also manage investments of the federal Thrift Savings Plan. As long as these managers were selected, retained, and perhaps even compensated based on their skill in matching as closely as possible the performance of broad market indexes, competitive pressures would do much to ensure that individual managers did not manipulate their investment authority to curry favor with government officials.[126] Such a structure should also make it difficult for trust fund administrators surreptitiously to establish alternative investment criteria on their own initiative.

Thus, to a considerable degree, privatization can be structured to impose institutional barriers to insulate investment management from political pressures. Structural restraints of this sort cannot, however, guarantee Congress will not subsequently enact new legislation establishing political criteria for trust fund

124. One could, I suppose, distinguish between government actions designed to enhance corporate performance and initiatives intended for collateral purposes unrelated to shareholder return. In practice, however, this distinction is hard to maintain, as it will often be possible to recharacterize collateral purposes as having a positive effect on performance. For this reason, my analysis makes no distinction between appropriate and inappropriate government initiatives in corporate governance.

125. I gather that is how my fellow discussant Warren Batts interprets the analysis.

126. For this competition to succeed, it would be desirable for the trust fund's portfolio to be divided into several pieces, perhaps a half a dozen, and to have the contracts subject to renewal periodically. In addition to making it easier to police management fees and account performance, dividing up the portfolio would reduce the volume of holdings of any manager. To the extent one is concerned about the overall size of the funds portfolio, investment managers could be limited to holding no more than 1 percent of the overall market.

investments or even imposing such criteria in the first place, notwithstanding the recommendation of expert advisers to pursue the sort of hands-off strategy that Angelis suggests.

Assessing this risk is a matter of political prediction and, as such, inherently debatable. From my perspective as a student of financial regulation, it is by no means clear that Congress would choose to interfere with trust fund investment management in the ways outlined in the Angelis paper. Most financial intermediaries—even those such as registered investment companies and private pension plans that are regulated exclusively at the federal level—are not subject to politically motivated restraints on investment, at least not of the sort. Angelis discusses,[127] even though there have been, from time to time, politicians who have expressed an interest in imposing such requirements.[128] The one substantial exception to this point is the Community Reinvestment Act of 1977, which requires federally insured depository institutions to serve the credit needs of local low- and middle-income borrowers. Although originally understood as an initiative to prevent red-lining in certain credit markets, the CRA is sometimes characterized as a federal credit allocation scheme. So, the field of federal financial institutions regulation does offer an example of social financial engineering. The statute is, however, extremely controversial in the banking community and has been widely criticized in the industry.

But, let's suppose that Congress overcame these structural impediments and proposed to play politics with trust fund investments along the lines that Angelis fears. How bad would it be? The paper focuses our attention on several distinct harms: one is a potential deterioration in return on fund investments—that is an injury to the fund itself—and the second is an interference with corporate management—that is an interference in the real economy.

Concerns about the Rate of Return

Let me begin with concerns about the rate of return. Suppose Congress were to limit trust fund equity investments to the S&P 500 minus firms engaged in the sale of tobacco. It is certainly conceivable that such a limitation could

---

127. To be sure, some analysts characterize portfolio restrictions as motivated to serve the political interests of management. See Roe (1994). But these restrictions also serve the more public-spirited goal of enhancing diversification.

128. The states, in contrast, have demonstrated somewhat greater interest in imposing politically motivated investment restrictions, both on insurance companies and banks. See, for example, *Metropolitan Life* v. *Ward*, 470 U.S. 869 (1985) (reviewing states' requirements that insurance companies invest locally). This difference between state and federal tendencies in this area may suggest that state experiences with public pension fund restrictions may not be a reliable guide of the political economy at the federal level.

impair the returns of the fund's equity investments.[129] However regrettable, this potential loss of economic return is not necessarily a ground for prohibiting trust fund investments in equity markets. If one accepts rate of return as the relevant metric,[130] the critical question is not whether a politically constrained stock index would underperform a pure index; rather the question is whether politicians would sufficiently mismanage the trust fund's equity investments to reduce the fund's return from its current all-Treasury investment posture.

One cannot answer this question with confidence. But, if one looks at the available data, there is some ground for hope. Throughout this conference and in the Advisory Council's report released last year, the conventional assumption is that the real long-term rate of return on equity investments will be on the order of 7 percent a year, whereas the equivalent return on current trust fund holdings is 2.3 percent or 2.4 percent. So, under the assumption that the expected real rate of return on equity investments is 450 basis points above expected returns on the trust fund's current portfolio—and that's the assumption that drives the privatization proposals analyzed in the paper—the relevant question is whether the cost of politically constrained baskets of equities would eat up all of this differential.[131] If one examines the empirical literature on the costs of social investing, much of which is summarized in Angelis's paper, one finds an estimated effect of 1 or 2 percentage points.[132] That is less than half of the assumed differential.[133] To be sure, one can find illustrations of states (and foreign governments) making spectacularly poor investments with public pension assets. But, as far as I can tell, these errors occur when the assets have been directly under government control and allocated to specific politically favored investments. The costs of a politically constrained portfolio index would likely, at least in my view, be substantially less severe.

Manipulation of Voting Rights for Political Ends

A distinct question is whether large trust fund investments in equity markets might introduce political considerations into fundamental issues of corporate

129. Although it is also possible that, at least in some markets, such a restriction could improve returns.

130. And this is a contested point, as discussed in chapter 4. by John Geanakoplos, Olivia Mitchell, and John P. Zeldes.

131. This figure would be lower but still substantial if privatized funds were divided between bonds and equity.

132. See Romano (1993); see also Mitchell and Hsin (1994).

133. Let us return to the CRA illustration for a moment. If one asks the question of how much this most visible form of federal credit allocation has cost, the answer is that it has a relatively small impact on the overall performance of depository institutions. Even critics of the statute estimate its

governance. Several members of the Advisory Committee took this concern seriously enough to recommend that trust fund voting rights be cleansed: either through the statutory elimination of those voting rights (for securities held by the trust fund), or through the adoption of a voting convention that mirrors the votes of other shareholders.[134]

An important contribution of the Angelis paper is its attempt to understand the ramifications of cleansing the voting rights of what could become a potentially large block of securities. I would like to focus on one component of his argument here: the possibility that cleansing voting rights would tend to entrench management and weaken the mechanisms of shareholder control.[135] In raising this concern, Angelis postulates a public firm with a large block of stock under management control—say, 25 percent of outstanding shares. If the trust fund were to take another 25 percent of that company's shares out of circulation, management's share of the voting shares that retained voting rights would rise to 33 percent, and its ability to block outside bids would be enhanced.

In many public companies, however, management controls no such substantial block of votes. Where activist institutional shareholders own several significant shares—say 3 to 5 percent blocks—the introduction of a large block of cleansed trust fund shares will enhance the power of outsiders, presumably

---

cost at on the order of twelve basis points of industry assets (estimating the direct costs of CRA compliance), further suggesting, at least to me, that the worst-case effects of social investment are likely to eat up only a small fraction of the increase in rates of return that privatization of fund assets would be expected to generate. See Independent Bankers Association of America (1993).

134. See Advisory Council on Social Security (1997a, p. 26). Although much anecdotal evidence at the state level has supported the view that government pension plans are prone to shareholder activism, it is not clear that this phenomenon would be replicated at the federal level with Social Security trust fund assets, particularly if voting rights were delegated to private investment managers, as they are with the federal Thrift Savings Plan. Moreover, if, as I have suggested, the resources were divided up among multiple advisers, voting power would be more diffuse, and no single manager could speak for all trust fund shares. See note 126. In this section, however, I accept the assumption that concern over corporate governance issues necessitates a cleansing of voting rights and then ask the question of whether cleansing the shares would have an adverse effect on corporate governance.

135. Space and time constraints prevent me from exploring a second potential problem of cleansing "voting rights": the possibility that this loss of rights would cause the trust fund to "lose" the premium associated with voting. In essence, this point is another worry about "rate of return": divesting voting rights will detract from fund performance. Whether or not the divestiture of voting rights will have this effect is, it seems to me, a difficult question of economics. The voting rights need not, after all, be lost forever and could reemerge when sold to other parties. There would, moreover, be many other aspects of privatization—most notably the entrance of such a large and long-term investor in the equity markets—that could, it would seem to me, have even larger effects on equity returns, and these might easily swamp the voting rights issue. In any event, many of these effects would, presumably, be incorporated into equity prices as soon as the parameters of the privatization proposal were adopted and well before the trust fund acquired any shares.

improving the market's ability to monitor shareholders. In essence, the cost of seeking corporate control will decline, at least for those companies in which activist institutional shareholders already have substantial blocks.

A separate and intriguing question is the effect of cleansed voting rights for companies in which neither management nor outsiders have large consolidated holdings. Although the matter is hardly free from doubt, I believe the answer must turn on the issue of whose shares the trust fund purchases. If we knew, for example, that the trust fund were to purchase its shares solely from individual investors, who are the least likely to participate actively in corporate governance issues, then the cleansing of their voting rights would tend to improve management discipline, because the remaining shareholders would be proportionately more activist. If it is the activists who sell out, however, the effect could easily be in the other direction.

Just as the macroeconomic effects of Social Security privatization depend on how the public adjusts its savings and investment patterns in response to the change, so too it seems to me do the corporate governance ramifications of the proposal depend on how the ownership patterns of public corporations are affected. It seems entirely plausible, as Angelis suggests, that for some corporations there may be an entrenchment of management, but for many others it may cause an increase in shareholder discipline. To answer this question, one would need to examine with greater care the ownership structures of the companies in which the fund was to invest and also determine to the extent possible the identity of shareholders whom the trust fund would succeed.

Political Influence Could Also Reach Individual Accounts

A final point I would like to address are the implications of this paper for the debate over whether Social Security should retain its current defined-benefit format or move to a defined-contribution format. Several of the Advisory Council members who support the Individual Account plan—a defined-contribution alternative—did so partially on the grounds that the risks of political interference were too great if equity investment were made in a defined-benefit format.[136]

One of the most interesting aspects of the Angelis paper is that its analysis does not for the most part turn on whether the investments are made in defined-benefit or defined-contribution form. After all, the primary lines of defense against political manipulation that the paper considers are: first, dele-

---

136. See Advisory Council on Social Security (1997a, p. 155) (statement of Edward M. Gramlich and Marc M. Twinney).

gation of investment management to private firms selected by a politically independent board and second, limitations of account investments to broad market indexes, such as the S&P 500. (I would also add a requirement that the funds be delegated to multiple managers so that intermanager comparisons on costs and performance would be possible.) All of these first-line structural restraints could be imposed whether or not the investments were held directly by the trust fund or allocated to individual accounts. Similarly, the voting rights of equity investments could be cleansed whether held in individual accounts or directly by the fund.[137]

The temptations for political intervention also appear largely symmetric. With both a defined-benefit plan and a defined-contribution plan organized along the lines of the Federal Thrift Savings Plan, politicians will face the temptation of manipulating a large body of capital market investments to fulfill social goals. To be sure, one might suppose that there would be strong public resistance to political efforts to interfere with returns on individual accounts.[138] But given the special role of the Social Security trust fund in our public debate, one might imagine equally strong opposition to political attempts to exploit trust fund assets for the benefit of "special interests." This political resistance could be enhanced if there were clear indexes—such as an undiluted market index—against which the costs of social engineering of trust fund assets could be measured.

So, one important lesson of the Angelis paper is that, at least in choosing between direct trust fund investment and the individual account approach, concerns over political interference in investment strategy do not point strongly in one direction or the other.[139]

Regulating a Privatized Social Security System

The need to constrain political interference in asset management is, however, only one of the regulatory challenges of Social Security privatization. A separate, and from my perspective even more important, concern is the amount

137. As described in some detail in the following paragraphs, one could also combine substantial restraints on financial risk with a defined-contribution privatization proposal.

138. This was perhaps my intuition and I gather that of Theodore Angelis, but it is interesting to note that my fellow discussant, Francis Cavanaugh, has the opposite intuition—that politicians might be more inclined to impose political considerations on individual account plans.

139. On the other hand, if one were concerned that privatization of Social Security was likely to prompt inappropriate government intervention when the capital markets fall, it is not clear to me whether such an action would be more likely with the Maintain Benefit approach (where the government shoulders the risk) or with an Individual Account approach (where individuals bear the losses directly).

of financial risk that participants in a privatized Social Security system would assume, particularly if privatization were implemented with IRA-style, personal security accounts.[140] This section reviews the regulatory challenges of privatization and then considers the kinds of regulatory regimes that could be deployed to mitigate those challenges.

Regulatory Challenges for a Privatized Social Security System

Granting Social Security participants unbridled discretion to invest all or a substantial portion of their Social Security contributions raises a host of regulatory challenges. In light of the number of participants involved—many of whom will be first-time investors—and the aggregate amount of assets available for management, the potential for abuse and overreaching will be great. The sort of scam-artists and scoundrels that have perpetuated penny-stock fraud and boiler-room operations will be attracted to individual Social Security accounts like moths to a flame. At a minimum, millions of participants—even those who restrict their investments to bank CDs and money market funds—may overpay for investment services, particularly in the early years as the market for account management works itself out, and some will undoubtedly suffer from outright fraud. Even if instances of wrongdoing were limited to a few percent of participants, the absolute number of abuses could be extremely high.

Fraud aside, the actual returns received on individual Social Security accounts may be much more problematic than many privatization proposals suggest. For the most part, discussions of Social Security privatization proceed on the assumption that average rates of return on capital market investments will exceed the risk-free rate paid on government securities and substantially beat the implicit return on current Social Security contributions. Even if this is true on average, actual returns on individual accounts will vary. Returns on many individual accounts will fall below the average.[141] Indeed, if individuals are given any substantial latitude in determining how to invest their Social Security accounts, it is all but certain that some participants will do worse on their investments than they would under the current Social Security system. By assuming financial risks, participants will experience variations in the rates of

---

140. Advisory Council on Social Security (1997a, pp. 30–33) (describing proposal for personal security accounts).

141. Depending how returns are distributed—for example, if the performance of the median account is below the average—more than half of all accounts will do worse than the average. See, for example, Shoven (1998) (reporting data on a large number of hypothetical portfolios in which mean returns exceed median returns).

return earned on their accounts. Put differently, privatizing Social Security will not offer participants a costless exchange of low returns for high returns. Rather, it offers a trade-off between the current system's low average, no-variance returns and a new system's higher-average, higher-variance returns.

Absent effective regulatory safeguards, several factors could contribute to variation in returns on individual accounts, including the following:

VARIATIONS IN ADMINISTRATIVE COSTS. As has been noted elsewhere, individual accounts would have relatively high administrative costs: both in terms of the direct fees paid to account managers and in terms of indirect costs from account managers obtaining less than optimal execution practices, brokerage commissions, and other services.[142] One effect of high administrative costs would be to lower average performance on individual accounts, but high costs can also generate variations in return. The level of administrative costs could vary considerably across individual accounts. The wealthy (with other assets available for management) could easily find themselves paying much lower administrative costs than poorer participants. In the financial markets, service providers often reduce fees in order to reach wealthier customers to whom other products might be marketed. Similarly, sophisticated participants can be expected to search for lower cost providers better than those who lack investment experience. In addition costs for smaller accounts would likely be higher, as a percentage of assets under management, than costs for larger accounts.

OTHER SOURCES OF VARIATIONS IN FINANCIAL PERFORMANCE. A variety of factors could lead to variations in the rate of return on individual account performance. From my perspective there are four principal sources of such variation:

—Intergenerational variation. Because the private capital markets do not outperform risk-free portfolios in a uniform manner, some generations will do better than others with their individual accounts. Those whose retirement years fall in a period of low asset prices will fare worse than those who retire in strong markets. Thus each generational cohort will not necessarily earn the long-run average market return.

—Variation from asset allocation decisions. Even those within the same generational cohort will experience substantially different rates of return. The degree of variation will increase the greater the choice of investments available to account participants. If one considers the closest current analog to individual

142. Some indirect costs may not show up directly in administration fees but will tend to lower portfolio performance over time. Less than optimal execution practices, for example, will have this effect.

accounts—401(k) plans—the data reveal considerable variation in the ways in which individuals invest their accounts: with some investing little in the stock market and others completely invested in the equities.[143] Different decisions about how to allocate account assets will lead to substantial differences in performance of accounts over time.

—Variation from differences in portfolio balancing strategies. Portfolio rebalancing decisions will exacerbate variations in performance. Consider two individuals of the same generation with the same level of contributions to an individual account. Suppose both invest only in either diversified stock funds or diversified bond funds, moving back and forth based on their own sense of which market is likely to perform better in the next quarter. Depending on the skill and luck with which they move their accounts between these two asset classes, these two individuals could enjoy dramatically different rates of return, even though they both followed the same asset allocation strategy. If a person made particularly bad decisions in this regard—constantly selling low and buying high—it is quite possible for that person to experience poor account performance even though both bonds and stock performed well over all. Differences in allocation strategies translate into variations in return, that is, financial risk.

—Variation from the selection of investment managers. Finally, even within asset classes, there are likely to be substantial differences in financial performance over time. If one looks to the most common vehicle for individual investment in the stock market—stock mutual funds—one also sees considerable variation in performance between the best and worst funds over any period of observations. So even with individuals in the same generational cohort with the same allocation and timing strategy—100 percent investment in the stock market all the time—there is likely to be variation in performance, unless the individuals used funds based on the same market index or otherwise equivalent portfolios.

As a result of all the foregoing factors, the actual rate of returns for a large number of participants in individual accounts could be expected to fall well short of average returns for certain asset classes. It is, moreover, quite possible that some fraction of individual account participants will do less well than the implicit rate of return currently generated on OASDI contributions.[144]

143. See Employee Benefit Research Institute (1996).
144. In a recent paper relying on Monte Carlo simulations, Zvi Bodie and Dwight B. Crane demonstrate how standard retirement investment strategies might be expected to underperform the government risk-free rate of return under various circumstances. See Bodie and Crane (1998, pp. 11–14). Part of the public debate over Social Security reform should, in my view, entail an extension of this sort of analysis to present the expected distribution of returns from competing proposals for privatization. Such analyses would help counteract the current emphasis on predicted average returns.

Designing a Regulatory Structure to Mitigate the Risks of Privatization

From a regulatory perspective, the most interesting question about Social Security privatization is the extent to which privatization legislation should and could address the regulatory challenges of fraud, excessive administrative costs, and variations in returns across individual accounts. Numerous regulatory options are available, and many might be used to dampen the risks that privatization could impose on Social Security participants. Regulatory restraints would, however, limit the investment choices available to social security participants, and thus conflict with the goals of individual autonomy and freedom that underlie many privatization proposals. In the end, framers of privatization legislation must balance the need for regulatory protections against the desirability of enhancing participant autonomy.

ESTABLISHING THE LOCUS OF REGULATORY SUPERVISION. An initial question about regulating the privatization of Social Security is determining at which entities the regulation would be directed. As the contribution to Social Security individual accounts would presumably come from payroll taxes, a natural target of regulation could be employers. (ERISA's regulation of employer-sponsored pension plans provides a model for such a regulatory system.) One could imagine imposing a legal duty on all employers to offer their employees an appropriate investment vehicle or range of investment vehicles for their privatized Social Security accounts.[145]

There are, however, substantial drawbacks to an employer-based system of regulation. Most important, it would extend regulation to a huge number of entities: all employers in the United States. Besides straining supervisory resources, this approach would be costly and of dubious efficacy inasmuch as many employers are small businesses or individuals, lacking in the experience necessary to assume substantial responsibilities for overseeing investment management. As a result of the problems associated with comprehensive regulation of employers, I suspect that Social Security privatization regulation would have only limited application to employers, perhaps requiring only that whatever portion of their employees' Social Security contributions are earmarked for privatized accounts are transferred to eligible account managers in

145. The ERISA safe-harbor regulations establishing an appropriate range of choices for 401(k) accounts offer one model for national standards of eligibility. See ERISA § 404(c), 29 U.S.C.A. § 1104 (West 1998); 29 C.F.R. § 2550.404c-1 (1998) (implementing regulations). An approach of this sort would establish general parameters regarding the type of investment choices employers must offer their employees, but then allow individual employees considerable latitude in deciding how to allocate their retirement investments within these general parameters.

a timely manner.[146] Under such a system, the critical issue will be determining who is an eligible provider and under what restrictions will such account managers operate.

DEFINING ELIGIBILITY TO PROVIDE SERVICES TO PRIVATIZED ACCOUNTS. Eligibility to offer investment services to privatized Social Security accounts could be determined in any number of ways. At one extreme, the government could offer a limited number of investment choices, and all participants would have to choose among those options. This is, in essence, what the Advisory Council's Individual Account option would provide. Typically, however, privatization proposals contemplate that individual accounts will be managed by or invested in regulated financial intermediaries: that is, banks, insurance companies, investment companies, and perhaps registered broker-dealers or investment advisers. So, at the other end of the spectrum, a wide range of financial intermediaries could be eligible to offer privatized Social Security accounts.

Although all major categories of financial intermediaries in the United States are subject to supervision, the content and intensity of oversight varies considerably from sector to sector.[147] In some fields, supervision is extensive. For example, banks, insurance companies, and money market mutual funds are subject to strict investment restrictions and mandatory capital requirements. Social Security accounts invested directly in these intermediaries (through bank deposits, insurance policies, or money market mutual fund shares) should incur relatively low levels of financial risk.[148] Accounts invested through other intermediaries (registered broker-dealers, investment advisers, other investment companies, or even bank trust departments) would, however, assume higher degrees of financial risk. Existing regulatory safeguards in these other fields consist primarily of open-ended fiduciary standards and disclosure obligations, which are not designed to insulate investors from variations in returns, and experience shows that individuals who invest through these intermediaries enjoy widely different rates of return.

Besides exposing Social Security participants to a wide and potentially confusing range of investment choices, the supervisory difficulties in allowing all regulated intermediaries to manage Social Security accounts are daunting. Despite a recent flurry of large mergers, the American financial services industry remains highly fragmented; tens of thousand of regulated entities and indi-

146. It would also be appropriate to grant such obligations an appropriate priority should the employer become insolvent.

147. See Jackson and Symons (1998).

148. Certain bank and insurance products are protected by public insurance programs, although the accounts of those near and in retirement could easily exceed current coverage levels.

vidual offer financial services. Ensuring uniform oversight of such a large number of potential account managers would be a daunting challenge, particularly in policing abuses of fraud and overreaching, which typically necessitate labor-intensive investigations and individual prosecutions. This supervisory task would be greatly simplified if the number of eligible providers were limited in some substantial manner. While certain elements of the financial services industry would undoubtedly resist such restrictions, I would be inclined to limit eligibility for account management to a relatively small number of intermediaries with excellent records of supervisory compliance. To ease supervision and reduce the likelihood of compliance problems, the number of eligible providers could be restricted to, say, fifty or even fewer well-established and well-capitalized financial institutions, all of whom have substantial incentives to avoid supervisory problems. One would probably want to allow for new entrants every year or so, both to keep the system dynamic and to replace managers that merge or otherwise go out of business.

DEVELOPING A NEW LEVEL OF REGULATION FOR PRIVATIZED ACCOUNTS. However many financial intermediaries are ultimately authorized to manage individual retirement accounts, the question then arises about what legal regimes should govern the terms under which these intermediaries can accept individual Social Security accounts. Conceivably, privatization legislation relying exclusively on existing regulatory structures could be adequate to safeguard participant investments. (Accounts placed with insurance companies would be protected through insurance regulation; accounts with banks, through banking regulation, and so on.) This would, however, be a risky strategy both for account participants and, perhaps also, the financial services industry.[149] More likely, in my view, privatization legislation will include a meta-level of regulation to establish a new system of rules governing private Social Security account investments, thus ensuring some uniformity and consistency in regulation for all participants.[150]

149. The risk to the financial services industry is that problems with privatized Social Security accounts could lead to increased regulation of large portions of the financial services industry, not just those portions managing Social Security accounts.

150. This supplemental level of regulation could build on existing regulatory structures in various ways. For example, if one conceptualized eligible providers as advisers to Social Security participants, the regulatory structure could mandate that account assets could only be invested in certain kinds of regulated intermediaries: for example, well-capitalized FDIC-insured banks or mutual funds regulated under the Investment Company Act of 1940 with more than $1 billion in assets. The provider's selection of investment vehicles and recommendations to account participants would be governed by the meta-regulation I recommend, but the underlying investments would be regulated under existing regulatory systems—that is, bank regulation and the 1940 Act. Our private pension regulation system has elements of this sort of jurisdictional allocation for plan

Such an overarching regulatory structure might address any number of issues, but I would be inclined to focus on the following areas:

—Regulation of account fees and other administrative expenses. As explored above, the absolute amount and variation in fees charges on privatized Social Security accounts is a matter of potential concern. To maintain competitive pressure on these charges, privatization legislation could mandate disclosure rules comparable to those the Securities and Exchange Commission has developed for the mutual fund industry.[151] Care would have to be taken to ensure that these disclosures reflect indirect compensation, such as soft dollar arrangements and similar practices, whereby advisers can increase their revenues without direct charges to account participants. To the extent that there is concern over fee differentials across account participants, regulations might also establish a ceiling on maximum fees. More direct controls over fees are also conceivable, but as our experience with fixed commissions and insurance rate regulation has demonstrated, price controls of this sort are difficult and costly to administer effectively.

ESTABLISHING FIDUCIARY OBLIGATIONS TO PARTICIPANTS. Another potentially appropriate regulatory mechanism would be the imposition of a fiduciary obligation on the part of eligible providers to recommend only "suitable" investments to Social Security participants and otherwise act in the best interest of those participants. Analogs of open-ended obligations of this sort already exist in the field of securities regulation and pension law, but they do not exist in all sectors of the financial services industry.[152] Although unquestionably costs are associated with duties of this sort, such an obligation would establish important minimal standards of conduct and prohibit a wide range of abuses, which are difficult to proscribe prospectively.[153]

---

assets placed in guaranteed insurance accounts and certain regulated investment companies. See ERISA § 401(b)(1), (2), 29 U.S.C.A. § 1101(b)(1). Jackson and Symons (1998); see also Langbein and Wolk (1995, pp. 644–48) (describing jurisdictional compromise).

151. For a recent overview of SEC reforms in this area, see Proposed Amendment to Mutual Fund Registration Form, *Federal Register*, vol. 62 (March 10, 1997), pp. 10,898–01.

152. See, for example, NASD Conduct Rule 2310, reprinted in NASD Securities Dealers Manual (CCH) 4261 (1997); ERISA § 404(a)(1), 29 U.S.C.A. § 1104(a)(1). Jackson and Symons (1998).

153. Articulating the precise scope of such a duty is beyond the scope of this essay. Drafters of privatization legislation should, however, consider the extent to which participants will be permitted to waive these fiduciary obligations. Supposing, for example, that a participant wanted to invest his or her entire account in a single high-technology start-up firm—an investment strategy widely perceived to be unsuitable for a retirement account. Could the participant insist on such an investment? Should it make a difference that the participant's eligible provider recommended the stock

DIRECT REGULATION OF ACCOUNT INVESTMENTS. A more difficult question is the extent to which privatization legislation should more directly influence the investment decisions of account participants. One could rely solely on the protections afforded through an open-ended fiduciary duty imposed on eligible providers, supplemented with appropriate disclosures regarding the intermediaries' recommendations. There are, however, other regulatory alternatives: most notably, imposing mandatory portfolio restrictions on participant accounts or, less intrusively, simply requiring the eligible providers to make certain kinds of investments available to participants.[154] The restrictions discussed below could be imposed as either mandatory restrictions or required options.

—Diversified and lower-risk investments. The primary justification for attempting to narrow the range of possible investment is to reduce the financial risk that account participants assume. The greater the choice of investment, the greater the possibility for variations in return across participants and the more likely some group of participants will in fact do worse than they currently do with implicit rates of return on their Social Security contributions. At a minimum, it seems to me, it would be desirable to steer participants toward either diversified pooled accounts (for example, mutual funds, qualifying insurance products, and perhaps appropriately constrained trust accounts) or relatively low-risk instruments (inflation-indexed government bonds, bank CDs, regulated annuities). To simplify participant choice, the number of investment choices might also be restricted to a relatively small number for each type of investment.

—Indexed portfolios. Steering participants to diversified pools will not, however, eliminate all financial risk. Even within the U.S. stock market, diversified pools have heterogeneous returns, leading to financial risk for participants. One could substantially limit this sort of risk by requiring that the diversified pools be based on broad market indexes, albeit at the cost of denying supramarket returns for those lucky enough to invest in the more successful

---

for a portion of the participant's account? Other related issues, such as the extent to which Social Security accounts can be pledged or otherwise alienated, would also need to be addressed. See ERISA § 206(d), 29 U.S.C.A. § 1056(d). Jackson and Symons (1998).

The need for open-end fiduciary obligations would lessen if privatization regulation also included direct regulation of account investments, as already discussed. In that case, fiduciary protections would not need to extend to asset selection but might be appropriate for advisory services and other aspects of account management.

154. Traditional bank and insurance regulation has relied heavily on portfolio restrictions; ERISA's new safe-harbor rules for 401(k) accounts are an illustration of a regime that simply requires that certain investment options be made available. See note 145.

actively managed accounts.[155] (The use of indexed portfolios would also make it easier for participants to compare the past performance and administrative costs of different eligible service providers.)

—Limitations on rebalance and asset allocation decisions. Even limiting investments to indexed funds will not, however, reduce all forms of financial risk. As mentioned above, allocations of funds between indexes and timing decisions in switching between indexes presents residual risks, which could in theory be diminished through limitations on both allocation decisions and the timing of reallocating portfolios. Regulatory restrictions could discourage account participants from adjusting their portfolios too frequently. For example, participants could be precluded from changing investment strategies more frequently than once a year.

—Protection from intergenerational variation. Finally, to deal with the risks of intergenerational variation in returns, regulations could steer account participants into purchasing some sort of insurance, guaranteeing a minimal rate of return on their account balances.[156] Insurance companies have for many years offered similar products, in the form of variable annuities with guaranteed minimum rates of return, and it is conceivable that similar products could be developed for privatized Social Security accounts.[157]

ALLOCATION OF SUPERVISORY JURISDICTION. A final question of regulatory design is the allocation of regulatory jurisdiction over privatized Social Security accounts. There are two important dimensions of jurisdiction: the authority to promulgate regulations and the authority to enforce those regulations. Both functions could be centralized with the Social Security Administration or some other appropriate agency. Or, the jurisdiction could be divided between the

---

155. Largely because of the problems associated with direct participant investment in the market place, some privatization proposals—most notably the Individual Account and Maintain Benefit proposals of last year's Advisory Council report—specify that privatization should take the form of investments in broad market-based indexes, for example, on the S&P 500 or other recognized indexes.

156. As discussed above, one very important risk that indexes do not eliminate is the possibility that stock returns will underperform historic averages—that is, intergenerational risk discussed above. It remains possible that the real rate of returns on stocks will be substandard during any particular period. It is, in theory, possible to design an investment product that eliminates some of the downside risk of stock market investments through some form of dynamic hedging strategy.

157. Although it might be difficult to devise a regulation that would require equity investments of PSA-style accounts to be hedged in this way, if the stock portfolios were centrally managed (as in the Maintain Benefit or Individual Account proposals), hedging strategies of this sort might be both feasible and desirable. For a discussion of hedging strategies of this sort, see Gordon (1997); see also Bodie and Crane (1998).

Social Security Administration and the various regulatory agencies with primary supervisory responsibility over the financial intermediaries licensed to be eligible providers. For example, the SSA could promulgate a system of regulation that the bank regulators would impose on banks, insurance regulators impose on insurance companies, and so on. Alternatively, both supervisory functions could be delegated to the primary regulators, allowing a number of agencies to issue authoritative (and potentially conflicting) interpretations of the enabling statute. Our financial system has illustrations of each approach to allocating jurisdiction,[158] although in this context—where an important public goal would be to encourage participants to make comparisons across sectors of the financial services industry—I believe centralization/uniformity of rule-making functions (of the sort that would define disclosure standards for performance and administrative fees) would be desirable.

The Role of Regulatory Safeguards in the Debate over Social Security Reform

As this menu of regulatory restraints reveals, it is possible both to adopt a PSA-style privatization proposal and at the same time adopt regulatory structures that will substantially constrain the financial risks that participants will assume. As a practical matter, the more of these constraints one imposes, the more sensible it would be to rely on an individual account-style approach where the government itself provides the investment choices. After all, a full menu of regulatory restraints will leave very little room for market competition, while entailing substantial supervisory and compliance costs. Indeed, to the extent one were to impose the full menu of regulatory constraints on Social Security participants—that is, mandating that equity investments be hedged to mitigate intergenerational variations in returns—one would have come very close to converting a defined-contribution program into a defined-benefit plan. At that point, I would question whether it would make a good deal more sense to go with a true defined-benefit plan, such as the Advisory Council's Maintain Benefit approach, which is likely to be a good deal more straightforward to implement and administer.

If, however, the framers of a privatized Social Security system seek some compromise between the current defined-benefit program and a new PSA-style initiative, a number of intermediate regulatory solutions are available. Regulatory structures could steer participants toward certain investment choices without formally mandating them, while at the same time prohibiting or at least

158. See Fein (1995) (reviewing various examples of jurisdictional coordination).

strongly discouraging clearly inappropriate investment choices. While these intermediate solutions will necessarily expose participants to some financial risk, appropriately structured regulatory restraints can reduce the number and severity of potential bad outcomes.[159] Though not a complete substitute for the kind of social insurance the Social Security system currently provides, regulatory safeguards can dampen the volatility of a privatized Social Security system, thereby protecting the interests of future Social Security participants and their beneficiaries.

As the national debate on Social Security reform turns to the various privatization proposals, discussions should include careful attention to the efficacy and completeness of the regulatory system that competing proposals contemplate. Rather than focusing solely on the average rate of return a particular proposal contemplates, analysts should also consider the full distribution of returns that participants can be expected to realize over time. The regulatory protections built into each proposal will have a substantial effect on these expected distributions. Carefully constructed and sensibly administered regulations can do much to soften the potentially harsh realities of Social Security reform.

Ian Lanoff, discussant

SOME OF YOU MUST be asking yourselves: "Why are we being subjected to a speech by a Washington lawyer?" I am sorry. My background has prepared me to examine the kinds of issues that are addressed in the paper by Theodore J. Angelis. During the Carter administration, I was head of the ERISA program at the U.S. Department of Labor. While there, I developed the rules and regulations on investments by private sector pension plans.

Later, after I had left that position, I was hired by the Department of Labor, which oversees the federal Thrift Savings Plan, to examine some complaints alleging fiduciary law violations that had been filed by one of the board members.

Finally, I represent many state and municipal public employee pension funds. I have been very much in the middle of some of the social investing controversies in the 1980s, of the South Africa divestiture controversy, and, just recently, the tobacco divestiture controversy.

What I intend to do today is to examine the three options that the Social Security Advisory Council proposed and measure them against the four threats to Social Security investing in equity markets that Angelis identified in his paper. The four threats are a social investing threat, a corporate governance or

---

159. As suggested above, see note 144. Monte Carlo simulations offer one technique for evaluating the distributional implications of various reform proposals. Alternative regulatory restraints could and, in my view, should also be evaluated in this manner.

shareholder activism threat, an international investment threat, which is somewhat akin to both the social investing threat and the corporate governance threat, and increased concerns on the part of the federal and state governments about overregulation of Social Security if it begins to make investments in private markets.

My conclusion is—and I agree with Cavanaugh—that the Maintain Benefits approach, which allows for investment by the Social Security board in a stock index fund selected by Congress, would minimize the risk under each of these four threats. In addition, I think the Maintain Benefits approach has a couple of other advantages. If one looks at every single individual and the investment risk that each would be subject to under, say, the Personal Security Account option, then I agree with Howell Jackson that some individuals will face risks and take risks that may lead to losses in their accounts. With the Maintain Benefits plan, every individual in the country who is working or retired will be taking exactly the same risk. It will be easy to measure and to know that risk.

Second, I have heard some economists talk—and I am not one myself—but I believe I understand what they are saying when they talk about increased savings by privatizing Social Security in some way. It seems to me that one advantage of the Maintain Benefits approach is that one is guaranteed that a certain fraction of Social Security assets will be invested in equities. In the Personal Security Account approach, however, there is no guarantee that participants in the Social Security system will invest in equities. I am also concerned that if there is no Social Security benefit system that people perceive as being safe, then, even in their current 401(k)s, people are going to become more conservative and less likely to invest in equities in their 401(k)s.

Let me briefly talk about the threats that Angelis identified and then talk about how I measure each of the options against those threats. The Maintain Benefits plan is basically a defined-benefit plan that is similar to most large corporate plans and most state public plans. This means that a single individual or a board of trustees makes the investment decisions on behalf of all the people covered by a plan. The way the Maintain Benefits plan would work, as I understand it or, if not, as I think it should be modified, would be for Congress to select a specific equity index. Congress has to be careful in selecting the index because a lot of people out there are selling modified or enhanced indexes. That scares me. Congress should choose an S&P 500 index or a Russell 2000 index. That should be spelled out in legislation. The individual or the board that makes decisions would therefore make decisions only about the choice of managers. They would not make decisions about different investments. This restrictive approach would provide a great deal of safety.

An additional level of safety could be what the Thrift Savings Plan legislation already provides. The fiduciary provisions in ERISA—prudence and loyalty to participants and beneficiaries—should apply directly to the individual or the board that is choosing the investment managers that would provide the index services. Unlike the Thrift Savings Plan, I would recommend that the Labor Department or some other agency be given authority to sue those who choose the investment managers. These people should have personal liability just like those who run private sector pension plans or state and municipal public pension plans.

With this approach—the defined-benefit approach restricted to index funds—there will not be any worry about social investing with economically targeted investments or pet projects. There simply would be no room for those kinds of investments. In any event, in my experience, social investing by pension funds is a minimal issue. This is true even for the kinds that are cited as a threat, such as divestiture from companies operating in South Africa of from tobacco companies. It has only occurred in a few plans, and when it has, it is almost always the legislature that is to blame, or it is elected officials who serve as sole trustee or constitute a majority of a board. This will not happen under Social Security because of the scrutiny investments will receive.

Second, with respect to corporate governance, there have been objections raised about the government getting into the position of questioning corporate behavior. The solution is simple. Just as the Thrift Savings Plan is not allowed to vote shares, Congress could enact similar provisions for the Social Security board under the Maintain Benefits approach. The way the Thrift Savings Plan handles this task is to have the managers vote the shares. That is the way almost every pension fund in the country, public or private, operates today, except for a few like CalPERS. In my experience, these managers—because they are fiduciaries, because they have reputations to protect, and because they are personally liable if they are imprudent—will not buckle under pressure. And I am not aware of any managers voting shares in ways that advance social, or union, or any other kind of objectives to which government regulators might object.

The international investment threat can also be easily eliminated. Congress can simply prohibit or restrict the Social Security Board from making overseas investments. There is no natural law and nothing in the Constitution that requires that international investments be part of a portfolio. If the Maintain Benefits plan is adopted, it will not be its objective to make a killing or to take huge risks to achieve large gains. The idea is to achieve a higher return than what Social Security returns today. The Angelis paper deals at great length with diversification. Diversification is just a function of prudence. If Congress decides that for whatever reason foreign investments should not be part of the portfolio, diversification would not overrule that. So, I see absolutely no problem with international investments. I see Congress having legitimate concerns about interference in the operation of foreign governments. That is an absolutely logical basis for Congress to restrict investments so that there are no international investments. In terms of government regulatory troubles, I just do not see what they would be, based on what I just said about the other three threats if this approach were taken.

In terms of the second approach, the Individual Accounts plan is like a 401(k) plan in which a private employer selects options. That is the way the Thrift Savings Plan operates. I could see it as a viable option, but I do have concerns. My biggest concern is that the largest part of an individual's retirement income would be based upon personal savings—individual accounts in Social Security, individual accounts in 401(k) type plans, and traditional personal savings. Instead of a three-legged stool, consisting of Social Security, pension plan, and traditional personal savings, there would be a one-legged stool.

Concerns about social investing with respect to a 401(k) type of plan should be no less than for a defined-benefit plan. One of the examples that Angelis gives in his paper is of Governor John Engler of Michigan who persuaded the legislature—and I understand it has now been reversed—to adopt a defined-contribution plan for public employees in the state rather than a defined-benefit plan. One of the arguments he made was that there would not be any social investing with a defined-contribution plan. I would like to ask the governor the following questions: if the auto industry took a dive, might he be tempted to form a fund to bail out the auto industry in Michigan and make that fund one of the options in the defined-contribution plan? If he did so, wouldn't workers and retirees be put under enormous pressure by politicians, their unions, and their employers to invest a part of their retirement assets in this particular investment fund? Importantly, the individual investor, unlike plan trustees, might not have fiduciary law restrictions to protect them against such pressure. That, to me, would represent an investment in a pet project—the worst kind of social investing.

In looking at corporate governance, I expect that Congress will delegate proxy voting responsibilities to fund managers. I hope that individual investors will be smart enough to allow their fund managers to vote their shares. But I am concerned about the pressures that might be brought to bear upon individual account owners to vote their shares in specific ways in situations involving corporate takeovers or corporate downsizing. Finally, I agree with Howell Jackson on worries about government overregulation. The government is going to become involved if individual choice is allowed because the government is going to have to design a way to educate people. It is going to have to figure out ways to educate every worker and retiree about the different options that are going to be available under the defined-contribution plan. Believe me, that is going to be a big job. Who will do it?

The Personal Security Account plan, or what I would label "a broker in every living room" is the least desirable choice of the three when measured against the threats posed in Angelis's paper. Think about the risk—the investment risk—of allowing every worker and every retiree in this country to be making choices based on recommendations by brokers. It gives me great concern.

As for social investing and corporate governance, this is the worst choice because it places individuals in a position to be pressured without any protection of fiduciary law. The Personal Security Account plan is the only plan that creates a problem with foreign investments. Under the other two plans, there would be no foreign investments. Under this plan, if people are allowed to invest in every type of investment, then brokers could sell investments in overseas funds. I can visualize some brokers selling derivatives, based on foreign currency movements, to unwary investors. Who would stop them? Then, again, I agree with Jackson that, maybe the government would try to intervene. Then, not only would there be a broker in every living room, there would be big government in every living room.

References

Advisory Council on Social Security. 1997a. *Report of the 1994–1996 Advisory Council on Social Security: Vol. 1: Findings and Recommendations.* Washington: Government Printing Office.

_____. 1997b. *Report of the 1994–1996 Advisory Council on Social Security: Vol. 2: Reports of the Technical Panels.* Washington: Government Printing Office.

American Law Institute. 1992. *Restatement (Third) of Trusts.* St Paul: The Institute.

Anand, Vineeta. 1997. "Funds Flexing Muscles Early in Proxy Battles." *Pensions and Investments* (March 17): 20.

Bagley, Constance E., and Berger, David J. 1997. "Proxy Contests and Corporate Control: Strategic Considerations." *Corporate Practice Series (BNA),* vol. 69, Washington: Bureau of National Affairs.

Biggs, John H. 1996. "Corporate Governance Assessment." *Director's Monthly* 20 (10):1–6.

Black, Bernhard S. 1990. "Shareholder Passivity Reexamined." *Michigan Law Review* 89 (3): 520–608.

Bodie, Zvi, and Dwight B. Crane. 1998. *The Design and Production of New Retirement Savings Products.* Working Paper 98-070. Harvard Business School Division of Research (January).

California Public Employees' Retirement System. 1995. "Domestic Proxy Voting Policies." January 17.

Cavanaugh, Francis. 1996. *The Truth about the National Debt: Five Myths and One Reality.* Harvard University Business School Press.

Coffee Jr., John C. 1994. "The SEC and the Institutional Investor: A Half-Time Report." *Cardozo Law Review* 15 (4): 837–907.

———. 1997. "Investor Capitalism: How Money Managers Are Changing the Face of Corporate America." *Michigan Law Review* 95 (6): 1970–89.

Committee for Economic Development. 1997. *Fixing Social Security.* New York.

"CREF Withholds Support for Disney Compensation Plan and Directors." 1997. PR Newswire, *available in* Westlaw, February 21.

Cross, Patrick S. 1993. "Economically Targeted Investments—Can Public Pension Plans Do Good and Do Well?" *Indiana Law Journal* 68(3): 931–76.

Crystal, Graef. 1992. *In Search of Excess.* Norton.

Diamond, Peter. 1997. "Macroeconomic Aspects of Social Security Reform." *Brookings Papers on Economic Activity*, September.

Easterbrook, Frank, and Fischel, Daniel. 1983. "Voting in Corporate Law." *Journal of Law and Economics* 26(2): 395–427.

Employee Benefit Research Institute. 1996. "Worker Investment Decisions: An Analysis of Large 401(k) Plan Data." EBRI Issue 176. August.

Even, William E., and MacPherson, David A. 1997. *Freed from FICA.* New York: Third Millennium.

Fama, Eugene F., and French, Kenneth R. 1992. "The Cross-Section of Expected Stock Returns." *Journal of Finance* 47 (2): 427–65.

———. 1993. "Common Risk Factors in the Returns on Stocks and Bonds." *Journal of Financial Economics* 33 (February): 3–56.

Fein, Melanie L. 1995. "Functional Regulation: A Concept for Glass-Steagall Reform?" *Stanford Journal of Law, Business, and Finance* 2 (Fall):89–128.

Fisch, Jill E. 1993. "From Legitimacy to Logic: Reconstructing Proxy Regulation." *Vanderbilt Law Review* 46 (5): 1129–99.

Franecki, David. 1997. "Pension Panel Says Corporate Governance's Issues Won't Fade." *Dow Jones News Service*, March 19.

Gordon, Jeffrey N. 1997. "Employees, Pensions, and the New Economic Order." *Columbia Law Review* 97(June):1519–66.

Gordon, Lilli, and Pound, John. 1993. "Active Investing in the U.S. Equity Market: Past Performance and Future Prospects." Unpublished manuscript (January).

Gramlich, Edward M. 1997. "Mending But Not Ending Social Security: The Individual Accounts Plan." *Benefits Quarterly*, third quarter: 25–28.

Haddock, David D., and Macey, Jonathan R. 1987. "Regulation on Demand." *Journal of Law and Economics* 30(2): 311–52.

Hammond, P. Brett, and Warshawsky, Mark J. 1997. "Investing Social Security Funds in Stocks." *Benefits Quarterly*, third quarter: 52–65.

Hemmerick, Steve, and Schwimmer, Anne. 1992. "States' Pension Grabs Fought." *Pensions and Investments*, August 17.

Hirschman, Albert O. 1970. *Exit, Voice, and Loyalty.* Harvard University Press.

Hsin, Ping-Lung, and Mitchell, Olivia. 1995. "Public Sector Pensions: Can They Meet the Challenge?" In *Retirement Trends*, proceedings of the forty-seventh annual conference of the IRRA.

Ibbotson, Roger G., and Brinson, Gary P. 1987. *Investment Markets: Gaining the Performance Advantage.* McGraw-Hill.

Independent Bankers Association of America. 1993. "Regulatory Burden: The Cost to Community Banks." January. Washington.

Jackson, Howell E., and Edward S. Symons. 1998. *The Regulation of Financial Institutions.* West Publishing.

Jensen, Michael. 1986. "Agency Costs of Free Cash Flow, Corporate Finance, and Takeovers." *American Economic Review* 76(2): 323–29.

Jensen, Michael, and Ruback, Richard. 1983. "The Market for Corporate Control: The Scientific Evidence." *Journal of Finance* 11 (1): 5–50.

Koppes, Richard H., and Reilly, Maureen L. 1996. "An Ounce of Prevention: Meeting the Fiduciary Duty to Monitor an Index Fund through Relationship Investing." *Journal of Corporate Law* 20 (3): 413–49.

Langbein, John H. 1996. "The Uniform Prudent Investor Act and the Future of Trust Investing," *Iowa Law Review* 81(3): 641–69.

_____. 1997. Remarks at the Power and Influence of Pensions and Mutual Funds Conference, February 21. In *Westlaw*, Dow Jones Money Management Alert file.

Langbein, John H., and Wolk, Bruce A. 1995. *Pension and Employee Benefit Law.* Westbury, New York: Foundation Press.

Lanoff, Ian. 1997. "If the Social Security Trust Fund Were to Be Invested in Stocks, How Could the Voting Rights Be Exercised?" Unpublished manuscript.

Lavelle, Marianne. 1991. "FDIC Legal Program Criticized." *National Law Journal*, November 25.

Litvak, Lawrence, 1981. *Pension Funds and Economic Renewal.* Washington: Council of State Planning Agencies.

Malkiel, Burton. 1993. *A Random Walk Down Wall Street.* Norton.

Mitchell, Olivia, and Ping Lung Hsin. 1994. *Public Pension Governance and Performance.* Working Paper Series 94-1. Pension Research Council. Philadelphia.

_____. 1997. "Public Pension Governance and Performance." In *The Economics of Pensions*, edited by Salvador Valdes-Prieto. Cambridge University Press.

Moore, Cynthia L. 1995. *Protecting Retirees' Money.* Arlington, Va.: National Council on Teacher Retirement.

National Conference of Commissioners on Uniform State Laws. 1997. *Uniform Management of Public Employee Retirement Systems Act.*

Nesbitt, Stephen L. 1994. "Long-Term Rewards of Shareholder Activism: A Study of the 'CalPERS' Effect." *Journal of Applied Corporate Finance* 6 (Winter): 75.

Pound, John. 1993a. "Creating Relationships between Institutional Investors and Corporations." Presented at the Conference on Relational Investing: Possibilities, Patterns and Problems, sponsored by the Columbia University Law School's Center for Law and Economic Studies (April).

_____. 1993b. "The Rise of the Political Model of Corporate Governance and Corporate Control." *New York University Law Review* 68 (5):1003–71.

Reilly, Maureen. 1997. "California Public Employees' Retirement System: Why Corporate Governance Today?" *Practicing Law Institute Corporate Law and Practice Course Handbook Series* 985 (April): 979–98.

Roberts, Douglas B., and Matthew J. Hanley. 1997. "Defined Contribution 'Right' for Public Plans." *Pensions and Investments*, March 31.

Roe, Mark J. 1991. "Political Elements in the Creation of a Mutual Fund Industry." *University of Pennsylvania Law Review* 139 (6):1469–1511.

———. 1994. *Strong Managers, Weak Owners.* Princeton University Press.

Romano, Roberta. 1993. "Public Pension Fund Activism in Corporate Governance Reconsidered." *Columbia Law Review* 93 (4): 795–853.

———. 1996. "Corporate Law and Corporate Governance." *Industrial and Corporate Change* 5(2): 277–339.

Schwartz, Alan. 1986. "Search Theory and the Tender Offer Auction." *Journal of Law, Economics, and Organizations* 2(2): 229–53.

Schwimmer, Anne. 1992. "Connecticut's Deal a Bust." *Pensions and Investments*, March 30.

Shleifer, Andrei, and Robert W. Vishny. 1997. "A Survey of Corporate Governance." *Journal of Finance* 52 (2): 737–83.

Shoven, John B. 1998. *The Location and Allocation of Assets in Pension and Conventional Savings Accounts.* Working Paper. Cambridge, Mass.: National Bureau of Economic Research (March).

Slater, David W. 1997. *Prudence and Performance: Managing the Proposed CPP Investment Board.* Toronto: C.D. Howe Institute.

Smith, Thomas A. 1997. "Institutions and Entrepreneurs in American Corporate Finance." *California Law Review* 30 (1): 1–78.

Stanton, Thomas H. 1997. "Institutional Factors to Consider with Respect to Proposals to Invest Social Security Funds in Equity Securities." In *Report of the 1994–1996 Advisory Council: Reports of the Technical Panels.* Washington: Government Printing Office.

U.S. General Accounting Office. 1992. *Pension Plans: Investments in Affordable Housing with Government Assistance.* Washington: Government Printing Office.

U.S. House Committee on Ways and Means and Committee on Education and Labor. 1983. *Public Employee Pension Benefit Plans: Joint Hearing before the Subcommittee on Oversight of the House Ways and Means Committee and the Subcommittee on Labor-Management Relations of the House Committee on Education and Labor.* 98 Cong. 1 sess. November 15 (statement of Alicia H. Munnell). Washington: Government Printing Office.

U.S. Securities and Exchange Commission. 1989. *Order Approving Proposed Rule Change.* Exchange Act Release 34-27,035. July 14.

———. 1991. *Regulation of Securityholder Communications.* Exchange Act Release 34-29, 315, June 17.

U.S. Senate Committee on Governmental Affairs. 1985. *Federal Employees' Retirement System: Hearing before the Committee on Governmental Affairs on S. 1527,* 99 Cong. 1 sess. September 11 (statement of Senator Stevens). Washington: Government Printing Office.

Wahal, Sunil. 1996. "Pension Fund Activism and Firm Performance." *Journal of Finance* 31 (1): 1–23.

Walters, Jonathan. 1992. "The Pension Fund Grab of '91." *Governing*, February, p. 18.

Zingales, Luigi. 1995. "What Determines the Value of Corporate Votes." *Quarterly Journal of Economics* 110(4): 1047–73.

Zorn, Paul. 1997. *1997 Survey of State and Local Government Retirement Systems.* Chicago: Public Pension Coordinating Council.

7

Public Opinion and
the Politics of Reforming
Social Security

THE PAPERS in this chapter look at the role that public
opinion and politics will play in Social Security reform.
The first paper describes Americans' attitudes toward Social Security and
toward alternative reform strategies. The second paper documents the politics
of past Social Security changes as a prelude to exploring how the political
process is likely to work this time around.

Myths and Misunderstandings about
Public Opinion toward Social Security
Lawrence R. Jacobs and Robert Y. Shapiro

POLICYMAKERS, PUNDITS, AND news audiences are bom-
barded every day with new public opinion polls and journalists' reports on the
state of Americans' thinking about Social Security. To interpret the information,
political observers rely on four assumptions about public thinking on Social
Security. The first is that the public really does not know much, if anything,
about Social Security. The clear implication is that the public's preferences
should be tracked as a practical political matter but should be discounted as an
influence on policy discussions.

No single poll on the public's attitude toward Social Security has received
more eye-opening attention than Third Millennium's UFO poll of eighteen to

We gratefully acknowledge the research assistance of Eric Ostermeier and James Smartt and a
grant from the Pew Charitable Trusts. We also appreciate the thoughtful comments of Eric Kingson.

thirty-four-year-olds in September 1994. Journalists (and policymakers) followed Third Millennium's lead and pitched the poll as suggesting that young Americans considered UFOs more likely than the prospect of collecting Social Security.[1] Third Millennium's UFO poll and its widespread use by journalists and policymakers illustrate the second assumption: Americans' confidence in the future of Social Security is dramatically changing, escaping like air from a punctured balloon. Public support for Social Security will decline dramatically now that confidence has collapsed.

The third assumption of political observers is that Americans are now turning toward radical change and would privatize Social Security as the best hope for restoring its future. Anne Willette, for example, opened her October 1, 1996, story for *USA Today* by heralding a poll that purported to demonstrate that almost 60 percent of Americans "want to invest some of their Social Security taxes themselves—even though they might end up with less money at retirement. Americans, particularly younger workers, are watching out for their interests and demanding their 'money's worth.'"

The final assumption is that the generations are at war over Social Security. Staving off the collapse of Social Security is the goal of self-serving seniors who are disregarding the interests of younger Americans. In a November 1994 broadcast, ABC's Jim Angle flagged younger Americans' "deep doubts about generational fairness."

We evaluated the validity of these four assumptions about public opinion by reviewing hundreds of responses to survey questions from the 1970s to the fall of 1997. We were especially interested in survey items that were worded in an identical or similar manner over a long period of time. As is well known, poll results are extremely sensitive to the wording of questions; survey responses can be an artifact of how poll questions are phrased. Examining similarly worded questions allows us to identify genuine patterns and trends in public opinion.

The conclusion of our analysis is that the evidence on public opinion is at odds with important aspects of the conventional presumptions regarding Americans' thinking about Social Security. The public is, in fact, better informed about Social Security than commonly presumed. Areas where the public is wrong often represent plausible conclusions based on the available information. The public may simply be echoing the choices presented to it. Although large proportions of citizens understand Social Security's operations, this knowledge is generally much more prevalent among the more affluent and educated.

1. Third Millennium, "Social Security: The Credibility Gap," survey by Frank Luntz and Mark Siegel (New York, September 1994).

In addition, Third Millennium's notorious UFO report is both misleading and provides no new information about public opinion—Americans have had low confidence in Social Security since the 1970s. Despite their low confidence, the public's support has remained strong, according to available trend data.

The third assumption that Americans welcome the opportunity to restructure Social Security similarly lacks a clear grounding in the available evidence. Responses to balanced survey questions show no support for individualized privatization. Politicians who emphasize this kind of structural reform place themselves in the vulnerable position of pressing an option that a comparatively well-informed public opposes.

The fourth assumption of intergenerational warfare is overstated. Although seniors are more sensitive to threats to Social Security, younger Americans are consistently just as supportive (if not more so) of the overall program. Forgotten in the rush to condemn seniors as "greedy geezers" are the differences that divide the elderly. Opinion surveys suggest that education, economic circumstances, and other factors both divide seniors and draw them together with other segments of the population including younger cohorts. A broad cross-section of Americans support Social Security not because it satisfies a simple calculation of its "money's worth" to any one individual but because it provides an insurance against the risk of low income in retirement and a protection from bearing the burden of financially drained parents.

What the Public Knows

Although Americans' overall political knowledge is "modest at best," Social Security is an exception.[2] The public appears to know more about Social Security than about national defense or basic government institutions. Thus, while the public cannot be characterized as a fully informed citizenry, its knowledge of Social Security is much higher than widely assumed. Surveys since 1973 show that at least half of the Americans questioned have consistently reported that they are "very" or "fairly" well informed.[3] The degree to

2. Delli Carpini and Keeter (1996).

3. These results are confirmed by several additional surveys conducted in 1997, which reported that nearly 60 percent of Americans felt confident in their understanding and knowledge about the program. A March 1997 *Washington Post* poll asked: "Would you say you know a lot, a fair amount, very little, or nothing about Social Security?" Five percent selected "a lot," 51 percent "fair amount," 40 percent "not too well informed," and 4 percent "not at all informed." The Employee Benefit Research Institute (EBRI) asked: "Would you say that you are very confident, somewhat confident, not too confident or not at all confident . . . that you have a good understanding of how the Social Security system works." 21 percent selected "very confident," 41 percent "somewhat confident," 23 percent "not too confident," 13 percent "not at all confident," and 2 percent reported "not knowing."

which Americans perceive themselves as informed varies significantly by age and somewhat by education and income. Seniors consistently rank themselves the highest and those below 30 the lowest. But Social Security is apparently sufficiently well understood through interpersonal contacts and media coverage to counteract the typical advantage of the affluent.[4]

Americans' confidence in their knowledge apparently springs from the information they receive through the media. Princeton surveys in January and February 1997 found that about half or more of Americans report following news reports on Social Security "very" or "fairly" closely.[5] Of course, whether Americans' confidence in their understanding of Social Security is justified remains a separate issue; the public may be overestimating its competence or the information conveyed to the public by policymakers and journalists may be inaccurate.

The evidence suggests that the public's confidence is not unwarranted. Many of the basic rules and procedures of the Social Security system are known to half or more of the public. Eight surveys since 1978 indicate that generally two-thirds or more of Americans accurately understand that Social Security is a pay-as-you-go system.

A collection of individual survey items since the 1970s reveals that a majority or a solid plurality of the public accurately understands important facts about Social Security (table 7-1). The public recognizes that their funds are invested in government bonds rather than in stocks or placed in a bank account; that exhaustion of the trust fund in 2029 will result in fewer assets and reduced benefits rather than the system becoming completely broke and unable to pay any benefits; and that its future financial problems stem from fewer workers and increased life expectancy. These are comparatively detailed and technical issues.

Over a third of the items in table 7-1, however, point to gaps in the public's understanding. Only one or perhaps three in ten Americans understand that Social Security is one of the federal budget's most expensive items; fraud and abuse have not caused the program's financial trouble; and that Social Security is not facing financial difficulty because it is a "Ponzi scheme" to finance other programs.

Although Americans are wrong on these facts, their responses are either plausible or reflect the information that policymakers and journalists have fed them. For instance, the public's false impression that Social Security is poorly

4. An alternative hypothesis is that lower-income groups are more likely to deceive themselves about a program that they have heard of but which they do not understand to the same depth as the more affluent.

5. The proportion who indicated that they followed Social Security "very" or "fairly" closely in the news fell from 64 percent in January 1997 to 49 percent in February.

Table 7-1. *Knowledge of Social Security*

Survey item	Percent correct
Social Security does not provide job training (1974)	89
Medicare is part of Social Security system (1974)	75
Social Security payroll taxes collected from workers today are used to pay benefits for current retirees (1997)	68
Social Security program faces financial difficulties because fewer workers will be available to pay Social Security taxes (1997)	59
Exhaustion of the Social Security trust fund means that the system will have fewer assets and will have to pay out benefits at a reduced level (1997)	57
Social Security is calculated as part of the total federal budget when the federal government calculates the budget deficit (1997)	50
Social Security trust fund invests in government treasury bonds (1997)	49
Social Security program faces financial difficulties because people on Social Security are living longer so they cost the program more money (1997)	47
Food stamps are not part of Social Security (1979)	41
Not all federal employees pay Social Security (1979)	37
Social Security is one of the two largest areas of spending by the federal government (1995)	33
Social Security is one of the top two federal budget expenses (1989)	27
What is Social Security tax rate (1979)	25
Social Security's financial difficulties result from money in its trust fund being spent on other programs (1997)	9
Social Security's financial difficulties result from its trust fund being invested unwisely (1997)	8
Social Security's financial difficulties do not result from fraud and abuse (1997)	7

Sources: See text.

administered likely stems from a general distrust of government and from the media's widespread coverage of administrative slipups; Social Security is guilty simply by association with government. In fact, less than 1 percent of Social Security outlays are consumed by administrative costs; and independent auditors have never charged that its rolls of retirees are bloated by bureaucratic bumbling and government incompetence. Yet only 7 percent realize that Social Security's financial problems do not stem from fraud and abuse.[6]

The public also errs in believing that foreign aid and food stamps are more costly than Social Security in the federal budget, an impression created by politicians and the news media. The 1996 presidential election, for instance,

6. Similar results were reported in a 1997 survey by the Public Agenda Foundation, which showed that 84 percent believed that "the government is mismanaging Social Security so badly that the money is going to waste," and 67 percent are convinced that "too many people are cheating the program." See Public Agenda Foundation, "Miles to Go: A Status Report on Americans' Plans for Retirement" (New York, 1997).

cautiously steered clear of Social Security but gave ample play to the burden on taxpayers of funding welfare and—in the Republican primaries—foreign "give-aways." With this background, concluding that food stamps and foreign aid are significant budgetary burdens is not so far-fetched.

Other Social Security issues on which the public appears off base are actually points of contention on which reasonable people disagree. For instance, only 8 percent of Americans do not attribute Social Security's financial difficulties to unwise investments. But, of course, observers are deeply divided over funding and investment issues. Some advocate accumulating a larger reserve and investing in stock. Others favor continuing Social Security's pay-as-you-go system, which operates with a small contingency reserve and invested in government bonds.

Still other cases of apparent public errors may result from ambiguous question wording. For example, a March 1997 survey by the *Washington Post* asked respondents if the average annual benefit that Social Security paid to retired workers was less than $10,000 a year, $10,000–$20,000 a year, $20,000 to $30,000, or more than $30,000. Thirty-eight percent chose the first category and 49 percent the second. The correct answer is not straightforward. It depends on whether the question is interpreted as referring to couples or nonmarried beneficiaries; the average Social Security benefit in 1992 was just over $10,000 for couples and a bit under 10,000 for nonmarried individuals.

In short, Americans' knowledge about Social Security is far from complete and certainly does not conform to the ideal of a democratic citizen, but it is more extensive than is commonly assumed, and wrong answers are often reasonable conclusions based on available information.

Differences in Knowledge

Americans' knowledge about Social Security and other political issues varies in striking ways. The distribution of political knowledge parallels the clustering of economic and social resources; the most affluent and educated tend to be the most knowledgeable.[7]

Table 7-2 presents the percentage of respondents correctly answering factual questions about Social Security based on their education, income, and age. Michael Delli Carpini and Scott Keeter find that "education is the strongest single predictor of political knowledge."[8] Education transmits specific infor-

---

7. We suspect that the income differences would be found in a multivariate analysis to largely reflect education difference.

8. Delli Carpini and Keeter (1996).

mation, instills the cognitive skills for effective learning, and stimulates students about politics, which leads to exposure to more information.

The better educated are more likely to understand accurately that the program is financed on a pay-as-you-go basis, that it is included in calculation of the federal budget, and other aspects of the program. For example, understanding that Social Security revenues are invested in government bonds jumps from 38 percent among individuals who did not graduate from high school to 64 percent among those who earned graduate degrees.

The advantage of education is somewhat muted for cases in which policymakers and journalists have provided limited or misleading information. For example, only a small fraction of the most educated understood the inaccuracy of claims that Social Security is hobbled by fraud, diversion of its funds to other programs, and unwise investments.

High-income individuals have a better grasp of Social Security's operations than lower-income individuals. For instance, only 38 percent of the poorest understood that Social Security revenues were invested in government bonds, while 62 percent of the most affluent recognized this important fact. The discrepancy between the high and low-income groups for many of the items in table 7-2 parallel the differences in knowledge found among better and less well educated. Income disparities may reinforce educational advantages in knowledge about Social Security.

Research on political knowledge demonstrates that age boosts understanding.[9] Education comes by passing through the human life cycle, which produces a range of experiences such as retiring or helping aging parents plan their finances, or by living through unique world events such as World War II or the Great Depression—events that mold the attitudes of that generation for the rest of their lives.

The survey results on Social Security provide only mixed evidence that age enhances knowledge. Only two of the eight items in table 7-2 indicate that age boosts knowledge. Older Americans were more aware that Social Security's problems stemmed from people living longer rather than from unwise investments, but even here knowledge dropped off for individuals above 70. Seniors were also less likely to appreciate the program's pay-as-you-go nature.

The Mixed Implications of Political Knowledge

The large proportion of Americans who understand many of the basic facts about Social Security demonstrate that they are equipped to reach informed

9. Delli Carpini and Keeter (1996).

Table 7-2. *Knowledge of Social Security according to Respondents' Education, Income, and Age*

Percent

Items pertaining to Social Security	Knowledge by education				
	Less than high school graduate	High school graduate	Some College	College graduate	Post-graduate
Pay-as-you-go	47	62	76	81	88
Part of budget in calculating deficit	43	49	46	58	51
Trust fund invests in government bonds	38	44	48	60	64
Faces difficulties because fewer workers to pay taxes	56	50	57	71	72
Faces difficulties because people are living longer	32	42	42	60	71
Difficulties not caused by fraud and abuse by recipients	3	6	7	8	15
Difficulties not caused by money in fund spent on other programs	5	6	8	14	16
Difficulties not caused by unwise investments of money in fund	9	6	9	9	9

Items pertaining to Social Security	Knowledge by income					
	Less than $10,000	$10,000–$20,000	$20,000–$30,000	$30,000–$50,000	$50,000–$70,000	More than $70,000
Pay-as-you-go	50	57	61	75	81	80
Part of budget in calculating deficit	51	50	54	50	46	52
Trust fund invests in government bonds	38	43	45	50	58	62
Faces difficulties because fewer workers to pay taxes	54	57	52	60	63	69
Faces difficulties because people are living longer	42	35	38	50	58	63
Difficulties not caused by fraud and abuse by recipients	4	7	8	7	9	9
Difficulties not caused by money in fund spent on other programs	6	7	7	9	11	16
Difficulties not caused by unwise investments of money in fund	8	5	7	8	11	8

| | Knowledge by age | | | | | |
	18–29	30–39	40–49	50–59	60–69	70+
Pay-as-you-go	66	75	75	77	46	54
Part of budget in calculating deficit	51	48	53	43	51	53
Trust fund invests in government bonds	47	52	50	51	44	47
Faces difficulties because fewer workers to pay taxes	55	60	59	58	65	56
Faces difficulties because people are living longer	30	41	58	56	58	44
Difficulties not caused by fraud and abuse by recipients	4	9	11	8	5	5
Difficulties not caused by money in fund spent on other programs	9	9	13	7	5	7
Difficulties not caused by unwise investments of money in fund	5	9	7	7	9	11

Source: See text.

choices and a basic understanding of the terms of debate. But knowledge is unequally held. The more affluent and better educated hold an advantage in being able to perceive and act on their self-interest or their notions of the public interest. The poor and less well educated are less well equipped and therefore compete at a significant disadvantage. For example, the less advantaged are less well equipped to understand that privatization could endanger their interests by threatening the redistributive impact of Social Security benefits.

Ironically, the advantage of education may be somewhat offset by the possibility of inaccurate information or manipulation. Because the better educated are more attuned to elite debate and media coverage, they may be especially vulnerable to being misled by incorrect information.[10] For instance, table 7-2 showed that the best educated were only marginally better informed than the least educated on the causes of Social Security's financial difficulties; this may partly stem from the incorrect statements of policymakers and journalists.

An Old Story: Low Confidence but Strong Support

The Third Millennium's UFO survey has become the flagship for the presumption that confidence in Social Security has collapsed. The UFO survey, however, has been falsely sold. Journalists conveyed the impression that respondents had weighed the relative likelihood of UFOs existing and Social Security surviving and concluded that UFOs were more probable. In fact, the survey never offered respondents a direct comparison; instead, it offered two separate questions, with the Social Security question appearing fifth and the UFO question fourteenth (as the survey's last substantive question before some standard demographic items).

A 1997 survey by the Employee Benefit Research Institute (EBRI) offered respondents the direct choice that Third Millennium falsely claimed to have posed. EBRI asked, "Which do you have greater confidence in: receiving Social Security benefits after retirement or alien life exists in outer space?" EBRI found that Americans overwhelmingly sided with Social Security over UFOs by a whopping margin of 71 percent to 26 percent. (Even among Generation X, respondents aged 33 or younger, the margin remained a stunning 63 percent to 33 percent).

Third Millennium not only misrepresented its results on UFOs and Social Security but also recounted an old story about public opinion. Confidence in Social Security's future has been low since the late 1970s. Confidence in the future of the program stood at 65 percent in 1975 but steadily dropped to

10. Page and Shapiro (1992).

32 percent by 1982 and has never returned to its earliest levels; presently it has stabilized at around 40 percent. Confidence in Social Security's future has been low for two decades. Weak confidence is not a new development.[11]

Low confidence in Social Security is concentrated in certain segments of the population. According to five surveys conducted by the *New York Times* and CBS, the most confident are seniors and those respondents with less income and education (many of whom are seniors). Seniors are already receiving benefits and therefore have tangible reasons for confidence, and individuals with less income or education harbor low expectations. High-income earners are particularly uncertain, while the most educated are members of younger cohorts, who were likely influenced by the dire warnings issued by policymakers and highlighted by journalists.

The superior confidence of the seniors and, to a lesser extent, the less well-educated remains stable between 1989 and 1997. However, the least well off, who expressed relatively higher confidence through 1995, are no longer more hopeful of Social Security's future than other income groups.

High Support

No survey question has repeatedly asked Americans over time if they support Social Security. The only modest exception occurred in the two surveys by the CATO Institute in spring 1996, which found that about two-thirds of Americans were "very" or "mostly" favorable toward Social Security.

Nevertheless, indirect survey questions confirm sustained and very strong support for Social Security. A series of questions have been asked of respondents over a number of years whether "we [are] spending too much, too little, or about the right amount on . . . Social Security." Table 7-3 indicates two very important points. First, an extraordinary 9 out of 10 Americans support the view that spending on Social Security is "about right" or "too little." Second, the high support has been remarkably stable even though 7 percent of respondents shifted from the "too little" to the "about right" category since 1986.

When Americans have been asked to set spending priorities in the federal budget, they have expressed overwhelming support for maintaining or expanding the program. Support remains enormous and opposition to cutting back massive. Table 7-4 indicates that since the mid-1980s fewer than 1 out of 10 Americans have favored decreasing Social Security's funding as they

11. Measuring Americans' confidence is sensitive to whether they are asked about receiving "the benefits you expect," the "future of the Social Security system," or more modestly, receiving "some benefits." Moreover, while Americans have low confidence in the general future of the program, a 1997 EBRI survey found that 58 percent believed they would receive some payment.

Table 7-3. *Spending on Social Security, 1984–96, Selected Years*

Percent unless otherwise noted

Date of survey	Response				
	Too little	About right	Too much	Don't know	N
April 1984	51	35	9	5	968
April 1985	52	38	7	3	1,534
April 1986	56	36	6	3	1,470
April 1987	55	35	6	4	1,466
April 1988	53	38	6	4	1,481
April 1989	54	37	4	5	1,537
April 1990	49	40	6	5	1,372
April 1991	52	39	4	5	1,517
April 1993	44	43	7	6	1,606
April 1994	47	41	7	5	2,992
May 1996	49	38	8	6	2,904

Question posed by NORC-GSS: We are faced with many problems in this country, none of which can be solved easily or inexpensively. I'm going to name some of these problems, and for each one I'd like you to tell me whether you think we're spending too much money on it, too little money, or about the right amount. Are we spending too much, too little, or about the right amount on . . . Social Security?

Source: National Opinion Research Center, General Social Surveys (NORC-GSS).

have wrestled with the competing demands on the federal budget, though more than a 10 percent shift has occurred from the "increased" to the "about right" categories.

Table 7-5 presents a series of surveys that used quite different wording to ask Americans whether the federal budget deficit should be reduced by cutting spending on Social Security. During the past fifteen years of surveys, two-thirds of Americans or more have opposed cutting the program to achieve budget reductions. Fiscal conservatives harbor similar views. Six polls in the mid-1990s asked respondents after they indicated support for a balanced budget if they would favor cuts in Social Security to achieve it; between 58 percent and 71 percent opposed balancing the budget if it meant cuts in Social Security.

A nearly identical pattern of steadfast support for Social Security appears in surveys on benefit reductions as a means to trim the federal budget. Table 7-6 reveals that since 1982 majorities of 61 percent to 78 percent have opposed reductions in cost-of-living adjustments (COLAs) to reduce the federal budget deficit, though the proportions favoring the reform have increased over time. Although not presented, other surveys find similar opposition to cuts in Social Security to reduce taxes.

Table 7-4. *Federal Budget Priorities, 1984–97, Selected Years*

Percent unless otherwise noted

Survey and date	Response					
	Increased	Same	Decreased	Cut out entirely (voluntary)	Don't know	N
NES 1984[a]	51	44	4	. . .	2	1,924
NES 1986	64	31	3	. . .	2	2,165
NES 1988	58	37	3	[b]	2	2,032
NES 1990	62	33	3	. . .	2	1,992
NES 1992	48	46.5	4	[b]	1	2,473
NES November 1994	51	43	5	. .	2	1,795
PSRA[c] December 1994	46	45	7	. . .	2	1,511
PSRA[c] May 1997	44	46	7	. . .	3	1,228

Question posed by NES, PSRA: If you had a say in making up the federal budget this year, for which of the following programs would you like to see spending increased and for which would you like to see spending decreased: Should federal spending on . . . Social Security be increased, decreased, or kept about the same?

Source: Surveys by National Election Studies (NES) and Princeton Survey Research Associates (PSRA).

a. Omits "of the following."

b. Less than 0.5 percent.

c. "If you were making up the federal budget this year, would you increase spending for Social Security, decrease spending for Social Security, or keep spending the same for this?"

The public has been more open to taxing the Social Security benefits of the wealthy as a means for reducing the federal budget deficit. Table 7-7 presents six differently worded questions that show majorities of Americans in every survey but two agreeing to tax the benefits of the wealthy. Americans have sent a strong and sustained message to budget cutters: while taxing the wealthy is acceptable, the basic structure of Social Security is off-limits in the competition for federal funding.

The public supports Social Security benefits for seniors because it represents an insurance against the risk of low income in retirement, a right earned by paying in during working years, and a protection from the burden of financially drained parents. Americans do not view the program in terms of individual profit and loss like a private investment, but rather they see it as a protection like fire insurance against known risks. For example, a 1997 survey by the Public Agenda Foundation found that 84 percent of the public agreed that Social Security "forces people who would otherwise neglect to save for their retirement to at least save something for it, and that 77 percent of the public

Table 7-5. *Cutting the Federal Budget by Reducing Spending on Social Security, 1981–97, Selected Years*

Percent

	Response	
Survey and date	Favor	Oppose
Gallup January 1981	21	79
Harris August 1981[a]	18	82
Harris September 1981[b]	22	78
Gallup January 1983[c]	13	87
Gallup Summer 1984[d]	14	86
Time-YSW December 1984[e]	9	91
YSW May 1985[e]	13	87
Kaiser/Harvard November 1994[f]	17	83
LAT January 1995[g]	12	86
Roper February 1995[h]	14	85
Harris May 1995[i]	19	79
ABC May 1995[j]	11	88
ABC-WP September 1995[k]	16	83
ABC-WP January 1996[k]	26	71
WP March 1997[l]	29	70

Original question posed by Gallup: Do you favor or oppose a cut in federal government spending for Social Security?

Sources: Surveys by Gallup Organization; Louis Harris and Associates; *Time* magazine surveys by Yankelovich, Skelly, and White (YSW); Henry J. Kaiser Family Foundation/Harvard School of Public Health, survey by KRC Communications (Kaiser/Harvard); *Los Angeles Times* (LAT); Roper Organization/Roper Starch Worldwide (after 1993); ABC; American Broadcasting Company/ *Washington Post* (ABC-WP).

Note: N's of at least 850.

a. Now let me ask you if the only way to have a chance to balance the federal budget by 1984 was to make sharp cuts in Social Security benefits, would you favor cutting Social Security or would you favor not balancing the federal budget?

b. President Reagan wants to balance the federal budget by 1984, but says he has to cut $75 billion in order to make the budget balance. If the only way to have a chance to balance the federal budget by 1984 were to make sharp cuts in . . . Social Security . . . would you favor such cuts, or would you favor not balancing the federal budget?

c. It is estimated that the federal government will have a deficit of as much as $200 billion for fiscal 1984—that is, it will spend more than it takes in—unless some steps are taken to reduce the deficit. Basically, there are only a few ways this deficit can be reduced. Please tell me whether you approve or disapprove of each of the following . . . Make cuts in "entitlement" programs such as Social Security, and the like.

d. Same as note c, except, It is estimated that the federal government will have a deficit of as much as $185 billion for fiscal 1985. . . .

e. Asked of registered voters. People have suggested making spending cuts in specific program areas in order to reduce the federal budget deficit. I am going to read you a list of programs. For each, please tell me whether you favor spending cuts to reduce the deficit or oppose spending cuts . . . Social Security.

f. Asked of adults who voted in the 1994 elections. A number of policies have been proposed in order to reduce the federal deficit. If the next Congress decides to address the problem of the deficit, would you favor or oppose each of the following policies that might be proposed? Decrease spending on Social Security. . . .

g. (As you may know, there is much discussion in Washington about which programs should be cut back in order to reduce the federal budget deficit.) Do you think the government should cut back spending . . . on Social Security?

h. (There is talk in Washington about cutting back certain programs to reduce the federal budget deficit. I'm going to read you a list of areas where possible cuts could be made.) Should the federal government cut back spending . . . on Social Security?

i. (A number of spending reductions have been proposed in order to balance the federal budget and avoid raising taxes). Would you favor or oppose making major spending reductions in . . . Social Security?

j. In order to balance the federal budget deficit in seven years would you favor or oppose cutting . . . the growth of spending on social security?

k. In order to reduce the federal budget deficit, should the government cut spending on . . . Social Security?

l. (Please tell me whether you favor or oppose reductions in future spending on Social Security for each of the following purposes). Would you favor or oppose reductions . . . to balance the federal budget?

polled supported the program because it guarantees a minimal income even if you face financial disaster in retirement."[12] A 1996 survey reported similarly lopsided majorities in all age groups who supported Social Security as insurance "just in case" it is needed.[13]

Social Security is also considered a benefit that is earned rather than doled out on the basis of need. Although a 1997 *Washington Post* survey found that 64 percent favored "reducing benefits paid to upper-income retirees in the future" in order to strengthen Social Security's finances, evidence indicates that the public favors the principle that all Social Security contributors earn a right to its benefits. Princeton Survey Research Associates discovered in a January 1996 survey that 63 percent of Americans approved of having their "tax dollars used to help pay" for the Social Security benefits of better-off retirees. Tellingly, the young were more supportive than seniors.[14] Americans

12. Public Agenda Foundation, "Miles to Go." DYG found a similar pattern in its two surveys in 1995 and 1996. "Social Security and Medicare: An Ongoing Study of Public Values and Attitudes," conducted by DYG, Inc., for the American Association of Retired Persons (AARP), Washington (Fall 1996).

13. DYG Inc., for the AARP, "Social Security and Medicare: An Ongoing Study of Public Values and Attitudes," fall 1996. DYG in its surveys for the AARP found that 70 percent to 80 percent of Americans agreed that "everyone who pays into Social Security should receive it, no matter what other income they have."

14. Princeton Survey Research Associates asked: ("As a taxpayer, please tell me whether you generally approve or disapprove of having your tax dollars used to help pay for each of the following). What about . . . Social Security for better off retired people?"

Table 7-6. *Cutting Federal Budget Deficit by Reducing Cost-of-Living Increase, 1982–95, Selected Years*

Percent

	Response		
Survey and date	Good idea, willing, favor	Bad idea, not willing, oppose	Don't know
CBS-NYT May 1982	31	61	8
CBS-NYT January 1985[a]	23	73	4
ABC-WP May 1985[b]	19	78	2
CBS-NYT November 1987[a]	22	73	5
Time February 1988[c]	29	66	5
Kaiser-Harvard November 1994[d]	26	74	. . .
Roper February 1995[e]	34	62	4
CNN-*Time*-YP May 1995[f]	34	62	4

Original question posed by CBS-NYT: In order to reduce the size of the federal budget deficit, would you be willing to have the government reduce scheduled cost-of-living increases in Social Security?

Sources: See table 7-5 for names of groups conducting surveys; and Columbia Broadcasting System/*New York Times* (CBS-NYT); *Time* magazine-Cable News Network, surveys by Yankelovich Partners (CNN-*Time*-YP).

Note: *N*'s of at least 800.

a. In order to reduce the size of the federal budget deficit, would you be willing to have the government reduce scheduled cost-of-living increases in Social Security or not?

b. Do you think the government should give people a smaller Social Security cost-of-living increase than they are now scheduled to get as a way of reducing the budget deficit, or not?

c. Do you favor or oppose the following proposals to reduce the federal budet deficit? Reducing cost-of-living increases in Social Security payments.

d. Asked of adults who voted in the 1994 elections. A number of policies have been proposed in order to reduce the federal deficit. If the next Congress decides to address the problem of the deficit, would you favor or oppose each of the following policies that might be proposed? Reduce the annual cost of living increases in Social Security.

e. In addition to these areas, some are suggesting that the amount of the annual increases in Social Security benefits—called COLAs—be reduced to help cut the federal budget deficit. As part of an overall plan to balance the budget, would you favor or oppose each of the following? . . . Lowering increases in Social Security benefits (COLAs) to about 2% for each of the next two years?

f. (Please tell me whether you favor or oppose each of the following to reduce the budget deficit) . . . Reducing the cost-of-living increases in Social Security benefits in 1999.

consider canceling benefits to any retirees to be tantamount—as participants in the National Issues Forum explained—to "breaking the promise." These surveys combined with the evidence on public support for taxing the benefits of the wealthy suggest that the public is reaching a subtle distinction: they acknowledge the principle that the wealthy—like all others who have paid in—have earned Social Security benefits like other contributors but favor tax-

Table 7-7. *Tax Benefits of the Wealthy to Reduce Budget*

Percent

	Response				
Survey and date	Favor, support	Oppose	It depends	Not sure, don't know, refused	N
Time-YCS February 1988	56	39	. . .	5	1,824
Harris October 1992[a]	58	40	. . .	1	1,248
USNWR January 1993[b]	49	46	3	2	1,005
Newsweek January 1993[c]	67	31	. . .	2	774
YP December 1994[d]	57	38	. . .	5	800
Time-CNN-WP March 1997[e]	64	34	. . .	2	1,309

Original question posed by Time/YCS: Do you favor or oppose the following proposals to reduce the federal budget deficit? Increasing taxes on Social Security payments going to wealthy Americans.

Sources: See tables 7-5 and 7-6 for names of groups conducting surveys; and Yankelovich Clancy Shulman (YCS); *U.S. News and World Report* (USNWR), survey by Princeton Research Associates; and Yankelovich Partners (YP).

a. I'm going to read you a number of steps that Ross Perot has proposed which he says will help reduce the federal deficit. For each statement, tell me if you favor or oppose it. . . . Increasing the tax on Social Security income for upper-income recipients.

b. As president, Bill Clinton will probably be forced to make tough choices. Would you favor or oppose each of the following choices that he might make in order to reduce the federal deficit? . . . Increase taxes on Social Security benefits for upper-income older people.

c. To help reduce the federal budget deficit, please tell me if you would support or oppose each of the following. . . . New taxes on Social Security benefits for the wealthy.

d. Do you favor or oppose requiring Social Security recipients who have higher incomes to pay federal income taxes on a larger share of their Social Security payments?

e. In order to keep the Social Security program financially sound in the future, would you favor or oppose each of the following proposals? . . . Reducing benefits paid to upper-income retirees in the future?

ing those benefits as an extension of the principle that allows taxation of private pensions.

Another source of Social Security's support is that working Americans count on it to support their retired parents. DYG surveys in 1985, 1995, and 1996 confirmed that three-quarters of Americans supported Social Security because it relieved them of the financial burden of caring for their parents.[15]

Americans from quite varied personal circumstances express substantial support for Social Security, and even the differences among groups defy

15. Conducted by DYG, Inc., for the AARP, "Social Security and Medicare: An Ongoing Study of Public Values and Attitudes" (Fall 1996).

Table 7-8. *Opposition to Spending Reductions on Social Security according to Education, Income, and Age*

Percent opposed

Demographic group	January 1995[a]	September 1995[b]	January 1996[b]	March 1997[c]
Education				
Less than high school graduate	94	88	85	70
High school graduate	90	88	75	68
Some college	85	85	72	69
College graduate	79	74	62	71
Postgraduate	67	66	44	73
Income				
Less than $10,000	90[d]	94[e]	78[e]	54
$10,000–$20,000	...	89[f]	81[f]	74
$20,000–$30,000	93	90	79	75
$30,000–$50,000	88	82	69	67
$50,000–$70,000	83[g]	74	63	67
Greater than $70,000	73[h]	68	57	73
Age				
18–29	83	83	74	60
30–39	86	84	74	69
40–49	81	80	68	70
50–59	88	85	65	73
60–69	92	82	73	80
70+	93	84	72	70

Sources: *Los Angeles Times*, January 1995; ABC/*Washington Post*, September 1995 and January 1996; and *Washington Post*, March 1997.

a. (As you may know, there is much discussion in Washington about which programs should be cut back in order to reduce the federal budget deficit.) Do you think the government should cut back spending . . . on Social Security?

b. In order to reduce the federal budgt deficit, should the government cut spending on . . . Social Security?

c. In order to balance the federal budget in seven years, would you favor or oppose cutting the growth of spending on Social Security?

d. Less than $20,000.

e. Less than $12,000.

f. From $12,000 to $20,000.

g. From $50,000 to $60,000.

h. Greater than $60,000.

straightforward classification. Tables 7-8 and 7-9 use different survey items to tell a similar tale: generally super majorities of 70 percent to 90 percent of Americans from different educational, income, and age backgrounds opposed reductions in Social Security spending to reduce the federal budget deficit. Within this overall consensus, however, some standard differences emerge. Individuals who were better educated, more affluent, and younger were less

Table 7-9. *Support for Spending on Social Security by Demographic Groups*

Percent indicating spending "too little" or "about right" on Social Security[a]

Demographic group	February 1991	February 1993	January 1994	February 1996
Education				
Less than high school graduate	83	91	90	89
High school graduate	90	90	90	90
Some college	91	87	88	86
College graduate	88	84	82	81
Postgraduate	87	76	85	77
Income				
Less than $15,000	91	90	88	86
$15,000–$20,000	96	84	87	92
$20,000–$30,000	94	90	92	88
$30,000–$50,000	89	88	87	88
$50,000–$70,000	90	84	88	87
More than $70,000	84	83	87	80
Age				
18–29	88	85	83	85
30–39	89	87	87	83
40–49	89	86	89	84
50–59	92	88	89	90
60–69	93	92	91	95
70+	96	87	92	90

a. *Question posed by NORC:* (We are faced with many problems in this country, none of which can be solved easily or inexpensively. I'm going to name some of these problems, and for each one I'd like you to tell me whether you think we're spending too much money on it, too little money, or about the right amount.) Are we spending too much, too little, or about the right amount on . . . Social Security?

Source: National Opinion Research Center (NORC).

opposed to spending cuts. However, a 1997 survey finds the most advantaged reverse positions and become possibly the greatest defenders of Social Security, perhaps because of a growing sense that the federal budget is under greater control.[16] Variations in question wordings complicate comparisons over time.

These views defy any presumption of self-interest. Repeatedly, seniors, the affluent, and the better educated depart from their expected positions to offer strenuous support for Social Security. The better educated were more protective of Social Security spending in 1991 (table 7-9) and 1997 (table7-8) than the least well educated. The most affluent were equally opposed to cuts in 1994 as

16. Table 7-9 also offers evidence that the most advantaged can be strong defenders of Social Security, despite what would seem to be their self-interest. See Cook and Barrett (1992).

the poorest (table 7-9). Despite breathless media accounts of intergenerational warfare, the younger cohorts were as protective of Social Security spending (if not more so) as the oldest in 1993 (table 7-8), 1995, and 1996 (table 7-9).

Further evidence that Americans persistently act against their narrow self-interest is available in a series of individual surveys in 1997. A March 1997 *Washington Post* survey reported that the young were the most concerned that Social Security benefits to average retirees were so small that they needed to struggle to get by; older groups were least likely to hold this view. A February 1997 *Los Angeles Times* survey found that the young were the most supportive of the existing arrangements for financing Social Security, with no clear differences among educational and income groups.[17]

The Public Remains Supportive Despite Its Low Confidence

A common assumption is that low confidence in Social Security's future erodes support for the program. The conventional wisdom is that as confidence drops, support dips. In fact, figure 7-1 reveals that neither low confidence or downward shifts in confidence consistently coincide with declining support. Confidence crashed from the 60 percent to 50 percent range in the mid-1970s to 39 percent in 1979 and then 32 percent in 1982, yet support for the program did not change appreciably. The 1990s also produced a similar pattern in which confidence plummeted but support remained relatively steady.

The conventional wisdom that the public's backing for Social Security is crumbling under the strain of low confidence is simply not supported by available evidence. The explanation for this apparent paradox lies in three factors that extend far beyond the particular challenges facing Social Security: economic anxieties, mistrust of government, and disproportionately negative news coverage of Social Security. Super majorities support Social Security but fear that politicians or an economic downturn will ruin it.[18]

Indeed, overwhelming proportions of Americans fear that economic bad news will hurt their financial situation in retirement. A 1997 survey by the Public Agenda Foundation found that 79 percent worried about inflation, 74 percent were concerned about high health care costs, and 66 percent expected a souring economy to undermine retirement plans.[19]

17. The survey asked: "Under the existing Social Security plan workers and their employers each contribute equally to total payroll taxes of 12.4 percent which is paid on $65,400 of workers' annual salary. Do you favor or oppose the existing Social Security plan?" Sixty-four percent favored the existing arrangement, and 29 percent opposed it.

18. Reno and Friedland (1997).

19. Public Agenda Foundation, "Miles to Go."

Figure 7-1. *Support of and Confidence in Social Security, 1976–96*

Percent support, confident

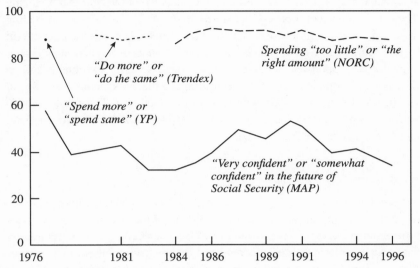

Sources: Yankelovich Partners (YP); Trendex; National Opinion Research Center (NORC); and Monitoring Attitudes of the Public by the American Council of Life Insurance (MAP), surveys by Yankelovich, Skelly, and White (1975–82), and the Roper Organization/Roper Starch Worldwide (1983–94).

The confidence of Americans in Social Security is unavoidably colored by their distrust of government in general. Confidence in government in general recently has been at or near its all-time lows, with the most disaffected concentrated among the young (who are the least confident in Social Security). The National Issues Forum (NIF), which convened focus groups around the country, found in 1997 that general "cynicism about government competence and trustworthiness" has fueled specific concerns about Social Security's ability to handle the retirement of baby boomers. NIF participants simply assumed that politicians would "play politics" with Social Security.[20] A 40-year-old New Mexico man captured the pervasive skepticism toward government when he complained in a Public Agenda Foundation study, "I don't think the politicians up there should have any control over it—I don't trust them."[21] Concern about Social Security is a symptom of a larger problem.

20. National Issues Forum Report on the Issues, "The National Piggybank: Does Our Retirement System Need Fixing?" conducted by John Doble Research Associates (Englewood Cliffs, N.J., 1997).
21. Public Agenda Foundation, "Miles to Go," p. 24.

Finally, the media's systematic framing of Social Security in terms of its problems and unending need for change can only increase Americans' anxiety about whether it will be there for them. Our analysis for the National Academy of Social Insurance of thousands of stories in the Associated Press and leading broadcast and print outlets between 1977 and 1994 found a persistent pattern: Social Security received large but relatively brief bursts of extensive media coverage that disproportionately zeroed in on Social Security's problems and on the need to reform the program.[22] The message in the mass media is that Social Security is difficult to sustain without constant doctoring. The public's confidence in Social Security, then, is most likely a function of dread of government, media coverage, and economic fears.

Reforming Social Security

Although the public recognizes the need to close Social Security's financing gap, it is not clamoring for a complete overhaul of the system and hardly sees the program as facing a crisis. Scattered polls do detect the public's recognition that changes will be needed to strengthen the program's future finances. For instance, Hart/Teeter surveys in January and September 1997 found that a steady 83 percent agreed "major changes" will be necessary at some point to "guarantee the future financial stability of the system."[23] But the public does not consider Social Security an urgent crisis. When Americans have been asked in open-ended questions to identify the most important problems facing the country, Social Security has failed to show up at any point in the 1990s as one of the top five problems—even when it has been lumped together with Medicare.[24] An October 1997 Harris survey found that taxes, education, health care (but not Medicare), crime, welfare and the federal budget deficit all ranked higher than Social Security as the most important issues for the government to address.

CATO's two surveys in the spring of 1996 found that fewer than 20 percent perceived Social Security as needing "radical change," with another quarter anticipating "major change."[25] Half of Americans concluded that the program needed only "minor change" or "only some change." Parallel results were found by differently worded questions in a December 1996 *Time*/CNN poll and a March 1997 *Washington Post* survey: both found a third of Americans classify-

---

22. Jacobs and Shapiro (1995); Jacobs, Watts, and Shapiro (1995).

23. Found in the Roper Database, Rutger Center, Storrs, Connecticut. The full question was "Do you think it will be necessary to make major changes in the way the system operates in order to guarantee the future financial stability of the system?"

24. Gallup Polls, 1990–98, *The Gallup Poll,* and press releases.

25. Found in the Roper Database, Rutger Center, Storrs, Connecticut (March and June 1996).

ing Social Security as facing a "crisis" and a half or more of Americans sizing the situation up as "a problem but not a crisis." The lack of fervor is especially apparent by way of comparison with health care, where a steady 80 percent to 90 percent of Americans believe that radical or major change is required.

Main Street Is Not Buying Privatization

The two CATO surveys conducted in spring 1996 appear to provide the strongest support for reforming Social Security to establish individual investments in the stock market. They report that two-thirds of Americans favor individualized privatization. A January 1997 survey by Princeton Survey Research Associates found that as a means for keeping Social Security financially sound 71 percent favored "letting individuals decide how some of their own Social Security contributions are invested." The young and better educated were most receptive to this reform.

But the CATO items are problematic and the Princeton questions are a limited measure of the public's full evaluation of privatization for two reasons. First, the question wordings are not balanced. Investing in the stock market poses both rewards and risks. Indeed, the Vanguard Group devoted a 1997 report to its customers to sternly warning against "unrealistic expectations" that have blinded investors to the fact that "risk is the inseparable companion of reward, and the risk of investing in stocks [is] considerable."[26] To probe the public's views on privatization requires asking balanced questions that pose the potential rewards and risks of equity investments. The CATO questions fail to mention risk altogether and instead ask respondents if they favor reforms allowing Social Security funds to be invested in a personal retirement account and passed on to heirs as an inheritance—all without imposing any reduction in current benefits.

Second, in the jargon of survey researchers, CATO's results are distorted by "context effects." A large body of research has established that the wording of one question can readily influence respondents' reaction to questions that immediately follow. Before questioning respondents about a privatization proposal, CATO's surveys ask seven questions about different components of their privatization proposal—none of which convey a balanced perspective on equity investments. The seven lead-up questions prime respondents to focus on the most positive aspects of reform.

The public's initial enthusiasm for privatization fades and then turns to overwhelming opposition as respondents are offered more balanced information.

26. "Remarkable Returns May Raise Unrealistic Expectations," *In the Vanguard* (Winter 1997), p.1.

Polls in December 1996 and January 1997 by NBC/*Wall Street Journal* found that respondents split when informed that stock investment of Social Security contributions could produce benefits that are "higher or lower than expected."[27] The young, better educated, and more affluent remained supportive of privatization—though even their absolute levels of support dropped from their earlier euphoria. Still another set of polls by NBC/*Wall Street Journal* in January 1997 found that a majority of respondents opposed the reform. One item found that 57 percent focused on the danger of individuals investing in the stock market when explicitly asked to weigh the "risk of losing money" against the "potential of higher returns."[28] Still another item reported that 61 percent concluded that the costs of individuals investing in the stock market outweighed its benefits when informed of the transitional costs of honoring the commitments to current retirees.[29]

The NBC/*Wall Street Journal* surveys indicate that informing respondents of a fuller set of questions raised by privatization dramatically changed the proposal's support among the educated and younger cohorts. The more educated cross over from supporters to the proposal's most ardent opponents. The young remained the most open to market risk but become the most turned off by having to shoulder the transitional costs.

A final set of survey questions offered respondents a balanced choice and found the strongest opposition to privatization. Surveys by *Time*/CNN and the *Washington Post* ask respondents if they would favor privatization as a way to make money or oppose it because it increased risks. The results presented in

27. The question asked: "There is a proposal that would allow people to invest some of their Social Security payroll contributions in the stock market. This change means that when people retire, their benefits could either be higher or lower than expected, depending on the stock market's performance. Would you favor or oppose this proposal to allow people to invest their Social Security payroll contributions in the stock market?" The December poll found that 46 percent favored the proposal and 44 percent opposed; the January poll found a 48-46 split.

28. The question asked: "There is a proposal that would allow people to invest some of their Social Security payroll contributions in the stock market. This change means that when people retire, their benefits could either be higher or lower than expected, depending on the stock market's performance. Thinking about the possibility of investing some of your Social Security payroll contributions in the stock market, which one of the following statements would you say best describes your opinion? Statement A: The risk of losing money in the stock market outweighs the potential of higher returns from investing in the stock market. Statement B: The potential of higher returns from investing in the stock market outweighs the risk of losing money in the stock market." Thirty-seven percent indicated that the potential returns outweigh the risk.

29. The question asks: "This proposal to allow people to invest Social Security contributions in the stock market also includes an increase in the payroll tax for current employees, as well as an increase in the federal deficit, so that benefits to current retirees also can be maintained. Do you think the benefits of allowing people to invest Social Security contributions in the stock market outweigh these costs of higher payroll taxes and deficits, or do you think the costs outweigh the benefits?" Twenty-two percent believed that the benefits outweigh the cost.

Table 7-10. *Response to the Possibility of Privatization*

Percent

Survey and date	Favor	Oppose	Not sure
Time-CNN December 1996	36	56	8
WP March 1997	35	63	2

Question: Some people favor investing a portion of Social Security tax funds in the stock market because this might lead to higher investment returns. Other people oppose this idea because they say the stock market is too unpredictable. What is your opinion? Do you favor or oppose investing a portion of the tax money collected for Social Security in the stock market?

Sources: *Time* magazine, Cable News Network (Time-CNN); and *Washington Post* (WP).

table 7-10 suggest that between 56 percent and 63 percent of Americans oppose privatization.

The better educated and more affluent are more open to transforming Social Security to allow stock investment, though even this group remains split on privatization. Table 7-11 presents the demographic breakdown for the March 1997 *Washington Post* survey in table 7-10. It indicates significant differences in the degree of opposition to investing Social Security taxes. The less well educated and the poor are almost twice as likely (70 to 80 percent) to oppose it as postgraduates and the most affluent (47 percent.) But it is striking that even individuals who are most likely to gain from equity investment remain divided. In addition, seniors are the most fervent opponents of the reform, but the young are nearly as apprehensive. Misgivings among age groups are widely shared.

An additional puzzle about investment remains. The surveys by *Time*/CNN and the *Washington Post* report that large majorities oppose privatization, but equally large majorities also favor allowing individuals (rather than the government) to invest their Social Security taxes as they wish. The question wording here, however, is critical. The question asks: "If some Social Security tax funds are invested in the stock market, which do you favor . . . having the government make this investment in a broad index fund, or allowing individuals to invest part of their portion however they would like?" The question presumes the very issue that the balanced frame items raises—that private investment is enacted. The question tells respondents to assume that "some Social Security tax funds are invested in the stock market." The answer to the puzzle is that Americans oppose equity investment but, if policymakers adopt it, they might then prefer to control their own investments.

The public's reaction to proposals regarding individual investment accounts as opposed to government investment in the stock market is difficult. The available

Table 7-11. *Investing in Stock Market by Demographic Groups*

Demographic group	Percent opposed
Education	
Less than high school graduate	74
High school graduate	72
Some college	58
College graduate	51
Postgraduate	47
Income	
Less than $10,000	80
$10,000–$20,000	71
$20,000–$30,000	70
$30,000–$50,000	60
$50,000–$70,000	51
Greater than $70,000	47
Age	
18–29	60
30–39	66
40–49	56
50–59	67
60–69	69
70+	65

Question posed by the Washington Post: Some people favor investing a portion of Social Security tax funds in the stock market because this might lead to higher investment returns. Other people oppose this idea because they say the stock market is too unpredictable. What is your opinion? Do you favor or oppose investing a portion of the tax money collected for Social Security in the stock market?

Sources: *Washington Post.*

data shed little light on this issue and on the issue of funding options. In addition, the public's views could evolve if they were presented with trade-offs between cutting benefits and one or more of the investment and privatization options. If investments were to be enacted, the public appears to prefer individual control over their investments, although the available data suggest that the inevitable transition costs could significantly depress the initial support for this option.

Mixed Evaluations of Incremental Reforms

Americans have not reached any consensus about the kind of incremental reforms that policymakers are weighing as alternatives to investment and privatization options. Americans' preferences toward the usual menu of incremental adjustments—reducing benefits and increasing taxes—are mixed.

Americans do not support hiking the retirement age as a means for strengthening Social Security's finances (table 7-12). In recent surveys, more than 60 percent of Americans reject this option. The public is more divided on the issue of reducing Social Security's costs by lowering the program's automatic COLAs. Two surveys by NBC/*Wall Street Journal* show that in December 1996 Americans favored reducing the COLA by a margin of 47 percent to 43 percent; an altered question in March 1997 found that the public opposed the change by a 53 percent to 37 percent margin.[30] Finally, as mentioned earlier, a March 1997 *Washington Post* survey indicates that 64 percent favor scaling back (but not canceling) the benefits of upper-income retirees in order to strengthen the program's finances.

Evidence on Americans' willingness to pay higher taxes is also mixed. A February 1996 CBS/*NYT* poll found that 52 percent opposed paying higher Social Security taxes to strengthen the program's financial future; by March 1997, opposition appeared greater (61 percent) in a somewhat differently worded *Washington Post* question.[31] The public's distrust of government may be fueling resistance to tax hikes. A participant in the National Issues Forum captured the sentiment of many Americans when she complained that "raising taxes won't solve the problem because [elected officials] won't use the money for Social Security;" though a young man added that "I'd pay more money now if I knew [it] would be there when I retire."[32]

When the public is forced to wrestle with the trade-offs facing policymakers, they prefer tax hikes to benefit cuts. A 1997 survey sponsored by the EBRI forced Americans to choose between increasing payroll taxes on workers or

30. The December 1996 survey may have been more attractive to respondents because it did not mention that reducing the CPI would "raise some future income taxes" as the March 1997 survey did (it also did not add the view of economists). The March 1997 survey asked: "There is now a proposal to reduce the government's official measure of inflation, called the Consumer Price Index, which some economists believe does not accurately reflect price increases. This will reduce future cost-of-living increases in such programs as Social Security and veterans' benefits, but also will reduce the federal deficit and raise some future income taxes. Do you strongly favor, somewhat favor, somewhat oppose, or strongly oppose reducing the Consumer Price Index in this manner?" The December 1996 question asked: "There is now a proposal to reduce the government's official measure of inflation, called the Consumer Price Index. This will reduce future cost-of-living increases in such programs as Social Security and veterans' benefits, but also will reduce the federal deficit. Do you strongly favor, somewhat favor, somewhat oppose, or strongly oppose reducing the Consumer Price Index in this manner?"

31. The CBS/*New York Times* question asked: "To make sure future Social Security benefits continue to be at least as good as today's benefits, would you favor or oppose paying higher Social Security taxes?" The *Washington Post* question posed: "In order to keep the Social Security program financially sound in the future, would you favor or oppose each of the following proposals? . . . Having everyone pay more in Social Security taxes?"

32. National Issues Forum Report on the Issues, "The National Piggybank: Does Our Retirement System Need Fixing?" conducted by John Doble Research Associates (1997).

Table 7-12. *Raising Retirement Age*

Percent

Survey and date	Response		
	Favor	*Oppose*	*Don't know, no answer*
Gallup October 1977[a]	30	64	7
MAP June 1979	19	74	7
MAP June 1981[b]	26	59	14
CBS-NYT July 1981[c]	50	42	8
NCA July 1981[d]	35	59	6
Harris August 1981[e]	33	65	2
ORC September 1981[f]	44	52	4
Roper July 1982[g]	21	70	9
Harris November 1982[h]	41	58	1
LAT November 1982[i]	45	52	3
Gallup November 1982[j]	30	63	7
NBC-AP November 1982[k]	44	50	6
Time-YSW December 1982[l]	42	54	4
CBS-NYT January 1983[m]	39	57	4
A-S April 1983[n]	44	45	11
NBC-WSJ January 1993[o]	20	77	3
Kaiser-Harvard November 1994[p]	39	61	. . .
PSRA January 1997[q]	31	64	5

Question posed by the American Council of Life Insurance, 1979: Currently, people can begin receiving full Social Security benefits at age 65. Some people are suggesting gradually raising, over the next 25 years or so, the age for full benefits to age 67 or 68 as a way to make the system financially sound. Do you favor this proposal or oppose it?

Sources: Monitoring Attitudes of the Public (MAP) by the American Council of Life Insurance, surveys by Yankelovich, Skelly, and White (1975–82); CBS-*New York Times* (CBS-NYT); National Council on the Aging, survey by Louis Harris and Associates (NCA); Louis Harris and Associates (Harris); Opinion Research Corporation (ORC); Roper Organization; *Los Angeles Times* (LAT); National Broadcasting Corporation-Associated Press (NBC-AP); *Time* magazine, Yankelovich, Skelly, and White (*Time*-YSW); Columbia Broadcasting System-*New York Times* (CBS-NYT); Audits and Surveys for the Merit Report (A-S); National Broadcasting Corporation-*Wall Street Journal* (NBC-WSJ); Henry J. Kaiser Family Foundation/Harvard School of Public Health, survey by KRC Communications (Kaiser-Harvard); and Princeton Survey Research Associates (PSRA).

Note: *N*'s of at least 750.

a. It has been proposed that as a cost saving measure the retirement age for Social Security be increased from 65 to 68. Would you favor or oppose such a change?

b. I am going to read you a number of proposals that have been made for changes in the Social Security system. For each proposal, I would like you to tell me whether you favor it, oppose it, or if you are uncertain. Gradually raise the age at which people receive full retirement benefits from age 65 to 68, beginning in the year 2000.

c. To save money, would you favor or oppose increasing the age at which people were eligible to receive full Social Security benefits from 65 to 68, if that change became effective 20 years from now?

d. A number of recommendations have been made to help the Social Security system. Please tell me whether you strongly approve, approve, disapprove, or strongly disapprove of each of the following recommendations? . . . Gradually raise the retirement age for full Social Security benefits from 65 to 68 years of age.

e. As you know, there is much discussion about changing Social Security to put that system on a sounder financial basis. Let me ask you about some proposals that have been made for Social Security changes. Would favor or oppose . . . changing the age from 65 to 68 that people can go on Social Security with full benefits, by the year 1990.

f. There have been many suggestions made for dealing with the problems of the Social Security system. I'm going to read some of these and, for each one, please tell me whether you strongly favor, mildly favor, mildly oppose, or strongly oppose the idea. Slowly increase the age of eligibility for full retirement benefits from 65 to 68.

g. Experts have said that in a few years there won't be enough money coming in from Social Security taxes to pay for the money going out in benefits. Here are some suggestions that have been made for coping with the problem of the rising cost of Social Security. (Card shown respondent.) For each one, would you tell me whether it is something you would be willing to see done, or not willing to see done? . . . Raise the age at which people are eligible to get Social Security benefits from 65 to 68.

h. Same as note d, except " . . . you approve or disapprove . . . "

i. Would you approve of gradually increasing the retirement age for Social Security benefits, or would you disapprove of that? (Wait for an answer.) Do you feel strongly about that, or not so strongly?

j. As I read off some of the ways Social Security could help pay its way, please tell me whether you approve or disapprove of each one: . . . Gradually increase the age at which people become eligible to receive Social Security benefits?

k. As you may know, the Social Security system cannot make all the current payments that are due without making changes of some sort in the way the system operates. I'd like to ask you a few questions about some specific proposals that have been made for changing the system . . . Next, would you favor or oppose gradually increasing the age at which people can retire with full Social Security benefits?

l. Asked of registered voters. There are a number of other proposals for dealing with the social security problem; I'd like to know how you feel about each one. Do you favor or oppose moving retirement age to 67 or 68?

m. The Social Security system is spending more money to pay benefits than it is taking from Social Security taxes. We want your opinion about some of the proposals that have been made to solve this. To solve the Social Security problem would you be willing or not willing to raise the age at which people are eligible for full benefits from 65 years old to 68?

n. The Congress has passed a four-part package to ensure the future funding of the Social Security system. We'd like to get your reactions to each of the four parts. First, the retirement age at which you can get full benefits will be raised to age 66 by the year 2009 and to age 67 by the year 2027. Do you: favor this strongly, favor this somewhat, oppose this somewhat, oppose this strongly?

o. Do you think that the government should gradually raise the retirement age so that people qualify for full Social Security benefits at age 67 rather than at age 65, or should the age for receiving Social Security benefits be kept at 65?

p. Asked of adults who voted in 1994 elections. A number of policies have been proposed in order to reduce the federal deficit. If the next Congress decides to address the problem of the deficit, would you favor or oppose each of the following policies that might be proposed? Increase the retirement age for Social Security from 65 to 67 years of age. . . .

q. I'm going to read you some proposals to change Social Security to keep the system financially sound in the future. Please tell me whether you would generally favor or oppose each proposed change that I read. What about this proposal . . . gradually increasing the retirement age for Social Security from 65 to 69 without affecting people now receiving benefits?

decreasing benefit levels for retirees, and found that 63 percent chose the former while only 32 percent opted for the latter. The views of retired and nonretired Americans did not differ significantly.[33]

Of course, new polls may find support for additional incremental reforms that are just beginning to receive attention. For instance, future surveys may find that the public favors, as President Clinton has proposed, spending part of the projected budget surplus to strengthen Social Security's financial future. How this translates into policy remains confusing. The public may also support boosting the base on which Social Security taxes are paid.

More successful respondents—as measured by educational and income attainment—are relatively more supportive of strengthening Social Security's future finances by reducing benefits. The elderly are sensitive to direct threats to their immediate circumstances. Although the preferences of different income and age groups is often consistent with self-interest, the affluent and elderly repeatedly take positions that contradict their narrow personal stakes. One of the most striking patterns is the opposition of all groups to scaling back Social Security. Failure to find a rigid battle line between seniors and younger cohorts confirms a significant body of previous research.[34]

Most segments of society consistently reject benefit reductions as an appropriate strategy for strengthening Social Security's finances. Table 7-13 shows that opposition to hiking retirement age is strong in all groups but especially among the less well educated, the poorest, and the youngest—all groups who stand to lose the most from any change. Table 7-14 reveals a more complex picture of opposition to reducing the cost-of-living-adjustment resulting from a downward adjustment in the consumer price index (CPI). Seniors and the lower income groups (especially in 1997) strongly rejected the option. But the better educated are only slightly less opposed than the less well educated, and those earning above $50,000 in 1996 were more protective of the existing COLA than the lower-income groups.

The attitudes of different age groups also defy simple categories. Table 7-14 suggests that seniors are protecting their self-interest by leading the opposition against reducing the COLA; such a change represents a direct threat to their retirement. While the young are the most opposed to raising the retirement age, seniors (who are most likely retired) are the least. Table 7-15 indicates that seniors agreed with the youngest cohort in favoring a reduction in the benefits of upper-income retirees, and that the lowest income group, who would be least affected by the reform, were the least supportive.

33. Employee Benefit Research Institute, "Survey on Retirement Confidence," Wave VII, 1997.
34. Page and Shapiro (1992); MacManus (1996); Rhodebeck (1993, pp. 342–64).

Table 7-13. *Strengthen Finances by Increasing Retirement Age, by Demographic Groups*

Percent opposed

Demographic group	January 1997[a]	March 1997[b]
Education		
Less than high school graduate	73	60
High school graduate	65	54
Some college	68	50
College graduate	57	44
Postgraduate	49	46
Income		
Less than $10,000		57
$10,000–$20,000		51
$20,000–$30,000		54
$30,000–$50,000		49
$50,000–$70,000		48
Greater than $70,000		54
Age		
18–29	65	55
30–39	69	53
40–49	66	57
50–59	68	52
60–69	60	48
70+	52	35

a. *Question posed by PSRA:* I'm going to read you some proposals to change Social Security to keep the system financially sound in the future. Please tell me whether you would generally favor or oppose each proposed change that I read. What about this proposal . . . gradually increasing the retirement age for Social Security from 65 to 69 without affecting people now receiving benefits.
b. *Question posed by WP:* (In order to keep the Social Security program financially sound in the future, would you favor or oppose each of the following proposals?) . . . Gradually increasing the retirement age for Social Security without affecting people now receiving benefits.

Source: Princeton Survey Research Associates (PSRA) and *Washington Post* (WP).

Reforming Social Security poses significant political risks, especially to Democrats who are perceived by the public as defenders of the program. Reforms that are unpopular with the public and are identified with Democrats would undermine confidence in the Democrats' ability to handle this issue. This decline in confidence appears to be taking place.

Since November 1994, a series of six surveys by NBC and the *Wall Street Journal*, and Princeton Research Associates and *Newsweek* indicate that the Democrats have generally held a steady edge in public trust. Americans' views have changed, however, as President Clinton has inched toward embracing

Table 7-14. *Strengthen Finances by Reducing Consumer Price Index,*
by Demographic Groups

Percent opposed

Demographic group	December 1996	March 1997
Education		
Less than high school graduate	46	45
High school graduate	41	60
Some college	46	56
College graduate	37	45
Postgraduate	44	43
Income		
Less than $10,000	32	64
$10,000–$20,000	34	55
$20,000–$30,000	47	53
$30,000–$50,000	41	59
$50,000–$70,000	47	50
Greater than $70,000	40	44
Age		
18–29	29	45
30–39	37	49
40–49	49	57
50–59	54	61
60+	51	59

Question posed by NBC-WSJ: There is now a proposal to reduce the government's
offical measure of inflation, called the Consumer Price Index. This will reduce future
cost-of-living increases in such programs as Social Security and veterans' benefits, but
also will reduce the federal deficit. Do you strongly favor, somewhat favor, somewhat
oppose, or strongly oppose reducing the Consumer Price Index in this manner?

Source: National Broadcasting Corporation-*Wall Street Journal.*

Social Security reform and many Democrats embraced the balanced budget
amendment despite warnings of the danger to Social Security. A growing number of Americans have concluded that neither party can be trusted to handle the
program. In little over two years, the proportion expressing confidence in neither party has jumped from 15 percent to a steady 22 percent in 1997.

Conclusion

Americans will be deluged with a burst of media coverage as the debate on
Social Security heats up. Several patterns appear likely. Americans are unlikely
to support a wholesale replacing of the current Social Security system with a
new privatized one. The combination of risk aversion, stock market fluctua-

Table 7-15. *Reducing Benefits to Upper-Income Retirees,*
by Demographic Groups

Demographic group	Percent in favor March 1997
Education	
Less than high school graduate	55
High school graduate	61
Some college	66
College graduate	70
Postgraduate	72
Income	
Less than $10,000	53
$10,000–$20,000	59
$20,000–$30,000	69
$30,000–$50,000	69
$50,000–$70,000	66
Greater than $70,000	63
Age	
18–29	60
30–39	64
40–49	71
50–59	65
60–69	61
70+	59

Question posed by the Washington Post: (In order to keep the Social Security program financially sound in the future, would you favor or oppose each of the following proposals?) . . . Reducing benefits paid to upper-income retirees in the future?

Source: *Washington Post.*

tions, and overwhelming support for the existing program guarantee significant resistance.

Americans, however, appear open to some reform short of wholesale changes. But even the usual menu of incremental adjustments will require concerted leadership and compromise solutions that unify political leaders. Whether Americans will ultimately support reform of Social Security will depend primarily on their reaction to the content and acrimony of the debate, and the media's portrayal of the debate.

If the past is any guide, journalists and policymakers should try to avoid two pitfalls. First, political activists are now preparing for policy debates by using polls to carefully calibrate their public presentations to win over public support. Combatants in the imminent Social Security debate are likely to frame the issues in ways that are most likely to sway Americans.

It is entirely predictable that the research on public opinion will define the terms on which the public debate is fought. As we have indicated, framing privatization in terms that stress increased choice and room for individual independence can boost support for it; by contrast, highlighting the risks of stock investments and the costs of the transition can pull the rug out on privatization.

The upcoming Social Security debate is likely to challenge seriously the presumption that politicians pander to public opinion when they make policy. The public, as discussed earlier, does not rank Social Security as a pressing crisis and is opposed to privatization and quite ambivalent regarding incremental changes. If politicians slavishly followed public opinion, they probably would pass on the issue of Social Security reform. But President Clinton and members of Congress are moving forward and will work to direct public opinion toward their preferred proposals. The presumption of pandering will be flipped on its head: instead of public opinion research driving policy decisions, policy decisions will drive public opinion research toward identifying the most effective language and arguments for presenting the preferred policy.

The second pitfall involves the media, who will communicate the debate to Americans. Whether Americans' knowledge about Social Security will deepen depends on journalists forgoing excessive coverage of the political fight in favor of coverage of substantive issues. Previous debates over Social Security suggest that journalists have typically bypassed substance in favor of disproportionate coverage of conflict and crisis.

The fact that political activists will be fighting for public opinion gives journalists an especially important responsibility to fully report the state of public thinking. Our recent "poll watch," which evaluated media reporting on public opinion toward entitlements, suggests that journalists load their stories with shallow references to polls as a quick frame of reference—the journalistic equivalent of a drive-by shooting. Nearly 40 percent of references to polls that we examined offered no actual evidence at all. Only a quarter of the references discussed survey results in an in-depth manner as the main focus of a story. In addition, polls were often briefly cited in a rapid-fire delivery. Over 80 percent of the references to them consumed the equivalent of ten lines of newspaper text or less; half of the references were five lines or less. It was rare for poll results to receive much genuine discussion.

Journalists have too often settled for generic characterizations of "poll after poll" and to vacuous references to "strong" or "weak" public attitudes, which leaves the audience helpless to evaluate the public's preferences on its own. Journalists ought to present far more fully the multiple and competing concerns that Americans bring to their evaluations. Let policymakers wrestle with aligning their preferences with those of the public.

The Political Feasibility of
Social Security Reform
R. Douglas Arnold

WHAT ARE THE CHANCES that Congress and the president will tackle the Social Security problem and enact reforms within the next several years? Does it seem more likely that they would adopt a comprehensive new system for retirement security or that they would approve more modest adjustments to the current system, returning the program to actuarial balance without altering its fundamental character? Are some kinds of reforms more politically attractive than others? These are important questions that deserve careful answers. This paper addresses these questions within a general discussion of the political feasibility of alternative schemes for reforming Social Security.

Policy analysts often avoid questions of political feasibility, preferring to design programs that they believe will best achieve certain ends, while leaving it to politicians to "do the right thing." Sometimes this works nicely and elected politicians enact analysts' handiwork. Quite frequently, however, the absence of early political analysis leads to unhappy outcomes. Sometimes Congress rejects not only the proposed policy but the notion of doing anything at all. Some would argue that this is what happened with President Bill Clinton's health care package. A comprehensive plan designed by policy specialists without proper attention to political feasibility drove health care reform off the governmental agenda. A second possibility is that Congress may start with policy analysts' most-preferred policy but quickly transform it into something that is unrecognizable to its early advocates and unlikely to achieve their intended purpose. The 89th Congress did this with President Lyndon Johnson's proposal to concentrate large sums of money in a few Model Cities by insisting that smaller sums be dispersed among 150 cities.[35] A third possibility is that Congress may adopt a proposal that seems attractive, only to have the program's supporting coalition unravel once the program begins operating. Congress enacted the Medicare Catastrophic Coverage Act by overwhelming margins in 1988, for example, only to reverse itself a year

A previous version of this chapter was published in *Political Science Quarterly*, vol. 113 (Summer 1998), pp. 213–40, and is reprinted with permission. I am grateful to Peter Diamond, Josh Goldstein, and Virginia Reno for helpful advice and comments. I have also profited from conversations with my colleagues on the Panel on Privatization of Social Security of the National Academy of Social Insurance and with the graduate students in the Arnold-Goldstein workshop on Social Security reform.
    35. See Arnold (1979, pp. 165–206).

later and repeal the entire program after beneficiaries protested the way costs were allocated.[36]

Early attention to the political feasibility of alternative schemes for reforming Social Security seems especially appropriate given the stakes. This is no ordinary program. Social Security is the cornerstone of retirement security for most Americans, with 60 percent of retirees drawing more than half their retirement income from this one program.[37] The long-term problems of Social Security are serious, however, and most experts counsel that the sooner Congress and the president fix these problems the better. Given these stakes, it makes sense to map carefully the political terrain that lies ahead, so that policy advocates do not make the kinds of mistakes that drive reform off the governmental agenda or push necessary changes far into the future.

Political Analysis

Before addressing the central question of political feasibility, it is important to understand what political science can—and cannot—accomplish. Political scientists have no special expertise in predicting the behavior of specific individuals. They have no tools for forecasting what Bill Clinton, Newt Gingrich, or Dick Gephardt will decide to do tomorrow morning, where each will come down on a particular proposal, or whether, in the midst of difficult negotiations, one of them will decide to be intransigent or accommodating, visionary or parochial, statesmanlike or petty. What individuals chose to do, and especially how institutional leaders decide to behave, will surely affect decisions about Social Security, but unfortunately political scientists have no special tools for analyzing these things.

Political scientists do have tools for analyzing how lots of politicians—say the 535 members of the House and Senate—might behave when they choose among specific policy options. Analysis is possible for large groups of legislators because many of the idiosyncrasies that seem so pronounced when one focuses on individuals disappear when summed across several hundred legislators. Analysis is also aided by the fact that legislators face similar problems year after year. Politicians establish habits for dealing with recurrent problems, and these habits shape how they deal with just about every problem that comes their way.

Some observers of Congress emphasize all the changes that occur on Capitol Hill. Electoral tides sweep one party in, the other out. Retirements and

---

36. For an excellent account, see Himelfarb (1995).
37. Advisory Council (1997b, p. 287).

electoral defeats change the cast of characters. Political scientists tend to emphasize constancy on the Hill. The sources of constancy are two, one institutional, the other electoral. The institutional fact is that Congress is a majoritarian institution in which legislators are equals. No legislator has constitutional authority over another; leaders serve at the pleasure of members; individual legislators are free to support or reject any alternative put before them. The electoral fact is that legislators retain their seats by their individual efforts to please their constituents. A seat in Congress is an individual franchise. As a consequence, legislators are extraordinarily attentive to what they hear from constituents, careful about how they deal with organized interests, and cautious when they cast major votes, calculating how specific votes might look in the middle of the next campaign if challengers decide to focus attention on them.[38]

The Agenda

Why is Social Security on the agenda for the first time in fifteen years? Why are policymakers considering modifying or replacing the program? Social Security was once such a regular item on the governmental agenda that no detailed explanation was really required. Between 1935 and 1973, Congress and the president enacted twenty-five Social Security laws—more than one bill every two years—as they transformed a relatively small retirement program, with initial tax rates of 1 percent each on employees and employers, into the mature program we know today, with tax rates of 6.2 percent.[39] During the final six years of this period, Social Security was constantly on the agenda, as Congress and the president responded to unusually high inflation by raising benefits seven times. Finally, in 1972, they placed Social Security on automatic pilot by enacting a provision that each year adjusts the wage base for changes in average wages and retirement benefits for changes in the consumer price index.

The 1972 law essentially removed Social Security from the regular governmental agenda. The program had reached maturity, and particularly as the economy stalled, there were no further pressures to expand it. Although insulated from inflation, Social Security was still vulnerable to other economic shocks and to long-term demographic changes. Social Security has returned to the governmental agenda only twice since 1972, each time because of actuarial imbalances. It first returned in 1975, after actuaries calculated that the program was

38. On how the electoral connection shapes legislators' voting decisions, see Mayhew (1974), Kingdon (1989), and Arnold (1990).

39. For a summary of Social Security legislation, 1935 to 1977, see Derthick (1979, pp. 429–32).

facing a deficit within three years. The sources of the problem were two: some mistakes in drafting the original adjustment formula, which overcompensated for inflation, and economic stagnation, which reduced revenues below their projections. After two years of debate, Congress and the president enacted a 1977 bill that phased in tax increases and recalibrated the inflation adjustment. Four years later Social Security was again back on the governmental agenda when actuaries forecasted both short-term and long-term deficits. After two years of intense effort, Congress and the president adopted the 1983 reform bill, this time just a few months before the trust fund would have run dry and current revenues would have been insufficient to cover benefit checks. This bill included both tax increases for current workers and benefit cuts for future retirees.[40]

What is unusual about Social Security today is that it is *not* facing a short-term deficit. Indeed, the trust fund is larger than ever and growing steadily. The problem is entirely long term. Government actuaries calculate that the system can pay all benefits until about 2032, after which the trust fund will be empty and current revenues will cover only about three-quarters of promised benefits.[41] The lack of any short-term crisis has profound implications for the politics of Social Security reform. First, there is nothing to force politicians to come to agreement about how to reform the system. Everyone may agree that reform is necessary, and that early reform is desirable, but there is nothing to *compel* early action. No one doubted the urgency of reform in the early 1980s, yet it took two years and the prospect that benefit checks were about to be curtailed before politicians agreed to a specific package of reforms. Nothing focuses politicians' minds on problem solving and compromise more than the prospect that their constituents might be deprived of benefits at daybreak.

The lack of a short-term crisis has also made it possible for policymakers to consider comprehensive reforms of Social Security rather than the incremental fixes that are typical when the well is about to run dry. Although Social Security has long had its critics, it has been difficult for these critics to get their ideas and proposals on the table. Either Social Security was flourishing and no one wanted to hear from a spoilsport, or Social Security was facing a short-term crisis and no one had time to reinvent the system. The opportunity to develop and consider comprehensive reforms does not suggest that these plans have any advantage over more incremental reforms, only that for the first time since 1935

40. For the story of the 1983 reform, see Light (1995).

41. Two years ago, when the Advisory Council on Social Security was preparing its recommendations, the projected date of insolvency was 2029. For the most recent projections, see Board of Trustees (1998, p. 4).

policymakers are open to considering alternative approaches to retirement security.

Policy Options

There is no shortage of plans for reforming Social Security.[42] In January 1997, the Advisory Council on Social Security proposed three separate plans, commonly referred to as Maintain Benefits (MB), Individual Accounts (IA), and Personal Security Accounts (PSA).[43] Each plan was supported by a minority of the thirteen-member council. Other plans on the table include those associated with prominent organizations (for example, the Cato Institute), those drafted by various groups of scholars (Kotlikoff-Sachs), and those already introduced in Congress (Kerrey-Simpson).[44] The following discussion concentrates on five plans that represent the range of alternatives. Rather than using the confusing and overlapping names provided by their champions—personal security systems, personal security accounts, individual accounts, and the like—it is simpler to refer to them by the names of their principal advocates: the Ball plan, the Gramlich plan, the Weaver-Schieber plan, the Kotlikoff-Sachs plan, and the Ferrara-Cato plan.[45] A final section examines two recent proposals: the Kasich plan and the Moynihan plan.[46]

Although these five reform plans differ in many important respects, ranging from their basic organizing principles to myriad details of implementation, two differences are fundamental to questions about political feasibility. The plans differ in the extent to which they provide for advance funding of retirement benefits. They also differ in how all of this advance funding should be invested, whether in a centrally managed fund, where risks and rewards are shared, or in various types of private accounts, where individual workers select investment options and bear the risks and rewards individually.

---

42. On the various approaches to reforming Social Security, see Diamond (1996) and Gramlich (1996).

43. See Advisory Council (1997a).

44. For a useful table summarizing the elements of seven plans, see Employee Benefit Research Institute (1996b).

45. The Ball, Gramlich, and Weaver-Schieber plans are presented in Advisory Council (1997a). The other two plans are described in Kotlikoff and Sachs (1997a ,1997b); Ferrara (1997).

46. Robert M. Ball, Edward M. Gramlich, Carolyn L. Weaver, and Sylvester J. Schieber were members of the thirteen-member Advisory Council on Social Security (1994–96). Laurence J. Kotlikoff is professor of economics at Boston University, Jeffrey Sachs is professor of economics at Harvard University, and Peter J. Ferrara is an associate scholar at the Cato Institute. Bob Kerrey (D-Nebr.) and Daniel Patrick Moynihan (D-N.Y.) are senators, Alan K. Simpson (R-Wyo.) is a former senator, and John Kasich (R-Ohio) is a House member.

Today's Social Security system is essentially a pay-as-you-go transfer program, with the contributions of current workers paying for the retirement benefits of current retirees. Although the system has a trust fund, it is relatively small and designed more to smooth out demographic fluctuations than to accumulate vast sums for investment.[47] The trust fund is currently accumulating extra funds while members of the baby boom generation are in their working years, but these reserves will be drawn down during their retirement years. The trust fund is invested exclusively in bonds of the U.S. government.

All five reform plans move Social Security in the direction of advance funding. Four plans include some type of individual accounts. The largest faction on the Advisory Council advocates a Maintain Benefits plan (the Ball plan) that would retain most of the system's pay-as-you-go character, while incorporating adjustments that would allow the trust fund to grow larger, be invested more aggressively, and thereby play a greater role in financing benefits.[48] At the other end of the spectrum, both the Kotlikoff-Sachs proposal and the Ferrara-Cato plan would phase out most of the current pay-as-you-go system and replace it with an advance-funded plan in which workers' contributions would be squirreled away in individual investment accounts. Another of the Advisory Council's proposals, the Weaver-Schieber plan, occupies a midpoint between these two extremes, with about half of all benefits provided by advance-funded, individually directed Personal Security Accounts and the other half by a variant of the current pay-as-you-go system. The third of the Advisory Council's proposals, the Gramlich plan, occupies some of the space between the Ball and Weaver-Schieber plans, grafting a smaller version of advance-funded Individual Accounts on top of a reduced pay-as-you-go system.

The debate is vigorous between those who propose to privatize all or part of Social Security by establishing individual accounts and those who seek to preserve a collective system where risks and rewards are shared. At least for the purists—the complete privatizers and the strict preservationists—the debate reflects fundamentally different conceptions of what Social Security should be. The complete privatizers envision Social Security as just another pension plan. They believe that workers should be allowed to control how their compulsory contributions are invested just as they currently control how their voluntary contributions to IRA or 401(k) accounts are invested. They celebrate the fact

47. The trust fund is currently equal to about 1.7 years of benefit payments. See Board of Trustees (1998, p. 127).

48. Under present law, the trust fund would decline to zero in 2032, whereas under the Ball plan the trust fund would grow to about 4.5 years' worth of benefits and then stabilize around that level. A fund of this magnitude could provide investment earnings equivalent to what an additional 2 percent payroll tax would supply. See Advisory Council (1997a, pp. 172, 184).

that risk and reward would be concentrated on individuals. The preservationists insist on viewing Social Security as social insurance rather than just another pension plan. They believe that it is essential to have a collective system that provides a guaranteed floor of retirement security for all Americans and that protects each individual from the risk of having inadequate retirement income. They believe that the current system is appropriately sized and that benefits should not be reduced.

If the debate were simply between the strict preservationists and the complete privatizers, then the preservationists would almost certainly prevail. Completely dissolving the safety net of social insurance and allowing individuals to manage all of their retirement assets is not a serious option given the broad public support for the idea of Social Security. But there are plenty of intermediate positions between strict preservation and complete privatization. The Gramlich and Weaver-Schieber plans, for example, are hybrids that call for partial privatization. They propose scaling back the size of the defined-benefit system and creating a parallel defined-contribution system that allows for some individual choice.

Social Security has long been conceived as part of a three-legged stool—the other two legs being employer-provided pensions and private savings—where the three legs together support the retirement needs of Americans. The partial privatizers are essentially asking whether the social insurance leg is too large. Although the question is always legitimate, it is especially so given all the changes that have occurred during the past two decades in the other two legs.[49] When the question was last raised in the 1960s and 1970s, a strong bipartisan consensus developed in favor of expanding the Social Security system. Today, as the deep divisions within the Advisory Council demonstrate, no consensus exists on the appropriate size of Social Security—at least in its current form.

Conflicts over the question of privatizing Social Security are intense. Questions about the appropriate size and scope of government are inherently ideological, partisan, and conflictual. But the whole question of moving toward advance funding is itself politically troublesome. Although questions about advance funding may appear tame by comparison to questions about establishing individual accounts, since advance funding ignites neither ideological nor partisan passions, a careful analysis of the politics of moving toward advance funding demonstrates the fallacy of this conclusion. Advance funding is troublesome for politicians of every partisan and ideological persuasion. Since advance funding is an essential component of every proposal for privatizing

49. See Cutler (1996).

even a portion of Social Security, this makes adopting privatization more difficult politically than the ideological conflict between individual choice and
social insurance suggests.[50]

The Politics of Funding Decisions

Advance-funded retirement systems have several advantages over pay-as-
you-go systems. Among other things, they promote national savings, and thus
economic growth, and they help insulate the financing of retirement plans from
the effects of large demographic shifts.[51] From a political perspective, however,
they have one large liability: they deliver no benefits in the near term for which
politicians can claim credit. As their name implies, the costs are now, the benefits far in the future. Few politicians enjoy imposing costs on their constituents
without also delivering some fairly immediate benefits—especially if there is
an easier way.[52]

Social Security actually began as an advance-funded system.[53] The original
plan, enacted in 1935, imposed a 1 percent payroll tax but promised no retirement benefits until 1942. Perhaps the costs were sufficiently small that they
were not seen as a major political liability; perhaps it helped that contributors
were promised that they could start collecting retirement benefits in just a few
years. By 1939 policymakers had begun the transformation to a pay-as-you-go
system, first by accelerating workers' eligibility for benefit payments to 1940,
then by adjusting benefits upward so that retirees received far more than their
own contributions could have earned, and finally by postponing planned tax
increases so that the trust fund would remain only a small buffer, not a large
investment fund.

The transformation from an advance-funded system to a pay-as-you-go system was easily accomplished because it united a diverse coalition of interests.
Program enthusiasts sought to deliver more benefits to retirees as soon as possible. Many legislators sought to minimize the tax burden on current workers

---

50. Advance funding is not logically necessary for privatization. For example, Latvia created a
privatized but unfunded pension system. But such hybrid schemes are both rare and difficult to
explain to politicians and citizens. On the distinction between privatization and advance funding,
see chap. 4, Geanakoplos, Mitchell, and Zeldes, in this volume.

51. On the economics of advance funding, see Diamond (1997).

52. Politicians are not the only people who behave in this fashion. Many consumers use install-
ment debt to maximize current benefits and minimize current costs. Perhaps politicians adopted
advance funding for Social Security in the 1930s because advance funding better corresponded
with the values of the day, just as the subsequent movement toward pay-as-you-go funding corresponded with the buy-now-pay-later mentality of the 1960s and 1970s.

53. For a superb political analysis of Social Security from 1935 to 1977, see Derthick (1979).

by deferring tax increases until they were absolutely necessary to fund current retirees' benefits.[54] And some conservatives were opposed to a large trust fund, fearing, according to Sen. Arthur Vandenberg (R-Mich.), "such an unmanageable accumulation of funds in one place in a democracy."[55] The same political logic that allowed for the transformation to a pay-as-you-go system also fueled the program's vast expansion over the next three decades. Because workers greatly outnumbered retirees, modest increases in the payroll tax, phased in gradually, covered large increases in retirement benefits.[56] The incremental costs for workers were small, the incremental benefits for retirees large.

Although policymakers gradually replaced an advance-funded system with a pay-as-you-go system, they retained the original rhetoric. They spoke in the common language of insurance, not in economists' language of transfer payments. The vocabulary of insurance was not only familiar, it was in many respects appropriate because policymakers were creating *rights* to benefits for workers who paid their dues.[57] Most people do not understand exactly how various types of insurance are funded, including casualty, health, and life insurance. What they do know is that by paying premiums they acquire rights to have future losses covered by insurance companies. By using similar language for retirement security, policymakers created similar rights. These new rights were stated not in a legal contract, to be enforced by the courts, but as a social contract, to be enforced by elected politicians subject to the court of public opinion. Mere transfer payments could be eliminated by future politicians, but Social Security benefits were different. They were earned rights, and no future politician could eliminate them without the consent of those who had paid their dues.[58]

The Politics of Advance Funding

Moving from the original advance-funded Social Security system to a pay-as-you-go system was relatively easy. Accelerating benefits and postponing costs is one of the easiest things that politicians do. The difficulties arise when

54. Derthick (1979, p. 215).

55. Derthick (1979, p. 232).

56. The number of workers per beneficiary declined from forty-two in 1945, to seventeen in 1950, nine in 1955, five in 1960, and four in 1965. It reached its current level of 3.3 workers per beneficiary in 1975. See Board of Trustees (1998, p. 122).

57. According to Martha Derthick, "Social Security was presented to the public as a program in which the worker takes care of his own future, gets back at least what he has paid for, and is entitled to get it back as a right." Derthick (1979, p. 289).

58. All of the reform plans recognize the sanctity of these rights. Even the plans that seek to replace the current Social Security system with something completely different recognize that they must provide benefits over the next six or seven decades for all workers and retirees who have been part of the pay-as-you-go system.

one attempts to reverse gears and reestablish advance funding as the organizing principle for retirement security. In order to do so, one must fund both systems for a while, simultaneously setting aside money for current workers while honoring all the existing obligations to retirees, near retirees, and indeed all those who have paid substantial sums into the current system. These obligations are immense. One estimate is that the program's unfunded liability to current workers and retirees is in the neighborhood of $9 trillion.[59]

The Kotlikoff-Sachs plan is clearest about what it would require to satisfy existing obligations while concurrently allowing workers to direct their own contributions into individual investment accounts. They propose a federal sales tax that "would begin below 10 percent and would decline to a permanent level of roughly 2 percent within 40 years."[60] Since the permanent tax of 2 percent is to fund a safety net for the poor, the remainder, perhaps 7 or 8 percent initially, is to pay transition costs. The political difficulties of establishing such a large tax are clear. First, it would be the largest new tax in American history, imposed at a time when "no new taxes" seems closer to the governing philosophy. Second, it would procure for the federal portfolio a form of taxation long reserved for states and localities. They would resist any invasion of their turf. Third, a sales tax, unlike the current payroll tax, would be a tax on retired citizens. It is not likely to be popular with retirees or with the American Association of Retired Persons, a group that probably has the power to scuttle any plan that it finds unacceptable.[61] Finally, members of Congress still recount the tale of how Al Ullman (D-Ore.), chairman of House Ways and Means, was defeated at the polls after championing a national value-added tax as the solution to the federal deficit.[62] Creating a new broad-based tax is more difficult for politicians than increasing an existing one. In short, both the size and the form of the transition tax proposed by Kotlikoff and Sachs highlight some of the political difficulties associated with moving toward an advance-funded system.

The proponents of advance funding are not naive. They know that neither citizens nor policymakers will be attracted by transition costs of this magni-

59. Recalibrated in terms of taxes, it would require a tax of 1.5 percent of taxable payrolls for about seventy years to eliminate an unfunded liability of $9 trillion. See Advisory Council (1997a, p.109).

60. Kotlikoff and Sachs (1997a, 1997b).

61. Kotlikoff and Sachs note that the poorest senior citizens—those who are totally dependent on Social Security—would be insulated from the new tax, because Social Security benefits would continue to be indexed for price changes. All other senior citizens, however, would suffer declines in their living standards because other forms of retirement income are not indexed. Although Kotlikoff and Sachs argue that compelling senior citizens to pay a share of Social Security's unfunded liability is "intergenerationally equitable," it is not an argument that many elected politicians are likely to find appealing.

62. See Arnold (1990, pp. 45–46).

tude. Their argument is that the benefits of moving to advance funding would be immense and that the benefits would more than justify the admittedly large costs. The principal advantage of advance funding is that it would increase national savings and these savings would stimulate economic growth.[63] A second advantage is that workers would eventually pay less for a given bundle of retirement benefits, because their benefits would be based on their own contributions as well as earnings on these contributions.

Estimating the costs and benefits of moving to an advance-funded system may demonstrate beyond a reasonable doubt that total benefits would eventually exceed total costs. The problem is that neither citizens nor politicians tend to evaluate policy alternatives by comparing total costs and benefits over an extended period of time.[64] Politics is much more about the timing and incidence of costs and benefits than about totals, and much more about the degree to which specific costs and benefits can be traced to politicians' individual actions. Because it is easier for citizens and politicians to estimate the incidence of costs and benefits in the short term, and because it is easier for citizens to connect short-term costs and benefits to politicians' individual actions, politics invariably revolves around these short-term effects. Both citizens and politicians tend to undervalue long-term effects when they evaluate policy alternatives.

Applying this logic to the Kotlikoff and Sachs plan, one sees that all workers and many retirees would incur large costs in the short term, and these costs would be directly traceable to the actions of individual legislators who supported their imposition. In contrast, the benefits would either be diffuse benefits, such as economic growth, or somewhat higher retirement benefits that would appear only in the long term. Most citizens would never trace either type of benefit to the actions that individual legislators took years before to produce them. In short, legislators could face electoral retribution for imposing easily traceable early-order costs, while it is doubtful that they would ever be rewarded for delivering such general benefits as economic growth and prosperity or such later-order benefits as the higher investment returns of individual retirement accounts.

Transition Costs

The point is not that it is impossible to reestablish a Social Security system based on advance funding. The point is that it is not yet in legislators' self-

63. On the effect of Social Security reform on private and national saving, see Engen and Gale (1997).
64. For a full theoretical treatment of the issues in this paragraph and the next, see Arnold (1990).

interest to impose the necessary transition costs. Reform is possible only when large majorities of Americans come to understand and accept the nature of the sacrifices that would be required to pay for the transition. Legislators will not enact this kind of reform just because they believe that advance funding is a good idea. Most legislators are unwilling to forfeit their careers to advance even a very good idea. Proponents of these reforms need to be honest with the American people, stating that whatever large benefits would be generated by adopting an advance-funded system would not be immediate. The benefits would be long term; and until then, workers (and perhaps retirees) would pay increased costs.

Some proponents of privatizing Social Security claim that large majorities of Americans already support full-scale privatization. Michael Tanner reports on a 1996 poll in which 69 percent of registered voters supported a detailed privatization plan, while a mere 12 percent opposed it.[65] Although the poll appears to have been professionally administered in terms of sample size and the like, the 200-word description of a privatized system that prefaced the actual question failed to mention transition costs. It summarized all the benefits of privatization, along with "no reduction in benefits for current Social Security recipients"; but it neglected to mention the sacrifices required to pay for both systems. Politicians will not be fooled by such nonsense. Polls that emphasize benefits and ignore costs tell us nothing more profound than that everyone likes a free lunch.

Proponents of advance funding need to be clear and precise about the transition costs. Kotlikoff and Sachs pass this test with ease. In contrast, the Ferrara-Cato plan attempts to show that "the transition can be financed without new taxes and without cutting benefits for today's recipients."[66] The miracle of a costless transition is justified in nearly a dozen ways, my favorite being: "Any remaining transition costs should be financed by cutting other government spending, much of which is wasteful and even counterproductive. Reducing it will not amount to a significant cost."[67] Ferrara has in mind cutting about $60 billion a year.[68] No matter how insignificant he believes these expenditures to be, cutting budgets is never an easy task, especially after the extensive budget cutting of the past decade. It is a mistake to pretend that there are no significant transition costs.

65. See Tanner (1996, pp. 4–5).
66. Ferrara (1997, p. 1).
67. Ferrara (1997, p. 14).
68. It is reminiscent of the magic asterisk in President Ronald Reagan's first budget that also referred to unspecified future expenditure cuts of $60 billion annually. It was far easier to assume that such cuts would be made than to make them. See Greider (1982, p. 36).

The proponents of moving toward an advance-funded system also need to be clear about *who* will pay for the transition. The notion that everybody— and every age cohort—can be better off during the transition is implausible. Martin Feldstein poses the distributional question starkly: "During the transition, which are the age groups that win and which are the age groups that lose?"[69] Feldstein and Samwick analyzed one possible transition scheme and concluded that it would take about nineteen years for the cost of funding two systems to drop below the cost of funding the current system alone.[70] The bottom line by age cohort: "Those who are retired when the transition begins are completely unaffected. Those who are at least 45 years old will always face a higher combined mix of taxes and PRA [Personal Retirement Account] contributions. Those who are younger will face a higher mix for 19 years and then a lower mix. The younger they are, the more likely that the present value of the combined payments will be lower in the transition than in the baseline."[71]

More studies of this type would be useful, with additional studies investigating alternative transition schemes and making alternative assumptions about economic returns. Although it may also be useful to estimate the distributional effects of increased economic growth, these estimates need to be separate from estimates of the distributional effects of transition costs. The transition costs are certain and directly traceable to legislators' actions, whereas increased economic growth is more speculative and completely untraceable to legislators' decisions.

The reason why proponents of advance funding must be clear about who would pay for the transition is that opponents are certain to focus on the issue of costs. Pretending that everyone will profit is implausible and could easily undermine the legitimacy of a reform proposal. That was the fatal error made by the proponents of the Medicare Catastrophic Coverage Act of 1988, who failed to prepare senior citizens for the fact that some of them would be worse off.[72] A better strategic model for enacting advance funding would be the decade-long effort to balance the federal budget. No one pretended that the transition to a balanced budget was costless. The debate was about who should sacrifice, who should pay higher taxes, and who should have their favorite benefit programs shaved, slashed, or terminated.

Policymakers can also modify the incidence of transition costs. Total costs may be fixed, but their incidence by income and age is a matter of choice.

69. Feldstein (1997, p. 20).
70. Feldstein and Samwick (1996); Feldstein (1997, p. 11).
71. Feldstein (1997, p. 21).
72. Himelfarb (1995).

Policymakers can also choose to phase in transition costs gradually. Advocates of advance funding often recommend that taxpayers swallow large doses of bitter medicine as quickly as possible so that the benefits would accrue rapidly. Politicians are more likely to prefer gradual transitions, beginning with small doses and slowly increasing the dosage over time. Gradualism was the approach that policymakers adopted in 1935 when they first instituted Social Security. Gradualism was also the approach that policymakers employed over the past decade when they moved the federal budget toward balance. Establishing what should be the proper transition period is not a matter in which policy experts have a comparative advantage, other than to show the relationship between the pace of sacrifice and the likely flow of benefits. The length of the transition period is a political choice, and it is best left to politicians who are skilled in estimating the rate at which their constituents can tolerate increased costs.

The General Problem of Costs

The analysis of the politics of replacing the current pay-as-you-go system with one based on advance funding has focused on transition costs because these costs are the principal impediment to reform. Imposing costs is a general problem, however, and one that all reformers must face. The current system is not adequately funded and there is no way to fix it without imposing costs on either today's generations or future generations. Before analyzing how other reform plans propose to apportion these costs, it will prove useful to examine how policymakers have allocated Social Security costs in the past.

Policymakers' aversion to imposing costs is not unique to the 1990s. From the very inception of Social Security, policymakers have been careful about how they apportioned costs. Gradualism has been the key to every single decision about costs from 1935 to 1983. The original Social Security Act, which imposed a payroll tax of 1 percent beginning in 1937, contained a gradual schedule for increasing the tax to 3 percent in 1949. But even this twelve-year schedule proved too rapid for politicians. Congress repeatedly slowed the schedule, moving the first scheduled increase from 1940 to 1950, and moving the original 3 percent ceiling to 1960.[73] Although Congress eventually increased the payroll tax to 6.2 percent, this was accomplished in twenty separate steps, averaging only 0.26 percentage point a step. Over the entire fifty-four-year period required for reaching the present tax rate, Congress increased taxes by less than 0.10 per-

---

73. Derthick (1979, pp. 429–31); Board of Trustees (1998, p. 33).

centage point a year.[74] In short, policymakers increased costs as slowly and imperceptibly as possible.

The initial decision to impose identical payroll taxes on workers and employers was another way to make costs less perceptible. Economists can argue all they want about whether workers ultimately pay the employers' share too with forgone wages, but politicians know that workers perceive only the part that is deducted from their wages. Workers are unlikely to perceive either the employers' share or something as nebulous as forgone wages. The one group that would have noticed that they were paying both employee and employer taxes was spared having to do so. From 1951 to 1983, self-employed workers paid only about three-quarters of the combined employee and employer rates.[75] Only under the pressure to find revenue to rescue Social Security in 1983 did Congress eliminate the special rate for self-employed workers, and even then, Congress created a seven-year transition period before the self-employed were brought up to parity with the combined tax rates for ordinary workers.[76]

The 1983 reform bill was a masterpiece at imposing costs as gradually and imperceptibly as possible.[77] The seven-year phase-in of both parity for the self-employed and a higher payroll tax for everyone was accompanied by reducing benefits for retirees in the distant future.[78] The normal retirement age was increased from 65 to 67, and early retirement benefits were cut from 80 percent to 70 percent of full benefits (both changes phased in between 2003 and 2027). Even current retirees had their benefits reduced modestly. Cost-of-living adjustments were delayed for six months for all retirees, and upper-income retirees had some of their tax-free Social Security benefits transformed into taxable

74. Only four of the twenty tax increases between 1937 and 1990 were as large as 0.5 percentage point (1950, 1954, 1960, 1963). For a list of tax rates by year, see Board of Trustees (1998, pp. 33–34).

75. Congress began charging self-employed workers 75 percent of the combined rate, but it allowed the rate to dip as low as 69 percent between 1973 and 1980. See Board of Trustees (1998, p. 33).

76. Actually, Congress established parity in tax rates effective 1984, but it also granted self-employed workers an income tax credit to offset part of the increase. The credit was not phased out until 1990. Self-employed workers are currently allowed to deduct the "employers" half of the payroll tax from taxable income, just like any other employer. Of course, this tax deduction is much less valuable than either the original reduced tax rate for self-employed workers or the transitional tax credit. See Congressional Quarterly (1984, p. 662).

77. Light (1995); Congressional Quarterly (1984, pp. 658–63).

78. Strictly speaking, legislators voted to accelerate the imposition of tax increases that were originally passed in 1977 and scheduled to be phased in between 1979 and 1990. Since the acceleration generated about $40 billion in additional revenues, it was a genuine tax increase, even if it did not raise the 1990 rate above what it would have become in the absence of the reform bill. See Light (1995, p. 180).

income. It was a classic share-the-pain strategy, imposing costs on workers and retirees alike. But the pain was administered as slowly as possible.

Advisory Council Plans

Each of the three Advisory Council Plans is a complicated amalgam of individual provisions for restoring actuarial balance. Each has a different plan for apportioning costs among workers, retirees, and future retirees. The most striking difference among the plans, however, is how they propose to increase taxes on workers and employers. Although all three plans propose increasing Social Security revenues by about 1.6 percent of covered payrolls, they differ in who would pay the incremental costs and when the payments would begin. The Gramlich plan would require an immediate increase in workers' contributions of 1.6 percent of earnings; employers would face no additional costs. The Weaver-Schieber plan would require an immediate increase in workers' and employers' contributions of 0.76 percentage point each; both increases would be eliminated after seventy-two years. The Ball plan would require that both workers' and employers' contributions increase 0.8 percentage point in the year 2045.

The Gramlich plan is most out of line with how Congress has apportioned Social Security costs in the past. Workers would bear directly all the incremental costs. The traditional parity between workers' and employers' contributions would be broken for the first time since the program's inception. It is hard to imagine any political advantages in breaking a link that has long been accepted by both business and labor, especially given the enormous political liabilities of doing so. As sure as the sun rises, opponents would claim that the provision was designed to soak poor- and middle-income workers while protecting rich corporations from sharing the burden. Arguments that imposing costs directly on workers was a better way to increase national savings would fall on millions of deaf ears, as would arguments that workers eventually pay employers' share of the payroll tax through forgone wages. Breaking the link between workers' and employers' contributions would also increase the likelihood of partisan conflict, because one party has long been associated with business, the other with labor.

Moreover, by concentrating all of the incremental costs directly on workers, the Gramlich plan would require an enormous increase in workers' contributions. An immediate increase of 1.6 percentage points in workers' contributions is more than three times greater than any increase in the history of Social Security.[79] It amounts to a 26 percent increase in the current payroll tax of

79. See note 74.

6.2 percentage points. At least on that count, the Weaver-Schieber plan is more attractive. By retaining the traditional link between workers' and employers' contributions, their plan would require an increase in workers' payments of only 0.76 percent of earnings. But even that rate is much larger than any increase in the history of Social Security. The point is not that it would be impossible for legislators to approve either the Gramlich or Weaver-Schieber rates. The point is that the designers of these two plans have made it unusually difficult for legislators to impose the level of costs that are essential for restoring actuarial soundness and moving toward advance funding. Recall that in 1983, when the well was about to run dry, legislators required a seven-year phase-in for an 0.8 percentage point increase in workers' contributions. Why, when the well is not scheduled to run dry until 2032, would legislators approve an *immediate* increase of either 1.6 or 0.76 percentage points? Why not employ the age-old strategy of gradualism?

Strictly speaking, the 1.6 percent increase in workers' payments under the Gramlich plan would not be a tax. According to the plan's proponents, it would be a contribution. Workers' contributions would be held by the government in individual accounts that would be invested in one or more indexed stock or bond funds; at retirement, both the contributions and the investment earnings would be used to purchase indexed annuities. Calling the payment a contribution, rather than a tax, however, does not transform fundamentally the politics of imposing pain. When the government mandates that workers forgo current consumption, it makes more difference how much consumption is to be forgone than what the mandatory payment is called.[80] When the government mandates that workers keep their contributions in government-approved accounts until retirement and then mandates that the contributions be used to purchase government-approved annuities, the difference between a contribution and a tax becomes even narrower.

The assumption that citizens prefer making mandatory contributions to individual accounts over paying a higher payroll tax would be on firmer ground if the actual choice were between alternative payments of approximately equal size. Direct ownership is highly valued in American society; and, all else equal, people might prefer sending their money to individually named accounts rather than to a giant collective account. The problem is that no one is being asked to choose between a tax and a contribution of the same magnitude. The choice is between an immediate contribution of 1.6 percent of wages under the Gramlich plan and a tax half as large and imposed a half century later under the Ball plan.

80. If the current Social Security system were somehow dissolved and the 6.2 percent payroll tax were transformed into a mandatory 6.2 percent contribution, would citizens across the land celebrate the elimination of a 6.2 percent tax?

If citizens really do prefer a large, immediate, mandatory contribution to a much smaller tax imposed far in the future (and no reliable evidence exists one way or the other), then it must be because they believe that the benefits from a contribution to an individual account are vastly more *certain* than the benefits from a tax. The appropriate question is how much extra are citizens willing to pay to increase their sense of confidence that benefits will be delivered far in the future? Since advance funding is crucial to establishing individual accounts, this is just a variant of the more general question concerning how much citizens are willing to pay to finance the transition to advance funding.

The Weaver-Schieber plan makes an even greater commitment to advance funding through defined-contribution accounts. It would redirect into personal security accounts 5 percentage points of the 6.2 percent that workers currently pay in Social Security taxes, while adopting a temporary transition tax of 0.76 percentage point each on employees and employers to cover obligations under the current pay-as-you-go system. As previously discussed, the Weaver-Schieber plan has a more politically realistic mechanism for increasing taxes than the Gramlich plan because it retains the current parity between employer and employee contributions that allows workers' direct contributions to be half as large. The fact that the transition tax would be temporary is also a nice feature, but a seventy-two-year transition period offers no political advantages, because all the benefits would be enjoyed by generations not yet born.

The Ball plan requires no immediate tax increase because it takes only a tiny step toward advance funding. Advance funding appears in this plan not by establishing individual investment accounts and finding new revenue to fill them, but by incorporating various small adjustments that would allow the current trust fund to grow larger and be invested more aggressively. The eventual tax increase of 0.8 percentage point each for workers and employers in 2045 is designed more to keep Social Security from again drifting out of balance as life spans continue to increase than it is to provide additional revenue for advance funding. Legislators should have no trouble approving a deferred tax increase of this magnitude, since the tax would never be imposed during their watch.

Despite the similarities among the three plans, with each proposing to increase Social Security revenues by about 1.6 percent of covered payrolls, the plans propose strikingly different routes toward that target. Surprisingly, the Gramlich plan, which was designed to be a moderate alternative between the other two, is the least graceful in imposing new taxes. The Weaver-Schieber plan, which proposes the most radical redesign of Social Security, is more politically adept at dealing with transition costs, because it retains the traditional parity between workers' and employers' contributions. And the Ball plan shows that it might be possible to incorporate additional advance funding in the current system without increasing taxes in the near term.

Other Costs

The analysis of the various reform plans has focused heavily on how they raise new revenue, because this is the most difficult aspect of moving toward advance funding. Imposing large, traceable, early-order costs on citizens is one of the toughest things that elected officials ever do. The three reform plans impose lots of other costs too, but none of these provisions are quite as difficult to accomplish as raising taxes for all workers. For example, all three plans forcibly enroll in the Social Security system all new state and local government workers. The three plans wisely steer clear of forcing current state and local employees to join the system, since such a provision would impose large, traceable, early-order costs on a well-organized group of workers that is politically active. By limiting the provision to newly hired workers—people who are not yet aware of their condition—the plans minimize the probability of electoral retribution. Current estimates are that this provision alone would eliminate about 10 percent of Social Security's long-range actuarial imbalance, in part because young government workers would contribute for many years before collecting benefits, and in part because many of these workers would have received some Social Security benefits anyway, based on other employment before, during, or after government service.[81]

All three plans would also impose costs on current retirees and future retirees. Current retirees would bear the lighter burden. None of the plans would directly reduce their benefits—something that would be large and noticeable to all. Instead, the plans would gradually alter the way in which Social Security benefits are taxed, and then redirect the consequent income tax revenues into the Social Security trust fund. Gradualism and the fact that these tax provisions would affect only some retirees help to make them politically more palatable. These provisions also continue a trend, initiated in the 1983 reform plan and expanded in the 1993 budget bill, to tax as ordinary income a portion of Social Security benefits. All that is at stake is the precise location of an already existing line between taxable and tax-free benefits.

The three plans use various means for imposing costs on future retirees. The Ball plan proposes changing the benefit formula. The proposed change would be gradual and, given that most people do not understand the benefit formula anyway, future retirees would be unlikely to trace their slightly diminished

81. Advisory Council (1997a, pp. 20, 181–83).

incomes to legislators' actions.[82] The Gramlich plan proposes even larger changes in the benefit formula, as well as gradual increases in the normal retirement age. The Weaver-Schieber plan proposes gradually replacing the current benefit formula with a flat-rate benefit beginning with workers younger than 55. Finally, all three plans would subject future retirees to the same kinds of gradual changes in the way Social Security benefits are taxed that would first affect current retirees.

All three plans seem to accept the notion that reducing benefits should be a gradual process. Gradualism allows everyone to readjust their affairs, and it minimizes the chances that anyone would notice any dramatic reduction in benefits that might stimulate a search for politicians to hold accountable. The surprise is that the Gramlich and Weaver-Schieber plans do not recognize the same political need to impose tax increases as gradually as possible. Perhaps in their zeal to move toward an advance-funded system as rapidly as possible they neglected the political imperative to impose all pain as slowly and imperceptibly as possible.

Investment Decisions

The three plans differ most significantly in how they propose to invest all this advance funding. Before discussing the investment options, it is important to note that we are now entering terra incognita. Congress has had plenty of experience deciding how to raise payroll taxes, adjust benefit levels, extend retirement ages, and restrict tax exemptions; and these past experiences help to inform an analysis of how legislators might handle similar provisions today. But Congress has never before chosen between polar opposites such as the Weaver-Schieber plan, which introduces defined-contribution accounts with individual control over investment and distribution, and the Ball plan, which seeks to preserve the essential character of the current defined-benefit system. The Ball and the Weaver-Schieber plans clearly rest on very different philosophies about how to organize a public pension system and about the trade-offs between universal retirement security and the importance of individual choice. What is yet to be determined is how these differences will play out politically.

The Ball plan has the advantage of familiarity. People can judge the proposed incremental changes against a well-known entity. The overall package is right out of the 1983 playbook. It is a carefully calibrated collection of incre-

---

82. The proposal is to increase the benefit computation period from thirty-five to thirty-eight years, which would reduce benefits by an average of 3 percent. Advisory Council (1997a, p. 25).

mental changes that would not be very popular individually but that many people can accept as a package deal in order to preserve a highly valued program. The one innovation is the proposal to consider investing the trust fund in the stock market.[83] This is also the plan's most controversial provision. The controversy has nothing to do with the riskiness of the stock market. Given that most private pension funds and most state and local pension funds are heavily invested in the stock market, it is difficult to sustain an argument that the largest pension fund in the country should be denied the higher yields of equities or the substantial advantages of diversification. The controversy is about whether it is healthy for the federal government to own a larger share of corporate America than any other shareholder. Under one plausible scenario, the Social Security trust fund would own about 5 percent of all corporate equities by the year 2020.[84] Direct investments of this magnitude could give the government power in corporate affairs beyond what it already exercises with its tax and regulatory authority.

It is relatively easy to devise mechanisms to allow the federal government to invest in private equities without acquiring additional power over private corporations. The government could decide to invest only in index funds and it could renounce all voting rights.[85] It could create a governing board that is as far removed from politics as possible—something like the Federal Reserve Board. Indeed, it seems likely that any plan to invest trust fund assets in the stock market would have to include these kinds of procedures in order to forestall the overwhelming opposition of corporations, corporate executives, and millions of citizens who believe that the federal government has no business using investment decisions or voting rights to interfere with corporate affairs.

The problem is that government cannot permanently establish a policy of passive investing or passive voting, because a future law can always repeal an existing one. No Congress can bind succeeding Congresses. So, the question boils down to whether citizens are comfortable with a plan that includes the possibility that a future Congress might interfere with investment decisions or corporate governance. The issue is sufficiently new that it requires an active debate about how serious is the problem, how large is the probability

83. Although the Ball plan does not explicitly endorse investing in equities, the actuarial projections that compare it with the other two Advisory Council plans assume that 40 percent of the trust fund would be invested in equities by 2015. Without this assumption, the Ball plan would be underfunded and additional tax increases or benefit cuts would be required. See Advisory Council (1997a, pp. 80–86, 166).

84. Hammond and Warshawsky (1997).

85. In cases where nonvoting is equivalent to voting on one side or the other, the government could vote its shares neutrally.

of governmental interference, and how best to forestall it.[86] The best protection against governmental interference is not just a well-designed set of procedures but public support for the notion that the federal government should remain a passive investor. Public support would help to forestall future efforts to modify governmental procedures. Vigorous advocacy of this position by a diverse group of interests is the best way to create such support.

The proponents of the Weaver-Schieber plan are convinced that the consequences of governmental interference in corporate affairs are so serious that they oppose any trust fund investment in the stock market.[87] Their alternative solution is to redirect 5 percentage points of the payroll tax into personal security accounts that individual workers would select and control. The model for this approach is something like 401(k) pension plans or individual retirement accounts (IRAs). Their approach is almost certain to guarantee that the federal government would have no direct influence over investment decisions or corporate governance.

Two controversies surround this approach. First, would it be worth the additional costs to establish, administer, and maintain millions of personal security accounts, rather than maintaining a single, centrally managed trust fund, especially if the principal reason for personal accounts is simply to prevent any possibility of governmental interference with investment decisions and corporate governance? The extra costs would be substantial, both for employers, who would direct contributions to the appropriate individual accounts, and for workers who would have some fraction of their contributions consumed by annual maintenance charges.[88] The first cost would be a special problem for small employers and for those with lots of part-time workers; the second cost would be a special problem for workers at the bottom of the wage distribution and for part-time workers. One measure of the magnitude of the total costs is the enthusiasm of Wall Street firms for individual accounts. On Wall Street these costs are counted as benefits.

The second controversy is whether it makes sense to have millions of workers making separate investment decisions in a public pension program that would continue to be the foundation of retirement security for most Americans. Are all workers capable of making sound investment decisions? What happens if some workers mismanage their investments or fail to annuitize their account balances at retirement and end up dramatically worse off? The proponents of the

86. See Theodore J. Angelis, chap. 6 in this volume, and Howell E. Jackson, chap. 6 in this volume. On activism by state and local pension funds, see Romano (1993).

87. Advisory Council (1997a, pp. 126–31).

88. On the administrative costs for various types of retirement systems, see Mitchell (1996).

Weaver-Schieber plan are remarkably sanguine about the ability of workers to manage decisions about investment and annuitization.[89] Empirical studies are less supportive of the notion that individuals make sound investment decisions.[90]

The two controversies together introduce questions of fairness across income classes, educational brackets, and the like. Would the poor pay disproportionate administrative costs because their contributions are so small? Does the plan favor well-educated workers or workers with particular skills because they are better able to manage their financial affairs? These are important political questions that have not been part of the Social Security debate since the program's inception. They are also the kinds of questions that tend to divide the two parties.

The Gramlich plan occupies the middle ground on investment decisions, annuitization, and the trade-off between individual choice and retirement security. The plan maintains more of the current defined-benefit system and squirrels away in individual accounts only about one-third as much money as the Weaver-Schieber plan (1.6 percent of earnings rather than 5 percent). The proposal also restricts individuals to only a few centrally managed investment options and requires full annuitization of account balances at retirement. The plan clearly comes down more heavily on the side of retirement security rather than maximizing individual choice.[91] But it does so by increasing the possibility that a future Congress might abandon passive investing or choose to exercise its voting rights. Under the Gramlich plan, the possibility of government interference is less than it is for the Ball plan, because the new accounts would belong to named individuals; but the protection is not as great as it is in the Weaver-Schieber plan, where the accounts would not be centrally managed at all.[92]

89. Advisory Council (1997a, pp. 114–17).

90. See Poterba and Wise (1996); Employee Benefit Research Institute (1996a); Diamond (1997).

91. The philosophical differences are best observed as the proponents of one plan critique another plan. Weaver, Schieber, and others on the Gramlich plan: "Our first concern is that this option simply contains far more restrictions on workers' choices than we deem necessary or desirable. The option sharply limits workers' investment choices. . . . The plan also forces workers to annuitize their full accumulations at retirement." Gramlich and Twinney on the Weaver-Schieber plan: "The PSA plan permits workers attaining age 62 full access to their accounts that have been accumulated over an entire working career. The government is in effect saying to people that it does not trust them to save for the future when they are younger than 62, so it requires them to hold PSAs. But once these people become 62 they suddenly become wise and responsible, and the government no longer requires them to preserve their assets beyond that date." Advisory Council (1997a, pp. 129, 157).

92. Advisory Council (1997a, pp. 129–31); Diamond (1997).

Political Packaging

Most of the alternative schemes for reforming Social Security have been designed by experts on Social Security. Although Congress and the president could choose to adopt one of these prepackaged plans, they are more likely to design their own package. They need to design a plan that can appeal to a diverse coalition of interests in Congress and across the country. Although the exact mechanism for drafting such a plan has yet to be determined, it is likely that the drafters will be dominated by political experts who are skilled at assembling coalitions for difficult issues.

The menu of options available to policymakers is much greater than the prepackaged plans discussed above, or even all the specific provisions contained in these plans. Policymakers can choose to modify tax rates, benefit formulas, transition schedules, retirement ages, cost-of-living adjustments, tax exemptions, investment options, annuitization rules, and the balance between individual and collective accounts in an extraordinary number of ways and still return Social Security to actuarial balance.[93] Indeed, the amateur policymaker can design quite a few alternative plans just by choosing provisions from a menu of alternatives that the Social Security actuaries prepared for the Advisory Council.[94] For each of eighty-two separate provisions, the actuaries have estimated the impact on Social Security's long-range actuarial balance.[95] Policymakers can ask the actuaries to provide similar estimates for any other provisions that they find appealing.

Rank-and-file legislators will never have the opportunity to vote on all the individual provisions that are part of a final package. A reform package will probably be assembled by a presidential commission, a bipartisan executive-legislative panel, the House Ways and Means Committee, or the Senate Finance Committee; and then legislators will be given the opportunity to approve or reject the final package. Many of the provisions will be individually distasteful, and legislators would never approve them if they had to vote on them one by one. Many legislators would fear electoral retribution for imposing specific costs on citizens that they could easily trace back to legislators' individual roll-call votes. Instead, the package will be framed as an overall plan to rescue Social Security, one that imposes significant costs on lots of people, but that does so fairly and in order to achieve a common and popular end.

93. For a discussion of the range of options for dealing with the actuarial imbalance, see Advisory Council (1997b, pp. 63–92).

94. Advisory Council (1997a, pp. 231–39).

95. The aim is to pick a set of alternatives that together amount to 2.17 percent of taxable payrolls over the next seventy-five years (the estimated difference between Social Security's revenues and expenses).

The job of the drafters is to design a plan that both citizens and legislators perceive to be fair. Public opinion will surely be important to how legislators decide, but the consequential opinions will not be the snap judgments reflected in polls taken about abstract proposals. The opinions that matter will be those that evolve during the period when Congress and the president focus on specific proposals. Citizens' opinions will be shaped by politicians' rhetoric, by the actions of interest groups and the champions of various causes, and by the way the mass media cover the unfolding story. Also relevant is how legislators anticipate that public opinion might evolve after a plan is approved and implemented.[96]

The Search for New Options

Given that the greatest impediment to privatization is the need to fund two systems for a while, politicians who favor full or partial privatization are actively searching for ways to reduce the transition costs. One approach is to dedicate all or part of the federal government's looming surpluses to reducing these costs. President Clinton stimulated a search for policy alternatives of this type when he declared in his 1998 State of the Union address that Congress should reserve every penny of the surplus for saving Social Security. His proposal was probably designed to block Republican legislators from adopting a new round of tax cuts and to give all legislators a strong incentive to solve the Social Security problem before dissipating the surplus on their favorite spending programs. No matter what his intent, Clinton's proposal is not neutral toward the various approaches to reform. It advances the cause of privatization—or at least partial privatization—more than it helps those who seek to maintain the current system.

To be sure, budget surpluses could be used to help shore up the current system. But the system is not in desperate need of revenue in the near term. Although Social Security clearly needs to have its revenue and benefit streams recalibrated to forestall long-term problems caused by demographic shifts, an infusion of cash today would only postpone the day of reckoning. A second problem is that Congress needs to devise a mechanism that can effectively reserve the looming surpluses for Social Security. The surpluses will occur not in the operating budget, where deficits continue to be large, but in the unified budget, where annual surpluses in the Social Security account mask annual deficits in the operating accounts. The challenge is to create a mechanism—no smoke and mirrors allowed—that allows surpluses in the unified budget to benefit Social Security when the surpluses are already attributable to surpluses in the Social Security accounts. The challenge is also to prevent future politicians

---

96. On how legislators anticipate future preferences, see Arnold (1990).

from dismantling the mechanism the next time they need revenue for the operating budget.

The situation is very different for the proponents of partial privatization. They have a desperate need for additional revenue in the near term to reduce the costs of funding two systems. Federal surpluses are just the windfall they need to fund part of the transition. One proponent has already designed a clever mechanism that not only diverts surpluses to this end but also prevents future politicians from redirecting the accrued surpluses to other ends. In March 1998, John Kasich (R-Ohio), chair of the House Budget Committee, proposed placing most of the surplus into individual retirement accounts for each worker. Individuals could choose how to invest these funds from a list of government-approved options; they could not withdraw funds before retirement.

The Kasich plan has several political advantages. First, it jump starts privatization by creating and funding individual accounts before Congress and the president settle all the long-term issues about Social Security reform, including whether to create a new defined-contribution system of individual accounts and what should be the balance between this new system and the current system. Once all these individual accounts are established, however, they provide both a precedent and the infrastructure for investing a potion of workers' payroll taxes in individual accounts. It is stealth privatization. Second, the Kasich plan launches privatization without Congress first having to increase taxes. It avoids the principal stumbling block in other privatization plans. Third, by placing the accrued surpluses in individual accounts, the plan places the money beyond the reach of future politicians who might be tempted to use it for other ends. Finally, it allows Republicans to claim that they have delivered another round of tax cuts, the only difference being that taxpayers cannot spend this particular windfall until retirement. It is a clever political package that makes the transition to partial privatization much easier, especially for those Republicans who consider that raising taxes is heresy.[97]

Senator Daniel Patrick Moynihan (D-N.Y.), the senior Democrat on the Senate Finance Committee, has proposed a different route to partial privatization. Not only does his plan avoid the need for a tax increase, it allows for an immediate tax cut. Moynihan proposes reducing the current payroll tax from 12.4 percent to 10.4 percent and allowing workers to use the 2 percent cut to establish voluntary personal savings accounts. Moynihan avoids any transition costs by reducing benefits and by returning Social Security to its pay-as-you-go roots, with just a

97. On April 1, 1998, in the first test of the popularity of this proposal, the Senate adopted, 51-49, a nonbinding resolution calling for dedicating the 1998 budget surplus to establishing Social Security personal retirement accounts. The vote revealed deep partisan divisions. Republicans supported the resolution, 49-6; Democrats opposed it, 43-2.

small contingency reserve. Reversing the planned growth in the trust fund means that the tax rate would eventually drift upward as the baby boom generation retires; but the eventual tax increase would be relatively modest, because the benefit cuts between now and then are quite large. The cuts include lowering cost-of-living adjustments by 1 percentage point a year for current and future retirees, taxing Social Security benefits under the same rules used for private pensions, and continuing to increase the retirement age as life expectancy increases.

The Moynihan plan for partial privatization has much in common with the Gramlich plan. Both plans create a system of individual accounts that would coexist with a slimmed-down version of the current defined-benefit plan. The principal difference between the two plans reflects the authors' occupational roots. Gramlich, the economist, views with alarm the low rate of national savings; he has devised a plan that would increase national savings as quickly as possible by requiring a contribution of 1.6 percent of taxable wages to an individual investment account. Moynihan, the practicing politician, sees little support among other practicing politicians for forcibly extracting that much additional revenue from workers. So, his individual accounts are to be voluntary, and the combined voluntary contribution and mandatory tax are to be no larger than the current tax rate. All the pain in Moynihan's plan is in the future—benefit reductions that are phased in gradually and a series of relatively small tax increases that are imposed in the distant future.

The Prospects for Reform

The most important political fact about the Social Security program is that it is the status quo alternative. Do nothing and the program continues. Permanently established in law, Social Security requires neither annual appropriations nor any other type of regular political maintenance. Until Congress and the president agree on how to change the program, payroll taxes keep rolling in and benefit payments keep flowing out, all according to the tax and benefit formulas that were last revised in 1983. To be sure, the current formulas are not sustainable in perpetuity. Annual revenues, supplemented by the trust fund, are adequate to cover all benefit payments for only the next three decades. From a politician's perspective, however, three decades is a very long time.

The one position that virtually everyone who studies Social Security shares is that reforming Social Security expeditiously is preferable to waiting until the problem becomes more severe. No matter how painful some of the remedies seem today, each remedy becomes more expensive as time marches on. If Congress chooses the traditional remedy of raising taxes, it could restore actuarial balance over the next seventy-five years by increasing the payroll tax by

1.3 percentage points each for employees and employers no later than 2002. If it waits another twenty years, it would need to increase the payroll tax by 2 percentage points each. Alternatively, if Congress decides to restore actuarial balance by reducing benefits for new retirees, it would need to reduce benefits by 21 percent beginning in 2002, but by 34 percent beginning in 2022.[98] Delay is even tougher for the proponents of advance funding. Each year the unfunded liability grows larger. Eventually the combined cost of supporting two systems becomes prohibitive. If Congress does nothing until the trust fund is exhausted in 2032, it would require a payroll tax of 8.9 percent each for employees and employers just to pay the next year's promised benefits, plus whatever Congress decides should be set aside for a new advance-funded system.[99]

Those who seek to preserve something like the current system are advantaged by the fact that Social Security is a well-known and popular program. Although preserving the current system would require difficult decisions about increasing taxes, cutting benefits, or extending the retirement age, these are decisions about which Congress has a great deal of experience. Skeptics sometimes argue that times have changed and that it is no longer possible for Congress to enact these traditional remedies. What the skeptics fail to appreciate is that it was always difficult for legislators to increase payroll taxes and cut benefits. Politicians struggled to save the system in 1983. No one wanted to enact the remedies that legislators eventually approved. The argument that times have changed is also undermined by the fact that during the past half dozen years Congress has approved both tax increases and benefit cuts for the rest of the federal budget. Many people were equally skeptical that Congress could enact those painful provisions.

Those who seek to replace the current defined-benefit system with a defined-contribution system have the tougher row to hoe. They are attempting to sell something new and different, and innovation is a difficult sell in any political system. To be sure, their cause is helped by the obvious similarities with such devices as individual retirement accounts, 401(k) plans, and mutual funds. It would have been inconceivable to enact something like the Weaver-Schieber plan or the Kotlikoff-Sachs plan in 1935. The greatest impediment to establishing individual accounts, however, is the need to fund two systems for a while. There is no free lunch here. If citizens want the benefits of an advance-funded system, with or without individual accounts, they must either increase their retirement contributions or accept a reduction in benefits. The closest thing to a free lunch is the unexpected surplus in the federal budget that could be used to fund part of the transition cost.

98. Advisory Council (1997b, p. 66).
99. Board of Trustees (1998, p. 108).

Although it is encouraging to see that President Clinton featured Social Security reform in his State of the Union address, proposed a White House conference for December 1998, and called for congressional action during 1999, it is impossible to overstate the obstacles to timely reform. The principal obstacle is the lack of a consensus on what Social Security should be. The debate today is not merely about tax rates and benefit levels—the traditional arena for Social Security politics. It is about the basic structure of the system. Altering the structure of any government program is always difficult, but it is especially so for a program that affects virtually everyone in American society.

A second obstacle to timely reform is the lack of an action-forcing crisis. Compromise is easiest when the failure to compromise creates a disaster. Essential to the reform of Social Security in 1983 was the fact that the trust fund was empty and revenues were insufficient to cover all benefit checks. No one wanted to be held accountable for reduced Social Security benefits. Essential to the annual budgetary agreements between Congress and the president is that failure to agree can lead to a government shutdown—a consequence that some politicians found appealing before they tried it several times. Unfortunately, the next action-forcing crisis for Social Security is penciled in for 2032.

Social Security reform today requires that political leaders come together and search for common ground. The search must be bipartisan, not simply because both Democrats and Republicans must join together to enact a reform plan, but because a bipartisan agreement is essential to selling a compromise plan to the American people. The chance that the American people will embrace a reform plan is far greater if Republican and Democratic leaders agree that the plan is fair than if they resort to partisan bickering as they did when they considered health care reform.

No one can know today the exact contours of a plan that Republican and Democratic leaders might design months or years from now. What seems certain, however, is that politicians will pay special attention to how costs are imposed. Partial privatization may well be part of a compromise plan, but only if its advocates can devise acceptable ways of funding the transition to advance-funded individual accounts.

Susan Dentzer, discussant

THE PAPERS BY Lawrence R. Jacobs and Robert Y. Shapiro and by R. Douglas Arnold constitute two very interesting presentations. The subject—public opinion and Social Security—is very close to my heart. In my former life as economics columnist for *U.S. News and World Report*, I found that whenever I got "lonely" for reader contact or felt too isolated from the public, the fastest way to remedy this problem was to write a column about Social Security because that would often generate about 150 letters the week after the column ran.

Many of these letters were generally from people who would write about what I called their "little coffers in Washington"—the little boxes where they believed their Social Security payroll contributions were stored, so that they could ultimately withdraw them, dollar by dollar, when they retired. Most of the letters were usually from people complaining about their Social Security surpluses being "stolen" by politicians or invested in "worthless IOUs." On a few occasions I had some fun by talking to people who were complaining about these worthless IOUs and quizzing them about their personal holdings—usually extensive—of U.S. Treasury securities!

As a result, I have spent a lot of time thinking about the level of public knowledge and understanding of Social Security, and on that basis I am less confident that the public understands as much about the system as Jacobs and Shapiro believe. I suppose it is possible that only the unwashed and ill-informed were reading my columns and responding to them, while the really smart and savvy members of the public are actually in the majority!

At any rate, today I would like to speak mainly about the role of the press and the news media in general in the Social Security reform debate. I very much want to echo the challenge that Jacobs and Shapiro offer in their paper: "Whether Americans' knowledge about Social Security will be deepened depends on journalists passing up excessive coverage of the political fight in favor of substantial coverage." It will not come as a shock to any of you, given what we have been reading about in the newspapers recently, that much of what the press writes about Washington is driven by the personalities in the news, rather than the substance of the issues at hand. That is fine when the stories really are about personalities, but it is not sufficient when the stories are fundamentally about public policy choices such as those that involve Social Security. In these stories, the real issues, as Arnold writes, are about "who should sacrifice, who should pay higher taxes, and who should have their favorite benefit programs shaved, slashed or terminated."

These are much harder stories for the press to write, and they are also tough to sell to many editors. Thus, it is no wonder that so many of us shy away from the meaty substantive and analysis-driven coverage about Social Security reform. Our model "story" is like the movie *Air Force One*: the hit film that starred the dashing Harrison Ford as the fearless president battling Russian nationalist terrorists who commandeered his plane. The film demanded plenty of suspension of disbelief from viewers, as actor Ford did everything from dangling from the plane while attached to a cable to dispatching the bad guys all by himself with an automatic weapon.

In reality, of course, the real-life "movie" of Bill Clinton's presidency, or of any presidency, is in many ways less heroic. In Clinton, for example, we have a president who among other things got skewered on health care reform and could not—or did not—halt two shutdowns of the government. Those of us who have watched these scenes up close have trouble imagining any real president in the Harrisonian role of commando in chief. Yet as journalists, we still insist on reporting many stories in purely personal terms—framing both events and policy debates as personal successes or failures of the president. This view is illogical, and with respect to the Social Security reform debate in particular, irresponsible. Let me offer a few notions about how we in the press could do better.

First of all, as the papers by Jacobs and Shapiro and Arnold suggest, we must do a better job of framing the issues that are at stake in the Social Security reform debate. This could be done in many ways, but in the interest of time today let me focus on just one: our need to frame the story in terms of the word "aging."

In a sense, this need should be self-evident. Yet I was struck in reading the Jacobs and Shapiro paper by the little support among the public for hiking the retirement age. I view this sentiment as partially an indication that we in the press have not been doing our job in reporting fully the demographic underpinnings of the potential problem of Social Security underfunding. Much of the public arguably understands the story of the baby boom followed by the baby bust. But I do not think it fully comprehends the equally important story of increasing longevity as a contributor to Social Security's potential future funding problems.

We have a responsibility to put this in terms that the baby boomers themselves can understand—to wit, that life expectancy at age 65 has increased 18 percent since 1970 alone. In other words, since the Vietnam-era confrontation at Kent State, we have had almost a one-fifth increase in life expectancy, on top of spectacular increases in longevity even earlier in the century. We in the press ought to do a better job of explaining this change, and of getting across the notion that Social Security reform in part means bringing a six-decade-old program up to date with these huge increases in longevity. Not only is this true on its face but conveying this information to the public would also help to correct the widespread misperception that Social Security's problems stem mainly from fraud and abuse or from the nefarious mistakes of policymakers.

Second, we in the press must not take sides in the Social Security reform debate. Once we have framed the issues, we inevitably have to move on to reporting and writing about potential policy responses or solutions, but we must do so in the context of conveying the notion that we do not have any truly perfect public policy options. There are only choices to be made among various trade-offs that will lead to different outcomes. Some of these outcomes are foreseeable, and some are not.

A prime example of what we should not do is a cover story that ran in *Time* magazine three years ago, with the cover line of "Social Insecurity." The argument of the piece was that it was time to scrap the Social Security system and, in effect, to privatize it. This was a provocative article, and it was just about the only substantial piece of coverage on Social Security that *Time* did during that period. Yet the story also contained errors of fact and was highly tendentious. If Jacobs is right, and public support for Social Security is as deep and broad as he suggests, millions of potential readers were probably turned off immediately by the story's supposition that it was time to scrap the program. As a result, an important chance to educate them was lost.

Although both sides of the Social Security reform are tendentious issues, the balance tilts at this point in favor of the pro-privatization forces in the popular press. Jacobs and Shapiro observed in their paper that the most affluent and educated people are most knowledgeable about Social Security. A perverse corollary to this is at work in the press: the most "yuppified" journalists and those who are earning the highest incomes seem most eager to extol the virtues of privatizing or partially privatizing the system. Put another way, the large white, male, aging coterie of Washington columnists tends to write favorably about privatization because these journalists believe that what will arguably be good for them personally will also be good for the entire nation. These are people who tend toward libertarianism, who feel comfortable making investment decisions. Some of them even write columns about investing on the side!

Tendentiousness on these issues may have a place within the advocacy press, and for opinion writers at places like the *New Republic* and the *National Review*, but the mainstream press should avoid the cover stories that crow about how Social Security is irretrievably broken. It should also avoid the other extreme—the Mother Jones approach that labels any privatization or partial privatization proposals as simply the result of the stealthy machinations of Wall Street.

Third, the press should acknowledge the uncertainties and resist unequivocal doom-and-gloom scenarios about the future of Social Security. This will be tough going, since to date the doom-and-gloom school appears to have thoroughly captured and dominated much of the press and public opinion. A case in point is the many books and treatises written by investment banker Peter Peterson, which have been excerpted time and again in many publications, including ones where I have worked. Now, as we all know, projections about the potential future underfunding of Social Security are not necessarily wrong; it's just that we cannot say with 100 percent certainty that they are right, either. We do not know whether any of the most dire fiscal outcomes that we think might come to pass will in fact come to pass. We cannot say what the future will look like.

Few policymakers will admit this publicly, so it is up to journalists to help fill this void. After all, as the National Academy of Social Insurance's own Robert Myers, formerly deputy commissioner of Social Security, has pointed out in congressional testimony, under the low-cost estimate of Social Security prepared by the system's actuaries, the program is projected to experience no long-range financing problem whatsoever. Yet when was the last time you read in the popular press that under some plausible—if not especially likely— circumstances, Social Security might never be in trouble at all? I confess that not even I have raised this possibility in any of my written work to date on Social Security. Those of us who have lived through the last several years in Washington, when almost all prognosticators in and out of government have made huge errors in forecasting the size of the federal budget deficit, should understand the great uncertainty built into all such projections and should make the public fully aware of this uncertainty.

Finally, the press must avoid the *Air Force One* syndrome that I mentioned at the outset of my talk. This syndrome represents an insistence on framing all policy disputes in personal terms—for example, as a test case of whether President Clinton or anybody in Congress will have the "guts" to take on Social Security and touch the supposed "third rail" of politics. Personality, of course, matters in politics, but this is just too important a debate to focus on such a small part of the coming story.

I'll close by repeating a line from Hugh Heclo's paper presented earlier in this book, to the effect that "In any democratic system . . . the great political sin is not to teach people about reality." Over the next year in particular, as the process of educating the public about Social Security reform gets under way, teaching people about reality should be one of journalists' primary tasks. I would simply ask members of the National Academy to help us in this effort. If our experience in health care reform during the early 1990s is any guide, many reporters without much prior knowledge of Social Security will ulti- mately be assigned to cover the debate. Thus the National Academy will have plenty to do in educating us before we can get around to educating the public. As Jacobs and Shapiro wrote in their paper, "Social Security is surrounded by a moat of jargon, but it is not rocket science." To continue the metaphor, please help all of us in the press cross the moat of jargon to the Holy Grail that awaits us in the castle of understanding.

Edward Gramlich, discussant

THESE TWO PAPERS were written in as lively a manner as they were delivered. Even though some of the words were a little painful personally, the papers are interesting and represent different ways of attacking the same political question.

Lawrence R. Jacobs and Robert Y. Shapiro analyze polls, and R. Douglas Arnold talks about the first principles of politics on how to reform Social Security.

In discussing years of polling results, the Jacobs-Shapiro paper takes on four presumptions about Social Security. The authors are positive and talk about the glass being half full. However, one could argue that the glass is half empty as well.

The first presumption is that the public is not well informed about Social Security. Jacobs and Shapiro feel the public is well informed. The basic facts are as follows. One poll contains self-reports—that is, pollers ask, "Are you well informed?" and respondents say if they are. Self-reports indicate that only 57 percent are well informed. That does not seem terribly high for a self-report-type question. The second fact is responses to multiple choice tests about Social Security: "Is it one of the two largest federal programs?" It is certainly that, but only 33 percent of the people say it is. "Do Social Security's problems stem from waste, fraud, abuse?" Ninety-three percent of the people say that they do. Those of you who are informed about Social Security would beg to differ on that point. Finally, Social Security spending is probably twenty times the level of the sum of foreign aid and food stamps, but most people say that it is less. In short, people may be well informed about Social Security in some dimensions, but they are not very well informed in other dimensions. If we view ourselves as teachers, we have work to do.

The second presumption involves confidence and support. Jacobs and Shapiro point out a difference between confidence and support. Confidence is measured by a question such as "Are you confident that Social Security will be there for you?" Although the numbers fluctuate, right now yes responses are at a 40 percent level. That does not seem unusually high as a number indicating confidence. We are all greatly reassured to know that more people are confident about Social Security than they are about the existence of UFOs, but confidence is still low.

Support for Social Security, however, is high. I think we can figure out why. The question is asked, "Do you support Social Security?" We all start thinking about our parents and what they would do without Social Security. Of course we support Social Security. The program provides a lot of social protections.

Nobody is questioning those social protections. We all believe in them deeply. So a support question is likely to elicit such emotional responses.

But a better way to ask these types of questions would be, "At the margin, would you do this, that, or the other thing?" If pollers ask those kinds of questions, they will not get emotional support. They will get people making marginal calculations. Jacobs and Shapiro did not analyze any questions that really test these marginal calculations. These questions would probably elicit responses a little bit less ebullient in terms of support for Social Security.

The third presumption is, "Do you support changes in Social Security?" Questioners ask about a number of technical changes. One is limiting the adjustment to the consumer price index. One is switching to privatization. One is changing the retirement age. One is reducing benefits for upper-income people. Limiting the CPI adjustment is favored by about a third of the respondents. Privatization is favored by about a third of the respondents. Changing the retirement age is fine with about 30 percent. Reducing benefits for upper-income recipients is agreeable to about 60 percent, though Jacobs and Shapiro do not give a summary number.

Another group that has done these types of tests, the Concord Coalition, has a better way to deal with these questions. The coalition assembles focus groups of, say, ten people, and tells them, "Your job is to get the budget deficit down to zero." (The coalition did this in the days when the budget deficit was much different from zero.) The members of the group are given options. You can do this to the Post Office. You can do that to military spending. You can do this to various other programs. People in the group then discuss and gradually work out budget adjustment plans.

Pollers could do the same thing with Social Security: "The trust fund is out of balance by x amount. We ought to bring it into balance. We could do this and it would save this amount. We could do that and save that amount, and so forth." A focus group could come up with Social Security reform plans. They might feature a little bit of adjustment here and a little bit of adjustment there. But, at least on an entering level, these percentages are probably big enough to get to a set of agreed-on changes in Social Security.

The last presumption that Jacobs and Shapiro talked about was not discussed verbally and not much in the paper. It is, "Is there an intergenerational war or conflict?" I never thought that anybody felt there was an intergenerational war or conflict. What does exist is differences in polling results. The differences are not huge, but there are differences.

Arnold talks about principles of political salesmanship for, or packaging of, Social Security reform. I do not mind political packaging, but we have to keep in mind the very thin line between packaging and plain old dishonesty. In some cases, packaging represents relatively harmless window dressing. In other cases the window dressing could be harmful.

One relatively harmless issue involves the payroll tax. It is assessed half on workers and half on employers. What economists will assert is that under a wide range of assumptions the part assessed on employers is largely paid by workers in the form of lower wages than would otherwise be the case. So, when economists talk about this matter, they usually slide right over the employer-employee distinction. It is simply not that important. I would say that this point is an example of harmless window dressing. A fully honest person might be more candid and say: "The taxes are all paid by workers. Let us assess them on workers." However, if it takes window dressing to get the political compromise for a successful program, then so be it. It is not a whole lot worse to assess part of the tax on employers.

In other cases the dictates of packaging cannot be dismissed so easily. One is the national saving issue. We have to raise national saving for Social Security. I will assert that, as an economist.

Does it help to have a very phased-in, gradual rise in the payroll tax rate? No, it does not help much. We have to raise contributions soon. We have to raise them, in particular, before the baby boomers start retiring. Here the interests of political packaging are quite at variance with the interests of what we really have to do to deal with Social Security.

Another question is transition cost. There, Arnold is on my side. He is critical of the Ferraro group because it, in effect, downplays transition costs. The group does not tell people what the transition costs are even though they are large. We both agree that groups that want to have Social Security plans that entail transition costs ought to be required to be clear about what the costs are.

Arnold criticizes my own Social Security reform plan for not being very "graceful." It is not graceful for two reasons. The add-on individual accounts raise national saving now. It involves an abrupt increase of 1.6 percent of the taxable payrolls. The second reason is that the add-on is paid entirely by workers.

Frankly, I knew this measure would not be popular. But I do feel that this change should be made. We have to be clear to workers that they have to save more. Advisory Council members and politicians have different rules. An Advisory Council gets one chance to say what it thinks should be done about a program. The incentive is to try to be perfectly clear, recognizing that it may be a political downer.

But just to prove I can do it, let me tell you what I would do if I were into political packaging. I would make three points about my plan. The first involves benefit cuts. These are very slow and gradual benefit cuts. Arnold applauds that. Actually, the reason for gradualism—and this is true of all the plans from the Advisory Council—is that it is just unfair to people to give them a set of Social Security rules and then slash their benefits if they had already retired, or even slash them a whole lot if they were approaching retirement age. Benefit cuts should be phased in gradually so as not to invalidate people's retirement plans and generate notches. In this case, the interests of sensible policy conform to those of political window dressing. If I were a politician and advertising my plan, I would make the point over and over that this third-rail analogy does not really apply to my plan or, indeed, to the other two plans of the Advisory Council, because they make no benefit cuts for current retirees. Benefits grow more slowly over time for those not yet retired and fairly well off.

The second point I would make is that my plan really does not have any explicit transition costs. Those could be huge, and the fact that my plan does not have them is an attractive feature.

The third point—the downer on my plan—is the add-on individual accounts or the defined-contribution accounts. This could be dealt with in several ways. First, about a third of the work force is undersaving, in the sense of having very little prospective pension income on top of Social Security. This is not a huge fraction of the work force. Voluntary mechanisms could get this third of the work force to save more. Large firms might be induced to put all their employees into their defined-contribution plans, or make other such changes, and avoid mandating the add-on saving. Tax privileges might not be conferred unless there were reasonably full participation. Second, in terms of window dressing, this could be called "private pension reform" and not Social Security reform, because the problem is that the private pensions on top of Social Security are inadequate. Third, as Arnold suggests, these add-ons could be paid partly by the employers.

These policies could be packaged more attractively but, from the standpoint of the Advisory Commission, it was more important to be clear about the problem with the system and what it would take to fix it.

Paul Light, discussant

THIS CONFERENCE TAKES PLACE almost fifteen years to the day after the National Commission on Social Security Reform completed its work in rescuing the program from its impending shortfall in 1983. Even now, the rescue brings back, through misty water color, memories of the way things were when Alan Greenspan, chairman of the commission, and his fourteen colleagues put together a miraculous last-second package designed to restore the program to fiscal balance. The question today is whether America can look forward to another rescue some time later this year or early in the next. The answer depends in large measure on what Americans want. Let me draw three quick observations about the state of public opinion as one considers the possibility of another Greenspan-esque Social Security rescue.

First, we need to be very careful about how we talk with the American public about this issue. (My grantmaking portfolio has nothing to do with Social Security; it is mostly about electoral reform and government performance and civic engagement of young Americans). Notwithstanding the relative calm of the American public regarding the Monica Lewinsky–Bill Clinton scandal, Americans tend to react quite extremely to Social Security.

My reading of the data is that confidence is low, because Americans are generally fearful about Social Security. Enough buzz abounds about the future problems of the program to produce an anxiety underneath the high support.

Second, I think we ought to be careful about what we talk about with the American public. I read Larry Jacobs's analysis and other analyses to say that we ought to talk about broad values with the American public as it relates to Social Security and stay away from the specifics of the program.

Third, I think we ought to be careful what we ask the American public for in this conversation. I do not think that the American public is well prepared today. I do not think that members of the public will be prepared by the end of the year to come up with a consensus that would be revealed in a series of cross-sectional surveys, however well designed they may be.

I believe that Americans want the system protected. They have some opinions here and there about how they would like to see it done; underneath all of this, the American public expects us to do our job. Period. They expect us to come to a consensus and talk to them honestly about what is going on, but the American public neither expects nor is capable of engaging in the debate about bend points, and so on.

Now, let us discuss 1983. Can we recreate that enormous momentum that produced the 1983 agreement? As you know, Speaker Newt Gingrich has endorsed creating another commission, and President Clinton is talking about a national dialogue that would lead to a White House Conference that would lead to a summit. Could that produce an agreement by the end of this year or early next year?

Bob Myers is still available to help them. I am sure he would volunteer in a second. That would be a real advantage. I think the 1983 commission had all the right players. It had all the right analysis in no small part due to Bob. It even had a crisis that had an action-forcing character to it. It did produce a result that we might all admire. However, let me mention two myths and two realities about the 1983 rescue.

A first myth about the 1983 rescue was that it was a triumph of rational science over raw politics. It was not. A great deal of raw politics lurked underneath the surface of the 1983 debate. We have heard some conversation today such as "Well, it would be best if we just stick to the substance." However, politics surrounds Social Security. People are going to fight hard about issues, and I would report on it—in context, of course. But the stakes are big now and they were big in 1983, and politics is important. The second myth about 1983 is that the American public was not well engaged in the debate. There was a lot of hysteria about Social Security. Remember the 1982 campaign involved a tremendous amount of demagoging on the issue. I am not sure the American public needs to be deeply engaged in the debate, but I do believe that engaging in a broad conversation about the values that Americans bring to bear on the issue will make it easier to accomplish change this time around.

Two realities about the 1983 debate create a caution about what we can expect this year. First, in 1983 Social Security had a clearly defined problem. In fact, one of the major contributions of the Greenspan Commission was to produce an agreement on the nature of the problem. In the short term, the shortfall was $150 to $200 billion, and the long-term problem was 1.8 percent of taxable payroll. Having that clearly defined benchmark against which to struggle was helpful. It was helpful to have to face the short-term problem and, then, to attach the long-term reforms to it.

Second, the 1983 agreements reflected a good deal of hard and secret bargaining. Ultimately, somebody has got to sit down and work out a deal here. It is a mistake to create expectations that everything must be done in public—and I am a believer in the American public. I think the American public can handle a great deal of challenge and is more rational than ordinarily believed. The parties need a venue in which hard bargaining can occur without the intense inspection of the media. I do not know how the media would feel about that. I would suggest that President Clinton reserve Blair House right now for late December of 1998, and early January, and make sure that he puts a good solid rope around the house to keep the media out. Perhaps this national conversation may provide the cover to achieve some kind of agreement. The missing piece in all of this ultimately is the lack of urgency for an agreement. I do not see how that can be resolved just yet.

At any rate, I do believe that we are on the cusp of an important national conversation and I am delighted to have been asked to comment on it.

References

Advisory Council on Social Security. 1997a. *Report of the 1994-1996 Advisory Council on Social Security: Vol. 1: Findings and Recommendations.* Washington: Government Printing Office.

_____. 1997b. *Report of the 1994-1996 Advisory Council on Social Security: Vol: 2: Reports of the Technical Panels.* Washington: Government Printing Office.

Arnold, R. Douglas. 1979. *Congress and the Bureaucracy: A Theory of Influence.* Yale University Press.

_____. 1990. *The Logic of Congressional Action.* Yale University Press.

Board of Trustees of the Federal Old-Age and Survivors Insurance and Disability Insurance Trust Funds. 1998. *The 1998 Annual Report.* Washington: Government Printing Office.

Congressional Quarterly. 1984. *Congressional Quarterly Almanac, 1983.* Washington: Congressional Quarterly.

Cook, Fay Lomax, and Edith Barrett. 1992. *Support for the American Welfare State.* Columbia University Press.

Cutler, David. 1996. "Reexamining the Three-Legged Stool." In *Social Security: What Role for the Future?* edited by Peter Diamond, David Lindeman, and Howard Young, 125–49. Brookings.

Delli Carpini, Michael, and Scott Keeter. 1996. *What Americans Know about Politics and Why It Matters.* Yale University Press.

Derthick, Martha. 1979. *Policymaking for Social Security.* Brookings.

Diamond, Peter. 1996. "Proposals to Restructure Social Security." *Journal of Economic Perspectives* 10 (3): 67–88.

_____. 1997. "Macroeconomic Aspects of Social Security Reform." *Brookings Papers on Economic Activity* 2: 1–87.

Employee Benefit Research Institute. 1996a. "Worker Investment Decisions: An Analysis of Large 401(k) Plan Data." *EBRI Issue Brief Number 176,* August.

_____. 1996b. "Keeping Track of Social Security Reform Proposals: A Summary." *EBRI Notes* 17 (11): 1–8.

Engen, Eric M., and William G. Gale. 1997. "Effects of Social Security Reform on Private and National Saving." In *Social Security Reform: Links to Saving, Investment, and Growth,* edited by Steven A. Sass and Robert K. Triest, 103–42. Boston: Federal Reserve Bank of Boston.

Feldstein, Martin. 1997. *Transition to a Fully Funded Pension System: Five Economic Issues.* NBER Working Paper 6149. Cambridge, Mass.: National Bureau of Economic Research.

Feldstein, Martin, and Andrew Samwick. 1996. *The Transition Path in Privatizing Social Security.* NBER Working Paper 5761. Cambridge, Mass.: National Bureau of Economic Research.

Ferrara, Peter J. 1997. A Plan for Privatizing Social Security. *The Cato Project on Social Security Privatization.* Washington: Cato Institute.

Gramlich, Edward M. 1996. "Different Approaches for Dealing with Social Security." *Journal of Economic Perspectives* 10 (3): 55–66.

Greider, William. 1982. *The Education of David Stockman and Other Americans.* E. P. Dutton.

Hammond, P. Brett, and Mark J. Warshawsky. 1997. "Investing Social Security Funds in Stocks." *Benefits Quarterly* 13 (3): 52–65.

Himelfarb, Richard. 1995. *Catastrophic Politics: The Rise and Fall of the Medicare Catastrophic Coverage Act of 1988.* Pennsylvania State University Press.

Jacobs, Lawrence, and Robert Shapiro. 1995. *The News Media's Coverage of Social Security.* Report prepared for the National Academy of Social Insurance (March).

Jacobs, Lawrence, Mark Watts, and Robert Shapiro. 1995. "Media Coverage and Public Views of Social Security." *Public Perspective* 6 (April-May): 9–10, 48–49.

Kingdon, John W. 1989. *Congressmen's Voting Decisions*, 3d ed. University of Michigan Press.

Kotlikoff, Laurence J., and Jeffrey D. Sachs. 1997a. "The Personal Security System: A Framework for Reforming Social Security." Presented to the Subcommittee on Social Security, House Committee on Ways and Means, *Hearings on the Future of Social Security for This Generation and the Next*, 105 Cong. 1 sess. March 6.

_____. 1997b. "It's High Time to Privatize." *Brookings Review* 15 (3): 16–22.

Light, Paul. 1995. *Still Artful Work: The Continuing Politics of Social Security Reform*, 2d ed. McGraw-Hill.

MacManus, Susan. 1996. *Young v. Old: Generational Combat in the 21st Century.* Westview Press.

Mayhew, David R. 1974. *Congress: The Electoral Connection.* Yale University Press.

Mitchell, Olivia S. 1996. *Administrative Costs in Public and Private Retirement Systems.* NBER Working Paper 5734. Cambridge, Mass.: National Bureau of Economic Research.

Page, Benjamin, and Robert Y. Shapiro. 1992. *The Rational Public: Fifty Years of Trends in Americans' Policy Preferences.* University of Chicago Press.

Poterba, James M., and David A. Wise. 1996. *Individual Financial Decisions in Retirement Saving Plans and the Provision of Resources for Retirement.* NBER Working Paper 5762. Cambridge, Mass.: National Bureau of Economic Research.

Reno, Virginia, and Robert Friedland. 1997. "Strong Support but Low Confidence: What Explains the Contradiction." In *Social Security in the 21st Century*, edited by Eric Kingson and James Schulz, 178–94. Oxford University Press.

Rhodebeck, Laurie. 1993. "The Politics of Greed? Political Preferences among the Elderly." *Journal of Politics* 55 (May): 342–64.

Romano, Roberta. 1993. "Public Pension Fund Activism in Corporate Governance Reconsidered." *Columbia Law Review* 93 (4): 795–853.

Tanner, Michael. 1996. *Public Opinion and Social Security Privatization. The Cato Project on Social Security Privatization.* Washington: Cato Institute.

Contributors

Henry J. Aaron
The Brookings Institution

Theodore J. Angelis
J. D. candidate
Yale University Law School

R. Douglas Arnold
Woodrow Wilson School of Public
and International Affairs
Princeton University

Warren L. Batts
Chairman and Chief Executive
Officer, ret'd.
Tupperware Corporation

Michael J. Boskin
Hoover Institution
Stanford University

Francis X. Cavanaugh
Public Finance consultant
Washington, D.C.

Susan Dentzer
Journalist
Washington, D.C.

Peter A. Diamond
Massachusetts Institute of
Technology

Richard Disney
Queen Mary and Westfield
College
University of London

John Geanakoplos
Yale University

Edward Gramlich
Board of Governors
Federal Reserve System

Michael J. Graetz
Yale University Law School

Hugh Heclo
George Mason University

Karen C. Holden
University of Wisconsin-Madison

Howell E. Jackson
Harvard University Law School

Lawrence R. Jacobs
University of Minnesota

Regina T. Jefferson
Catholic University of America
School of Law

Ian Lanoff
Groom Law Group, Chartered
Washington, D.C.

Paul Light
The Pew Charitable Trusts and
  University of Minnesota

Olivia Mitchell
The Wharton School
University of Pennsylvania

Alicia H. Munnell
Carroll School of Management
Boston College

John Myles
Institute on Aging
Florida State University

Dallas L. Salisbury
Employee Benefit Research
  Institute

Sylvester J. Schieber
Watson Wyatt Worldwide

Winfried Schmähl
University of Bremen

Robert Y. Shapiro
Columbia University

Lawrence H. Thompson
The Urban Institute

David Walker
Wes-Can Consultants

R. Kent Weaver
The Brookings Institution

Stephen P. Zeldes
Columbia University

Cathleen Zick
University of Utah

Conference Program

**National Academy of Social Insurance
Tenth Annual Conference and Membership Meeting**

**Framing the Social Security Debate:
Values, Politics, and Economics
January 29–30, 1998**

Thursday, January 29, 1998

9:00–9:15	Welcome and Introduction
	John Palmer, Maxwell School, Syracuse University, and Academy President
9:15–10:30	Session I. *Values, Politics, and Economics in Social Security Reform*
	Why is Social Security reform on the agenda? What are the issues for national savings, productivity, and economic growth? What values are at stake? How do political risks and realities affect Social Security reform? How will changes affect the security of retirement income in the future?
	Chair: Ann L. Combs, William M. Mercer, Inc.
	Michael J. Boskin,* Stanford University, co-chair of Academy Panel on Social Security Privatization, "A Framework for Considering Social Security Reform"

Peter A. Diamond,* Massachusetts Institute of
Technology, co-chair of Academy Panel on Social
Security Privatization, "Economics of Social Security
Reform—An Overview"

Hugh Heclo,* George Mason University, "A Political
Science Perspective on Social Security Reform"

10:30–10:45   Break

10:45–11:20   Session IIa. *Pensions and Savings: In What Form?*

How do pensions and savings fit with Social
Security? How are private pensions changing and
why? What are the implications for Social Security in
providing retirement income security?

Chair: Nancy J. Altman, consultant

Presenter: Dallas L. Salisbury,* Employee Benefit
Research Institute

Discussant: Regina T. Jefferson, Catholic University
Law School

11:20–11:45   Introduction of Social Security Advisory Board

The Honorable Stanford G. Ross, chair

12:00–1:00   Keynote Address
The Honorable Lawrence H. Summers,*
Deputy Secretary of the Treasury Department

1:15–3:00   Session IIb. *Social Security: In What Form?*

Two plans of the 1996 Advisory Council on Social
Security would shift part of Social Security to individual savings or defined-contribution (DC) accounts.
How would such a shift affect the risks workers face
over their lifetimes? The relation between workers'
benefits and contributions? The income security of
women and widows in old age?

Chair: Janice M. Gregory, ERISA Industry
Committee

Presenters:

Lawrence H. Thompson, The Urban Institute, "Individual Uncertainty in Retirement Income Planning Under Different Public Pension Regimes"

John Geanakoplos,* Yale University, Olivia Mitchell,* University of Pennsylvania, and Stephen P. Zeldes,* Columbia University, "Would a Privatized Social Security System Really Have a Higher Rate of Return?"

Karen C. Holden, University of Wisconsin, "Insuring against the Consequences of Widowhood in a Reformed Social Security System"

Discussants:
Sylvester J. Schieber,* Watson Wyatt Worldwide
Henry Aaron, The Brookings Institution

3:15–5:00   Session III. *Insights from Social Security Reform Abroad*

How are other advanced industrial countries reforming their old-age pension systems to adapt to an aging population? What can be learned from different approaches taken in Canada, the United Kingdom, Australia, Germany, and other advanced industrial countries?

Chair: Keith G. Banting, Harvard University

Presenter: Kent Weaver, The Brookings Institution, "The Politics of Pensions: Lessons from Abroad"

Discussants:
Richard Disney, Institute for Fiscal Studies, London
John Myles, Florida State University
Winfried Schmähl, University of Bremen, Germany
David Walker, Special Advisor to the Minister of
    Finance, Canada

6:30–8:30   Dinner

Heinz Dissertation Award Presentation, Joseph F. Quinn, chair

Dinner Address: Bruce Vladeck, "Should Medicare
Stay Part of Social Security?"

Friday, January 30, 1998

8:45–9:45   Roundtable Discussions

Unemployment Insurance—Chairs: Richard Hobbie
and Wayne Vroman

Children's Health Security—Chairs: Gerard
Fergerson, John Holahan, and Judith Moore

Medicare Public Understanding—Chairs: Stuart
Butler and Ted Marmor

Health Care Financing Issues Abroad—Chairs: Debra
Chollet and William Hsiao

Americans Discuss Social Security—Chair: Carolyn
Lukensmeyer

10:00–10:30   Keynote Address
The Honorable Jim McCrery (R-La.)

10:30–12:00   Session IV. *Public Investment in Private Markets*

Two proposals from the 1996 Advisory Council envision investing part of Social Security funds in private
markets on a model similar to the federal employees'
Thrift Savings Plan (TSP). One plan would invest
part of the aggregate trust funds in private equities;
another plan would have workers invest individual
accounts in their choice of government-managed
stocks or bond funds. Why are these plans proposed?
What new issues are posed by public management of
investments in private markets?

Chair: Roberta Romano, Yale University Law School

Issues paper: Theodore J. Angelis, Yale University
Law School, "Investing Public Money in Private
Markets: What Are the Right Questions?"

Commentary:
Warren L. Batts, retired chairman and CEO,
    Tupperware, and past chairman,
    National Association of Manufacturers
Francis X. Cavanaugh, retired executive director, TSP
Howell Jackson, Harvard Law School
Ian Lanoff,* Groom Law Group, Chartered,
    Washington, D.C.

12:00–1:00   Luncheon Address

The Honorable Kenneth S. Apfel,* Commissioner of
Social Security Administration

1:15–3:00   Session V. *Public Opinion and the Politics of
Reforming Social Security*

What do Americans know, believe, and care about
Social Security? How do their views differ by age
and income, and over time? How do public perceptions influence policymaking? How might views
change as the policy debate unfolds? What are the
implications for long-term political stability in Social
Security?

Chair: Martha Derthick, University of Virginia

Presenters:
Lawrence R. Jacobs, University of Minnesota, and
Robert Y. Shapiro, Columbia University, "Myths
and Misunderstandings about Public Opinion
toward Social Security: Knowledge, Support and
Reformism"

R. Douglas Arnold,* Princeton University, "The
Political Feasibility of Social Security Reform"

Discussants:
Susan Dentzer, journalist
Edward Gramlich, Federal Reserve Board of
Governors
Paul Light, The Pew Charitable Trusts

3:00–3:30   Wrap-Up by Conference Co-chairs

                       R. Douglas Arnold, Professor of Politics and Public
                         Affairs, Princeton University
                       Michael J. Graetz, Justus S. Hotchkiss Professor of
                         Law, Yale University
                       Alicia H. Munnell, Peter F. Drucker Professor of
                         Management Sciences, Boston College

* Member, Academy Panel on Privatization of Social Security

Index

Action-forcing mechanisms: effect on pension reform, 217–18, 235. *See also* Pension reform pressures

Administrative costs for pension systems: Australia, 51–52; Chile, 51, 52, 226; for deposit system, 56–57; in government selected portfolios, 50–51, 56, 57; impact on rate of return, 176–77, 179, 226, 337; Individual Accounts (IA) proposal, 288, 324–25; Personal Security Accounts (PSA) proposal, 6, 51–57, 317, 326, 410; regulating, 51, 55–56, 226, 342; Thrift Savings Plan (TSP), 322, 323; United Kingdom, 52–55; U.S. Social Security, 13, 55, 325–26, 359

Advanced funded systems. *See* Prefunded public pension design

Advisory Council on Social Security, 27, 393. *See also* Individual Accounts (IA) proposal; Maintain Benefits (MB) proposal; Personal Savings Account (PSA) proposal

Altmeyer, Arthur, 172–73

Angle, Jim, 356

Annuity purchases: conversion risks, 41–42, 86; ERISA requirements, 159–61; individual decisionmaking, 5–6, 45–48, 166–68; as intergenerational variation protection, 344; *1990* payment amounts, 103

Approved Personal Pension (United Kingdom), 230, 231

Argentina, 136

Artoni, Robert, 243

Asset accumulation: risks in defined-contribution plans, 5, 40–43, 107–11, 132–34; simulations of economic risks, 10, 123, 125–29; U.S. statistics, 84. *See also* Saving rate

Australia: delayed retirement incentives, 206; disability insurance, 227; elderly population statistics, 191; government pension obligations, 16, 240–41; means testing, 188, 207, 245; pension coverage expansion as reform, 208, 216, 217, 225, 239–40, 246; pension fund competition, 227; retirement age increase, 202; role of labor in pension reform, 211, 240, 245–46; saving rate, 318; taxation of benefits, 207

Austria, retirement age, 202

Averting the Old Age Crisis (World Bank), 200

Ball plan. *See* Maintain Benefits (MB) proposal

Battle, Ken, 223

Benefit expectations: impact on pension reform, 15, 76–78, 215–17, 223, 225, 232, 235, 237, 397

Birth rate declines: impact on benefit levels, 119–20, 135; impact on pension